A2-Level Psychology for AQA A

The Complete Course for AQA A2

Contents

Unit 4

Section 10: Psychology in Action

Section 11: Research Methods

Exam Help

Reference

Published by CGP

Editors:
Katherine Craig, Ceara Hayden, Edmund Robinson, Camilla Simson.

Contributors:
Radha Bellur, Lauren Burns, Richard Carciofo, Elisa M Gray, Nigel Holt, Christine Johnson, Kate Robson, Denise Say, Stuart Wilson.

ISBN: 978 1 84762 796 4

With thanks to Mark Billingham, Sharon Cooper, Mary Falkner, Andrew Gallacher, Rosie McCurrie, Glenn Rogers, Hayley Thompson and Karen Wells for the proofreading.
With thanks to Anna Lupton for the copyright research.

Groovy website: www.cgpbooks.co.uk

Printed by Elanders Ltd, Newcastle upon Tyne.
Jolly bits of clipart from CorelDRAW®

How to Use This Book

Learning Objectives

These tell you exactly what you need to learn, or be able to do, for the exam.

Exam Tips

There are tips throughout the book to help with all sorts of things to do with answering exam questions.

How Science Works

This book covers How Science Works. The scientific process is described at the front of the book and Unit 4: Section 11 is a whole section on research methods.

Learning Objectives:
- Know the psychological explanations of obesity.
- Know the biological explanations of obesity, including neural and evolutionary explanations.

Exam Tip
You only need to know about one eating disorder. So choose anorexia nervosa, bulimia nervosa or obesity and learn everything you need to know about that one.

5. Obesity

Obesity rates are rising dramatically — so much so that obesity is now an epidemic in the UK. Obesity has lots of health implications and understanding the possible causes and explanations may help us to prevent it from increasing.

What is obesity?

A person is classed as obese if they have an abnormally high **body mass index** (BMI) of 30 kg/m² or higher. This is about 20% above normal for their height and body frame, i.e. they're carrying too much **adipose** (fatty) tissue. Obesity is generally caused by a person taking in more calories (food) than they burn off (by exercise), but there are some genetic conditions and medications that can increase the risk of obesity.

It's estimated that by 2050 over half of the people in the UK will be obese. This is pretty worrying when you consider that it's already one of the leading preventable causes of death worldwide — it increases the risk of illnesses like heart disease, diabetes and cancer. The most effective way to treat obesity is with a sensible diet and plenty of exercise. However, increasingly people are turning to quick fixes —'miracle' pills or surgery such as stomach stapling, gastric band fitting or gastric bypass surgery.

Measuring obesity

Body mass index is a measurement of height relative to weight.
A normal BMI is between 18.5 and 25.
The equation to work it out is:

$$\text{BMI} = \frac{\text{Weight } (kg)}{\text{Height}^2\ (m^2)}$$

BMI	Weight
Below 18.5	Underweight
18.5 - 24.9	Healthy
25 - 29.9	Overweight
Over 30	Obese

Figure 1: *Table showing weight categories.*

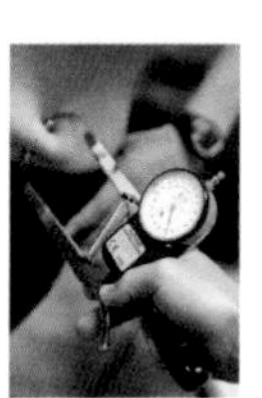

Figure 2: *In addition to BMI, health professionals use a skin fold test to measure obesity.*

Example
Shehan is 1.68 m tall. He weighs 89 kg. We can work out his BMI using the calculation below:

$$\text{BMI} = \frac{\text{Weight } (kg)}{\text{Height}^2\ (m^2)} \quad \text{BMI} = \frac{89}{1.68^2} \quad \text{BMI} = \frac{89}{2.8224} \quad \text{BMI} = 31.53$$

Based on this calculation, he has a BMI of 31.53 and is therefore, obese.

Biological explanations

Genetic causes
Some studies have shown that there is a genetic element to obesity.

Key study of adoption studies and obesity — Stunkard et al (1986)

Method: The weight of 540 adult adoptees from Denmark was compared with that of both their biological and adoptive parents. The adoptees were split into 4 weight classes — thin, median, overweight and obese.

Results: There was a strong relationship between the weight of the adoptees and that of their biological parents. There was no relationship between the weight of the adoptees and their adoptive parents in any of the weight classes.

84 Unit 3: Section 5 Eating Behaviour

Examples

- These are here to help you understand the theory.
- You don't need to learn them unless it says so in the text.

- Psychological conditions. A number of psychological conditions can cause insomnia. For example, depression, post-traumatic stress disorder and generalised anxiety disorder can all cause insomnia through secondary side effects.
- Stress or anxiety. Worrying about something causes anxiety (higher bodily arousal), which may in turn cause insomnia. Failure to get to sleep can cause frustration, which creates more anxiety, making it even harder to get to sleep and producing a vicious circle.
- Medication. Some medications may have side effects which disrupt sleep. Also, medications taken to improve sleep may cause problems if their effects are too long-lasting (leaving the person sleepy the next day), or if their effects wear off too early. Some people may become dependent on sleeping pills and suffer even worse insomnia if they stop taking them.

Example
Liz is suffering from post-traumatic stress disorder after being involved in a car crash. She has trouble sleeping, which is diagnosed as secondary insomnia.

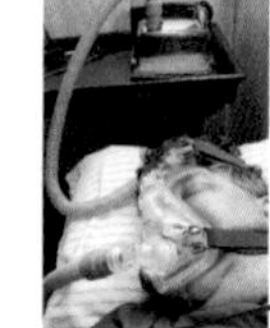

Figure 2: *Sleep apnoea in obese people is treated using special masks to unblock airways.*

Problems with research
Research into insomnia is difficult as there are many variables that can cause or influence the condition. This problem is compounded by the fact that some of the variables are hard to control. Much of the research that's been done has produced correlational evidence rather than showing cause and effect.

Tip: Sleepwalking is also called somnambulism.

Sleepwalking

Sleepwalking is a disorder associated with stage 3 and stage 4 sleep. It affects approximately 15% of children and 2% of adults. The causes of sleepwalking are not fully known but it's thought it can be triggered by **sleep deprivation** (especially in people with a history of sleepwalking), an irregular sleep schedule, stress or anxiety or some drugs, e.g. anti-psychotics or stimulants.

Real World Connection
Jules Lowe was a 32 year old man from Manchester who was tried for murder in 2003. He claimed he could not recall committing the crime and must have been sleepwalking. Despite being found 'not guilty' of murder he has been indefinitely secured in a psychiatric hospital.

Key study of sleepwalking — Dauvilliers et al (2005)

Method: Dauvilliers et al asked 256 people who had been diagnosed with a sleep disorder to detail their family history of sleep disorders, as well as a summary of their sleeping habits. They compared these results to a control group, who were acting as a baseline measurement.

Results: Dauvilliers et al's study suggests there may be a genetic component to sleepwalking — they found higher concordance rates for the disorder in identical twins than in non-identical twins.

Conclusion: Sleepwalking has a genetic link.

Tip: Sleepwalking is often more common in children. However, this could be because children spend longer in stages 3 and 4 of sleep — when the behaviour is more likely to occur.

Additional study of sleepwalking — Hublin et al (1997)

Hublin et al had also conducted a study by looking at the concordance rates of sleepwalking in identical twins. They found the rates to be approximately 66% for boys and 57% for girls, which confirms that there is certainly some genetic component. However, as the rates are not 100% there must also be other factors which influence sleepwalking.

Tip: See page 144 for more about concordance rates.

Unit 3: Section 1 Biological Rhythms and Sleep 19

Studies

- There are lots of psychological studies throughout the book. There are plenty of details about the methods, results and conclusions, as well as some evaluation points.
- Some are labelled as 'key studies' and others as 'additional studies'. If you're pushed for time, just focus on the key studies.
- Also, don't worry if your teacher has taught you about different studies in your lessons — as long as they're on the right topic, using any studies in your exam answers is fine.

Tips

These are here to help you understand the theory.

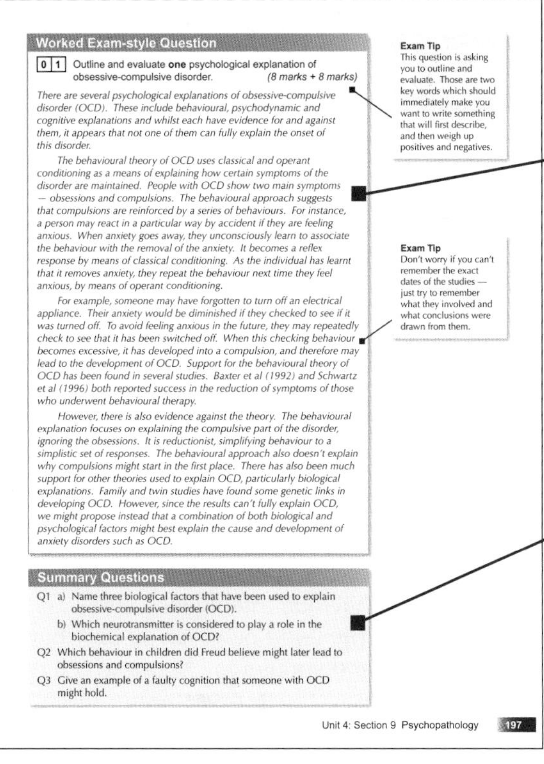

Worked Exam-style Question

0 1 Outline and evaluate **one** psychological explanation of obsessive-compulsive disorder. *(8 marks + 8 marks)*

There are several psychological explanations of obsessive-compulsive disorder (OCD). These include behavioural, psychodynamic and cognitive explanations and whilst each have evidence for and against them, it appears that not one of them can fully explain the onset of this disorder.

The behavioural theory of OCD uses classical and operant conditioning as a means of explaining how certain symptoms of the disorder are maintained. People with OCD show two main symptoms — obsessions and compulsions. The behavioural approach suggests that compulsions are reinforced by a series of behaviours. For instance, a person may react in a particular way by accident if they are feeling anxious. When anxiety goes away, they unconsciously learn to associate the behaviour with the removal of the anxiety. It becomes a reflex response by means of classical conditioning. As the individual has learnt that it removes anxiety, they repeat the behaviour next time they feel anxious, by means of operant conditioning.

For example, someone may have forgotten to turn off an electrical appliance. Their anxiety would be diminished if they checked to see if it was turned off. To avoid feeling anxious in the future, they may repeatedly check to see that it has been switched off. When this checking behaviour becomes excessive, it has developed into a compulsion, and therefore may lead to the development of OCD. Support for the behavioural theory of OCD has been found in several studies. Baxter et al (1992) and Schwartz et al (1996) both reported success in the reduction of symptoms of those who underwent behavioural therapy.

However, there is also evidence against the theory. The behavioural explanation focuses on explaining the compulsive part of the disorder, ignoring the obsessions. It is reductionist, simplifying behaviour to a simplistic set of responses. The behavioural approach also doesn't explain why compulsions might start in the first place. There has also been much support for other theories used to explain OCD, particularly biological explanations. Family and twin studies have found some genetic links in developing OCD. However, since the results can't fully explain OCD, we might propose instead that a combination of both biological and psychological factors might best explain the cause and development of anxiety disorders such as OCD.

Exam Tip
This question is asking you to outline and evaluate. Those are two key words which should immediately make you want to write something that will first describe, and then weigh up positives and negatives.

Exam Tip
Don't worry if you can't remember the exact dates of the studies — just try to remember what they involved and what conclusions were drawn from them.

Summary Questions

Q1 a) Name three biological factors that have been used to explain obsessive-compulsive disorder (OCD).
b) Which neurotransmitter is considered to play a role in the biochemical explanation of OCD?

Q2 Which behaviour in children did Freud believe might later lead to obsessions and compulsions?

Q3 Give an example of a faulty cognition that someone with OCD might hold.

Unit 4: Section 9 Psychopathology 197

Worked Exam Questions

- These are the sorts of questions that could come up in the exams.
- There's an example answer, plus tips on answering the question (and other questions like it).
- Don't just learn these answers though — you'll need to tailor your exam answers to the specific questions asked in the exam.

Summary Questions

- There are a lot of facts to learn for A2 Psychology — these questions are here to test that you know it all.
- All the answers are in the back of the book.

Glossary

There's a glossary at the back of the book full of all the definitions you need to know for the exam, plus loads of other useful words.

Exam Help

There's a section at the back of the book stuffed full of things to help with your exams.

Section Summaries

You'll find a useful summary of the key facts at the end of each section.

Exam-style Questions

- Practising exam-style questions is really important — you'll find some at the end of each section.
- They're the same style as the ones you'll get in the real exams — you'll be used to shorter questions from AS, but A2 uses longer answer questions to give you the chance to apply your understanding and knowledge of psychology.
- In the back of the book you'll find loads of help with answering the questions. There are explanations of what you'll get marks for, and lots of hints and tips about what to include and how to structure your answers.

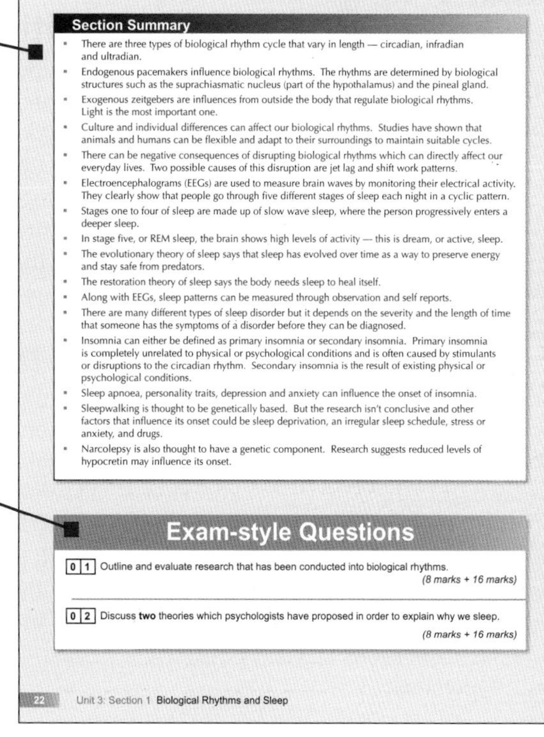

Section Summary

- There are three types of biological rhythm cycle that vary in length — circadian, infradian and ultradian.
- Endogenous pacemakers influence biological rhythms. The rhythms are determined by biological structures such as the suprachiasmatic nucleus (part of the hypothalamus) and the pineal gland.
- Exogenous zeitgebers are influences from outside the body that regulate biological rhythms. Light is the most important one.
- Culture and individual differences can affect our biological rhythms. Studies have shown that animals and humans can be flexible and adapt to their surroundings to maintain suitable cycles.
- There can be negative consequences of disrupting biological rhythms which can directly affect our everyday lives. Two possible causes of this disruption are jet lag and shift work patterns.
- Electroencephalograms (EEGs) are used to measure brain waves by monitoring their electrical activity. They clearly show that people go through five different stages of sleep each night in a cyclic pattern.
- Stages one to four of sleep are made up of slow wave sleep, where the person progressively enters a deeper sleep.
- In stage five, or REM sleep, the brain shows high levels of activity — this is dream, or active, sleep.
- The evolutionary theory of sleep says that sleep has evolved over time as a way to preserve energy and stay safe from predators.
- The restoration theory of sleep says the body needs sleep to heal itself.
- Along with EEGs, sleep patterns can be measured through observation and self reports.
- There are many different types of sleep disorder but it depends on the severity and the length of time that someone has the symptoms of a disorder before they can be diagnosed.
- Insomnia can either be defined as primary insomnia or secondary insomnia. Primary insomnia is completely unrelated to physical or psychological conditions and is often caused by stimulants or disruptions to the circadian rhythm. Secondary insomnia is the result of existing physical or psychological conditions.
- Sleep apnoea, personality traits, depression and anxiety can influence the onset of insomnia.
- Sleepwalking is thought to be genetically based. But the research isn't conclusive and other factors that influence its onset could be sleep deprivation, an irregular sleep schedule, stress or anxiety, and drugs.
- Narcolepsy is also thought to have a genetic component. Research suggests reduced levels of hypocretin may influence its onset.

Exam-style Questions

0 1 Outline and evaluate research that has been conducted into biological rhythms. *(8 marks + 16 marks)*

0 2 Discuss **two** theories which psychologists have proposed in order to explain why we sleep. *(8 marks + 16 marks)*

22 Unit 3: Section 1 Biological Rhythms and Sleep

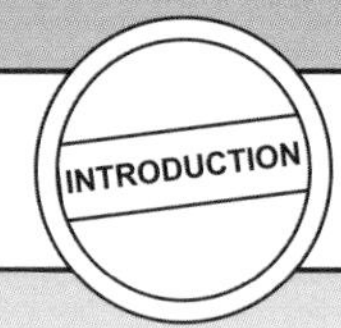

Introduction to A2 Psychology

A2 Psychology

So you've decided to study A2 Psychology. Good call. You might be wondering what exactly it's going to involve. The next few pages give you a bit of a taster of the stuff that you'll be studying...

Tip: You don't need to learn the stuff on these pages — it's just here as a good introduction to the things that you're going to be meeting during A2 Psychology.

A2 Psychology is made up of two units

A2 Psychology is made up of two units — imaginatively named Unit 3 and Unit 4.

Unit 3

Unit 3 contains eight topics — Biological Rhythms and Sleep, Perception, Gender, Relationships, Aggression, Eating Behaviour, Intelligence and Learning, and Cognition and Development. The good news is you only have to answer questions on three of these topics and you get to choose which ones you do.

Tip: There's load more information about the A2 exams in the 'Exam Help' section. Check out pages 296-301.

Unit 4

Unit 4 covers Psychopathology (where you'll have to choose one disorder to study out of three) and Psychology in Action (where you'll study one application of psychology from a choice of three). There's also a visit to the old favourite, Research Methods.

Tip: Psychology is a science, so researchers have to follow the scientific process when they're coming up with new theories. See pages 5-6 for more about the scientific process.

You learnt about the different approaches that are used to study psychology during AS level. You'll need these again for A2, so here's a quick recap:

The cognitive approach

Cognitive psychologists focus on internal processes to understand behaviour, such as how we perceive or remember things. They compare the human mind to a computer system, so they use computer models to try to understand human cognition (thinking). Using concepts from information processing, cognitive psychologists describe the brain as a processor — it receives input, processes it, and produces an output. Obviously it's ridiculously more complicated, but the general idea is the same. Cognitive psychology studies are often laboratory-based and artificial, so they can lack validity in the real world (ecological validity).

A big area of research in the cognitive approach is perception. Gregory (1966) proposed a theory which suggests that our brain tries to process information by treating the stimuli around us as hypotheses. Our brain tests these hypotheses within different contexts using our stored knowledge. However, other researchers disagree. Gibson (1979) suggested that stored knowledge is not required to make sense of a situation. Instead he argued that stimuli provide visual information which allows us to make sense of the world directly from what we see around us. You'll find out a lot more about perception in Unit 3: Section 2 (pages 23-37).

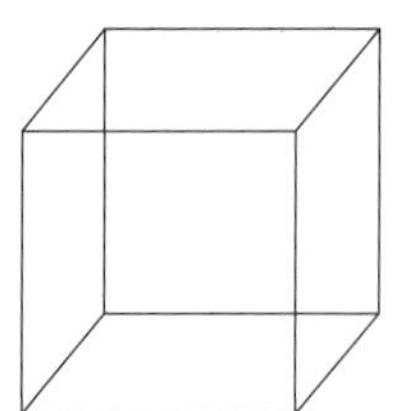

Figure 1: *A visual illusion called a Necker cube. As you look at it your perception of which face is the front face changes. According to Gregory (1966), this is your brain testing out different hypotheses.*

Developmental psychology

You covered developmental psychology at AS level and it's back again for A2. Bet you're pleased about that. Developmental psychology is a bit of a jumble of ideas from different approaches. It deals with how people develop and change over their lifetime. It also involves looking at how children are qualitatively different to adults in their understanding, abilities and feelings.

Researchers like Piaget and Samuel and Bryant looked at children's cognitive development. They studied the way children approach problems depending on their age and the stage of development they've reached. They found that the brain appears to have a timetable of what we can do and when we can do it — e.g. children don't start speaking or progress with potty training until they reach a certain stage of development.

A lot of this research has real world applications — for example, knowledge about children's cognitive development can be applied to education. The work of developmental psychologists has changed the way a lot of subjects are taught. For example, Bruner's spiral curriculum (see page 127) is commonly used across the educational system.

Unit 3 includes some developmental psychology — for example, you look at the development of moral understanding (knowing right from wrong) and social cognition (understanding self and others, and being able to see things from other people's perspective).

Tip: Developmental psychology involves conducting research on young children which can sometimes be a bit tricky. There are also ethical issues involved as children can't give informed consent — permission must be obtained from a parent. There's more about ethics on pages 260-262 in the research methods section.

Figure 2: *Conducting psychological research on children can be difficult.*

The biological approach

The biological approach explains behaviour as a product of nature. It involves three key assumptions:

- Human behaviour can be explained by looking at internal, biological stuff, like hormones and the nervous system.
- Experimental research that uses animals can be generalised to human behaviour.
- Abnormal behaviour can be removed using biological treatments — e.g. medication for mental illness such as schizophrenia.

So, as far as this approach is concerned, it's what's inside that counts... Researchers look at genetics, hormones, the brain and the nervous system to explain behaviour. It's very scientific — research is mostly carried out in laboratory experiments. Common research techniques include animal studies, brain scans and correlational studies.

For example, biological psychologists have tried to explain aggression. Research has suggested that an area of the brain called the amygdala plays an important role in aggressive behaviour. Animal studies have shown that electrical stimulation of different parts of the amygdala can either cause or reduce aggression, while a review study by Mpakopoulou et al (2008) showed that surgically disconnecting the amygdala from the rest of the brain can cause people to become less aggressive.

Other research has shown a link between aggressive behaviour and the hormone testosterone. Brook et al (2001) found a positive correlation between testosterone and aggression, while Tennes and Kreye (1985) showed that cortisol (a hormone believed to reduce the level of testosterone) was lower in aggressive children.

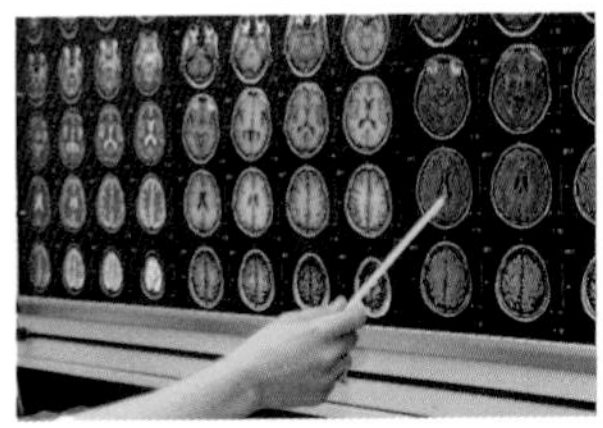

Figure 3: *Brain scanning allows psychologists to study the structure and functioning of the brain (see page 139).*

Tip: You can read more about explanations of aggression in Unit 3: Section 4 (starting on page 52).

Tip: Correlational studies identify relationships between variables (see page 255).

Individual differences

Individual differences is another one that's made up of bits from loads of approaches. The main thing that researchers want to find out is how and why we're all different from each other. You might think it's pretty obvious that we're all different, but psychologists have got to find something to fill the day.

In the individual differences approach, the theories of why we're all different come from various different approaches. For example, we might be depressed because of genetic factors (the biological approach), or it might be down to irrational or negative thoughts (the cognitive approach).

Tip: You can read more about depression and other psychological disorders in Unit 4: Section 9 — Psychopathology (pages 144-202).

Other areas of psychology tend to assume that people are broadly the same — e.g. developmental psychologists assume that we all go through the same basic stages of development. A big area of research in the individual differences approach is abnormality. Deviation from the norm is okay to a point, but societies have difficulties dealing with people who are considered to be very abnormal.

Because of this, an important issue to bear in mind is how normality is defined, and whether anyone has the right to decide that someone else is abnormal. Several different definitions have been suggested — abnormality can be seen as a deviation from social norms, it could be a failure to function adequately in day-to-day life, or it could be defined by using a tick-list of symptoms. To complicate matters, culture and time often affect the way that things are defined. To some cultures, or in certain times, someone's behaviour could seem perfectly normal — however, to other cultures, or in other times, the same behaviour could be deemed to be abnormal.

Tip: If you've covered something before at AS level, it doesn't hurt to go back and have a quick look to remind yourself what you learned. It might make new topics in this book easier to learn.

Social psychology

Last one, hurrah. Social psychology isn't new to you either — you covered it for AS. This approach is all about how we interact with each other and how we influence each other's thoughts, feelings and behaviour — either as individuals or as groups.

Major areas of research include conformity and obedience. Probably the most famous experiment in social psychology is Milgram's Behavioural Study of Obedience (1963). In the experiment he tested people's obedience by asking participants to give someone electric shocks if they made mistakes in a learning task. Most of his participants carried on giving the shocks, even when they thought they were causing harm. He concluded that most people will follow orders even if it means doing something they don't think is right. Pretty scary stuff. Other areas of research include persuasion, attitudes and relationships.

***Figure 4:** Parents can influence their child's gender identity with their own behaviour.*

Gender is a big area of research in social psychology. According to this approach we learn gender-typical behaviours by observing and copying the behaviour of people around us, or through operant conditioning. For example, if a child gets rewarded for a certain behaviour, e.g. by praise and attention, they are more likely to repeat that behaviour. In this way our parents and peers can influence the development of our gender identity.

Common research methods in social psychology include correlational studies, observational studies and experimental methods. If you don't remember what these are don't stress — there's a whole section on research methods starting on page 251.

1. The Scientific Process

Developing and testing scientific ideas is done in a certain way for all sciences. These pages will give you the low-down on everything you need to know.

What happens in the scientific process?

Science tries to explain how and why things happen — it answers questions. It's all about seeking and gaining knowledge about the world around us. Scientists do this by asking questions and suggesting answers and then testing them, to see if they're correct — this is the scientific process.

- Ask a question — make an observation and ask why or how it happens.
- Suggest an answer, or part of an answer, by forming a **theory** (a possible explanation of the observations).
- Make a prediction or **hypothesis** — a specific testable statement, based on the theory, about what will happen in a test situation.
- Carry out a test — to provide evidence that will support the prediction (or help to disprove it).

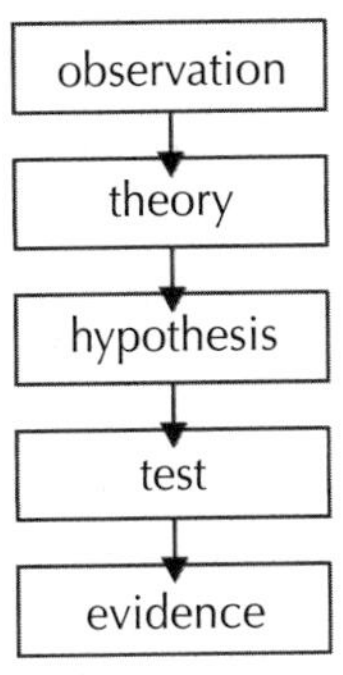

Figure 1: *The process of forming and testing a hypothesis.*

Example

- You might have seen someone give an obviously wrong answer to a task in front of a group of people, just because everyone else in that group has already given that answer. So, your question could be, "Why do people sometimes give obviously wrong answers when they're in a group of people?"
- You might form a theory that they do this to appear normal, and to avoid being excluded or rejected from the group.
- Your hypothesis might then be, "People carrying out an unambiguous task will give an incorrect answer to be consistent with the majority."
- To test this, you might put a participant in a group with some confederates (people who are 'in' on the experiment) who give a deliberately wrong answer to an easy task. You would then observe whether the participant also gives the wrong answer, or whether they resist the influences of conformity.

Tip: Most theories that you come across in books and journals has been through this process. Loads of evidence needs to be collected before a theory can be accepted.

Suggesting explanations is all very well and good, but if there's no way to test them then it just ain't science. A theory is only scientific if it can be tested.

Peer review

Peer review is a process used to ensure the integrity of published scientific work. Before publication, scientific work is sent to experts in that field (peers) so they can assess the quality of the work. This process helps to keep scientists honest — e.g. you can't 'sex-up' your conclusions if the data doesn't support it, because it won't pass peer review.

Tip: Peer review is an important part of the scientific process. It takes place in all areas of science, not just psychology.

Examples

These pieces of research wouldn't pass peer review:

- 80% of schizophrenia patients show a significant improvement in their symptoms after using a new treatment for schizophrenia, so the researchers conclude that it'll help everyone with schizophrenia. However — the researchers can't conclude this because they'd be ignoring the 20% of patients who didn't show an improvement.
- A researcher conducting a survey into whether local people are for or against a new housing development carries out his survey at a meeting held by people campaigning against new housing developments. However — his results will be biased, so he can't draw any reliable conclusions from his data.

Peer review helps to validate conclusions — it means published theories, data and conclusions are more trustworthy. But it can't guarantee that the conclusions are 100% right. More rounds of predicting and testing are needed before they can be taken as 'fact'.

Sometimes mistakes are made and bad science is published. Peer review isn't perfect but it's probably the best way for scientists to self-regulate their work and to ensure reliable scientific work is published.

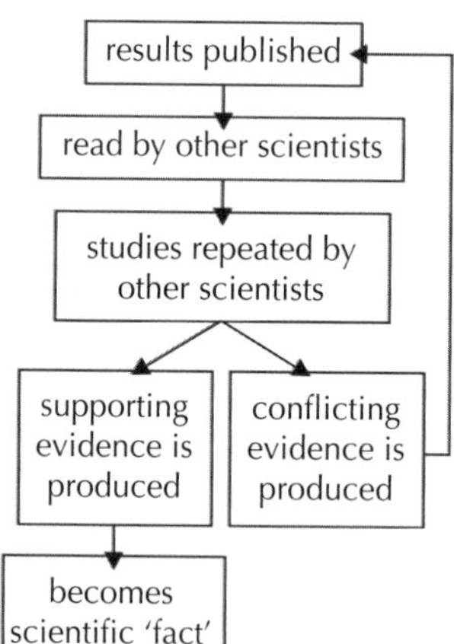

Figure 2: *The process of testing theories by collecting more evidence.*

Testing theories

Science is all about testing theories. It starts off with one experiment backing up a prediction and theory. It ends up with most scientists agreeing with it and you learning it. Stirring stuff. This is how the magical process takes place:

- The results are published — scientists need to let others know about their work, so they try to get their results published in **scientific journals**. These are just like normal magazines, only they contain scientific reports (called papers) instead of celebrity gossip. All work must undergo peer review before it's published.
- Other scientists read the published theories and results, and try to repeat them — this involves repeating the exact experiments, and using the theory to make new predictions that are tested by new experiments.
- If all the experiments in all the world provide evidence to back it up, the theory is thought of as scientific 'fact' (for now).
- If new evidence comes to light that conflicts with the current evidence the theory is questioned all over again. More rounds of testing will be carried out to see which evidence, and so which theory, prevails.

Figure 3: *Studies are replicated by other psychologists — if they come up with the same results, it provides more support for the conclusion.*

Accepting theories

If the evidence supports a theory, it's accepted — for now. Our currently accepted theories have survived this 'trial by evidence'. They've been tested over and over and over and each time the results have backed them up. BUT, and this is a big but, they never become totally undisputable fact. Scientific breakthroughs or advances could provide new ways to question and test a theory, which could lead to changes and challenges to it. Then the testing starts all over again...

And this, my friend, is the tentative nature of scientific knowledge — it's always changing and evolving.

Tip: The key thing to remember here is that just because theories are published in journals and books, they never become hard fact — there's always the chance that conflicting evidence could one day be found.

2. The Role of Science

Science isn't just done so that we know more and more stuff. We can use the knowledge we gain to improve our lives.

Making decisions

Lots of scientific work eventually leads to important discoveries that could benefit humankind. Oh yes. These results are used by society (that's you, me and everyone else) to make decisions about the way we live. All sections of society use scientific evidence to make decisions:

- Politicians use science to devise policy.

Example

Cognitive behavioural therapy is available on the NHS because there's evidence to show it can help people with depression.

- Private organisations use science to determine what to make or develop.

Example

Evidence has shown that the number of people being diagnosed with depression is increasing, so drugs companies might put more money into this area of research.

- Individuals also use science to make decisions about their own lives.

Example

Government guidelines were changed in 2010 to reduce the maximum recommended amount of salt people should eat per day. This was due to the results of a study showing that reducing salt could significantly reduce heart disease. However, even if evidence suggests that we should eat less salt, it's up to individuals to decide whether they take that advice or not.

Real World Connection

Psychologists don't just do research for the fun of it. For example, psychologists study mental disorders in order to try to discover the causes and also to develop effective treatments. Our knowledge of many disorders has been massively increased due to studies that have been carried out.

Influences on decision making

Making decisions in science isn't straightforward. Other factors can influence decisions about science or the way science is used.

Economic factors

Society has to consider the cost of implementing changes based on scientific conclusions.

Example

The NHS can't afford the most expensive drugs without sacrificing something else. Sometimes they decide to use a less expensive drug despite evidence showing there's a more effective one.

Scientific research is expensive so companies won't always be able to afford to develop new ideas.

Example

Developing new drugs is costly, so pharmaceutical companies often only invest in drugs that are likely to make money.

Figure 1: *Pharmaceutical companies will only mass produce drugs that are known to be effective and are likely to make money.*

Social factors

Decisions affect people's lives. How psychologists decide what's normal and what's abnormal affects how people are treated.

Tip: The DSM is the Diagnostic and Statistical Manual of Mental Disorders. It contains details of all known mental disorders and includes criteria that must be present for a person to be diagnosed. There have been many versions of the DSM — it's updated and republished to include newly discovered disorders and also to remove others which are no longer considered to be disorders.

Example

Homosexuality was defined as an abnormal behaviour until fairly recently — it was included in the DSM-II, but removed and replaced with 'sexual orientation disturbance' when the manual was revised for a later printing. This was again changed for the publication of the DSM-III — a new category called 'ego dystonic homosexuality' was included. However, in 1986, the diagnosis was finally completely removed and replaced with a broader category called 'sexual disorders not otherwise specified'. This category was more in line with what's currently classed as abnormal behaviour, as symptoms include a very distressed state caused by an unwanted sexual orientation.

Environmental factors

Some scientific research and breakthroughs might affect the environment. Not everyone thinks the benefits are worth the possible environmental damage.

Example

Scientists have only tested a very small percentage of tropical plants for medicinal purposes, but many of them are already used in drugs. For example, a muscle relaxant used in Parkinson's disease is derived from a plant called curare liana. Scientists believe unexplored regions of the world like remote parts of rainforests might contain many more untapped drug resources. But some people think we shouldn't exploit these regions because any interesting finds may lead to deforestation and reduced biodiversity in these areas.

Figure 2: A test tube containing the extract from a curare plant.

Being responsible

Science has to be responsible in many ways. Yes, you've guessed it — **ethics**. Scientists aren't allowed to test something just because they can. They have to think about the ethical considerations surrounding the experiment design and how the results could affect society.

Design

Experiments have to be carefully designed and run to avoid any ethical issues.

Examples

- Experiments involving animals are tightly controlled and monitored.
- Studies are checked to ensure they aren't placing individuals in unnecessary danger.
- If a study shows a drug has a highly beneficial effect, it's stopped and those in the placebo (negative) group are given the drug too.

Tip: There's more information about ethics in psychology on pages 260-262. The British Psychological Society have a very strict set of guidelines that all experiments and studies must stick to.

Results

Psychologists have to be careful how they use the results of their studies.

Example

Scientists' understanding of some genetic disorders (e.g. autism) could lead to tests to detect members of the population that carry the genes for them. But would people want to know?

Society does have a say in what experiments take place. Controversial experiments involving ethical issues have to be approved by scientific and ethics councils before they are allowed to be carried out.

Unit 3 Section 1: Biological Rhythms and Sleep

1. Biological Rhythm Cycles

Some people might claim to have no sense of rhythm. But in fact, everyone has biological rhythms which help with sleep patterns, eating behaviours and other important actions. Read on to find out more...

Learning Objectives:
- Know about circadian, infradian and ultradian rhythms, including the role of endogenous pacemakers and of exogenous zeitgebers in the control of circadian rhythms.
- Know about the disruption of biological rhythms, for example shift work and jet lag.

Different cycles
Biological rhythms can be classified according to how long their cycle lasts.

Circadian rhythms
These have cycles that generally occur once every 24 hours.

Examples
- We will usually go through the sleep-waking cycle once every day.
- Core body temperature tends to peak mid-afternoon and reach a low in the early hours of the morning, at around 4.00-4.30am.
- Heart rate dips during the night and peaks around mid-morning.

Infradian rhythms
These have cycles that occur less than once every day.

Example

The menstrual cycle occurs less than once every day. Sabbagh and Barnard (1984) found that when women live together their menstrual cycles may synchronise. It isn't clear why, but it may be linked to pheromones (chemicals that can affect the behaviour or physiology of others).

Figure 1: *Migration is another example of an infradian rhythm.*

Ultradian rhythms
Theses have cycles that occur more than once every 24 hours.

Examples
- Eating — usually every four hours.
- Smoking / drinking caffeine — for those who are addicted.
- Sleeping — the sleep cycle has several repeating stages of light and deep sleep (see page 13). Research using EEGs (electroencephalograms) to monitor brain activity during sleep has shown that a regular sleep pattern is really important. Disrupting these cycles can have very serious consequences.

Real World Connection
People who suffer from Seasonal Affective Disorder (SAD) have a lower mood in the winter months than during the summer. Researchers believe this is due to the reduced light levels in winter, suggesting that those with SAD are showing evidence of an infradian rhythm. See page 10 to read a study on SAD.

Tip: See pages 10-11 for more about the serious consequences of disrupting ultradian rhythms.

Biological rhythm regulation
Biological rhythms are regulated by internal and external influences.

The timing of biological rhythms is determined by factors both inside and outside our bodies.

Endogenous pacemakers
Some aspects of our biological rhythms are set by genetically determined biological structures and mechanisms within the body.

Tip: Lots of research is based on animal studies and so generalisation to humans can be an issue. Even though animals and humans have a similar brain structure, we are still very different.

Tip: A lesion is damage to an organ or other body part, and can be intentionally created.

Real World Connection
In support for both endogenous and exogenous factors, Terman (1988) conducted a study investigating SAD in American patients. He found that incidences of SAD were five times higher in a northern state compared with a southern state. He believed this was directly correlated to the reduced light levels up north during the winter months. But there are other factors which may have influenced his results, such as standard of living.

Figure 2: Innuit hunters spend half their year in total darkness and half in permanent daylight. But this doesn't affect sleeping habits.

The suprachiasmatic nucleus (SCN), part of the hypothalamus, seems to act as an internal clock to keep the body on an approximate 24-hour sleep-waking cycle. It is sensitive to light and regulates the pineal gland, which secretes melatonin — a hormone which seems to induce sleep. When there is less light, more melatonin is produced. When there is more light, secretion is reduced and waking occurs.

Examples

Stephan and Zucker (1972) conducted one of the first studies into circadian rhythms of rats after damage to the SCN. When the rats' SCNs were damaged they were less likely to have normal drinking and sleeping patterns than the control group.

Other research has been conducted since. Menaker et al (1978) lesioned this structure in hamsters — their sleep-waking cycle was disrupted.

Exogenous zeitgebers

These are influences outside of the body that act like a prompt, which may trigger a biological rhythm. Light is the most important zeitgeber.

Example

Siffre (1972) spent six months in a cave. He had no clocks and no natural light as zeitgebers. His sleep-waking cycle extended from a 24-hour to a 25-30 hour cycle. It therefore seems that natural light is needed to fine-tune our normal 24-hour cycle. However, Siffre's study, along with some other similar pieces of research, is based on a single participant, which means the results are hard to generalise.

Endogenous and exogenous factors

Endogenous and exogenous factors interact to regulate the timing of our biological rhythms. In some cases, endogenous factors may completely determine a cycle.

- Pengelly and Fisher (1957) found that squirrels will hibernate even when kept in laboratory conditions very different from their natural environment. However, many animals can react more flexibly, especially humans who are able to adapt to their surroundings. We can make ourselves stay awake and change the environment to suit our needs, e.g. by using artificial light.
- Cultural factors are also important. For example, Innuit hunters often live in permanent daylight or permanent night-time but can maintain regular daily sleep cycles — so the cycle can't just be determined by levels of light acting on the pineal gland.
- Individual differences can also affect the rhythms. Aschoff and Wever (1976) found that in a group of people isolated from daylight, some maintained their regular sleep-waking cycles. Other members of the group displayed their own very extreme idiosyncrasies, e.g. 29 hours awake followed by 21 hours asleep. This also shows that factors must interact to control or influence biological rhythms.

Disrupting biological rhythms

Disrupting biological rhythms can have negative consequences.

In the natural environment, zeitgebers normally change slowly, e.g. light levels during the year change gradually. However, in modern society, zeitgebers can change quickly. This can have negative effects on our ability to function — slowing reaction times, impairing problem-solving skills, and limiting our ability to concentrate.

Jet lag

Jet planes allow fast travel to different time zones. Leaving the UK at 9am means that you'd get to New York at about 4pm UK time. New York is 5 hours behind the UK, so the local time would be about 11am. Consequently you'll feel sleepy at an earlier (local) time. If you then went to sleep you would wake-up earlier and be out of sync with local timing. It appears easiest to adapt by forcing yourself to stay awake.

It can take about a week to fully synchronise to a new time zone. Wegman et al (1986) found that travelling east to west (phase delay) seems easier to adapt to than travelling west to east (phase advance). This is because phase delay is like going to bed later — phase advance is more difficult as it's like having to get up earlier.

Example

Schwartz et al (1995) found that baseball teams from the east coast of the USA got better results travelling to play in the west than teams based in the west did when travelling to play in the east.

Real World Connection
Melatonin has been studied to see if it's a good treatment for jet lag. In a review, Arendt and Deacon (1997) reported that 50% of participants who took 5mg of fast-acting melatonin didn't experience jet lag after travelling. Take a look back at page 10 to remind yourself about the role of melatonin on biological rhythms.

Shift work

Modern work patterns mean some people work shifts throughout the 24-hour period, disrupting their sleep cycle.

Key study of shift work — Czeisler et al (1982)

Method: Czeisler et al (1982) studied workers at a factory whose shift patterns appeared to cause sleep and health problems. The researchers recommended 21-day shifts (allowing more time for workers to adapt), and changing shifts forward in time (phase delay). The employees had previously worked a backwards rotation — working during the nights for the first week, late afternoons in the second week and only mornings during the third week (phase advance).
They would then restart the pattern again in the fourth week.

Results: After implementing the changes, productivity and job satisfaction increased.

Additional study of shift patterns — Gordon et al (1986)

Gordon et al (1986) investigated the working habits of police officers in Philadelphia. He found that after changing their shift patterns to a phase delay cycle from a phase advance cycle, they were much more productive, less likely to fall asleep while at work and reported fewer accidents.

Tip: Sometimes the effects of jet lag or shift work can be so bad that they get classified as sleep disorders. There's more on pages 18-20 about other disorders of sleep.

Real World Connection
Lots of people have jobs that involve shift work and this can have many implications on their lives. Moore-Ede (1993) estimated that, within the USA alone, over $77 billion is spent on health care due to accidents from shift workers. Lorries also have the highest accident rates between 1am and 7am when our bodies are naturally telling us to sleep.

Research on biological rhythms

Research on biological rhythms has limitations.

Findings from animal studies can't accurately be generalised to humans — humans have greater adaptability. Studies that have deprived humans of natural light have still allowed artificial light, which may give many of the benefits of natural light — this reduces the validity of these studies.

Tip: Individual differences always crop up in psychology — studying something as complicated as the mind makes it hard to generalise any study.

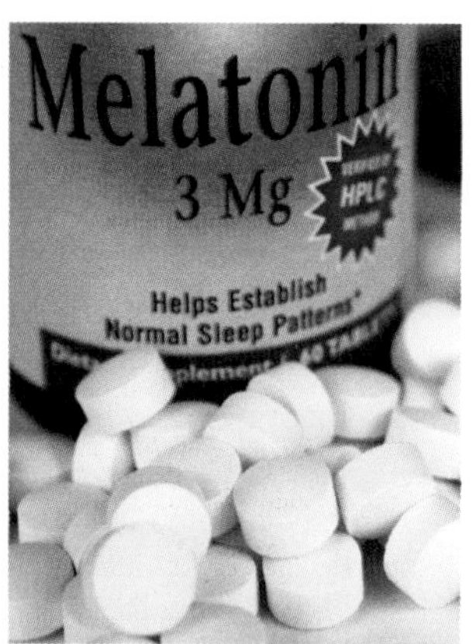

Figure 3: *Drugs such as melatonin are sometimes used to help sleep deprivation.*

Things like individual differences need further study. Some people are more alert early in the day, and others later on, and the speed with which we adapt to disruptions can vary. It's difficult to determine whether a person's lifestyle is a cause or effect of their biological rhythms.

If we fully understand what causes the problems linked to jet lag and shift work, we can minimise or avoid them, reducing accidents in work environments. However, there are different ways to deal with these problems, e.g. taking time to naturally adjust, or using drugs to reduce the effects of sleep deprivation.

Worked Exam-style Question

0 1 Using examples, identify the differences between circadian, infradian and ultradian rhythms. *(8 marks)*

Biological rhythms can be split into three different categories, depending on how long they last. They can vary from once every 24 hours, to less than once every day, to more than once every day and they can be used to categorise a lot of our everyday behaviours.

A circadian rhythm is a cycle that happens every 24 hours. Circadian rhythms can apply to systems that we might not even be aware of consciously, such as breathing, heart rate, metabolism and temperature. In regards to core body temperature, it is usually highest in the mid-afternoon and lowest at around 4.00-4.30am. One of the most obvious cycles that has a circadian rhythm is the sleep-wake cycle which we usually go through once a day.

Infradian rhythms occur a lot less frequently than circadian rhythms over a fixed period of time. One example is the female menstrual cycle, which is cyclic over one month. Another example is Seasonal Affective Disorder (SAD), where sufferers experience mild depression during the winter and then are free from symptoms in the summer. This is thought to be due to changes in the amount of light they are receiving naturally throughout the year.

Finally, ultradian rhythm cycles happen the most frequently — occurring more than once each day. For example, we tend to eat approximately every four hours. Likewise, the different stages of sleep can be considered to have ultradian rhythms as we cycle through them several times during a night's sleep.

Exam Tip
For this question, you're just recalling facts and examples. You should aim to answer questions like this fairly quickly, giving you time for the more tricky 'evaluate' and 'discuss' questions which require a bit more thinking about.

Exam Tip
Using real life examples is testing your ability to apply psychology to the wider world.

Summary Questions

Q1 Give an example of an infradian rhythm.

Q2 Give an example of an exogenous zeitgeber.

Q3 Describe how endogenous and exogenous factors influence sleep.

Q4 Declan has to travel all over the world for work.

a) Why might he experience jet lag on his journey from London, England to Atlanta, USA?

b) Should he go to bed early or stay up late to help him cope with the effects of the jet lag?

Q5 Give one problem with using animal studies within biological rhythm research.

2. Sleep States

There are several theories about the purpose of sleep and its different stages.

Learning Objectives:

- Understand the nature of sleep including stages of sleep and lifespan changes in sleep.
- Know about the functions of sleep, including evolutionary and restoration explanations.

Brain activity

Sleep can be split into stages of different brain activity. Electroencephalograms (EEGs) measure electrical activity in the brain, and are used to record the stages of sleep.

Adults pass through the stages about five times a night, with each cycle lasting about 90 minutes. Who'd have thought we were so busy... As you fall into deeper sleep, brain activity becomes higher voltage and lower frequency. After stage 4 the cycle reverses back through stages 3 and 2. A period of active sleep occurs instead of stage 1.

During the active stage, metabolic activity increases, and the body appears almost paralysed except for rapid eye movement (REM). The EEG pattern is almost like when you're awake. The cycle is repeated about five times during the night, but we only enter stages 3 and 4 in the first two. Periods of REM increase with each cycle. These are the stages of sleep:

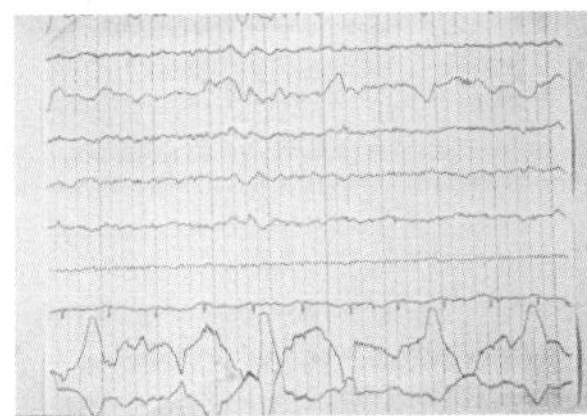

Figure 1: *An EEG print-out can show the brainwaves of a sleeping person.*

	Stage of sleep	Characteristics	EEG wave pattern
Slow wave sleep (SWS)	Stage 1	A bit like deep relaxation, with lowered heart rate, muscle tension and temperature. It's quite easy to wake people up.	
	Stage 2	Has slower and larger EEG waves, with some quick bursts of high frequency waves called sleep spindles.	
	Stage 3	Has even larger, slower waves. Heart rate continues to fall, as does body temperature.	
	Stage 4	Has the largest, slowest waves of all, because it's the deepest stage of sleep. Metabolic activity is pretty low in general, and the sleeper is very hard to wake.	
Active sleep	REM sleep	The most active part of sleep but muscles are often paralysed. There's vivid dreaming and eye movements in this stage.	

Tip: Stages 1-4 are known as non-REM sleep (NREM). They are all slow wave sleep (SWS) states.

Theories of sleep

Evolutionary approaches

These relate to the environment, evolution and survival of the fittest.

Examples

- Webb (1968) suggested that everyday sleep is similar to hibernation — sleep conserves energy at times when it's harder to get resources (i.e. at night time). Using energy would be inefficient.
- Berger and Phillips (1995) showed that when food was hard to find and the temperature was lower, animals tended to sleep more. They believed this was an effective way of saving precious energy sources.
- Meddis (1977) suggested that sleep helps keep animals safe. By being quiet and still, they are less likely to attract predators (especially at night). However, sleep also makes animals vulnerable to predators if discovered.

Not sleeping at all would be very advantageous, but as it seems to occur in all animals, it must have an important function — although how much sleep animals have varies. Animals that graze often and must avoid predators sleep less, while predators, that don't eat as frequently and aren't hunted, sleep more.

The evolutionary approach, focusing on survival and environmental adaptation, is useful for understanding how and why behaviours occur. Behaviours have evolved to help survival and adapt us to our environment.

Evolution occurs over long periods so it's hard to test theories about why some behaviours have been naturally selected. So, it's difficult to prove them wrong, making them less useful from a scientific perspective.

Tip: The evolutionary approach doesn't explain why animals sleep, just when they sleep. For instance, many animals are nocturnal (they sleep during the day) in order to avoid being eaten at night when their predators are hunting.

Figure 2: *Evolution may explain why some animals hibernate.*

Tip: One problem with the evolutionary approach is that it can be contradictory. It provides explanations for why animals might sleep for both longer and shorter periods of time. Animals might sleep longer to stay still and out of trouble, but they could also avoid danger by sleeping less and staying more alert.

Restoration approaches

These suggest that sleep restores the body's ability to function, after being busy during the day. Oswald (1980) suggested that SWS/non-REM sleep is for restoring bodily functions linked to physical activity, and REM sleep is for restoring brain functions.

Horne (1988) distinguished between two types of sleep: core sleep, which is made up of stage 4 SWS (for body restoration) and REM sleep (for brain restoration), and optional sleep, which is made up of the other sleep stages. Although optional sleep is not necessary, having it can help to conserve energy.

Key study of restoration approaches — Horne and Pettitt (1985)

Method: Horne and Pettitt (1985) investigated restoration by stopping the body from recovering using sleep deprivation. The researchers split the participants into three different groups. They tested whether or not sleep deprivation would affect performance on an auditory task.
Group 1 were sleep-deprived for 72 hours and not given a reward incentive for finishing the challenge. Group 2 were sleep-deprived but were given a reward if they finished. Group 3 were not sleep-deprived nor given a reward.

Results: Those in Group 2 (who all had rewards) and Group 3 performed equally well on the auditory task. Those in Group 1 performed much worse.

Conclusion:	Rewards can overcome sleep deprivation.
Evaluation:	There were only five participants in each group. As the sample size was so small it is hard to generalise the results to a wider population.

It seems that important brain and body restoration occurs during sleep. Babies, whose brains are developing, spend more time in REM sleep and release more growth hormone during SWS. Shapiro et al (1981) found that long-distance runners had more SWS after a race, implying that the exercise increased the need for bodily restoration.

However, Horne and Minard's (1985) study found that when participants did physical and cognitive activity they fell asleep more quickly, but did not sleep for longer. It may be that there was a reduction in the amount of optional sleep that they had.

Tip: Research has also provided evidence that goes against the restoration process. Ryback and Lewis (1971) monitored healthy students who spent six weeks just lying in bed. While the theory says that they shouldn't have needed as much sleep, the results showed the participants didn't change their sleep patterns at all.

Techniques used in sleep research

The following equipment and techniques are often used in sleep laboratories:

- Equipment such as EEGs measure electrical activity in the brain and provide quantitative reports which can easily be compared to others. They have high reliability and changes in sleep stages can be easily identified.
- Other equipment used includes EOGs (electrooculograms) which measure the electrical activity of the eyes, and EMGs (electromyograms) which measure the electrical activity in muscles.
- Self reports involve participants keeping a record of their dreams or estimating their length. They're useful for gaining information which couldn't be collected in any other way, but they're limited by the accuracy of recall.
- Observations of patterns and directions of eye movements can be recorded and related to sleep stages. Variables, such as noise and distraction, are controlled to increase the reliability of the research. However, research in sleep laboratories creates an artificial environment, which may affect the participants' sleep patterns and so reduce validity.

Figure 3: *EEGs are a useful way to measure brain activity during sleep.*

Sleeping patterns

The amount we sleep and our patterns of sleep change as we get older. The older we get the less we tend to sleep — babies sleep up to 20 hours a day, whilst most adults average 7-8 hours and people over 50 average only 6 hours.

Key study of sleeping patterns — Ohayon et al (2004)

Method:	Ohayon et al (2004) collected the results of lots of different studies into the sleeping patterns of people aged from 5-102.
Results:	They found that as people got older, sleep in stages 1 and 2 increased, but the deeper sleep in stages 3 and 4 decreased.
Conclusion:	Sleep patterns do change with age.

Tip: Older people are often more prone to sleep disorders. Take a look at pages 18-20 to find out more.

Tip: These types of laboratory experiments, although useful, often lack ecological validity. Take a look at page 257 to read more about ecological validity.

Key study of sleeping patterns — Kleitman (1963)

Kleitman was a key contributor in investigating and categorising the different stages of sleep. He found that newborn babies may spend 8-9 hours every day in REM sleep. Children have less REM sleep than infants, and adults have less than children. Kleitman concluded that as we get older we tend to have less REM sleep.

Tip: There's more on sleep disorders coming up on pages 18-20.

Key study of sleeping patterns — Kales and Kales (1974)

Kales and Kales conducted a comprehensive review of various laboratory experiments, observations and psychological evaluations into sleep and sleep disorders. Sleepwalking was shown to be more common in men than in women and also seemed to run in families. Kales and Kales also found that elderly people are more likely to wake up several times during their night's sleep than younger people.

Evaluation of research into sleep patterns

Most evidence for changes in sleep patterns comes from laboratory research using EEG recordings. These recordings are obtained by attaching electrodes to participants. This creates an unfamiliar sleeping environment for the participants, which may disrupt their usual sleep patterns.

However, Empson (1989) suggests that after the first night participants adjust to the conditions and their sleep is representative of their usual patterns.

More research is needed to find out the reasons for lifespan changes in sleep. For example, REM sleep in childhood may be linked to brain development.

Worked Exam-style Questions

Exam Tip
Questions for Unit 3 are worth 24 marks each — so this shorter one would be part of a larger question in the real exam.

0 1 Outline and evaluate the evolutionary approach to sleep.
(6 marks)

The evolutionary approach to sleep looks at the environment, evolution and survival of the fittest to try to explain the reasons why people and animals sleep. One theory suggests that sleep is useful to conserve energy. Webb (1968) likened everyday sleep to hibernation. He said that when it is harder to get certain resources, such as food, it makes sense to save up energy and then use it at a time when it is most needed. Meddis (1977) said that the purpose of sleep is to provide safety. When animals stay asleep, they are less likely to be vulnerable to dangers of the outside world, for example predators.

Exam Tip
One really good way of evaluating an approach is by showing that there are conflicting findings. A lot of psychological research provides contradictory results which can lead to debate within the subject.

However, there is also evidence that contradicts the finding that suggests animals sleep to 'keep safe'. For instance, creatures that graze a lot tend to be prey species, so they have to find ways to avoid their predators. One way of avoiding them is by sleeping less than their predators who eat a lot less often.

The conflicting research shows that we still have a lot to learn about the role of sleep. Whilst the evolutionary approach is useful for trying to understand why and how behaviour occurs, it is hard to scientifically test the theory. Also, as some sleep research has been carried out on animals, it is difficult to generalise the results to humans.

As an alternative explanation, the restoration approach also explains the role of sleep. It suggests that the purpose of sleep is to allow the body to recover and restore some of its energy that it lost during the day. This explanation may answer some of the problems of the evolutionary approach, for example, the fact that it doesn't explain why people sleep.

---

0 2 Outline the four different stages of non-REM sleep. *(6 marks)*

Adults normally go through the four stages of non-REM sleep five times a night. The stages are marked by different brain wave patterns and can be measured through an EEG.

Stage one is characterised by a low heart rate which allows temperature to drop. It is a bit like deep relaxation and people can easily be awoken from this stage. Next is stage two, where people drift into a slightly deeper sleep. There are slower brain waves in this stage but sometimes there are high frequency bursts of energy known as sleep spindles. Stage three is a deeper sleep again, with brain waves continually slowing down. Stage four is the deepest stage of sleep. It has very large, slow waves and everything in the body has slowed down. Metabolic activity is very low and the sleeper is often hard to wake during this stage.

Exam Tip
This question is only worth six marks, so don't spend too long describing each of the stages in loads of detail.

Exam Tip
The question only asks for non-REM sleep, so there's no point writing about REM sleep in your answer.

---

0 3 Describe a study investigating the restoration approach to sleep. *(4 marks)*

Horne and Pettitt (1985) investigated the restoration theory of sleep by depriving three different groups of sleep to see if this impaired their ability to complete an auditory task. Group 1 were sleep deprived for 72 hours and not given a reward for completing the task. Group 2 were given a reward if they completed the task after being sleep deprived for 72 hours. Group 3 were not sleep deprived but were also not given a reward.

The results showed that those who had rewards, despite being sleep deprived, did equally as well as those who had experienced no sleep deprivation. These findings illustrate that perhaps sleep deprivation and the need for restoration can be overridden by the prospect of a reward.

Exam Tip
Remember that psychology studies set out to find evidence to support a researcher's theory. As we can never be 100% sure about anything in science, we can talk about studies that disprove a theory and ones that provide support for it.

Summary Questions

Q1 What is REM sleep?

Q2 What is the difference between core and optional sleep?

Q3 Name three techniques used in sleep research.

Q4 Amy's EEG shows waves that are fairly steady except several large sleep spindle spikes. What stage of sleep is she likely to be in?

Q5 Evaluate the restoration theory of sleep.

3. Disorders of Sleep

Learning Objective:

- Understand the explanations for sleep disorders, including insomnia, sleepwalking and narcolepsy.

Everyone, at some point, is likely to have a bad night's sleep. But when people regularly experience problems with their sleep, they may have a sleep disorder.

Insomnia

People with **insomnia** have difficulty falling asleep, difficulty staying asleep, or both. They may feel sleepy and irritable during the day, with impaired concentration — this can affect their daily life and their relationships. Insomnia may be acute, lasting a few nights, or chronic, lasting for weeks, months or years. Research has suggested that about 10% of adults may suffer from chronic insomnia.

Tip: Some people feel the need to complete certain rituals before they go to sleep. This can vary amongst individuals but may include acts such as ensuring all the lights are switched off, getting your clothes ready for the morning or even just reading before turning off the light. If any of these routines are disrupted, it can often lead to temporary insomnia.

Influences on insomnia

An episode of insomnia can be influenced by many factors. For example:

Sleep apnoea

This is a condition where a person's airways become temporarily blocked whilst they are sleeping, causing their breathing to be interrupted. This disrupts their sleep pattern — either causing a person to wake up or to move into a lighter stage of sleep. **Sleep apnoea** is linked to snoring and may be caused by various abnormalities in brain or respiratory functioning. It's also linked to obesity — especially in males.

Personality traits

Characteristics like being overly sensitive, worrying, having a very serious attitude to life issues and being overly dependent on other people can lead to insomnia.

Figure 1: *Shift workers, such as miners, often have insomnia because of their irregular work hours.*

Depression and anxiety

These increase emotional arousal — which may then increase physiological arousal, causing insomnia.

Types of insomnia

Primary insomnia

Primary insomnia is insomnia that isn't linked to any existing physical or psychological conditions. Instead, it may be caused by:

- Stimulants. Stimulants such as caffeine or nicotine increase arousal and can lead to insomnia. This can also lead to a vicious circle of frustration and anxiety.
- Disruptions to circadian rhythm. Jet lag, shift work and sleeping at irregular times (e.g. staying-up late at weekends) may all disrupt sleep patterns and lead to insomnia.

Example

Tom sleeps really irregular hours, going to bed really late and sleeping in during the day. This has caused him to have primary insomnia.

Tip: One way of tackling both primary and secondary insomnia is through **sleep hygiene**. This doesn't mean making sure you're clean before bed — it means all the things people can do to help them sleep, such as creating a peaceful environment, eliminating any stress and avoiding caffeine at night.

Secondary insomnia

Secondary insomnia is the result of existing physical or psychological conditions. For example:

- Physical complaints. A number of physical complaints such as arthritis, diabetes and asthma can cause insomnia.

- Psychological conditions. A number of psychological conditions can cause insomnia. For example, depression, post-traumatic stress disorder and generalised anxiety disorder can all cause insomnia through secondary side effects.
- Stress or anxiety. Worrying about something causes anxiety (higher bodily arousal), which may in turn cause insomnia. Failure to get to sleep can cause frustration, which creates more anxiety, making it even harder to get to sleep and producing a vicious circle.
- Medication. Some medications may have side effects which disrupt sleep. Also, medications taken to improve sleep may cause problems if their effects are too long-lasting (leaving the person sleepy the next day), or if their effects wear off too early. Some people may become dependent on sleeping pills and suffer even worse insomnia if they stop taking them.

Example

Liz is suffering from post-traumatic stress disorder after being involved in a car crash. She has trouble sleeping, which is diagnosed as secondary insomnia.

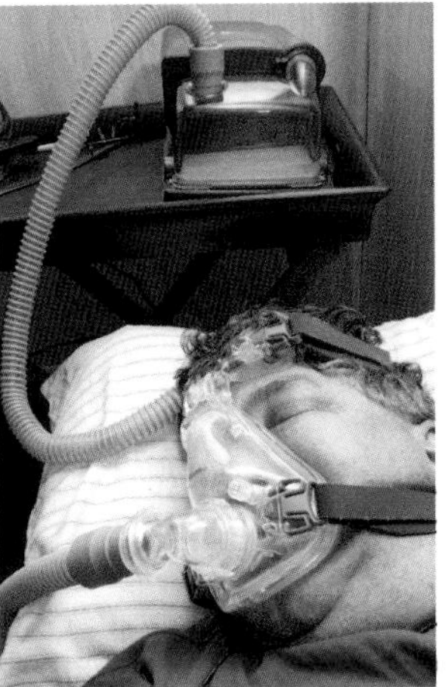

Figure 2: *Sleep apnoea in obese people is treated using special masks to unblock airways.*

Tip: Sleepwalking is also called somnambulism.

Problems with research

Research into insomnia is difficult as there are many variables that can cause or influence the condition. This problem is compounded by the fact that some of the variables are hard to control. Much of the research that's been done has produced correlational evidence rather than showing cause and effect.

Sleepwalking

Sleepwalking is a disorder associated with stage 3 and stage 4 sleep. It affects approximately 15% of children and 2% of adults. The causes of sleepwalking are not fully known but it's thought it can be triggered by **sleep deprivation** (especially in people with a history of sleepwalking), an irregular sleep schedule, stress or anxiety or some drugs, e.g. anti-psychotics or stimulants.

Real World Connection

Jules Lowe was a 32 year old man from Manchester who was tried for murder in 2003. He claimed he could not recall committing the crime and must have been sleepwalking. Despite being found 'not guilty' of murder he has been indefinitely secured in a psychiatric hospital.

Key study of sleepwalking — Dauvilliers et al (2005)

Method: Dauvilliers et al asked 256 people who had been diagnosed with a sleep disorder to detail their family history of sleep disorders, as well as a summary of their sleeping habits. They compared these results to a control group, who were acting as a baseline measurement.

Results: Dauvilliers et al's study suggests there may be a genetic component to sleepwalking — they found higher concordance rates for the disorder in identical twins than in non-identical twins.

Conclusion: Sleepwalking has a genetic link.

Tip: Sleepwalking is often more common in children. However, this could be because children spend longer in stages 3 and 4 of sleep — when the behaviour is more likely to occur.

Additional study of sleepwalking — Hublin et al (1997)

Hublin et al had also conducted a study by looking at the concordance rates of sleepwalking in identical twins. They found the rates to be approximately 66% for boys and 57% for girls, which confirms that there is certainly some genetic component. However, as the rates are not 100% there must also be other factors which influence sleepwalking.

Tip: See page 144 for more about concordance rates.

Tip: Narcolepsy a neurological disorder. It is not a psychological condition.

Tip: Usually the hypothalamus stops making hypocretin at night, which could explain why we fall asleep.

Narcolepsy

Narcolepsy is a disorder causing sudden episodes of day-time sleepiness, leading to a person falling asleep for a short period of time (seconds or minutes). They may also experience features of sleep such as weak muscles (cataplexy) and dream-like imagery. Narcolepsy affects 0.02-0.06% of the population, most of whom develop the condition in early adulthood. The causes of narcolepsy may include:

Reduced levels of hypocretin

Hypocretin is a chemical made in the hypothalamus that's involved in regulating arousal levels. It's thought narcolepsy may be caused by the body's immune system attacking the cells that produce hypocretin, reducing the body's ability to regulate sleep.

Key study of hypocretin — Thannickal et al (2000)

Thannickal et al examined the brains of four narcoleptic patients who had died 4-12 years earlier. They found that there were between 85-95% less hypocretin neurones in these brains in comparison to 12 brains of people who had not suffered from narcolepsy.

Exam Tip
Concordance rates give us a great insight into whether a psychological issue can be explained by nature or nurture.

Genetics

Studies have shown a 25-31% concordance rate for the condition between identical twins — this suggests a genetic link. This concordance rate is fairly low, so environmental influences must also be important. It could be that a virus, e.g. that causes measles, may trigger a genetic predisposition to narcolepsy. So a person would need the genetic predisposition for narcolepsy as well as contact with the virus before developing the condition — meaning the cause would be both genetic and environmental.

Exam Tip
You can choose any two sleep disorders for this question, and there are certainly lots to choose from. To prepare for the exam, make sure you are comfortable writing about all of them.

Exam Tip
When you're asked to outline a disorder, it's a good idea to talk about its symptoms, its prevalence and how it's thought to be caused.

Worked Exam-style Questions

0 1 Outline **two** different sleep disorders.

(8 marks)

Two sleep disorders that can directly impact on the lives of many people are sleepwalking and narcolepsy. Sleepwalking is a sleep disorder which occurs in stages 3 and 4 of sleep. It can happen as a result of sleep deprivation, an irregular sleep schedule, stress or anxiety, or even drugs. It has been reported to occur more often in males than females, and more in children than in adults. Dauvilliers et al (2005) proposed a strong genetic link to the disorder in their investigation into the family histories of 256 people with sleep disorders.

Narcolepsy is a sleep disorder where sufferers fall asleep during the day, for a short period of time. Sufferers might also find they have weak muscles and experience dream-like imagery. Narcolepsy affects less than 1% of the population, and the condition usually develops in early adulthood. Hypocretin is believed to be involved in the disorder. This chemical is made by the hypothalamus and is involved in regulating arousal levels. The hypothalamus stops making hypocretin at night, which is why people sleep during those hours. In narcolepsy, it's thought that the body's immune system might attack the cells that produce hypocretin, reducing the ability to regulate sleep.

0 2 Alice is a junior doctor and has just finished a series of night shifts. She is now having trouble sleeping. Suggest how her work schedule could have led to insomnia and describe other factors which may have also contributed to her sleep disorder.

(8 marks)

As Alice has been doing night shifts, she will have disrupted her natural sleep-wake cycle which can lead to primary insomnia. She will be sleeping irregular hours, sleeping during the day and working at night which means her circadian rhythms will have been disrupted. As a result, she could be left feeling sleepy, irritable and with impaired concentration.

If she is particularly sensitive, or a worrier, this might also contribute to her insomnia. Those who experience increased emotional arousal through depression or anxiety are more likely to suffer from insomnia as it can also increase physiological arousal.

There are several other factors which could also lead to insomnia. For example, sleep apnoea is a condition where a person's airways become temporarily blocked whilst they are sleeping, interrupting their breathing and sleep pattern. Although it is more common in males, and more frequent in those who are obese, if Alice suffers from this it may be contributing to her insomnia.

A final factor that might be influencing Alice's insomnia is the use of stimulants. Stimulants, such as caffeine or nicotine, increase arousal and can lead to anxiety. If Alice smokes or drinks coffee, this may be leading to her insomnia.

Overall, there are several factors which can lead to insomnia, and it might not just be her work shifts that have led to Alice's disorder.

Exam Tip

Although the question doesn't tell you much about Alice or her work, you can make other suggestions about her lifestyle as long as you justify them in your answer.

Summary Questions

Q1 a) What is the difference between primary and secondary insomnia?

b) Give one reason for why someone might have primary insomnia.

c) Give one reason for why someone might have secondary insomnia.

Q2 Ralph has just been prescribed some medication to alleviate his hayfever. It has left him often awake through the night and irritable during the day. What type of sleep disorder might he have?

Q3 Why is research into insomnia sometimes difficult?

Q4 a) Give one symptom of narcolepsy.

b) It's been found that narcolepsy has a concordance rate of between 25-31%. What does this mean in terms of explaining the causes of this sleep disorder?

Section Summary

- There are three types of biological rhythm cycle that vary in length — circadian, infradian and ultradian.
- Endogenous pacemakers influence biological rhythms. The rhythms are determined by biological structures such as the suprachiasmatic nucleus (part of the hypothalamus) and the pineal gland.
- Exogenous zeitgebers are influences from outside the body that regulate biological rhythms. Light is the most important one.
- Culture and individual differences can affect our biological rhythms. Studies have shown that animals and humans can be flexible and adapt to their surroundings to maintain suitable cycles.
- There can be negative consequences of disrupting biological rhythms which can directly affect our everyday lives. Two possible causes of this disruption are jet lag and shift work patterns.
- Electroencephalograms (EEGs) are used to measure brain waves by monitoring their electrical activity. They clearly show that people go through five different stages of sleep each night in a cyclic pattern.
- Stages one to four of sleep are made up of slow wave sleep, where the person progressively enters a deeper sleep.
- In stage five, or REM sleep, the brain shows high levels of activity — this is dream, or active, sleep.
- The evolutionary theory of sleep says that sleep has evolved over time as a way to preserve energy and stay safe from predators.
- The restoration theory of sleep says the body needs sleep to heal itself.
- Along with EEGs, sleep patterns can be measured through observation and self reports.
- There are many different types of sleep disorder but it depends on the severity and the length of time that someone has the symptoms of a disorder before they can be diagnosed.
- Insomnia can either be defined as primary insomnia or secondary insomnia. Primary insomnia is completely unrelated to physical or psychological conditions and is often caused by stimulants or disruptions to the circadian rhythm. Secondary insomnia is the result of existing physical or psychological conditions.
- Sleep apnoea, personality traits, depression and anxiety can influence the onset of insomnia.
- Sleepwalking is thought to be genetically based. But the research isn't conclusive and other factors that influence its onset could be sleep deprivation, an irregular sleep schedule, stress or anxiety, and drugs.
- Narcolepsy is also thought to have a genetic component. Research suggests reduced levels of hypocretin may influence its onset.

Exam-style Questions

0 1 Outline and evaluate research that has been conducted into biological rhythms.

(8 marks + 16 marks)

---

0 2 Discuss **two** theories which psychologists have proposed in order to explain why we sleep.

(8 marks + 16 marks)

Unit 3 Section 2: Perception

1. Theories of Perception

Perception is our way of sensing and understanding everything around us. Several theories try to explain how perception lets us process what we experience in our surroundings.

Learning Objective:

- Know the theories of perceptual organisation, including Gibson's bottom up/direct theory of perception and Gregory's top down/indirect theory of perception.

Giving meaning to stimuli

- Our senses are constantly detecting stimuli in the environment around us.
- The information the stimuli provide has to be processed in order to make sense of it. This processing is known as perception.
- Theories of how the information is understood are known as theories of perception. You need to know about two of them — Gibson's direct theory and Gregory's indirect theory.

Gibson's direct theory

Gibson's (1979) direct theory of perception takes a bottom up approach. 'Bottom up' means information is put together to make sense of it. We take in information, piece by piece, and process it in such a way that we can understand it.

Gibson's theory of perception suggests that stimuli provide visual information which allow people to make sense of the world directly from what they see. Previously stored knowledge isn't needed — the information provided by the stimuli is enough. Gibson argues that this is possible because of the large amount of information provided by the optic array.

The optic array

The optic array is the pattern of light that enters the eye, allowing things to be seen. It's a really complicated pattern — it's made up of all the light rays reflecting off all the objects and surfaces in view, so it holds lots of information. To make things even more complex, it changes each time you move. The optic array gives rise to texture gradients, horizon ratios and optic flow patterns. These are all involved in perception.

Tip: Texture gradients make objects that are close to us appear more detailed than objects that are further away (Figure 1). Objects further away appear smoother.

Figure 1: *The texture of a field or meadow appears to be smoother further away.*

Texture gradients

Objects that are far away take up less of the optic array and are closer together than objects that are near. This is known as the texture gradient. It provides information on the depth and distance of objects.

Example

When we look at something like grass, we can see the details much more clearly when it's close compared to when it's far away.

Horizon ratios

Objects that are the same height are cut in the same place by the horizon, regardless of how far away they are. This is known as a horizon ratio and provides us with information on the size and distance of objects.

Tip: As the houses are the same size, the horizon line cuts each house in the same place (Figure 2).

Figure 2: Objects of the same size/height always meet the horizon at the same point.

Optic flow patterns

As we move, the place we're moving towards appears to be stationary whilst other objects appear to move past us. Objects that are close to us seem to be moving quickly, whilst those far away seem to move much more slowly. For example, when you travel in a car, signposts and nearby buildings zoom by in comparison to mountain ranges in the distance. This is due to changes in the optic array as we move. These are known as optic flow patterns. They give us information on the position and depth of objects.

Although the optic array changes when a person moves, the information provided by texture gradients, horizon ratios and optic flow remains constant. This enables us to perceive the world around us.

The optic array explains our perception of the position of objects relative to each other. However, it doesn't address how we're able to perceive what objects are or how they should be used. Gibson proposed that we perceive how an object should be used from the object itself.

Examples

An object affords (offers) itself to certain behaviours, e.g. a bed affords itself to being laid down on. The affordances of objects can change depending on the circumstances, e.g. a box might afford itself to storing something or to being stood on to reach a high object.

Real World Connection
Gibson's research into optic flow patterns has real world applications. When you approach a roundabout in a car, you often see lines on the road that get closer together. This is to give the driver the impression that they are travelling faster than they actually are so they slow down.

Comments on Gibson's theory

Gibson studied perception in real world situations, so his theory has ecological validity. His theory also has practical applications — the concept of optic flow has been used to help train pilots. However, the idea of affordances has been criticised. Many psychologists believe that the uses of some objects can't be perceived without drawing on stored knowledge or experience.

Gregory's indirect theory

A different approach to perception is Gregory's top down theory. 'Top down' means perception is steered by context and prior knowledge. Using our past experiences allows us to quickly categorise and interpret what we are seeing, a bit like deciphering a code.

Figure 3: Gibson was particularly interested in trying to find out how pilots perceived the runway as they came in to land.

Example

There are times when we have to use our prior knowledge to help us understand what we're seeing. Deciphering messy handwriting can be difficult. But if we use the context of the sentence, it is easier to decode what each word says. For instance, someone's 'lo' may look like a 'b', or their 'g' may look like an '9':

The bakery is cbsed

9.00am — 9iraffe feeding

But by using our past knowledge, we can make a guess that what looks like 'cbsed' actually says 'closed' and '9iraffe' says 'giraffe'.

Tip: Gibson's approach takes a more reductionist view of perception. It breaks it down into smaller parts, whereas Gregory's approach looks at the whole picture.

Gregory's (1966) indirect theory of perception suggests that stimuli often don't provide the cognitive system with enough information for it to make sense of a situation.

This could be because the stimuli are ambiguous or because the information they provide is limited. Instead, stimuli are treated as hypotheses which are tested within different contexts using stored knowledge. Visual illusions provide support for Gregory's theory:

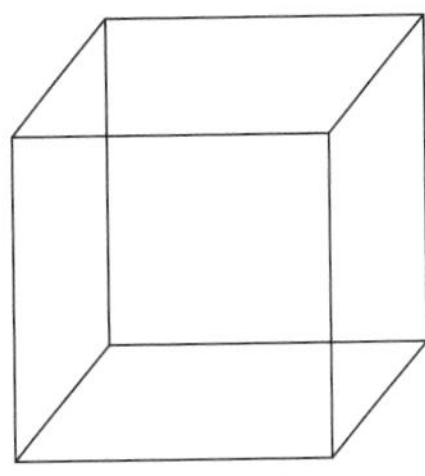

Figure 4: *A Necker cube*

The diagram on the left shows a Necker cube. As you look at it your perception of which face is the front face changes. Gregory suggests that this is your brain testing different hypotheses. As there's no context to help you decide which the front face is, your brain continues to switch between them. This supports Gregory's theory that stimuli alone don't always provide enough information for the cognitive system to work out what's going on.

Real World Connection
There are many other examples of ambiguous diagrams similar to the Necker cube (Figure 4). They show that sometimes we do need a context to be able to interpret the objects for what they are.

Key study of Gregory's indirect theory — Palmer (1975)

Method: Participants were shown an image of a scene, such as a bedroom. They were then shown images in quick succession, each showing an object that was either related to the scene (e.g. a bed), or unrelated (e.g. a musical instrument) and asked to identify them.

Results: Participants correctly identified over 80% of the related images, but only around 50% of the unrelated ones.

Conclusion: Top down processing has been used by the participants. Experience and memory play a significant role in perception, supporting Gregory's indirect theory of perception.

Evaluation: This was a very well controlled study but the task and the setting were artificial meaning it lacks ecological validity. The participants were also all undergraduate students, representing a similar demographic of interests, backgrounds and ages. Therefore, findings for this group of people may not be relevant if extended to a wider population.

Tip: It's easy to get mixed up with Gibson's and Gregory's theories. One way of remembering which theory belongs to whom, is to remember that Gibson's theory is bottom-up (they both contain the letter 'b').

Tip: A lot of psychology experiments are conducted on undergraduate students, because of a lot of research takes place in universities. Whilst doing so can provide a large sample size, it's often not possible to generalise the findings to a wider population.

Additional study of Gregory's indirect theory — Johansson (1973)

Johansson devised an experiment in which he attached lights to various body parts of an actor. In a dark room, with just the lights shining, the participants were unable to determine what the dots represented when the actor remained still. But as soon as the actor started to walk, they guessed correctly that the lights formed the shape of a person.

The results of Johansson's experiment support Gregory's theory, that our previous knowledge and experiences help us to identify what we're seeing.

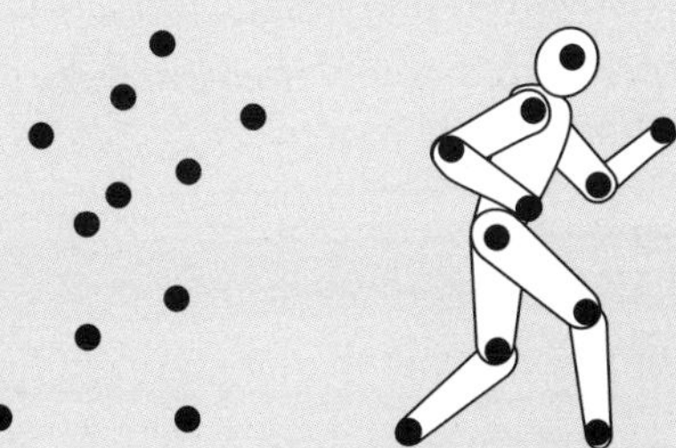

Figure 5: *The pattern of dots on the left is unrecognisable on a static actor. When attached to a walking actor, the human form quickly becomes obvious.*

Figure 6: Optical illusions and ambiguous diagrams were one of Gregory's interests used to support his theory.

Comments on Gregory's theory

There's plenty of evidence to support Gregory's theory — however, it's based on laboratory experiments so lacks ecological validity. The theory can explain errors in perception — for example, those caused by optical illusions. However, many psychologists reckon that if perception is based entirely on hypothesis testing we would make more errors in perception than we do.

A combination of processes

Many psychologists believe that perception stems from a combination of top down and bottom up processes. Bottom up processes are most likely when the information provided by stimuli is unambiguous and plentiful. Top down processes become more dominant when the amount or the quality of information provided by stimuli is reduced. We become more dependent on stored knowledge and past experiences. When this happens, unconscious 'educated guesses' play a greater part in perception.

Worked Exam-style Questions

0 1 Describe and evaluate Gibson's (1979) direct theory of perception. *(4 marks + 4 marks)*

Gibson proposed that perception was a bottom up process. This means that information is gathered from the world and then pieced together in order to make sense of it. Gibson suggested that this information comes from the optic array. This is a complicated pattern of light that enters the eye and gives rise to texture gradients, horizon ratios and optic flow patterns. These are all involved in perception. The brain decodes the optic array in order to make sense of the world around us. He went on to say that we don't need to use any previous knowledge or experience in this process because we get so much information from what we see.

Gibson based his theory on real life observations and therefore it has high ecological validity. Gibson's theory has also contributed to real world applications such as the training of pilots. The fact that it can be successfully applied in these ways provides a great deal of support for the theory. Much of the criticism of Gibson's theory comes from the fact that psychologists say we need prior knowledge to perceive objects — a large feature of Gregory's indirect theory of perception.

Many research studies have used visual illusions to support Gregory's theory, and therefore disprove Gibson's theory. These have shown that we do need prior knowledge in order to perceive objects. For instance, Palmer (1975) showed that top down processing was used when participants were asked to identify a quick succession of images that were either related or unrelated to a scene that they'd previously been shown. However, unlike the research into Gibson's theory, this experiment lacks ecological validity as it involved unrealistic laboratory work.

Overall, Gibson provides a comprehensive theory that describes perception using a bottom up approach.

Exam Tip
The specification asks you to know about both Gibson and Gregory's theories so make sure you don't get them confused.

Exam Tip
When evaluating these theories, you can always compare them to contrasting ideas. Just make sure you stay focused on the question.

Summary Questions

Q1 Name one phenomenon (other than texture gradients) that the optic array gives rise to.

Q2 What support is there for Gregory's (1966) theory of perception?

Q3 Does Gregory's theory adopt a top down or bottom up approach?

2. Development of Perception

The nature-nurture debate features a lot in research on perception.
It offers us two different explanations of how we perceive the world around us.

Learning Objectives:
- Understand the development of perceptional abilities, including depth/ distance and visual constancies.
- Know about perceptual development, including infant and cross-cultural research.

Studies on the development of perception

There's been much debate over whether our perceptual abilities are innate (inbuilt) or are learned through experience. In other words, whether they're down to nature or nurture. Studies have been carried out to investigate the development of perceptual abilities such as depth perception and visual constancies.

Depth perception

Some studies suggest depth perception is innate. Depth perception allows us to change a 2D image on the retina (the inner lining of the eye) into 3D information. We do this using cues such as relative size, texture gradients and optic flow patterns (see pages 23-24).

Key study of depth perception — Gibson and Walk (1960)

Method: A 'visual cliff' was created using a layer of glass with two levels of a checkerboard pattern underneath. The shallow level had the pattern just below the glass, the deep level had the pattern four feet below. 36 six-month old babies were placed on the shallow side and encouraged by their mothers to crawl on to the deep side.

Results: Most babies wouldn't crawl on to the deep side of the visual cliff.

Conclusion: Babies can perceive depth so depth perception is the result of nature, not nurture.

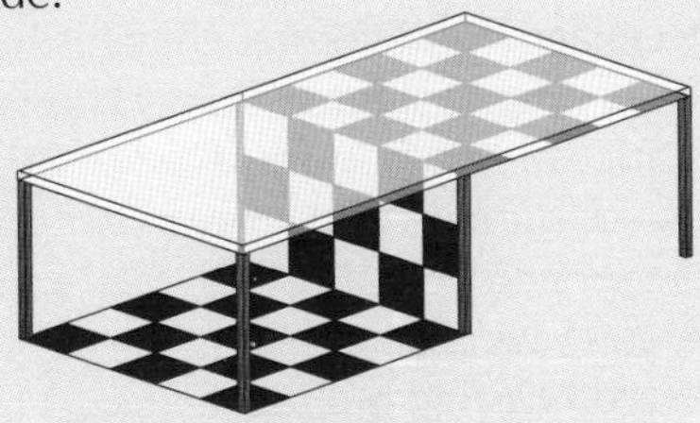

***Figure 1:** The visual cliff used in Gibson and Walk's experiment.*

Evaluation: The validity of this study is questionable as the babies were six months old and could have learnt depth perception by this age. Campos (1970) tested babies by measuring their heart rate when they were on different sides of the cliff. He found that the heart rate of two-month old babies (who couldn't crawl) was the same on both sides, suggesting they didn't perceive any change in depth. Nine-month old babies (who could crawl) had a increased heart rate on the deep side, suggesting they had learned depth perception, i.e. through nurture.

Tip: The babies had to be old enough to be able to crawl — but they could have learnt depth perception during that time.

***Figure 2:** Gibson and Walk's visual cliff experiment provided evidence for depth perception as an innate mechanism.*

Additional study of depth perception — Granrud and Yonas (1984)

Granrud and Yonas wanted to explore further whether depth perception is innate or learnt. They showed infants a series of different cards, one of which showed a depth cue, the others didn't.

Exam Tip
Psychology studies are never usually 100% conclusive. Evidence usually comes up that contradicts the theories. If you're evaluating a theory in an answer, you could give some evidence that contradicts it.

They found that only infants older than seven months preferred the cards with the depth cue (where one card looked nearer the infant than the others). They were more likely to reach for items on the cards that seemed closer. Those who were five months showed no preference, which contradicts the idea that depth perception is innate.

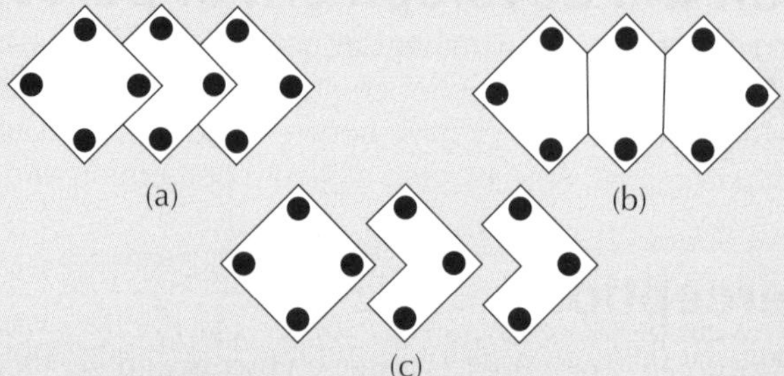

Figure 3: *The cards used in Granrud and Yonas's (1984) experiment. Older babies were more likely to reach for set (a) because they show a depth cue.*

Visual constancies

Studies have suggested that visual constancies are innate. As you look at an object, an image of it forms on the retina, allowing it to be seen. The closer an object is, the larger the image it creates on the retina. However, when the brain interprets the image it's able to identify the object as being closer rather than larger. This is known as **size constancy**.

Similarly, when an object is rotated, e.g. a door opening, the shape of the image on the retina changes but the brain doesn't interpret this as the object changing shape. This is known as **shape constancy**. Size and shape constancy are both visual constancies and important perceptual abilities. Several studies have been carried out to determine whether visual constancy is a result of nature or nurture:

Figure 5: *An example of shape constancy — the picture is still the same, just at a different angle.*

Figure 4: *Shape constancy tells us that the windows are actually the same shape — the angle makes them look different.*

Tip: It can be hard to scientifically test babies and their behaviours because a lot of their head movements are involuntary.

Tip: Research using infants often raises ethical issues. Consent has to be given by their parents or caregivers and any undue distress must be carefully monitored.

Key study of shape constancy in babies — Slater and Morrison (1985)

Method: Newborn babies were shown a square held at different angles. At some angles the image on the retina would be a trapezium. Once the baby was familiar with the square they were shown a trapezium alongside it (Figure 6).

Figure 6: *The infants were shown a square at different angles, before being shown a square next to a trapezium.*

Results: The babies were more likely to look at the new trapezium than the square.

Conclusion: Babies can distinguish between the trapezium and the square held at an orientation where it looks like a trapezium.
So, babies have an innate ability to apply shape constancy to objects.

Key study of size constancy in babies — Bower (1964, 1966)

Method: Two-month-old babies were conditioned to look at a 30 cm cube held 1 m away from them, by being given a reward each time they looked at it. Once they could do this they were presented with new stimuli. Firstly they were shown a 90 cm cube held 1 m away. This would create a larger retinal image than the original cube. Then they were shown a 90 cm cube held 3 m away, producing the same size retinal image as the original. Lastly, the original 30 cm cube was held at a distance of 3 m, producing a smaller retinal image than before.

Results: The babies preferred to look at the original 30 cm cube held at a distance of 3 m than the 90 cm cubes.

Conclusion: Babies can distinguish between objects of different sizes regardless of the size of the image they create on the retina. So, babies have an innate ability to apply size constancy to objects.

Tip: It's important that a study's results can be replicated as a test of reliability.
This is one reason why Bower conducted several experiments.

Tip: Biological factors might also influence how people perceive different things.
For instance, some drugs can cause people to perceive the world in a different way by causing hallucinations.

Cross-cultural studies

If perceptual abilities are the result of nature they're likely to be present in everyone regardless of culture. However, if they're the result of nurture they're likely to vary between people of different cultures. So, cross-cultural studies can help to determine whether perceptual abilities are the result of nature or nurture:

The Müller-Lyer illusion

This shows two lines of the same length that can appear to be different lengths due to inward or outward facing arrow heads (see Figure 7).

Tip: Cross-cultural research can often be biased — the researcher's own culture can influence how they see the different cultures they are studying.

Key study of perception across cultures — Segall et al (1966)

Method: Segall et al (1966) showed the illusion (Figure 7) to a sample of urban South Africans and a sample of rural Zulus.

Results: Most of the urban South Africans identified the line with the inwardly pointing arrows (a) as being longer than the line with the outwardly pointing arrows (b). The Zulus were less susceptible to the illusion, with a high proportion identifying the lines as being the same length.

Conclusion: Segall suggested that the urban South Africans, who were used to an environment dominated by straight lines (e.g. in buildings, furniture, roads, etc.), interpreted the diagram in 3D.

Tip: The Müller-Lyer illusion was used in Segall et al's (1966) investigation.

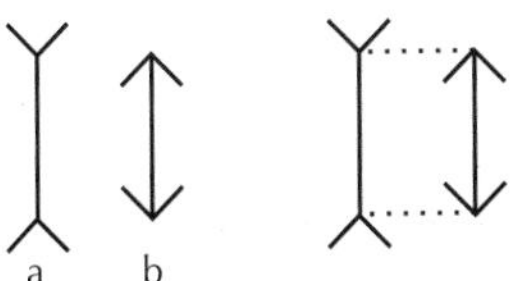

Figure 7: *The Müller-Lyer illusion.*

Real World Connection
Another example of an illusion is the Ponzo illusion (Figure 9). When two identically sized objects are placed between a set of converging lines, the one nearest the point often appears bigger. This illusion is said to explain why the moon sometimes looks bigger when it is closer to the horizon.

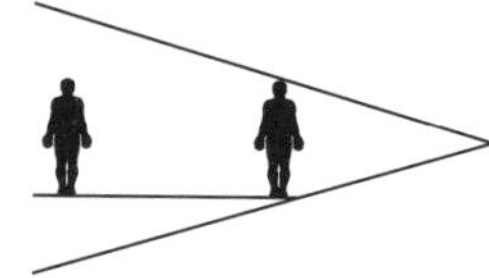

Figure 9: The Ponzo illusion.

In 3D, line 'a' resembles an object receding away from the observer (e.g. the inner corner of a room, see Figure 8). Line 'b' resembles an object projecting towards the observer (e.g. the outer corner of a building).

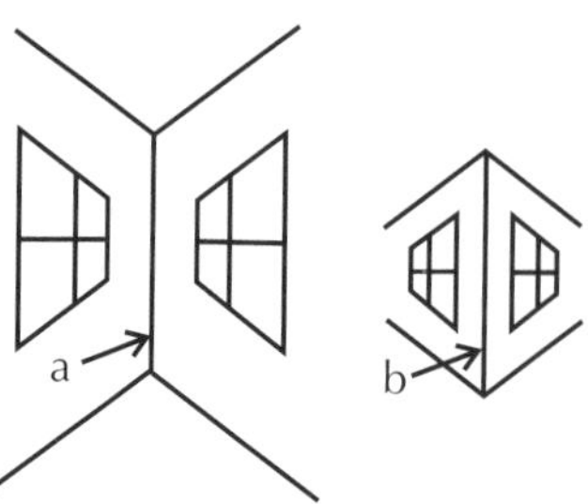

Figure 8: 3D version of the Müller-Lyer illusion

As line 'a' appears to recede away from the observer the brain interprets it as being further away than line 'b'. So, the brain interprets line 'a' as being larger than the image it forms on the retina (size constancy) and perceives it to be longer than line 'b'.

The Zulu people were less familiar with buildings made from straight lines — their huts were circular. Segall suggested that they saw the lines in 2D, so didn't apply size constancy and didn't perceive any difference in the length of the lines.

He saw this difference in perception across cultures as evidence that perceptual abilities are developed in response to the environment, i.e. perception is the result of nurture.

Additional study of perception across cultures — Turnbull (1961)

Turnbull reported an account following his stay with the BaMbuti pygmies in the Congo. The tribe were forest dwellers and therefore they were used to being surrounded by vegetation and dense trees. One day, Turnbull took his guide, Kenge, out of the forest allowing him to see things from a great distance for the first time, because his view was now unrestricted. He was able to see a herd of over 100 buffalo in the distance. Kenge asked, "What insects are those?"

Turnbull explained they were actually buffalo, twice the size that Kenge was used to seeing within his natural environment. When they got closer, Kenge was amazed to find Turnbull was speaking the truth and believed some form of witchcraft had taken place to 'make' the buffalo grow in size.

From this example, it has been suggested that perception of the outside world does seem to be influenced by the environment we grow up in, supporting the nurture side of the debate.

Tip: Turnbull wasn't really doing a study into perception across cultures. He was an anthropologist studying pygmies. He just noted down these observations while studying them.

Figure 10: Knowing that the size of an animal will appear to increase as you get nearer is an example of size constancy.

Worked Exam-style Questions

0 1 Discuss how research into visual constancies has helped our understanding of perceptual development. *(4 marks + 4 marks)*

Visual constancies include shape and size constancy. They allow us to interpret objects that appear to change in shape or size depending where we are standing, or what context we see them in. We can use visual constancies to understand that the objects themselves are staying constant. Lots of studies have tried to investigate whether visual constancies are developed over time, as a result of our environment, or whether they are innate. This is known as the nature-nurture debate.

One study which looked at shape constancy was Slater and Morrison's (1985) investigation. They showed babies squares held at different angles, one of which resulted in a trapezium-shaped retinal

Exam Tip
Make sure you start by defining what visual constancies are, and providing some examples.

image. They then showed the babies a square and a trapezium and found that the babies were more likely to look at the new trapezium than the square. As the infants had shown that they could distinguish between two different objects, and that a trapezium was not just a square at a different angle, it was concluded that babies do have an innate ability to apply shape constancy to objects.

Similarly, Bower (1964, 1966) proposed that size constancy is also innate. His experiments involved babies looking at cubes different distances away. They showed that infants could distinguish between objects of different sizes despite the retina images still being the same.

Both of these experiments suggest that visual constancies are innate, but some studies provide contradictory results and suggest that behaviour and perception are influenced by nurture. For example, Segall et al's study of the Zulu people provided results which suggested that perception differs across cultures, and therefore is not innate.

To summarise, research has not showed conclusively whether perceptual development is down to nature or nurture and so the debate is still ongoing.

Exam Tip
Don't forget to briefly explain the study, rather than just listing the name of the researchers. It shows you've really learnt what you need to know.

Exam Tip
Using studies with different outcomes show a balanced and well-rounded answer.

---

0 2 Discuss how cross-cultural research has contributed to our understanding of perceptual development.

(4 marks + 4 marks)

Cross-cultural research can be used by psychologists to investigate whether something is the result of nature (our biological make-up and genetics) or nurture (our environment and upbringing).

Segall et al (1966) showed that rural Zulu people were much less likely to be 'tricked' by the Müller-Lyer illusion than urban South Africans because they lived in an environment where straight lines were much less common. His research provides evidence against the suggestion that perception is innate. Instead, the findings support the idea that perception is a process that is learnt, and therefore is dependent on the environment that someone lives in. Turnbull (1961) also gives support for the idea that perception is something gained from our environment with his cross-cultural research. He looked at the BaMbuti tribe where he recorded the case of one of the local men not understanding the size differences in animals observed from different distances.

This cross-cultural research has been important in providing evidence for the nurture side of the perceptual development debate. As these two studies have shown though, more research would be beneficial. Cross-cultural research is often biased because it relies on the observations and conclusions drawn by the experimenter. A researcher's own culture and perceptions of the world can often influence this.

Exam Tip
Evaluating cross-cultural research as a whole method is a good way to pick up some of the AO3 evaluation marks within this answer.

Summary Questions

Q1 Tori wants to replicate Gibson and Walk's (1960) 'visual cliff' study.

a) What is she trying to investigate?

b) If she got the same results as them, what could she conclude?

c) Give one criticism of this Gibson and Walk's study.

Q2 What is shape constancy?

Learning Objectives:

- Understand Bruce and Young's theory of face recognition, including case studies and explanations of prosopagnosia.

3. Face Recognition and Visual Agnosia

We often take face recognition for granted, but for some people, recognising faces can be difficult. Research using these people can help us understand face perception better.

Bruce and Young's (1986) theory

Face recognition is an important perceptual ability — allowing us to form relationships and function socially. It lets us tell the difference between thousands of faces, even though they have the same basic features, e.g. eyes. We're also able to identify familiar faces — those of friends, family or famous people. Bruce and Young (1986) suggest that the process of face recognition is different from recognition of other objects.

Tip: Agnosia is another way of saying 'loss of recognition'.

Key study of face recognition — Tanaka and Farah (1993)

Method: Participants were shown a series of houses and faces. They were then presented with two stimuli — either two face or house parts by themselves, or two whole faces or houses. Participants were asked to say which one they'd seen before.

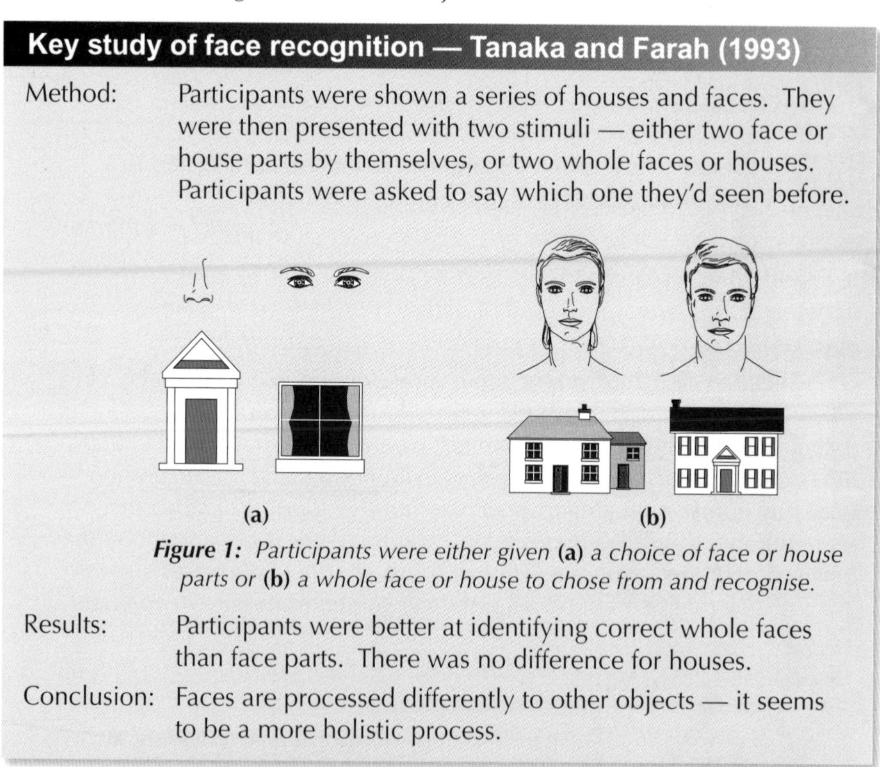

Figure 1: *Participants were either given* **(a)** *a choice of face or house parts or* **(b)** *a whole face or house to chose from and recognise.*

Results: Participants were better at identifying correct whole faces than face parts. There was no difference for houses.

Conclusion: Faces are processed differently to other objects — it seems to be a more holistic process.

Real World Connection
People's skill in recognising faces might not be completely to do with the processing involved, but with the familiarity that comes from seeing so many faces every day. Diamond and Carey (1986) used a similar method to Yin's (1969) study, but showed inverted dogs and human faces to both a control group and a dog-breeding group. They found that the dog-breeders experienced just as much difficulty in identifying the inverted dogs as they did the faces, suggesting that familiarity may be behind face recognition.

Additional study of face recognition — Yin (1969)

Method: One of the first experiments into the differences between face recognition and object recognition was conducted by Yin. He asked participants to look at a series of inverted (upside down) and upright faces alongside a series of inverted and upright objects and identify ones they had previously seen.

Results: Participants were worse at identifying inverted faces than inverted objects.

Conclusion: Face recognition involves a different process to object recognition.

Bruce and Young's (1986) model outlines a number of different components involved in face recognition:

- **Structural encoding** — Physical features are interpreted to determine basic information (e.g. age, gender). This allows a structural model of the face to be built up.
- **Expression analysis** — Facial features are analysed to work out the person's emotional state.
- **Facial speech analysis** — Facial movements (e.g. lip movements) are used to help interpret speech.
- **Directed visual processing** — Processing of specific features (e.g. whether the person has a beard).
- **Face recognition units** — These contain information about the structure of familiar faces.
- **Person identity nodes** — These contain information known about the person (e.g. their job, interests).
- **Name generation** — This helps us to retrieve the name of a familiar person and relate it to their face.
- **Cognitive system** — This contains extra information (e.g. the context in which a face is likely to be seen). It also helps determine which of the other components involved in face recognition are activated.

Bruce and Young suggested that some of these components are activated in a specific sequence, whilst others can work in parallel with each other. The diagram below shows how they suggest the components are linked.

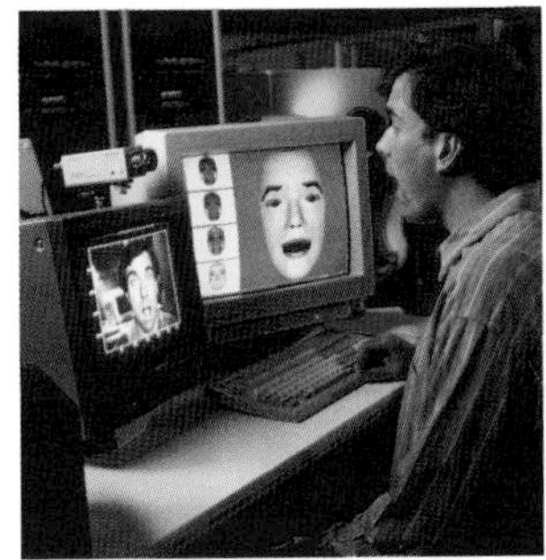

Figure 2: Researchers investigating how we process faces often use scientific equipment such as this expression analysis software.

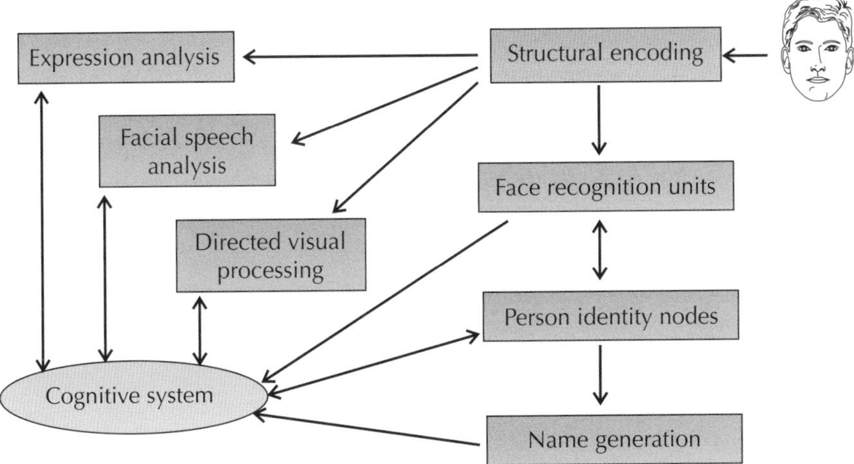

Figure 3: *Face recognition involves lots of different interactive parts.*

Tip: One of the criticisms of Bruce and Young's (1986) model is that the components within the model are not always fully explained.

For example, structural encoding is always the first component to be activated. After this either face recognition units, facial speech analysis, expression analysis or direct visual processing may be activated. These components work in parallel.

However, person identity nodes can only be activated after the face recognition units, and only after this can name generation be activated. These components work in sequence. Makes sense — you can't come up with information about someone until you've realised they're familiar.

Real World Connection
Bruce and Young's theory can explain everyday situations in which we can recognise people from many different angles.

The components

Bruce and Young's model proposes that we use different components to process new and familiar faces.

- They suggest that processing of a new face involves structural encoding, expression analysis, facial speech analysis and directed visual processing.
- Recognition of familiar faces uses structural encoding, face recognition units, person identity nodes and name generation.

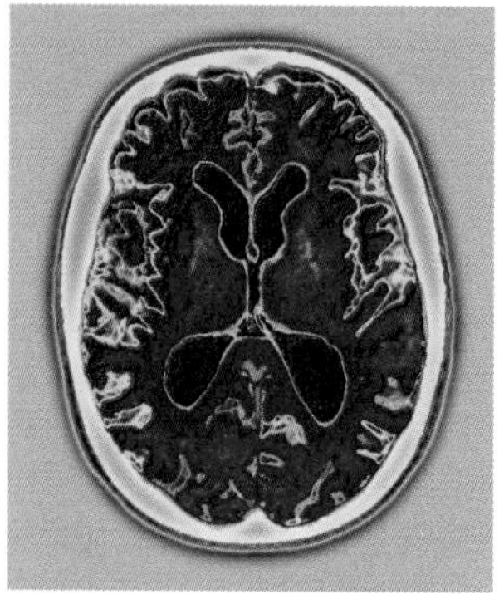

Figure 4: Someone suffering from Alzheimer's may experience prosopagnosia. This explains why they can't always recognise loved ones.

Tip: If someone is born with prosopagnosia, or it develops slowly over time, it is often hard to diagnose. This is because these people don't realise that their ability to recognise faces is impaired. They learn to develop other cues, such as depending on voice recognition, to help them remember who people are.

Real World Connection
It's quite hard to find people with prosopagnosia to study, which is why there is limited research within this area. However, with the use of the internet and modern technology, finding patients within the real world is becoming easier.

People with prosopagnosia

Prosopagnosia is a condition where people have difficulty recognising familiar faces. It's usually caused by brain damage, but some evidence suggests that it could also be congenital (present at birth). There are different types of prosopagnosia, with the most serious forms leaving people unable to recognise their spouse, close family and friends. Some patients can't even recognise their own face. Some studies of prosopagnosia have provided support for Bruce and Young's model of face recognition:

Key study of prosopagnosia — Farah (1994)

Method: Farah studied a patient (LH) who developed prosopagnosia as a result of brain damage caused by a car crash. Along with a control group of participants who didn't have prosopagnosia, he was shown pictures of faces and pairs of spectacles and then given a recognition memory test.

Results: LH performed as well as the control group in recognising spectacles but much worse than the control group in recognising the faces.

Conclusion: This suggests that prosopagnosia is caused by damage to the area of the brain involved in face recognition but not object recognition.

Evaluation: This supports Bruce and Young's proposal that face recognition and object recognition are separate processes.

Additional study of prosopagnosia — Mathison et al (2011)

Method: Mathison et al reported the case of a 7 year old boy who was believed to have developmental prosopagnosia. They conducted a series of face recognition tests along with tasks in which he had to identify emotions and recognise other objects.

Results: On the face recognition tasks, the boy scored 46.8%. In comparison, the average score for children his age is 80% and, if he had guessed all the answers, an average score due to chance would have been 50%. There was no difference found in his scores on the other tasks when compared to average scores for his age.

Conclusion: Face and object recognition appear to be different processes.

Additional study of prosopagnosia — Kurucz and Feldmar (1979)

Kurucz and Feldmar saw a patient with prosopagnosia who was unable to identify familiar faces but could interpret the emotional state of the person. This suggests that recognition of familiar faces and interpretation of emotional states are processes that work independently of each other. This supports Bruce and Young's concept of expression analysis and face recognition units as separate components that work in parallel with each other — one can be functional even if the other isn't.

These case studies suggest that the various types of prosopagnosia are caused by problems with one or more of the components of Bruce and Young's model. For example, the patient in Kurucz and Feldmar's study would have suffered damage to face recognition units or person identity nodes but not to the expression analysis component.

Evaluation of Bruce and Young's model

Some studies suggest that Bruce and Young's model isn't accurate.

Example

de Haan et al (1991) found that, when given the names and faces of famous people, a patient with amnesia was able to correctly match 88% of the faces to the names even though they couldn't give any other information about the person. This doesn't support Bruce and Young's model — the study suggests that activation of face recognition units was followed by name generation, bypassing person identity nodes entirely.

Worked Exam-style Questions

0 1 Discuss the research into Bruce and Young's model of face recognition. *(4 marks + 4 marks)*

Bruce and Young (1986) proposed a theory that suggested face and object recognition are separate processes. Their model of face recognition involves many different components which work together to allow people to perceive faces and recognise the people to whom they belong. Their theory has been supported by several studies, mainly involving people with prosopagnosia. This is a disorder where people cannot recognise faces. By studying people with this disorder, it can be concluded that if face perception is impaired but object recognition is not, then the two processes must be separate.

Research by Farah (1994) has provided support for Bruce and Young's theory. Farah investigated the case of a brain damaged patient, LH, who had prosopagnosia. After developing the disorder following a car accident, LH could no longer recognise faces but could still recognise everyday objects, supporting the idea that face and object recognition are separate processes.

However, much of the research to support Bruce and Young's theory relies on case studies, and therefore it is hard to generalise the results to a wider population. There is also research which contradicts their model. de Haan et al (1991) found that people with amnesia were still able to

Exam Tip

The question asks you to discuss research. So, don't just describe studies — the key is to also explain how they provide support for (or contradict) Bruce and Young's theory.

Exam Tip

If you're evaluating a study, you can talk about its methodology. Take a look at page 279 for more on case studies.

give names to faces, and that they just couldn't give any further information about the person. This suggests that face recognition doesn't follow Bruce and Young's model, which proposed that names cannot be retrieved without information about the person first being activated.

To summarise, no conclusive evidence has been found to say for definite whether or not Bruce and Young's model is correct. More research is needed in order to be certain that object recognition and face recognition occur by different processes, and also to be certain that the information and components involved in face recognition are accessed in the order that Bruce and Young proposed.

---

0 2 Outline one limitation of Bruce and Young's theory.

(4 marks)

Exam Tip
When you're talking about limitations, use studies which have contradicted the original theory to point out why it's not quite right.

Bruce and Young's theory cannot account for some observations that have been found in other studies. For example, de Haan et al (1991) found that when given the names and faces of famous people, amnesiacs could still correctly match the two, indicating that face recognition was still functioning even in those with brain damage.

These findings do not support Bruce and Young's model because the research suggests that face recognition units are followed by name generation. In Bruce and Young's model, name generation cannot be accessed until the face recognition units have been activated.

Summary Questions

Q1 Steven has difficulty recognising faces. Using your knowledge of face recognition, give one suggestion of what could be wrong.

Q2 Name two components of Bruce and Young's theory used:

a) when processing new faces.

b) when processing familiar faces.

Q3 Adam was taking part in a psychology experiment where he was presented with either isolated facial features or actual faces. He had to identify if he'd seen the features previously.

a) According to Bruce and Young, why would he do better at identifying the features if they were part of a face context?

b) What would happen if the stimuli were houses and house features instead of faces and facial features?

Section Summary

- There are two main theories of perception outlined by Gibson (1979) and Gregory (1966).
- Gibson's direct theory takes a bottom up approach, claiming that information is put together, piece by piece, ready for us to interpret it. Gibson's theory suggests that the optic array gives us all of this information — texture gradients, horizon ratios and optic flow patterns all contribute to perception.
- Gregory's indirect theory involves top down processing. He claims that previous knowledge and past experiences are used to help us make sense of what we see. Gregory's theory uses evidence from visual illusions as support for this type of processing.
- Perception may actually involve a combination of aspects of both Gibson's and Gregory's theories.
- Studying the development of perception allows researchers to investigate whether perception is innate, or whether it develops as a result of our environment and upbringing.
- Depth perception studies involving infants, such as Gibson and Walk's (1960) study involving a 'visual cliff', suggest that depth perception is innate. However, Campos (1970) found contradictory results, suggesting perception is not innate and is learnt.
- Granrud and Yonas's (1984) experiment found 5-month-old infants were no more likely to reach for something that appeared closer, suggesting that perception is not innate and is learnt after this age.
- Research into visual constancies has also shown that perception may be innate. Size and shape constancy are terms used to describe our understanding that the size and shape of an object stay the same, even though they may look different when viewed at an alternative angle.
- Evidence for size and shape constancy in infants has been found in studies by Slater and Morrison (1985) and Bower (1964, 1966).
- Cross-cultural research provides further evidence for the nature-nurture debate within developmental perception. Segall et al (1966) and Turnbull (1961) both showed that the environment someone is raised in does contribute to how they perceive objects.
- Face recognition seems to use different processing methods to object recognition.
- Bruce and Young (1986) developed a theory which supported this claim and their model outlines how faces are processed within the brain. These components include structural encoding, expression analysis, facial speech analysis, directed visual processing, face recognition units, person identity nodes, and name generation, all leading into the cognitive system.
- Prosopagnosia is a disorder which can be used as evidence to support the suggestion that face recognition is different from object recognition. Sufferers cannot recognise faces but are often able to recognise other objects normally.

Exam-style Questions

0 1 Describe what is meant by the condition prosopagnosia.

(4 marks)

0 2 Discuss how prosopagnosia research has contributed to our understanding of perception.

(4 + 16 marks)

Learning Objectives:

- Know about theories of the formation, maintenance and breakdown of romantic relationships.
- Understand reward/need satisfaction and the social exchange theory.

***Figure 1:** Relationships provide rewards that satisfy our social needs.*

1. Formation, Maintenance and Breakdown

Psychologists have theories about the formation, maintenance and breakdown of romantic relationships. Useful stuff. Who'd have thought that studying A2-Level psychology would make you a dating expert...

Starting a relationship

There are a lot of factors which determine how a relationship forms in the first place. These include:

- Contact (it's pretty hard to form a relationship without it).
- Physical appearance — how someone looks and acts can initially make them attractive to us.
- Similarity — having a lot in common with someone, (i.e. enjoying the same things, having similar moral values and backgrounds, etc.) often kick starts a relationship.

Kerckhoff and Davis (1962) explain the development of relationships using the **filter model**. Initially we have a 'field of availables' — potential people to form a relationship with. We narrow these people down to a smaller 'field of desirables' by applying certain filters. Once we have narrowed down our choices, we evaluate them on these factors to see if they're compatible.

Example

We tend to be attracted to people who have similar socio/demographic backgrounds, attitudes, values and emotional needs to ourselves.

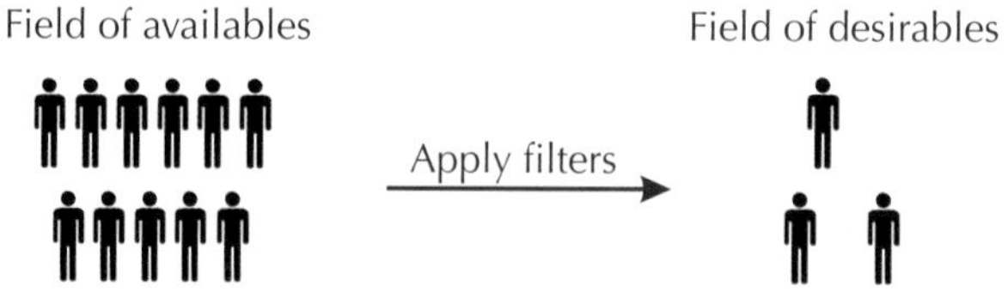

Field of availables → Apply filters → Field of desirables

***Figure 2:** The filter model lets us narrow down our choices for potential partners.*

Forming and maintaining relationships

Reward/need satisfaction theory

We may form relationships for selfish reasons. Reward/need satisfaction theory, which comes from the behaviourist approach, states that we form friendships and relationships to receive rewards or reinforcement from others. Relationships provide rewards that satisfy our social needs.

Examples

- Rewards include things like approval, sex, status, love, money, respect, agreement with our opinions, smiling, information, etc.
- Our social needs are things like self-esteem, affiliation, dependency, influence, etc.

Receiving rewards and having our needs satisfied, motivates us to continue the relationship. So, in terms of operant conditioning, being in a relationship is positively reinforced because it is rewarding.

Byrne and Clore's (1970) **Reinforcement-Affect theory** suggests that both operant and classical conditioning play a part in relationships. The theory states that we learn to associate people with positive or enjoyable situations, even if they are not directly rewarding us in these instances.

Tip: Remember — operant conditioning occurs when organisms learn to associate particular behaviours with particular consequences. Classical conditioning occurs when a stimulus produces a response in an organism because it's become associated with another stimulus which normally produces that response (see page 107).

Matching hypothesis

Walster et al (1966) developed the idea that people tend to choose partners who are considered to be as equally attractive as themselves. They suggested this was because people have realistic expectations and are more likely to be a good match. Murstein (1972) provided evidence in a study where 197 couples were rated on attractiveness. A high correlation in attractiveness between the couples who were in long term relationships was found.

Economic theories

Economic theories consider relationships to be a trading process.

Social Exchange Theory (Thibaut and Kelley, 1959) suggests that people try to maximise rewards (e.g. attention, self-esteem, happiness) from a relationship and minimise costs (e.g. time, effort, emotional support). If the relationship is to continue, then the rewards must not be outweighed by the costs — we should end up in profit. So, relationships are formed using a sort of 'cost-benefit' analysis. But if we are striving to get more and give less, this may result in an unequal relationship.

Equity theory suggests that people expect relationships to be fair and equal. They want to receive rewards from relationships that are in balance with the rewards they provide for the other person. If a relationship is unequal or unfair then it produces discomfort and distress in both partners, even if you are the one getting more and giving less. The disadvantaged person may try to make things fairer if it seems possible.

Real World Connection

The theories outlining how relationships are formed don't have to be about romantic relationships. They can also apply to friendships. Cash and Derlega (1978) found that the matching hypothesis applied to friendship groups — they tended to contain people of a similar level of attractiveness.

Comments

- The theories are often simplistic in trying to describe how relationships are formed. Relationships are actually quite complex.
- They don't consider cultural and gender factors, which may cause people to treat relationships in different ways.

Tip: It's difficult to define what rewards and costs might be since these will differ between people.

Perception of relationships

Relationships can be perceived very differently. People within a relationship may have different feelings about the relationship and have different levels of satisfaction.

Key studies on perception of relationships

Hatfield et al (1979) asked newlyweds to assess what they and their partner contributed to the relationship and their level of contentment with the marriage. The least satisfied were those who were under-benefited (unhappy about giving the most). The next least satisfied were those who were over-benefited (perhaps they felt a bit guilty about giving the least). Equal relationships were the most satisfactory.

There may be sex differences in how we feel about unequal relationships. Argyle (1988) found that over-benefited men were almost as satisfied as those in equitable marriages. Over-benefited women, however, were much less satisfied than women in equal relationships.

Figure 3: *If a relationship is unequal or unfair it produces discomfort and distress in both partners.*

Theories of relationship formation can also give an insight into relationship maintenance. A relationship in which your needs are satisfied would be important for you to protect and maintain. In the same sense, equity theory says that people in an unbalanced, unfair relationship may attempt to change things in order for the balance to be restored.

Breakdown of relationships

These are some common reasons for the breakdown of a relationship:

- dissatisfaction or boredom with the relationship
- breaking agreed rules (e.g. being faithful, confidentiality)
- interference from other relationships (e.g. family or friends)
- abuse (e.g. violence, drugs, alcohol)
- an attractive alternative relationship exists
- costs outweigh benefits
- conflict or dispute (e.g. over finances)
- jealousy over a real or imagined rival.

Theories suggest relationships end in stages:

Tip: Lee's model doesn't look at why the relationship broke down in the first place — it just describes the stages of a relationship breakdown.

Key study of the breakdown of relationships — Lee (1984)

Lee (1984) conducted interviews with over 100 couples who had broken up. Five stages were identified in the process of the breakdown of a relationship:

1. Dissatisfaction in one or both partners
2. Exposing the dissatisfaction and identifying problems
3. Negotiating the exposed problems
4. Resolution — attempting to solve problems
5. Termination of the relationship if no resolution

Not all couples went through all the stages. It seems that less intimate relationships may progress to the termination stage more quickly. Stronger relationships took longer to go through the stages and took longer to get over.

Duck (1988) developed a four-phase model of the ending of an intimate relationship:

1. **Intra-psychic phase** — inside the head of one person. *One partner becomes dissatisfied with the relationship.*

2. **Dyadic phase** — between two people. *The other partner is told about the dissatisfaction.*

3. **Social phase** — beyond the couple. *The break-up is made public to friends and family. Implications are discussed (e.g. care of children). The relationship can still be saved here (e.g. intervention of family, external marital support).*

4. **Grave-dressing phase** — finishing the relationship completely. *The ex-partners organise their lives post-relationship. They tell their own version of the break-up and of their current relationship with their ex.*

Figure 4: *One partner becomes dissatisfied with the relationship in the intra-psychic phase.*

Comments

The theories don't take individual differences into account and research evidence suggests these models don't show how complex relationship dissolution can be. Rusbult and Zembrodt (1983) said some people in relationship breakdowns actively lead the process (to resolve the problems or speed up the ending). Others are passive (believing things will resolve themselves). Akert (1992) said people who do the breaking up are less likely to be upset and show physical symptoms (e.g. loss of appetite and sleep) — not surprising really. Finally, these theories don't take cultural differences in relationships into account (see page 48).

Tip: In Duck's (1988) model, one phase clearly leads onto the next as a threshold point is reached. For example, the intra-psychic phase becomes the dyadic phase when the dissatisfied partner reaches a point where they tell their partner they're unhappy with the relationship. Similarly, the dyadic phase becomes the social phase when the couple decide to make the break up public.

Worked Exam-style Question

0 1 Outline theories of the maintenance of relationships. *(8 marks)*

The reward/need satisfaction theory suggests that relationships allow us to receive rewards and reinforcement from others. For example, we maintain friendships and relationships to receive rewards or reinforcement from others, which satisfies our social needs. Rewards include things like approval, sex, status, love, money, respect, agreement with our opinions, smiling and information. Our social needs are things like self-esteem, affiliation, dependency and influence.

Receiving rewards and having our needs satisfied, motivates us to continue the relationship. In terms of operant conditioning, (i.e. learning to associate particular behaviours with particular consequences) being in a relationship is positively reinforced because it is rewarding.

The Social Exchange Theory, proposed by Thibaut & Kelley (1959), suggests that people try to maximise rewards (e.g. attention, self-esteem and happiness) from a relationship and minimise costs (e.g. time, effort and emotional support). If the relationship is to continue, then the rewards must not be outweighed by the costs — we should end up in profit. So, relationships are maintained using a sort of 'cost-benefit' analysis. However, if we are striving to get more and give less, this may result in an unequal relationship.

Exam Tip
It's a good idea to give examples to show the sorts of things you mean.

Exam Tip
Unit 3 exam questions are always worth 24 marks. So there would be a second part to this question worth 16 marks.

Summary Questions

Q1 Suggest three factors that determine how a relationship gets started in the first place.

Q2 According to Kerckhoff and Davis (1962) what is the 'field of availables'?

Q3 Suggest three reasons for the breakdown of a relationship.

Q4 According to Lee (1984), what is the fourth stage in the breakdown of a relationship?

Q5 a) Deirdre and Ken are in a long term relationship. Deirdre has been unhappy with the relationship for a while, but has yet to tell Ken. According to Duck's (1988) model, what phase is Deirdre in?

b) Deirdre eventually tells Ken she is unhappy. What phase of Duck's model are Deirdre and Ken in now?

c) Deirdre and Ken go their local pub and tell all of their friends the news. What phase of Duck's model are Deirdre and Ken in now?

Learning Objectives:

- Understand evolutionary explanations of human reproductive behaviour.
- Know about the relationship between sexual selection and human reproductive behaviour.
- Know about sex differences in parental investment.

2. Reproductive Behaviour

No, these pages aren't all about sex. They do explain why you might find the guy/girl sat opposite attractive though. Read on Casanova...

Sexual selection and reproductive behaviours

Sexual selection explains certain reproductive behaviours. Within a species there are certain characteristics that increase an individual's mating potential.

Example

Female peacocks find the long, brightly coloured tails of male peacocks attractive. Males with very brightly coloured tails are more noticeable to predators. Those with very long tails find it difficult to escape from predators. So, long, brightly coloured tails reduce male peacocks' chances of surviving. However, as female peacocks are attracted to this feature, males with long, brightly coloured tails have a higher chance of reproducing and passing their genes on to the next generation than other males. This means that the characteristic evolves in the species even though it reduces the survival chances.

Figure 1: A male peacock's long, brightly coloured tail attracts female peacocks. This male with the 'best' tail is more likely to reproduce and pass his genes on to the next generation.

This evolution of characteristics which increase an individual's mating potential is known as sexual selection. In humans, characteristics affecting attractiveness include physical and mental health and some physical features. These influence potential mates as they indicate ability to reproduce and provide for offspring.

Types of sexual selection

Intrasexual selection

Intrasexual selection is the evolution of characteristics that enable an individual to compete with their rivals. Animals with 'better' characteristics are able to survive to reproduce and pass on their genes to their offspring.

Intersexual selection

Intersexual selection is the evolution of characteristics that are attractive to a mate (e.g. the peacock's tail). Animals with more attractive characteristics are more likely to mate, and will therefore pass on their genes to their offspring.

Sperm competition

Sperm competition is a form of intrasexual selection. Short's (1979) Sperm Competition Theory suggests that males are motivated to ensure that their sperm is successful in fertilisation and compete against other males to make this happen. This has resulted in males evolving to release large amounts of sperm during ejaculation. This is a form of intrasexual selection and increases the likelihood of successful fertilisation.

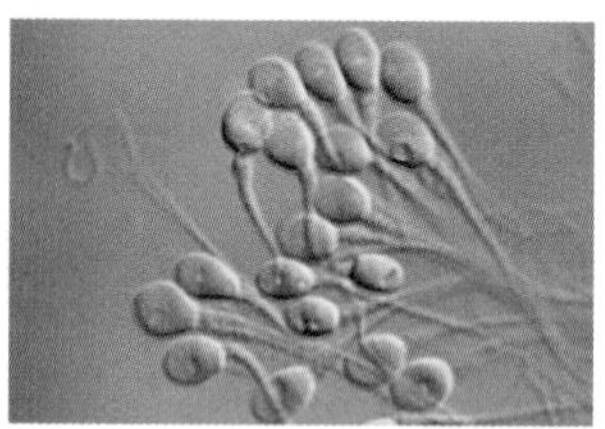

Figure 2: Sperm competition is a form of intrasexual selection.

Cross cultural research

Buss (1989) carried out cross cultural research into intersexual selection. This study shows one key difference in partner selection between genders.

Key study on differences in intersexual selection — Buss (1989)

Method:	Questionnaires were used to collect data from over 10 000 men and women from 37 different cultural groups. The questionnaires covered demographic information such

	as age, gender and marital status. They also asked about preferences for variables such as marriage, age differences and characteristics in a mate (e.g. intelligence, sociability and financial prospects).
Results:	Women valued variables associated with gaining resources (e.g. money, safe environment) more highly than men. Men valued variables associated with reproductive capacity (e.g. youth) more highly than women.
Conclusion:	Historically, women have had limited access to the resources needed to provide for themselves and their offspring. So, they've evolved to select mates who can provide these resources. Men have been limited by access to fertile women, and so have evolved to be attracted to women with a high likelihood of reproducing.
Evaluation:	The study supports an evolutionary explanation of gender differences in sexual selection. Similar findings were found across a range of different cultures. However, it wasn't a truly representative study as it was hard to include rural and less educated populations. The study also didn't take social influences on mate selection into account. For example, changes in society mean that women in many cultures are now able to provide for themselves and their offspring, and aren't as dependent on men for resources. Also, homosexual relationships aren't explained, as reproduction isn't a goal in same-sex relationships.

***Figure 3:** According to the study by Buss (1989), women value variables such as providing a safe environment more highly than men, who value variables associated with reproductive capacity.*

Tip: The study by Buss was conducted in 1989. Although it's not all that long ago, attitudes have changed quite a lot since. For example, 'working mums' and 'stay at home dads' are more common now than they were in the eighties.

Additional study on differences in intersexual selection — Buss and Schmitt (1993)

A study by Buss and Schmitt (1993) highlighted gender differences relating to reproductive behaviour. When participants were asked how many sexual partners they would ideally have in the next two years, it was found that on average men wanted 8 partners, while women wanted just one. When asked how many sexual partners they would ideally have in a lifetime, women wanted 4-5 — men wanted 18 partners on average. This can be explained by intersexual selection. Males want to have lots of offspring so their genes get passed on to as many children as possible.

Parental investment

Parental investment can be explained in terms of evolution.
Parental investment refers to any time, effort and energy that a parent puts towards the conception, gestation and rearing of a child that reduces their ability to invest in other offspring. In species where gestation is short and offspring become independent quickly, less parental investment is needed. However, in humans, parental investment is more demanding — gestation takes nine months and children don't become independent for many years. Sex differences are an evolutionary factor that affects parental investment.

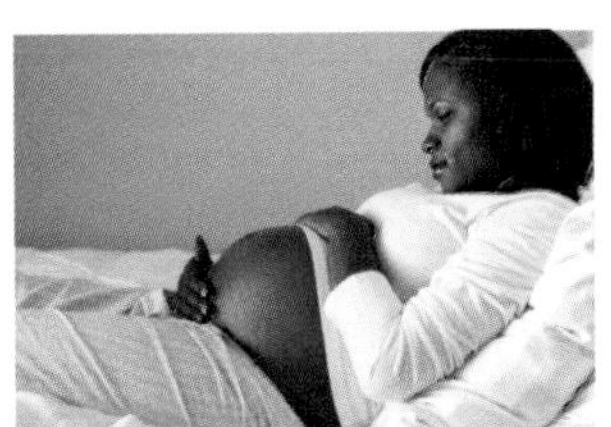

***Figure 4:** Parental investment is greater in women as they have a bigger role to play in the development of their offspring.*

Sex differences

Parental investment in humans shows sex differences. Men only need to be involved at conception whilst women also have to invest during pregnancy. There are differences when the offspring is born too, e.g. women may invest

Figure 5: Parental investment may also be higher in women as the number of children they can have is limited.

Tip: The stronger males passing their genes on is similar in principle to the peacock example on page 42 — peacocks with bigger tails are more likely to successfully reproduce and pass their genes on. As a result peacocks have evolved to have large attractive tails.

Figure 6: Men are generally bigger than women. In terms of intersexual selection, those who are strong and aggressive are more likely to win female attention.

Exam Tip
This question lets you pick the study you want to talk about. Choose one that you know enough about, since there are lots of marks up for grabs.

in breast-feeding. Historically, men provided protection, shelter and other resources (e.g. food) whilst women invested more time and energy in the day-to-day care of children. The number of children women can have is limited so they're likely to invest heavily in the survival of each one. Men can have many more children so investment in each individual is less important.

Trivers (1972) suggests the sex that invests most in the offspring (usually females) will discriminate when choosing a mate. The sex that invests least (usually males) will compete more for the higher investing mates. Trivers' parental investment theory explains why men are usually bigger than women. Men who were strong and aggressive were more likely to win the competition for a higher investing female. This meant that their genes were more likely to stay in the gene pool. Trivers' theory also offers an explanation for differences in sexual promiscuity between men and women. Men are more willing to engage in one-night stands and to have sex with lots of different partners, whereas women are more choosy. Trivers argued that this was because the parental investment per child is usually much lower for men than for women. Men need to make as many offspring as possible whereas women need to find a mate who will protect their offspring.

Not all psychologists agree that parental investment theories explain the differences in reproductive behaviour between men and women. Some women are willing to have one-night stands, and get involved with short-term relationships.

It's possible that culture has also played a big role in shaping human reproductive behaviour. For example, it's often seen as socially acceptable for men to be promiscuous, but promiscuous women are shunned. Buss (2000) accepts evolutionary explanations for reproductive behaviour, but points out that sexual discrimination in women and sexual competition in men could be problematic for modern relationships.

Worked Exam-style Question

0 1 Outline and evaluate research into sexual selection.
(8 marks + 8 marks)

Buss (1989) conducted cross-cultural research into intersexual selection. They gathered information from over 10 000 men and women from 37 different cultural groups. They used questionnaires to gather data, including demographic information such as age, gender and marital status. The questionnaires also asked about preferences for variables such as marriage, age differences and characteristics in a mate (e.g. intelligence, sociability and financial prospects).

■ *It was found that women had a clear preference for factors from which they would gain resources (e.g. money, a safe environment). In contrast, men tended to base their preferences on factors linked to reproductive capacity (for example, youth).*

The study concluded that as, historically, women have had limited access to the resources needed to provide for themselves and their offspring, they're likely to have evolved to select mates who can provide these resources. In contrast, men have been limited in terms of their access to fertile women, and have evolved to be attracted to women with a high likelihood of reproducing.

The study supports an evolutionary explanation of gender differences in sexual selection. Similar findings were found across a range of cultures, making the conclusion more robust.

However, the study does have limitations. It had a biased sample — it didn't use participants from a rural or less educated background, which makes it hard to apply generalisations from the results to the wider population. Also, the time and context in which the research was conducted may have been important, and the results may not reflect today's population. Nowadays, many women across different cultures are able to provide for themselves and their offspring, and aren't as dependent on men for resources. Also, the study and its conclusions can't account for homosexual relationships where reproduction isn't a goal.

The study made use of questionnaires, a form of self report. Individuals may have wished to present themselves in a good light to the researchers and therefore may not have answered questions truthfully, which could have affected the results of the study.

To summarise, Buss's study was useful in investigating sexual selection. It provides support for the evolutionary approach, and using cross-cultural methods, allows results to be generalised to wider populations. However, since it does have limitations, further research into this topic area would still be needed in order to draw firm conclusions about sexual selection.

Exam Tip
The best way to evaluate a study is to go through its methodology and pick out the good points and the bad points.

Summary Questions

Q1 The males of a certain species of antelope have very large horns. These horns are very easily spotted by predators. Use your scientific knowledge to suggest how the large horns of the antelope may have evolved.

Q2 Explain the difference between 'intrasexual selection' and 'intersexual selection.'

Q3 a) What type of sexual selection is sperm competition?

b) According to Short's (1979) Sperm Competition Theory, what have males evolved to do in order to increase the likelihood of successful fertilisation?

Q4 What is meant by the term 'parental investment'?

Q5 Give two possible reasons why parental investment is greater in women than in men.

Q6 According to Trivers's (1972) parental investment theory, how are gender differences in sexual promiscuity explained?

3. Adult Relationships

Learning Objectives:
- Understand the influence of childhood on adult relationships.
- Understand the influence of culture on romantic relationships.

It's likely that our ability to form successful adult relationships is affected by the relationships we form and observe when we are young. Our adult relationships can also be affected by culture...

Attachment theory and adult relationships

Ainsworth's attachment theory

In the 1970s, Ainsworth used the Strange Situation to investigate attachment. From her studies, she found three different types of attachment were present:

- Secure attachment — there's a strong bond between the child and its caregiver. If they're separated, the infant becomes distressed. However, when they're reunited, the child is easily comforted by the caregiver.
- Insecure-resistant — the child is often uneasy around their caregiver, but becomes upset if they're separated. Comfort can't be given by strangers, and it's also often resisted from the caregiver. Children who show this style of attachment both accept and reject social interaction and intimacy.
- Insecure-avoidant — if they're separated from their caregiver, the child doesn't become particularly distressed, and can usually be comforted by a stranger. This type of attachment is shown by children who generally avoid social interaction and intimacy with others.

Tip: Bowlby called this the 'continuity hypothesis' — i.e. early relationships influence later relationships.

Ainsworth's attachment types caused lots of further research into how childhood attachment may influence relationships later in life.

Adult relationships

Hazen and Shaver (1987) linked attachment theory to adult relationships. Childhood experiences can influence adult relationships as they provide examples of how to behave. Hazen and Shaver (1987) noticed similarities between the attachments infants form with their caregivers and the behaviour shown by adults in romantic relationships. They investigated the link between the attachment type individuals showed as children and the way they felt about adult relationships:

Figure 1: *Studies have shown that people who experienced parental divorce during childhood have more negative attitudes towards relationships in adulthood.*

Key study on attachment and adult relationships — Hazen and Shaver (1987)

Method: A 'love quiz' questionnaire was published in a newspaper. It consisted of questions relating to the one most important romantic relationship experienced in a person's life.
The questions were designed to classify an individual as one of Ainsworth's attachment types. The questionnaire also contained questions which aimed to assess the participant's childhood relationships with their caregivers.

Results: The attachment type that an individual had shown as a child was significantly related to how they felt about adult relationships. Those who showed a secure attachment type in childhood were more likely to enjoy secure relationships as an adult. Those with an insecure-avoidant attachment type in childhood were more likely to find it difficult to trust people in adult relationships. Those with an insecure-resistant attachment type in childhood were more likely to feel anxious in adult relationships and find it hard to get others as close to them as they wanted.

Tip: You covered attachment and Ainsworth's strange situation at AS-Level. Take a look back if you need a reminder.

Conclusion: Relationships formed with parents during childhood affect relationships in adulthood.

Evaluation: The study was based on self-report data which is subjective and therefore may be unreliable. The data was also retrospective, further reducing the reliability of the study. Also, because the study relied on people replying to a newspaper article, the sample might not be representative of the whole population.

Additional study on attachment and adult relationships — Feeney and Noller (1990)

Method: 374 students (62 male and 212 female) were asked to complete a self-report questionnaire which covered details such as relationship history, their attachment to their parents, and their level of self-esteem amongst other things.

Results: Those who had secure parental attachments were more likely to be in a serious, long-term romantic relationship than those who had an insecure attachment with their caregiver.

Conclusion: Parental attachment influences later adult relationships.

Evaluation: The sample was gender biased in that there were far more females than males and so the results can't be generalised to the entire population. Also, self-report data makes the results unreliable due to social desirability bias and inaccurate memory.

Parental divorce and adult relationships

Many studies show that people who experienced parental divorce during childhood have more negative attitudes towards relationships than those who didn't experience parental divorce.

Examples

These negative attitudes include being less optimistic about having a successful relationship, feeling less trustful of partners, having a more favourable attitude towards divorce and a more negative attitude towards marriage.

Silvestri (1991) found that having divorced parents significantly increased an individual's own chances of getting divorced. Johnston and Thomas (1996) suggest that this could be because individuals model their adult behaviour on their parents' behaviour. Alternatively, it could be a result of learnt negative behaviour, disruption caused by family tension, or separation from a parent or siblings during normal child developmental stages. If one parent is absent the child doesn't have a template on which to model their own adult relationships. Franklin et al (1990) found that this can create problems with children's future adult relationships.

Not all children of divorced parents go on to have unsuccessful adult relationships. There are many factors which can influence the long-term effects, e.g. quality of relationship with parents and support after divorce. This research can be used to minimise the effect of divorce on children.

Tip: A lot of the research into relationships has involved artificial situations or depended on self-report questionnaires. However, Fraley and Shaver (1998) conducted a naturalistic observation in an airport to look at how couples with different attachment types dealt with leaving their partners when boarding a plane. Participants completed a questionnaire first to determine their attachment type. They showed that couples who were separating at the airport were more likely to show attachment behaviours than those not separating. They also found that women classed as insecure-avoidant were likely to show less attachment behaviour than those classed as other attachment types.

Real World Connection

Researching the causes of adult relationship problems can provide psychologists with important information that can be used to help minimise the effects of potentially harmful events, such as divorce, on children.

Peer interaction in adolescence and adult relationships

Figure 2: *Interaction with our peers during adolescence helps us to develop skills that are important for our adult relationships.*

Many studies have shown that children who have secure attachments are more socially skilled and confident, and therefore are more likely to be 'popular' at school.

Key studies of peer interaction

Arnett (2007) suggests that friendships with peers during childhood and adolescence give opportunities to develop the skills needed to form successful adult relationships. These include how to resolve conflict and how to take on different roles needed in relationships. Collins and van Dulmen (2006) support this theory and also suggest that relationships with peers give individuals the opportunity to learn behaviours and expectations involved in relationships. So, experiences during childhood and adolescence influence the quality of adult relationships.

Cultural attitudes to relationships

Different cultures have different attitudes to relationships. Western societies tend to be individualist and Eastern societies tend to be collectivist. A collectivist society sees the individual as part of an interdependent social group. Obligations to others and the good of the group are very important. Relationships are more likely to be non-voluntary (e.g. arranged marriages), where marriage joins families as well as individuals. Extended families are more likely to live together, providing support for each other.

In Western societies, the emphasis is on the individual's freedom, achievements and rights. So relationships are formed for individual happiness and are mostly voluntary, where a person chooses their partner for themselves.

The attitudes and values of cultures affect relationships. Hsu (1981) stated that Western cultures value change and new things, but that Eastern cultures value ancestry, history and continuity. Values affect relationships in different parts of the world.

Tip: Arranged marriages are where a husband or wife is chosen for a person rather than them choosing for themselves. Coupling is often arranged by the couple's parents and, in some cultures, there is no choice in the matter. In other cultures, the process allows more choice — a person can meet, and has opportunity to decline, a prospective partner. Arranged marriages are permanent — shame may be brought on the family if a marriage does not last. Often in collectivist societies, an arranged marriage is not just a union between the couple — it is seen that the whole extended family 'marries' the other extended family.

Duration

Relationships are more likely to be permanent in non-Western cultures. In Western societies, we are more likely to split up and have new relationships.

Marriage

Arranged marriages are often associated with collectivist cultures, and involve whole families. Arranged marriages also seem to have more stability than those based on 'romantic love'. However, De Munck (1996) found that in a Sri Lankan community with an emphasis on arranged marriages, romantic love was still considered when choosing a partner.

Ghuman (1994) stated that arranged marriages were common among Hindus, Muslims and Sikhs in Britain, but Goodwin (1997) found that only 9% of Hindu marriages he studied were arranged.

Levine et al (1995) found a higher percentage of people from collectivist societies would marry a person with the right qualities whom they didn't love, compared to members of individualistic societies.

Attempts have been made to find out how successful arranged marriages are, in comparison to 'chosen/love' marriages (marriages where the couple have selected each other on the basis of 'romantic love').

Key studies on the success of arranged marriages

Gupta and Singh (1982) conducted a longitudinal study on 100 professional couples living in India. 50 of the couples were produced from arranged marriages, and 50 were from 'love marriages'. Couples were asked to complete rating scales stating how much they currently 'liked' and 'loved' their partner after one, five and ten years of marriage.

It was found that in love marriages, liking and love were high at the start of the marriage, but decreased as time progressed. In contrast, arranged marriages had lower love and like ratings initially, but as time passed both love and liking increased. After ten years, arranged marriages actually exceeded the 'love marriages' in both love and liking.

However, a study by Xiaohe and Whyte (1990) found contradictory results — their findings showed that women in love matches, were much more satisfied with their relationships than women in arranged marriages.

Figure 3: *Arranged marriages are commonly associated with collectivist societies.*

Divorce

Goodwin (1999) calculated the US divorce rate to be 40-50%. However, the Chinese regard divorce as shameful to the families involved as much as the divorcing couple so fewer marriages end in divorce. This is beginning to change though, as a result of westernisation.

The role of religion is also a key cultural factor in determining how marriage and divorce are seen:

Examples

- In the Roman Catholic Church, divorce is not recognised as marriage is seen as an act that has been created by God and can't be broken. In most countries, if a marriage doesn't work out you can still have a civil divorce — but within the Catholic Church the marriage would still exist.
- Islam allows divorce, but there are rules and regulations that must be followed to allow it to go ahead. According to the Qur'an, it is not desired and should be a last resort.

Tip: It's hard to generalise the results of Xiahoe and Whyte's (1990) study to a wider population as the study was carried out in just one country.

Real World Connection

Social class is another factor that might influence divorce rates. Haskey (1987) conducted a study where the results showed that divorce rates of couples in England and Wales were much higher in those from unskilled and lower socio-economic backgrounds, than in the professional classes.

Worked Exam-style Question

0 1 Discuss the influence of childhood experiences on adult relationships.

(8 marks + 16 marks)

Childhood experiences are thought to be important in shaping who we become as adults. This includes the relationships we have as adults. Research has shown that childhood attachment behaviours can influence attachments and relationships in later life. Hazen and Shaver (1987) believed that childhood experiences can influence adult relationships because they provide examples of how to behave. They believed that the attachment an infant has with its parents can later influence and determine its behaviour in romantic relationships as an adult.

To investigate this theory, a 'love quiz' questionnaire was published in a newspaper consisting of questions relating to the one most important romantic relationship experienced in a person's life. The questions were designed to assess which of Ainsworth's attachment types each participant displayed. The questionnaire also contained questions to assess the participant's childhood relationships with their caregivers.

Exam Tip

A2 questions tend to be quite broad, but make sure you stay focused in your answer. Writing a quick plan of what you want to say before you start will help keep you on track.

Exam Tip
Apply your knowledge of research methods in psychology when evaluating studies — you can criticise studies by talking about things such as their sampling methods.

Exam Tip
As this question is really broad it's a great opportunity to drop in a load of studies and show off your knowledge.

It was found that there was a significant correlation between the attachment type people reported as a child and how they felt about adult relationships. For instance, those who showed a secure attachment type in childhood were more likely to have a secure relationship as an adult. People who were wary and not trustful of others as an adult were those who had experienced an anxious-avoidant attachment relationship in childhood. Finally, those with an anxious-resistant attachment type in childhood were more likely to feel anxious in adult relationships and find it hard to get others as close to them as they wanted. The researchers concluded that childhood relationships with caregivers do appear to directly affect the type of relationships that they form as adults.

However, there are several criticisms of this work. Firstly, the data was gathered from self-report questionnaires. These rely on people remembering things from the past which can be unreliable and subjective. Also, the sample for this research was taken from people who responded to a particular newspaper article. This means the sample is unlikely to be representative of the whole population and therefore, the results cannot be generalised.

Another childhood experience that can affect future adult relationships is divorce. Many studies show that people who experienced parental divorce during childhood have more negative attitudes towards relationships than those who didn't experience parental divorce. These negative attitudes include being less optimistic about having a successful relationship, feeling less trustful of partners, having a more favourable attitude towards divorce and a more negative attitude towards marriage. Silvestri (1991) found that having divorced parents significantly increased an individual's own chances of getting divorced. Johnston and Thomas (1996) suggest that this could be because individuals model their adult behaviour on their parents' behaviour.

Alternatively, it could be a result of learnt negative behaviour, disruption caused by family tension, or separation from a parent or siblings during normal child developmental stages. If one parent is absent the child doesn't have a template on which to model their own adult relationships. Franklin et al (1990) found that this can create problems with children's future adult relationships. However, not all children of divorced parents go on to have unsuccessful adult relationships. There are many factors which can influence the long-term effects, e.g. quality of relationship with parents and support after divorce.

Overall, it would seem that childhood experiences can influence later relationships, but that the way in which this happens is still unclear.

Summary Questions

Q1 Name Ainsworth's three types of attachment.

Q2 Why did Arnett (2007) think that childhood friendships with peers are important?

Q3 a) Give two typical features of a collectivist society.

b) Which type of society tends to be collectivist, Eastern or Western?

Q4 Outline a study which looked at arranged marriages.

Q5 How might divorce rates be influenced by cultural factors?

Section Summary

- There are a lot of factors that determine how a relationship starts in the first place. Kerckhoff and Davis (1962) produced a 'filter model' in order to describe how relationships develop.
- Reward/need satisfaction theory is a view that we take part in relationships for selfish reasons — relationships provide rewards that satisfy our social needs.
- Economic theories consider relationships to be a trading process.
- There are many reasons why relationships might break down. These include things like dissatisfaction or boredom with the relationship, breaking agreed rules (e.g. being faithful, confidentiality), etc.
- Some theories suggest that relationships end in stages. Lee (1984) provided evidence for a five-stage process, while Duck (1988) developed a four-phase model.
- Sexual selection is the evolution of characteristics which are attractive to potential mates. Types of sexual selection include intersexual and intrasexual selection.
- Buss (1989) carried out cross-cultural research and found gender differences in intersexual selection — men preferred variables associated with reproductive capacity, while women valued variables associated with gaining resources. The study supports an evolutionary explanation of gender differences in sexual selection.
- Gender differences are also seen in parental investment. Women show greater parental investment than men because they have a bigger role to play in the biological development of their offspring, and also because the number of children they can have is limited in comparison to men.
- Trivers (1972) used parental investment theory to explain sex differences in selecting a mate, and differences in sexual promiscuity between men and women.
- Our childhood experiences can affect our ability to form adult relationships. Hazen and Shaver (1987) linked attachment theory to adult relationships, showing that relationships formed with parents during childhood affect relationships in adulthood.
- Many studies show that experiencing parental divorce as a child affects our ability to form successful adult relationships.
- Peer interaction in childhood is an opportunity to develop the skills needed in adult relationships.
- Western societies tend to be individualist and Eastern societies tend to be collectivist. They also have different attitudes towards adult relationships. These differences can affect the duration of relationships, as well as attitudes towards marriage and divorce.
- Arranged marriages are more common in collectivist societies. Attempts to measure the success of arranged marriages have produced conflicting results. Gupta and Singh (1989) produced evidence suggesting they can be highly successful, but findings by Xiaohe and Whyte (1990) disagree.

Exam-style Questions

0 1 Discuss theories behind the formation and/or maintenance of relationships.

(8 marks + 16 marks)

---

0 2 Discuss how culture influences adult relationships.

(8 marks + 16 marks)

Unit 3 Section 4: Aggression

1. Social Theories of Aggression

Learning Objectives:

- Know the social psychological theories of aggression, for example, social learning theory and deindividuation.
- Know about institutional aggression.

Aggression is behaviour intended to harm — including physical and psychological harm. It's important that we try to understand why it exists and what it is for, in order to find ways to prevent it.

Deindividuation theory

One social psychological theory of aggression suggests we're disinhibited and more likely to display aggressive behaviour when we're an anonymous part of a crowd. People may feel less personal responsibility and less fear of public disapproval when they're part of the group. Festinger et al (1952) coined the term **deindividuation** to describe this state.

There's some real-world evidence for this effect:

Examples

- Mullen (1986) analysed newspaper reports of lynch mob violence in the US. The more people there were in the mob, the greater the level of violence.
- Mann (1981) analysed 21 reports of suicides and identified ten cases where a crowd had baited the person threatening suicide (e.g. shouting 'jump'). Baiting was more likely to happen at night, when the crowd was at a distance and when the crowd was large (more than 300 people).
- Silke (2003) analysed accounts of attacks in Northern Ireland and found that, out of 500 people involved, 206 were disguised, and that the disguised attackers were the people who conducted the most violent acts.

Real World Connection
The August 2011 riots in London could be explained using deindividuation theory. Those who took part in the lootings and arson may have been less inhibited whilst disguised in hooded tops and masks. In feeling less responsible for their actions, they would be more likely to behave aggressively.

***Figure 1:** Deindividuation may have been a factor in the 2011 London riots.*

Research studies have also supported deindividuation:

Examples

- Zimbardo (1969) showed that anonymity affects behaviour. Participants in his study believed they were administering shocks to another participant in a learning experiment. Individuated participants wore normal clothes, large name badges and were introduced to each other. Deindividuated participants wore coats with hoods, were instructed in groups and weren't referred to by name. The more anonymous participants administered more and longer shocks.
- Diener et al (1976) observed 1300 trick-or-treating children in the US. If they were anonymous (in costumes, masks or large groups) they were more likely to steal money and sweets.

This evidence supports the idea that deindividuation increases aggression. But there are also examples of it having no effect or even reducing aggression. For example, individuals in crowds at religious festivals often express goodwill to others. It could be that being in a group means that you conform to group norms. If group norms are **prosocial**, the individual may behave that way too.

Tip: Sometimes people may feel <u>less</u> anonymous in groups than if they are alone. This may explain why groups can sometimes reduce aggression — people are afraid others in the group may be watching them.

Social learning theory

Social learning theory says behaviours are learnt in two ways:

- Directly through reinforcement. **Positive reinforcement** is where a certain behaviour leads to a reward, making the behaviour more likely in the future. **Negative reinforcement** is where a certain behaviour helps to avoid an unpleasant consequence, so it's more likely to be repeated in the future.

Example
Rewards, such as money, can be gained after aggressive behaviour. E.g. Shaun broke into the newsagents and stole some money.

- Indirectly by seeing others being rewarded or punished for behaviours (**vicarious learning**).

Example
Eric Harris and Dylan Klebold carried out the Columbine High School massacre in which 13 people were killed. They were both alleged to be fans of violent video games, which some people have linked to the massacre. Seeing characters in video games being rewarded for violent behaviour could encourage aggression in the players themselves through vicarious reinforcement.

Bandura (1965) conducted the Bobo doll experiment to investigate whether aggressive behaviour can be learnt through reinforcement and punishment.

Key study of the social learning theory of aggression — Bandura (1965)

Method:	In a controlled observation with an independent measures design, children watched a video of a male or female model behaving aggressively towards a Bobo doll. Their behaviour was distinctive — e.g. they used a hammer or shouted certain things. The children either saw the model being told off (punished) or being rewarded with sweets (reinforced). In a control condition, the model was neither rewarded nor punished. The children were then allowed to play in a room of toys, including the Bobo doll.
Results:	Children who'd seen the model being rewarded and those in the control condition imitated more aggressive behaviours than those who saw the model being punished.
Conclusion:	Children learn aggressive behaviour through observation and imitation, particularly if it's rewarded.
Evaluation:	The models used distinctive actions that the children were unlikely to produce spontaneously, meaning that Bandura could be sure that imitation was taking place. However, the conditions were pretty artificial — it's unlikely that children would see adults behaving aggressively towards toys in real life, so the study lacks ecological validity. The study also didn't consider the differences between playfighting and aggression towards other people. The previous behaviour of the children wasn't considered, and no follow-up was done to see if the aggressive behaviour was long-term.

Tip: Social learning theory says that an individual's experiences can explain their aggressive behaviour.

Figure 2: Video games are thought to influence aggressive behaviour through vicarious reinforcement.

Tip: A Bobo doll is an inflatable figure with a weight in the bottom.

Figure 3: A Bobo doll, as used by Bandura.

Tip: Violent films and computer games are controversial and when they are linked with events such as the Columbine High School massacre, their effects can seem alarming. However, several meta-analyses have shown that the effects of violent video games on aggression may actually be much less significant.

Correlations between aggressive behaviour and violent video games have been shown by some studies, but the relationship isn't necessarily causal — it may just be that more aggressive individuals have a preference for more violent games — not surprising really...

Tip: Although there are some limitations of the research into the influence of media violence on aggressive behaviour, there have been some useful findings. For example, it has shown that not all people are affected by the media, and therefore, there must be other factors that influence aggressive behaviour.

Additional study of the social learning theory of aggression — Paik and Comstock (1994)

Method: Paik and Comstock conducted a meta-analysis investigating the impact of media violence on behaviour. They analysed the results of 217 different studies dating from 1957 to 1990.

Results: The results showed that there was an overall significant correlation between watching violent television and films and violent behaviour. The correlation for men was slightly stronger than for women, and those who watched violent cartoons and fantasy programmes also showed more aggressive behaviour than people who watched other types of films and programmes.

Conclusion: There is a correlation between aggressive behaviour and watching violent media images.

Evaluation: Although this review was large and included many studies, lots of the experiments took place in laboratories and may therefore have lacked ecological validity. The results also only show a correlation, and not a causal relationship — it might just be that people who are more aggressive are also more likely to choose more violent and aggressive media.

Institutional aggression

Institutional aggression is the term used to describe aggression within an institutional environment (e.g. in prisons or the military) — it's often caused by social factors rather than people's personal feelings. For example, Zimbardo's (1973) prison experiment showed that when people adopted artificial roles as 'prison guards', they were unnecessarily aggressive towards the 'prisoners'.

Tip: An institution is a place that is governed by a person, or group, with authority. They usually have strict social guidelines. They can include places such as schools, prisons and hospitals.

Key study of institutional aggression — Zimbardo (1973)

Method: 24 male participants were divided into two groups at random and labelled as either a 'prisoner' or a 'guard'. They were then placed in a simulated prison at Stanford University and observed by the research team.

Results: At the start of the experiment, both 'guards' and 'prisoners' adopted their roles quickly. The 'guards' became authoritative whilst the 'prisoners' were obedient. Because the aggression shown by the 'guards' became too extreme, the experiment had to be stopped early.

Conclusion: An institutional environment can cause people to conform to perceived roles within particular situations.

Evaluation: The sample used within this experiment was not representative of the population — it consisted of just young, male undergraduate students, so the results can't be generalised to the whole population. Whilst the experiment was highly unethical and caused a lot of distress, it has stimulated a lot of research into behaviour and aggression.

Acceptable institutional aggression

Aggression doesn't always involve red faces, bulging eyes and throbbing veins. It can be calm, organised, and even respectable. Certain groups in society are actually relied on to show aggression, so the rest of us don't have to...

Aggression in the police force

To uphold the rules and norms of society the police are allowed to use aggression against people breaking the law. In this situation, aggression can be seen as a prosocial behaviour and many people think the threat of police aggression is critical in maintaining order in society.

To make sure their aggressive behaviours are controlled and appropriate to the situation police officers have to go through training — uncontrolled police aggression or abuse of police power isn't tolerated by society. The Independent Police Complaints Commission helps make sure that police aggression is controlled and appropriate by holding police officers accountable for their actions.

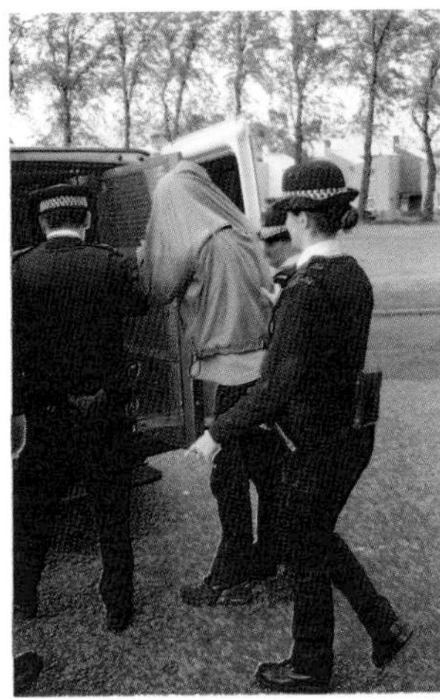

Figure 4: *The police sometimes use aggressive techniques to keep us safe.*

Aggression in the military

Wars are usually started and coordinated by politicians. Their motivations may be very different to those of the soldiers who join up to fight. For example, a soldier may join the military in order to become part of a group and feel a sense of belonging, leading to increased self-esteem.

Aggression, or the threat of aggression, is an important feature of a soldier's job. However, like in the police force, the aggression needs to be controlled and used for specific purposes only. For this reason soldiers receive training on when to behave aggressively and what types of aggression are appropriate. For example, the use of guns to return enemy fire is deemed acceptable, but violence towards prisoners and innocent civilians is not.

However, organised aggression isn't always respectable or accepted by society. Terrorist groups are an example of aggressive organisations that aren't tolerated by society.

Tip: Institutional aggression can vary depending on situational forces and individualistic factors. Situational forces are factors that exist within the environment, such as the nature of the authority figure and whether deindividuation is occurring. Individualistic factors include the personality characteristics such as the morals of the individuals involved.

Aggression in terrorist groups

People who join terrorist organisations may be motivated by a wide range of reasons, including the sense of belonging that comes with joining a group. Many join believing it will bring them certain benefits.

Example

Young Palestinians living in poverty are often recruited as suicide bombers with the promise of glory in the afterlife.

The difference between military organisations and terrorist groups is relative, depending on who the target of aggression is — enemy soldiers or civilians.

Worked Exam-style Questions

0 1 Outline how social learning theory might explain aggression.

(4 marks)

Social learning theory proposes that behaviour, including aggression, can be learnt in two ways. It can be learnt directly through reinforcement, which can be both positive and negative. Alternatively, it can be learnt indirectly, through seeing other people being rewarded or punished for their behaviour. This indirect learning is known as vicarious learning. Various pieces of research have provided support for theses ideas.

Exam Tip

It's often a good idea to scribble down a brief plan to outline what you'll include in your answer.

Exam Tip
Try to support the points that you make with examples. Making links with everyday life shows that you really understand what you're talking about.

Direct reinforcement can be positive — i.e. the behaviour leads to a reward, making the behaviour more likely in the future. For instance, if a child pushes their little brother out of the way to get the last ice lolly and their parent still gives it to them, then they are more likely to repeat the behaviour as they have been rewarded for it. Direct reinforcement can also be negative — a behaviour which helps to avoid an unpleasant consequence is more likely to be repeated in the future.

Indirect, or vicarious, reinforcement is the idea that reinforcement of aggressive behaviour can come from watching others being rewarded or punished. Bandura (1965) illustrated this theory very effectively through his Bobo doll experiment. He showed that children can learn aggressive behaviour through observation and imitation after watching a model behaving aggressively towards a Bobo doll. The children either saw the model being told off (punished) or being rewarded with sweets (reinforced). Children who'd seen the model being rewarded imitated more aggressive behaviours than those who saw the model being punished, providing evidence for the idea that children can learn aggressive behaviour through indirect, or vicarious, reinforcement.

Summary Questions

Q1 What is deindividuation theory?

Q2 What were the findings of the study by Diener et al (1976)?

Q3 What research design was used in Bandura's (1965) study of the social learning theory of aggression?

Q4 Outline the results of Paik and Comstock's (1994) study of the social learning theory of aggression.

Q5 What is institutional aggression?

Q6 Who were the participants in Zimbardo's (1973) prison experiment?

Q7 Give an instance of acceptable institutional aggression.

2. Biological Explanations of Aggression

Some people are more aggressive than others. While some differences in behaviour may be explained by our environment, some may be a result of biological factors.

Genetic factors

Species of various animals have been **selectively bred** to produce highly aggressive individuals — e.g. Doberman dogs were originally bred by humans to behave aggressively towards intruders so they can be used as guard dogs.

This ability to select the most aggressive dogs and breed them together to give new generations with the same aggressive tendencies suggests that there are specific genes that determine levels of aggression.

In humans, evidence for a genetic component to aggression comes from twin studies and adoption studies, where criminality is used as a measure of aggression.

Key study of genetic influences on aggression — Mednick et al (1984)

Method: A concordance analysis of 14 427 Danish adoptees was conducted. Rates of concordance for criminality between the adoptees and their adopted and biological parents were compared.

Results: 13.5% of adoptees with parents (adoptive or biological) without a criminal conviction had a criminal conviction themselves, compared to 14.7% of adoptees with at least one criminally convicted adoptive parent, 20% of adoptees with at least one criminally convicted biological parent, and 24.5% of adoptees with at least one convicted adoptive and one convicted biological parent.

Conclusion: A genetic link is supported. However, the concordance rates are quite low, suggesting that there are other factors that lead to criminality.

Evaluation: Adoption studies allow separation of the genetic and environmental influences. However, criminal convictions may not be a valid indicator of aggression — the convictions could have been for non-violent crimes. Also, just because a person has not been convicted of a crime doesn't necessarily mean that they have never committed one.

Additional study of genetic influences on aggression — Rutter et al (1990)

Method: Rutter et al (1990) conducted a meta-analysis to look at aggressive behaviour in twins. They used studies which had looked at concordance rates of criminal behaviour in identical (MZ) and non-identical (DZ) twins.

Results: In DZ twins there was a 13-22% concordance rate of criminal behaviour. In MZ twins, this was higher, with

Learning Objectives:

- Understand the biological explanations of aggression.
- Know about the neural and hormonal mechanisms in aggression.
- Know about the genetic factors in aggressive behaviour.

Tip: Concordance rates show us how likely it is that a certain trait is shared by two individuals.

Real World Connection
Dmitri Belyaev was one of the first scientists to specially breed animals to create desired characteristics. His research into reducing the aggressiveness of silver foxes took 18 years but successfully concluded that aggression does seem to have some sort of genetic link.

Figure 1: *Belyaev and his silver foxes.*

Tip: Twin and adoption studies are useful because they give us a clearer picture of the role of genetics.

concordance rates ranging from 26-51%.

Conclusion: Since concordance rates are higher in MZ twins than DZ twins, there appears to be a genetic component to aggressive behaviour.

Key study of genetic influences on aggression — Christiansen (1977)

Method: A concordance analysis of all 3586 pairs of twins born between 1881 and 1910 in a region of Denmark was conducted. From this sample, 926 individuals were registered by the police for criminal activity. Identical (MZ) and non-identical (DZ) twins were compared for the rate at which both twins of the pair were registered.

Results: Male MZ twins showed 35% concordance for criminality, compared to the 12% concordance shown between DZ twins. Female MZ twins showed 21% concordance compared to 8% for DZ twins.

Conclusion: There's a genetic component to aggressive behaviour.

Evaluation: Genetics can't be the only factor, as the concordance rate for MZ twins (who share all of their genetic material) wasn't 100%. In previous twin studies, samples have been used where at least one twin had committed a crime. This gave inflated concordance rates. However, by studying all the twins born in a specified time frame, this study gives a more representative rate of concordance. As with all twin studies, shared environment for MZ twins is a confounding variable. As with Mednick et al's (1984) study, there may be cases of criminal behaviour that haven't been reported, which would mean that the results aren't accurate.

Real World Connection

An amygdalotomy is a procedure which involves disconnecting the amygdala (see Figure 2) from the rest of the brain. Studies have shown that, following the procedure, many patients experience a loss of emotion and become a lot less aggressive. Mpakopoulou et al (2008) conducted a review looking at studies investigating aggression in patients before and after an amygdalotomy. Of the 13 papers they looked at, they found that overall, aggressive behaviours in those who'd had an amygdalotomy had decreased between 33 and 100% with no impact on the patients' learning or intelligence.

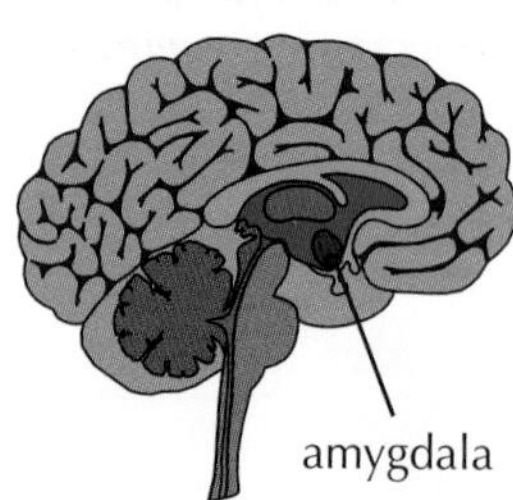

Figure 2: *The location of the amygdala in the brain.*

Neural factors in aggression

Different areas of the brain, including the temporal lobe and the limbic system, have been linked to different forms of aggressive behaviour. One part of the limbic system, the amygdala, has been found to have a particularly strong connection to aggression.

Animal studies have shown that electrical stimulation of different parts of the amygdala can either cause or reduce aggression.

Example

Lesions to the amygdala have been found to cause cats to attack, but caused dogs to become more submissive and less aggressive — they needed more stimulation to provoke a response.

There is some evidence for the role of the amygdala in human aggression too.

Example

Charles Whitman, a sniper who killed 14 innocent people and wounded 31 others, left a note that pleaded for his brain to be examined after death for possible dysfunction. An autopsy showed that he had a temporal lobe tumour, pressing on his amygdala.

Hormones involved in aggression

High levels of **testosterone** (an androgen) are linked to aggression.

Levels of testosterone have been compared in males and females, and in violent and non-violent criminals. Males in general, and violent criminals in particular, have higher levels of testosterone. This may explain their higher levels of aggression. However, there's a problem with establishing cause and effect — this data is only correlational. Another factor could be causing aggressive behaviour, or it could be that being aggressive raises levels of testosterone.

Real World Connection
Taking drugs, or drinking alcohol, may also affect the brain and lead to aggression. Fortier et al (2011) have shown that alcohol misuse can lead to brain damage, particularly in the frontal areas of the brain. This can subsequently lead to aggressive behaviour, supporting the theory that aggression has a biological link.

Key study of hormones and aggression — Brook et al (2001)

Method: Brook et al (2001) conducted a meta-analysis of 45 studies, to study the relationship between testosterone and aggression.

Results: They found a weak positive correlation of 0.14 between testosterone and aggressive behaviour.

Conclusion: Testosterone may be related to aggressive behaviour.

Evaluation: A large sample of studies were used, increasing the reliability of the results. However, because this was a correlational study, cause and effect can't be established.

Tip: A positive correlation means that as one variable increases, so does another. The value of a positive correlation can range between 0 and +1. The closer to 1 it is, the stronger the link between the two variables.

Additional study of hormones and aggression — Tennes and Kreye (1985)

Method: Tennes and Kreye (1985) wanted to investigate the relationship between cortisol and aggression. They measured the cortisol levels of 70 schoolchildren over several days to get baseline measurements and also took readings of cortisol levels on days where children were sitting tests. Observations of the children's behaviour were also made.

Results: Lower levels of cortisol were found in more aggressive schoolchildren.

Conclusion: Cortisol plays a role in aggressive behaviour.

Evaluation: The relationship between cortisol and aggression is only correlational — we can't say there's a causal relationship based on the results from this study. Also, the results may not necessarily be relevant in different contexts or age groups.

Figure 3: *Levels of cortisol are thought to be lower in more aggressive schoolchildren.*

Van Goozen et al (1994) studied the effects of testosterone directly. This avoided having to depend on correlational data, which made it easier to establish cause and effect.

Key study of hormones and aggression — Van Goozen et al (1994)

Method: In a repeated measures design, 35 female-to-male and 15 male-to-female transsexuals completed questionnaires to assess proneness to aggression. They completed the

Tip: Van Goozen et al's (1994) study only used a small sample size — this makes the results less reliable.

Real World Connection
Whilst there is lots of evidence for the biological link to aggression, in particular the role of hormones, we still have to consider individual differences. Harrison et al (2000) conducted a study where they injected 56 men with testosterone. They found that, despite all having the same extra amount of the hormone, not all men showed the same aggressive behaviours whilst playing a frustrating computer game. Individual differences, such as personality characteristics, do appear to play some role in determining behaviour.

questionnaires before and after receiving hormone treatment to 'change' their sex. Female-to-male transsexuals were given testosterone (an androgen) and male-to-female transsexuals were given anti-androgens. Treatment lasted 3 months.

Results: Female-to-male transsexuals reported an increase in aggression proneness, whereas male-to-female transsexuals reported a decrease.

Conclusion: Levels of testosterone determine the likelihood of displaying aggressive behaviours.

Evaluation: By controlling levels of testosterone experimentally, the direction of cause and effect between testosterone and aggression can be established. However, self-report measures of aggression were used, which are subjective and so may not be valid. The participants may have been conforming to stereotypes of their new gender roles by expressing an increase or decrease in aggression.

Worked Exam-style Question

0 1 Outline biological explanations of aggression. *(8 marks)*

One biological explanation for aggression focuses on the role of genetics. This theory suggests that aggressive behaviour has a hereditary component and is therefore passed on to offspring in the genes, rather than being a product of environmental factors.

Studies into the role of different structures in the brain have provided another biological explanation of aggression. Different areas of the brain, including the temporal lobe and the limbic system, have been linked to aggressive behaviour. In particular, a part of the limbic system called the amygdala has been found to have a strong connection to aggression. Animal studies have shown that electrical stimulation of different parts of the amygdala can either cause or reduce aggression, while some human studies have shown that disconnecting the amygdala from the rest of the brain (a process known as an amygdalotomy) can reduce aggression in humans.

Various hormones have also been linked to aggressive behaviour. Studies suggest that high levels of the androgen testosterone may increase aggression. Low levels of cortisol, another hormone, have also been linked to aggression.

Exam Tip
In this question you're asked to outline biological explanations of aggression. Don't take your answer any further by evaluating the theories — you won't get any extra marks if you do.

Summary Questions

Q1 Which areas of the brain are thought to be involved in aggression?

Q2 Name one hormone that is believed to be related to aggression.

Q3 Describe the method used by Van Goozen et al (1994) to study aggression in sex-change participants.

3. Evolutionary Explanations of Aggression

There are lots of examples of how aggression in animals is necessary for their survival. This might mean evolution has a strong part to play in aggression.

Learning Objectives:

- Know the evolutionary explanations of human aggression, including infidelity and jealousy.
- Understand the evolutionary explanations of group display in humans, for example, sport and warfare.

Lorenz's evolutionary explanation

Lorenz proposed a theory of aggression based on animal behaviour. He used the idea of natural selection (that only the best adapted will survive and pass on their genes) to explain how the behaviour of animals is shaped.
Lorenz suggested his theory could also be applied to humans.

- Aggression is an innate tendency that's triggered by environmental stimuli.
- Aggression is an adaptive response. An individual will be more likely to pass on their genes if they're able to gain the upper hand in competition for food, mates or territory.
- Aggression is ritualised. A behaviour won't be passed on in the genes if it gets an animal killed before it produces offspring. So, there are ritual behaviours in place to stop confrontations being fatal.

Figure 1: *Fighting amongst deer is an evolutionary display of aggression as they fight for a mate.*

Example

Wolves end a fight by the loser exposing his jugular vein as a sign of submission. This puts the winner in prime position to kill their rival, but in fact the winner takes no further action. If animals were routinely killed during everyday power struggles or mating contests, it's likely the species would become extinct.

Lorenz's theory has been criticised on the fact that aggression isn't always adaptive and ritualised — there are many species that do fight to the death. Also, the relevance of the theory to humans is limited, as cultural influences are highly influential in the expression of aggression.

Example

A person's religious beliefs may shape their actions, as may the availability of weapons or the occurrence of war. However, an evolutionary approach may be relevant in explaining some aggressive human responses.

Jealousy is a form of aggression

Jealousy is a form of aggression to deter a partner's infidelity. In a survey by Kinsey (1948), 50% of married men and 26% of married women reported having had sex with somebody else while married.

Infidelity can be seen as an evolutionary adaptive strategy for a man to increase the quantity of offspring carrying his genes, and for a woman to improve the quality of her offspring. However, it's obviously not in the genetic interests of their partners to be cheated on — it won't be their genes being passed on to the next generation. Indicators that a partner is being unfaithful often lead to jealous rage. Jealousy has been explained as a product of evolution, although this response is triggered differently in each sex.

Tip: Kinsey's (1948) study was a long time ago. It is possible that trends and ideas in terms of what men and women expect from relationships have changed. The study also only considers men and women who admitted to infidelity — the actual rates could have been much higher. Kinsey's work has been criticised for using participants from non-representative samples (e.g. including responses from a disproportionate number of prisoners), meaning that his conclusions may not be fair.

Key study of sex differences in jealousy — Buss et al (1992)

Method: This was a cross-cultural questionnaire study. Participants were presented with the hypothetical scenario that someone

Tip: Cross-cultural studies are good for investigating whether or not something has a biological basis. If a trait can be found across many different cultures, it is a good indication that it's got a strong biological explanation and isn't dependent on cultural or environmental factors.

Tip: People can often lie on questionnaires to show themselves in a better light and therefore the data might not be truly reliable.

they were in a serious, committed romantic relationship with had become interested in someone else. They were asked what would distress them more — imagining their partner forming a deep emotional attachment to that other person, or enjoying passionate sexual intercourse with the person.

Results: Across all studies, more men than women reported sexual infidelity to be most upsetting. On average, 51% of the men versus 22% of the women chose this to be more distressing than emotional infidelity.

Conclusion: Men's jealousy is innately triggered by the threat of uncertainty over the paternity of children produced within the relationship. However, women are more threatened by emotional involvement as it could mean being left for another woman, and so reducing the resources available to her children.

Evaluation: The fact that the evidence was consistent across different cultures suggests that these different responses are innate rather than learned. However, the fact that the questionnaires were based around a hypothetical situation, and the responses available to the participants were multiple choice, means that the validity of the results is questionable — they may not accurately reflect what participants would actually do if they found themselves in that situation.

Additional study of sex differences in jealousy — Haden and Hojjat (2006)

Haden and Hojjat (2006) conducted a study to look at the differences between men and women in their aggressive responses to hypothetical and real betrayal situations. They discovered that more people were more verbally aggressive after a hypothetical romantic betrayal than a hypothetical friendship betrayal. In real life situations, they acted equally as aggressively in romantic and friendship relationships and there were no gender differences.

Group aggression

Aggression can be used by groups to establish dominance in status or to gain better resources. Warfare and sport are two examples of group displays of aggression in humans. There's an evolutionary explanation for them both:

Warfare

Buss and Shackelford (1997) suggest that aggression is an adaptive response as it encourages the reproductive success of the species. Sexual selection means that we choose between prospective mates who we will breed with. Aggression through warfare is one way to eliminate rivals and increase the likelihood of our genes being passed on. According to Waller (2002), terrorist attacks and genocides can be explained by evolutionary theory. Because humans have evolved living in groups, a sense of 'them' and 'us' has become important to us. Warfare and other violence against 'outsiders' are ways of defining the boundaries of our groups.

Tinbergen (1968) pointed out that aggression in humans doesn't always have an adaptive survival function. Humans are one of the few species that use aggression purely to cause harm. Tinbergen said that advances in technology mean we're now able to fight each other from long distances. In face-to-face aggression we use signals of appeasement and submission (e.g. emotional tears blur vision and so reduce the efficiency of attack and defence — this acts as a signal of submission to the opponent). In modern warfare, these signals no longer apply as we can't clearly see our opponent. In other words, changes in technology have outstripped the evolution of adaptive behaviour.

Sport

Podaliri and Balestri (1998) studied Italian football supporters.

Key study of aggression in sport — Podaliri and Balestri (1998)

They found that aggressive chants and aggressive behaviour strengthened the cultural identity of the different supporters, so that the differences between the groups were emphasised.

They argued that being associated with the winning team at a football match gives us increased status and makes us more attractive to potential partners. This has adaptive value because we increase the likelihood of genes from our group being passed on — aggressive behaviour has survival value.

A weakness of this approach is that similar levels of aggression are rare in supporters of other types of sports. Also the role of testosterone (see page 59) and social learning theory (see page 53) aren't considered.

Figure 2: *Some sports, such as underwater hockey, have fewer reports of spectator violence than sports such as football.*

Worked Exam-style Question

0 1 Outline and evaluate evolutionary explanations of aggression.

(8 marks + 16 marks)

Evolutionary explanations of aggression state that aggressive behaviour is an adaptive response to help individuals to survive long enough to reproduce and pass on their genes.

Lorenz proposed an evolutionary explanation of aggression based on observations of animals. Animals often compete aggressively for food, territory and mates — so being more aggressive makes animals better competitors and more likely to survive and reproduce. Lorenz also argued that aggression between individuals of the same species is ritualised in animals to prevent aggressive encounters from becoming fatal and the species from becoming extinct — meaning that controlled aggression is an adaptive response and an advantageous trait for a species to have. Even though evidence of ritualised aggression (e.g. in wolves) provides support for Lorenz's ideas, his critics point out that aggression can be disadvantageous as it isn't always ritualised and many species do fight to the death. Critics of Lorenz's evolutionary explanation of aggression also argue that it is largely irrelevant when explaining human aggression. They argue that an evolutionary explanation can't account for cultural and religious factors, which are often very influential on the expression of aggression in humans.

Exam Tip
Illustrating your answer using examples is a great way to pick up extra marks.

Exam Tip
Make it clear where you're talking about human aggression, or where you're referring to animal aggression — it might be obvious to you, but it helps to make things really clear for the examiner.

Other flaws of the evolutionary explanation have also been pointed out. For instance, Tinbergen (1968) pointed out that aggression in humans doesn't always have an adaptive survival function — humans can use aggression purely to cause harm. It also seems that technology has outstripped the evolution of adaptive behaviour. Advances in technology mean we're now able to fight each other from long distances, so we can't clearly see our opponents. This means that signals of appeasement and submission produced during face-to-face aggression may no longer apply. It could be that free will plays more of a part in aggressive behaviour than evolutionary biological factors.

Jealousy in humans can be seen as a form of aggression used to deter a partner's infidelity. In a survey by Kinsey (1948), 50% of married men and 26% of married women reported having had sex with somebody else while married. This infidelity can be seen as an evolutionary adaptive strategy for a man to increase the quantity of offspring carrying his genes, and for a woman to improve the quality of her offspring. However, it's obviously not in the genetic interests of their partners to be cheated on — it won't be their genes being passed on to the next generation. In this case, jealousy is potentially produced as a product of evolution. This point is supported by the results of a cross-cultural study by Buss et al (1992) in which participants were presented with the hypothetical scenario that someone they were in a serious, committed romantic relationship with had become interested in someone else. It was found that women were more concerned with the emotional infidelity, whereas men were more distressed by sexual infidelity.

Exam Tip
Theories in psychology will always be supported, or contradicted by research. Being able to talk about this will get you AO2 and AO3 marks.

The results of this study support Lorenz's evolutionary explanation of aggression — they suggest that men's jealousy is innately triggered by the threat of uncertainty over the paternity of children produced within the relationship, whereas women are more threatened by emotional involvement as it could mean being left for another woman, and so reducing the resources available to her children. The findings of this study were consistent across different cultures suggesting that these different responses are innate rather than learned, providing further support for Lorenz's theory. However, the validity of this study is low, as the questionnaires were based around a hypothetical situation, and the responses available to the participants were multiple choice, so the results may not accurately reflect what participants would actually do if they found themselves in that situation.

Exam Tip
Don't forget to write a concluding statement, summarising what you've written. It'll round your answer off nicely.

In conclusion, although some researchers have provided evidence that contradicts an evolutionary theory of aggression, Lorenz's work has provided a good explanation with lots of support.

Summary Questions

Q1 According to Lorenz, why is aggression an adaptive response?

Q2 a) What was the conclusion of Buss et al's (1992) research?

b) Provide one evaluative point about Buss et al's (1992) study.

Q3 Louis recently played in a Korfball match. Towards the end of the match, the crowd chanted increasingly aggressively. How might an evolutionary psychologist explain this behaviour?

Q4 Outline a study which investigated aggression in sport.

Section Summary

- Aggression can be both a physical and psychological act and there are several theories to explain it — social theories, biological theories and evolutionary theories.
- Social theories of aggression include deindividuation theory and social learning theory.
- According to deindividuation theory, being anonymous encourages aggression. The theory has been supported by numerous research studies such as Zimbardo's (1969) study, where disguised participants were more likely to give an electric shock to another participant.
- Social learning theory says behaviours are learnt in two ways — directly through reinforcements (rewards and punishments) or indirectly by seeing others being rewarded or punished.
- Bandura (1965) conducted a famous experiment using a Bobo doll to show that vicarious learning (indirect social learning) could influence aggressive behaviour.
- Institutional aggression is aggressive behaviour within an institutional environment (e.g. in prison or the military).
- There are acceptable forms of institutional aggression (e.g. in the police force and the military).
- Biological explanations of aggression focus on genetic influences, the brain itself and the role of hormones.
- Studies looking at the heritability of aggressive behaviour have suggested that although aggression has some genetic basis, other factors must also contribute to aggressive behaviour.
- The amygdala, which is part of the limbic system, has been shown to influence aggressive behaviour. Other parts of the limbic system and the temporal lobe are also believed to be linked to aggression.
- Hormones have also been investigated in relation to aggression. Testosterone levels have been found to be higher in more violent criminals. Low levels of cortisol have been linked to an increase in aggressive behaviour.
- The evolutionary explanation of aggression proposes that aggression is a survival tactic to ensure that animals live to reproduce and pass on their genes.
- Jealousy is a form of aggression, seen as an evolutionary response to infidelity.
- Group aggression is a way for groups to establish dominance in status or to gain better resources. Examples include warfare or aggressive behaviour between sports fans of opposing teams.

Exam-style Questions

0 1 Outline neural and hormonal mechanisms of aggression.

(8 marks)

0 2 Evaluate neural and hormonal explanations of aggressive behaviour.

(16 marks)

---

0 3 Outline and evaluate infidelity and jealousy as evolutionary explanations for human aggression.

(8 marks + 16 marks)

---

0 4 Describe and evaluate social psychological theories of aggression.

(8 marks + 16 marks)

Unit 3 Section 5: Eating Behaviour

Learning Objectives:

- Understand factors influencing attitudes to food and eating behaviour, for example cultural influences, mood and health concerns.
- Know about the success and failure of dieting.

1. Factors Influencing Eating Behaviour

We all have to eat. But people's behaviour around food can differ. There are several reasons why people vary in their attitudes to food.

Cultural influence

Cultural influence affects attitudes towards food and size.

In the UK today we tend to assume that you have to be skinny to be beautiful. But that's actually quite a recent idea. Throughout human history, being voluptuous (curvy) was considered an attractive trait in a potential partner — it signalled health and access to plentiful resources in times of scarcity. People were proud to gorge themselves on food and drink because it signalled their wealth and status.

However, in the last 40 years the 'supermodel' and 'size zero' figure has become popular in Western culture. Highly profitable diet, exercise and surgery industries have sprung up as a result of this popularity. In many other places big is still seen as best though.

Tip: One reason we tend to prefer our own culture's food is because of exposure and social learning. Take a look at page 83 for more on this.

Examples

In many African cultures plump females are regarded as wiser and more fertile, in Asian cultures weight is often still linked to affluence and success, and Pacific Islanders (Hawaiians/Samoans) equate large physical size in both genders with beauty and status.

Food is also an important part of many religions:

Examples

- Some fast to show devotion (e.g. Muslim Ramadan).
- Some feast to celebrate important events (e.g. Christian Christmas).
- Some forbid certain foods (e.g. Judaism — pork isn't eaten).
- Some incorporate food in rituals (e.g. Catholicism — communion wafers).

Figure 1: *Celebrations are often linked to certain foods.*

Different cultures attach different meanings to foods and eating forms a major part of many celebrations and ceremonies worldwide. Imagine birthdays without cake, or Christmas without sprouts...

Attitudes to food

Effect of mood

Attitudes to food can be affected by mood. Anyone who has been unable to eat when stressed or who has 'pigged out' on junk food when they're feeling down will know that mood and food are linked. Also, a reduced appetite or bad diet, caused by a lack of motivation, is a common symptom of depression.

Tip: Depression can be both a cause and symptom of different eating behaviours.

If you don't have the energy to prepare healthy meals you might be more likely to resort to unhealthy pre-packaged ready meals and quick snacks. Some people may impulsively 'comfort eat' or binge eat in the hope that a quick indulgence will make them feel better — usually choosing foods high in carbohydrates, fat, sugar and salt to provide that quick 'hit'. This can lead to a vicious cycle of mood swings caused by unnatural highs and lows in blood sugar levels, which trigger further cravings.

Key study of stress and eating — Conner et al (1999)

Method: A group of 60 students were asked to record every minor life hassle for a week. They scored each hassle on a 3 point scale alongside the number of snacks they ate.

Results: There was a direct positive correlation between the number of life hassles and the number of snacks consumed within a week. There were no differences between genders.

Conclusion: Attitudes to food may be influenced by mood.

Evaluation: The students may have guessed what the researchers were investigating. This can cause people to change their behaviours — this is responding to demand characteristics.

Tip: A life hassle is something that causes people distress and affects their everyday life — for example, starting a new school can be a stressful event. An altered routine, the prospect of making new friends and getting used to new surroundings can all affect someone's everyday life.

Additional studies of stress and eating

More support for the link between an increase in stress and changes in eating behaviour comes from Gibson's (2006) study. They found that when their participants reported higher levels of stress, they also reported a higher intake of carbohydrates and sugary foods.

However, not all research suggests a positive relationship between stress and eating behaviour. Sometimes people can stop, or reduce, their food intake when they are anxious. Popper et al (1989) studied the behaviour of marines and found that when they were in highly stressful situations, their eating levels dramatically decreased.

Tip: Foods high in carbohydrates and sugar help boost mood by working on the serotonin system. People with depression often have less serotonin which may be why there seems to be a link between food and mood.

Effect of emotional intelligence

Psychologists are currently investigating the role **emotional intelligence** (EI) plays in the relationship between mood and eating behaviour. They believe that people with a high level of personal EI make better food choices and are less likely to use food to regulate their mood. These people are also less likely to find that their appetite is affected (reduced or increased) by stress.

Tip: Emotional intelligence is the ability to recognise and manage your own emotions and those of other people.

Key study of EI — Costarelli et al (2009)

Method: 92 Greek female students were given questionnaires about their attitudes to eating. They also had to provide an account of their eating behaviour and do an EI test.

Results: Those who were classified as having disordered eating patterns had a lower EI than those not classified as having disordered eating patterns.

Conclusion: EI is linked to eating behaviour.

Evaluation: The sample wasn't representative as only young, female, Greek students were used. The results, therefore, can't be generalised. The study also relied on self-reporting, which means the results may not be completely accurate.

Tip: You can read more about anorexia on page 76 and bulimia on page 81.

Real World Connection

Dieting programmes such as Weight Watchers® get a lot of mixed press in their effectiveness at helping people lose weight. Jebb et al (2011) used a large sample to see whether people enrolled in a Weight Watchers programme were more likely to lose weight than those who followed a standard medical plan. They split up 722 obese patients into two random groups — Weight Watchers or medical care. They then monitored them for one year. Those in the Weight Watchers programme lost twice as much weight, concluding that schemes such as these really can be successful.

Health concerns

Health concerns (e.g. high blood pressure) can affect what and how much we eat. However, eating healthily can become an obsession for some people:

Example

Orthorexia is an eating disorder where people survive on a highly restricted diet to try and avoid anything they think might be 'unhealthy'. This can range from pesticides, herbicides, artificial additives or genetically modified ingredients to fats, animal products, or anything except raw fruit and vegetables. In extreme cases this can lead to **malnutrition** or even death.

More familiar examples of eating disorders include anorexia and bulimia. Sometimes these can begin with a desire to lose weight and be more healthy, which then gets out of hand and becomes a dangerous obsession.

Dieting

Dieting doesn't always lead to weight loss. It's not as easy as just going on a diet and watching the weight drop off. Whether a person succeeds in losing weight depends on things like motivation, willpower, genetics, lifestyle and medical conditions (e.g. diabetes or thyroid problems). Other factors include:

Support and encouragement

Eating is often a part of social interaction, so many experts think dieting should be too. Informing friends and family of weight loss goals should help reduce the temptations of food and encourage positive reinforcement (and punishment) from others. Lots of dieters also join a weight loss group or diet with a friend or partner to maintain motivation.

But this approach doesn't work for everyone — some people find constant monitoring by others stressful and use secretive binge eating as a defence mechanism.

Key study of dieting — Wardle and Beales (1988)

Method: 27 women who had been classified as obese were split into three groups. Group 1 followed a diet plan (high restraint), Group 2 followed an exercise plan (low restraint) and Group 3 acted as the control group. All three groups followed the plans for seven weeks. At week four, all participants were asked to go to the laboratory where their food intake was monitored before and after a pre-load. At week six, they were asked to return to the laboratory and their food intake was monitored again. However, this time they had to complete a stressful test beforehand.

Results: Participants in Group 1 (the dieting group) ate a lot more during the laboratory sessions than the other groups.

Conclusion: Those who feel highly restrained are more likely to overcompensate with food when put in a stressful situation. These results do seem to support the connection between stress and overeating.

Evaluation: This experiment was highly controlled and, using a non-student sample, could represent the wider population. However, the sample size is very small and most of the experiment took place in an unnatural setting, meaning it lacks ecological validity.

Tip: Pre-load methods are used a lot in experiments investigating eating behaviour. They usually involve giving people different foods or drinks with varying calories to see how this affects their later eating behaviour.

Additional study of dieting — Polivy and Herman (1999)

Method: Polivy and Herman (1999) wanted to investigate what would happen if dieters were caused distress. They investigated female students, some of whom were dieters, and told them they had either succeeded or failed a certain cognitive task. Some were then given ice-cream to eat at their leisure.

Results: Compared to the control group, the participants who were dieting were more likely to blame their distress on eating the ice-cream available to them, rather than their failure on the task.

Conclusion: This study provides evidence for the masking hypothesis to explain failure of dieting — dieters blame their emotions on eating behaviour rather than a real reason for their distress.

Evaluation: The task was not very realistic and so the study lacks ecological validity. It also didn't consider other factors in peoples' lives and their individual differences which may have influenced the results. Certain people respond to failure in different ways.

Tip: The masking hypothesis explains what happens when people use one behaviour to disguise how they are really feeling. In terms of eating, people may binge eat and blame their distress on what they've just eaten rather than facing up to the real issue.

Physiological changes due to dieting

Your body has evolved to cope with chronic food shortages by lowering your metabolic rate and protecting fat stores in times of starvation. Extreme dieting triggers this response. If you then return to normal eating you end up with more excess calories than before which are then converted to fat. To overcome the feeling of deprivation during the diet people often also overeat afterwards, which gives an even bigger weight gain. You may then start another, even more restrictive diet to undo the weight gain. But this will just reduce the metabolic rate further and so the pattern of 'yo-yo' dieting continues.

Figure 2: *Yo-yo dieting can be difficult for many people.*

Key study of the psychological effects of dieting — Polivy and Herman (1975)

Method: In a study with an independent measures design, samples of dieting and non-dieting students were placed in three 'pre-load' conditions — drinking either one or two glasses of milkshake or nothing at all. They were then given unlimited supplies of ice cream.

Results: The non-dieters ate less ice cream the more milkshakes they had drunk. The dieters ate more ice cream the more milkshakes they had drunk.

Conclusion: Drinking the milkshake had damaged the dieters' determination — they gave in to total indulgence after failure. This is known as 'the counter-regulation effect'.

Evaluation: These findings support what we already know about dieting (the 'diet starts tomorrow' mentality). Follow-up studies have found that many people have an 'all-or-nothing' mentality to dieting — if they break the diet they tend to see it as immediate failure and so eat as much as they like.

Figure 3: *Commercial weight loss programmes have been shown to be highly effective.*

Exam Tip
Unit 3 exam questions always contain 24 marks. These questions would both have other parts to them.

Exam Tip
Although there are other influences on attitudes to food and eating, the question only asks you to describe the role of culture. Don't waste time talking about things that won't get you any marks.

Exam Tip
Culture has many different aspects. This can include religion.

Exam Tip
It's OK to use the abbreviated forms of words, such as 'EI' in your answers — as long as you've defined it first.

Exam Tip
Although EI isn't on the specification, the examiners would be able to award marks for 'alternative' factors in this question. If you mention something in your answer which isn't on the specification, just make sure you explain it thoroughly.

Worked Exam-style Questions

0 1 Describe the influence of culture on attitudes to food and eating behaviour. *(8 marks)*

Our culture is made up of social norms and rules, which guide our behaviour. All sorts of behaviours, including eating behaviour, can be influenced by cultural factors.

Over time, the idea of what 'beautiful' is has changed. Historically, curvy women were regarded as attractive. Being large signalled good health and access to plenty of resources and wealth. However, over time, things have changed. Due to Western culture, there has been a rise in the notion that 'thin is beautiful'. Supermodels are becoming thinner and a lot of emphasis has been put on diets, exercise and even surgery to help people get their 'ideal' body shape. As a result, attitudes towards food and eating have changed. However, cultures across the world see food in different ways. In Africa, there is still very much the idea that big is best — overweight females are seen as being wiser and more fertile. Likewise, in Asia, overweight people signify wealth and success.

Religion is also an important part of culture that influences people's attitudes toward food. For example, Jews are forbidden from eating pork. Muslims take part in Ramadan, where they fast to show devotion. Many cultures feast to celebrate important events. For example, Christmas is often celebrated with particular foods. This confirms that eating patterns are certainly culturally dependent and are related to social norms.

Overall, culture shapes the way we live our lives. Through historic perceptions of what it means to be attractive, along with religious teachings and traditions in regards to food, culture does seem to influence food and eating behaviours.

0 2 Describe and explain one factor which can affect attitudes to food. *(4 marks)*

There are several factors which can affect attitudes to food, but one of these is emotional intelligence (EI). EI is the idea that people can manage their own emotions, as well as those of other people. In recognising your emotions you are likely to make better food choices and therefore, less likely to rely on food as a way of regulating mood. As a result, everyday situations that might cause stress or anxiety are less likely to affect the eating patterns of people with a high EI.

Psychologists have researched the link between EI and eating behaviour and, as Costarelli et al (2009) have shown, those with a higher EI are less likely to have disordered eating behaviours.

Summary Questions

Q1 Give an example of how eating behaviour may be affected by mood.

Q2 What is orthorexia?

Q3 Gina has been told she needs to lose some weight. She has tried dieting but without much success.

a) What could be one possible explanation for her failure to diet?

b) Give one other factor which might make Gina's dieting experience more successful.

2. Biological Explanations of Eating Behaviour

Eating behaviour can be explained using a biological approach. There are parts of our bodies that naturally tell us when to eat and when to stop.

Learning Objectives:
- Understand the neural mechanisms involved in controlling eating behaviour.
- Understand the evolutionary explanations of food preference.

Neural mechanisms

Neural mechanisms control eating and satiation. The hypothalamus is a gland in the brain responsible for homeostasis (keeping conditions in the body constant). It helps to regulate things like temperature, circadian rhythms and intake of food and drink. The ventromedial nucleus (VMN) and the lateral nucleus (LN) are the parts of the hypothalamus that are thought to be involved in food regulation.

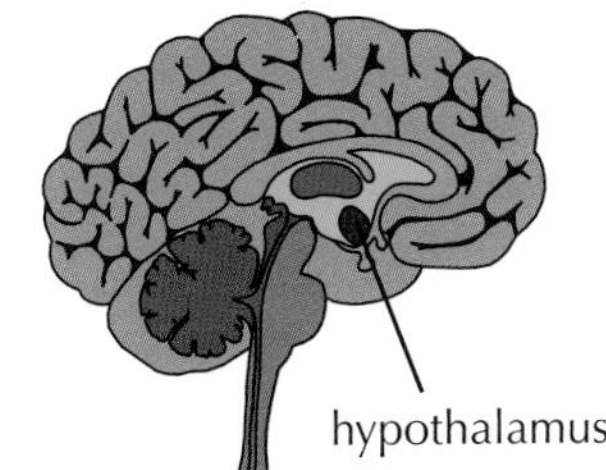

***Figure 1**: The hypothalamus is the finger-nail sized part of the brain responsible for keeping conditions in the body constant.*

The ventromedial nucleus

The **ventromedial nucleus** is the satiety centre. Satiety is the unconscious physiological process that stops you eating. The VMN provides the signal to stop eating when it picks up hormonal messages.

Tip: Satiation just means feeling full.

Example

When food is being digested the level of the hormone CCK in the bloodstream is high. This stimulates receptors in the VMN.

Tip: CCK stands for cholecystokinin.

Experimental electrical stimulation of the VMN has been shown to reduce food intake. Malfunctions in the VMN may cause obesity. This was demonstrated by Baylis et al (1996).

Tip: The VMN is also called the ventromedial hypothalamus.

Key study of VMN lesioning in rats — Baylis et al (1996)

Method:	Two symmetrical lesions (injuries) were made in the VMN of eight male and five female rats. Their body weight was later compared with age-matched controls.
Results:	The rats with lesions in their VMN had become obese, while the control rats had not.
Conclusion:	Lesions in the VMN cause hyperphagia (overeating) and obesity, so the VMN must play a role in satiation.
Evaluation:	This was a very small sample using only one breed of rat, so the findings can't be generalised. Also, other tissues surrounding the VMN might have been damaged when the lesions were created, so it might not necessarily just be the VMN that is involved.

Tip: There are often problems with generalising the results from animal studies. Just because something was shown to be true for one species, it doesn't necessarily mean that it will apply to other species (like humans).

Additional study of VMN lesioning in rats — Gold (1973)

Gold (1973) lesioned the VMN of a sample of rats. Unlike other findings, he discovered that just lesioning this part of the brain did not result in overeating. Overeating only happened when other areas of the brain were damaged as well. However, his findings have not been replicated since which means they might not be that reliable.

The lateral nucleus

The **lateral nucleus** is the hunger centre. When the body's blood sugar level drops, homeostatic responses kick in to help restore the equilibrium. Receptors in the LN detect the drop in blood sugar. This then causes neurons to fire that create the sensation of hunger. The person is driven to eat and blood glucose levels increase. Receptors then send a hormonal message to the VMN to give the sensation of fullness (see page 71).

Tip: The LN is also called the lateral hypothalamus.

Damage to the LN can reduce food intake. For example, chemical lesions are known to produce aphagia (failure to eat). However, as with VMN studies, there may be methodological problems muddying the water.

The VMN and LN work very close together, controlling the body's hunger and satiety signals (see Figure 2).

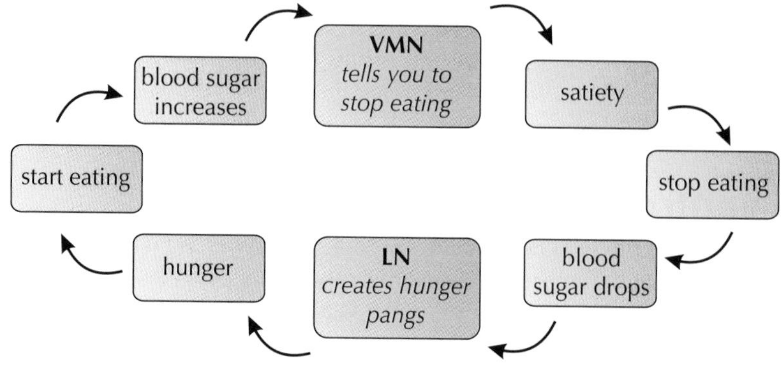

Figure 2: Diagram showing the hunger-satiety cycle.

Figure 3: Studies which require lesions frequently use mice and rats to show the neural mechanisms involved in eating behaviour.

Key study of LN lesioning in rats — Winn et al (1990)

Method:	The toxin NMDA was used to make lesions in the LN of rats. A small dose (lesions in LN only) and a large dose (lesions spread to adjacent areas) condition was used, and there was also a control group.
Results:	Rats that had the small dose of NMDA showed no changes in their eating behaviour after a brief recovery period. However, rats that had the large dose showed long-term deficits in their eating behaviour.
Conclusion:	Damage to the hypothalamus impairs feeding responses, but the LN may not have as much of an effect as previously thought.
Evaluation:	This research is useful as it shows that the localisation of brain function is more complex than originally thought. However, this was an exploratory study to test whether NMDA was an effective toxin for use on the hypothalamus and wasn't originally intended to investigate hunger. Therefore, all the relevant variables may not have been controlled, reducing the reliability of the results.

Real World Connection
Kluver-Bucy syndrome is a disorder in which certain parts of the sufferer's brain are damaged. As one of the symptoms includes overeating, and sometimes even eating inappropriate objects, the damage further suggests that neural mechanisms are involved in eating behaviour. However, these sufferers do have other problems and so the link is still unclear.

Ghrelin

The stomach also sends a hormonal message to the brain when it's empty. This hormone is called ghrelin. The hungrier you are, the more ghrelin you secrete.

Key study of ghrelin and eating behaviour — Cummings et al (2004)

Method: Six male participants were asked to record their hunger levels every 30 minutes after they were given lunch. Their ghrelin levels were monitored every five minutes using blood samples.

Results: Immediately after they had eaten, ghrelin levels fell in all of the participants. It was at the lowest point 70 minutes after they'd eaten. There was a correlation in most of the participants between hunger level and the amount of ghrelin recorded in their blood.

Conclusion: Ghrelin does seem to signal appetite and hunger in humans.

Evaluation: This experiment used a small sample size and only used male participants so the results can't be generalised to a wider population. Although the results only provide a correlation rather than a cause and effect relationship, they do support other findings linking ghrelin to eating behaviour.

Evolutionary reasons for food preference

There are evolutionary reasons for food preferences. People need food to survive and throughout history it's been a driving force for evolution. This can help explain why so many people would rather have a chocolate eclair than a slice of grapefruit.

Tip: Evolutionary theory assumes that behaviour is shaped by our environment and adapts over time to ensure survival.

Why we like sweet stuff...

Harris (1987) found that newborn babies have a preference for sweet things and dislike bitter things. These preferences and dislikes are universal, suggesting a genetic (therefore evolutionary) explanation. Early mammals were frugivores (ate mainly fruit). Sweet food now triggers the release of the pleasure-inducing brain chemical dopamine which acts as a reinforcer.

Most poisons have a strong bitter taste — so our dislike of this type of taste could be a survival reflex.

Tip: Dopamine is a neurotransmitter that works on the reward system of the brain.

Why we prefer food that's bad for us...

Burnham and Phelan (2000) suggest that a preference for fatty foods would have helped our ancestors survive in times of food scarcity — these foods are full of energy-giving calories. Even though food is no longer scarce, we're still programmed to stuff ourselves with burgers and cakes when they're available in order to build up fat reserves in case there's ever a shortage.

Again, dopamine may act as a reinforcing reward.

Figure 4: *We still prefer unhealthy foods despite having access to food that's better for us.*

Why we like our meat spicy...

Sherman and Hash (2001) analysed almost 7000 recipes from 36 countries and found that meat dishes contained far more spices than vegetable dishes. They hypothesised that this was because spices have antimicrobial properties — meat is more vulnerable to being infested with bacteria and fungi than vegetables are. This may also explain why people in hot climates tend to eat more spicy food — microbes grow faster in warmer conditions.

Why we won't eat green bananas or mouldy bread...

We've learned to avoid food that seems unripe or mouldy. Knowledge passed on from other people as well as our own experiences tell us that good food means life and bad food means death (or at least a dodgy tummy and wasted energy).

Tip: Spicy foods are eaten in some cultures rather than others. Take a look back at page 66 to read more about cultural impacts on food and eating behaviour.

Evaluation of the evolutionary approach

The evolutionary approach explains eating behaviours as adaptive traits that have been evolved over time to help humans survive. But there are several criticisms to the approach — it doesn't consider people's free will, it is reductionist as behaviour is explained as a set of responses to the environment and it ignores both cultural or social influences on eating behaviour.

Worked Exam-style Questions

0 1 Outline evolutionary reasons for food preferences. *(8 marks)*

Food, especially safe food, is necessary for survival, and so one of the explanations for why food preferences have developed comes from the evolutionary approach.

Children often prefer sweet foods and dislike bitter flavours. Harris (1987) conducted a research study looking at child food preferences and confirmed this was the case all around the world. Because it was a cross-cultural study, we can presume that food preferences at a young age are biologically determined. This means it is likely to have an evolutionary explanation. Secondly, avoiding foods that are bad for us is going to help us survive. Poisons are often bitter and unpleasant and so our dislike of bitter, unpleasant tastes is highly likely to be a survival reflex.

> **Exam Tip**
> Cross-cultural studies can show that something must be genetically based because it's unaffected by environmental differences.

Burnham and Phelan (2000) suggested that historically, foods high in fat which we now consider to be bad for us, may have actually helped us survive. This is because these foods are high in energy-giving calories and were therefore needed to build up our fat reserves in case there was a shortage of food. Now, for many people in our culture, food scarcity is no longer problematic, and we no longer need such an intake of high calorie foods. However, people seem 'programmed' to still eat them in case food scarcity hits again.

> **Exam Tip**
> Illustrating your answer with a study shows you have read around the pure facts.

Finally, the evolutionary approach may explain why we prefer spicy foods over non-spicy foods. Spices have antibacterial properties and therefore, having a preference for spiced meats is an adaptive trait that offers a survival advantage as you're less likely to get ill from spiced meats than non-spiced ones.

The evolutionary approach accounts for our food preferences by stating that, in order to survive, we needed high calorie food that would not make us ill. Some of these preferences have still stayed with us today and cross-cultural research can confirm the biological and evolutionary basis of these assumptions.

> **Exam Tip**
> Provide a succinct summary to wrap up everything you've said.

---

0 2 Outline and evaluate the role of neural mechanisms involved in controlling eating behaviour. *(4 marks + 12 marks)*

One neural mechanism that controls eating behaviour involves the ventromedial nucleus (VMN), which is part of the hypothalamus. The VMN plays a vital role in controlling satiety signals, which tell the body when to stop eating. This is an unconscious physiological process. When food is being digested, the level of the hormone CCK is high. The VMN is stimulated and sends a message to stop the body taking in food.

> **Exam Tip**
> Giving support for your statements reinforces the facts you've just given in your answer.

Support for the role of the VMN has come from studies which have directly stimulated this part of the brain. This results in a reduced food intake. Conversely, if the VMN has been lesioned, as Baylis et al (1996) showed in their rat experiment, satiety signals were not received and the rats could not control their eating habits. Consequently, they ended up obese.

Another neural mechanism that controls eating behaviour involves the lateral nucleus (LN). This is known as the hunger centre, and our bodies know to replenish our blood sugar supply when receptors in the LN detect that blood sugar levels have dropped.

Exam Tip
You can abbreviate long, scientific names to shorter initials, such as VMN and LN, as long as they are fully named to begin with.

Winn et al (1990) conducted a study looking at the role of the LN in hunger using rats. In their experiment, they either lesioned just the LN or larger areas, involving other adjacent parts of the brain. They compared these rats to a control group with no lesions. They found that the rats who had a large lesion were likely to eat much less whereas the rats who had only LN damage showed no change in their eating. Therefore, it was concluded that the LN alone might not be directly responsible for eating behaviour, and the localisation of brain function is more complicated.

The LN and the VMN work together in relation to hunger and eating behaviour. Over time, after the VMN has told you to stop eating, your blood sugar will start to drop. The LN then creates hunger pangs. This hunger means you start eating again which increases your blood sugar until, once again the VMN detects that it is time to stop eating. This cycle is called the hunger-satiety cycle.

Exam Tip
If you can remember the diagram on page 72 it will help you to outline how the VMN and LN link together. If you can show this in your answer, you'll really impress the examiner.

Finally, the role of ghrelin, a hormone secreted by the stomach, is also thought to be involved in eating behaviour. Ghrelin sends a message to the brain when the stomach is empty; the hungrier someone is, the more they secrete. A study by Cummings et al (2004) looked at the hunger levels of six male participants in relation to their ghrelin levels. They found a correlation between how hungry the participants were and the levels of ghrelin in their body. However, the study population was small and gender biased, and the results therefore cannot be generalised to the wider population.

Although there is lots of research into neural mechanisms in eating behaviour, several other approaches provide alternative explanations. The evolutionary approach suggests that eating behaviours have adapted as a survival mechanism. However, like the neural mechanisms theory, it is reductionist, deterministic and cannot account for people's free will in explaining eating behaviour.

Overall, there are several neural mechanisms which are thought to be involved in eating behaviour. The VMN, LN and ghrelin all seem to play a significant role, although the evidence is mixed. It is clearly a complicated process and more scientific research is needed to fully understand the process.

Exam Tip
As with lots of psychology research, there are often inconclusive results which means further research is needed.

Summary Questions

Q1 What is homeostasis?

Q2 a) Outline the procedure of one study which illustrates the role of the ventromedial nucleus.

b) Give one limitation of the study.

Q3 Which part of the hypothalamus controls satiety?

Q4 What does the lateral nucleus do in relation to eating behaviour?

3. Anorexia Nervosa

As people have become increasingly conscious of their weight, cases of anorexia nervosa have increased. It can have really serious consequences.

What is anorexia nervosa?

Anorexia nervosa leads to significant weight loss. Anorexia nervosa is one of the most common eating disorders in the UK. About 90% of cases are females aged 13–18 years old. About 1 in 250 females and 1 in 2000 males in the UK between 15 and 30 suffer from anorexia. It involves a dramatic reduction in the amount of food eaten, leading to significant weight loss.

The DSM-IV (the main diagnostic manual for mental disorders) describes four main characteristics of anorexia:

1. Low weight

Anorexia is characterised by a refusal to maintain a normal body weight. This is usually classified as consistently weighing less than 85% of the expected weight for their build, age and height.

2. Anxiety

Anorexics are very fearful of gaining weight or getting fat even when they're seriously underweight.

3. Body-image distortion

People with anorexia have distorted self-perception.
They believe they're overweight even when very thin, judge themselves based largely on their weight and refuse to accept the seriousness of their condition.

4. Amenorrhoea

Females usually stop menstruating due to their low body weight.
Missing three consecutive periods is a clinical characteristic of the disorder.

Biological explanations

Genetic explanations

Genetic explanations have been suggested for anorexia nervosa.

Key study of concordance rates in twins — Holland et al (1988)

Method:	Concordance rates (extent to which twins share the same traits) were studied in 45 pairs of twins. At least one twin of each pair had been diagnosed as having anorexia nervosa — the study examined how often the other twin also suffered from the disorder.
Results:	The concordance rate was 56% for identical (MZ) twins and only 5% for non-identical (DZ) twins.
Conclusion:	Anorexia has a genetic basis, since MZ twins, who share all of their genetic material, have a higher concordance rate than DZ twins, who only share half of their genetic material.
Evaluation:	Identical twins share 100% of their genetic material, so other factors must also be involved in causing anorexia nervosa as the concordance rate was only 56%. The higher concordance in MZ twins could be due to environmental rather than genetic factors, as looking the same may lead to more shared experiences.

Learning Objectives:

- Know the psychological explanations of anorexia nervosa.
- Know the biological explanations of anorexia nervosa, including neural and evolutionary explanations.

Exam Tip
You only need to answer questions about one eating disorder. So choose anorexia nervosa, bulimia nervosa or obesity and learn everything you need to know about that one.

Tip: See page 149 for more about the DSM-IV.

Tip: Eating disorders involve abnormal patterns of eating that are harmful to the affected person.

Figure 1: *Body distortion is one of the main symptoms of anorexia nervosa.*

Neural causes

Researchers have suggested that anorexia nervosa may be due to damage to the hypothalamus, specifically the lateral nucleus (the area of the brain responsible for controlling hunger). Lesion studies show that damage to this area can produce aphagia (a failure to eat) in animals, and recent research suggests that anorexics have reduced blood flow to this area. But it hasn't yet been proven whether this is a cause or an effect of the disorder.

Anorexics often also have abnormally high levels of the neurotransmitter serotonin and this causes abnormally high levels of anxiety. Serotonin production is stimulated by biological components (amino acids) in food, so starvation may actually make anorexics feel better. But again, it's not clear whether these serotonin levels are a cause or an effect of the disorder.

Tip: Take a look back at page 72 to remind yourself about the lateral nucleus's role in eating.

Tip: Whilst biological explanations for anorexia nervosa do have some support, they would suggest that both men and women should, in theory, be just as likely to have the illness as each other. However, more women than men are reported to suffer from the disorder.

Key study of serotonin in anorexia nervosa — Kaye et al (2005)

Method:	Kaye et al (2005) used brain imaging scans to compare the neurotransmitter receptors in the brains of patients with anorexia nervosa with a set of control patients.
Results:	There were significant differences between the serotonin levels in the brains of the patients with anorexia nervosa in comparison to the control group. This was the same even after they had recovered and gained more weight.
Conclusion:	There is a relationship between serotonin levels and anorexia nervosa. Because there are still differences between those with anorexia and those without even after weight gain, this only provides evidence for a correlational relationship between anorexia and a disrupted serotonin system.
Evaluation:	The results don't conclusively show that altered serotonin levels cause the disorder. It could be that severe weight loss has a long term impact on the serotonin system in the brain.

Figure 2: *Evolutionary psychologists claim that since our ancestors travelled long distances without much food, our bodies can adapt to being starved.*

Evolutionary approach

The evolutionary approach looks back at our ancestors to explain why anorexia nervosa exists. Guisinger (2003) suggested that a long time ago, our hunter-gatherer ancestors often had to move rapidly from place to place in search of food. If someone is starved, and lacking in energy, their bodies wouldn't normally be able to cope with so much travelling around.

As evolutionary psychologists, such as Guisinger, have argued, the body adapted to this starvation mode and allowed hunter-gatherers to move around despite being underweight. As some anorexics show, starvation can lead to high levels of restlessness and energy, despite having little food. This would have helped hunter-gatherers to survive.

Tip: Evolutionary theory states that maladaptive behaviours should decrease as we evolve. However, anorexia nervosa rates are on the rise, meaning that other factors must be involved.

Psychodynamic explanations

The psychodynamic approach suggests unconscious motivations. Anorexia nervosa may be...

A reaction to sexual abuse

If a person is sexually abused they may then loathe their body for appearing attractive to an abuser — anorexia nervosa is a way to help destroy the body and so make it less attractive to others.

Tip: It's really hard to establish cause and effect in eating disorder research. It's difficult to separate out what is a cause and what is a symptom.

Tip: A lot of evidence for the psychodynamic approach comes from case studies. As these only usually look at single individuals, it's hard to generalise the findings.

A reluctance to take on adult responsibilities

Anorexia nervosa prevents females developing breasts or hips — instead of gaining a womanly shape they remain physically childlike and so are able to remain dependent on their parents for longer.

A reflection of low self-esteem

Very low self-esteem may cause a person to believe their needs (in this case food) to be wrong in some way, or that they're not worthy of having food. They then deny themselves food.

A battle against controlling parents

Bruch (1978) found that parents of anorexics tend to be domineering. Anorexia might be an attempt to regain some control by manipulating the one thing they have control of — their body.

Remember though — it's hard to find **empirical evidence** for theories like these, and there are many counter arguments, e.g. not everyone with anorexia nervosa has experienced sexual abuse or has controlling parents.

The behavioural approach

The behavioural approach suggests conditioning may be the cause.

Tip: Remember from AS: classical conditioning is all about learning associations and operant conditioning is about positive and negative reinforcement.

Classical conditioning

Leitenberg et al (1968) claimed that anorexia nervosa could be a result of someone learning to associate eating with anxiety — often to phobic proportions. For example, being bullied whilst eating lunch at school. Losing weight helps to reduce that anxiety.

Operant conditioning

Praise and admiration for initial weight loss acts as positive reinforcement for more extreme food avoidance. A constant feeling of hunger then acts as a reward in itself. Gilbert (1986) reported that anorexics experience pleasure and pride as a result of not eating. The guilt associated with eating is lessened (negative reinforcement), as well as the fear that their weight will attract negative attention (punishment).

Figure 3: Popular culture is full of images that suggest 'thin is beautiful'.

The role of the media

Some researchers think that the media might be to blame for eating disorders. The media floods us with images of thin models, unintentionally suggesting the idea that 'thin is beautiful'. Lots of researchers have tried to prove that anorexia nervosa can be caused by this media impact, but they've yet to provide conclusive evidence. Also, it can't explain why, despite all receiving the same media messages in the Western world, not everyone develops an eating disorder.

Key study of media influences — Keel and Klump (2003)

Method:	A review of all of studies looking at anorexia nervosa and the role of media influences was conducted. The review looked at studies conducted all over the world to get an idea of how culture might affect the results.
Results:	Anorexia nervosa was found in all countries, but the more Westernised the influences were in a country, the higher the rates of anorexia nervosa.
Conclusion:	Western media may have a role in determining anorexia nervosa prevalence rates, but because it's present in all countries, there must be other factors too.

Other researchers have tried to come up with more conclusive results.

Additional study of media influence — Becker et al (2002)

Method: Becker et al's naturalistic experiment used a sample of teenage girls from Fiji. They looked at a community that had previously had no television or Western influences at all and measured the rates of eating disorders in groups given a television compared to those not given a TV.

Results: They found that more girls in the TV exposure group later developed eating disorder tendencies than those left without a TV.

Conclusion: There is a direct link between Western influences from a TV on eating disorder behaviours.

Evaluation: None of the teenagers from the study were ever officially diagnosed with eating disorders — they just showed indicators of developing eating disorders. There are also ethical issues within this research. Purposefully introducing Western influences to a culture with the knowledge that it may cause eating disorders could be seen as highly unethical.

It seems that there are many explanations for anorexia nervosa but each approach has limitations. The evolutionary approach is considered too deterministic, the psychodynamic approach is often deemed unscientific and the behavioural approach is too reductionist. It seems likely that a combination of these theories will provide the best explanation for eating disorders.

Worked Exam-style Question

0 1 Outline and evaluate explanations for anorexia nervosa.

(8 marks + 16 marks)

Research into the causes of anorexia nervosa has not been completely conclusive. There are many different theories to explain it, two of which are the biological and the behavioural theories. The biological approach suggests that anorexia nervosa may have either a genetic, neural or an evolutionary cause.

Firstly, there is research into the genetic approach which suggests that there is a genetic influence in anorexia nervosa. For example, Holland et al (1988) conducted a twin study to look at the concordance rates of identical and non-identical twins with anorexia nervosa. 56% of identical twins both had anorexia nervosa, compared with 5% for non-identical twins. The findings therefore support the idea that genetic factors must be involved, but since the concordance rate for identical twins was not 100%, we cannot conclude that genetic factors are solely to blame for the disorder. It could be that the environmental factors, such as education and media influence involved in the twins' upbringing may have contributed to the higher rates of anorexia nervosa in identical twins.

Neural causes may also explain anorexia nervosa. Brain damage, particularly to the hypothalamus and lateral nucleus have been shown to be linked to anorexia nervosa. These are areas that have been linked to regulating eating behaviour. Damage to the lateral nucleus can produce a failure to eat in animals, and research has also suggested that people with

Exam Tip
Knowing about several different explanations of anorexia nervosa is really useful if you're asked to evaluate one of them. You can use the others to suggest why it might not be such a good explanation after all.

Tip: Connan et al (2003) suggested that anorexia nervosa is caused by a genetic predisposition, later triggered by social and behavioural influences. This idea combines the biological and psychological approaches and seems to account for the various prevalence rates across the world.

Exam Tip
Don't forget that these first 8 marks will be for giving AO1 details, whilst the remaining 16 marks will be for AO2 and AO3, evaluative comments.

Exam Tip
You need to make sure you show you can evaluate what you're writing about if you're asked to do so.

Exam Tip
You can use your knowledge about eating behaviour and the brain for this part of the answer.

anorexia may have a reduced blood flow to this area. Serotonin has also been found to be higher in those with anorexia and this causes high levels of anxiety. Serotonin production is stimulated by amino acids in food, so starvation could make anorexics feel better. Kaye et al (2005) researched the link between serotonin and those with anorexia nervosa. They supported the idea that starvation leads to an altered level of serotonin. However, this relationship was correlational and doesn't show cause and effect. It could be that anorexia causes the altered serotonin level.

The evolutionary theory is another biological explanation for the disorder. Guisinger (2003) suggested that, historically, our hunter-gatherer ancestors would have faced food shortages. However, they still had to travel from place to place. In order to carry out their everyday tasks on very little food, they had to adapt to function using a 'starvation mode'. The restlessness and energy found in some people with anorexia provides evidence for the fact that hunter-gatherers could remain active with very little food. However, this theory doesn't explain why more women than men have the disorder, and why, if it is now a maladaptive trait, anorexia rates are rising and not declining.

Exam Tip
There are loads of different explanations for the biological approach to anorexia nervosa — if you can talk about a few of them and evaluate them, you'll have a really well-rounded answer.

Another explanation for anorexia nervosa comes from the behavioural approach. It suggests that eating behaviours could be the result of learning and reinforcement.

One of the effects of anorexia nervosa is anxiety. The behavioural approach says that anxiety can be a learned response, gained through classical conditioning. Leitenberg et al (1986) claimed that people can develop phobias through associating eating with anxiety. This then leads them to stop eating to avoid anxiety, leading to anorexia nervosa.

Similarly, operant conditioning explains why people who diet sometimes develop an eating disorder. When weight is lost, people get praise from others suggesting that they look great. This positive feedback acts as a reward and makes them continue to lose weight. Likewise, a feeling of hunger can act as the reward. Gilbert (1986) showed that anorexics gained a sense of achievement when they didn't eat; this also encouraged them not to eat. The guilt that a person might feel after eating is lessened through negative reinforcement when they starve themselves. Any fear that their weight will attract unwanted negative attention will act as a punishment, also preventing eating.

In conclusion, all of the explanations for anorexia nervosa have good and bad points. There is currently no single explanation which can fully explain anorexia nervosa, suggesting that it could be a combination of different factors. This is because the evolutionary approach is deterministic, the psychodynamic approach isn't very scientific and the behavioural approach is reductionist. However, when combining all of these approaches, a clearer understanding of anorexia nervosa can be used to explain the onset of this eating disorder.

Exam Tip
Finish off your answer by providing a short, but concise, summary of everything you've written.

Summary Questions

Q1 a) What is amenorrhoea?

b) Name two other effects of anorexia nervosa.

Q2 What role may serotonin have in people with anorexia nervosa?

Q3 Briefly outline a psychodynamic explanation for anorexia nervosa.

4. Bulimia Nervosa

One eating disorder that is becoming increasingly common is bulimia nervosa. This is where people are dissatisfied with their body shape, resulting in disrupted and irregular eating habits.

What is bulimia nervosa?

Bulimia nervosa involves a pattern of binge eating followed by some kind of purge so that weight isn't gained — for example by inducing vomiting, doing excessive exercise or using laxatives. So, the person's weight fluctuates but stays within a normal range.

The DSM-IV (the main diagnostic manual for mental disorders, see page 149) describes five main characteristics of bulimia:

1. Bingeing

Eating a large quantity of food in a short time frame. During a binge the person feels out of control, i.e. they can't stop themselves from eating.

2. Purging

After bingeing the person tries to prevent weight gain. This may involve vomiting, using laxatives, not eating for a long period of time or excessive exercise.

3. Frequent bingeing and purging

The binge-purge cycle needs to have been repeated about twice a week for at least 3 months before a diagnosis of bulimia is given.

4. Distorted self-evaluation

People suffering from bulimia judge themselves based largely on their body shape and weight.

5. Separate condition to anorexia

Bulimia isn't just a feature of anorexia, it can exist as a condition on its own.

Biological explanations

Genetic explanations

Kendler et al (1991) studied over 1000 pairs of twins where at least one twin had bulimia nervosa and found concordance rates of 23% in identical twins and 9% in non-identical twins. Although this suggests genetics may play a part in bulimia nervosa, it can't be the full story. As identical twins share all of their genetic material, a concordance rate of 100% would be expected if genetics were the only factor.

Neural causes

Neural causes have also been investigated.

Key study of the role of cholecystokinin (CCK) — Kissileff et al (1996)

Method:	25 people with bulimia nervosa and 18 controls were asked to binge eat (i.e. eat as much as they could in one sitting).
Results:	The participants with bulimia nervosa consumed an average of 3500 calories whereas the controls only managed 1500 calories on average. The participants with bulimia nervosa

Learning Objectives:

- Know the psychological explanations of bulimia nervosa.
- Know the biological explanations of bulimia nervosa, including neural and evolutionary explanations.

Exam Tip

You only need to know about one eating disorder. So choose anorexia nervosa, bulimia nervosa or obesity and learn everything you need to know about that one.

Tip: Eating disorders involve abnormal patterns of eating that are harmful to the affected person.

Figure 1: *Nighttime bingeing is a common occurrence in bulimics.*

Tip: Concordance rates tell you how frequently twins share the same trait.

	were also found to have depressed levels of CCK (a hormone related to satiety, see page 71).
Conclusion:	Depleted levels of CCK allowed bulimic patients to carry on eating without feeling full.
Evaluation:	This would seem to fit with the enhanced appetite that many bulimics report and their pattern of overeating. However, a lot of the research into the effects of CCK on satiety is based on animal models, so there's no guarantee that the same findings apply to humans. The study also used a fairly small sample size, so it might not be valid to generalise the results to the whole population.

Tip: Animal testing is used a lot as a research method in psychology — there's more about this on pages 146-147.

It's also been found that bulimics often have abnormally low levels of the neurotransmitter serotonin leading to bouts of abnormally low mood. Serotonin production is stimulated by biological components (amino acids) in food, and so overeating may actually make bulimics feel temporarily better — although it later leads to guilt and purging.

Tip: One limitation of the evolutionary explanation of bulimia is doesn't provide a concrete explanation into why people with the disorder purge.

Evolutionary explanation

The evolutionary approach to bulimia suggests that bingeing is an adaptive response to a lack of food. However, our ancestors lived on an unreliable food source. When they received food, they may not have known where their next meal was going to come from and so bingeing would have been the only option to ensure survival.

Real World Connection
One type of therapy used in eating disorders is family therapy, involving the parents and siblings of the person affected. Le Grange et al (2007) investigated whether supportive parents decreased the recovery time of their bulimic teenagers. They found that in the group who had family therapy, approximately 40% of bulimics stopped their binge-purge behaviour. Out of the group who only had standard psychotherapy, only around 18% recovered.

The psychodynamic approach

The psychodynamic approach says bulimia is a defence mechanism. Bulimia nervosa may be...

A reaction to sexual abuse

The binge-purge cycle helps to express self-disgust for attracting an abuser by punishing the body. Wonderlich et al (1996) interviewed 1099 American women and found a correlation between childhood sexual abuse, dissatisfaction with appearance and bulimia. 16-33% of cases of significant bulimia could be attributed to sexual abuse in childhood.

A result of emotional damage from poor parental relationships

According to Halmi (1995), bulimics often mistake their emotions for hunger, as poor parental relationships stunted their ability to distinguish between internal needs and feelings.

A defence mechanism to help guard against trauma

Bulimia is often triggered by a specific traumatic event, e.g. a divorce or long-term illness. Bulimics may try to block out unhappy feelings by indulging in overeating.

Theories from the psychodynamic approach are difficult to find empirical evidence for, and there are many counter arguments. For example, not everyone with bulimia has experienced sexual abuse or suffered a trauma that could be pinpointed as a trigger.

Tip: Becker et al (2002) did a study that looked at the causes of eating disorders in girls in Fiji. You could use it in questions about bulimia nervosa so look back to page 79.

The behavioural approach

The behavioural approach suggests bulimia is learned.

Operant conditioning

Bulimics often have poor eating habits before they develop the disorder fully, e.g. they often reduce their food intake as part of a diet, then overeat to compensate for their deprivation. Both of these behaviours would bring about positive reinforcement — praise for weight loss and satisfaction from indulgence. However, overeating may lead to anxiety (a punishment) which is then reduced by purging (negative reinforcement). This makes the purging behaviour more likely to happen again.

Social learning theory

Hamilton and Waller (1993) found that bulimics overestimated their own size and shape after seeing fashion magazine photos. Rodin (1991) found that they often had mothers who also had the disorder, or who constantly dieted. This would suggest that exposure to models who are positively reinforced for their weight loss may lead to imitation. However, not everyone who comes into contact with possible models goes on to develop the disorder — so social learning theory can't be the full story.

Tip: This is an example of vicarious reinforcement. Bandura (see page 53) Came up with this idea of indirect reinforcement — we're more likely to imitate a person who is reinforced for their behaviour.

Worked Exam-style Question

0 1 Discuss the biological approach to explaining bulimia nervosa.
(4 marks + 4 marks)

The biological approach to explaining bulimia nervosa suggests that the eating disorder may either be a result of genetics, neural causes or as a result of evolution. To provide evidence for a genetic cause, methods generally involve twin studies. These use concordance rates to assess whether bulimia nervosa is inherited, and therefore genetic, or if it is a result of the environment. Kendler et al (1991) studied over 1000 sets of twins where at least one twin had bulimia. In identical twins, who share 100% of their genetic material, he found a 23% concordance rate. This means that there does seem to be some genetic link, but because the concordance rate is not 100% genes are not the only cause of the disorder.

To investigate neural causes, Kissileff et al (1996) looked at the role of cholecystokinin (CCK). CCK is the hormone related to satiety — it tells the body when it is full. They studied 25 people with bulimia nervosa and compared them to 18 control patients who were asked to binge eat. Those with the eating disorder were able to consume over double the calories that the controls could manage. The group with bulimia nervosa also had much lower levels of CCK. This experiment concluded that these depleted levels of CCK allow bulimic patients to continue eating without feeling ill. However, there were problems with this experiment which reduces the amount of trust that we can put in the explanation.

For example, the sample was very small, making it hard to generalise the results to a wider population. Secondly, we still don't know whether the lack of CCK is a cause or effect of the eating disorder. More research would be needed, in an experimental setting, to determine which comes first in those with bulimia nervosa.

Exam Tip
The answer for this question should include an equal split of AO1 and AO2 marks.

Exam Tip
If you can't remember the full name for cholecystokinin, just writing CCK will be fine.

Exam Tip
You could also talk about the fact that there's no completely conclusive evidence for the biological explanation. Psychological explanations, such as operant conditioning and social learning could provide a better model — it could even be a mixture of factors from different approaches.

Summary Questions

Q1 Give two psychodynamic explanations for bulimia.

Q2 Give three characteristics of bulimia nervosa.

Q3 Define bingeing and purging.

Q4 Explain how bulimia nervosa may be a result of operant conditioning.

Learning Objectives:

- Know the psychological explanations of obesity.
- Know the biological explanations of obesity, including neural and evolutionary explanations.

Exam Tip
You only need to know about one eating disorder. So choose anorexia nervosa, bulimia nervosa or obesity and learn everything you need to know about that one.

5. Obesity

Obesity rates are rising dramatically — so much so that obesity is now an epidemic in the UK. Obesity has lots of health implications and understanding the possible causes and explanations may help us to prevent it from increasing.

What is obesity?

A person is classed as obese if they have an abnormally high **body mass index** (BMI) of 30 kg/m^2 or higher. This is about 20% above normal for their height and body frame, i.e. they're carrying too much **adipose** (fatty) tissue. Obesity is generally caused by a person taking in more calories (food) than they burn off (by exercise), but there are some genetic conditions and medications that can increase the risk of obesity.

It's estimated that by 2050 over half of the people in the UK will be obese. This is pretty worrying when you consider that it's already one of the leading preventable causes of death worldwide — it increases the risk of illnesses like heart disease, diabetes and cancer. The most effective way to treat obesity is with a sensible diet and plenty of exercise. However, increasingly people are turning to quick fixes —'miracle' pills or surgery such as stomach stapling, gastric band fitting or gastric bypass surgery.

Measuring obesity

Body mass index is a measurement of height relative to weight.
A normal BMI is between 18.5 and 25.
The equation to work it out is:

$$\text{BMI} = \frac{\text{Weight } (kg)}{\text{Height}^2\ (m^2)}$$

BMI	Weight
Below 18.5	Underweight
18.5 - 24.9	Healthy
25 - 29.9	Overweight
Over 30	Obese

Figure 1: *Table showing weight categories.*

Example

Shehan is 1.68 m tall. He weighs 89 kg. We can work out his BMI using the calculation below:

$$\text{BMI} = \frac{\text{Weight } (kg)}{\text{Height}^2\ (m^2)} \qquad \text{BMI} = \frac{89}{1.68^2} \qquad \text{BMI} = \frac{89}{2.8224} \qquad \text{BMI} = 31.53$$

Based on this calculation, he has a BMI of 31.53 and is therefore, obese.

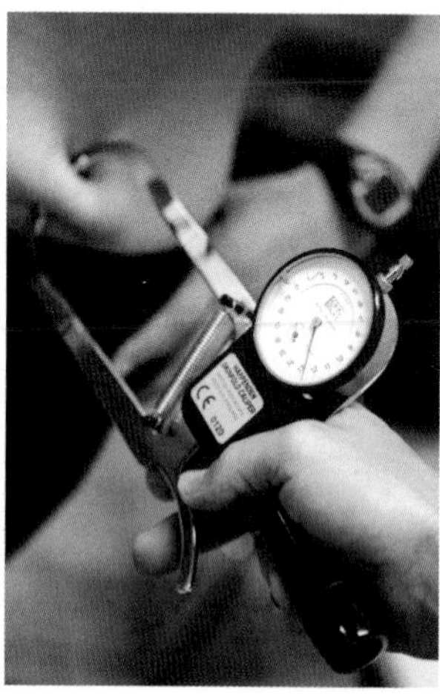

Figure 2: *In addition to BMI, health professionals use a skin fold test to measure obesity.*

Biological explanations

Genetic causes

Some studies have shown that there is a genetic element to obesity.

Key study of adoption studies and obesity — Stunkard et al (1986)

Method:	The weight of 540 adult adoptees from Denmark was compared with that of both their biological and adoptive parents. The adoptees were split into 4 weight classes — thin, median, overweight and obese.
Results:	There was a strong relationship between the weight of the adoptees and that of their biological parents. There was no relationship between the weight of the adoptees and their adoptive parents in any of the weight classes.

Conclusion:	Genetic influences have an important role in determining adult weight — environment seems to have little effect.
Evaluation:	This finding is supported by other biological versus adoptive relative research and even by some twin studies. However, it's probably too reductionist to say that genetics alone are responsible for obesity. Also, the participants were all from Denmark, so the results can't be generalised to the whole population.

Neural activity

In some cases obesity is caused by a chemical problem.

Key study of leptin and obesity — Montague et al (1997)

Method:	Two severely obese children (male and female cousins) were studied — a large proportion of their total body weight was made up of adipose (fatty) tissue.
Results:	A mutation on the part of their DNA responsible for controlling their supply of **leptin** was found — they didn't produce enough leptin. Leptin is a protein produced by adipose tissue which provides a neural signal that fat reserves in the body are full.
Conclusion:	Their leptin deficiency had caused the children's obesity. They did not have enough of this chemical to cause neural activity to suppress appetite in the normal way.
Evaluation:	A number of trials in which obese patients were given doses of leptin have had very little success. Research now suggests that most people with obesity in fact have high levels of leptin — they're just resistant to its effects. This was a case study of only two children, so although it revealed a lot about their particular situation, the findings weren't relevant to the majority of obese people.

Evolutionary explanation

Obesity may also have an evolutionary explanation. During hard times and when food was scarce, it was wise to have a store of fat in the body as a reserve. James Neel (1962) suggested that there was a gene that would allow hunter-gatherers to put on weight quickly when food was plentiful — he called this the **thrifty gene**. Having the 'thrifty gene' would be advantageous for hunter-gatherers during times of food shortage.

Key study of the evolutionary approach to obesity — Ravelli et al (1976)

Method:	The BMIs of 18-year old Dutch men were collected in a naturalistic observation. The stage of pregnancy their mothers were in during the time of the Dutch famine of 1944 was also recorded. It was believed that if the mothers were subject to starvation during the first two trimesters of the pregnancy, when the baby's hypothalamus is developing, the offspring would be more likely to be obese in later life. At this stage, the hypothalamus would signal that a state of starvation is likely, and once the child is born, they would

Tip: Taking in more calories than you burn off leads to obesity. The reverse is true for weight loss.

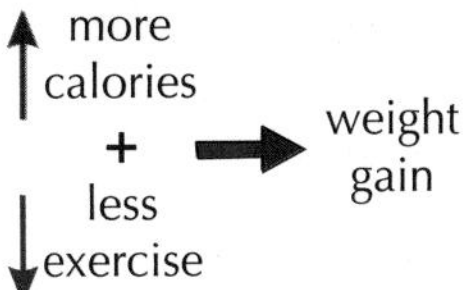

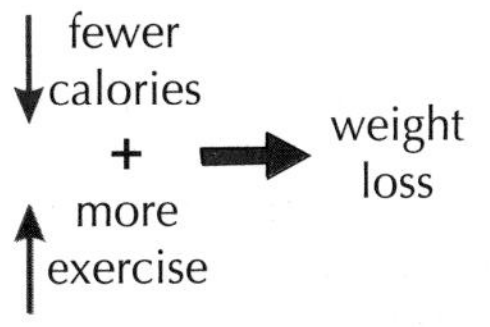

Figure 3: *The obese mouse was missing a gene that makes leptin.*

Tip: Lots of studies into the role of leptin in obesity have involved mice. Halaas et al (1995) looked at mice who were missing the gene that makes leptin. They concluded that these mice didn't have any satiety signals telling them when to stop eating and so they were obese. Halaas et al found that when they were given injections of leptin, they appeared to be able to control their eating and their weight returned to a normal level.

Figure 4: *Factors such as famine can influence later obesity, according to evolutionary psychologists.*

	be more likely to eat to obesity.
Results:	Women whose first two trimesters of their pregnancy fell at the same time as the famine did have 18-year old sons with higher obesity rates.
Conclusion:	There does appear to be an evolutionary basis for obesity.
Evaluation:	This study uses naturalistic data and therefore, has high ecological validity. The results only show correlation, not cause, so obesity could be caused by another factor. For example, the study didn't consider birth weight which may have influenced adult weight.

Tip: As you learnt at AS-Level, part of Freud's psychodynamic approach was all about disruptions and fixations during the stages of development which can cause problems in later life.

Tip: Socio-psychological factors, such as the availability of fast food, an increase in TV and video games, and a decrease in physical activity might all play a big part in obesity.

Real World Connection
Obesity research is really relevant in the world today. In the UK, over half of the adult population and over a third of the child population is classed as overweight or obese. It can have huge impacts on people's health and wellbeing, and can lead to long-term and life-limiting conditions such as diabetes. A lot of current research focuses on obesity reduction and management, including national campaigns into eating healthily.

The psychodynamic approach

The psychodynamic approach links obesity with emotional conflict. Obesity may be...

The result of an oral fixation

It's been suggested that obese people experienced trauma at the oral stage of psychosexual development, and so developed a fixation there. This means that they derive pleasure from food and are unable to delay gratification, as they're ruled primarily by the id (the pleasure principle).

A reflection on the lack of coping skills

Lots of people binge eat as a result of stress — it's a form of denial used to escape negative feelings that the person can't cope with.

Due to our thanatos instinct (death drive)

Psychodynamic psychologists believe that attempting to eat ourselves to death reflects the unconscious human desire for self-destruction.

Parental overfeeding may be a reaction to trauma

Parents who have experienced the death of a child are sometimes prone to overfeeding remaining or subsequent children to the point of morbid obesity. They feel unable to deprive the child of anything.

The behavioural approach

The behavioural approach suggests obesity is conditioned.

Children learn from an early age to associate eating with happiness (i.e. classical conditioning) for several reasons:

- Parents or teachers may use food to reinforce good behaviour, e.g. sweets as rewards. Parents may praise children for clearing their plate or punish them for wasting food at mealtimes. Advertisers use brightly coloured packaging, friendly characters and free gift giveaways. Celebrations are always accompanied by food, e.g. birthday parties. In classical conditioning, the food is available at the same time as the reward.
- As adults they may then overeat to try to recapture these happy emotions (positive reinforcement) or to remove a negative state such as sadness, anger or boredom (negative reinforcement). So, operant conditioning is also in effect.

Evaluation of approaches to obesity

Each psychological approach to obesity has limitations — the biological explanation is reductionist, the evolutionary approach is deterministic and the psychodynamic approach is unscientific. So, it could be a combination of theories which best explains the onset of this eating disorder.

Psychodynamic theories are difficult to find empirical evidence for. Also, there are many counter arguments. For example, not everyone who is obese has parents who experienced a trauma.

Worked Exam-style Questions

0 1 Describe the evolutionary theory of obesity. *(4 marks)*

Evolutionary psychologists explain obesity by looking at our ancestors in their hunter-gatherer states. Food supplies may have been scarce and it was often unknown where people would get their next meal from. As a result, people would have had to eat lots when it was available and store this as fat reserves for a time when food wasn't readily available.

Even though we are now in a society where food is relatively plentiful and accessible, the mechanisms within our bodies are still driven to cause us to overeat and store fat. Neal (1962) suggested that there was a 'thrifty gene' which allowed hunter-gatherers to easily put on weight when food was plentiful. This would be an advantage during subsequent food shortages. It may be that this gene still exists today. Research by Ravelli et al (1976) suggested that if a mother was pregnant during a period of starvation, their child was more likely to be obese later in life. This could be due to the infant's brain development telling them that they need to develop compensatory eating behaviour.

---

0 2 Outline **one** psychological theory of obesity. *(4 marks)*

Obesity may be determined by our past experiences according to the psychodynamic theory. Using Freud's developmental stages, obesity can be explained in terms of it being the result of an oral fixation. It has been proposed that people who experienced trauma during the oral stage of development developed a fixation there and derive pleasure from food. They're unable to delay gratification because they are too heavily controlled by the id.

The psychodynamic theory also suggests that obesity may exist because of a lack of coping skills. People often turn to eating when they are stressed and this is believed to be a way of them denying their real problems.

Similarly, the psychodynamic theory also suggests that an unconscious desire for us to 'eat ourselves to death' is an obese person's inner death drive, or thanatos instinct.

Finally, the psychodynamic theory states that obesity may be caused by the parents. This may be the case in parents who have lost children and so feel particularly cautious about the wellbeing of their other children. In these cases, they do not want to deny their child anything and so they end up overfeeding them.

Summary Questions

Q1 How would you classify someone as obese?

Q2 Why is it important to try to prevent obesity rates increasing?

Q3 Which chemical has been found to be linked with obesity in animals?

Q4 Give one way that the behavioural approach might suggest how a link between food and happiness is created.

Exam Tip
In the exam, the question won't specify which eating disorder you should talk about. Instead, it'll say something like "describe the evolutionary theory of one eating disorder" which would allow you to chose which one you want to talk about.

Exam Tip
Using different research studies is a great way to describe the theories of eating behaviours. Make sure you know a couple for each disorder.

Exam Tip
Each Unit 3 exam question is worth 24 marks so there'd be other parts to these questions.

Exam Tip
At A2-Level you're expected to bring in knowledge that you may have learnt at AS. Freud's theories of personality and developmental stages crop up everywhere.

Section Summary

- There are many different factors that influence eating behaviour — these include culture, mood, emotional intelligence and health concerns.
- Dieting is one method of weight regulation, but it doesn't always work. If people have support and encouragement, they are more likely to lose weight.
- Yo-yo dieting can happen as a result of the change of metabolic rates when people start dieting. As dieting effects how the body stores calories, weight gain and loss can happen at different rates.
- Biological explanations of eating behaviour suggest that eating is controlled by neural mechanisms. The ventromedial nucleus (VMN) and the lateral nucleus (LN) in the hypothalamus tell us when to start and stop eating.
- The VMN is the satiety centre and tells us to stop eating when we're full. The lateral nucleus does the opposite — it's the hunger centre that tells us when we need to eat.
- Evolutionary theories try to explain the reasons we like different types of food. They suggest that a lot of our food preferences can be traced back to times when we ate for survival, rather than pleasure.
- Three of the most common eating disorders are anorexia nervosa, bulimia nervosa and obesity.
- Anorexia nervosa is an eating disorder characterised by low weight, anxiety, body-image distortion and amenorrhoea.
- Bulimia nervosa is an eating disorder characterised by bingeing, purging, frequent bingeing and purging and a distorted self-evaluation. It is a separate condition to anorexia nervosa.
- Obesity is an eating disorder. BMI is used to classify people as obese — those who have a body mass index of 30 kg/m^2 or higher fall into this category.
- Psychological explanations for anorexia nervosa, bulimia nervosa and obesity suggest that behaviour is a result of interactions with others and past experiences.
- Biological explanations for anorexia nervosa, bulimia nervosa and obesity suggest that behaviour is a result of neural causes, genetic factors and chemical imbalances, affecting different parts of the brain.
- Evolutionary explanations for anorexia nervosa, bulimia nervosa and obesity suggest that eating behaviours have developed as a survival mechanism over time.
- But there's not yet an agreed cause for any of the eating disorders.

Exam-style Questions

0 1 Choose one eating disorder and outline its characteristics.

(8 marks)

0 2 Evaluate explanations of the eating disorder you chose for part (a).

(16 marks)

---

0 3 Outline factors that influence attitudes to food and eating behaviour.

(8 marks)

0 4 Describe and evaluate the evolutionary explanations for food preferences

(8 marks)

0 5 Evaluate research into the neural mechanisms involved in controlling eating behaviour.

(8 marks)

1. Psychological Influences on Gender

Your sex is whether you are biologically male or female, whereas your gender is how you identify yourself as being either masculine or feminine. The development of gender has been explained in many ways.

Learning Objectives:
- Know about cognitive developmental theory, including Kohlberg.
- Know about gender schema theory.

Cognitive developmental theory

Gender is the way someone acts and identifies themselves — the behavioural characteristics that make a person masculine or feminine.

Cognitive developmental theory was first proposed by Piaget. It suggests that children's thoughts and views on the world change as they develop. Many theories use Piaget's ideas to explain how ideas about gender change with age.

Tip: For more on Piaget's cognitive developmental theory, see page 118.

Kohlberg's (1966) theory

Kohlberg's (1966) **theory of gender consistency** is part of his wider cognitive developmental theory. It identifies three stages of gender development:

Gender identity

The child is aware that they're male or female, but think their gender might change (e.g. by wearing opposite sex clothes). This stage usually occurs between the ages of 2 and 3½ years old.

Gender stability

The child realises that their gender will remain fixed over time (e.g. boys will become men). However, they may think that gender can change in different situations (e.g. when doing an 'opposite-sex activity'). This stage usually occurs between the ages of 3½ and 4½.

Gender consistency

The child is aware that gender remains fixed in different situations (e.g. cross dressing doesn't change gender). This usually occurs between the ages of 4½ and 7.

Figure 1: *Between the ages of 4½ and 7, children are often aware of their 'gender role'.*

Key study of the cognitive development of gender — Ruble et al (1981)

Method: 50 male and 50 female children between the ages of four and six were asked to watch a TV commercial advertising a new toy that had previously been rated as 'gender neutral'. The advert featured either two girls or two boys playing with the toy. After the participants were shown the advert, they were then given a chance to play alone with a set of toys, which included the gender neutral toy, and were observed remotely.

Tip: If something is 'gender neutral', it isn't seen to be either stereotypically masculine or feminine.

Tip: Look back at the previous page to remind yourself what gender consistency means.

Tip: Gender appropriate behaviours are often culturally determined. For instance, in the UK, it may be stereotypical for young girls to play with dolls and young boys to play with cars.

Figure 2: Gender stereotypes might influence what toys boys and girls play with.

Exam Tip
Both Kohlberg's theory of gender consistency and the gender schema theory are specifically mentioned in the specification — this means you could be asked directly about them in the exam. Make sure you know the details.

Results:	Older children (those with a higher awareness of gender consistency) played with the gender neutral toy for less time if they had watched the advert featuring opposite sex children compared with the advert featuring the same sex children.
Conclusion:	The older a child is, the more influenced they are by gender roles.
Evaluation:	The study didn't look at the children's behaviour before the experiment — it may be that younger children have had less TV exposure to begin with and might therefore be less likely to be influenced by watching the behaviour of the children in the advert. Also, older children could have been influenced in their gender beliefs by other factors.

Additional studies of the cognitive development of gender

There is other experimental evidence that supports Kohlberg's theory. For example, a study by McConaghy (1979) asked children in Kohlberg's gender stability stage to identify the gender of dolls. Children were more likely to use the dolls' clothing rather than their genitals as an indicator for gender, suggesting that children in the gender stability stage believe that changing the situation (e.g. clothing) can also cause gender to change.

Munroe et al's (1984) study found the same stages in children from different cultures.

Despite some evidence supporting Kohlberg's theory, his ideas have been criticised for ignoring the effects of social influences and conditioning. Other critics point out that Kohlberg's theory describes what happens, but is unable to explain why.

Gender schema theory

Martin and Halverson's (1981) **gender schema theory** combines cognitive developmental theory and social learning theory to suggest how gender stereotyping helps children learn what is and what isn't appropriate for their gender. It proposes that, by the age of three, children have developed a basic **gender identity**. They also have a gender schema which contains the child's ideas about **gender appropriate behaviour**.

Through observation, children continue to learn gender appropriate behaviours and add them to their schema. A child's gender schema is based on the concept of an **in-group** and an **out-group**. Activities, objects and behaviours associated with their own sex are seen as in-group. Those associated with the opposite sex are out-group.

Example

A boy might label objects such as cars and trousers as in-group and objects like dolls and skirts as out-group.

Through reference to their in-group/out-group schema, children will show a bias towards in-group behaviours.

Key study of parental attitudes to gender behaviours — Tenenbaum and Leaper (2002)

Method:	A meta-analysis of 43 studies was conducted, which looked at the relationship between a parent's attitude to gender behaviours and their children's gender beliefs.

Results:	They found that parents with traditional views on gender appropriate behaviours had children with more traditional beliefs about gender behaviours than parents with less traditional views.
Conclusion:	Parents can influence the development of their child's gender identity.
Evaluation:	This study ignores the role of genetics — it could be that, as parents and children share genetic material, biological factors might influence the development of gender thinking.

Tip: You'll read more about biological explanations of gender on pages 94-96.

Having a gender schema can help children to manage all the information that they're exposed to. They can focus on processing information related to their in-group and filter out information related to their out-group.

However, there are also disadvantages — reinforcing stereotypical gender roles can discourage children from showing interest in things related to their out-group. This can limit their opportunities and lead to discrimination.

There is some evidence to support gender schema theory. For example, Bradbard et al (1986) gave children unfamiliar toys and found they were more likely to play with them (and remember them) if they were described as being for their own gender rather than the other.

As children get older they are capable of more complex cognition and understand that their gender doesn't limit them rigidly to in-group objects and behaviours.

Tip: Visual preference tasks are often used to measure infant development. An infant might be shown two pictures, for example, one of a boy playing with cars and one of a girl playing with dolls. The infant is then observed to see which card they look at for the longest.

Additional studies of gender schema theory — Campbell et al (2000, 2004)

Method 1:	Campbell et al (2000) investigated the visual preferences of children aged 3 months, 9 months and 18 months.
Results:	They found that all children preferred watching the male pictures, but at 9 months, male participants were significantly more likely to watch a male image and toys than female participants.
Conclusion:	Gender-defined schemas appear to develop at an early age.
Evaluation:	Because the study was longitudinal, individual differences between participants were unlikely to account for any differences in the choice of visual preferences in each group of children.
Method 2:	Campbell et al (2004) used a longitudinal design to monitor the behaviour of infants at 24 months and 36 months. They asked them to identify, from a photo album, the girl/boy in the photo, the girl's/boy's toy and the girl's/boy's activity.
Results:	94% of the 36 month olds could label the correct sex and over 50% stereotyped behaviours and toys. At 24 months, only 20% identified stereotyped behaviours and toys.
Conclusion:	Between the ages of 2 and 3, gender stereotypes seem to develop very quickly.
Evaluation:	Once again, as a longitudinal study, the results have a high level of validity since individual differences between participants are less likely to influence the results.

Figure 3: A photo on a visual preference task could show a boy playing with a truck.

Psychological androgyny

People who don't fit gender stereotypes show psychological androgyny.

Key study of psychological androgyny — Bem (1974)

Bem (1974) developed a self-report questionnaire known as the Sex Role Inventory by asking 50 male and 50 female students to rate personality traits (e.g. shyness) as being either masculine or feminine.

The most highly rated masculine, feminine and neutral words were then used to form a questionnaire, which aimed to measure the mix of stereotypically masculine and feminine traits present in an individual. Individuals rate themselves for these traits on a scale of 1 to 7. Those who score highly for both masculine and feminine traits are said to be psychologically androgynous.

Tip: Bem's Sex Role Inventory is also referred to as the BSRI.

Bem suggests that androgyny is advantageous in society as it means people have the traits needed to cope with a range of situations. Those who score highly on only one scale have a more limited range of skills. Several studies suggest that environmental factors are the cause of psychological androgyny.

Example

Weisner and Wilson-Mitchell (1990) compared children raised in families that put an emphasis on traditional gender roles with children raised in families that actively downplayed traditional gender roles. They found that androgyny was higher in children who had been encouraged to ignore traditional gender roles.

Tip: Have a look at page 98 for more about the role parents play in gender development.

Other researchers have suggested that androgyny is more likely to be a lifestyle choice. Psychologically androgenous people have the advantage of being able to use the best masculine traits as well as the best feminine traits, which offers obvious advantages.

Gender dysphoria

Gender dysphoria is a mental disorder which causes a person to feel that they're biologically one gender but psychologically the other — they feel that they're trapped in the wrong body. For example, a boy may behave effeminately, want to wear female clothes and have a baby. There has been a suggestion that gender dysphoria could form part of other mental health illnesses.

Tip: Gender dysphoria is also known as gender identity disorder.

Tip: Sex identity and gender identity are completely different. Sex identity is physically being either male or female. Gender identity is feeling either masculine or feminine.

Key study of gender dysphoria — Cole et al (1997)

Method:	318 males and 117 females, each who'd been diagnosed with gender dysphoria, were asked to complete a set of questionnaires recording their mental health.
Results:	Less than 10% of the sample had a mental health illness (not including gender dysphoria), but this rate doesn't significantly differ from the general population.
Conclusion:	Individuals with gender dysphoria often have no other diagnosed mental disorders — so gender dysphoria should be considered as being separate from other psychiatric illnesses.
Evaluation:	The sample used in this study was not representative of

Tip: People with long term gender dysphoria can also be described as 'transsexuals'.

the general population as it contained a disproportionate number of males. This inconsistency could have skewed the results as prevalence rates of mental illnesses differ between males and females.

Some studies have indicated that gender dysphoria could be caused by parental psychiatric problems or absent fathers.

Additional study of gender dysphoria — Rekers and Kilgus (1997)

Rekers and Kilgus (1997) studied families where offspring had gender dysphoria and found that:

- 80% of the gender dysphoria sufferers had mothers with mental health problems.
- 45% had fathers with mental health problems.
- 37% of sufferers had absent fathers (or no male role model).

However not all children who experience these problems during childhood go on to develop gender dysphoria — so there must be other explanations.

Worked Exam-style Question

0 1 Outline the cognitive developmental theory of gender.

(4 marks)

Kohlberg (1966) developed the cognitive developmental theory of gender consistency. He outlined three stages of development that children go through and affect their view of themselves as masculine or feminine. These stages are gender identity, gender stability and gender consistency.

The first stage, gender identity, is where a child is aware of themselves as being male or female, but they still think this can change if they behave like the opposite sex. For instance, by wearing opposite sex clothes they may believe that they become the opposite sex. It occurs between the ages of 2 and 3½.

The next stage, gender stability, develops between the ages of 3½ and 4½. This is when a child realises they will stay the same gender over time, for instance a girl will become a woman. However, they still may think that gender can change in different situations, for example, they may think that gender is dependent on external appearance, i.e. a child is a girl because she wears a dress.

Finally, gender consistency occurs between the ages of 4½ and 7 and is when a child realises that gender stays constant both over time and within different situations.

Exam Tip
In the introduction, give a brief summary of Kohlberg's (1966) theory and then go on to explain each part in more detail.

Exam Tip
If you can remember the ages when each stage occurs, it will show the examiner you really understand that you're talking about how gender develops over childhood.

Summary Questions

Q1 Define 'gender'.

Q2 a) According to Martin and Halverson's (1981) gender schema theory, what should children have developed by the age of three?

b) According to the researchers, what is a child's gender schema based on?

Q3 Outline a study investigating gender dysphoria.

2. Biological Influences on Gender

Learning Objectives:

- Know about the role of hormones and genes in gender development.
- Know about evolutionary explanations of gender.
- Know about the biosocial approach to gender development including gender dysphoria.

The biological explanation of gender says that it's our biological make-up which determines if we're male or female.

Genes and hormones

Gender development is affected by genes and hormones.

Sex chromosomes

Females have a pair of X chromosomes — XX. So all ova contain a single X chromosome. Males have one X chromosome and one Y chromosome in each body cell — XY. This means sperm may contain either an X chromosome or a Y chromosome. It's the Y chromosome that leads to male development.

If an ovum is fertilised by a Y carrying sperm, the offspring will be XY (male). If an ovum is fertilised by an X carrying sperm the offspring will be XX (female). Which sperm fertilises the ova is determined by chance.

Some humans are born with variations in the standard sex chromosome pattern. Studies of people with such variations indicate that gender differences can be caused by different sex chromosomes in males and females.

Tip: Chromosomes contain genes which control the development of all our characteristics, such as gender, hair colour, etc.

Example

In Klinefelter's syndrome males are born with XXY sex chromosomes — they have an extra X chromosome. Males with this syndrome are sterile and tend to be less muscular and have less facial and body hair. They can have problems using language to express themselves and may have trouble with social interaction.

Tip: Sex chromosomes cause hormones to be released by the gonads in the embryos. These hormones determine the sex of the embryo as it develops. The SRY gene on the Y-chromosome determines the actual sex of a child, causing an embryo to be male. So if it doesn't initiate the male hormones, the embryo will be female.

Hormone levels

The major male and female hormones are **androgens** and **oestrogens**. Both types of hormone are present in males and females, but in very different amounts. Men produce more testosterone (an androgen) each day than females, and females produce more oestrogens than males. However, some humans produce smaller or larger quantities of these hormones than normal.

Example

Sometimes people are born with much more testosterone than normal — a particular form of a syndrome called **CAH**.

- This form of CAH can cause early sexual development in males, but doesn't have much of an effect otherwise.
- The behaviour of girls with this type of CAH tends to be masculinised — they have a preference for playing with boys' toys and enjoy 'tomboyish' activities.
- Physically, girls tend to look more masculine. Their growth is fast and puberty can happen early.
- CAH can also cause physical abnormalities such as ambiguous genitalia. This can make it difficult to tell whether someone is male or female at birth.

Tip: CAH stands for 'congenital adrenal hyperplasia'.

Case studies of conditions like this suggest that the effect of testosterone on the developing brain is responsible for the differences in gender behaviour.

Evolutionary explanations

Gender roles are the behaviours seen as appropriate for one sex and not the other. For example, traditional gender roles would include men being the breadwinner and women staying at home to bring up the children. Many psychologists believe that gender roles originally developed through evolution. For example:

- Shields (1975) suggests that men and women evolved to have roles that complemented each other — dividing the behaviours necessary for survival.
- Buss (1995) suggested that the different behaviours shown by men and women are the result of different reproduction strategies.

Figure 1: *The evolutionary approach is based on the idea that men were traditionally hunters while women stayed at home to look after the children.*

Example

Trivers (1972) suggests that women invest more in offspring than men do and so discriminate more when choosing a mate. This could lead to some stereotypically female behaviours, e.g. coyness. In contrast, men have to compete for mates so demonstrate more aggressive behaviours.

The biosocial approach

The biosocial approach explains gender development as a result of both biological and social factors. Money and Ehrhardt's (1972) biosocial theory of gender has two main aspects:

- During foetal development, genetics and physiological changes (such as the inheritance of an X or Y chromosome and the presence of hormones like testosterone) lead to the development of male or female physical characteristics.
- Once the baby is born people react differently to it depending on its gender — it's given a social label. This labelling means that males and females are treated differently from birth and learn different attitudes and behaviours as a result — they are socialised in different ways.

Money and Ehrhardt suggest that the social labelling of infants and children has a greater influence on their behaviour than physiological differences do.

Smith and Lloyd (1978) investigated differences in behaviour towards male and female babies:

Real World Connection

Some people might argue that we still hold the same gender roles as our ancestors and that men should go out and work and women should stay home to look after the children. However, the number of working women has risen hugely over the past few decades, suggesting that gender is not completely determined by evolutionary factors.

Key study of behaviour towards male and female babies — Smith and Lloyd (1978)

Method:	A sample of recent mothers were asked to play with an unfamiliar baby. A variety of toys were available for them to use. A number of babies were used in the experiment — some were male and some were female. They were dressed up in gendered clothing and given a male or female name.
Results:	Participants were likely to offer gender stereotyped toys to the baby they played with. According to the sex they perceived the baby to be (based on its clothing and the name that it had been given) they also used different verbal

Tip: Take a look back at page 94 to read more about the role of chromosomes in determining sex.

Figure 2: *Traditionally, parents tend to dress baby boys in blue and girls in pink.*

Tip: The biosocial approach creates a more realistic explanation for gender — one that combines biological and social influences.

communication styles. Boys were given encouragement for motor activity and girls were more likely to be spoken to calmly and in a soothing manner.

Conclusion: People's behaviour towards babies alters depending on the babies' perceived gender.

Evaluation: This study supports the biosocial theory, showing that people react differently to boys and girls. This imposes different ideas of what it is to be a boy or a girl on the baby, i.e. they are socialised differently and so learn to behave according to a particular gender role. However, the participants might have shown demand characteristics — they could have worked out the purpose of the experiment and acted to fit in with it.

Gender dysphoria

Although gender dysphoria (see page 92) is currently classed as a psychiatric condition, recent studies have suggested a biological cause. For example, Hare et al (2009) showed a link between male-female gender dysphoria and low testosterone activity in the developing brain. This could cause the development of a female gender identity.

The biosocial approach has also been used to explain gender dysphoria. To investigate this explanation, Money and Ehrhardt looked at case studies of individuals who had undergone transgender operations in order to see how much of an influence biology and social interaction have on gender development. One example is Money's 1975 study of David Reimer:

Tip: Transgender operations involve surgery to make genitals more appropriate to the desired gender.

Key study of gender dysphoria — Money (1975)

Method: Money carried out a case study into a boy, Bruce Reimer, who had accidently had his penis burnt off during a circumcision in infancy. Money advised Bruce's parents that the boy could be surgically changed into a girl and brought up as a female. This was done, and Bruce was renamed Brenda and brought up as a girl from the age of 18 months.

Results: According to Money, for the first part of her life, Brenda seemed to act more like a girl than a boy. However, as she grew up, she preferred to play with boys' toys, became 'tomboyish' and felt socially isolated from other girls. Eventually, at the age of 14, Brenda learned about her past and chose to return to living as a male. He called himself 'David', and lived the life of a male for some years after. However, David later became deeply unhappy and committed suicide.

Conclusion: Bringing up a boy as a girl doesn't work — especially when the boy has been exposed to normal amounts of testosterone during development.

Evaluation: All seemed to go well at first, and people were surprised by the idea that people might be born gender-neutral. However, many allegations were made that Money did not reveal the true events and that Brenda was never happy as a girl. Also, this case study does not rule out the possibility that a boy with an abnormality in testosterone levels might provide different results. If it was testosterone that caused Brenda to remain psychologically male, then having a lack of testosterone could mean that a boy could feasibly be brought up as a girl. 'David' was brought up as a boy for the first year and a half of his life. This could have had a significant impact on his later feelings about his gender. Perhaps if he had been brought up as a girl from a younger age the results would have been different. This study also has ethical issues — it's been suggested that Money encouraged the parents to consider a sex change for their son for the benefit of his own research.

Money and Ehrhardt conducted other case studies of people with biological disorders that result in ambiguous genitalia which aren't clearly either male or female. From their research they identified a sensitive period lasting until around the third year of life. During this time, change in gender will not cause any psychological harm. After this age there is a much greater likelihood of distress and psychological damage. However, this suggestion has been criticised because the small number of case studies used may not be representative of everybody in these circumstances.

Worked Exam-style Questions

0 1 Outline the role of hormones in gender development.

(4 marks)

Exam Tip
All questions for Unit 3 in A2 psychology are worth 24 marks. This means this'd form part of a longer question.

The biological approach to explaining gender development suggests that hormones may play a key role in determining whether people see themselves as male or female. Males and females have both male and female hormones which are called androgens and oestrogens, but they have them in different amounts. Men tend to have more androgens (e.g. testosterone) while women have more oestrogen.

As studies have shown, having different levels of these hormones can lead to someone being either particularly masculine or feminine. For instance, a condition called congenital adrenal hyperplasia (CAH) exists, whereby sufferers are born with much more testosterone than normal. Male CAH sufferers experience early sexual development. However, female sufferers tend to be more 'masculinised' — they typically prefer playing with boyish toys, they grow faster and have a more masculine appearance.

Exam Tip
You don't have to remember the full name for CAH — it's fine to use the abbreviation.

Summary Questions

Q1 a) Females have a pair of X chromosomes — XX. What sex chromosomes do males have?

b) What is Klinefelter's syndrome?

Q2 Laura is a strong, independent woman and the main breadwinner of the home. Her partner Frank stays home to cook and clean. How might this go against the evolutionary explanation of gender?

Q3 Outline Money and Ehrhardt's (1972) biosocial theory of gender.

Q4 Describe Smith and Lloyd's (1978) experiment into adult behaviour towards male and female babies.

3. Social Influences on Gender

Learning Objectives:

- Know about the social influences on gender, for example, the influence of parents, peers, schools and media.
- Know about the cultural influences on gender role.

We're all influenced by the world around us, and this can have a huge impact on shaping our gender identity.

Parents and peers

Social learning theory suggests that we learn by observing and copying the behaviour of people around us. This learning can be passive (when the behaviour is simply watched and copied) or it can be active (when the behaviour is reinforced by rewards or discouraged by punishments).

Gender typical behaviours can be learnt this way, with males copying the behaviour of other males and females copying behaviour of other females. For example, girls may imitate the behaviour of their mothers — the behaviour becomes part of their idea of the female gender role. There's also evidence that parents and peers react differently to children depending on their gender:

Parents

Parents can shape their child's gender identity with their own behaviour through operant conditioning. When a child gets rewarded for a certain behaviour, through praise and attention, they are more likely to continue to act that way.

Tip: Take a look back at page 90 to read more about parental influence on gender development in a study by Tenenbaum and Leaper (2002).

Example

Positive reinforcement may encourage gender stereotyped behaviour:

"Rachel was told she looked beautiful in the new dress she wore to a school friend's birthday party. When she put on new trousers, no one noticed".

Figure 1: Parents often act as role models to their children to help define gender roles.

Key study on parental influence on gender — Rubin et al (1974)

Method:	Rubin et al created a list of paired adjectives. The researchers then asked thirty pairs of parents, half with sons and half with daughters, to chose the adjective from each pair which most closely described their child. The infants were weighed and measured to ensure that all infants were roughly the same weight and height.
Results:	Rubin et al found that fathers used words like 'soft' and 'beautiful' to describe newborn daughters and 'strong' and 'firm' to describe sons.
Conclusion:	Parents apply gender stereotyping to their children despite there being no physical differences between children at that age.
Evaluation:	Gender roles may have changed since this study was conducted in the 1970s and so the results can't be generalised to our current society.

Additional studies on parental influence on gender

Culp et al (1983) found that women treated babies differently according to how they were dressed — talking more to those dressed as girls and smiling more at those dressed as boys.

Hron-Stewart's (1988) study found that adults were quicker to comfort a crying baby girl than a crying baby boy, expecting boys to be hardier and braver. Also, mothers were more likely to help a daughter complete a task than a son.

Peers

Peer relationships may also influence gender development.

Key study of peer influence on gender — Fagot (1977)

Method: 106 boys and 101 girls were observed in a preschool classroom whilst playing with each other. The reactions of peers and teachers were then measured.

Results: When boys conducted stereotypically feminine play behaviour, they were criticised by both peers and teachers. In comparison, girls who engaged in stereotypically masculine behaviour were criticised less.

Conclusion: Peer criticism differs depending on the gender of the individual.

Evaluation: This study has high ecological validity since it is a naturalistic observation and takes place in a real life setting.

Additional studies of peer influence on gender

Maccoby and Jacklin (1987) found that children as young as three prefer same-sex playmates. Maccoby (1990) found that when children organise their own activities they tend to segregate themselves according to their gender.

Serbin et al (1984) suggest that girls try and influence situations by polite suggestion whilst boys use direct commands. Lamb and Roopnarine's (1979) study of nursery behaviours found that children encouraged gender appropriate behaviour and criticised gender inappropriate behaviour.

Tip: It's been suggested that peers might actually be a lot more influential than parents in determining a child's gender development. Further studies are needed to see if this might be the case.

The different behaviours that girls and boys observe and experience can lead to development of gender roles.

The media

TV, films, magazines and computer games usually show gender stereotypical behaviour. Several studies have shown that the behaviour displayed in these media can influence gender roles. For example, some studies have shown that the more TV a child watches the more stereotypical their views on gender are.

***Figure 2**: The amount of TV a child is exposed to may shape their ideas of gender.*

Key study of media influence on gender stereotypes — Williams (1986)

Method: Williams (1986) carried out a two year natural experiment in Canada. She looked at the effect of introducing TV to a town (Notel), by comparing it to a nearby town that already had TV (Multitel). At the start of the experiment, gender stereotyping was much greater in Multitel than Notel.

Results:	Williams found that gender stereotypes of Notel children increased and became more like those of Multitel children after the introduction of TV.
Conclusion:	The media do appear to influence sex role stereotypes in children.

Tip: Remember — correlation does not mean causation. Take a look at page 255 to read more about correlation and causation.

Additional studies of media influence on gender roles

There have been lots of studies into the role of media on gender roles. Leary's (1982) correlational study suggested that the more TV a child watched, the more likely they were to have stereotypes about different gender roles — supporting the findings of Williams's (1986) study.

Peirce (1993) looked at the content of magazines for teenage girls. They showed that over half of the articles portrayed females as being dependent on men and unable to deal with their own issues.

Hurst (2006) interviewed boys asking them what they thought 'masculinity' meant and they replied using words exaggerated in media representations of men, such as 'sporty' and 'risk takers'.

Both of these studies illustrate that media representations of male and female characteristics are narrow and certainly may influence the gender development in their readers.

Figure 3: *Teenagers can easily be influenced by magazines, as well as their peers.*

School influence

The attitude of schools and teachers can influence gender roles. For example, if teachers hold gender stereotypes this may influence their beliefs about the abilities and preferences of girls and boys.

Bigler (1995) compared students in classes that were divided by gender with students in classes where gender wasn't emphasised. Students divided by gender were more likely to have stronger gender stereotypes and a stronger belief that all males are similar and all females are similar.

Tip: In school, children are also heavily influenced by their peers. For more on peer influence on gender, see page 99.

Cross-cultural research

Cross-cultural research has been carried out to identify how gender roles differ between cultures. Cross-cultural research can also help us to understand the causes of gender roles — if roles are similar in different cultures it suggests a biological explanation. However, if they vary between cultures a social explanation of gender roles is more likely.

Tip: Studies in the Western world seem to dominate the literature — remember this when evaluating the research because it means the results often can't be generalised to other cultures.

Key study of cross-cultural research on gender roles — Whiting and Edwards (1988)

Method:	Whiting and Edwards observed the behaviour of children in the USA, Mexico, Japan, India, the Philippines and Kenya.
Results:	They found that gender behaviour was very similar to Western stereotypes and that there were clear differences between male and female behaviour. For example, girls were more caring than boys, and boys were more aggressive than girls. In societies where children were expected to work to contribute towards the family, there were further gender differences. Girls were more likely to look after younger siblings and do domestic work, whilst boys were

	more likely to look after animals and were less likely to work within the home.
Conclusion:	Similar gender roles are found across cultures, suggesting that there's a biological explanation.
Evaluation:	As this study compared lots of different children across the world it would have been expensive and time consuming, although it was truly representative of a global population.

Responsibility for childcare

Katz and Konner (1981) looked at 80 different cultures — they found that in 90% of them women had the main responsibility for child rearing. This gender division has implications for men and women in terms of occupation, finance and mobility. D'Andrade (1966) looked at information from 224 societies to investigate what types of tasks and jobs were performed by males and females. He found that:

- Men were more likely to travel further from the home, and be involved in weapon making, metal work and hunting.
- Women were more likely to make and repair clothes, prepare and cook food, and make objects for use in the home.

Segal (1983) suggested that the differences in activities associated with gender roles are related to the differences in involvement in childcare.

Worked Exam-style Question

0 1 Describe social influences on gender. *(4 marks)*

Psychologists have investigated many social factors which could influence gender. Social learning theory proposes that behaviour is learnt through observation, and by copying others. Gender typical behaviours can be learnt this way, with males copying masculine behaviours and females copying feminine behaviours. This can often take place in families, e.g. with sons copying the behaviours and attitudes of their fathers. In this way, a child's gender can be influenced by the actions of their parents.

Parents can also shape their child's gender identity with their own behaviour through operant conditioning. For instance, rewards and praise for acting in a gender-stereotyped way are often used in everyday situations and so behaviour is reinforced. In the same way, a child's peers can also have an effect on a child's gender, e.g. Gavin wore a pink t-shirt to the cinema and his friends laughed at him. When he wore his blue t-shirt, no one noticed.

The media may also influence a child's perception of gender roles. TV, films, magazines and computer games usually show gender stereotypical behaviour, which can influence a child's perception of gender roles.

Summary Questions

Q1 Outline a study which investigated parental influence on gender.

Q2 Describe Williams's (1986) study of Notel and Multitel.

Real World Connection
Margaret Mead (1935) carried out a thorough study of gender roles in different cultures. She looked at three different tribes in Papua New Guinea and showed that each tribe had a different role for men and women. Not only were the gender roles of each tribe different to the Western world, they were also different to each other. In one tribe, both men and women were very feminine, in another, both sexes were masculine and in the third, they showed the reverse of Western definitions. Her study clearly shows that gender roles do appear to be influenced by our culture and environment, and aren't controlled by our biology.

Exam Tip
There are loads of things you could write about for this question. Don't worry if the things written here aren't what you would have picked.

Exam Tip
If you can't think of any studies to support your answer, then try and give an example that helps to explain the point that you are making.

Section Summary

- There are several approaches to explaining how gender develops — these include psychological, biological, biosocial and social explanations.
- Gender is how we think of ourselves in terms of being masculine or feminine. Sex is the physical fact of us being either biologically male or female.
- Cognitive development theories of gender state that gender ideas change with age. As we get older, we go through different stages with different ideas of what it means to be male or female.
- Kohlberg (1966) proposed a cognitive development theory that highlighted three different stages of gender development — gender identity, gender stability and gender consistency.
- Martin and Halverson's (1981) gender schema theory suggests that children's gender identity is affected by what they learn from the environment. They add gender appropriate behaviours to a schema of what it is to be male or female.
- The biological approach says that biological factors make you act in either a masculine or feminine way and that genes and hormones determine a person's gender. Males and females are biologically very different — they have different sex chromosomes and different levels of hormones.
- Evolutionary theorists suggest that gender roles have developed to ensure survival, which is why males and females have roles that are different and complement each other. Since females become pregnant, they usually stay home to care for the children leaving the men to develop skills that will enable them to hunt and provide for the family.
- The biosocial approach combines biological and social explanations for gender development. It has been supported by studies such as Smith and Lloyd (1978) who showed that adults change their behaviour towards children depending on the biological sex of the child.
- Gender dysphoria is where people feel that they're the opposite gender to that which they were biologically born as. It's been linked to parental psychiatric problems and absent fathers, but has also been explained using a biosocial approach.
- Through social learning, parents, peers, teachers and the media can influence gender roles. People can develop ideas of gender by observation and imitation, and through conditioning and reinforcement.
- Cross-cultural studies have provided mixed evidence into whether gender roles are biologically or socially determined. Some studies have shown that gender roles are consistent across different cultures while other studies have shown that they can differ significantly.

Exam-style Questions

0 1 Outline how the evolutionary approach explains gender.

(8 marks)

0 2 Evaluate the evidence for biological influences on gender development.

(16 marks)

1. Theories of Intelligence

Several theories in psychology try to explain how intelligence developed and what it actually is. There seems to be more to it than getting good marks.

The learning approach

The learning approach to intelligence suggests intelligent behaviours are developed through conditioning. For this to happen there needs to be an initial change in behaviour that's then rewarded. This is known as reinforcement and encourages the person to repeat the behaviour.

Examples

- Skinner taught pigeons to play ping-pong by providing positive reinforcement in stages — for standing on the court, then for touching the ball, then for hitting it correctly, etc.
- Intelligent human behaviours, e.g. driving a car or writing, can be learnt in the same way. For instance, we may learn to ride a bike through conditioning — every time we fall off, this acts as a negative reinforcement until we learn to balance and stay on.

This approach has been criticised for being **reductionist** — it takes something as complex as intelligence and reduces it down to simple learning processes of stimulus and response reactions. More understanding is needed of what cognitive abilities are involved in intelligence and what biological and environmental factors influence individual differences in intelligence.

The psychometric approach

The psychometric approach involves measuring intelligence to produce an intelligence quotient (IQ) score. This is done through intelligence tests that are focused on mathematical ability and abstract, logical reasoning.

Spearman

Spearman (1904) found that people who did well on one kind of test, e.g. arithmetic, usually did well in other kinds of tests, e.g. spatial reasoning. In other words, their test scores showed a positive correlation. So, he proposed that everyone has a **general intelligence** that's genetically determined and unchangeable. He termed this 'g'. He also suggested that people develop specific abilities, 's', which are influenced by learning. This can explain why, for example, some people are better at maths than at English.

Cattell

Cattell (1963, 1971) expanded on Spearman's theory of general intelligence by splitting it up into two parts — **crystallised intelligence (Gc)** and **fluid intelligence (Gf)**. Gc requires people to use their previous knowledge and learning, whereas Gf involves reasoning and information processing with no prior knowledge needed.

Thurstone

Thurstone (1938) argued against the concept of 'g', claiming that there are 7 independent groups of **primary mental abilities** rather than one general

Learning Objectives:

- Understand psychometric theories of intelligence, for example, Spearman, Cattel and Thurstone.
- Understand information processing theories of intelligence, for example, Sternberg and Gardner.

Figure 1: *Skinner's pigeons.*

Tip: 'Psychometrics' is the word used to describe how psychologists measure the differences between people. It is more concerned with measuring intelligence than actually defining it.

Tip: To remember the difference between crystallised intelligence and fluid intelligence, think of crystallised as being more solid based on something concrete. Fluid intelligence is looser and less dependent on other things.

intelligence. He tested over 200 students using almost 60 different tests and determined seven mental abilities:

- Numerical — solving numerical problems.
- Verbal — understanding words and sentences.
- Spatial — visualising relationships between shapes and mentally manipulating objects to see them from different perspectives.
- Word fluency — talking rapidly and being able to understand words in different contexts, such as rhymes, anagrams, etc.
- Memory — learning and recalling information.
- Perception — seeing the differences and similarities between things.
- Reasoning — finding the rules to solve a problem.

Figure 2: *Musical ability is difficult to measure.*

Comments

- There are many issues with the use of IQ tests. Many things, e.g. musical ability, are difficult to measure. Also, tests may be biased towards one culture.
- Developmental factors are not considered by the psychometric approach — 'g' may be influenced by education and nutrition, which could promote or impair the development of intelligence.

The information processing approach

The information processing approach to intelligence focuses on the use of a set of cognitive processes.

Sternberg's (1985) triarchic model

Tip: Sternberg's (1985) triarchic model splits up intelligence into three parts:

Intelligence

Contextual | Experiential | Componential

Contextual intelligence can only be assessed when the environment has been considered. With experiential intelligence, people often do better on tests they have done before. Componential intelligence relates more deeply with information processing.

Sternberg (1985) proposed that intelligence is made up of three different skills:

- Componential intelligence (analytical) — the ability to solve problems, see solutions, monitor and plan.
- Experiential intelligence (creative) — the ability to react to stimuli and develop ideas, either new or familiar.
- Contextual intelligence (practical) — the ability to adjust to different environments and contexts.

Combining these skills together makes up Sternberg's **triarchic model of intelligence**. He then further divided up componential intelligence into three more components. These are the cognitive processes that underlie intelligence:

- Metacomponents — planning and control processes used in problem solving and decision making.
- Performance components — processes that allow us to carry out actions, e.g. memorising, calculating, etc.
- Knowledge acquisition components — processes used to learn new information.

Comments on Sternberg's model

Sternberg's model allows for the influence of both internal and external factors on intelligence. It also addresses intelligence in relation to practical, real-life scenarios rather than just academic contexts.

However, Gottfredson (2003) argues that Sternberg's concept of practical intelligence is faulty — it simply represents a set of skills developed to cope with a particular environment, rather than a kind of intelligence.

Gardner's (1985) multiple intelligences theory

Traditionally, intelligence has been seen as a single concept, emphasising verbal, logical and mathematical skills. Gardner's theory of multiple intelligences suggests that we have several different kinds of intelligence. These each involve different cognitive structures so are independent of each other, although they do interact. So, a person could have a high level of ability in some areas of intelligence, but a low level in other areas.

Gardner initially identified seven kinds of intelligence. In 1997 he added an eighth to his model:

- Logical-mathematical — ability in mathematics and logical and abstract reasoning.
- Verbal-linguistic — speaking, reading, writing and the ability to learn languages.
- Visual-spatial — ability in mental visualisation and art.
- Musical — abilities relating to sound, rhythm and tone.
- Bodily kinaesthetic — use of body, e.g. athletic and dance ability.
- Intrapersonal — associated with self-understanding, feelings, motivations and objectives.
- Interpersonal — social skills, empathy and ability to cooperate with others.
- Naturalistic — the ability to understand and act in the natural world, e.g. classifying plants or rock types.

Figure 3: *Professional athletes have a very high level of bodily kinaesthetic intelligence.*

Tip: Gardner studied several remarkable individuals to provide examples for each of his kinds of intelligence. These might help you remember all the different types:

Logical-mathematical — Einstein (mathematician, physicist).

Verbal-linguistic — TS Eliot (poet).

Visual-spatial — Picasso (artist).

Musical — Stravinsky (composer).

Bodily kinaesthetic — Martha Graham (dancer).

Intrapersonal — Ghandi (leader).

Interpersonal — Freud (psychiatrist).

Naturalistic — Darwin (naturalist).

Comments on Gardner's theory

- Gardner's theory is based on a range of research methods, including psychometric tests and case studies of people who have low IQ scores but high ability in particular kinds of intelligence. For example, Horwitz et al (1965) found that some people who were considered to have low intelligence could rapidly calculate the day of the week that a particular date fell on.
- The concept of multiple intelligences can be applied to education. This would give a broader approach than the traditional emphasis on verbal and mathematical skills. It can also help teachers to understand the best ways for different students to learn things.
- Autistic savants can illustrate how multi-dimensional intelligence can be, in further support of Gardner's theory. Savants are those who have been diagnosed with autistic spectrum disorder and they often perform badly in standardised IQ tests. However, they do show vastly superior skills in many other areas such as maths or art.
- The theory has been criticised because some aspects are vague, e.g. intrapersonal and musical intelligence are difficult to define. They're also difficult to measure precisely. Also, some people believe that some of the types of intelligence identified by Gardner are really just names for talents or personality traits, rather than a kind of intelligence.

Example

Sacks (1995) described the case of Stephen Wiltshire, well known for his phenomenal artistic ability. Despite his autism, Stephen is able to produce detailed and accurate drawings of scenes after seeing them just once. According to Gardner's theory, he shows a deficit in interpersonal intelligence but has extremely high visual-spatial intelligence.

Exam Tip
The question just asks you to outline one psychometric theory so all you need to do is provide a brief summary of the theory with no evaluation.

Exam Tip
Your answer for this question should include half AO1 points and half AO2 points.

Exam Tip
Start your answer by showing the examiner that you know what psychometric theories of intelligence are.

Exam Tip
Don't forget to cover the 'evaluate' part of the question too. Even if you write a really good answer covering the 'outline' part, you can't get all the marks unless you answer the question fully.

Exam Tip
At A2-Level the exam questions for psychology are always worth 24 marks each. That means there would be other parts to these questions.

Worked Exam-style Questions

0 1 Outline **one** psychometric theory of intelligence.

(4 marks)

Spearman used a psychometric approach to measure intelligence based on mathematical ability, abstract and logical reasoning. He found that usually if someone did well on one test, they also performed highly on others. This meant that everyone had a general intelligence that is genetically determined and therefore, not changeable. He labelled this 'g' and said that, in addition to 'g', people also have a specific skill set which marks them as being different to others. He called this 's' and these skills are influenced by learning.

---

0 2 Outline and evaluate **one** psychometric theory of intelligence.

(4 marks + 4 marks)

Psychometric theories of intelligence involve measuring intelligence levels through a series of tests. This gives an intelligence quotient (IQ) score which allows psychologists to look at the differences between people. The tests often involve different types of skills, mainly mathematical ability, abstract tasks and logical reasoning.

One psychometric theory of intelligence was proposed by Thurstone. Previously, Spearman had suggested that people have one overall 'general intelligence', but instead, Thurstone thought people had primary mental abilities across seven different areas. These were numerical, verbal, spatial, word fluency, memory, perception and reasoning skills. From a series of almost 60 different tests, Thurstone created these categories after compiling the results from tests completed by over 200 students.

However, there are several issues with Thurstone's theory and with the use of intelligence tests within the psychometric approach. Many things, such as musical and sporting abilities, are very difficult to measure. Tests might also be biased towards one culture. Finally, the psychometric approach does not consider different developmental factors. It may be that intelligence is influenced by education and nutrition. Both of these factors might either promote intelligence or cause it to suffer.

There are several other theories of intelligence which can be used to provide an alternative view of intelligence and may overcome the problems of psychometric theories. These include the information processing theories which considers the environment and practical, real-life influences on the intelligence in people a lot more than the psychometric approach.

Summary Questions

Q1 Name two of Thurstone's primary mental abilities.

Q2 What were the two types of intelligence in Cattell's theory?

Q3 Name one information processing theory of intelligence.

Q4 Catherine is very artistic whilst Steven is really good at maths. According to Gardner:

a) What kind of intelligence does Catherine have?

b) What kind of intelligence does Steven have?

2. Animal Learning and Intelligence

Lots of research has been conducted to see whether animals have the same types and levels of intelligence as us humans. The results are interesting...

Learning Objectives:

- Know about simple learning (classical and operant conditioning) and its role in the behaviour of non-human animals.
- Know about intelligence in non-human animals, for example, self-recognition, social learning and Machiavellian intelligence.

Types of learning

Psychologists have used behaviourist ideas of conditioning to explain how people learn. It would seem that both humans and non-human animals can learn in this way. Learning can either take place through classical conditioning or operant conditioning.

Classical conditioning

Classical conditioning occurs when a stimulus produces a response in an organism because it's become associated with another stimulus which normally produces that response. Animals can be classically conditioned.

Example

When dogs see food, they salivate. This is an automatic, unlearned response — a reflex. The food is an unconditioned stimulus (UCS) and salivation is an unconditioned response (UCR). Pavlov (1927) studied laboratory dogs that always received their food after a bell was rung. After a while the dogs would salivate when the bell was rung (before getting the food) as they associated the bell with food. The bell had become a conditioned stimulus (CS), and salivation had become a conditioned response (CR).

Before conditioning
A certain stimulus, e.g. food (unconditioned stimulus, UCS) —triggers→ a natural reflex, e.g. salivation (unconditioned response, UCR)

During conditioning
UCS repeatedly presented with another stimulus, e.g. a bell (neutral stimulus) —triggers→ salivation (unconditioned response, UCR)

After conditioning
Over time the bell presented by itself (conditioned stimulus, CS) —triggers→ salivation (conditioned response, CR)

Tip: Unconditioned responses are just natural reflexes.

Figure 1: *Pavlov's dogs may just be showing a learned response, rather than any form of intelligence.*

The principles of classical conditioning are:

- **Generalisation** — when stimuli similar to the original CS (e.g. a bell with a different pitch) produce the CR (e.g. salivating).
- **Discrimination** — when stimuli similar to the original CS don't produce the CR. This can be achieved by withholding the UCS (e.g. food) when the similar stimulus is used. The animal will begin to discriminate between the CS and the similar stimulus and will only respond to the CS.
- **Extinction** — when the CR (e.g. salivating) isn't produced as a result of the CS (e.g. bell). This happens when the CS is repeatedly presented without the UCS (e.g. food) following it.
- **Spontaneous recovery** — when a previously extinct CR is produced in response to the CS. This happens when the CS is presented again after a period of time during which it's not been used.

Tip: Don't confuse punishment with negative reinforcement. Punishment stops behaviour, whereas negative reinforcement uses the act of taking away something bad to reinforce, and so increase, behaviour.

Real World Connection
Punishments and reinforcements happen all the time in everyday situations. For example:

Positive reinforcement — giving a chocolate bar to a well-behaved child to encourage future good behaviour.

Negative reinforcement — being told by the teacher that you'll have no extra homework if you pass your test.

Positive punishment — giving out a detention after someone's handed in homework late to stop them handing it in late in future.

Negative punishment — taking away a child's pocket money if they're naughty to discourage future naughty behaviour.

Figure 3: A Skinner box has become a well recognised piece of equipment to measure learned behaviour.

- **Higher order conditioning** — when a new CS (e.g. a light) produces the CR because the animal associates it with the original CS. This can be achieved by consistently presenting the new CS before the original CS.

It's important to make sure that the CS happens at the right time. If the CS is given after the UCS, rather than before, the conditioning tends to be less effective. This is called backward conditioning.

Operant conditioning

Operant conditioning occurs when organisms learn to associate particular behaviours with particular consequences. Positive consequences encourage them to repeat the behaviour, negative consequences discourage them from repeating the behaviour.

Operant conditioning can involve positive reinforcement, negative reinforcement or punishment (see Figure 2). Positive reinforcement occurs when the behaviour produces a positive outcome, e.g. food, so the behaviour is reinforced and likely to be repeated. Negative reinforcement occurs when the behaviour removes a negative stimulus, e.g. pain, so the behaviour is reinforced and likely to be repeated. Punishment occurs when the behaviour is punished, e.g. electric shock, deterring the animal from repeating it.

	Positive stimulus	**Negative stimulus**
Stimulus added *In response to behaviour*	Encourages behaviour *positive reinforcement*	Discourages behaviour *positive punishment*
Stimulus removed *In response to behaviour*	Discourages behaviour *negative punishment*	Encourages behaviour *negative reinforcement*

Figure 2: *Using reinforcement and punishment to shape behaviour.*

Operant conditioning can be used to teach animals certain behaviours:

Example

Skinner (1938) studied laboratory rats to see if they could learn behaviour through operant conditioning. He placed the rats in boxes containing a lever. Pushing the lever provided the rat with food pellets — a positive consequence. Over time, the rats pushed the lever more frequently as they associated the behaviour with the reward of food.

Comments

- Most research into conditioning has involved animals. This means generalising to humans is difficult. More research into human conditioning would be useful.
- Different species have different capacities for learning by conditioning. Some may also learn by simple observation, with no reinforcement involved.
- Genetics seem to influence and limit what different species can learn by conditioning.

Example

Breland and Breland (1951) gave food to pigs when they carried wooden coins (in their mouths) to a 'piggy bank'. However, they started to drop them on the floor and push them towards the bank with their snout (showing an instinctive foraging behaviour), so taking longer to get the food.

- A lot of the experiments into intelligence in animals may be seen as unethical. Nowadays, studies have to conduct a cost-benefit analysis of whether it's acceptable to use and to ensure that the animals are well looked after.

Figure 4: *Researchers have found it difficult to condition certain animals — instinctive behaviours can often take over.*

Non-human animal intelligence

Self-recognition, social learning and Machiavellian intelligence are all seen as evidence of intelligence.

Self-recognition

Self-recognition may be assessed by the mark test — an animal is anaesthetised and red dye is put on its forehead. Later, the animal is placed in front of a mirror. If it touches the mark on its head as opposed to the image in the mirror, it provides evidence that it identifies the image in the mirror as itself. A few animals, e.g. chimpanzees, have shown self-recognition. However, Heyes (1994) claims that this doesn't prove that they're self-aware in the same way that humans are.

Key study of self-recognition — Povinelli et al (1997)

Method: The researchers painted a mark above the eyes and ears of a group of chimpanzees who had previously been made familiar with mirrors. A baseline measurement was taken of the number of times the chimpanzees touched their painted face parts. They were then shown mirrors to view the marks and then their behaviour was monitored again to see how frequently they touched their face.

Results: After looking in the mirror, the chimpanzees all touched their painted body parts significantly more than before they had seen a mirror, and more than any other body part.

Conclusion: As their behaviour increased after seeing their reflections, it would appear that self-recognition does exist in non-human animals.

Evaluation: This experiment doesn't prove that self-recognition exists — it could just be that the chimpanzee can distinguish between their physical self and the outside world.

Tip: Baseline measurements are often taken before participants take part in a study. It allows for a fairer comparison before and after the experimental condition.

Tip: Research into non-human animal intelligence usually involves either an observational study or a laboratory experiment.

Machiavellian intelligence

Machiavellian intelligence is the ability to manipulate social situations to reach a goal. For an animal to do this it needs to have theory of mind — an ability to imagine the world from the perspective of others. Theory of mind allows animals to attribute behaviour to intentions, beliefs and feelings, and enables them to deceive others.

Key study of laboratory experiment — Woodruff and Premack (1979)

Method: Chimpanzees watched as a trainer placed food under one of two containers, both of which were out of their reach. One of two trainers then entered. One trainer wore a green coat, the other a white coat. If the chimps were able to guide the green-coated trainer to where the food was, they were given the food. If they guided the white-coated trainer to the food, the trainer kept the food. However, if the white-coated

Tip: A lot of the research into animal intelligence has focused on the great apes. This is because they are our closest non-human ancestors and therefore, the results can be generalised a bit more reliably. The findings from other animals have been less conclusive.

Tip: Investigating theory of mind in non-human animals can be tricky as they don't have language capabilities like we do. This means that the researchers have to infer from an animal's behaviour whether they have theory of mind abilities or not.

trainer did not find the food, it would be given to the chimp.

Results: After repeating the test several times, all of the chimps learned to guide the green-coated trainer to the food. Some of the chimps intentionally deceived the white-coated trainer, pointing to the opposite container to where the food was, whilst the rest withheld information about the location of the food.

Conclusion: Chimps have theory of mind and are able to deceive.

Evaluation: The chimps may have learnt to guide the green-coated trainer to the food through conditioning (with food acting as a positive reinforcer) rather than actively attempting to deceive the white-coated trainer. This doesn't require a theory of mind so wouldn't be an example of Machiavellian intelligence.

Additional studies of Machiavellian intelligence

Byrne and Whiten (1988) also explored the idea of Machiavellian intelligence. Between them they observed many different cases of primate behaviour. They showed that great apes were able to deceive each other in order to get something they desired.

Byrne and Whiten (1990, 1992) had previously showed this with their account of a non-dominant male sneaking off to mate with a female behind a rock. Both apes 'pretended' to be eating in order to provide a distraction to what they were really up to.

Harcourt (1992) proposed the idea that certain non-human species could form alliances based on their 'intelligent' understanding of whether it would benefit them. Despite other animals forming bonds with each other, only animals more closely related to us, such as baboons and great apes seemed to form alliances based on their desire to gain something from the relationship. This shows elements of both Machiavellian intelligence and theory of mind.

Figure 5: *Chimpanzees may form alliances as a way of getting what they want. This could be food or other resources.*

Social learning

Social learning occurs when an animal copies behaviour that it sees another animal receive a benefit from. This is known as **vicarious reinforcement**. Kawai's (1965) naturalistic observations of macaque monkeys showed that one of them started to wash potatoes in the sea before eating them. Other monkeys soon seemed to imitate this.

Figure 6: *Even younger chimpanzees have been found to understand what tools are used for.*

Key study of social learning — Tomasello (1987)

Method: Two different groups of chimpanzees were studied — one group were 4-6 years old and the others were 8-9 years old. He then split these into two further groups so there was an experimental group and a control group for each age bracket. The chimps were all given a tool which could be used to reach some food placed out of reach. In the experimental group, the chimps were shown an adult chimp

	using the tool in a particular way to retrieve the piece of food. The control group were not shown how to use the tool.
Results:	Younger chimps learnt to use the tool to get the food, whereas the older chimps didn't. However, the exact technique used by the younger chimps was not the same as what they saw the adult doing.
Conclusion:	Imitation and social learning do seem to be taking place. However, only the results of the action, not the action itself, are imitated.
Evaluation:	The study relies on a human interpretation of the events. We can only presume that the chimps imitated the goal of the actions, but because we can only guess, this makes the results unreliable.

However, Nagell et al (1993) suggest that animals may just notice environmental features that others are interacting with, so also explore them and learn by trial and error.

Example

A study by Hinde and Fisher (1949) initially provided evidence for social learning theory. They reported, through observations, a sudden and rapid increase in the number of blue tits pecking through foil bottle tops in London during the 1940s. However, Sherry and Galef (1984) conducted an experiment where they split up two groups of chickadees. One group saw another chickadee breaking open the foil top to the milk bottle, while the other group just saw an already opened milk bottle. They found that both groups were subsequently equally as quick at opening the milk bottle when presented with a closed one. This study therefore provided evidence against the social learning theory.

Figure 7: *Imitation may just be trial and error.*

Tip: A chickadee is just a small type of bird — but don't worry, you won't be asked specifically about them in the exam.

Worked Exam-style Questions

0 1 Discuss the role of conditioning in learning in non-human animals.

(8 marks + 8 marks)

Both classical and operant conditioning can be used to explain animal behaviour. Founded in the behavioural approach, classical conditioning describes how a stimulus can become associated with a response that already exists. For instance, as Pavlov (1927) showed in his classical conditioning experiment with dogs, pairing a bell with food eventually results in the dogs automatically salivating when they hear a bell. Whilst this behaviour isn't intelligence, it goes to show that certain behaviours can be learnt by animals.

Operant conditioning occurs when a behaviour and consequence become associated with each other, either encouraging or discouraging future behaviour. For example, Skinner (1938) developed a device called a 'Skinner box' containing a lever which would provide food pellets when pushed. He then placed rats inside and watched them as they investigated how to get the food. After pressing it by accident at first, the rats soon learnt that pressing the lever would give them food and they gradually pushed it more frequently. This is evidence of positive

Exam Tip
You really need to make sure you know the difference between classical and operant conditioning for questions like this.

reinforcement where a behaviour produces a positive outcome. Operant conditioning also involves negative reinforcement. This is where behaviour removes a negative stimulus. For example, not giving out punishments to a dog when it performs a trick, would allow it to learn that performing good tricks is a good behaviour. Punishment can also be involved. This is where a stimulus can stop a behaviour. For instance, receiving an electric shock after pressing a certain button will ensure the button isn't pressed again.

Like classical conditioning, operant conditioning suggests that learning in animals happens by learning associations. However, there have been problems with the research in this area. A lot of the experiments have been conducted on animals and therefore, can't be generalised to humans. One way to improve on this would be to conduct more research in natural conditions on humans, using methods such as field studies.

Exam Tip
Don't forget about the limitations of using animals in experiments — it's a key criticism in lots of psychology experiments.

Exam Tip
If you expand on criticisms by suggesting improvements or how problems might be solved, you're showing the examiner that you are able to critically analyse research studies thoroughly.

Secondly, different species seem to respond to conditioning in different ways. This means that, to some degree, different levels of learning must exist and some animals may simply learn by observation without any reinforcement.

Also, there does seem to be a genetic link which suggests learning behaviours are not completely influenced by reactions to the environment. Finally, the use of animals in experiments could be seen as unethical. The researchers must conduct a cost-benefit analysis and follow strict guidelines to ensure the welfare of the animals.

---

0 | 2 Outline how self-recognition studies have been used to explore intelligence in non-human animals.

(4 marks)

Exam Tip
It is a good idea to define any key terms in the question, just to show the examiner you do know what you're talking about.

Self-recognition, where an animal is self-aware, is seen as evidence of intelligence. This concept has been studied using a technique known as the 'mark test'. The researchers paint a mark on an animal's face while they are anaesthetised and then place them in front of a mirror. If the animal touches the mark, this is taken as proof that they understand the animal in the reflection is them.

Summary Questions

Q1 In terms of classical conditioning,
  a) define spontaneous recovery.
  b) define extinction.

Q2 a) Give an everyday example of negative reinforcement.
  b) Give an everyday example of positive punishment.
  c) Explain the difference between reinforcement and punishment.

Q3 What is Machiavellian intelligence?

Q4 What is vicarious reinforcement?

3. Human Intelligence

Humans are (usually) more intelligent than other species, but our levels of intelligence differ. There are many reasons why this might be the case.

Learning Objectives:

- Know about evolutionary factors in the development of human intelligence, for example, ecological demands, social complexity and brain size.
- Know about genetic and environmental factors associated with intelligence test performance, including the influence of culture.

Evolutionary factors

Darwin's (1859) theory of natural selection suggests that characteristics that increase an animal's chances of surviving and reproducing are likely to be passed from one generation to the next. If intelligence is beneficial to survival, the most intelligent members of a population are the most likely to survive and reproduce. This gives rise to intelligent offspring, who are also likely to survive and reproduce. In this way the species evolves over time to become more intelligent.

Humans are a highly intelligent species. This suggests that intelligence is a characteristic that's been beneficial to the survival of humans and has evolved through natural selection. Several factors may have contributed to the evolution of human intelligence. For example:

Ecological demands

The ecological demands of the environment may have stimulated the development of intelligence.

Examples

- A hunter-gatherer or foraging lifestyle requires memory and navigational skills, so higher intelligence levels would be beneficial for survival.
- Animals that merely graze in large areas of land, with little stimulation or need to search for their food, are likely to have lower levels of intelligence.
- Arboreal primates (those that live in trees) survive on fruit and nuts and use a complex set of navigational skills to forage for their food. Once they have found their food, they often have to determine how to break open the nuts, using more problem solving skills and therefore, increasing the intelligence of the primate family.

***Figure 1:** This long-tailed macaque is known for eating crabs — foraging behaviour that requires lots of skill.*

Our ancestors would first have foraged for food, but then later started to hunt. They were likely to have developed tools and, as hunting would require the cooperation of a group, social skills would have also developed. Over time, intelligence would have grown through developments in these behaviours.

Social complexity

Humans are social animals. Living in groups could have contributed to the development of intelligence. The social complexity of group living may help survival, e.g. by giving protection from predators and cooperation when hunting. However, social living also creates competition and conflict, e.g. for a mate.

Successful social living is more likely if animals are intelligent and have theory of mind, allowing them to understand others' intentions and feelings. This also allows for Machiavellian intelligence — where individuals and groups can deceive others for their own advantage. There is some evidence that social complexity and intelligence are linked:

- Other animals considered to be intelligent, e.g. primates and dolphins, also live in social groups.
- Cosmides and Tooby (1992) found that people are better at solving logical

Tip: Look back at page 109 to read more about Machiavellian intelligence.

problems if they are put in terms of everyday social situations, rather than presented in an abstract form. This suggests that intelligence may have evolved to deal with social situations. However, it's not clear which evolved first — intelligence or group living.

Dunbar (1992) proposed that in primates brain size is proportional to social group size. The more sociable we are, the greater level of intelligence we'd need to interact with others, and the larger our brain size.

Brain size

Jerison (1973), found a positive correlation between body size and brain size in animals. However, humans have brains seven times larger than expected for a mammal of our size.

Early hominids had a brain size of about 600 cubic centimetres. This remained relatively constant for 1.5 million years before doubling in size over the last 0.5 million years. This is despite the fact that larger brains require more energy and make childbirth more difficult and dangerous. However, these evolutionary costs are balanced by increased intelligence. Higher intelligence requires more brain cells and possibly more specialised brain areas — and so bigger brains evolved. Research on brain size as a proportion of body size supports this theory. Willerman et al (1991) used MRI scanning to measure the brain size of college students. Those with higher IQ scores had larger brains (proportionate to body size). However, a limited, unrepresentative sample was used, meaning that it's hard to generalise the results. Also the type of IQ test may have had an effect on the results.

Real World Connection
Dunbar (1992) says the maximum number of people we can keep up a social relationship with is 150. This is called 'Dunbar's number' and is thought to be between 100 and 200, but 150 is the generally accepted figure. He based his findings on research investigating the ideal sizes of various tribes and social groups across different cultures and species. Dunbar's number has been used to quantify various social group sizes such as the average number of people we send Christmas cards to and the number of friends we regularly communicate with on social networking sites. As he suggested this number of contacts is a universal figure, his research supports the evolutionary theory of intelligence.

Genetics and the environment

There's a lot of debate about the role genetic and environmental factors play in intelligence test scores. Closely related people, e.g. siblings, tend to have more highly correlated IQ scores than less closely related people, e.g. cousins.

However, environmental factors must influence intelligence to some extent otherwise identical twins would show a correlation of 1 — which they never do. Another way of testing for genetic influences is to compare the correlations adopted children show with their biological and adoptive relatives. A higher correlation with their biological relatives than with their adoptive relatives (whose environment they share) suggests a strong genetic link.

The influence of social class on intelligence is one environmental factor which has been investigated. Intelligence testing can be a sensitive issue. For example, in the past, the use of IQ tests led to a conclusion that White Americans are more intelligent than African-Americans, and that it was due to genetic differences. Environmental factors hadn't been considered.

Tip: Whether intelligence is caused by genetics and the environment is an example of the nature-nurture debate in psychology. The nature-nurture debate is all about whether behaviour is determined by our genes and biology (nature) or our environment (nurture).

Tip: Identical twins are often referred to as 'MZ' (monozygotic) and non-identical twins as 'DZ' (dizygotic).

Key studies of genetic and environmental influences

Bouchard et al (1990) conducted a large scale study where they followed MZ and DZ twins who had been separated at birth. They measured a huge number of factors, including IQ. For MZ twins raised apart, their IQ scores had a correlation of around 0.7. It was roughly 0.9 for those raised together. IQ seems to be influenced by both genes and the environment.

Bouchard and McGue (1981) did a meta analysis of 111 studies and found that the people with the highest IQ correlations were identical twins reared together. They showed a correlation of 0.86 compared to 0.6 for non-identical twins reared together. This suggests that intelligence is influenced by genetics.

But Schiff et al (1978) found that children from lower socio-economic backgrounds who were adopted into families with higher socio-economic status showed higher IQs than their biological relatives. This suggests that intelligence is affected by environmental factors. Also, Bouchard and McGue (1981) found that identical twins reared apart showed a lower correlation in IQ scores (0.72) than identical twins reared together. This supports the theory that environmental factors affect IQ.

Tip: Concordance rates can also be written as percentages, so 0.86 and 0.6 would be 86% and 60%.

So, genetics and environmental factors are both important in IQ test performance, and probably interact. For example, variations in intelligence caused by genetics could be compounded or reduced depending on the environment (e.g. quality of nutrition or education).

The Minnesota transracial adoption study — Scarr and Weinberg (1976)

Method: Scarr and Weinberg (1976) investigated the intelligence levels of over 100 black and mixed race adopted children. The children had been raised by upper-middle class, white parents with above-average IQ levels.

Results: The IQ of those raised by the adoptive families was higher than a set of control participants raised by their natural parents from a lower social class.

Conclusion: Social factors and the environment do appear to influence intelligence levels.

Tip: There are loads of other variables that may have affected the results of Scarr and Weinberg's (1976) experiment. The age at which the child was adopted, their natural birth parents' IQ, the school they went to, etc. may all have influenced the results.

Comments

Different studies have used different kinds of IQ test, making comparisons difficult. Closer relatives often share more similar environments (e.g. the same home) than more distantly related people. This makes it difficult to separate genetic influences from environmental influences.

Tip: See page 104 for the triarchic model.

The effect of culture

Sternberg's (1985) **triarchic model of intelligence** suggests that intelligence is shown by successfully adapting to the physical and social demands of the surrounding environment.

Key studies of the role of culture in intelligence

Sternberg et al (2001) found that some Kenyan children knew a huge amount about herbal medicines but didn't perform very well on normal IQ tests.

Other studies have looked at how intelligence is defined in different cultures. Sternberg and Yang (1997) suggested that Asian cultures were more likely to see intelligence as an understanding of others and knowing when to show your intelligence or not, whereas Western cultures used more quantitative skills such as verbal and numerical reasoning.

Figure 2: *This Indian doctor may not perform well on normal IQ tests, yet his knowledge of herbal medicines is vast.*

Tip: Mackintosh (1998) used a series of 'culture-free' non-verbal reasoning tests (tests which ask people to look for patterns and analyse shapes) to investigate the differences between races. He found that White Americans obtained better results than Black Americans, suggesting that there are genetic differences in intelligence. However, non-verbal tests are not necessarily 'culture-free' so the environment still may be an important contributing factor.

Das (1994) also looked at Eastern cultures, and concluded that Buddhists and Hindus were likely to attribute intelligence to feelings of awareness, mental effort and recognising others.

Example

In Zimbabwe, the word for intelligence is 'ngware'. This actually translates as 'prudent' or 'cautious', suggesting that this particular culture sees intelligence as a sign of knowing your social boundaries.

So intelligence must be understood in relation to the culture that a person lives in. In some cultures the ability to pass exams could be seen as evidence of intelligent behaviour, whilst in others the ability to hunt has greater value. Any intelligence testing that's carried out must take these differences into account.

Herrnstein and Murray (1994) conducted a study investigating the relationship between race and IQ. However, they were heavily criticised after concluding that genetic differences made some races more intelligent than others. It was thought they had confused race with social class.

Worked Exam-style Question

0 1 Discuss **one** evolutionary factor that may be related to the development of intelligence.

(4 marks + 4 marks)

Research has been conducted into the relationship between brain size and intelligence. Jerison (1973) found that there was a positive correlation between body size and brain size in animals, but that humans far exceeded what was expected of them. From research into early hominids, it seems that there's been an incredibly fast brain size evolution. Developments in hunting skills, such as tool use and cooperation with others, would have required a development in intelligence and so, over the past 0.5 million years, a larger brain has been linked to greater intelligence. This is because a larger brain contains more brain cells and probably has more specialised brain areas.

A more modern study has also been conducted where Willerman et al (1991) managed to show, using an MRI scanner, that those college students with higher IQs actually had larger brains. However, it's hard to generalise the results of this study as an unrepresentative sample was used. The type of IQ test also may have affected the results as some people are better at some elements of IQ tests than others.

The evolutionary approach is deterministic which takes away the idea of free will. It also doesn't consider the effect of the environment on intelligence, such as education, social background and culture.

Exam Tip
There are lots of examples you could use to talk about the relationship between brain size and intelligence. Choose one that you know really well so you've got plenty to say.

Exam Tip
This question is worth 8 marks, but it will form part of a 24 mark question. Make sure you pay attention to how many marks each part is worth so you spend the right amount of time on each.

Summary Questions

Q1 Suggest how arboreal primates may have increased the brain size of the primate family.

Q2 Name one evolutionary factor that may have influenced intelligence.

Q3 Outline a study investigating the genetic link in intelligence.

Q4 Give one example of how intelligence might differ between cultures.

Section Summary

- The learning approach suggests that intelligent behaviours are developed through conditioning.
- The psychometric approach to intelligence suggests that intelligence can be measured. Spearman, Cattell and Thurstone developed psychometric theories of intelligence.
- Spearman (1904) proposed that everyone has a general intelligence (g) and specific abilities. Cattell (1963, 1971) thought that intelligence can be split into two types — crystallised and fluid. Thurstone (1938) argued that there are seven different groups of mental abilities and these all combine to make up intelligence.
- The information processing approach tries to explain intelligence by focusing on the cognitive processes involved. Sternberg and Gardner developed theories within the information processing approach.
- Sternberg (1985) came up with a triarchic model which divided intelligence into three parts.
- Gardner (1985) identified eight different kinds of intelligence, involving different cognitive structures that are all independent.
- Animal learning can be explained using conditioning. Classical conditioning involves forming associations between stimuli, whereas operant conditioning involves associating particular behaviours with certain consequences.
- Non-human animals may show some kinds of intelligence. This can be shown as self-recognition, social learning and Machiavellian intelligence.
- Evolutionary factors, such as ecological demands, social complexity and brain size, may have affected the development of intelligence.
- It seems that human intelligence is influenced by both genetics and the environment.
- Human intelligence appears to be linked to culture. People have to adapt to the environment they live in, and this seems to influence how well they perform on IQ tests. Also, what's considered intelligent in one culture may not be the same in another.

Exam-style Questions

0 1 Outline **one** information processing theory of intelligence

(8 marks)

0 2 Evaluate the information processing approach to intelligence.

(16 marks)

---

0 3 "Human intelligence is controlled exclusively by genetic factors". Discuss this statement with reference to psychological research.

(8 marks + 16 marks)

1. Development of Thinking

Learning Objectives:
- Understand theories of cognitive development, including Piaget and Vygotsky.

Tip: 'Cognition' just means thinking.

Figure 1: *Jean Piaget, a psychologist famous for his work with children.*

Figure 2: *A baby undertaking an object permanence test.*

Tip: Make sure that you know and understand Piaget's stages of development before you move on. If you don't, the next few pages will be hard to follow.

A child's thinking changes and develops as they get older. Not surprisingly, this interests psychologists...

Piaget's theory of cognitive development

Piaget said that we're all born with the basics to allow cognitive progression — reflexes and senses. Piaget was interested in the development of **cognition** and so did loads of different intelligence tests on children. He observed that children of the same age kept making the same mistakes in the same tasks. Piaget therefore proposed that cognition progresses in stages. He reckoned that more complex abilities become possible as children move through stages of development as they get older:

1. **Sensorimotor stage (0–2 years)** — The child's knowledge is limited to what their senses tell them when they're exploring their surroundings. This exploration brings about an understanding of the concept of **object permanence** (if you put a towel over a toy, the toy is still there).
2. **Preoperational stage (2–7 years)** — The child has some language now, but makes logic mistakes — e.g. cats have four legs, so everything with four legs must be a cat. They typically can't do the three mountains task (see page 119) or conservation tasks (see pages 119-120). Children at this stage show egocentrism, irreversibility and centration (see page 119).
3. **Concrete operational stage (7–11 years)** — The child's use of logic improves and they can do conservation tasks. They no longer show egocentrism, irreversibility and centration but can't yet use **abstract reasoning** (reasoning in their head).
4. **Formal operational stage (11+ years)** — The child is much more advanced now, and can use abstract reasoning in problem solving. They can also use hypotheses and theoretical principles, and deal with hypothetical situations.

Schemas

Piaget used the idea of **schemas** a lot in his work. A schema contains all the information you know about an object, action or concept — e.g. the schema of a human face has two eyes, a mouth and a nose, and the schema of riding a bike contains all the movements you'd need to make. Schemas help you to organise and interpret information — new experiences are taken into our schemas (**assimilated**) and are **accommodated** by them. Accommodation just involves altering existing schemas.

Example

A child's schema for an apple may be an edible, green, hard sphere. A red apple challenges this schema. The new information is assimilated and accommodated — an apple is now an edible, hard sphere that is either green or red.

Piaget reckoned that children try to find a balance between assimilation and accommodation during cognitive development.

Experiments testing Piaget's theory

Piaget and Inhelder (1956) conducted the 'three mountains task' on children in order to provide evidence for Piaget's theory.

Key study of cognitive development — Piaget and Inhelder (1956)

Method: Piaget and Inhelder built a 3-D model of three mountains. The mountains had different landmarks on them — e.g. one had a cross on it, and another had a house. Piaget and Inhelder put a small doll on one of the mountains and then showed children photos of the mountains taken from various angles. The children were asked to pick the photo that matched what the doll could see.

Results: It was found that children at Piaget's preoperational stage (2–7 years old) picked the photo taken from their own perspective, rather than the one taken from the doll's perspective.

Conclusion: It was concluded that children at this stage were unable to put themselves in the doll's shoes.

Evaluation: The 'three mountains task' is quite abstract — being questioned on a 3-D model of mountains is quite an unfamiliar thing to happen for a child, therefore the study can be criticised for lacking ecological validity.

Figure 3: The set up used by Piaget and Inhelder (1956) in their three mountain task.

Piaget used the 'three mountains task' and other experiments as evidence that children at his preoperational stage have the following qualities:

- **Egocentrism** — they can only view the world from their own viewpoint. They're not sensitive to the fact that others may have different views or thoughts (as demonstrated by the 'three mountains task').
- **Irreversibility** — they don't understand that you can undo an action (e.g. that you can reform a sausage-shaped piece of clay into its original ball shape — see Figure 4).
- **Centration** — they focus on small aspects of a task, not the task as a whole.

Tip: Make sure you know what words like 'egocentrism' mean. It'll impress the examiner if you can use them in the exam — just make sure you use them correctly and in the right context.

Figure 4: Children at the preoperational stage don't understand irreversibility— e.g. that you can undo an action or change things back.

Later stages of cognition

Piaget showed how other skills develop in later stages:

1. Understanding of conservation

Conservation is the understanding that a set quantity stays the same, even if it looks different.

Example

If liquid is poured from a short, fat glass into a tall, thin glass, the amount of liquid is still the same (see Figure 5).

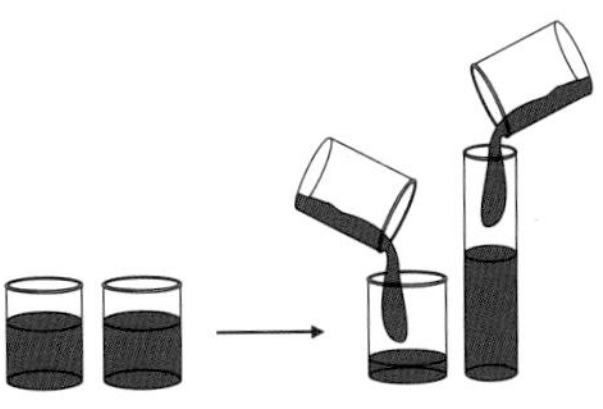

Figure 5: Liquid conservation task

Key study of conservation — Piaget and Szeminska (1952)

Method: Children were presented with two identical rows of counters and asked if both rows had the same number of counters. One of the rows of counters was then spread out and the question was repeated.

Results: Children at both the operational and preoperational stages could answer the first question correctly. When the counters were spread out and the question repeated, children at the preoperational stage answered incorrectly.

Conclusion: Children at the preoperational stage can't understand conservation.

Figure 6: *Children at the preoperational stage typically can't do conservation tasks.*

Children at the concrete operational stage can correctly identify that the amount of liquid or the number of counters stays the same even after they've been rearranged. But children at the preoperational stage will say that the spaced out row contains more counters or the tall glass more liquid.

Key study of conservation — McGarrigle and Donaldson (1974)

McGarrigle and Donaldson found that if a puppet (Naughty Teddy) 'accidentally' knocked the counters so that the row looked longer, even younger children at the preoperational stage said that the number of counters was the same. This suggests that they did understand conservation, which raises questions about Piaget and Szeminska's (1952) findings. Perhaps in their experiment, children were responding to demand characteristics — the change in the counters was obvious and deliberate, and the same question was asked twice, suggesting that a different response was expected the second time. When the counters were spread out 'accidently' by 'Naughty Teddy', children were more likely to focus on what had happened and answer correctly.

Figure 7: *The results of McGarrigle and Donaldson's 'Naughty Teddy' study brought Piaget and Szeminska's results into question.*

2. Problem solving abilities

Key study of problem solving abilities — the 'four beaker problem' — Piaget and Inhelder (1956)

Method: Piaget and Inhelder gave children four beakers, each containing a colourless liquid. When two of the liquids were mixed the liquid turned yellow. Children had to work out the right combination.

Results: Children at the formal operational stage used systematic testing of different mixtures, whereas children at the concrete operational stage used a random approach.

Conclusion: Children at the concrete operational stage do not display abstract reasoning.

Evaluation: Some researchers have argued that not everybody gets to the formal operational stage of systematic hypothesis testing, so it might not be a universal stage of development.

Evaluation of Piaget's theory

There's evidence for and against Piaget's stages of cognitive development:

- There's cross-cultural similarity in the stages — studies have suggested that children of all backgrounds progress through the stages in the same way, which provides support for Piaget's theory.
- Piaget underestimated abilities at each age — for example, the experiment with Naughty Teddy showed that preoperational children can in fact understand the concept of conservation.

Tip: Make sure you try to learn a few of the studies in this evaluation section. It looks really good in the exam if you can support a point you're making with experimental evidence.

- Other studies have found results that conflict with Piaget's. For instance, Bower and Wishart (1972) showed that object permanence was displayed in 1 month olds, whereas Piaget believed this stage of development didn't occur until 8 months.
- Hughes (1975) conducted a modified version of the 'three mountains task', instead using the concept of hiding a boy doll from two policeman dolls (see Figure 8). Hughes found that children aged as young as 4 years old were able to put themselves in the doll's shoes, whereas Piaget and Inhelder (1956) showed that children at the preoperational stage were egocentric — they couldn't put themselves in another's shoes.
- **Demand characteristics** may have affected Piaget's results. Asking a child the same question twice may be confusing, leading them to give a different answer. Rose and Blank (1974) conducted Piaget and Szeminska's counter conservation task, but only asked if there were the same number of counters after the transformation had taken place. When the study was conducted this way (rather than asking before and after as in Piaget and Szeminska's (1952) original study), it was found that Piaget's preoperational-aged children did much better. A study by Samuel and Bryant (1984) also found that children performed significantly better when only asked one question.
- Piaget said that practice and teaching wouldn't speed up progression through the stages but this isn't true — it's been found that teaching can help to move children on through the stages.
- Piaget didn't think that language was important in cognitive development. He thought you needed cognitive development first in order to allow language to develop. But other theorists, such as Vygotsky, take a different view on this, as you'll find out on page 122.

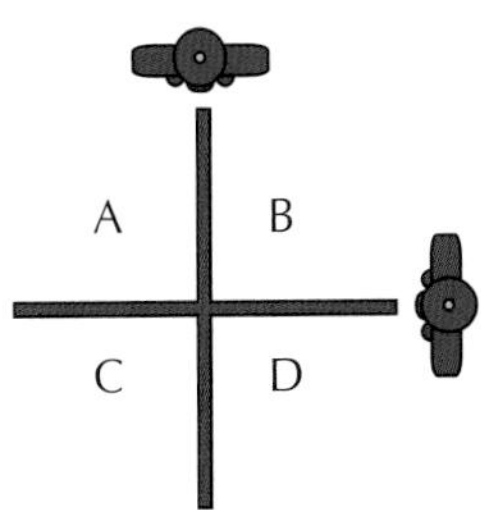

Figure 8: *The set-up used in the study by Hughes (1975). Children were asked to hide a boy doll so that he could not be seen by either of the policeman dolls.*

Tip: See pages 119-120 for the methodology used in Piaget and Szeminska's (1952) counter conservation task.

Vygotsky's theory of cognitive development

Vygotsky said there were two types of mental function — elementary and higher. **Elementary functions** can be thought of as innate reflexes, sensory abilities and certain types of memory. **Higher functions** include more complex tasks like language comprehension and decision-making.
Social and cultural factors play a necessary part in moving from one type of functioning to the other — it's the influence of others around you that drives cognitive development.

One of Vygotsky's ideas was the **zone of proximal development** (ZPD). This is the difference between the problem solving a child can do on their own and the problem solving they can do with a more able peer or adult. If your teacher has an idea of what your potential is, they can help you reach it by pushing and guiding. So it's interaction with the teacher that's important (unlike Piaget's idea that progression happens on its own). Instruction is social and driven by the teacher using language and cultural influences.
The intention is to help the child to be self-regulated and responsible for their own learning.

Figure 9: *Lev Vygotsky, a soviet psychologist.*

Figure 10: *The guidance of an adult can help a child reach their potential.*

Key study of the zone of proximal development — McNaughton and Leyland (1990)

Method: Children completed jigsaws of increasing levels of difficulty with guidance from their mother. They were observed during this, and the hardest jigsaw they completed was recorded. They then returned a week later and attempted a

Tip: The concept of the ZPD can be applied to education, see page 126.

	new set of jigsaws alone.
Results:	The highest jigsaw level reached by children in the second week was lower than in the first week.
Conclusion:	The guidance of an adult can increase a child's ability to complete a task, showing that guiding a child within their ZPD can improve their cognitive development.
Evaluation:	A jigsaw is a task that a child is likely to be familiar with, therefore the study has high ecological validity.

The role of language in cognitive development

Vygotsky suggests that language is a driving influence on cognitive development. Children first learn language as a means to communicate with caregivers. It's also a tool that allows adults to communicate social and cultural information to children.

As the child grows older they use language not only to communicate but also to guide their behaviour— they use **self-talk** (talking out loud) to regulate and direct themselves. This self-talk eventually becomes internalised and becomes silent **inner speech**. At this point the child has developed two very different forms of language — inner speech and external oral speech.

Oral speech is used socially for communication, whilst inner speech is a cognitive tool that allows individuals to direct and monitor their thoughts and behaviour. If someone finds a task difficult they may re-employ self-talk to exert greater control over their thoughts.

Tip: It doesn't look great in the exam if you can't spell the names of the important researchers. As far as names go, Vygotsky is a tricky one, so it's worth making an effort to learn it. Perhaps use the rhyme 'V-Y-got-sky' to help you.

Vygotsky's stages of development

Like Piaget, Vygotsky also came up with stages of development. Vygotsky's stages aren't as rigidly defined as Piaget's — they're broader areas of development (without specified ages) giving an idea of the stages children go through as their thinking matures (concept formation). He came up with these 4 stages after studying how children of various ages went about solving a problem:

1. **Vague syncretic stage** — trial and error methods are used, with no understanding of the underlying concepts.
2. **Complex stage** — use of strategies begins but they're not used successfully.
3. **Potential concept stage** — successful strategies are used but only one at a time.
4. **Mature concept stage** — lots of strategies used at the same time. Thinking becomes mature and developed.

Evaluation of Vygotsky's theory of cognitive development

Vygotsky carried out very few studies whilst coming up with his theory. However, other people have carried out studies that have provided evidence that supports Vygotsky's theory:

Key study supporting Vygotsky's theory — Berk (1994)	
Method:	75 children aged between 6 and 8 were observed working alone on maths problems. Their self-talk was observed and their progress in maths was analysed over time.

Results: On average, children displayed self-talk 60% of the time. Those who used more self-talk when solving maths problems did better in maths over the following year. Children who displayed self-talk relating to the task were generally focused and attentive. In contrast, children whose self-talk was not relevant to the task were more fidgety and overall less focused.

Conclusion: Self-talk is frequently used by children and task-related self-talk can help direct the child's thoughts, assisting in problem-solving.

Evaluation: The study has high ecological validity as it took place in a school — an environment that is familiar to children.

***Figure 11:** Self-talk can help direct a child's thoughts during problem-solving.*

Additional studies supporting Vygotsky's theory

Chi et al (1989) showed that pretending to talk to the author as you read (self-explanation) can help increase understanding. This is evidence for the use of speech in thought.

Gardner and Gardner (1969) found that with instruction animals can reach higher levels of functioning. This is evidence for the role of culture in learning.

Tip: If the studies by Chi et al and Berk are anything to go by, it could be useful to talk out loud to yourself when revising. Seriously, if there's something you don't understand, try explaining it to yourself out loud. You never know, it might help...

Another strength of Vygotsky's theory is that it can be successfully applied to education (see page 126). However, a major criticism of Vygotsky's theory is that it over-emphasises social and cultural factors in intelligence and ignores biological factors.

Bruner's theory of cognitive development

Bruner's (1966) theory focuses on representations of knowledge. He claimed that our brains use three modes of representation for knowledge:

Tip: Bruner's theory offers an alternative to Piaget and Vygotsky's ideas.

1. **The enactive mode** — At first, knowledge is only in the form of physical actions, i.e. learning by doing. For example, a baby's knowledge of a rattle would involve how to hold and shake it. Later, this mode is used to represent knowledge such as how to swim. So, knowledge just involves 'muscle memory'.
2. **The iconic mode** — At 2–6 years we begin to also store knowledge in the form of mental images involving different senses like vision, smell and touch. For example, our knowledge of what an apple is includes what it looks like and tastes like.
3. **The symbolic mode** — From about 7 years old we develop the ability to think in symbolic ways — we can store things as words and numbers. Language and thinking become strongly linked, e.g. we use language to talk about experiences. This allows us to mentally manipulate concepts and ideas, and to think in abstract ways.

***Figure 12:** According to Bruner, we learn by doing when we are in the enactive mode.*

Like Vygotsky, Bruner thought that language was very important for cognitive development. So, language instruction might help achieve understanding. However, Sinclair-de-Zwart (1969) found that although language appropriate for conservation tasks could be taught to children who couldn't conserve, most were still unsuccessful at the conservation tasks. Further development seems to be necessary before the next stage can be reached.

Evidence supporting Bruner's theory

Key study supporting Bruner's theory — Bruner and Kenney (1966)

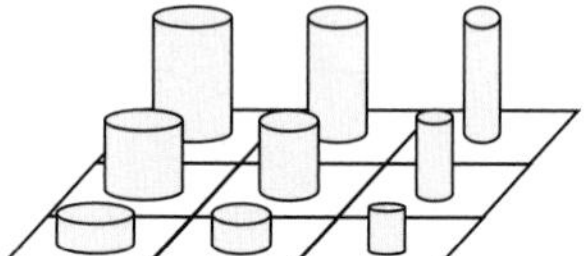
Figure 13: *The arrangement of glasses used by Bruner and Kenney (1966).*

Method: Children aged 5–7 were shown a grid with an arrangement of different sized glasses on it (see Figure 13). These were removed and the children had to replace them as they had been (requiring iconic thinking), or rearrange them, e.g. in a mirror image (requiring symbolic thinking).

Results: All the children replaced the glasses correctly, but only the older children could rearrange them. Children without the appropriate language to talk through the problem were only able to do the replacement task.

Conclusion: Mental manipulation of ideas requires symbolic representation, and children must have progressed to the symbolic mode of cognitive development in order to think in this way. Language is important for more complex thinking.

Evaluation: This was a laboratory experiment so there was good control over variables. However, all the study really showed was that older children can manage more complex tasks — so, this could also be used as support for Piaget or Vygotsky's theory.

Worked Exam-style Question

0 1 Describe **one** theory of cognitive development.

(8 marks)

Bruner's theory of cognitive development focuses on representations of knowledge and is seen as an alternative to the theories of Piaget and Vygotsky. Bruner claimed that our brains move through three modes of representation for knowledge during development. The first is the enactive mode. At first, knowledge is only in the form of physical actions, i.e. we learn by doing. For example, a baby's knowledge of a rattle would involve how to hold and shake it. Later, this mode represents knowledge such as how to swim. Here knowledge just involves 'muscle memory'.

The iconic mode is Bruner's second type of knowledge. At 2–6 years we store knowledge as mental images involving different senses like vision, smell and touch, e.g. our knowledge of an apple includes what it looks and tastes like.

This is followed by the symbolic mode. From about 7 years old, we are able to think in symbolic ways — we can store things as words and numbers. Here, language and thinking become strongly linked, for example, we use language to talk about experiences. This allows us to mentally manipulate concepts and ideas, and to think in abstract ways.

Exam Tip
Remember, questions in the Unit 3 exam are each worth 24 marks. This 8 mark question would just be part of a larger question. For more information see the 'Exam Help' section (pages 296-301).

Exam Tip
Giving an example illustrates the point you're making, so helps the examiner know what you're talking about.

0 2 Evaluate Piaget's theory of cognitive development.

(8 marks)

Piaget proposed a theory of cognitive development which suggests that more complex abilities become possible as children move through four stages of cognitive development as they get older. Piaget conducted a lot of experiments on children, which he then based his theory on. For instance, Piaget and Inhelder's (1956) 'three mountains task' provided evidence that children in the preoperational stage are egocentric, while Piaget and Szeminska's (1952) experiment on conservation using counters suggested that children in the preoperational stage are unable to understand conservation.

However, other studies have found results that conflict with Piaget's ideas and his evidence. For example, McGarrigle and Donaldson's (1974) 'Naughty Teddy' experiment showed that preoperational children could understand the concept of conservation, suggesting that perhaps Piaget's theory underestimated a child's abilities at each age. In addition, a modified version of the 'three mountains task' using a less abstract concept of hiding a boy doll from two policeman dolls by Hughes (1975) found that children aged as young as 4 years old were not egocentric. Again, this contradicts Piaget's ideas.

It has been suggested that some of the experiments that Piaget based his theory on may have been affected by demand characteristics. For instance, in Piaget and Szeminska's (1952) counter conservation experiment, children may have been inclined to respond differently after the counters were spread out simply because they were being asked the same question a second time, so assumed a different answer was expected. When Rose and Blank (1974) reproduced Piaget and Szeminska's experiment, but only asked if there were the same number of counters after the transformation had taken place, it was found that children at Piaget's preoperational stage did much better. Samuel and Bryant (1984) also found that children performed significantly better when only asked one question, providing further evidence that Piaget's results were subject to demand characteristics.

In summary, although there is support for Piaget's theory, the criticisms of the methodology used in his own research question the accuracy of his theory. More research is needed to conclusively say whether Piaget's theory is an accurate representation of cognitive development.

Exam Tip
There's a lot to say about Piaget, but don't just dive straight into your answer — take a minute to think about what the question is specifically asking about and what your answer needs to cover. If it helps, scribble down a quick plan.

Exam Tip
An evaluation doesn't just have to be criticisms or positive comments — you can weigh up both so that your answer is structured like an argument.

Summary Questions

Q1 Outline the characteristics of a child at Piaget's preoperational stage.

Q2 What were the results of Piaget and Inhelder's (1956) study using the 'four beaker problem'?

Q3 What is the zone of proximal development?

Q4 Outline the methodology used by McNaughton and Leyland (1990) in their study of the zone of proximal development.

Q5 Name Vygotsky's four stages of cognitive development.

Learning Objectives:

- Understand applications of cognitive development theories to education.

2. Applying the Theories to Education

Psychologists don't just make theories for fun. Theories of cognitive development can have real life practical applications, such as in education.

Implications of Piaget's theory for education

Piaget's theory suggests a child-centred approach to education, in which children can learn for themselves through their own experience.
It can be applied to find ways to help children learn more effectively:

- **Learning by discovery** — according to Piaget, when children encounter new experiences that their current schemas can't deal with adequately, they develop new schemas through the process of accommodation. This implies that providing opportunities to actively experience new things in a stimulating classroom with lots of different resources will help promote cognitive development.
- **Readiness** — Piaget claimed that development is limited by the process of maturation. So, children can't learn particular kinds of knowledge until they're ready to develop the necessary schemas. For example, a child at the preoperational stage isn't ready to understand conservation of volume.
- **Appropriate materials** — teachers must provide appropriate challenges, e.g. preoperational children should be given concrete examples of new ideas to help their understanding. Teachers must also be sensitive to developmental differences between students, because some children mature and learn more quickly than others.

Tip: Flick back to page 118 for a reminder of schemas and accommodation.

Figure 1: *Piaget believed that a stimulating classroom in which children can actively experience new things will promote cognitive development.*

The Plowden Report (1967)

The Plowden Report reviewed primary level education and made recommendations for UK schools. The report included research and surveys. Some of the recommendations it made were based on Piaget's theory.
For example, Piaget's ideas about discovery learning, readiness and a set sequence of developmental stages were used in the report. However, Piaget's theory isn't now as widely accepted as it once was. It's now known that children generally have more abilities than Piaget claimed, e.g. operational thinking may develop earlier than Piaget suggested.

Implications of Vygotsky's theory for education

Vygotsky's theory supports a teacher-guided approach and suggests that interactions with others are important in learning. In other words, other people are needed to stimulate cognitive development. For example, scaffolding is an important concept developed from Vygotsky's theory where other people assist a child's cognitive development.

Scaffolding is when a teacher, another adult or a more cognitively advanced child acts as an expert to guide the child. They do this by making suggestions or doing demonstrations to provide a framework by which the child learns to do a task. At first the child might need lots of help, but as they learn less help is needed and they can carry on learning independently.
For scaffolding to work it needs to take place within the child's zone of proximal development (ZPD) (see page 121).

Figure 2: *Vygotsky's theory led to the concept of scaffolding — a method where an 'expert' guides the child, providing a framework for their learning.*

Key study on scaffolding — Wood et al (1976)

Method:	Thirty children aged 3–5 were given the task of building a model and were observed. A tutor gave help to each child according to how well they were doing — the help was either in the form of showing or telling.
Results:	Scaffolding allowed the children to complete a task they wouldn't have been able to do alone. The effectiveness of the scaffolding was influenced by various factors, e.g. how the tutor simplified the task, and how they helped them identify important steps. Showing was used most when helping younger children, whilst telling was used more with the older children. Also, the older the child was the less scaffolding was needed for them to complete the task.
Conclusion:	Scaffolding can be helpful but consideration needs to be given to maximise its effectiveness.
Evaluation:	This study had fairly good ecological validity, but there was less control over variables, reducing reliability.

Figure 3: *In a study by Wood et al (1956), the effectiveness of scaffolding was studied. Children were observed building a model with the guidance of a tutor.*

Bruner's ideas for education

Bruner (1966) agreed with Vygotsky that social interaction is important for cognitive development, and he made some important suggestions for education:

The Spiral Curriculum

Although a child's age and level of development will limit what they can learn, Bruner argued that even difficult concepts can be introduced at an appropriate level from an early age. As the child grows the concept can be repeatedly revisited, each time in more depth — this will achieve a more complete and in-depth understanding. In this way, children can build up their knowledge, and the earlier learning should make the later learning easier.

Motivation

Bruner argued that children are more motivated to learn if they have an intrinsic interest in what they're studying. This is more of an incentive than external motivations like getting good marks. So teachers should encourage an active interest in topics and aim to come up with engaging ways to teach them.

Language

Through discussions in class, children can learn about other perspectives, and achieve deeper understanding.

Discovery Learning

Bruner emphasised that children should not just learn facts, but should learn by exploring and discovering facts. This also helps them to learn about the process of acquiring knowledge.

Bruner's ideas have been very influential — for example the use of a spiral curriculum is now quite common.

Real World Connection

The spiral curriculum is used in schools today. For instance, at primary school you may have been taught that plants need sunlight to grow. At secondary school this concept will have been revisited — you will have been taught the basic equation for photosynthesis. The concept is expanded on again at A-level, this time going into the chemical reactions that take place within the plant's cells. In this way the concept is repeatedly revisited, each time in more depth, until a comprehensive understanding is reached.

Evaluation of applying cognitive theories to education

Although theories of cognitive development have been usefully applied to education, there are often practical difficulties involved. For example, it can be very time-consuming to continually assess the ZPD of all the children in a class. Also, providing enough appropriate challenges and finding appropriate expert peer tutors can be a problem.

As more research is done and theories develop, the implications for education need to be regularly reviewed. For example, Sylva (1987) has suggested that Piaget's learning by discovery is not actually always the most effective approach and that his theory should not be relied on so heavily.

Exam Tip
This question would make up part of a bigger question worth a total of 24 marks.

Exam Tip
Students often write everything they know about a topic. Don't go mad — you don't have time and it won't get you extra marks.
Read the question and focus just on what it is asking for — and also pay attention to the number of marks a question is worth.

Worked Exam-style Questions

0 1 Discuss the application of theories of cognitive development to education. *(8 + 8 marks)*

Vygotsky's theory can be applied in schools as a teacher-guided approach. It suggests that interaction with other people is important in stimulating our cognitive development. This is illustrated by the concept of scaffolding, developed from Vygotsky's ideas.

Scaffolding is where a child's cognitive development is guided by another individual, i.e. a teacher, adult or a more cognitively advanced child acts as an expert to guide the child. They make suggestions or demonstrate to the child, which provides a framework that allows the child to learn how to do a task. At first they might need a lot of help, but with time less help is needed and they can carry on learning independently. Scaffolding needs to take place within a child's zone of proximal development — this is the difference between the problem solving ability of a child on their own and their problem solving ability when they have the guidance of a more able peer or adult.

A number of studies provide support for the benefits of using scaffolding techniques in education. For instance, Wood et al (1976), observed thirty children aged 3–5 attempting to build a model. A tutor gave help to each child according to how well they were doing. This help was either in the form of showing or telling. It was found that scaffolding allowed the children to complete a task they wouldn't have been able to do alone, and that the older the child was, the less scaffolding was needed. The effectiveness of the scaffolding was influenced by various factors, e.g. how the tutor simplified the task and how they helped the children identify important steps. Showing was used most when helping younger children, whilst telling was used more with the older children.

Overall, it would seem that applying Vygotsky's ideas to education can be helpful, but consideration needs to be given to maximise its effectiveness, i.e. ensuring scaffolding takes place within the child's zone of proximal development and choosing the correct type of scaffolding according to the age of the child, etc.

Bruner's theory of cognitive development led him to make some important suggestions for education. He proposed the spiral curriculum. This is the idea that difficult concepts can be introduced at an appropriate level from an early age, even though a child's age and level of development will limit what they can learn. As the child progresses the concept is revisited, each time in more depth, achieving a more complete understanding. This allows children to build up their knowledge with the earlier learning making the later learning easier. This concept has been widely used across education.

Bruner believed that children are more motivated to learn if they have an intrinsic interest in what they're studying — it's more of an incentive than external motivations like getting good marks. According to Bruner therefore, teachers should encourage an active interest in the topics they teach and aim to teach them in engaging ways.

Bruner also proposed that language plays an important role in education and that through discussions in class, children can learn about other perspectives, and achieve a deeper understanding of a topic.

Finally Bruner proposed 'discovery learning'. This is the idea that children should learn by exploring and discovering facts for themselves, which also helps them to learn about the process of acquiring knowledge.

Although theories of cognitive development have been usefully applied to education, there are often practical difficulties involved. For example, it can be very time-consuming to continually assess the zone of proximal development of all the children in a class and difficult to provide each child with an appropriate expert peer tutor. Also, providing enough appropriate challenges within the classroom can be problematic.

Summary Questions

Q1 What was the Plowden report?

Q2 a) Who can act as an 'expert guide' to a child in scaffolding?

b) Outline the process of scaffolding.

Q3 a) Outline the methodology used in Wood et al's (1976) scaffolding study.

b) What were the results of Wood et al's (1976) scaffolding study?

Q4 What was Bruner's idea of 'discovery learning'?

Q5 Give one practical difficulty associated with applying cognitive theories to education.

Learning Objectives:

- Understand Kohlberg's theory of moral understanding.

3. Development of Moral Understanding

We're not born knowing right from wrong — we develop moral understanding as we get older (which is probably why toddlers think it's OK to give their baby brother a haircut, or use mummy's lipstick to draw on the dog).

Kohlberg's theory of moral understanding

Kohlberg thought that moral understanding progresses in stages. He argued that your moral understanding increases as you grow older because at each stage you take more and more of the social world into account.

Kohlberg investigated this idea using a series of ten moral dilemma stories.

Tip: It's a good idea to learn one of these examples in case you get asked a question about Kohlberg's study in your exam.

Examples

The 'Heinz dilemma'. In the story, Heinz chose to break into a shop to steal expensive drugs to cure his dying wife. Should he have done this?

The 'brother's dilemma'. In this story, Joe's father promised that if Joe earned $50 he could go to camp, but then changed his mind and asked Joe for the money. Joe only gave him $10 and went to camp with the other $40. Alex, Joe's younger brother, knows the truth. Should he tell their father?

The participants of Kohlberg's (1963) study (which you can read more about on page 131) had to decide what the characters in the dilemmas should do, or discuss whether the characters responses were right or wrong. Kohlberg was interested in the participants' reasons for their decision, rather than the decision itself.

From the results of the study, Kohlberg came up with three levels of moral understanding — preconventional, conventional and postconventional. Each of these levels is made up of two stages:

Level 1 — Preconventional Morality

- **Stage 1 — Punishment and obedience orientation**
  Reasons for behaviour aren't taken into account. The only reason for not doing something is because you'll be punished. For example, Heinz shouldn't steal the drugs because he'll go to jail.
- **Stage 2 — Instrumental purpose orientation**
  Morality is based on meeting your own interests and getting what you want. For example, Heinz should steal the drugs because otherwise his wife will die and he'll be upset.

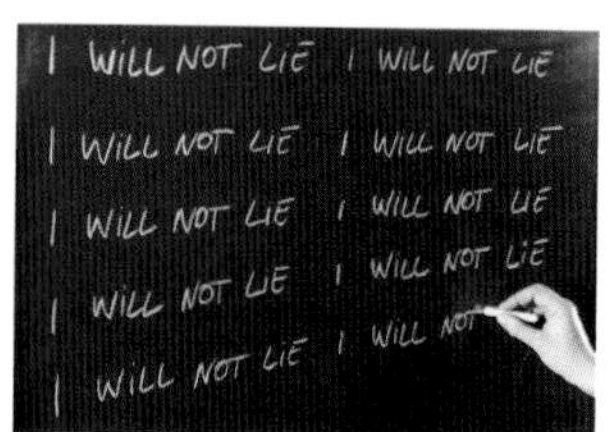

Figure 1: At stage 1 of Kohlberg's model of moral understanding, people behave morally simply in order to avoid punishment.

Level 2 — Conventional Morality

- **Stage 3 — Morality of interpersonal cooperation**
  You try to live up to the expectations of people who are important to you. Behaviour that improves your relationship with these people is seen as moral. For example, Heinz should steal the drugs as his family and friends would expect him to do everything he can to save his wife.
- **Stage 4 — Social-order orientation**
  Moral behaviour is behaviour that fits in with social norms, obligations and rules, e.g. following the law. Morality is seen in the context of society as a whole. For example, Heinz shouldn't steal the drugs because it's against the law, and laws should always be followed.

Level 3 — Postconventional Morality

- **Stage 5 — Social-contract orientation**
  Laws are seen as flexible in certain situations, and not all of equal

importance. Laws are only followed if they contribute towards the welfare of others. For example, Heinz should steal the drugs — although stealing is against the law, it's better to steal than to let his wife die.

- **Stage 6 — Universal ethical principles**
  You've developed your own set of abstract moral principles that you follow above those laid down by the law. For example, Heinz should steal the drugs as human life has a higher value than personal property.

Real World Connection
It can be argued that not many people reach Kohlberg's later stages of moral development. However there are a few famous examples of those who have... Nelson Mandela spent 27 years in prison as a result of crimes he committed as an anti-apartheid activist. Similarly, politician Aung San Suu Kyi spent around 15 years under house arrest as a result of her political actions in Burma, while Ghandi was imprisoned for many years following his non-violent civil rights campaign in India. All of these individuals followed their own moral principles above those set out by the law.

Key study of moral understanding — Kohlberg (1963)

Method: A sample of 72 American boys aged 10, 13 and 16 were each interviewed for approximately 2 hours. Each child was asked to think about a selection of moral dilemmas (e.g. the 'Heinz dilemma' — see page 130), and comment on the actions taken by the characters. They were then asked to justify their reasoning. Kohlberg recorded their answers.

Results: Kohlberg classified the children's responses into three groups. He used these to come up with three levels of moral understanding — preconventional morality, conventional morality and postconventional morality (see previous page). The answers of the younger children tended to fit into the preconventional level, whereas the answers of the older children tended to reflect the conventional stage. Few participants showed postconventional morality.
The participants appeared to be consistent in their thinking and presented similar answers to different moral dilemmas.

Conclusion: Children progress from a state of preconventional morality into a state of conventional morality. Only much later, if at all, do they show postconventional morality.

Evaluation: Participants had to come up with the responses themselves, rather than choosing from a list of possible responses. This meant that the responses were not influenced by any pre-existing ideas that Kohlberg may have had. However, in sorting the participants' responses into levels, Kohlberg may have shown some investigator bias. This study lacked ecological validity as the dilemmas were hypothetical, and showed gender bias as all the participants were boys. Also, the results of this study cannot be generalised to more collectivist cultures where the rights of the individual are more likely to come second to social obligations. Finally, as Kohlberg himself later pointed out, his study was limited as it did not allow for emotions such as guilt and empathy.

Tip: Western societies tend to be individualist and Eastern societies tend to be collectivist. In a collectivist society, the focus is on the social group and the community as a whole. The needs of the individual are viewed as less important.

Evaluation of Kohlberg's theory of moral understanding

Other researchers have reviewed and evaluated Kohlberg's work:

Additional studies on moral understanding

Sobesky (1983) found that using different versions of Heinz's dilemma (i.e. different consequences for Heinz and his wife of Heinz stealing or not stealing) changes the response of the reader. So an individual's response isn't fixed depending on the stage of moral development they're at, but changes according to the situation.

Kohlberg's study is culturally biased towards Western society. Snarey (1985) conducted a meta-analysis of 45 cross-cultural studies carried out across approximately 30 different countries. The findings of this meta-analysis suggested that Kohlberg's stages 1-4 are universal, but that stages 5-6 are not. According to Kohlberg's theory, this could be interpreted to mean that people in collectivist societies are less morally developed than those in individualist societies. However, this would simply be because they would score lower in Kohlberg's stages, as collectivist societies place more importance on the group as a whole, rather than the individual.

Kohlberg's theory can also be considered gender-biased — most of Kohlberg's work was carried out on US males, so his findings may not apply to other groups. Gilligan (1982) claimed that the theory was androcentric and focused too much on male-oriented ideas about justice rather than also taking into account other moral approaches that might appeal more to women.

Hart and Fegley (1995) found that some morally-driven people are not motivated by duty or by right and wrong, as Kohlberg suggested — some people are motivated to behave morally because it makes them feel good.

Tip: Remember — a meta-analysis is a study which combines the results of several studies all addressing a related topic.

Tip: Androcentric just means focused on men. Kohlberg's (1963) study only used male participants, so his results are androcentric. As Kohlberg based his theory of moral development on these results, it means that the theory as a whole can't really be generalised to females.

Worked Exam-style Question

0 1 Outline Kohlberg's theory of moral understanding.

(8 marks)

Kohlberg believed that moral understanding develops in stages. He believed that our moral understanding increases as we get older because at each stage we take more and more of the social world into consideration. He investigated this idea by conducting a study using a series of ten moral dilemma stories. The participants (children aged between 10 and 16) had to discuss what the characters in each story should do, or decide whether their actions were justified. Using the reasoning of the participants, Kohlberg came up with three levels of moral understanding — preconventional, conventional and postconventional. Each of these three levels is made up of two stages.

Level 1 — preconventional morality, consists of stage 1 and stage 2. Stage 1 is named punishment and obedience orientation. Here, reasons for behaviour aren't taken into account and the only reason for not doing something is fear of punishment. In stage 2 (instrumental purpose orientation), moral decisions are based on meeting your own interests and getting what you want.

Conventional morality is level 2 of Kohlberg's theory of moral development and is made up of stages 3 and 4. Stage 3 is called morality of interpersonal cooperation. Here individuals try to live up to the expectations of people who are important to them. Behaviour that improves their relationship with these people is seen as moral. In stage 4 (social-order orientation), morality is seen in the context of

Exam Tip
This question is an example of the kind of 8 mark question that would make up part of an 24 mark Unit 3 question.

Exam Tip
Remember to think about time management in the exam. Don't rush, but keep your eye on the clock to make sure you're allowing yourself enough time for all the questions. For more on exam technique see the 'Exam Help' section, pages 296-301.

society as a whole — behaviour that fits in with social norms, obligations and rules.

The final level of moral understanding is level 3 — postconventional morality. According to Kohlberg this occurs much later on and some people don't ever reach it. In stage 5 (social-contract orientation), laws are only followed if they contribute towards the welfare of others, and are seen as flexible in certain situations, and not all of equal importance. In stage 6 (universal ethical principles), people follow their own abstract set of moral principles above the law.

Summary Questions

Q1 Outline the 'brother's dilemma' used in Kohlberg's (1963) study.

Q2 According to Kohlberg's theory, what are the 3 levels of moral understanding?

Q3 Who were the participants in Kohlberg's (1963) study?

Q4 a) Give one advantage of the methodology used in Kohlberg's (1963) study of moral understanding.

b) Give one disadvantage of the methodology used in Kohlberg's (1963) study of moral understanding.

Q5 a) What research method was used in Snarey's (1985) study?

b) What were the findings of Snarey's (1985) study?

Q6 What were the findings of Hart and Fegley's (1995) study of morality?

Learning Objectives:

- Understand development of the child's sense of self, including Theory of Mind.
- Know about the development of children's understanding of others, including perspective taking, for example, Selman.

4. Development of Social Cognition

Social cognition is a term given to the cognitive processes that underlie social interactions. Developing social cognition allows us to understand ourselves and others, and to see how we, as a person, fit into society.

Sense of self

A **sense of self** develops during childhood. Having a sense of self includes things like being able to distinguish between self and others, and referring to each with appropriate language, having knowledge of our experiences, abilities, motivations, etc. and having ideas about body image.

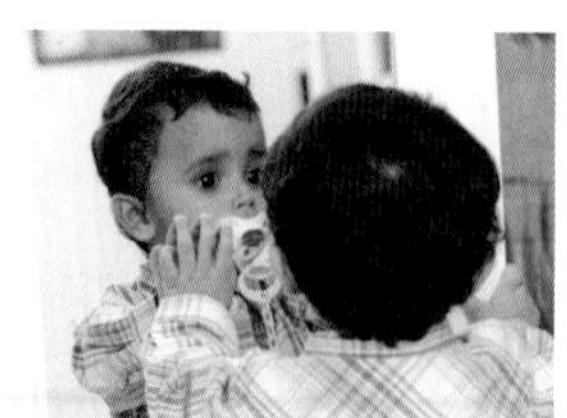

Figure 1: *Self recognition in a mirror indicates that a child has developed a sense of self.*

Key study of sense of self — Lewis and Brooks-Gunn (1979)

Method: 96 children aged from 9-24 months were observed for 90 seconds whilst sat on their mother's lap in front of a mirror. Unknown to the child, a smudge of red was then applied to their nose during a routine face wipe and the observation was repeated.
It was assumed that if the baby increased nose-touching in the second observation it was because they recognised themselves in the mirror and were surprised by the presence of a red mark which isn't normally there.

Results: Nose-touching increased during the second observation in the older children (21-24 months) — below 18 months the children typically ignored the mark.

Conclusion: By 2 years, children recognise themselves in a mirror, and therefore have developed a sense of self.

Evaluation: The use of mirrors and observation of motor activity is a clever way of getting around young infants' inability to verbally communicate. However, the study is based on the assumption that nose touching increases due to self-recognition, when in fact it may increase for another, unknown reason.

Tip: A similar test has been done on animals to see if they display self recognition — see page 109.

Additional studies of sense of self

Lewis and Brooks-Gunn (1979) also showed that children as young as 9 months spent more time studying and smiling at a photograph of themselves than photos of other children, when presented with an array of photos of children of a similar age. Children older than 15 months also said their own name when looking at the photograph and referred to the children on the other photos as 'baby'.

Povinelli et al (1996) conducted a study using video recordings. Children were recorded after having a sticker placed on their forehead. They found that 3-4 year olds removed the sticker from their heads when they spotted it on the video playback. However children aged 2 did not remove the sticker. However, this doesn't necessarily mean that they didn't recognise themselves — they may still have recognised themselves on the video, but didn't realise that the sticker would continue to exist.

Tip: Children are unable to give informed consent to participate in psychological research — their parents or guardian must give their permission instead. For more information on ethics in psychology see pages 260-262 in the research methods section.

Important stages during development include:

- **Existential self** — from about three months old we learn to distinguish self from non-self, and find out that we exist separately from other things. The development of object permanence (see page 118) may help this.
- **Categorical self** — from about two years old we start to use language to describe ourselves, using culturally defined categories, e.g. age, male/female, tall/short, etc. We are also described by other people in this way, which can influence our idea of ourself. For example, describing a child as 'clever' or 'naughty' could influence their self-esteem.
- **Identity crisis** — Erikson (1968) claimed that during adolescence, when going through body changes and starting to make plans for the future, we may try out different roles until we find our true identity.

Having a sense of self also involves being able to see yourself as others see you. This requires some understanding of the minds of others, and being able to see things from their perspective.

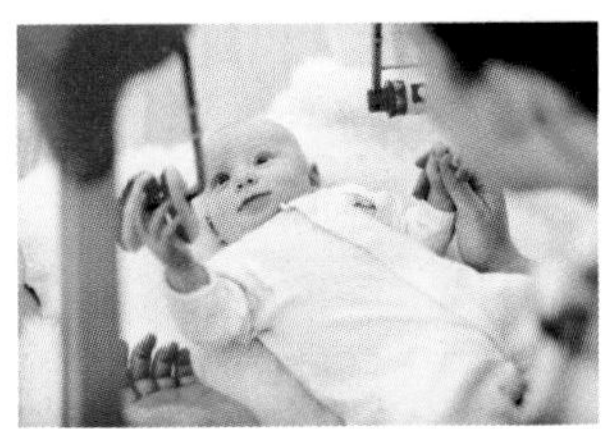

***Figure 2:** In the existential self stage of development, we begin to distinguish self from other objects.*

Theory of Mind (ToM)

Theory of Mind (ToM) is about understanding other people's minds. Humans have a unique ability to cooperate and carry out complex interactions. It's thought this is possible because we have a Theory of Mind. This involves understanding that we and others have minds with knowledge, feelings, beliefs, motivations, intentions, etc. We can explain and predict other people's behaviour by making inferences about their mental states. This includes the knowledge that others may have false beliefs about the world.

Real World Connection
A child who has not yet developed Theory of Mind can cause embarrassing situations for their parents, e.g. when they loudly state that the lady sat next to them on the bus is wearing a horrible hat.

Key study of ToM — Baron-Cohen et al (1985)

Method: Three groups of children were studied — children with autism with an average age of 12 years, children with Down's Syndrome with an average age of 11 years, and 'normal' children with an average age of 4 years. The experiment (see Figure 3) was carried out as follows:

1. The experiment used two dolls — Sally had a basket, Anne a box. Children were asked to name the dolls (the naming question).
2. Then Sally was seen to hide a marble in her basket and leave the room.
3. Anne took the marble and put it in her box.
4. Sally returned and the child was asked, 'Where will Sally look for her marble?' (belief question).

The correct response is to point to the basket, where Sally believes the marble to be. They were also asked, 'Where is the marble really?' (reality question) and 'Where was the marble in the beginning?' (memory question).
Each child was tested twice, with the marble in a different place the second time.

Results: All of the children got the naming, reality and memory questions correct. In the belief question, the children with Down's Syndrome scored 86%, the 'normal' children 85%, but the children with autism scored 20%.

Conclusion: The findings suggest that autistic children have an under-developed Theory of Mind, sometimes called

***Figure 3:** The Sally-Anne task used by Baron-Cohen et al (1985).*

mind-blindness. They seem unable to predict or understand the beliefs of others.

Evaluation: Dolls were used throughout the study, causing it to lack ecological validity. Also, children with autism may in fact have a more highly developed Theory of Mind and understand that dolls don't have beliefs.
Repeating the study by acting out the scenes with humans might show an increase in ability on the tasks. However, Leslie and Frith (1988) did a similar study with real people and not dolls and found the same pattern of results.

Tip: Autism is a developmental disorder. People with autism often can't understand other people's emotions and feelings, resulting in difficulties with social interaction.

Most children develop ToM at around four years old. However, the kind of questions asked in Baron-Cohen et al's false belief task may be difficult for younger children to understand. It seems that three-year-old children can pass some versions of the test, so Theory of Mind may actually develop earlier.

There's also disagreement about the development of ToM. It may have an innate basis, but nurture and experience are also likely to be important in its development.

Tip: The 'nature vs. nurture' debate pops up all over the place in psychology. It's all about whether we're born with an ability, or whether we develop it due to the environmental factors that we're exposed to.

Perspective-taking

One aspect of having a ToM is understanding that other people's perspectives can differ from your own. Children gradually become more skilful in their **perspective-taking** ability.

Key study on perspective-taking — Selman (1980)

Method: Selman told children a number of stories involving dilemmas. For example, one was about Holly, a girl who liked to climb trees but whose father had made her promise that she wouldn't. Holly's friend then asks her to rescue his cat from a tree. Selman asked the children various questions about how the characters would feel and what they should do, etc.

Results: From the children's answers, Selman identified five kinds of perspective-taking — undifferentiated and egocentric, differentiated and subjective, second-person and reciprocal, third-person and mutual, and in-depth and societal-symbolic (see below for more on the stages).

Conclusion: Selman concluded that as children go through these stages they become better able to understand that other people have different perspectives, and can use information to put themselves in other people's shoes.

Evaluation: As in Kohlberg's (1963) study on moral development (see pages 130-131), the study made use of hypothetical situations so the results lacked ecological validity.

Tip: The 'three mountains task' used by Piaget and Inhelder (1956) also requires perspective taking — the children have to imagine the mountains from the doll's perspective. Perspective taking is also needed in the policeman doll task by Hughes (1975). For more information on these studies see pages 119 and 121.

Selman's stages of perspective-taking

1. **Undifferentiated and egocentric**
   Up to about six years of age, children can separate self and other, but in a physical sense only. They don't perceive any psychological differences, seeing the other person in the same way they see an object.
2. **Differentiated and subjective**
   From five to nine, children understand that other people have different

perspectives because they have access to different information (i.e. know different things). However, only their own perspective is seen as important and they can't take the perspective of the other person.

3. **Second-person and reciprocal**
   Between seven and twelve, children can put themselves in someone else's shoes and view a situation from another's perspective. They also realise that other people can do the same.
4. **Third-person and mutual**
   Between ten and fifteen years old, children develop the ability to take the perspective of a third impartial person who's viewing an interaction between other people.
5. **In-depth and societal-symbolic**
   From about fourteen, children understand that third-party perspectives can be influenced by factors such as social or cultural values. They can see a situation from a variety of different perspectives, e.g. moral, legal, etc.

Real World Connection
Children in Selman's differentiated and subjective stage know that others have different perspectives, but they view their own perspective as most important. For instance, this little girl's mother doesn't want to buy cakes, but the little girl does, which in her eyes is more important.

Additional study of perspective-taking — Keller and Edelstein (1991)

Keller and Edelstein conducted a longitudinal study using 121 subjects, who were each tested when they were 7, 9, 12, and 15 years old. Participants had to make a choice about what a person should do in one of Selman's dilemmas — for example, in one scenario, a person has promised to meet her best friend, but receives a more attractive invitation from a new friend. The participants had to justify their answer, and also decide how they would deal with any undesirable consequences resulting from their choice.

It was found that the responses of the participants fell within Selman's stages of perspective taking, therefore this study provides support for Selman's model.

Selman's ideas about perspective-taking can have practical applications in education. For example, using multi-cultural materials and having class discussions can expose children to different perspectives. This may help to promote their perspective-taking ability.

Worked Exam-style Question

0 1 Outline what is meant by Theory of Mind. *(4 marks)*

Theory of Mind is about understanding other people's minds. It develops during childhood and allows us to cooperate and carry out complex interactions. This involves understanding that we and others have minds with independent knowledge, feelings, beliefs, motivations, intentions, etc. It gives us the ability to explain and predict other people's behaviour by making inferences about their mental states. This includes the knowledge that others may have false beliefs about the world.

Exam Tip
This is just worth 4 marks, so don't write a massive essay including everything you know about Theory of Mind. Stick to the key points, and keep your answer short and sharp.

---

0 2 Discuss the development of Theory of Mind. *(8 marks + 8 marks)*

Baron-Cohen et al (1985) conducted a study investigating false belief, in order to see if different groups of children had Theory of Mind. Their participants were children with autism with an average age of 12 years, children with Down's Syndrome with an average age of 11 years, and 'normal' children with an average age of 4 years.

■ The researchers used dolls in order to create a scenario, testing to see whether the children could put themselves in the dolls shoes, therefore displaying Theory of Mind. It was found that the majority of children with Down's Syndrome and the 'normal' children had Theory of Mind, but that many of the children with autism failed the test.

Exam Tip
This question gives you quite a lot of freedom. Pick the studies that you know most about — don't worry if it's not these ones.

From these findings, the researchers concluded that the majority of children develop Theory of Mind at around 4 years old and that autistic children may have an under-developed Theory of Mind. This means that they are unable to understand or predict others beliefs. Alternatively, the results may actually show that children with autism have a more highly developed Theory of Mind and understand that dolls don't have beliefs. However, Leslie and Frith (1988) replicated the study using real people and found a similar pattern of results, providing support for the conclusions drawn by Baron-Cohen et al. It's important to bear in mind, though, that the fact that Baron-Cohen et al's study used dolls, the ecological validity of the results is reduced.

One aspect of having a Theory of Mind is gaining the ability to understand that other people's perspectives can differ from your own. This is known as perspective taking. To test this, Selman (1980) questioned children about a number of stories involving dilemmas. From the children's answers, Selman identified five kinds of perspective-taking, which children go through as they become better able to understand that other people have different perspectives.

Keller and Edelstein (1991) conducted a longitudinal study in which participants had to make a choice about what a person should do in one of Selman's dilemmas. Their results identified stages similar to Selman's.

■ Research into Theory of Mind suggests that the majority of children develop Theory of Mind at around 4 years old, and that children go through a number of stages as they develop the ability to understand that other people have different perspectives.

Exam Tip
A concluding statement summarising the main points that you've made is a good way of rounding off your answer.

Summary Questions

Q1 Give three characteristics that a child with a sense of self displays.

Q2 Lewis and Brooks-Gunn (1979) investigated sense of self in children by putting a red mark on the child's nose. What were the results of the study?

Q3 a) At what age are children typically at during the 'categorical self' stage of development.

b) Describe this stage of development.

Q4 How did Selman (1980) investigate perspective taking in children?

Q5 a) Name Selman's first stage of perspective taking.

b) Typically how old are children at this stage?

Q6 Describe Selman's 'in-depth and societal-symbolic' stage of perspective taking.

Q7 Give an example of how Selman's ideas can be applied to education.

5. The Mirror Neuron System

Recent research suggests that biology may play a key role in social cognition.

Learning Objectives:
- Understand biological explanations of social cognition, including the role of the mirror neuron system.

A biological basis for social cognition

Neurons (nerve cells) in the cerebral cortex are organised into four main areas: the frontal, temporal, parietal and occipital lobes (see Figure 1). Different processes, such as visual perception, involve one or more of these lobes. Some areas of the brain seem to have very specialised roles in cognition.

It seems likely that many of our sophisticated social abilities, such as Theory of Mind, also involve complex brain mechanisms — these may have evolved as our brains and intelligence grew. Abilities like this could have been stimulated by our complex social living (see pages 113-114). Attempts have been made to connect findings from neuroscience and social psychology and combine them into more complete theories — this is known as **social neuroscience**.

frontal lobe
parietal lobe
occipital lobe
temporal lobe

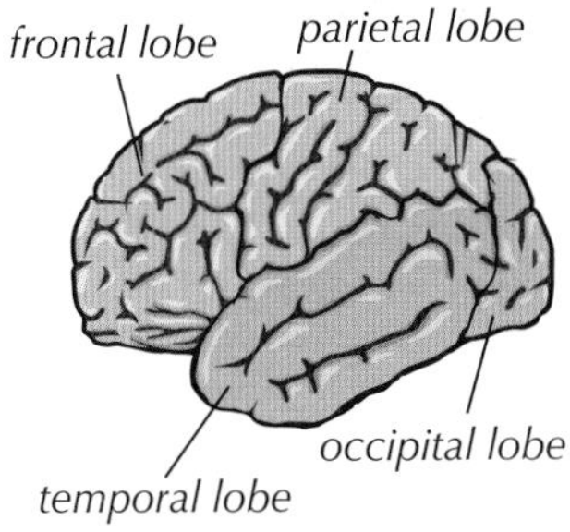

Figure 1: *The cerebral cortex, showing the different lobes of the brain.*

Mirror neurons

Mirror neurons are brain cells that are involved in performing an action, such as holding a cup. However, they're also active when you observe someone else doing the same action. So, whether you're actually holding a cup, or only observing someone else holding a cup, particular mirror neurons will be active.

Key study of mirror neurons — Di Pellegrino et al (1992)

Method: Electrodes were inserted into individual neurons in the premotor cortex of macaque monkeys.
When the monkeys reached for food, the activity in the neurons was recorded.

Results: The neurons were active when the monkeys reached for food, but also, unexpectedly, active when they observed someone else reach for food.

Conclusion: This was the first study to provide evidence for the existence of mirror neurons. Although the function of mirror neurons is not yet clear, they may help in understanding observed behaviour.

Evaluation: The experiment was not designed to study mirror neurons, so the information gathered about them was limited.
Also, this experiment involved inserting electrodes into animals' brains, which raises ethical issues.

Tip: The premotor cortex is located in the frontal lobe. It's responsible for planning and controlling limb movements.

Tip: For more on ethical issues in psychology see pages 260-262.

It's hard to record the activity of individual neurons in the brains of humans. So, studies have been done using brain scanning techniques such as **functional Magnetic Resonance Imaging (fMRI)**, which analyse brain activity during particular kinds of behaviours (see Figure 2).

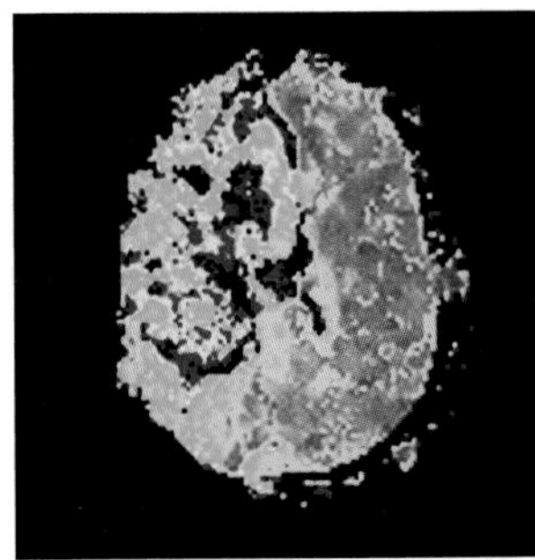

Figure 2: *fMRI shows brain activity by monitoring blood flow to different areas. Increased blood flow (represented by red/black) shows increased activity.*

Additional studies of mirror neurons

Iacoboni et al (1999) found that there are areas of the frontal and parietal cortex that are active when people carry out and observe actions.

Meister et al (2004) used fMRI to show that the same parietal lobe neurons were activated when participants played a piece of music on a silent piano, and when they imagined themselves playing the same piece.

Mirror neurons and social cognition

Mirror neurons may be important for social cognition. Neurons that are active both when you do something and when you see other people do the same thing may help you understand the behaviour of others.

Figure 3: *Fogassi et al (2005) recorded the activity of mirror neurons in macaque monkeys.*

Key study on mirror neurons and social cognition — Fogassi et al (2005)

Method: The activity of 41 mirror neurons in 2 macaque monkeys was recorded as they observed a person pick up an apple as if to eat it, or pick up the apple and place it in a cup.

Results: Different groups of neurons responded to the two outcomes (eat or place). Also, some neurons fired after the apple was picked up but before the second action (eat or place) was carried out.

Conclusion: Different patterns of response link with different behavioural objectives and some neurons seem to predict the intention of actions. So, mirror neurons may help to understand and predict the behaviour of others.

Evaluation: Animals may behave differently under lab conditions, meaning the experiment has low ecological validity. Also, the experiment was carried out on monkeys so it's difficult to generalise the results to humans — neurons in humans may not respond in the same way.

Experiments with humans using fMRI show that brain areas that are active when we feel particular emotions (e.g. happiness or pain) are also active when we see others feel the same emotion.

Additional study on mirror neurons and social cognition — Morrison et al (2004)

Morrison et al used fMRI to record participants' brain activity while they were given a painful poke to the hand with a blunt needle. They were then shown a video of someone receiving a needle prick to the hand, and their neural activity was compared.

It was found that the same neurons were activated when experiencing pain, and when watching someone else experience pain. This supports suggestions that mirror neurons may be involved in empathy.

The mirror neurons debate

The function and importance of mirror neurons is not yet fully understood. For example, they may be involved in imitation — but macaque monkeys (which have mirror neurons) have a limited ability for imitation learning. Also, mirror neurons are found in monkeys that don't seem to have Theory of Mind (ToM) in the same way that humans do.

Tip: See pages 135 if you're unsure what Theory of Mind is.

In addition, fMRI research shows that ToM tests activate brain regions that aren't generally thought to be part of the mirror neuron system. It may be that mirror neurons can be involved in learning by imitation, but that the development of ToM involves more than this.

More needs to be learnt about the development of mirror neurons. Falck-Ytter (2006) reckoned that mirror neurons start to develop during the first year of life. However, Meltzoff and Moore (1977) found that human infants can imitate facial expressions soon after birth. This could either suggest that mirror neurons have an innate basis, or else that imitation doesn't necessarily involve mirror neurons.

Figure 4: Meltzoff and Moore (1977) showed that infants display imitation soon after birth.

The role of social neuroscience

Social neuroscience is inter-disciplinary — it involves both biological and social concepts and theories. These different types of theories may mutually inform each other — biological research can help understand social processes better, and vice versa. This means we can understand behaviour at different levels of explanation.

This approach may bring important insights into human social cognition (e.g. the basis of empathy). Also, some conditions associated with developmental problems (e.g. autism) might be better understood.

However, animal experiments involve invasive methods, e.g. inserting electrodes into the brain — this raises ethical issues.

Worked Exam-style Question

0 1 Discuss the role of mirror neurons in social cognition.

(8 marks + 8 marks)

Mirror neurons are brain cells that are involved in performing an action, but that are also active when you observe someone else doing the same action. Mirror neurons may have an important role in social cognition, as neurons that are active both when you do something and when you see other people do the same thing may help you understand the behaviour of others. This is illustrated by Fogassi et al's (2005) study. In this study 2 macaque monkeys either watched a person pick up an apple as if to eat it (the 'eat' condition), or watched a person pick up an apple and place it in a cup (the 'place' condition). In both conditions the activity of 41 mirror neurons in the monkeys' brains were recorded.

Analysis of the monkeys' neural activity showed that different groups of neurons responded to the two conditions (eat or place). It was also observed that some neurons fired after the apple was picked up but before the second action (eat or place) took place. It was concluded that different behavioural objectives produce different patterns of response and that some neurons may predict the intention of actions. These findings suggest that mirror neurons could play a role in helping us to understand and predict the behaviour of others.

Experiments with humans using functional magnetic resonance imaging (fMRI) also suggest that the areas of the brain that are active when we feel particular experiences (e.g. happiness or pain) are also active when we observe others experiencing the same emotion. For example, in a study by Morrison et al (2004) participants had their hand painfully poked with a blunt needle, while fMRI was used to record their brain activity. Their neural activity was also recorded while they watched a video of someone else receiving a needle prick to the hand. When their neural activity was compared it was found that the same neurons were activated when experiencing pain and also when watching someone else experience pain. The findings of this study support suggestions that mirror neurons may play a role in empathy.

The function and importance of mirror neurons is not yet fully

Exam Tip
An introductory statement helps you set the scene and get into the flow of writing.

Exam Tip
If you are using a study as an example, make it obvious how it relates to the point that you are discussing. A summarising statement at the end of a description can be really helpful.

understood. For example, mirror neurons are present in monkeys that don't seem to have Theory of Mind in the same way that humans do. It's also believed that mirror neurons may be involved in imitation — for instance Meltzoff and Moore (1977) found that human infants can imitate facial expressions soon after birth, which could suggest that mirror neurons are present and active from birth. However monkeys have a limited ability for imitation learning, and yet they have mirror neurons. fMRI research also shows that Theory of Mind tests activate brain regions that aren't believed to be part of the mirror neuron system. These findings suggest that although mirror neurons can be involved in learning by imitation, development of Theory of Mind may involve more than just mirror neurons.

- *Although a lot has been discovered about mirror neurons so far, more research is needed before their role in social cognition is fully understood.*

Exam Tip
A concluding statement rounds off your answer nicely.

Summary Questions

Q1 Name the four lobes of the brain.

Q2 a) Describe the method used by Di Pellegrino et al (1992) to study mirror neurons.
b) What were the results of this study?
c) Why could this study be considered unethical?

Q3 Which areas of the brain did Iacoboni et al (1999) find to be active when people carry out and observe actions?

Q4 What were the two experimental conditions in the study by Meister et al (2004)?

Q5 According to Falck-Ytter (2006) when do mirror neurons start to develop?

Q6 Meltzoff and Moore (1977) found that human infants can imitate facial expressions soon after birth. What two things could this suggest about mirror neurons?

Section Summary

- Piaget conducted a range of intelligence tests on children in order to investigate cognitive development. He came up with a theory stating that there are four stages to cognitive development — the sensorimotor stage, the preoperational stage, the concrete operational stage and the formal operational stage. He believed that more complex abilities become possible as children move through the stages as they get older.
- Vygotsky also came up with a model of cognitive development, consisting of four stages — vague syncretic, complex, potential concept and mature concept. Vygotsky emphasised the effect of social and cultural factors — he believed that it's the influence of others around you along with language that drive cognitive development.
- Bruner's theory of cognitive development focused on representations of knowledge. He claimed that our brains use three modes of representation — the enactive mode, the iconic mode and the symbolic mode. Bruner also thought that language was very important for cognitive development.
- Piaget, Vygotsky and Bruner's theories of cognitive development can be applied to education. Piaget's theory suggests a child-centred approach to education, in which children can learn for themselves through their own experience. Vygotsky's theory suggests a teacher-guided approach and that interactions with others are important in learning. Bruner agreed with Vygotsky that social interaction is essential, and he made some important suggestions for education. For instance, his spiral curriculum concept is commonly used in schools.
- Kohlberg developed a theory of moral understanding by analysing children's responses to various moral dilemmas. He came up with three levels of moral understanding that children progress through — preconventional, conventional and postconventional.
- Social cognition involves things like perspective-taking, having a sense of self and a Theory of Mind.
- Research has shown that children can recognise themselves, and therefore have a sense of self, by around 2 years.
- Having a Theory of Mind allows us to understand other people's minds. Baron-Cohen et al (1985) conducted a study which suggested that children develop a Theory of Mind at around 4 years.
- Selman (1980) investigated perspective-taking by presenting children with various dilemmas. Through analysing their answers he identified five stages of perspective-taking— undifferentiated and egocentric, differentiated and subjective, second-person and reciprocal, third-person and mutual and in-depth and societal-symbolic.
- Social cognition may have a biological basis — it might be that mirror neurons are important in understanding and predicting the behaviour of others. However, their function and importance is not yet fully understood — further research is needed in this area.

Exam-style Questions

0 1 Outline and evaluate Vygotsky's theory of cognitive development.

(8 marks + 16 marks)

---

0 2 Describe research investigating the development of a child's sense of self.

(8 marks)

0 3 Evaluate Kohlberg's theory of moral understanding.

(16 marks)

Exam Tip
These next four pages will give you a good introduction to what clinical psychology is all about.

1. Clinical Psychology

Clinical psychology is all about diagnosing and treating mental health disorders. Research is done in a variety of different ways.

The role of clinical psychologists

Clinical psychology focuses on studying, explaining and treating emotional or behavioural disorders. Clinical psychologists assess patients using interviews, observations and psychological tests. They then help patients work through their problems, e.g. using talking therapies. Researchers gather primary and secondary data to improve understanding of mental disorders. Clinicians then apply this to individual cases to help them establish a clear diagnosis and decide upon the correct treatment for each individual.

Primary data is information collected during the researcher's direct observations of a patient, e.g. test results, answers to questionnaires, observation notes. **Secondary data** is information collected from other studies. This data can be used to check the validity of studies, or used to prove or disprove a new theory.

Tip: There's more on schizophrenia and twin studies on page 152.

Twin studies

Twin studies are used to find out if genetic factors influence the development of mental disorders. They involve looking at **concordance rates** — the chance that both twins will develop the mental disorder. Identical (MZ) twins share all their genetic material, and non-identical (DZ) twins share around half. So, if both MZ twins are more likely to develop schizophrenia (a higher concordance rate) than both DZ twins, it can be assumed that schizophrenia has a genetic cause. However, it can't be the full story unless concordance rates are 100% in MZ twins.

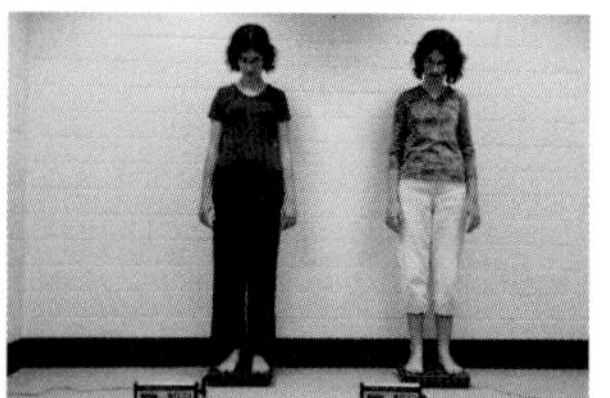

Figure 1: *Twin studies can help researchers to determine the genetic influence of mental disorders.*

Exam Tip
The examiner should know what you're talking about if you just refer to identical and non-identical twins as MZ and DZ twins. But make sure you know which is which if you're going to use these abbreviations.

Key twin study in clinical psychology — Gottesman and Shields (1966)

Method: Hospital records for the previous 16 years were examined to identify people with schizophrenia who had a twin. Around 40 sets of twins agreed to take part in the study, which was a natural experiment using independent measures.

Results: The concordance rate was about 48% for MZ twins and about 17% for DZ twins. The exact figures vary depending on the type of schizophrenia, but overall, MZ twins had a much higher concordance rate than DZ twins.

Conclusion: As the results for MZ twins are much higher, this suggests a genetic cause for schizophrenia.

Evaluation: The results for MZ twins don't show 100% concordance, which means that there must be other important factors that influence schizophrenia. Although the researchers had a large amount of data covering a long period of time, it's unlikely the study could be replicated until new data existed.

Strengths of twin studies

Twin studies contain rich data if they've used a case study method — researchers have the opportunity to study rare phenomena in a lot of detail. They often involve unique cases, so existing theories can be challenged, and ideas for future research can be suggested. They also have high ecological validity — the variables aren't manipulated so the findings should be true to real life.

Weaknesses of twin studies

Twin studies tend to report only correlational relationships — the researcher doesn't have much control over the variables, so the findings could be the result of a confounding variable. This means that it's difficult to establish cause and effect. There may be problems with ethics — it can be difficult to get informed consent if the subjects have a mental disorder. Finally, getting samples for case studies can be problematic. For example, identical twins are quite rare, so there aren't very many research opportunities. There's also an issue with generalisation — only using a small sample of twins means it's difficult to generalise the results to other people.

Tip: Onstad et al (1981) also looked at the concordance rates of schizophrenia between twins. Their results supported the findings of Gottesman and Shields (1966) — they found that if one MZ twin was diagnosed with schizophrenia, there was a 48% chance that the other twin would also have schizophrenia. DZ twins showed a 4% concordance rate.

Tip: Confounding variables are factors which might affect the results but which aren't controlled in the experiment — this could include the environment in which people grow up in.

Family studies

Family studies are used to see how likely it is a disorder will occur in one person if others in their family have it as well. They look at concordance rates between parents, children and siblings.

Example

Kendler et al (1985) looked at the risk of schizophrenia in first degree relatives of patients with schizophrenia. They found that individuals were at least 18 times more likely than controls to have schizophrenia if the first degree relative of a schizophrenic patient was also diagnosed with the disorder.

Strengths of family studies

Family studies are really useful — they provide important evidence that can be used to support the role of genetics and the environment in different psychological disorders. They can be objective — using DNA extraction techniques allows for reliable results.

Weaknesses of family studies

Family studies aren't always valid — they don't always report all of the variables which may be contributing to a certain disorder. For instance, they often ignore cultural or environmental influences, which may impact the onset of certain mental disorders — as well as genes first degree relatives also tend to share many environments and experiences. Family studies also rely on comparing people who are already diagnosed with the disorder — this means it can be hard to tell the difference between whether something is genetic or environmentally caused.

Tip: We get 50% of our genes from each of our parents, as do our siblings. So, 'first degree' relatives are parents, children and siblings that we share 50% of our genetic make-up with. 'Second degree' relatives are those which we share 25% of our genetic make-up with. These include grandparents, grandchildren, aunts, uncles, half-brothers and half-sisters.

Adoption studies

Adoption studies look at people who have been born to a parent who has a certain disorder but then raised by adoptive parents without the disorder.

Tip: Adoption studies are great for trying to separate out genetic and environmental factors. They provide support for the nature-nurture debate. Have a look at page 154 to read more about this.

Key adoption study in clinical psychology — Tienari (1987)

Method: In Finland, Tienari compared over 100 children whose biological mothers had schizophrenia with a set of matched controls whose biological parents didn't have schizophrenia. All of the children had been adopted before they were four years old and raised by non-schizophrenic parents. They were later observed to see how many had been diagnosed with schizophrenia.

Results: The children with schizophrenic mothers were much more likely to be schizophrenic in later life than those without a schizophrenic biological parent.

Conclusion: There does appear to be a genetic component to schizophrenia.

Evaluation: Not all children of biological parents with schizophrenia developed the disorder so the environment that the children were raised in by their adopted parents may have played some role in determining the onset of schizophrenia.

Figure 2: *Adoption studies are fairly uncommon, but really useful.*

Strengths of adoption studies

Adoption studies can help to show whether something seems to be genetically or environmentally determined. They are also ethical — rather than splitting up twins or families, they rely on situations that already exist. They also allow researchers to observe cases for long periods of time — this means we can get lots of detailed information about the same set of individuals over an extended period of time.

Weaknesses of adoption studies

Adoption studies don't always report at what age a child was adopted — this means that other factors and environmental influences may have already affected the child's behaviour and influenced the outcome of any results. Also, children are sometimes adopted because they are difficult or problematic, and therefore may have a mental disorder before they have been officially diagnosed, and before they have even been adopted. Finally, adoption studies usually rely on retrospective data — they often follow cases over a long period of time which means the definitions and diagnostic criteria of certain mental disorders might change.

Tip: Retrospective data is data that is gathered by asking people to think back to the past. It relies a lot on the accuracy of the person's memory.

Animal studies

Animal studies are used in clinical psychology because they allow researchers to carry out tests that couldn't be done on humans. However, using animals for research raises ethical issues.

Key study of animal studies in clinical psychology — Lipska et al (1993)

Method: This was a laboratory experiment that involved making lesions in rats' brains to see if they developed schizophrenia-like symptoms. Areas of the hippocampus associated with schizophrenia were damaged using an injection of ibotenic acid a week after the rats were born.

Results: The rats with a damaged hippocampus developed schizophrenia-like symptoms as their brains matured, e.g. hyperactivity, memory problems and a lack of response to rewards.

Conclusion: Damage to the hippocampus can lead to the onset of schizophrenia-like symptoms, which suggests that the hippocampus plays a role in the development of schizophrenia.

Evaluation: The variables in this experiment were tightly controlled, which means that it should be possible to establish cause and effect — the rats wouldn't have developed these symptoms if their brains hadn't been damaged. However, it's difficult to know how many symptoms of schizophrenia the rats were actually experiencing, because you can't establish whether they were having hallucinations or delusions.

Figure 3: *Rats are frequently used in psychology experiments.*

Strengths of animal research

One strength of animal research is that researchers can conduct experiments on animals that they couldn't do on humans because of ethical restraints, e.g. lesion studies. This means that clinical psychologists can investigate the causes of mental disorders, e.g. the effects of particular chemicals or social deprivation. They also don't need to get the animal's informed consent or worry about deception. Also, most animals used in research reproduce much more quickly than humans, so it's quicker and easier to carry out **longitudinal studies** of genetic influence, e.g. whether schizophrenia has a genetic cause. Finally, they're useful in terms of detachment — it's easier for researchers to be impartial with animal participants than with humans, so the results are more likely to be objective.

Tip: There's more information on ethics a bit later... take a look at page 260-262 if you want a sneaky peek.

Weaknesses of animal research

Humans and animals are qualitatively different, so there are problems with generalising the results from animal studies to humans. Substances can have different effects on different animals, e.g. morphine has a calming effect on humans, but it causes manic behaviour in cats. Language can also provide a barrier — animals don't have language, which is a vital part of human behaviour. In clinical psychology this means that animals can't describe their symptoms, so it's difficult to know whether they're experiencing any mental abnormalities.

Summary Questions

Q1 What does clinical psychology involve?

Q2 Give one way in which clinical psychologists might assess patients.

Q3 a) What is primary data?

b) What is secondary data?

Q4 Give one weakness of using adoption studies in clinical psychology.

Q5 Give one strength of using family studies in clinical psychology.

Q6 Briefly outline a study in clinical psychology that uses animals.

2. Schizophrenia

Schizophrenia literally means 'split mind' but it's actually not about having multiple personalities at all. Read on to find out more...

Learning Objectives:

- Know the clinical characteristics of schizophrenia.
- Understand the issues surrounding the classification and diagnosis of schizophrenia, including reliability and validity.

The impact on the mind

Schizophrenia disrupts the mind's ability to function. Schizophrenia is a thought process disorder. It's characterised by disruption to a person's perceptions, emotions and beliefs. The onset of schizophrenia can be acute (a sudden onset, where behaviour changes within a few days), or chronic (a gradual deterioration in mental health that develops slowly over time). Males and females are equally affected. In males schizophrenia usually develops in their late teens or early 20s, while females tend to develop it 4 or 5 years later. Overall, approximately 0.5% of the population is affected. It's thought that schizophrenia isn't a single disorder but that there are various subtypes — however, there still isn't an agreed definition.

Exam Tip
You only need to answer questions about one disorder in psychopathology. So choose schizophrenia, depression, phobic disorders or obsessive compulsive disorder and learn everything you need to know about that one.

Clinical characteristics

People with schizophrenia can experience a range of possible symptoms:

Perceptual symptoms

- Auditory hallucinations — hearing things that aren't there. People often hear voices saying abusive or critical things.
- Sometimes people see, smell or taste things that aren't there.

Social symptoms

- Social withdrawal — not taking part in or enjoying social situations. People might be aloof or avoid eye contact.

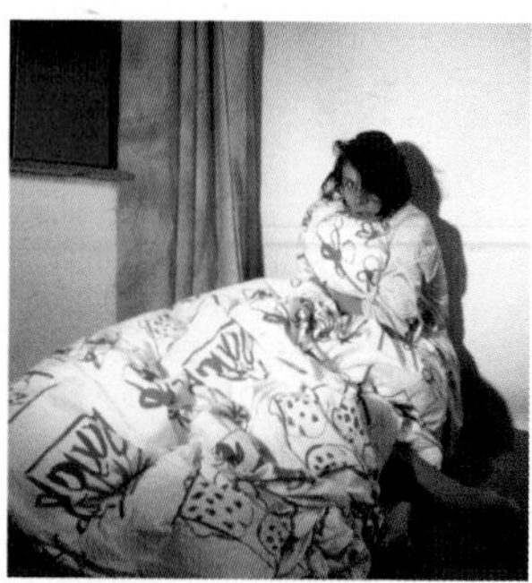

Figure 1: *Hallucinations can be very real for patients.*

Cognitive symptoms

- Delusions — believing things that aren't true. People can have delusions of grandeur (where they believe they're more important than they are, e.g. that they're the king) or of paranoia and persecution (where they believe people are out to get them). Some people with schizophrenia also experience delusions of control — they believe that their behaviour is being controlled by somebody else.
- Thought control — believing that your thoughts are being controlled. For example, thought insertion is when people feel that someone's putting thoughts into their heads. Withdrawal is when they believe that someone is removing their thoughts. They might also believe that people can read their thoughts — this is broadcasting.
- Language impairments — irrelevant and incoherent speech. People often show signs of cognitive distractibility, where they can't maintain a train of thought. They might also repeat sounds (echolalia), jumble their words (word salad), make nonsensical rhymes (clang associations) and invent words (neologisms).

Real World Connection
There are many famous people who suffer from schizophrenia. John Nash, a brilliant mathematician, was portrayed by Russell Crowe in the 2001 film "A Beautiful Mind". The film shows how a person can live, and be successful, despite suffering from a mental illness.

Affective / emotional symptoms

- Depressive symptoms — a lack of energy and interest in things, especially in personal care and hygiene.
- Lack of emotion — not reacting to typically emotional situations. This is also called emotional blunting.
- Inappropriate emotions — reacting in an inappropriate way, e.g. laughing at bad news.

Behavioural symptoms

- Stereotyped behaviours — continuously repeating actions, which are often strange and don't have a purpose.
- Psychomotor disturbance — not having control of your muscles. People may experience catatonia, where they sit in an awkward position for a long time. In this state people will sometimes stay in whatever position they're put in (so if you lift their arm over their head it'll stay like that until you move it back).
- Catatonic stupor — lying rigidly and not moving for long periods of time. People are conscious during these episodes and can remember what was going on around them, although they don't seem aware of it at the time.

Tip: Not all symptoms are present in all patients.

Type 1 and Type 2 symptoms

The symptoms of schizophrenia are sometimes categorised as **Type 1** or **Type 2**. Type 1 symptoms are **positive symptoms**. This is where people experience something, feel that something is happening to them, or display certain behaviours — e.g. hallucinations, delusions, jumbled speech. Type 2 symptoms are **negative symptoms**. This is where people have an absence of 'normal' behaviours — e.g. they're withdrawn, unresponsive and show a lack of emotion.

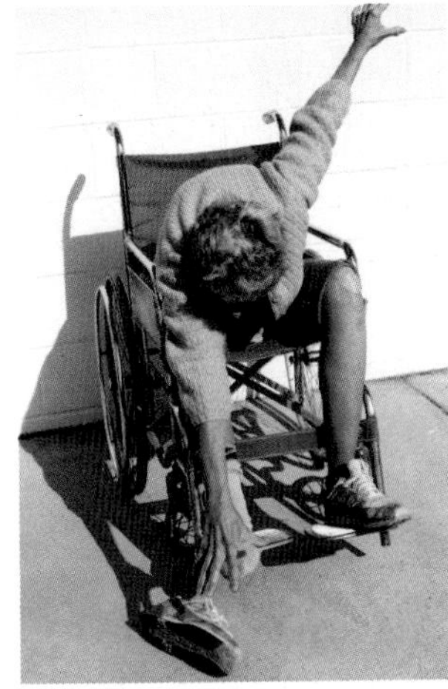

Figure 2: *Catatonic behaviour can cause patients to either be completely frozen or flail their limbs. This patient could stay like this for several hours.*

Subtypes of schizophrenia

Schizophrenia is usually split up into five different subtypes.

- Paranoid — patients experience hallucinations and delusions whilst their cognitive abilities remain unaffected.
- Catatonic — movement and behaviour is disturbed. Patients are either frozen rigid or they display excessive, over the top actions.
- Disorganised — speech and behaviour is often disorganised in these patients and their mood tends to be flat or inappropriate.
- Undifferentiated — patients show signs of schizophrenia but they don't show enough of one behaviour to categorise them fully.
- Residual — patients are generally getting better but continue to experience negative symptoms. These patients don't show any positive symptoms.

The DSM-IV

The DSM-IV is the fourth edition of the American Psychiatric Association's Diagnostic and Statistical Manual of Mental Disorders. It contains a list of mental health disorders. Individuals are rated on multiple axes / dimensions and diagnostic categories are used, e.g. personality disorders and psychosocial problems. It aims to give diagnosis of mental disorders reliability and validity:

Reliability

Reliability is how far the classification system produces the same diagnosis for a particular set of symptoms. In order for a classification system to be reliable the same diagnosis should be made each time it's used. This means that different clinicians should reach the same diagnosis.

Figure 3: *Eugen Bleuler, a Swiss psychiatrist, was the first person to coin the term 'schizophrenia'.*

Validity

Validity is whether the classification system is actually measuring what it aims to measure. There are three main types of validity. Descriptive validity is how similar individuals diagnosed with the disorder are. Aetiological validity is how similar the cause of the disorder is for each sufferer. Predictive validity is how useful the diagnostic categories are for predicting the right treatment.

For a person to be diagnosed as schizophrenic, the DSM-IV states that their symptoms must significantly impair reality testing — the ability to function in the real world. The symptoms have to have been present for at least six months.

Tip: There is also another diagnostic classification system called the ICD-10.

Problems with diagnoses

Problems with reliability

Schizophrenia diagnosis may be affected by cultural bias.

Example

Harrison et al (1984) showed that there was an over-diagnosis of schizophrenia in West Indian psychiatric patients in Bristol. No research has found any cause for this, so it suggests that the symptoms of ethnic minority patients are misinterpreted.

This questions the reliability of the diagnosis of schizophrenia — it suggests that patients can display the same symptoms but receive different diagnoses because of their ethnic background.

The method and procedures that psychiatrists use to assess patients within clinical psychology can also be subject to reliability issues.

Tip: The diagnosis of schizophrenia is pretty difficult because of the various subtypes, and also because each individual varies a lot in the symptoms they actually present. Many of the symptoms are also subjective — it's hard to quantify them.

Key study of reliability in diagnoses — McGorry et al (1995)

Method:	McGorry et al (1995) investigated the reliability of different diagnostic procedures. They used four different procedures and sets of criteria to diagnose 50 patients believed to have schizophrenia.
Results:	They found that there was only a 66-76% agreement rate between the different procedures.
Conclusion:	There are clear differences in the outcomes of using different procedures when diagnosing a patient with schizophrenia.
Evaluation:	This experiment has clear and important implications for the diagnosis of schizophrenia. It highlights the problems that could arise if someone with severe schizophrenia or psychotic symptoms didn't get the correct diagnosis because they wouldn't get the best possible care and treatment.

Real World Connection

Japanese medical professionals decided to change the name of schizophrenia in 2002 from a word which translates as 'mind-split-disease' to one which means 'integration disorder'. Sato (2006) conducted a study to see if this improved the reliability of diagnosing the illness, concluding that the new label has made it clearer, and therefore more reliable, to define what schizophrenia is.

Problems with validity

The validity of a diagnosis refers to whether the diagnosis really does define what is or isn't a disorder.

Example

Rosenhan (1973) conducted a study where people with no mental health problem got themselves admitted into a psychiatric unit by saying they heard voices — they became pseudopatients. Once they'd been admitted they behaved 'normally'. However, their behaviour was still seen as a symptom of their disorder by the staff in the unit. One pseudopatient who wrote in a diary was recorded as displaying 'writing behaviour'.

This questions the validity of the diagnosis of mental disorders — once people are labelled as having a disorder, all of their behaviour can be interpreted as being caused by the disorder.

However, as Bannister (1968) pointed out, each person diagnosed with schizophrenia may exhibit slightly different symptoms. This makes it really difficult to make a diagnosis of schizophrenia that is truly valid.

Finally, the medical phrasing and technical terms within classification systems can affect the validity of diagnosing mental health problems. Cultural differences create language barriers, meaning that professionals across the world may struggle to make the same diagnosis for a set of symptoms.

Worked Exam-style Question

0 1 Discuss the issue of validity in diagnosing schizophrenia.

(8 marks + 8 marks)

If a diagnostic procedure is valid, it should measure what it sets out to measure. There are three main types of validity. The first is descriptive validity. This looks at how similar the individuals are who have been diagnosed with the disorder. The second is aetiological validity which looks at how the disorder was caused and whether this is the same across different patients. Finally, predictive validity looks at whether the patient can be treated correctly based on the diagnosis given; in other words, how useful the diagnostic categories are for predicting the right treatment.

In diagnosing mental health disorders, particularly one as complex as schizophrenia, validity can be problematic since each individual case can vary. As Bannister (1968) concluded, each person who is diagnosed with the disorder may show a slightly different combination of symptoms. Schizophrenia has a very wide range of clinical characteristics, and each individual will vary a lot in the symptoms they present.

Rosenhan (1973) investigated the validity of diagnosing psychiatric patients by devising an experiment in which he asked people who had no mental health issues to pretend they were hearing voices in order to see if they would be admitted to a psychiatric unit and be diagnosed with schizophrenia. He found that, despite behaving normally once they'd been admitted, the label of schizophrenia stuck with them. One patient, who was merely writing notes, was reported to be displaying 'writing behaviour'. It appears that once people have been given a label, others have preconceptions as to what their behaviours should be. As has been shown, this influences the validity of the diagnosis of certain mental health disorders.

Overall, validity is a very important consideration in the diagnosis of mental health disorders as it can affect the diagnosis that is given. This has further implications on the care and treatment of these disorders; people need to be correctly diagnosed if they are to get the appropriate treatment.

Exam Tip
The marks in the exam will be split up to show you which are AO1 marks and which are AO2/3 marks — pay attention to the split.

Exam Tip
This question is worth 16 marks but since the questions on psychopathology in Unit 4 are worth 24 marks each, this would have another part worth 8 marks.

Exam Tip
It's always a good idea to start your answer by defining the key terms you're talking about.

Exam Tip
Giving examples of how diagnosing schizophrenia may be influenced by various factors to affect its validity will give you extra marks in the exam.

Exam Tip
This is a good question for talking about real life — think about how the issue might apply to people with schizophrenia.

Summary Questions

Q1 a) Give two cognitive symptoms of schizophrenia.
b) Give two behavioural symptoms of schizophrenia.

Q2 a) Give an example of a Type 1 symptom of schizophrenia.
b) Are Type 1 symptoms of schizophrenia classified as positive or negative symptoms?

Q3 What do psychologists mean by the reliability of a classification system?

Learning Objectives:

- Know the biological explanations of schizophrenia, for example, genetics and biochemistry.
- Know the psychological explanations of schizophrenia, for example, behavioural, cognitive, psychodynamic and socio-cultural.

3. Explanations of Schizophrenia

Because schizophrenia is such a complex disorder, it should come as no surprise that there are many different explanations of the disorder. As usual, it's the nature-nurture debate between biological and psychological theories.

Biological factors

Genetic factors (inherited tendencies)

Being genetically related to someone with schizophrenia can significantly increase a person's chances of developing it. Family and twin studies have looked at concordance rates:

Tip: Concordance rates show the chance that someone will develop a disorder if they're related to someone who has it.

Key studies of a genetic factor in schizophrenia

Gottesman (1991) reviewed about 40 twin studies and found that with identical (MZ) twins there was about a 48% chance of both being schizophrenic. With non-identical (DZ) twins there was about a 17% chance.

Adoption studies have found that when children are adopted because one or both of their biological parents has schizophrenia, the chance of them developing it is still the same as those with biological parents with schizophrenia who aren't adopted. This suggests that genetics are more significant than the environment. Shields (1962) found that MZ twins raised in different families still showed around 50% concordance.

Kety et al (1994) also provided support for a genetic explanation for schizophrenia. Their results suggested that there was a higher concordance rate in people with biological relatives with the disorder than a control group.

There is also evidence against genetic factors. No study has found a 100% concordance rate, so schizophrenia can't just be caused by genes. Shared environment may cause higher concordance rates in family studies because children imitate 'schizophrenic' behaviours from their relatives. This means other factors need to be considered, e.g. biochemical or psychological factors.

Tip: PET scans stand for 'positron emission tomography' scans. They produce images which show levels of brain activity.

Biochemical factors

Post-mortems and PET scans have shown that schizophrenics have abnormally high levels of the neurotransmitter dopamine. These findings led to the development of the dopamine hypothesis, which states that synapses that use dopamine as a neurotransmitter are overactive in the brains of people with schizophrenia. The evidence in support of this explanation of schizophrenia has come from the fact that antipsychotic drugs reduce the symptoms of schizophrenia by blocking dopamine receptors. This suggests that it's the overactive dopamine receptors causing the symptoms. Also, drugs like amphetamines, which increase dopamine function, can sometimes cause schizophrenia-like symptoms in people without schizophrenia.

Tip: Dopamine is found in the limbic system.

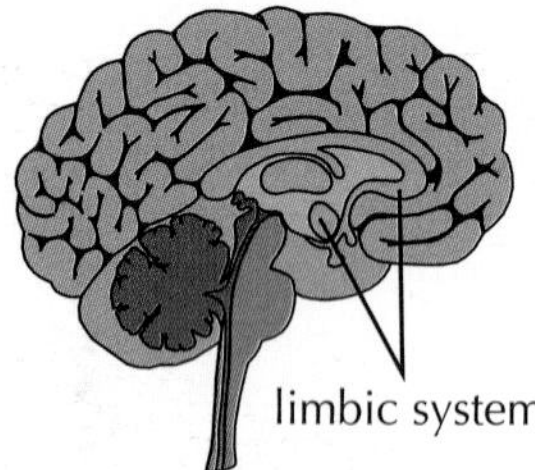

Figure 1: The limbic system includes the hypothalamus, thalamus, amygdala and hippocampus.

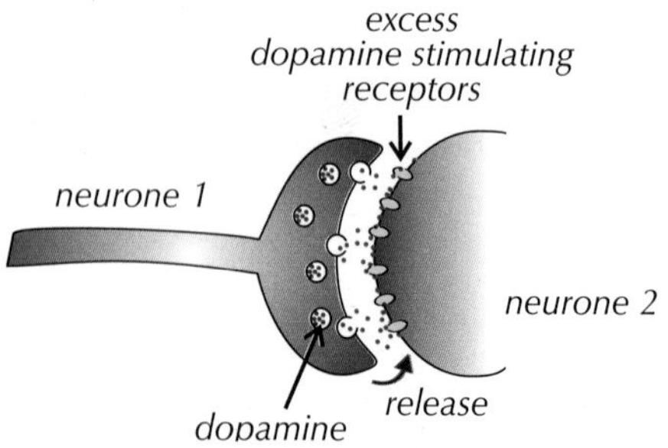

excess dopamine stimulating receptors
neurone 1
neurone 2
release
dopamine

Figure 2: The dopamine hypothesis states that people with schizophrenia have too much dopamine.

Examples

- Curran et al (2004) concluded that effects of taking illegal stimulant drugs were similar to that of schizophrenia. Since the illegal drugs work on the dopamine system, schizophrenia would also appear to have a link to dopamine.
- Chan et al (2010) conducted research into the rate of blinking in those with schizophrenia. They concluded that blink rate, which is said to be linked to the dopamine system in the brain, was significantly higher in patients with schizophrenia than controls.

Tip: The biochemical approach to schizophrenia is very reductionist — schizophrenia is a pretty complex mix of symptoms so it seems far too simplistic to explain it with just one neurotransmitter.

Evidence against the biochemical explanation includes how antipsychotic drugs only work on the positive symptoms of schizophrenia, e.g. hallucinations. This means that increased dopamine function doesn't explain negative symptoms like social withdrawal. The link with dopamine is correlational, so it doesn't show cause and effect. It may be that increased dopamine function is a symptom of schizophrenia, rather than a cause of it.

The actual role of dopamine in schizophrenia is still unclear:

Examples

- Davis et al (1991) found that dopamine levels vary across different areas of the brain — there appears to be high levels in the subcortical regions of the brain and low levels in the prefrontal cortex, which could explain both positive and negative symptoms.
- Remington (2008) investigated the possibility that a combination of dopamine and serotonin neurotransmitters are implicated in schizophrenia. However, more research is still needed in this area.

Tip: The most effective drug used to treat schizophrenia is clozapine. But since this affects the serotonin system more than influencing dopamine levels, you can use this as evidence against the dopamine hypothesis.

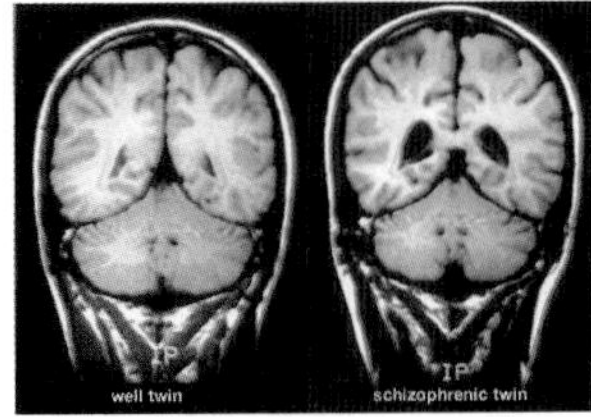

Figure 3: *The ventricles in schizophrenics' brains (right) have been found to be larger than those without the disorder.*

Neurological factors

Abnormal brain structure, caused by abnormal development, could be the cause of schizophrenia.

Key studies of neurological factors in schizophrenia

Johnstone et al (1976) compared the size of the ventricles (hollow areas) in schizophrenics' brains with non-schizophrenics' brains. They found that the people with schizophrenia had enlarged ventricles, which suggests that schizophrenia is linked to a loss of brain tissue. Buchsbaum (1990) carried out MRI scans on schizophrenics' brains and found abnormalities in the prefrontal cortex.

Tip: Studies have found these brain abnormalities, such as larger ventricles, more frequently in people with Type 2 symptoms.

Evidence against neurological factors includes the fact that non-schizophrenics can also have enlarged ventricles, which contradicts Johnstone's evidence. However, there's conflicting findings amongst schizophrenic patients too. These findings are correlational, so they don't show cause and effect. It may be that abnormal brain structure is a symptom of schizophrenia, rather than a cause of it.

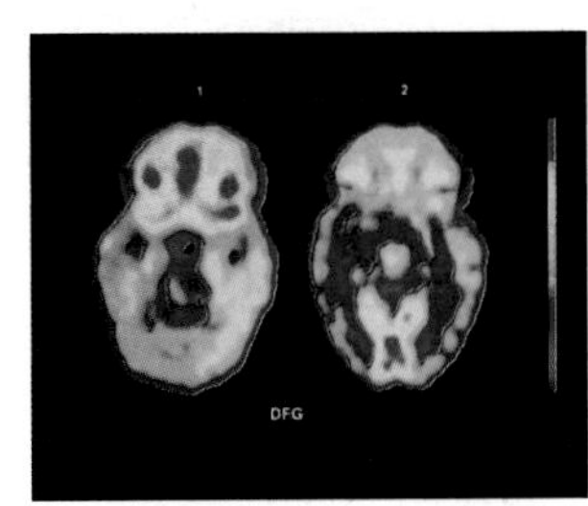

Figure 4: *Frontal lobe functioning is decreased in those with schizophrenia (right), as indicated by the green colouring.*

Psychological factors

Behavioural factors

Behaviourists argue that schizophrenia is learnt through operant conditioning. Someone may do something that gets a positive reaction or reward from others. This encourages the person to repeat the behaviour — it reinforces it.

Evidence for behavioural factors includes token economies, which use reinforcement to encourage 'normal' behaviours, which can help to treat schizophrenia (see page 158). This suggests that some of the behaviour could be learnt.

But... biological and psychological research suggests that schizophrenia isn't just a learnt behaviour.

Psychodynamic theory

Freud claimed that schizophrenia is caused by over-whelming anxiety. It's a defence mechanism involving regression into an early stage of development. Hallucinations are the ego's attempt to restore contact with reality.

There isn't any research evidence to support Freud's theory. Psychoanalysis isn't an effective treatment, which suggests that psychodynamic theory doesn't explain what causes schizophrenia.

However, Laing (1967) also argued that schizophrenics lose contact with reality as a way of coping with social pressure. He claimed that it was wrong to encourage schizophrenics to conform.

Socio-cultural factors

The social causation hypothesis states that people with low social status are more likely to suffer from schizophrenia than people with higher social status. It's thought that factors like poverty and discrimination cause high stress levels, and that this can cause schizophrenia.

Key studies of socio-cultural factors in schizophrenia

Harrison et al (2001) found that people who were born in deprived areas were more likely to develop schizophrenia. This suggests that factors like poverty, unemployment and crowding have an impact on schizophrenia.

Mortensen et al (1999) analysed data from over 1.7 million Danish people and found a relationship between where people were born and the prevalence rate of schizophrenia. The larger the town of birth, the more likely it was that someone would have the disorder.

But, these results are correlational, so they don't show cause and effect. The social drift hypothesis suggests that there are more people with schizophrenia in deprived areas because having schizophrenia gives them a lower social status, e.g. because they might be unemployed.

Cognitive factors

Cognitive psychologists argue that schizophrenia is caused by faulty information processing. This leads to delusions, thought interference, language impairment and memory problems.

Key study of faulty cognitive processing in schizophrenia — Frith (1992)

Frith (1992) outlined a faulty cognitive processing theory to explain schizophrenia. He proposed that people with schizophrenia struggle to see their own internal thoughts as thoughts produced by them, and not as auditory hallucinations. His findings were based on the discovery that patients with the disorder showed an inability to act of their own will, monitor their own involuntary actions or consider the actions and beliefs of others. However, Frith's theory ignores the role of the environment and has been criticised by other psychologists for being too reductionist.

Real World Connection
The biological and psychological explanations for schizophrenia are part of the nature-nurture debate. The nature-nurture debate crops up a lot within psychology. It tries to identify whether the causes of disorders, behaviours or actions are a direct result of our genes and biological make-up (nature) or the environment and social influences in which we're brought up in (nurture). In this case, the biological factors provide evidence for the nature side of the debate whilst the psychological factors provide evidence for nurture.

Tip: Frith's (1992) research links to the stuff on theory of mind — he says that those with schizophrenia don't have a fully working theory of mind. This means that they struggle to understand the different mental states of others, and also have trouble attributing their own thoughts to themselves. For example, whilst most people might attribute the internal dialogue "my parents want me to be polite" as coming from themselves, someone with schizophrenia may perceive it as an auditory hallucination coming from elsewhere. Take a look at page 135 for more on theory of mind.

Frith's findings were supported by other studies, such as the study by Brunet et al (2003). They looked at the activation of particular areas of the brain in people with and without schizophrenia. It was found that there were differences in blood flow in the brain when both sets of participants were asked to carry out a theory of mind task.

Neufeld (1978) compared the cognitive processes of people with schizophrenia with a control group. The participants with schizophrenia took longer to encode stimuli and showed short-term memory problems. This suggests that their ability to process information was impaired.

Many of the symptoms of schizophrenia involve cognitive impairment — one of these is showing attentional biases. For example, Bentall (1994) reported that people with schizophrenia were likely to show attentional biases towards objects that represented danger.

Example

A schizophrenic may be more likely to focus on a knife than another, more neutral object, such as a loaf of bread.

Bentall's research was based on the fact that paranoia is a symptom of some forms of schizophrenia. Cognitive tests examining attention, such as the Stroop test, also provided support for his theory. Bentall and Kaney (1989) found that schizophrenics took longer to process words that were paranoid in meaning compared to neutral words — this was said to be because they have an attentional bias towards such words.

Evidence against cognitive factors exists through biochemical research which suggests that cognitive problems are caused by increased dopamine function, rather than faulty information processing.

The diathesis-stress model

The diathesis-stress model combines both biological and psychological factors. It suggests that people who are biologically vulnerable to developing a mental disorder may be more likely to develop it if they are subjected to certain social or environmental stressors.

Lots of research has been conducted in this area. The fact that concordance rates in twin studies (see page 144) aren't 100% indicates that there does seem to be some genetic link, but that the environment must play a role as well.

Figure 7: *The diathesis-stress model.*

However, there is conflicting evidence for the model and studies can often be biased because the researchers want their findings to support the diathesis-stress model.

Tip: The Stroop test was devised by Stroop in 1935 as a method of investigating cognitive processing and attention. Participants have to state the colour of the text when presented with different coloured words (see Figure 5). People take longer when the colour of the text disagrees with the meaning of the word than when the colour and the word match. This is a sign that attentional processing is involved. In Bentall and Kaney's (1989) research, they found that it took schizophrenics longer than controls to identify the text colour of paranoid words.

Red	**Yellow**
Green	**Red**
Purple	**Green**

Figure 5: *Stimuli in the original Stroop test.*

Knife
Invaded
Mad

Figure 6: *Stimuli in the paranoid Stroop test.*

Tip: The diathesis-stress model is also known as the vulnerability-stress model. The larger the vulnerability, the smaller the stressor needed to trigger a disorder.

Figure 8: *Stress could trigger schizophrenia in the diathesis-stress model.*

Exam Tip
Start your answer off by choosing one biological explanation of schizophrenia and summarising what it means.

Exam Tip
Concordance rates provide really good evidence to support or disprove genetic theories of disorders.

Exam Tip
Finish off your answer with a brief conclusion that clearly summarises the key points you've just made.

Exam Tip
All psychopathology A2-Level exam questions are worth 24 marks. That means there'd be at least one other part to this question.

Worked Exam-style Questions

| 0 | 1 | Outline and evaluate **one** biological explanation of schizophrenia.

(8 marks)

The genetic explanation proposes that schizophrenia is an inherited disorder, caused by a genes passed on from parents. Psychologists use family, twin and adoption studies to see how likely it is that genetics plays a part in determining schizophrenia. They chiefly use concordance rates to work out the chance that someone will develop a disorder if a close family member also has it. For example, if there is a 100% concordance rate for the disorder in identical twin studies, we can conclude that there is a high chance the disorder is caused by genetic factors, since identical twins have exactly the same DNA. However, the results have not shown a 100% concordance rate, so there is evidence both for and against the role of genetics.

Gottesman (1991) reviewed concordance rates from many twin studies and found that there was just under a 50% chance of both identical twins having schizophrenia and just under 20% chance of both non-identical twins having it. Additionally, Shields (1962) had previously found very similar concordance rates of just under 50% for identical twins despite studying identical twins who had been raised apart. This suggests that there is certainly a genetic factor involved, but that it is not exclusively responsible for the onset of schizophrenia.

Because twins tend to be raised in very similar environments and children have been known to 'imitate' behaviours of those they are close to, it is hard to differentiate how much of their behaviour is a result of their environment and how much is caused by genetics. Therefore, other factors need to be considered in order to determine the causes of schizophrenia.

Summary Questions

Q1 Name one way psychologists can investigate the biochemical factors of schizophrenia.

Q2 What is the dopamine hypothesis?

Q3 Give one criticism of the neurological explanation of schizophrenia.

Q4 Give two psychological factors which can be used to explain schizophrenia.

Q5 a) What evidence supports the diathesis-stress model for schizophrenia?

b) Give one example of an environmental stressor used in the diathesis stress model for schizophrenia.

4. Treating Schizophrenia

As you've no doubt figured out, schizophrenia has loads of different symptoms and possible causes. This can make treating it quite difficult. Luckily there are many different treatments and often they're combined.

Learning Objectives:

- Know about the biological therapies for schizophrenia, including their evaluation in terms of appropriateness and effectiveness.
- Know about the psychological therapies for schizophrenia, for example, behavioural, psychodynamic and cognitive-behavioural, including their evaluation in terms of appropriateness and effectiveness.

Biological therapies

Traditionally, the biological treatment of schizophrenia involved techniques such as psychosurgery and electroconvulsive therapy (ECT). In the 1940s, psychosurgery was a popular technique, using a prefrontal lobotomy to separate the frontal lobe from the rest of the brain. This technique was used on those with severely violent and aggressive symptoms with success, but the side effects (which involved flat emotion, personality changes and social withdrawal) were horrific.

ECT involves placing electrodes on the head of a sedated patient and applying a voltage of around 250 V to stimulate the brain. This procedure isn't very well understood and, due to the negative side effects of personality changes and memory deficits, it's only used as a last resort.

Both of these biological therapies were a lot more common as early methods of treatment for schizophrenia. Nowadays, biological therapies involve more scientifically robust measures. For example, the biological approach to treating schizophrenia involves drug therapy. Treatment is based on the dopamine hypothesis (p.152) — the theory that schizophrenia is linked to increased dopamine activity in the brain. Antipsychotic drugs (neuroleptics) work by blocking dopamine receptors (see Figure 1).

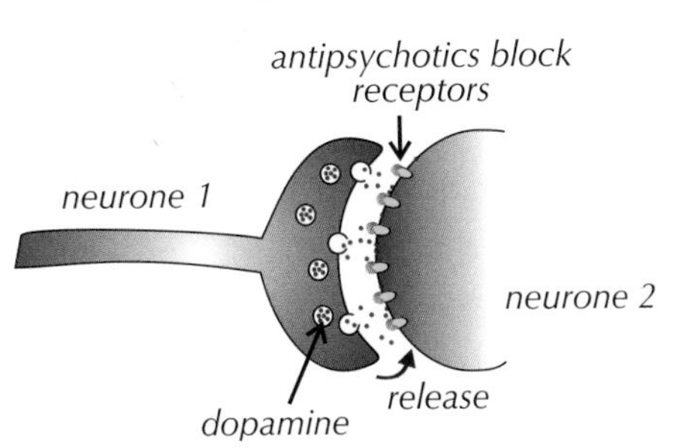

Figure 1: *Antipsychotic medication blocks dopamine receptors so neurone 2 is not stimulated.*

Tip: Antipsychotic drugs can be 'conventional' drugs, or 'atypical' drugs which also affect serotonin.

<u>Advantages</u>

Drug therapy is effective at reducing positive symptoms, e.g. hallucinations. It's successful for a large number of schizophrenia patients, meaning that more people can live in the community rather than being institutionalised. It's the most widely-used and effective form of treatment for schizophrenia. Almost all other treatments are used alongside drug therapy.

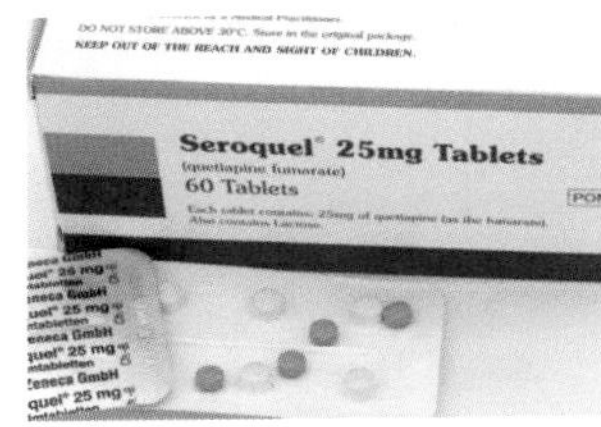

Figure 2: *Antipsychotic drugs are commonly used to treat schizophrenia.*

<u>Disadvantages</u>

Drug therapy isn't very effective for treating negative symptoms like social withdrawal. It treats the symptoms of schizophrenia but not the cause. Symptoms often come back if people stop taking antipsychotic drugs and this can lead to the 'revolving door phenomenon', where patients are constantly being discharged and re-admitted to hospital. There are ethical issues surrounding the use of drug therapy. Some people argue that drug treatment is a 'chemical straitjacket' — it doesn't really help the patient, it just controls their behaviour to make it more socially acceptable and easier to manage.

Most people will experience some short-term side effects when taking antipsychotic drugs, e.g. drowsiness, blurred vision, dry mouth, constipation and weight gain. Long-term side effects include increased risk of diabetes and tardive dyskinesia (involuntary repetitive movements that continue even

Exam Tip

When you're evaluating a treatment for schizophrenia, you can use the advantages of another treatment as disadvantages of the one you're evaluating.

Tip: Psychiatrists have to weigh up the pros and cons of drug treatments when deciding whether to use this sort of treatment on someone with schizophrenia.

after they've stopped taking the medication). Clinical trials have shown that as many as two-thirds of people stop taking antipsychotic drugs because of the side-effects. However, newer antipsychotic drugs seem to have fewer long-term side effects than the older ones.

Psychological therapies

Behavioural therapy

Behavioural treatment for schizophrenia is based on operant conditioning — learning through reinforcement. Token economies can help encourage people in psychiatric institutions to perform socially desirable behaviours, e.g. getting dressed and making their beds. Patients are given tokens which reinforce these behaviours — they can then exchange these for something they want, like sweets or cigarettes.

Figure 3: *Chocolate is a popular reward used in token economy programmes.*

Advantages

Token economy programmes can produce significant improvements in self care and desirable behaviour, even with chronic institutionalised schizophrenics.

Example

Ayllon and Azrin (1968) set up a token economy with schizophrenic patients in a psychiatric institution. They found that the amount of socially desirable behaviour increased — patients went from performing an average of 5 chores a day to around 40.

Tip: Behavioural therapies have been found to be most effective as a short term solution — the effects don't usually last for the long-term.

Disadvantages

Token economies are usually context specific so they might not transfer into the real world. Once people are away from institutions they often don't continue showing desirable behaviour, because there's nothing to reinforce it. The patients' behaviour might be superficial — they might only produce desirable behaviour if they're going to receive a token. There are ethical issues surrounding the use of behavioural therapy. It could be argued that it doesn't really help the patient, it just makes their behaviour more acceptable to other people.

Tip: Read more about the ethical implications of certain psychological research methods on pages 260-262.

Cognitive behavioural therapy

Cognitive behavioural therapy (CBT) is based on the assumption that patients can be helped by identifying and changing their 'faulty cognitions'. Schizophrenic patients are encouraged to reality-test their hallucinations and delusions.

Example

In reality-testing these hallucinations and delusions, schizophrenics may question and try to control the voices they hear. They do role-play exercises and homework to test out their 'faulty thinking' and are helped to see the consequences of thinking differently.

Through this they can gradually realise where the 'faults' in their thought patterns are, and can begin to change them.

Tip: Frith's (1992) work on information processing in those with schizophrenia appears on pages 154-155. CBT expands on this research by getting patients to understand that the voices they are hearing are their own, not put there by external sources.

Key study of CBT — Chadwick et al (1996)

Method:	Chadwick et al (1996) reported the case of Nigel, a man with schizophrenia who believed he had the ability to predict what people were about to say. Nigel himself asked to prove his 'power' to Chadwick's team and so they showed

	him over 50 video tapes of different scenarios, paused at certain intervals. Nigel was asked to predict what was going to happen next.
Results:	Nigel didn't get one prediction correct.
Conclusion:	Nigel concluded, through this reality testing form of CBT, that he didn't in fact hold any 'special power'.
Evaluation:	Although this is a case study, and therefore can't be generalised to a wider population, it does show that CBT can be successful in certain situations.

Tip: CBT gives the patient a chance to come to their own conclusion that they may have faulty thinking processes, rather than just being told they do by a psychologist.

Advantages

Sensky et al (2000) found that CBT was effective in treating schizophrenic patients who hadn't responded to drug treatment. It was helpful with positive and negative symptoms, and patients continued to improve 9 months after treatment had ended. CBT puts patients in charge of their own treatment by teaching them self-help strategies. This means there are fewer ethical issues than with other therapies (e.g. drug therapy).

Disadvantages

CBT only treats the symptoms of schizophrenia — it doesn't address the cause of the disorder. It's difficult to measure the effectiveness of CBT because it relies on self-report from the patient, and the therapist's opinions. This makes it less objective. Patients can become dependent on their therapist.

Real World Connection

Whilst there are many advantages to CBT, and evidence to support its effectiveness at treating schizophrenia, there have been cases where it might have had a negative effect. Kingdon and Turkington (1994) found that although 70% benefited, 30% of the patients they researched who'd undergone some form of CBT started to deteriorate following their treatment.

Social skills training

Social skills training (SST) allows patients to observe others who act appropriately, and then through modelling, reinforcement and role play they can copy their behaviour so they know how to act in certain situations. Patients would attend several sessions focusing on specific skills, e.g. conversation skills, time management and assertiveness.

Advantages

Bellack et al (2004) found that patients with schizophrenia were successfully able to learn social skills to help them outside hospital after undergoing SST.

Disadvantages

The therapy often uses situations which might not always be relevant to real life, meaning that the results can't be generalised. It overemphasises the behaviour of those with schizophrenia and underplays the role of cognitions.

Psychoanalysis

Psychoanalysis aims to identify the underlying cause of the mental disorder. This is done using different therapeutic techniques, e.g. dream analysis and free association. When the unconscious conflicts that are causing the problems are made conscious, the therapist and patient can discuss and try to resolve them. This will hopefully lead to the disorder being cured.

Figure 4: *Psychoanalysis is based on Freud's ideas including dream analysis.*

Advantages

It aims to treat the cause of the disorder, not just the symptoms. Patients have more control over their treatment than with other therapies, e.g. drug therapy.

Disadvantages

Other forms of treatment (e.g. CBT) have been found to be more effective. Patients are often unable to carry out the therapy, due to a lack of cognitive skills, etc. It's difficult to prove the effectiveness of psychotherapy — it's based on subjective data and the unconscious mind. There's also a risk that patients will develop false memories, e.g. of childhood abuse.

Tip: Drug therapy is often used alongside one of the psychological treatments.

Worked Exam-style Question

0 1 Outline and evaluate biological therapies for schizophrenia.

(8 marks + 8 marks)

There are several biological therapies that can be used in the treatment for schizophrenia. The biological explanation states that schizophrenia is the result of chemical imbalances or structural defects in the brain which result in the variety of symptoms seen in schizophrenia. There are several biological therapies which have been used to target this complex set of symptoms.

The original biological therapies that were used as early treatments of the disorder were prefrontal lobotomies and electroconvulsive therapy (ECT). They both involve procedures that alter the state of the brain in order to change the behaviour of those with schizophrenia. Prefrontal lobotomies involve separating the frontal lobe from the rest of the brain, whilst ECT involves a current of 250V being applied to the brain. However, both procedures left patients with permanent and irreversible changes in their behaviour, mood and personality which has large ethical implications. Since it's uncertain exactly how they work, these procedures are now rarely used and are only carried out as a last resort.

Exam Tip
When talking about the different treatments for schizophrenia, it'd be a good idea to mention which causal explanation they're based on. For example, in this answer you can talk about how the biological explanation for schizophrenia has led to the development of drugs which target the neurotransmitters thought to be involved.

Drug therapies are now the most common form of biological therapy used to treat schizophrenia, though they are often used alongside other forms of psychological therapies. Treatment is based on the dopamine hypothesis, which states that schizophrenics tend to have increased dopamine activity in the brain in comparison to non-schizophrenics. Antipsychotic drugs (neuroleptics) are used to combat this by blocking the dopamine receptors so that less dopamine activity can occur within the brain.

Exam Tip
If a question asks you to evaluate, make sure you weigh up the advantages and disadvantages of a treatment.

There are several advantages and disadvantages of biological therapies. Firstly, drug therapies have been shown to be successful in reducing positive symptoms, such as hallucinations, that people with schizophrenia experience. This means that fewer people with the disorder have to stay institutionalised and be cared for within a hospital — they're able to go out and live within the community.

However, drug therapies aren't good at treating negative symptoms such as social withdrawal. They also only treat the symptoms, not the cause, and symptoms often come back once drug therapy is stopped. The side effects, both short-term and long-term, of the drugs can also be severe and this has led many to discontinue using them.

Exam Tip
A brief summary shows the examiner you're organised and can write a well-structured answer.

Drug therapies are the most commonly used form of therapy today because of their effectiveness and by combining them with other psychological treatments, schizophrenia can be managed effectively.

Summary Questions

Q1 Explain how token economy programmes can be used to treat schizophrenia.

Q2 a) What does cognitive behavioural therapy (CBT) assume?
b) Give two disadvantages of CBT.

Q3 What is social skills training (SST)?

Q4 Give one advantage of psychotherapy.

5. Depression

Everyone has good days and bad days, but it becomes a lot more serious when the bad days start to impact on everyday life.

What is depression?

Depression is a mood disorder. Mood disorders are characterised by strong emotions, which can influence a person's ability to function normally. A mood disorder can affect a person's perceptions, thinking and behaviour. Depression is one of the most common mood disorders. There are many types, including:

- **Major depression** (unipolar disorder) — an episode of depression that can occur suddenly. Major depression can be reactive — caused by external factors, e.g. the death of a loved one. Or, it can be endogenous — caused by internal factors, e.g. neurological factors.
- **Manic depression** (bipolar disorder) — alternation between two mood extremes (mania and depression). The change in mood often occurs in regular cycles of days or weeks. Episodes of mania involve over-activity, rapid speech and feeling extremely happy or agitated. Episodes of depression involve the symptoms covered below.

Clinical characteristics

People with depression can experience a range of possible symptoms:

Physical / behavioural symptoms

- Sleep disturbances — insomnia (being unable to sleep) or hypersomnia (sleeping a lot more than usual).
- Change in appetite — people may eat more or less than usual, and gain or lose weight.
- Pain — especially headaches, joint ache and muscle ache.

Affective / emotional symptoms

- Extreme feelings of sadness, hopelessness and despair.
- Diurnal mood variation — changes in mood throughout the day, e.g. feeling worse in the morning.
- Anhedonia — no longer enjoying activities or hobbies that used to be pleasurable.

Cognitive symptoms

- Experiencing persistent negative beliefs about themselves and their abilities.
- Suicidal thoughts.
- Slower thought processes — difficulty concentrating and making decisions.

Social / motivational symptoms

- Lack of activity — social withdrawal and loss of sex drive.

The DSM-IV

The DSM-IV is the fourth edition of the American Psychiatric Association's Diagnostic and Statistical Manual of Mental Disorders. It contains a list of mental health disorders. Individuals are rated on multiple axes / dimensions and diagnostic categories are used, e.g. personality disorders and psychosocial problems. It aims to give diagnosis of mental disorders reliability and validity:

Learning Objectives:

- Know the clinical characteristics of depression.
- Understand the issues surrounding the classification and diagnosis of depression, including reliability and validity.

Exam Tip
You only need to answer questions about one disorder in psychopathology. So choose schizophrenia, depression, phobic disorders or obsessive compulsive disorder and learn everything you need to know about that one.

Real World Connection
Depression is one of the most common psychological disorders. Many great figures in history have suffered with depression, including Sir Winston Churchill.

Figure 1: *Many well known figures have suffered from depression.*

Tip: There is also another diagnostic classification system called the ICD-10.

Figure 2: When a depressed mood starts to impact on everyday life, such as school, then it may be more than just feeling down.

Tip: Lots of people suffer from depression alongside other disorders. This can make it difficult to diagnose because it's really hard to separate which symptoms are being caused by which disorder.

Real World Connection

Mackenzie et al (2011) conducted a study looking at the rates of undetected depression amongst American and Canadian university students. Through surveys, they found that although there were no significant differences between rates of depression in men and women, roughly one in every four students reported symptoms of depression, suggesting that the rates for depression are fairly high. This indicated that interventions are needed for potentially high rates of undetected depression.

Reliability

Reliability is how far the classification system produces the same diagnosis for a particular set of symptoms. In order for a classification system to be reliable the same diagnosis should be made each time it's used. This means that different clinicians should reach the same diagnosis.

Validity

Validity is whether the classification system is actually measuring what it aims to measure. Descriptive validity is how similar individuals diagnosed with the disorder are. Aetiological validity is how similar the cause of the disorder is for each sufferer. Predictive validity is how useful the diagnostic categories are for predicting the right treatment.

Types of depressive disorder

The DSM-IV identifies two main depressive disorders. These are **major depression** and **dysthymia**. The differences between the two are the length of time the symptoms persist for, and the level of depression felt by the sufferer. In major depression, a person's mood is so low that their everyday functioning is affected. However, for those with dysthymia, the depressive state is not as deep and some sufferers may have periods of relatively 'normal' mood, although they have a low mood on most days.

Problems with the reliability of diagnoses

For a person to be diagnosed with major depression, the DSM-IV states that at least five symptoms must have been present nearly every day for at least two weeks. However, the diagnosis of depression isn't always reliable — people displaying the same symptoms don't always get the same diagnosis.

Example

Women are twice as likely to be diagnosed with depression than men. There don't seem to be any clear reasons for why women would be more likely to suffer from depression than men. Some researchers have claimed that it's to do with hormonal differences between men and women. Others have said it's because of socio-cultural factors — the different ways that males and females are socialised means they react differently to stressful life events. However, it could be that clinicians expect more women to suffer from depression than men, so are more likely to diagnose a woman with depression than a man who displays the same symptoms.

Key study of the problems with the reliability of diagnoses — Keller et al (1995)

Method: Keller et al (1995) conducted a large study in which 524 patients were interviewed after reporting symptoms of depression. Using the DSM-IV classification system, health professionals from different sites were asked to diagnose the patients initially and then again six months later.

Results: Within the sites, the reliability of the diagnoses was categorised as 'good-to-excellent' in comparison to the reliability across different sites which was 'fair-to-good'. Over time the reliability of the diagnoses became 'poor-to-fair' for major depression.

Conclusion: Reliability may have been lower across time because the criteria of the DSM-IV are very strict. Certain symptoms, such as tiredness, may change a lot over time and depend on the time of year, the situation or even the time of day.

Evaluation: The large sample size makes the results fairly reliable.

Two other issues that may affect the reliability of diagnoses look at the situations in which people are diagnosed. If someone has symptoms of depression, they would visit a health professional to get a diagnosis. However, when they describe their symptoms, the health professional is then reliant on this retrospective report, which could be inaccurate. Additionally, health professionals often have limited time and resources. This could affect the reliability of their diagnosis.

Tip: Retrospective just means looking back into the past. Our memories aren't that reliable which is why retrospective reports can be problematic.

Problems with the validity of diagnoses

Rosenhan (1973) conducted a classic study that questioned the validity of the diagnosis of mental disorders. He believed that psychiatrists couldn't tell the difference between sane people and people with mental disorders. People who didn't have any kind of mental health problem got themselves admitted into a psychiatric unit by claiming they heard voices — they became pseudopatients. Once they'd been admitted they behaved 'normally'. However, their behaviour was still seen as a symptom of their disorder by the staff in the unit. For example, one pseudopatient who wrote in a diary was recorded as displaying 'writing behaviour'.

This questions the validity of the diagnosis of mental disorders — once people are labelled as having a disorder, all of their behaviour can be interpreted as being caused by the disorder.

Most diagnoses of depression are given by a GP. However, these health professionals are only trained in general medicine and so may lack the knowledge and the skills to identify those with depression. Since they have access to a patient's records, they may be unintentionally biased by past information about the patient when diagnosing their current symptoms.

Tip: Cultural differences, language barriers and the use of technical terms within classification systems can also affect the validity of diagnosing mental health problems.

Figure 3: A GP's lack of specialist training may compromise the validity of a diagnosis.

Worked Exam-style Question

0 1 Discuss the issues surrounding the classification and diagnosis of depression. *(8 marks + 16 marks)*

The American Psychiatric Association's Diagnostic and Statistical Manual of Mental Disorders (DSM-IV), is a classification system used to identify and diagnose mental health disorders. Patients are rated on multiple axes. If they fulfil certain criteria they're given a diagnosis.

However, diagnosing mental health disorders such as depression can be difficult. The DSM-IV outlines two main depressive disorders — major depression and dysthymia. They both have different sets of symptoms which have to be evident in the patient before they can be diagnosed. However, as with all mental health problems, there are issues in the reliability and validity of these diagnoses.

Reliability is the term used to describe how far a classification system arrives at the same diagnosis for a certain set of symptoms. So, the diagnosis should be the same each time it's used and different clinicians should come to the same diagnosis. For example, for a person to be diagnosed with depression, the DSM-IV says they must show at least five symptoms from a given list for at least two weeks, almost everyday. This can be difficult to do — people suffering with symptoms will visit a health professional to get a diagnosis but their list of symptoms and experiences of the past two weeks depends on their own reliability of their memory. This retrospective account of their symptoms can be inaccurate.

Exam Tip
This question is worth 24 marks — this breaks down into 8 marks for providing descriptions and factual information and 16 marks for evaluating and applying your knowledge.

Exam Tip
To organise your answer it's a good idea to make a brief plan to start with. Scribble down a quick outline of what you're going to write before you begin.

Exam Tip
Providing examples of studies shows you know your stuff. If you expand on this and say why a study supports or disproves something, then you're also showing you can apply your knowledge.

Exam Tip
Providing tips and ideas of how psychological research might progress shows you can apply your understanding of the issues within psychology.

Exam Tip
When you start a new line of thought in your answer, make sure you define what you're talking about.

Exam Tip
For big questions such as this, it's a good idea to finish with a clear summary — it doesn't have to be long, just a sentence or two will do.

Keller et al (1995) conducted a study which looked at the reliability of using the DSM-IV as a diagnostic tool for those with depression. They asked several health professionals to diagnose over 500 patients and make a follow-up diagnosis six months later. They found that whilst reliability was 'fair-to-good', the reliability of arriving at the same diagnosis after six months was only 'fair'. Their study showed that time can certainly alter the reliability of using the DSM-IV and that there must be various factors which influence why someone may or may not be diagnosed with depression after presenting their symptoms. These factors could include situational events (such as personal experiences that day), the time of day, or even their mood that week.

There are also socio-cultural and gender factors which might influence the reliability of a diagnosis of depression. Women are twice as likely to be diagnosed with depression than men, but there doesn't seem to be any scientific reason as to why this might be the case. More studies are needed to investigate whether this is because women react differently to stressful life events than men, or whether health professionals expect them to be depressed and so are more likely to diagnose depression in a woman even if a man reports the same symptoms.

Validity is another issue when classifying and diagnosing depression. Validity looks at whether the classification system actually measures what it aims to measure. There are three types of validity. Descriptive validity measures how similar individuals who are diagnosed with the disorder are, aetiological validity measures how similar the causes of the disorder are for each individual and predictive validity looks at how useful the diagnostic categories are for predicting the right treatment.

Rosenhan (1973) conducted a famous study where it was shown that psychiatrists weren't able to tell the difference between patients and pseudopatients, suggesting that the DSM-IV is not always reliable. In the study, people with no mental health problems claimed they were hearing voices and were admitted to a psychiatric unit. However, once they had been admitted, they behaved 'normally'. Despite this, their behaviour was still seen as a symptom of their disorder by the staff.

Also, most diagnoses of depression are given by a GP who isn't specially trained in identifying mental disorders. GPs are often rushed for time and dependent on previous medical notes and so they may be influenced by these constraints and provide an inaccurate diagnosis.

Overall, the reliability and validity of diagnoses leaves the DSM-IV open to a lot of criticism. However, it is still useful in providing a much needed classification of depression.

Summary Questions

Q1 What does endogenous mean?

Q2 Describe bipolar disorder.

Q3 Give two examples of affective / emotional symptoms of depression.

Q4 What is aetiological validity?

Q5 a) Give two types of depressive disorder categorised in the DSM-IV.

b) Outline the differences between these two depressive disorders.

6. Explanations of Depression

There isn't a single explanation that can fully account for depression. So, best to learn all of them so you're ready for whatever the examiner throws at you.

Biological factors

Genetic factors (inherited tendencies)

Being biologically related to someone who has depression seems to increase a person's chance of developing it. There is evidence for a genetic factor.

Key studies of a genetic factor in depression

Twin study

McGuffin et al (1996) found that if one identical (MZ) twin has major depressive disorder, then in about 46% of cases their twin is also diagnosed with it. For non-identical (DZ) twins the concordance rate is about 20%.

Adoption study

Wender et al (1986) studied the biological parents of adopted children who had major depressive disorder. The biological parents were eight times more likely to have depression than the children's adoptive parents.

Family study

Gershon's (1990) family study found that the rates of depression between first degree relatives were between 7-30% higher than those who had no family history of depression. This is significantly higher than rates in the general population.

The evidence against genetic factors includes the fact that the concordance rates found in twin studies aren't 100%, so genetics can't be the whole story. Environmental factors could also play a role. Genetic factors only seem to explain endogenous depression (depression caused by internal factors) — psychological factors seem to have more influence in the development of reactive depression. The samples used in the family, twin and adoption studies were often very small and so the results can't be generalised to the rest of the population.

Biochemical factors

Low levels of serotonin have been linked to depression. Kety (1975) developed the **permissive amine theory**, which states that serotonin controls the levels of the neurotransmitter noradrenaline. A low level of serotonin causes the level of noradrenaline to fluctuate — low levels of noradrenaline then cause depression, while high levels cause mania. Bunney et al (1972) further supported this idea in their study showing that noradrenaline levels fluctuate in those with bipolar depression, accounting for their alternative depressive and manic states.

The evidence for biochemical factors looks at how antidepressant drugs work by increasing the availability of serotonin at the synapses by preventing its reuptake or breakdown. This suggests that it's the low levels of serotonin that lead to depressive disorders. Post-mortems carried out on people who committed suicide have shown abnormally low levels of serotonin, suggesting that this may have caused their depression.

Learning Objectives:

- Know the biological explanations of depression, for example, genetics and biochemistry.
- Know the psychological explanations of depression, for example, behavioural, cognitive, psychodynamic and socio-cultural.

Exam Tip

If you're evaluating the explanations for depression then you can use the methodological strengths and weaknesses of the research methods (e.g. twin studies) to explain why there might be more confidence in some explanations over others.

Tip: Things like the effectiveness of drug treatments and the fact that depression has physical symptoms point towards a biological explanation.

Real World Connection
The biological and psychological explanations for depression are part of the nature-nurture debate. The nature-nurture debate crops up a lot within psychology. It tries to identify whether the causes of disorders, behaviours or actions are a direct result of our genes and biological make-up (nature) or the environment and social influences in which we're brought up in (nurture). In this case, the biological explanation provides evidence for the nature side of the debate whilst the psychological explanation provides evidence for nurture.

Figure 1: Moving house can be a stressful life event.

However, just because antidepressants relieve the symptoms, it doesn't mean they treat the cause. Low levels of serotonin could be a result of depression, not the cause. Psychological research has found alternative explanations for the cause of depression. The biochemical explanation is also deterministic and reductionist — it assumes people have no free will and, in reducing behaviour to a set of biological processes, could be viewed as over simplistic.

Psychological factors

Socio-cultural factors

Social psychologists focus on how depression can be triggered by something external, e.g. a bereavement or divorce.

Key study of socio-cultural factors in depression — Brown and Harris (1978)

Method:	Brown and Harris (1978) studied depression by interviewing housewives in London.
Results:	They found that 61% of the subjects with depression had recently experienced a stressful life event, compared with only 19% of the non-depressed subjects. Of the subjects who had experienced a stressful event but had a close friend, only 10% had depression. This can be compared with the 37% of depressed subjects who didn't have a close friend.
Conclusion:	These results suggest that depression is influenced by stressful life events and a lack of emotional support.
Evaluation:	Brown and Harris's study just shows a correlation, so you can't prove cause and effect. It could actually be that depression makes some stressful life events more likely to happen, e.g. someone might be more likely to lose their job or get divorced as a result of their depression.

The effect of social factors doesn't explain why some people experience endogenous depression (sudden depression that occurs because of internal factors). Other approaches might have better explanations.

Behavioural factors

Behaviourists reckon that depression develops when stressors (e.g. death of a loved one or being made redundant) lead to a lack of positive reinforcement. The attention that depressive behaviour then draws (e.g. sympathy from others) can then provide positive reinforcement, meaning the person learns to continue being depressed.

It may also be influenced by learned helplessness. This occurs when people learn not to try because they believe they'll never succeed. Seligman (1975) restrained dogs so that they couldn't avoid receiving electric shocks. Later when they could actually avoid the shocks they didn't even try — they displayed **learned helplessness**. This can be generalised to humans — when people aren't in control of stressful events they eventually learn not to try and improve them, causing them to become depressed.

Key study of behavioural factors in depression — Hiroto (1974)

Method: In this controlled experiment, Hiroto (1974) split up the participants into three separate groups. Group One were played a loud and obtrusive noise which they couldn't control. Group Two were played the same loud noise but they could turn it off. Group Three didn't hear any noise. Following this, each group was then presented with a series of loud bursts of noise and told they could prevent the noise from occurring if they were quick enough to push a lever. However, they weren't told which way to push the lever. Half were told it would be dependent on their skill, while the other half were informed that chance would decide if the noise switched off.

Results: Around four times as many participants from Group One, who'd previously had no control over the noise, failed to switch off the noise when it was presented in loud bursts. Also, participants who were told that stopping the noise was out of their control and due to chance performed significantly worse than those told their skill would help in quietening the sound.

Conclusion: Humans are vulnerable to learned helplessness and even just being told that something is out of their control can influence this negative state of mind.

Evaluation: Numerous other studies have also replicated similar findings and the theory of learned helplessness does seem to explain why people remain in negative situations, such as abusive relationships.

Figure 2: *In studies, loud, uncontrollable noises such as a pneumatic drills have been used to show how learned helplessness exists in humans.*

But, the behaviourist theory ignores the influence of biological factors. It also only explains reactive depression (depression caused by external events). It may be that biological factors are responsible for causing endogenous depression.

Cognitive factors

Abramson et al (1978) developed Seligman's (1975) **theory of learned helplessness** into a cognitive theory. They looked at people's thought processes in response to failure and stated that failure can be interpreted as:

- Internal (the person's fault) or external (caused by something else).
- Stable (likely to continue) or unstable (could easily change).
- Global (applies to all situations) or specific (just applies to this situation).

Depressed people may see failure as internal, global and stable (it's their fault, happens in all situations and won't change). This is just one example of a model of faulty cognitions — there are other models (see page 168).

In support of the cognitive explanation, Beck et al (1979) found that depressed people had negative thought processes — they exaggerated their weaknesses and played down their strengths. He called these **negative self-schemas** and claimed that they are caused as a result of experiencing a traumatic childhood event.

Tip: Abramson et al's (1978) expansion of Seligman's (1975) theory of learned helplessness is also known as the **hopelessness theory of depression**.

Tip: Lewinsohn et al (1985) came up with a similar cognitive theory of depression which shows how a cycle of depressive thoughts and actions deepen depression further:

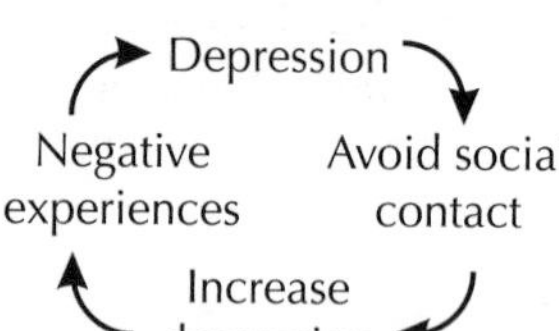

Figure 4: Lewinsohn's cognitive model of depression

Tip: You looked at Beck's cognitive model at AS, so look back if you want a reminder of any of the details.

Tip: Freud wasn't the only psychodynamic psychologist — lots of others supported the psychodynamic approach too.

Figure 5: Freud believed that a bad relationship between a parent and child could lead to depression in later life.

Tip: The diathesis-stress model is also known as the vulnerability-stress model. The larger the vulnerability, the smaller the stressor needed to trigger a disorder.

Examples

Traumatic events which could cause a negative self-schema may be:

- Bullying at school.
- Death of a close family member.

Beck identified a 'cognitive triad' of negative, automatic thoughts linked to depression (see Figure 3). These include negative views about:

- themselves (e.g. that they can't succeed at anything),
- the world (e.g. that they must be successful to be a good person),
- the future (e.g. that nothing will change).

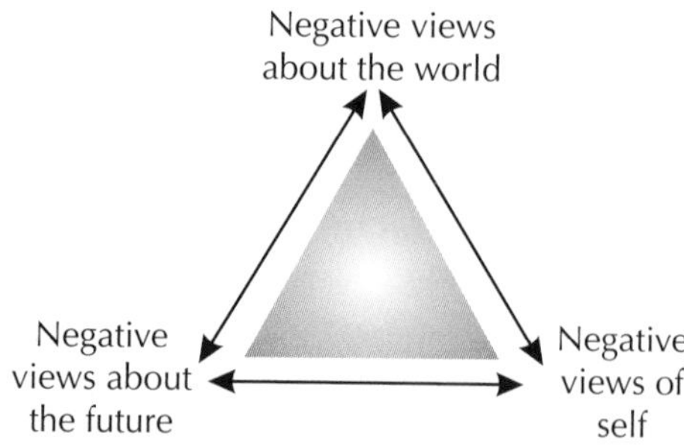

Figure 3: Beck's cognitive triad.

However, this theory is just based on a correlation — it doesn't prove cause and effect. It may be that negative thinking is actually the result of depression, not the cause of it. Instead, biological or other psychological factors could be the cause.

Psychodynamic theory

Freud claimed that if a child feels unloved by its parents it becomes angry. This creates guilt, so the anger is redirected towards the self. These feelings are repressed, but may later return following a stressful life event, causing depression.

Evidence comes from Brown and Harris (1978) who found that the women they interviewed were more likely to have depression if they experienced disrupted childhood attachments, especially if their mother had died. However, there isn't any research evidence to support Freud's theory, so it's unfalsifiable (impossible to prove wrong). It's also lacks scientific rigour because the unconscious mind is difficult to test. Also, the psychodynamic theory ignores the significance of other factors in causing depression, e.g. biological factors.

The diathesis-stress model

The diathesis-stress model (Figure 6) combines both biological and psychological factors. It suggests that people who are biologically vulnerable to developing a mental disorder may be more likely to develop it if they are subjected to certain social or environmental stressors.

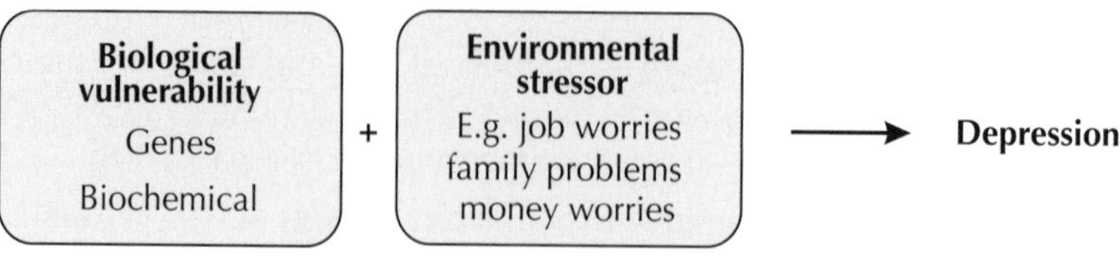

Figure 6: The diathesis-stress model.

Lots of research has been conducted in this area. The fact that concordance rates in twin studies (see page 144) aren't 100% indicates that there does seem to be some genetic link, but that the environment must play a role as well. Kendler et al (1995) provided support for the model as they showed that women who had experienced negative and stressful life events and who were vulnerable to depression, were more likely to suffer from depression later in life.

However, there is conflicting evidence for the model and studies can often be biased because the researchers want their findings to support the diathesis-stress model.

Figure 7: *Money worries could be a trigger for depression.*

Worked Exam-style Question

0 1 Outline cognitive explanations of depression. *(8 marks)*

There are many psychological explanations for depression and one of these uses cognitive factors to try and explain the symptoms. The cognitive approach uses the idea of negative thoughts and feelings creating a cycle of depression. Theories within this approach have support from various different studies.

Seligman (1975) developed the theory of learned helplessness which states that people often give up trying because they believe they won't succeed. These feelings have often been created through positive reinforcement. Abramson et al (1978) expanded upon this theory to develop it into a cognitive theory known as the hopelessness theory of depression involving faulty cognitions. In investigating people's thought processes when they experienced failure, they found that people interpreted this failure as internal, global and stable. That is, they believed failure was their fault, that it will happen to them in all situations all of the time, and it won't change.

Beck's cognitive triad is another cognitive theory involving the role of negative thought processes. He proposed that people have negative thought processes which exaggerate their weaknesses and play down their strengths. He called these negative self-schemas. Negative self schemas can be caused by traumatic events such as bullying at school or the death of a close family member. Events such as these can lead people to have continuously negative views. Their negative views of the world, themselves and the future all contribute to a negative perception of everything, a state of mind which would naturally lead to a depressed mood.

There are many theories of depression, but the cognitive theory provides an overview of the thought processes involved within this mental health disorder.

Exam Tip
As this question is only worth 8 marks, and all psychopathology exam questions at A2-Level are worth 24 marks, there'd be at least one other part to this question.

Exam Tip
Since this question is just asking you to outline the theory, the answer doesn't need any evaluation.

Summary Questions

Q1 Outline a study that explores whether genetic factors play a part in depression.

Q2 What is the permissive amine theory?

Q3 How did Seligman demonstrate learned helplessness in dogs?

Q4 Describe one piece of evidence against the psychodynamic explanation of depression.

Q5 What two factors does the diathesis-stress model combine in order to explain depression?

7. Treating Depression

There are many different treatments for depression based on the various explanations of the disorder. However, combining therapies has often proved to be the best.

Learning Objectives:
- Know about the biological therapies for depression, including their evaluation in terms of appropriateness and effectiveness.
- Know about the psychological therapies for depression, for example, behavioural, psychodynamic and cognitive-behavioural, including their evaluation in terms of appropriateness and effectiveness.

Tip: Therapy using drugs is also called chemotherapy.

Real World Connection
SSRIs and SNRIs are the most commonly prescribed antidepressants today. MAOIs and TCAs are older drugs and tend to cause more unpleasant and severe side effects. Because of this, lots of people who have been prescribed them stop taking them, which can just make the problem worse.

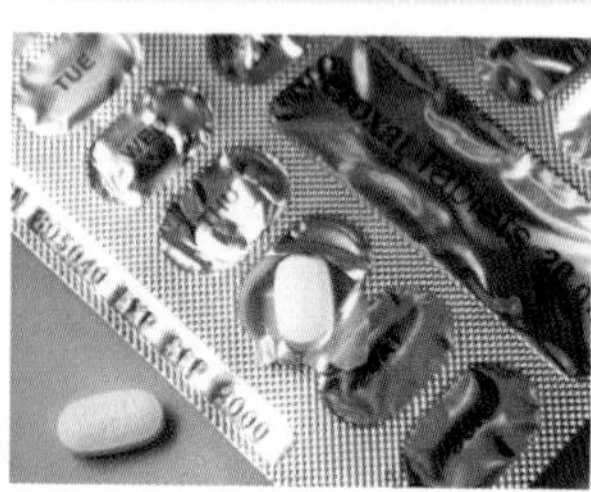

Figure 2: SSRIs, such as SEROXAT® and PROZAC®, are some of the most commonly prescribed antidepressants.

Biological therapies

Drug treatments

The biological approach to treating depression involves drug therapy. Treatment is based on altering the levels of serotonin and noradrenaline in the brain. These neurotransmitters regulate things like emotions, sleep patterns, sex drive and reaction to stress. There are four main types of antidepressant drugs:

- Monoamine oxidase inhibitors (MAOIs) increase the availability of serotonin and noradrenaline by preventing their breakdown.
- Tricyclic antidepressants (TCAs) increase the availability of serotonin and noradrenaline by preventing their reuptake.
- Selective serotonin reuptake inhibitors (SSRIs) increase the availability of serotonin by preventing its reuptake — see Figure 1.
- Serotonin and noradrenaline reuptake inhibitors (SNRIs) prevent the reuptake of serotonin and noradrenaline, so increase their availability.

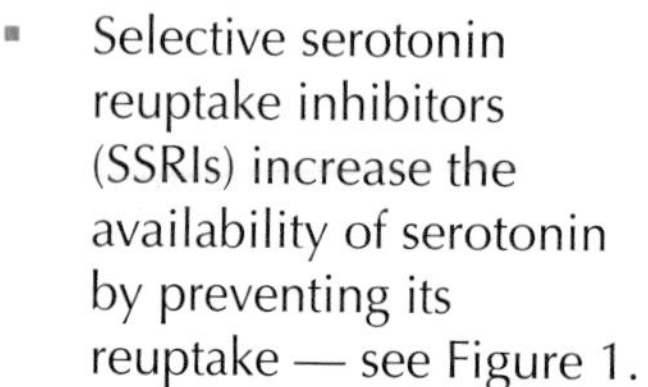

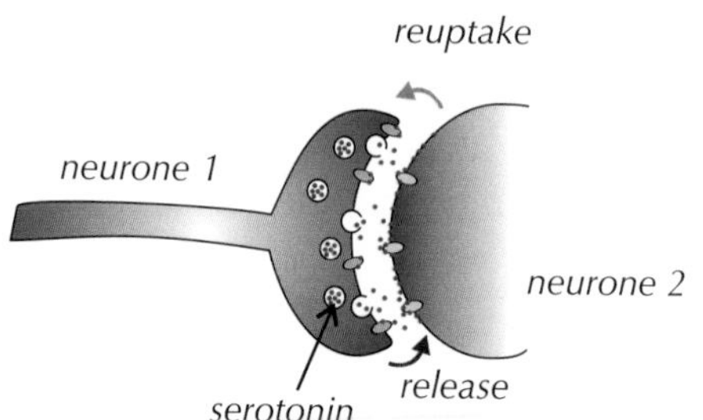

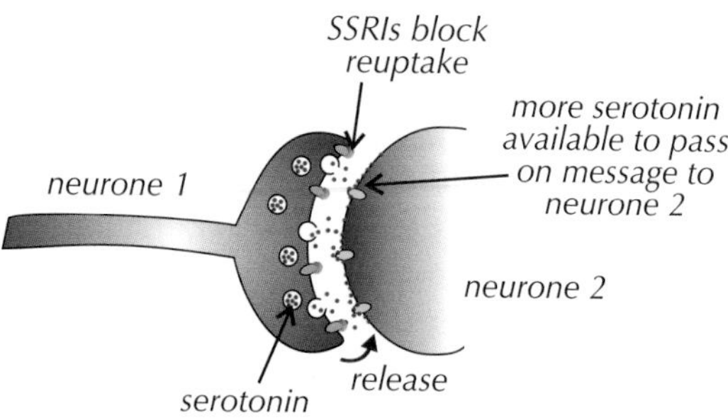

Figure 1: SSRIs are used in the treatment of depression to manage serotonin levels.

Advantages

Studies have shown that antidepressants are successful in reducing the symptoms of depression for more than half of patients. It's the most widely-used and effective form of treatment for depression. Psychological treatments are often used alongside drug therapy because antidepressants can remove some of the symptoms, allowing other therapies to focus on the cause of the depression.

Disadvantages

Antidepressants only treat the symptoms of depression. Other therapies are needed to try and tackle the cause of it. There are ethical issues surrounding the use of drug therapy. Some people argue that drug treatment is a 'chemical straitjacket' — it doesn't really help the patient, it just controls their behaviour to make it more socially acceptable and easier to manage. Antidepressants can have side effects, e.g. drowsiness, dry mouth, indigestion and nausea. They also take a few weeks to start working, which could be a disadvantage for someone with severe depression and who might be suicidal.

ECT and psychosurgery

Electroconvulsive therapy (ECT) and psychosurgery are two last-resort treatments for severe depression. ECT involves placing electrodes on the head of a sedated patient and uses a voltage of 250 V to stimulate the brain. This procedure is not very well understood and there are severe negative side effects such as personality changes and memory deficits. However, unlike in other mental health disorders, such as schizophrenia, its use as a treatment for severe depression has been supported due to its higher effectiveness. However, it is still unclear how and why the treatment works.

The use of psychosurgery as a treatment for depression has a controversial past. Before the development of antidepressant drugs, the 1930s saw lots of research into prefrontal lobotomies and other psychosurgical techniques. Nowadays, an **anterior cingulotomy** can be performed in cases of depression where drugs and other psychological therapies have failed. This involves cutting a lesion in the cingulate gyrus, part of the brain which connects the limbic system with the frontal lobe. Although it's been suggested that it's effective in about half of the cases, it can produce severe side effects such as seizures and, therefore, other treatments are preferable.

Tip: The cingulate gyrus is involved in processes such as learning and regulating emotion.

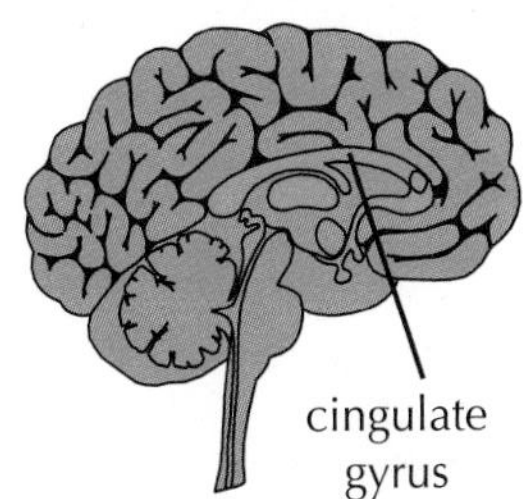

Figure 3: *Anterior cingulotomies are used as a last resort treatment.*

Psychological therapies

Psychoanalysis

Psychoanalysis aims to identify the underlying cause of the mental disorder. This is done using different therapeutic techniques, e.g. dream analysis and free association. When the unconscious conflicts that are causing the problems are made conscious, the therapist and patient can discuss and try to resolve them. This will hopefully lead to the disorder being cured.

<u>Advantages</u>

It aims to treat the cause of the disorder, not just the symptoms. Patients have more control over their treatment than with other therapies, e.g. drug therapy.

<u>Disadvantages</u>

Psychotherapy can be distressing for people because they're encouraged to recall traumatic events. This can sometimes be more difficult to deal with than the original symptoms. It's difficult to prove the effectiveness of psychotherapy because it's based on subjective data and the unconscious mind. There's also a risk that patients will develop false memories. Other forms of treatment, e.g. cognitive behavioural therapies (see page 172) and drug therapy have been found to be more effective.

Tip: Dream analysis assumes that our dreams contain an insight into our unconscious minds. Patients divulge their dreams to the therapist who then interprets the meaning. However, they could be misinterpreted and it is often hard to remember exactly what happened in our dreams.

Tip: Free association allows the patient to talk freely and 'let their mind wander'. The therapist interprets what they say, looking for patterns of association and key themes.

Key study of psychological therapies — Thase et al (1997)

Method: Thase et al (1997) conducted a meta-analysis to investigate whether psychotherapy was successful in treating major depression. They investigated the outcome of almost 600 patients with major depression who had either experienced just psychotherapy, just cognitive behavioural therapy or a combined treatment of psychotherapy and antidepressants.

Results: They found that in those with mild depression, there was no significant difference in the success of treatment between the single and joint therapies. However, in those with severe depression, treatment outcomes were much more successful in the patients who had received drugs alongside psychotherapy.

Tip: Psychotherapy allows for catharsis — the outpouring of emotion which is believed to 'cure' the patient.

Tip: As the name implies, cognitive behavioural therapy combines cognitive and behavioural therapies. It suggests that our thought processes, memories and perceptions of the world can affect how we behave.

Conclusion: Psychotherapy may be useful for mild depression, but a combination of treatments is better for those with major depression.

Evaluation: Conducting a meta-analysis allowed the researchers to collect a lot of data. This large amount of data makes the findings more reliable.

Cognitive behavioural therapies

There are several models that explain how faulty cognitions can lead to depression. For example:

- Ellis (1962) — The ABC model claims that disorders begin with an activating event (A) (e.g. a failed exam), leading to a belief (B) about why this happened. This may be rational (e.g. 'I didn't prepare well enough'), or irrational (e.g. 'I'm too stupid to pass exams'). The belief leads to a consequence (C). Rational beliefs produce adaptive (appropriate) consequences (e.g. more revision). Irrational beliefs produce maladaptive (bad and inappropriate) consequences (e.g. getting depressed).

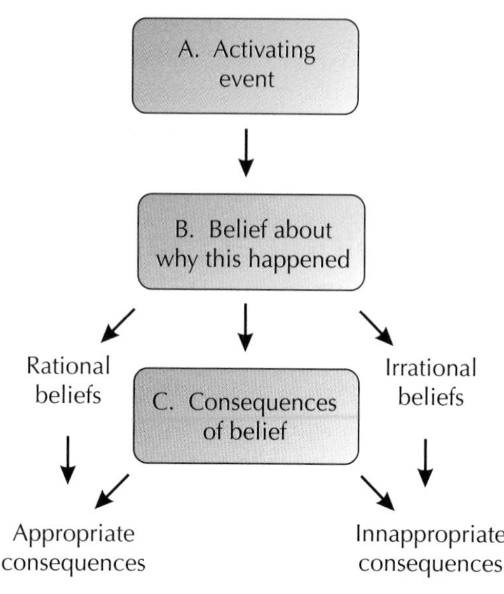

Figure 4: Flowchart showing Ellis's 'ABC model'.

- Beck (1963)'s cognitive triad links negative thoughts about the self, the world and the future with depression. People who have these negative thoughts exaggerate their weaknesses and play down their strengths.

Figure 5: Some beliefs may be rational and fully explain why someone failed an exam.

Tip: Take a look back at page 168 to see the diagram and explanation of Beck's cognitive triad.

Examples

- Negative view of the self — "I am worthless".
- Negative view of the world — "Everyone hates me".
- Negative view of the future — "I'll never be any good at anything".

Cognitive behavioural therapy (CBT) aims to identify and change the patient's faulty cognitions. This is generally what happens during CBT:

The therapist and client identify the client's faulty cognitions. Therapists sometimes encourage their clients to keep a diary so they can record their thought patterns, feelings and actions. The therapist tries to show that the cognitions aren't true, e.g. the client doesn't always fail at what they do. Together, they set goals to think in more positive or adaptive ways, e.g. focusing on things the client has succeeded at and trying to build on them Although the client may occasionally need to look back to past experiences, the treatment mainly focuses on the present situation.

Real World Connection

GPs often prescribe antidepressants to patients with depression. However, with the increase in support for therapies such as CBT, there is a need for this to become a possible treatment option too. In 2008, the government introduced the Improving Access to Psychological Therapies (IAPT) programme to help with this.

CBT helps to link the patient's thoughts, emotions, behaviours and feelings and allows them to take credit for changing their behaviour (Figure 7). Health professionals use this model, getting patients to explore how they are feeling and behaving. Often seeing it written down helps patients to understand how feelings can impact their behaviour and vice versa. There has been lots of research into the effectiveness of CBT as a tool in treating mental health problems, such as depression.

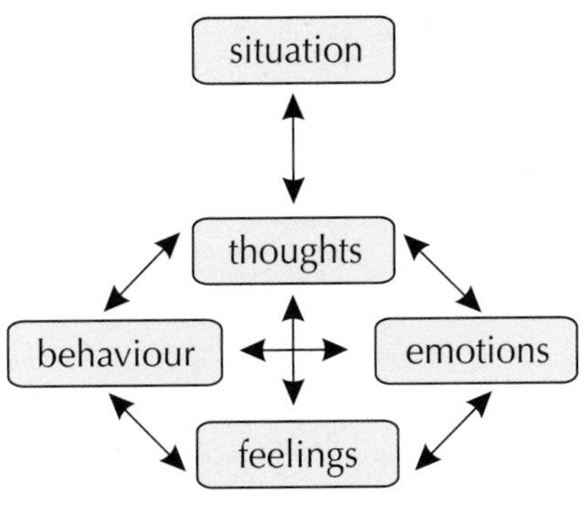

***Figure 7:** The CBT model used by psychiatrists.*

***Figure 6:** Patients are encouraged to keep a diary as part of CBT.*

Advantages

CBT empowers patients — it puts them in charge of their own treatment by teaching them self-help strategies. This means there are fewer ethical issues than with other therapies like drug therapy.

Key studies of CBT as a treatment for depression

Brandsma et al (1978) found that CBT is particularly effective for people who put a lot of pressure on themselves and feel guilty about being inadequate.

Dobson (1989) conducted a meta-analysis that concluded that, in the short term, CBT produced a higher success rate than drug or behaviour-based treatments.

Additionally, Hollon et al (2005) looked at the relapse rate of people with depression following CBT and drug therapies. Patients were initially either given antidepressants or CBT and then monitored over a twelve month period. Some patients stopped treatment over this time, whilst others didn't. Patients withdrawn from CBT were less likely to relapse than patients withdrawn from medication.

Tip: 'Relapse' is when someone suffers from a disorder again after previously recovering.

Disadvantages

Faulty cognitions might be the consequence of a disorder rather than its cause. For example, depression may be caused by a chemical imbalance in the brain, which causes people to think very negatively. Cognitive therapies may take a long time and may be more effective when combined with other approaches, e.g. drug therapy.

Tip: People are often treated with a combination of drugs and a psychological therapy. Different therapies suit different people so it seems like a good idea that psychiatrists treat people on a case-by-case basis.

Worked Exam-style Question

0 1 Discuss biological treatments for depression. *(24 marks)*

Depression has strong biological links. Following the research into genetic and biochemical explanations, it seems evident that there is a call for treatments which work on these factors. There are several different biological therapies which include drug therapy, psychosurgery and electroconvulsive therapy (ECT). They all have varying levels of success in terms of treating depression.

Firstly, drug therapies aim to alter the levels of serotonin and noradrenaline in the brains of patients, as the level of these

Exam Tip
You can pull in all the information you learnt about the explanations for depression into this answer — it'll make it a lot more complete and well thought out.

Exam Tip
The names for the antidepressants are long, but you can always use the abbreviations instead. Make sure you know what they do and how they work.

Exam Tip
Remembering something's advantages and disadvantages is a sure way to get loads of marks for discussion questions in the exam.

Exam Tip
Finish off your answer with a brief summary sentence to conclude what you've just said.

neurotransmitters are thought to be low in people with depression. Emotions, sleep patterns, sex drive and stress reactions are all characteristics which appear to be linked to these neurotransmitters. Drug treatments work on increasing these neurotransmitters within the brain.

There are four main types of antidepressants and each one works slightly differently. The older ones are the monoamine oxidase inhibitors, which increase serotonin and noradrenaline levels by preventing their breakdown, and the tricyclic antidepressants, which increase serotonin and noradrenaline levels by preventing their reuptake. More modern antidepressants are selective serotonin reuptake inhibitors, and serotonin and noradrenaline reuptake inhibitors. They both work by preventing the reuptake of the neurotransmitters and therefore, increasing their availability in the brain.

However, whilst these drugs seem to work fairly effectively, and studies have shown they are successful in more than half of all patients who take them, there are some disadvantages. Firstly, drug therapies only treat the symptoms and not the cause of depression. Secondly, there are ethical issues surrounding the use of drug therapy, notably that the drugs aren't giving the patient a chance to tackle their problems as the drugs are changing and controlling their behaviour. Finally, the side effects of the drugs can be unpleasant and include drowsiness, a dry mouth and nausea. Psychological treatments are often used alongside an antidepressant, because antidepressants can relieve some of the symptoms whilst other therapies focus on the cause.

ECT and psychosurgery are also biological treatments for depression. ECT involves a patient having electrodes placed on their head and a current of 250 V being used to stimulate their brain. Whilst it isn't really understood how it works, it has been shown to be a highly effective, immediate treatment, in those with severe depression. Additionally, psychosurgery is used as a last resort treatment for those with severe depression and involves a surgeon lesioning a particular area of the brain that separates the frontal lobe from other parts of the brain. This has also been shown to be effective. However, the side effects of both ECT and psychosurgery can be extreme and can include personality changes, seizures and memory loss.

Overall, biological therapies have been shown to be effective, but with the addition of other therapies such as psychological treatments, a more rounded and complete treatment programme can be established.

Summary Questions

Q1 Name two types of antidepressant drugs.

Q2 Psychotherapy can be used as a treatment for depression.

a) Give one advantage for this treatment approach.

b) Give one disadvantage for this treatment approach.

Q3 How is Ellis's (1962) ABC model used to treat depression?

Q4 Give an example of a piece of research that can be used to support the use of cognitive behavioural therapy in depression.

8. Phobic Disorders

It's perfectly normal to feel a bit anxious now and then. But when anxiety stops you from doing things you'd normally do, or if it happens all the time or about odd things, it may be a disorder.

What is a phobia?

A phobia is an example of an anxiety disorder. A phobia is an extreme, irrational fear of a particular object or situation. There are three types of phobia classified by the DSM-IV:

Specific phobias

This is a fear of specific objects or situations. There are five subtypes:

- Animal type (also called zoophobia, e.g. fear of spiders).
- Environmental dangers type (e.g. fear of water).
- Blood-injection-injury type (e.g. fear of needles).
- Situational type (e.g. fear of enclosed spaces or heights).
- 'Other' (any phobia that isn't covered in the categories above).

Specific phobias can lead to extreme behaviours and reactions, e.g. fainting, when someone is presented with the object or situation they fear. But they don't even have to be presented with it — merely the anticipation of an encounter can lead to a reaction.

Social phobia

This is the fear of being in social situations (e.g. eating in public or talking in front of a group of people). It's usually down to the possibility of being judged or being embarrassed.

Example

Celine avoided going on public transport because she was afraid of speaking to the bus driver. She was most concerned with the fact that other people on the bus might see her blush as she hands over her fare.

This is more than just being shy — things like public speaking scare a lot of people but social phobia is much more extreme. It's different to a specific phobia because it's mainly concerned with the reactions of others and what other people might think.

Agoraphobia

This is a fear of open spaces. It's specifically linked to the fear of having a panic attack in a public place and not being able to get away. It often develops as a result of other phobias, because the sufferer's afraid that they'll come across the source of their fear if they leave the house. Sweating, an increased heart rate, and an irrational and intense fear of dying are all symptoms of agoraphobia.

Clinical characteristics

The different types of phobia all have very similar clinical characteristics.

Cognitive symptoms

Irrational beliefs about the stimulus that causes fear. People often find it hard to concentrate because they're preoccupied by anxious thoughts.

Social symptoms

Avoiding social situations because they cause anxiety. This happens especially if someone has social phobia or agoraphobia.

Learning Objectives:

- Know the clinical characteristics of phobic disorders.
- Understand the issues surrounding the classification and diagnosis of phobic disorders, including reliability and validity.

Exam Tip

You only need to answer questions about one disorder in psychopathology. So choose schizophrenia, depression, phobic disorders or obsessive compulsive disorder and learn everything you need to know about that one.

Tip: There are two types of social phobia — generalised social phobia and specific social phobia. Generalised social phobia accounts for people who experience fear in all social situations. Specific social phobia only occurs in a particular location. For example, someone may be afraid of one particular shop.

Tip: Agoraphobia is actually diagnosed as 'panic disorder with agoraphobia'.

Tip: Lots of these symptoms are normal, automatic responses to things in the environment and certain events. But it's only when they're out of proportion that they become classed as part of a disorder.

Tip: The fight-or-flight response comes from our instinct to survive during a stressful situation. Prehistorically, encountering danger would lead someone to react by 'fight' or 'flight' (running away). By increasing adrenaline and heart rate, the body is getting itself ready.

Behavioural symptoms

Altering behaviour to avoid the feared object or situation, and trying to escape if it's encountered. People are often generally restless and easily startled.

Physical symptoms

Activation of the fight or flight response when the feared object or situation is encountered or thought about. This involves release of adrenaline, increased heart rate and breathing, and muscle tension.

Emotional symptoms

Anxiety and a feeling of dread.

Diagnostic criteria for phobias

The DSM-IV (see below) classifies a fear as a phobia if you can put a tick next to these criteria:

- There's significant prolonged fear of an object or situation.
- People experience an anxiety response (e.g. increased heart rate) if they're exposed to the phobic stimulus.
- Sufferers realise that their phobia is irrational and out of proportion to any actual danger. They may try to hide their phobia from other people, which can cause more anxiety.
- Sufferers go out of their way to avoid the phobic stimulus.
- The phobia disrupts their lives, e.g. they avoid social situations.

Figure 1: Acrophobia, or the fear of heights, is a common specific phobia.

The DSM-IV

The DSM-IV is the fourth edition of the American Psychiatric Association's Diagnostic and Statistical Manual of Mental Disorders. It contains a list of mental health disorders. Individuals are rated on multiple axes / dimensions and diagnostic categories are used, e.g. personality disorders and psychosocial problems. It aims to give diagnosis of mental disorders reliability and validity.

Reliability

Reliability is how far the classification system produces the same diagnosis for a particular set of symptoms. In order for a classification system to be reliable the same diagnosis should be made each time it's used. This means that different clinicians should reach the same diagnosis.

Validity

Validity is whether the classification system is actually measuring what it aims to measure. Descriptive validity is how similar individuals diagnosed with the disorder are. Aetiological validity is how similar the cause of the disorder is for each sufferer. Predictive validity is how useful the diagnostic categories are for predicting the right treatment.

Tip: There is also another diagnostic classification system called the ICD-10.

Problems with the validity of diagnoses

Rosenhan (1973) conducted a study where people who didn't have any kind of mental health problem got themselves admitted into a psychiatric unit — they became pseudopatients. Once they'd been admitted they behaved 'normally'. However, their behaviour was still seen as a symptom of their disorder by the staff in the unit. For example, one pseudopatient who wrote in a diary was recorded as displaying 'writing behaviour'. This questions the validity of the diagnosis of mental disorders — once people are labelled as having a disorder, all of their behaviour can be interpreted as being caused by the disorder.

Tip: Cultural differences, language barriers and the use of technical terms within classification systems can also affect the validity of diagnosing mental health problems.

Problems with the reliability of diagnoses

Clinicians can show bias when they're diagnosing mental disorders.

Example

Skre (1991) investigated the inter-rater reliability of three different clinicians asked to diagnose social phobias in patients. Each clinician was asked to diagnose patients from several audio tapes. The study found a correlation of over 0.7 between the diagnoses of the researchers, which is considered to be high within inter-rater reliability tests.

Figure 2: *It can sometimes be hard to distinguish between what is simply a fear of a situation, like crowds, and what is a disorder.*

Key study of validity and reliability problems in diagnosing phobias — LeBeau et al (2010)

LeBeau et al (2010) conducted a review to look at validity within the categories of specific phobias. They investigated the diagnostic procedures used to categorise different phobias. They reported that inter-rater reliability was 'very good' between health professionals who all diagnosed patients with specific phobias using the criteria set out in the DSM-IV. However, this was only the case when specific phobias were a patient's only disorder. In patients who they had other mental health problems, and a phobia wasn't the main cause of their symptoms, the reliability of the diagnoses decreased.

Tip: Inter-rater reliability describes how likely it is that one researcher will arrive at the same conclusion as another. The higher the inter-rater reliability, the more reliable the measure is.

Worked Exam-style Question

0 1 Outline the clinical characteristics of phobic disorders.

(4 marks)

Phobic disorders are characterised by several clinical characteristics. These are cognitive, social, behavioural, physical and emotional symptoms. Cognitive symptoms include irrational beliefs about certain events and situations which can lead to difficulty concentrating due to being preoccupied by anxious thoughts. Social symptoms include avoiding certain situations where there are lots of people. Behavioural symptoms are those where people change their behaviour in order to avoid encountering an object or situation that they're afraid of. Physical symptoms are those that come from the body — these can include the release of adrenaline or an increased heart rate after seeing a phobic object, such as a spider. Finally, emotional symptoms include feelings of anxiety and dread which, in the case of those with a phobic disorder, happen when the individual worries about meeting the phobic object or situation.

Exam Tip

This question is only asking for factual knowledge. Don't waste your time explaining characteristics — just stick to a description.

Exam Tip

This question is only worth 4 marks so it would make up part of a larger question. Questions in the psychopathology part of the A2 exam are worth 24 marks.

Summary Questions

Q1 Define 'phobia'.

Q2 Paul is afraid of needles. What type of specific phobia may he have?

Q3 What is agoraphobia?

Q4 Give two criteria that the DSM-IV lists to diagnose a phobic disorder.

Q5 a) What is aetiological validity?

b) What is predictive validity?

9. Explanations of Phobias

Learning Objectives:
- Know the biological explanations of phobic disorders, for example, genetics and biochemistry.
- Know the psychological explanations of phobic disorders, for example, behavioural, cognitive, psychodynamic and socio-cultural.

Phobias have been explained by many different factors. There are both biological and psychological theories to contend with, so see what you think.

Biological factors

Genetic factors (inherited tendencies)

Some phobias are much more common than others, and many of these are of things that can be dangerous to humans, e.g. snakes, spiders, heights. This suggests that humans have evolved a genetic predisposition to fear these things because it has survival value. This is **preparedness theory**. The assumption is that phobias have a genetic cause, so they should run in families, or be shared by identical twins who will have the same genes.

Key studies of a genetic factor in phobias

Using a family interview method, Reich and Yates (1988) found a higher rate of social phobias amongst relatives than other disorders. 6.6% of those with phobias had a relative with it too, compared to 0.4% of those with panic disorders.

Ost (1992) looked at those with specific phobias of blood and found that in over 60% of cases, they also had a first degree relative with the same disorder.

Fyer et al (1990) also conducted a family study looking at the rates of specific phobias in individuals if a first degree relative also had a specific phobia. They found that, out of 49 participants with a phobia, just over 30% had a relative with a similar condition.

Tip: Take a look back at page 145 to remind yourself of the advantages and disadvantages of family studies.

However, Torgerson (1983) found that identical (MZ) twins don't always share phobias. This suggests that other factors are also involved in causing phobias, e.g. psychological factors.

As a lot of the research in support of genetic factors uses family studies, imitation is likely to exist — people may copy others' behaviours and actions, therefore exhibiting similar phobias.

Tip: Biological theories explain why people can develop phobias without having had an associated bad experience.

Neurological factors

Neurological explanations of phobias suggest that our behaviour is caused by our instinctive fight-or-flight response. Studies using MRI scans have tried to determine which areas of the brain might be activated in phobic patients.

Key studies of neurological factors in phobias

Gray (1982) identified the behavioural inhibition system — a circuit in the limbic system in the brain that's linked to anxiety. When something unexpected and possibly dangerous happens, signals are sent to this area from the cortex. This causes anxiety which may make the person 'freeze'. How susceptible someone is to anxiety and panic may depend on how sensitive this circuit is.

Johnson et al (2000) did a longitudinal study showing that adolescents who smoked were 15 times more likely to develop anxiety disorders later in life, especially if they were heavy smokers. This may be due to the effects of nicotine, which may make areas of the brain more sensitive.

Tip: The behavioural inhibition system is believed to exist within the limbic system.

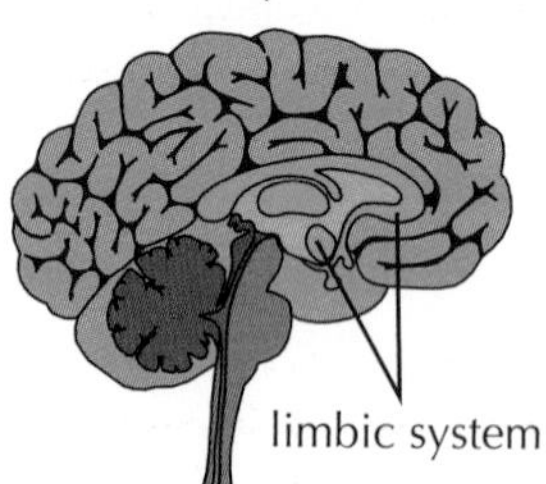

Figure 1: *The limbic system is linked to anxiety.*

However, Johnson et al's (2000) research is correlational — it doesn't prove that smoking caused the anxiety. This research doesn't take other factors into account. For example, behavioural research has shown that some phobias, especially specific phobias, can be learnt.

Biochemical factors

Neurotransmitters, including serotonin, dopamine, noradrenaline and gamma-aminobutyric acid (GABA), have all been found to be associated with anxiety. In normal functioning, GABA is released in response to high arousal. It has an inhibiting effect so it reduces arousal and therefore anxiety. The **GABA hypothesis** states that individuals with a phobic disorder may have low activity levels of GABA. This means that their neurones are not inhibited, leading to anxiety.

Evidence in support of this theory comes from successful drug treatments which work increasing the activity of GABA. For example, drugs such as Valium can lead to a reduction in anxiety because of the way it binds to the GABA receptors.

However, since not all drug treatments have been found to be successful, biochemical factors cannot exclusively explain phobias.

Psychological factors

Behavioural factors

Behaviourists believe that phobias are learnt through classical or operant conditioning.

Classical conditioning can be used especially to explain specific phobias. A previously neutral thing starts to trigger anxiety because it becomes associated with something frightening.

Key studies of behavioural factors in phobias

Watson and Rayner (1920) conducted a study on an 11-month-old boy called Little Albert. A loud noise was made every time he played with a white rat. He then began to associate the rat with the frightening noise, and showed fear when he saw it. The white rat was initially presented as a neutral stimulus (NS) and the noise as an unconditioned stimulus (UCS). By pairing the UCS and NS together, the rat becomes a conditioned stimulus (CS). An unconditioned fear response (UCR) initially occurs, but then the conditioned stimulus (CS) leads to a conditioned response (CR).

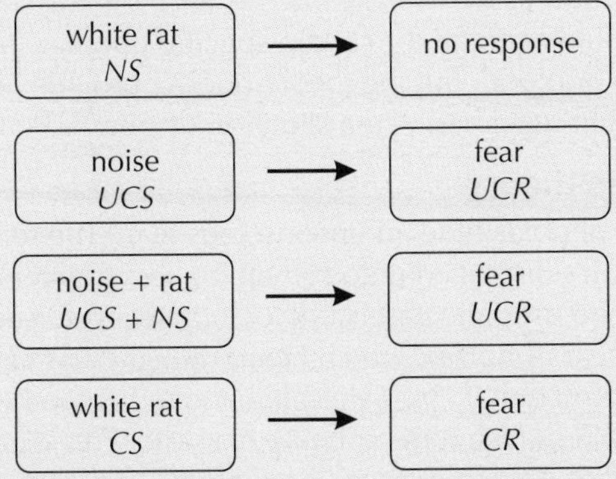

Barlow and Durand (1995) showed that in cases of individuals with a severe fear of driving, 50% of them had actually been involved in a road accident. Through classical conditioning, the road accident (an UCS) had turned driving into a CS for those now with the phobia.

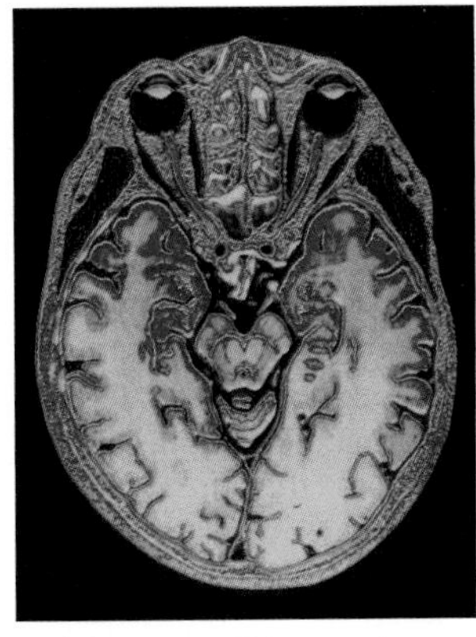

Figure 2: *MRI scans have been used to identify brain areas that are activated in those with phobias.*

Tip: The GABA hypothesis comes up again in the treatment section of phobic disorders on page 183.

Tip: There's more on conditioning on pages 107-108.

Figure 3: *Little Albert soon developed a phobia against white rats.*

Real World Connection

People report phobias of many different kinds — some of them might be more unusual than others, such as 'alliumphobia', a fear of garlic. However, as Ost (1987) found, different phobias tend to appear at different stages of people's lives. Animal phobias are more common in younger children, whilst agoraphobia occurs more in adulthood.

Operant conditioning can be used especially to explain social phobia and agoraphobia. A person's fear goes when they get away from the situation that causes fear. This is negative reinforcement — they learn to avoid the stimulus that causes anxiety because they feel better when they escape it.

Behavioural therapies are very effective at treating phobias by getting the person to change their response to the stimulus (see page 179). This suggests that they're treating the cause of the problem.

However, there is evidence against the behavioural explanation. Davey (1992) found that only 7% of spider phobics recalled having a traumatic experience with a spider. Similarly, Menzies and Clarke (1993) investigated children who had a phobia of water. They found that only one parent out of 50 (2%) could recall an episode of possible classical conditioning that could explain the onset of their child's phobia. This suggests that there could be other explanations, e.g. biological factors. (But just because they couldn't remember the experience, this doesn't mean it didn't happen.)

Real World Connection
The biological and psychological explanations for phobic disorders are part of the nature-nurture debate. The nature-nurture debate crops up a lot within psychology. It tries to identify whether the causes of disorders, behaviours or actions are a direct result of our genes and biological make-up (nature) or the environment and social influences in which we're brought up in (nurture). In this case, the biological explanation provides evidence for the nature side of the debate whilst the psychological explanation provides evidence for nurture.

Socio-cultural factors

It's thought that upbringing could affect the development of phobias.

Arrindell et al (1989) reported that people with social phobia claimed that their parents were controlling, over-protective and didn't show much affection. This suggests that upbringing can cause social phobia. Social learning theory states that behaviour is influenced by your environment and the people you grow up with. Children may see that a parent or older sibling is afraid of something and imitate their response.

Example

Bandura and Rosenthal (1966) asked participants to watch a model appear to receive electric shocks following the sound of a buzzer. The participants soon developed a physiological response associated with fear when they just heard the buzzer. Even though they weren't getting the electric shock themselves, they imitated a fear response, indicating a strong conditioned emotional response.

Figure 4: *Little Hans was afraid of horses — Freud said this was a phobia representing his fear of his father.*

But, the research on upbringing is correlational, and it relies on people's memory, which can be inaccurate. Other factors may be responsible, e.g. some people may have a biological pre-disposition that makes them more likely to develop phobias. Also, research has suggested that not all phobias are caused in the same way. Merckelbach et al (1996) discovered that learning theory could account for certain specific phobias, particularly ones involving animals or blood, but the theory doesn't provide an explanation as to why people might react badly to a situation or stimuli in the first place.

Psychodynamic theory

Freud argued that phobias hide an unconscious fear. The real fear creates so much anxiety that it's displaced onto something less frightening or embarrassing. Freud used the case study of Little Hans to support his theory. Little Hans had a fear of horses, which Freud thought was caused by Oedipal conflict. Freud claimed that Hans was attracted to his mother and frightened that his father would punish him for being his rival. This fear created so much anxiety and guilt that it was displaced onto horses, which were like Hans' father because they wore bridles (which looked like his beard) and had big penises. Right...

Tip: The Oedipal conflict suggests that children are unconsciously attracted to their opposite sex parents.

However, Freud's theories are unfalsifiable — they're unscientific because they can't be proved wrong. Hans had been very frightened by seeing a horse fall down in the street. It could be that this produced a phobia of horses through classical conditioning.

Figure 5: *Aerophobia is a fear of flying.*

Cognitive factors

Beck and Emery (1985) proposed that interactions between an anxious person's cognitive processes and their belief in their vulnerability makes them more likely to interpret stimuli as being threatening.

Example

Eimear is on a flight that experiences some bad turbulence. She has many anxious thoughts, and later believes that the next time she flies, the plane may crash. This could turn into a fear of flying.

Evidence for a cognitive explanation for phobias comes from Hope et al (1990) who showed participants words written in different colours. Participants with social phobia took longer to name the colour of social threat words (e.g. 'failure'). This suggests that they processed them in a different way.

But this doesn't show cause and effect — it could be that feeling vulnerable is a symptom of anxiety, not the cause of it. Phobias could be caused by other factors, e.g. biological factors.

Tip: It'd be useful to have a look at Beck's cognitive triad to see how negative thoughts about the world, ourselves and the future might all create anxiety. Take a look at page 172.

The diathesis-stress model

The diathesis-stress model (Figure 6) combines both biological and psychological factors. It suggests that people who are biologically vulnerable to developing a mental disorder may be more likely to develop it if they are subjected to certain social or environmental stressors.

Tip: The diathesis-stress model can also be referred to as the vulnerability-stress model. It says that the larger the vulnerability the smaller the stressor needed to cause a psychological disorder.

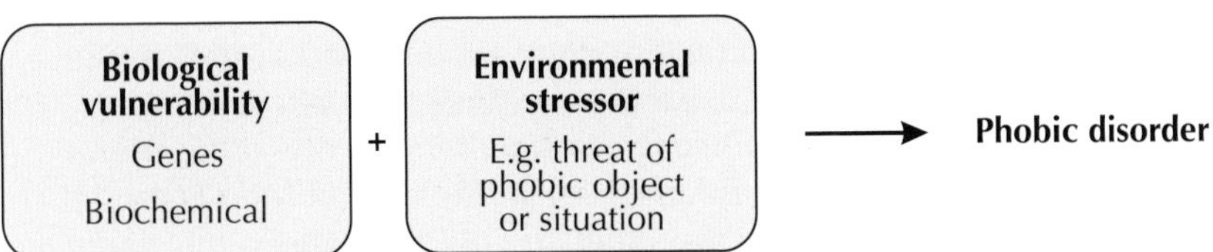

Figure 6: *The diathesis-stress model.*

Some research has been conducted in this area. The fact that concordance rates in twin studies (see page 144) aren't 100% indicates that there does seem to be some genetic link, but that the environment must play a role as well. Kleiner and Marshall (1987) investigated patients who had been diagnosed with agoraphobia. They found that over 80% of them had been through family problems before having their first panic attack.

However, lots of people experience traumatic events within their lives and yet they don't develop phobias. This must mean there are other factors involved.

Worked Exam-style Questions

0 1 Outline **one** biological explanation of phobias. *(4 marks)*

Because certain phobias are more common than others, some psychologists believe that there must be inherited traits which result in the onset of such disorders. Preparedness theory states that we have evolved to be afraid of things that might cause us harm, such as spiders, snakes and heights, and this is why people may have phobias of them.

Exam Tip
You won't be marked down if you don't remember the exact percentages in studies. You can get around the problem by using words such as 'about' or 'approximately' or 'over 60%'.

Research using family studies have been used to try to establish whether there is any truth in this assumption.

Reich and Yates (1988) showed that rates of social phobias were higher in families where someone else had it too. Likewise, Ost (1989) found that over 60% of people with a blood specific phobia were likely to have a first degree relatives who also had the anxiety disorder.

Exam Tip
For longer questions, it's a good idea to scribble down a quick plan of what you want to cover in your answer. It'll help you to stay focused when you start writing, and it's also a great way to make sure your answer is structured in a logical order.

| 0 | 2 | Outline and evaluate psychodynamic explanations for phobic disorders.

(8 marks + 8 marks)

The psychodynamic theory is a psychological theory which explains phobias using Freud's idea that phobias hide an unconscious fear. The real fear creates so much anxiety that we displace it onto something else which is less frightening or embarrassing. The research surrounding Freud's psychodynamic theory provides support and contradictions for this theory. Firstly, Freud's case study of Little Hans was used to support the theory. Little Hans came to Freud after revealing he had a fear of horses. After looking at Little Hans' relationship with his parents, Freud concluded that this fear of horses was a way for Little Hans to displace his actual fear. Freud believed that Hans was attracted to his mother and was frightened that his father would punish him for being his rival. This follows Freud's idea of the Oedipal conflict. The fear that Hans felt created so much anxiety and guilt that it became displaced on to horses.

Exam Tip
If you need reminding about the Oedipal conflict, take a look at page 180.

Because Freud's theories rely on case studies, personal experiences and a therapist interpreting situations, they are unscientific and cannot be proved wrong — they are unfalsifiable. There was also evidence against Freud's theory and this suggests that there may be other, more comprehensive explanations for phobias. In the case of Little Hans, he had seen a horse fall down in the street. It could have been this traumatic event which actually caused his phobia of horses, rather than a fear of his father. This would have occurred through classical conditioning. Studies such as the case of Little Albert by Watson and Rayner (1920) have provided ample support for the role of conditioning. This further disproves the psychodynamic explanation for phobias.

Exam Tip
To pick up more evaluation marks, you could also talk about how the biological approach contradicts what the psychodynamic approach proposes.

Overall, there's very little in the way of scientific evidence for the psychodynamic theory of phobic disorders. It would appear that there is a lot of evidence against it, and so it is likely that phobic disorders can be better explained by alternative explanations, such as the behavioural and biological approaches.

Summary Questions

Q1 Which part of the brain is linked to anxiety in the neurological explanation of phobic disorders?

Q2 Outline Watson and Rayner's (1920) study of Little Albert.

Q3 Give one criticism of the socio-cultural explanation for phobias.

Q4 How does the diathesis-stress model explain phobias?

10. Treating Phobic Disorders

Phobic disorders come in lots of different forms, as you'll have already seen. This means that psychologists have come up with multiple ways to treat them.

Learning Objectives:

- Know about the biological therapies for phobic disorders, including their evaluation in terms of appropriateness and effectiveness.
- Know about the psychological therapies for phobic disorders, for example, behavioural, psychodynamic and cognitive-behavioural, including their evaluation in terms of appropriateness and effectiveness.

Biological therapy

The biological approach to treating phobic disorders involves drug therapy. Anxiolytic drugs (e.g. tranquillisers) such as **benzodiazepines**, reduce anxiety by increasing the activity of the neurotransmitter GABA. GABA produces a feeling of calmness. Benzodiazepines act as a booster to allow the GABA to have a greater effect on the receiving neurone (see Figure 1).

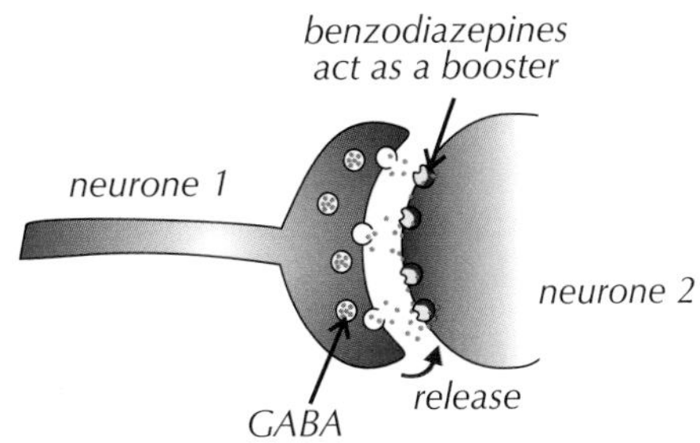

Figure 1: *Benzodiazepines increase GABA activity.*

Antidepressants, sometimes used for those with depression, can also be used. These include:

- Monoamine oxidase inhibitors (MAOIs), which increase the availability of serotonin and noradrenaline by preventing their breakdown.
- Selective serotonin reuptake inhibitors (SSRIs), which increase the availability of serotonin by preventing its reuptake.
- Serotonin and noradrenaline reuptake inhibitors (SNRIs), which prevent the reuptake of serotonin and noradrenaline, so increase their availability.

SSRIs are used most commonly for social phobia.

Tip: Therapy using drugs is also called chemotherapy.

Tip: GABA stands for gamma-aminobutyric acid. You can read a bit more about the GABA hypothesis on page 179.

Advantages

Benzodiazepines take effect very quickly. This means that they're good for treating phobias in the short term, e.g. before stressful events like exams.

Key studies of drug treatments for phobic disorders

Stein et al (1998) conducted a double-blind trial where over 180 patients with a social phobia were split into two groups. Group One were given a course of an SSRI antidepressant, whilst Group Two were given a placebo drug. They found that there was a significant improvement in Group One in terms of their social phobia. Over 50% of Group One showed reduced symptoms of anxiety and phobic symptoms, whereas just over 20% of Group Two improved.

Stein et al concluded that SSRIs are effective in reducing anxiety-related symptoms in those with social phobia in the short term. This experiment was highly controlled, allowing for an effective investigation into the role of an SSRI in phobic disorders. However, further investigation would be needed to assess the drug's effectiveness in the long term.

Davidson et al (1993) compared the effects of benzodiazepines with a placebo, and found that benzodiazepines were more effective at reducing the symptoms of social phobia.

Tip: A double-blind trial is an experiment where neither the patients nor the researchers know which experimental groups the participants are in. This element of control prevents the researchers from making biased interpretations or the participants from altering their behaviour, and makes the study far more reliable.

Tip: Placebos are just pills that do nothing at all. They're used to test if any effect happens just because people think they're being treated.

Real World Connection
The side effects of drugs such as benzodiazepines can be dangerous, not just to the person taking the drug, but to other people too. Thomas (1998) looked at the relationship between road accidents and benzodiazepines. The study concluded that accident rates were approximately double in those taking benzodiazepines in comparison to a control group.

Figure 2: *Drug treatments can have negative side effects — some which even compromise our safety.*

Tip: Exposure therapy is also known as flooding — it uses real situations to help people get over their fears. Implosion therapy is another type of flooding — this uses imagined situations.

Tip: One of the biggest benefits of social skills training is the lack of negative side effects, unlike those found with drug treatments.

Disadvantages

Benzodiazepines can cause side effects like drowsiness. They also cause physical and psychological dependency, so they can't be used long-term. The symptoms of phobias often return when people come off medication. Drug therapy only treats the symptoms of the disorder. Other therapies are needed to try and tackle the cause of it, e.g. behavioural therapies.

Psychological therapies

Behavioural therapies

Behavioural treatment for specific phobias is based on classical conditioning (learning through association). There are three techniques for treating specific phobias:

1. Systematic desensitisation

Systematic desensitisation works by using counter-conditioning so that the person learns to associate the phobic stimulus with relaxation rather than fear. Patients rank feared situations, from the least stressful (e.g. saying the word *spider*) to the most stressful (e.g. holding a spider). They are then taught relaxation techniques like deep breathing. The patient then imagines the anxiety-provoking situations, starting with the least stressful. They're encouraged to use the relaxation techniques and the process stops if they feel anxious. Patients will gradually be able to work through the feared situations on the list without feeling anxious.

2. Exposure therapy

This involves exposing the patient to the phobic stimulus straight away, without any relaxation or gradual build-up. This can be done in real life, or the patient can be asked to visualise it.

Example

Someone who was afraid of heights might imagine standing on top of a skyscraper. The patient is kept in this situation until the anxiety they feel at first has warn off. They realise that nothing bad has happened to them in this time, and their fear should be extinguished.

3. Social skills training

Social skills training (SST) involves modelling, rehearsal and behaviour reinforcement. Through a series of observations where patients can view and then imitate what is deemed to be 'appropriate' behaviour, they come to learn how they should be acting within a given situation. Through role play activities, homework tasks and feedback from the therapist, SST has been found to be an effective form of therapies for those with specific phobias. Shear and Beidel (1998) reported its success in patients with social anxiety.

Advantages of behavioural therapies

Behavioural therapy is very effective for treating specific phobias. Zinbarg et al (1992) found that systematic desensitisation was the most effective of the currently known methods for treating phobias. It works very quickly, e.g. Ost et al (1991) found that anxiety was reduced in 90% of patients with a specific phobia after just one session of therapy.

Disadvantages of behavioural therapies

There are ethical issues surrounding behavioural therapy — especially exposure therapy, as it causes patients a lot of anxiety. If patients drop out of the therapy before the fear has been extinguished, then it can end up causing more anxiety than before therapy started. Behavioural therapy only treats the symptoms of the disorder. Other therapies are needed to try and tackle the cause of it, e.g. cognitive behavioural therapy.

Cognitive behavioural therapy

Cognitive behavioural therapy (CBT) helps patients by identifying and changing their faulty cognitions. For example, many people with social phobia assume that they'll embarrass themselves in social situations, so think it's best to avoid them. Here's what generally happens during CBT:

- The therapist and client identify the client's faulty cognitions.
- The therapist tries to show that the cognitions aren't true, e.g. the client doesn't always embarrass themselves.
- Together, they set goals to think in more positive or adaptive ways, e.g. going to a party and talking to people they don't know. The aim is to prove to the client that their negative thoughts about what's going to happen are wrong, and so reduce their anxiety.

> **Tip:** A combination of treatment approaches may be used for people with phobic disorders.

Example

Yeltzen has a social phobia. He is trying to overcome it by working through a CBT course. Together, he and his therapist have identified his faulty cognitions, which include thoughts that people will laugh at him if he speaks up and that he's likely to embarrass himself in social situations. Yeltzen and his therapist then create positive goals for him to work towards, such as answering a question in class. Achieving this goal would reduce Yeltzen's anxiety, as it's likely he'd prove that his previous faulty cognitions were wrong.

Figure 3: Social phobias can stop people from enjoying themselves at parties.

Advantages

CBT is effective at treating phobias, e.g. Thorpe and Salkovskis (1997) found reduced anxiety in spider phobics after only one session of CBT. CBT empowers patients — it puts them in charge of their own treatment by teaching them self-help strategies. This means that it's a very ethical treatment. CBT is also a flexible treatment, which can be tailored to the needs of the individual. There are a range of options available, from group CBT sessions to individual sessions.

> **Tip:** CBT treatment usually takes between 12-20 weeks.

Disadvantages

Faulty cognitions might be the consequence of the disorder rather than its cause. For example, phobias may be caused by a chemical imbalance in the brain which leads to faulty thought processes. Patients can become dependent on their therapist. CBT is often time intensive and requires commitment from both the patient and the therapist.

> **Tip:** Dream analysis assumes that our dreams contain an insight into our unconscious minds. Patients divulge their dreams to the therapist who then interprets the meaning. However, they could be misinterpreted and it is often hard to remember exactly what happened in our dreams.

Psychotherapy

Psychotherapy aims to identify the underlying cause of the mental disorder. This is done using different therapeutic techniques, e.g. dream analysis and free association. When the unconscious conflicts that are causing the problems are made conscious, the therapist and patient can discuss and try to resolve them. This will hopefully lead to the disorder being cured.

Play therapy has been used, with some success, as a psychotherapy treatment for children. Therapists observe children playing with a large array of toys and, after interpreting their actions, they use their findings to engage with the child and help them overcome their phobias. Success has been found in several reports, including research by Santacruz et al (2006). They conducted an experiment comparing two play therapies with a control

> **Tip:** Free association allows the patient to talk freely and 'let their mind wander'. The therapist interprets what they say, looking for patterns of association and key themes.

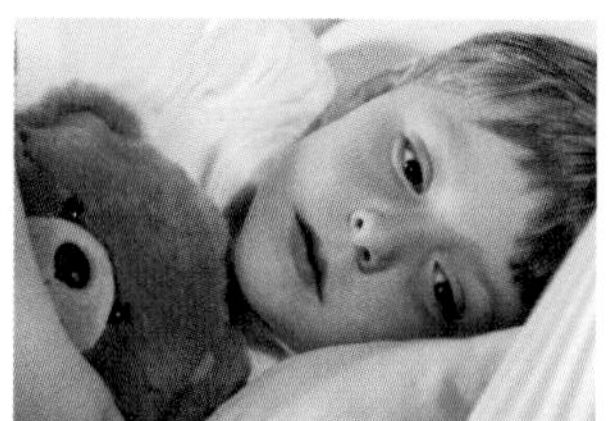

Figure 4: Play therapy has been found to be successful in treating darkness phobias in children.

group and found that those in the play therapy groups achieved a significant improvement in darkness phobia even up to 12 months later. Play therapy is one of the most successful therapies tailored specifically for children, suggesting that treatments may be age dependent.

Advantages

It aims to treat the cause of the disorder, not just the symptoms. Patients have more control over their treatment than with other therapies, e.g. drug therapy.

Key study of psychotherapy as a treatment for phobic disorders — Knijnik et al (2004)

Knijnik et al (2004) investigated 30 individuals who had been diagnosed with generalised social anxiety. In this controlled and blind trial, the participants were separated into two groups. Group One participated in a series of group psychotherapy sessions whilst Group Two participated in a group session which didn't involve psychotherapy. After twelve weeks, the results found that both groups had improved. However, those in Group One had improved significantly more than Group Two. These results support the idea that psychotherapy can be beneficial in treating phobias.

Tip: In a blind trial, the participants don't know what group they're in — this aims to prevent demand characteristics (see page 252).

Tip: A lot of mental health disorders are comorbid — this is where one disorder exists alongside another one, e.g. depression and a phobia. Treatments such as CBT can be used to treat both of them.

Disadvantages

Psychotherapy can be distressing for people because they're encouraged to recall traumatic events. This can sometimes be more difficult to deal with than the original symptoms. It's difficult to prove the effectiveness of psychotherapy — it's based on subjective data and the unconscious mind. There's also a risk that patients will develop false memories, e.g. of childhood abuse.

Worked Exam-style Questions

0 1 Evaluate the effectiveness of biological therapies in treating phobic disorders. *(8 marks)*

Biological therapies involve drug treatments to treat mental health conditions such as phobic disorders. They usually influence the levels and activity of the neurotransmitters in the patient's brain. There are several neurotransmitters which are believed to be involved in phobias, and treatment involves therapies that act upon these.

The main neurotransmitter involved in anxiety is GABA. GABA produces feelings of calmness, and drugs such as benzodiazepines have been found to reduce anxiety by increasing the amount of this neurotransmitter in the brain. Benzodiazepines act as a booster by allowing GABA to have an increased effect on receiving neurones. Results of a study by Davidson et al (1993) support this. The study involved participants who had been diagnosed with a social phobia, half of which were given the drug and the other half a placebo. There was a significant reduction in symptoms for those who had received the drug compared to the placebo. The use of benzodiazepines has been shown to be effective in the short term, as they act very quickly.

Likewise, Stein et al (1998) explored the role of antidepressants in treating people with anxiety disorders. They compared groups of social anxiety patients who received a selective serotonin reuptake inhibitor (SSRI) with a group who received a placebo drug. Their results showed

Exam Tip
When you're talking about the treatment of a disorder, it's a good idea to link it back to the explanation of the disorder that the treatment is based on.

Exam Tip
Including research in your answer is one way of supporting or disproving a theory. Here, the results of Davidson et al's study are used as evidence to support the theory.

over a 50% improvement in the symptoms for those who had received the SSRI. This was over double the rate of improvement found in those who had received the placebo drug. Stein's study was highly controlled, and used a double-blind design, so we can be fairly confident about the reliability of the results.

Overall, the effectiveness of drug treatments does appear to be positive. However, if benzodiazepines are used, there are some disadvantages which must be taken into consideration. The side effects include drowsiness, and physical and psychological dependency is another serious problem. Additionally, when a patient stops taking medication, the phobia may return, suggesting that drug treatment isn't completely successful in curing phobias. This is because the drugs appear to be only treating the symptoms, not the root cause of the disorder and so other treatment options may be necessary.

---

0 2 Outline one psychological therapy that is used to treat phobic disorders. *(4 marks)*

Phobic disorders can be treated with both biological and psychological therapies. One psychological therapy which has been found to be successful is cognitive behavioural therapy (CBT). CBT is based on the idea that people need help to change their faulty cognitions. For example, a patient might get help for a social phobia through sessions with a therapist. The therapist would help identify the patient's faulty cognitions, which might include the individual thinking that nobody likes them. These cognitions are then shown to be untrue. Goals are then established for the patient to work towards. The aim of the therapy is to allow patients to devise a set of challenges for themselves so that they can understand that their negative thoughts are wrong and their anxiety is not rational.

Exam Tip
Using words such as 'overall' and 'in conclusion' tell the examiner that you're about to summarise everything — this is a great way to add structure to your answer.

Exam Tip
Start off your answer with a brief sentence outlining the topic as a whole. Then you can narrow down your response from there.

Exam Tip
You can use abbreviations, such as CBT, in your answers. Just make sure you've defined them the first time you use them.

Exam Tip
Because A2-Level psychopathology exam questions are worth 24 marks, each of these questions would have other question parts with them.

Summary Questions

Q1 a) Describe how benzodiazepines are thought to work.

b) Give one disadvantage of using benzodiazepines.

Q2 a) What is systematic desensitisation?

b) Name one other behavioural therapy used in the treatment of phobic disorders.

Q3 Give one study which supports the use of psychotherapy as a treatment for people with a phobic disorder.

11. Obsessive-Compulsive Disorder

Learning Objectives:
- Know the clinical characteristics of obsessive-compulsive disorder.
- Understand the issues surrounding the classification and diagnosis of obsessive-compulsive disorder, including reliability and validity.

A lot of us have odd quirks and our own ways of doing things. But when this behaviour starts to affect daily life, a diagnosis of obsessive-compulsive disorder (OCD) might be made.

What is OCD?

Obsessive-compulsive disorder is a type of anxiety disorder that has two parts — **obsessions** and **compulsions**. Most people with OCD experience obsessions and compulsions that are linked to each other. For example, excessive worrying about catching germs (an obsession) may lead to excessive hand washing (a compulsion). Obsessive-compulsive disorder affects about 2% of the world's population. Sufferers usually develop the disorder in their late teens or early 20s. The disorder occurs equally in men and women and in all ethnic groups.

Exam Tip
You only need to answer questions about one disorder in psychopathology. So choose schizophrenia, depression, phobic disorders or obsessive compulsive disorder and learn everything you need to know about that one.

Obsessions

Obsessions are intrusive and persistent thoughts, images and impulses. They can range from worrying that you left the oven on to worrying that you might kill your parents. For thoughts like these to be classified as obsessions, the DSM-IV (see page 189) states they must meet the following criteria:

- Persistent and reoccurring thoughts, images or impulses that are unwanted and cause distress to the person experiencing them.

Example
Imagining that you've left the door unlocked and burglars are in your house.

Tip: Obsessions are the cognitive part of the disorder.

- The thoughts, images or impulses are more serious than just worrying too much.

Example
Continuing to focus mentally on the imaginary burglar, rather than dismissing it as an unlikely event.

- The person actively tries to ignore the thoughts, images or impulses but is unable to.
- The person is aware that the thoughts, images or impulses are created by their own mind and aren't the result of thought insertion (a symptom of some other disorders — see page 148).

Compulsions

Compulsions are physical or mental repetitive actions. For example, checking the door is locked nine times or repeating a certain phrase or prayer to neutralise an unwanted thought. The problem is that the action only reduces the anxiety caused by an obsession for a short time, which means that the obsession starts up again. The DSM-IV uses the following diagnostic criteria:

Figure 1: *Excessively checking you've turned the gas off could be classified as a compulsion.*

- The person repeats physical behaviours or mental acts that relate to an obsession. Sometimes the person has rules that they must follow strictly.

Example
A rule that you must check the door is locked ten times before you can leave home.

- The compulsions are meant to reduce anxiety or prevent a feared situation — in reality they're excessive or wouldn't actually stop a dreaded situation.

The DSM-IV states that if the obsessions or compulsions last more than an hour each day this is an indication of a clinical case of OCD. An alternative indication of OCD is if the obsessions and compulsions interfere with a person's ability to maintain a relationship, hold down a job or take part in social activities.

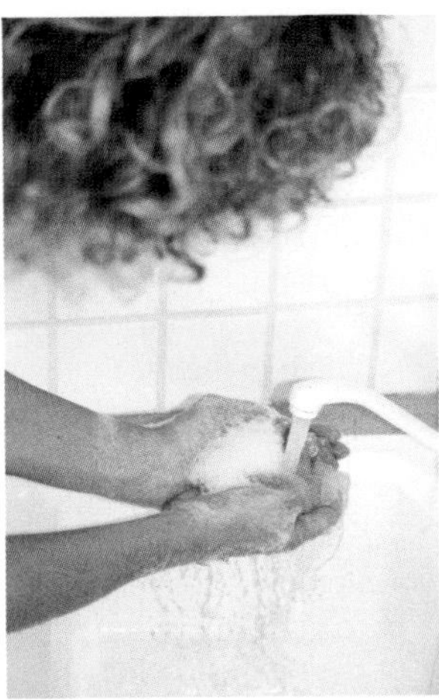

Figure 2: Washing your hands is 'normal' but when it becomes an obtrusive part of your life, it may be a symptom of OCD.

Types of OCD behaviours

There are several common types of OCD behaviours. Here are four:

Checking

This includes checking that the lights are off or that you have your purse.

Contamination

This involves a fear of catching germs by, say, going to a restaurant, touching door handles, shaking hands or using public toilets.

Hoarding

Keeping useless or worn-out objects, such as old newspapers or junk mail.

Symmetry and orderliness

Getting objects lined up 'just right', such as having all the tins in your food cupboard facing forward in exactly the same way, or everything on your desk arranged in a neat order in the right places, with everything at a specific angle.

The DSM-IV

The DSM-IV is the fourth edition of the American Psychiatric Association's Diagnostic and Statistical Manual of Mental Disorders. It contains a list of mental health disorders. Individuals are rated on multiple axes / dimensions and diagnostic categories are used, e.g. personality disorders and psychosocial problems. It aims to give diagnosis of mental disorders reliability and validity:

Tip: There is also another diagnostic classification system called the ICD-10.

Reliability

Reliability is how far the classification system produces the same diagnosis for a particular set of symptoms. In order for a classification system to be reliable the same diagnosis should be made each time it's used. This means that different clinicians should reach the same diagnosis.

Tip: There are many different ways to classify how reliable diagnostic tools are. Test/retest reliability is how likely it is that the same diagnosis will be given when a researcher diagnoses a patient once and then diagnoses them again at a later date. Inter-rater reliability looks at whether two separate researchers make the same diagnosis for a set of symptoms.

Validity

Validity is whether the classification system is actually measuring what it aims to measure.

- Descriptive validity — how similar individuals diagnosed with the disorder are.
- Aetiological validity — how similar the cause of the disorder is for each sufferer.
- Predictive validity — how useful the diagnostic categories are for predicting the right treatment.

Problems with the reliability of diagnoses

The DSM criteria can cause problems in diagnosing OCD. How do you decide objectively when it is that worrying too much about something actually becomes an obsession? Is there a clear point when a physical behaviour or mental act becomes a compulsion? People with other disorders, for example eating disorders, also experience obsessions and compulsions. This means that they could be misdiagnosed as having OCD.

Real World Connection
Obsessive compulsive personality disorder (OCPD) is often confused with OCD. This shows another problem in the reliability of diagnosing mental health problems. Both OCPD and OCD share some of the same symptoms — patients have difficulty in changing their beliefs and have high levels of anxiety and fear. But, there are key differences between the two disorders. People with OCPD don't really understand that their behaviours might not be 'normal' and therefore the worry this causes has less of an impact on everyday life.

Tip: Comorbidity is where one disorder exists alongside another one.

Example

Sometimes schizophrenic symptoms, such as obsessions, might be misdiagnosed as OCD. However, people with OCD have an awareness of reality and know their behaviours and thinking patterns are unusual. This isn't normally the case for those with schizophrenia.

Some people suffer from more than one disorder at once. When the two disorders have similar symptoms, it's hard to reliably give a diagnosis because it can be hard to tell which symptoms relate to which disorder. For example, the comorbidity rates of OCD with other mental health disorders is really high. Torres et al (2006) conducted a large scale investigation into OCD and found that out of over 8000 adults with the disorder, over 60% of them also had another mental health problem.

Diagnosing OCD can also lack reliability when assessing people who have been admitted to psychiatric units for problems such as substance abuse. Penick et al (1988) found that almost two thirds of patients who had been admitted for psychoactive substance abuse also had psychiatric symptoms. The drugs are likely to have altered their brain chemistry. But, once they're 'clean', their symptoms will stop and they won't show signs of mental health problems, such as OCD.

Key study of the problems with reliability of diagnoses — Steinberger and Schuch (2002)

Steinberger and Schuch (2002) looked at the reliability of diagnosing over 60 children with OCD using two different classification systems — the DSM-IV and the ICD-10. They found that each system resulted in different diagnoses, which indicates there are large differences between them. The results of the study highlighted how important it is that classification systems are consistent in defining which symptoms need to be present in order for a diagnosis of a mental health disorder to be made.

Problems with the validity of diagnoses

Figure 3: In Roshenhan's study, 'writing behaviour' was misinterpreted as a symptom.

Key study of the problems with validity of diagnoses — Rosenhan (1973)

Rosenhan (1973) conducted a study where people who didn't have any kind of mental health problem got themselves admitted into a psychiatric unit — they became pseudopatients. Once they'd been admitted they behaved 'normally'. However, their behaviour was still seen as a symptom of their disorder by the staff in the unit. For example, one pseudopatient who wrote in a diary was recorded as displaying 'writing behaviour'.

This questions the validity of the diagnosis of mental disorders — once people are labelled as having a disorder, all of their behaviour can be interpreted as being caused by the disorder.

Tip: A lot of mental health disorders go undetected because often people don't understand that their behaviour might be irrational or unusual.

Cultural factors

Culture may have an impact on the reliability and validity of a diagnosis. Symptoms such as fear of contamination and obsessive rituals may be culturally bound and therefore, using one classification system based on a Western perspective wouldn't be ideal.

Example

India still upholds a rigid caste system — they believe that those with high status exhibit 'purity', whereas those with a lower status are 'polluted'. Within this culture, it would not be deemed as unusual for a high status individual to feel 'contaminated' if they came into contact with a low status individual. This wouldn't be a sign of OCD — it's merely a culturally bound behaviour.

Tip: Culturally bound behaviours are those which have been shaped by people around us. They're what our culture accepts as a 'normal' way to act.

Williams et al (2005) conducted a study into OCD behaviours, and looked at the differences between Black, Hispanic and White people in America, both with and without OCD. They asked all participants to complete a survey to measure their levels of OCD behaviour. The researchers found that Black and Hispanic people scored the same as those with OCD when responding about their fears of animal contamination. However, this was thought to be because Black and Hispanic people were less likely to come into contact with animals in comparison to White people.

Figure 4: *India's caste system means people may naturally fear contamination from others.*

Finally, the medical phrasing and technical terms within classification systems can affect the validity of diagnosing mental health problems. Cultural differences create language barriers, meaning that professionals across the world may struggle to make the same diagnosis for a set of symptoms.

Worked Exam-style Questions

0 1 Discuss the issue of reliability which surrounds the classification of obsessive-compulsive disorder. *(8 marks)*

Reliability measures how likely it is that a classification system, such as the DSM-IV, provides the same diagnosis when given a certain set of symptoms. This can be a measure of how likely it is that, overtime, someone receives the same diagnosis from their clinician if they present the same symptoms. It can also be a measure of how likely different clinicians provide the same diagnosis after being presented with identical symptoms.

There are several issues with reliability when diagnosing obsessive-compulsive disorder (OCD). Firstly, it is very difficult to objectively assess the symptoms of mental health disorders, particularly those with symptoms of OCD. It's hard to distinguish when something such as obsessive worrying or checking behaviour becomes a symptom rather than a quirky personality trait. Not having a cut-off point which clearly defines a physical behaviour as being a genuine compulsion can compromise the reliability of a diagnosis.

Exam Tip
It's fine to use the abbreviated version of the disorder rather than write out the full name each time. Just make the abbreviation clear the first time you use it.

There are also issues relating to comorbidity. This is the idea that many people with mental health disorders don't just have one problem, but two or more at the same time. For example, people who suffer from OCD may also suffer from disorders such as depression. Distinguishing between two or more sets of symptoms can be difficult, and it could be the case that one mental health problem hides another.

Similarly, other disorders might show symptoms that are similar to OCD which means an incorrect diagnosis of OCD might be made. Eating disorders often involve obsessive behaviours, whilst people with

Exam Tip
You could also have outlined a study that illustrates a problem with the reliability of diagnoses — for example, Steinberger and Schuch (2002). However, as the question is only worth 8 marks, you've got to be careful not to go overboard and simply write everything you know about the topic. Unnecessary information won't get you any more marks and you may end up running out of time.

schizophrenia might also experience compulsions. Although there are guidelines within the DSM-IV to help distinguish between such closely related disorders, patients might not always present all of their symptoms which means the diagnosis is not always reliable.

---

0 2 Outline the clinical characteristics of obsessive-compulsive disorder. *(6 marks)*

Obsessive-compulsive disorder (OCD) is a type of anxiety disorder which affects about 2% of the world's population. It can be diagnosed by using the DSM-IV, which has criteria for the two components of the disorder — obsessions and compulsions.

Obsessions are intrusive and persistent thoughts, whereas compulsions are physical or mental actions. People with OCD tend to have obsessions and compulsions that are linked together.

During obsessions, patients experience images or feelings that cause distress. For instance, they might constantly be worried that their front door has been left unlocked and that they're going to get burgled. The DSM-IV states that the thoughts, images or impulses are more serious than just worrying — everyone worries from time to time, but when this affects daily life, the criteria is met. The person is unable to rationalise the worry, and so is continually thinking about it. Another characteristic is that the person may actively try to dismiss the distracting thoughts, but is unable to. Finally, for a diagnosis of OCD, the person must be aware that their obsessive thoughts are created by their own minds and are not inserted from elsewhere.

In terms of the DSM-IV, for behaviour to be classified as a compulsion the person must repeat a physical behaviour which relates to an obsession. For instance, checking a door is locked an excessive amount of times before leaving home. The compulsions are meant to reduce anxiety or prevent a feared situation, but in reality they're excessive and wouldn't actually stop the dreaded situation from happening.

Exam Tip
Both of these questions are worth less than 24 marks, which is how many the exam questions in A2-Level psychopathology are always worth. This means there'll be other parts to these questions.

Summary Questions

Q1 a) Give an example of how an obsession and compulsion may be linked to each other.
b) Give one of the DSM-IV criteria for each of these parts.
c) How long should these symptoms last in order for the OCD to be considered as a clinical case?

Q2 a) 'Symmetry and orderliness' is a common type of OCD behaviour. Give one example of a behaviour this could include.
b) Name three other types of OCD behaviours.

Q3 Define 'predictive validity'.

Q4 What is the DSM-IV?

12. Explanations of OCD

There are many explanations which try to account for the cause of OCD. However, since there is evidence both for and against each theory, not one explanation seems to be able to fully explain OCD.

Learning Objectives:

- Know the biological explanations of obsessive-compulsive disorder, for example, genetics, biochemistry.
- Know the psychological explanations of obsessive-compulsive disorder, for example, behavioural, cognitive, psychodynamic and socio-cultural.

Biological factors

Genetic factors (inherited tendencies)

Some researchers think that genetics plays a part in OCD. Studies have looked at concordance rates to see if being related to someone with OCD significantly increases your chances of developing the disorder.

Key studies of a genetic factor in OCD

Lenane (1990) conducted a family study which showed almost 30% of those with OCD also had a first degree relative with the disorder.

Billet et al (1998) did a meta-analysis of twin studies that had been carried out over a long period of time. They found that identical (MZ) twins had a concordance rate of 68% for OCD, compared to non-identical (DZ) twins who had a concordance rate of 31% for OCD.

Pauls et al (2005) found that 10% of people with a first degree relative with OCD also suffered from the disorder. This is compared to around 2% of people in the general population.

Tip: First degree relatives are parents, sons, daughters and siblings.

Tip: Concordance rates show the chance that someone will develop a disorder if they're related to someone who has it.

However, no study has found a 100% concordance rate for MZ twins, so genetics can't be the full story in OCD. Black et al (1992) found no increase in OCD prevalence in first degree relatives of OCD patients compared to a control group, therefore suggesting that the rates are not too different from the general population rate of OCD. It's possible that children imitate the obsessive and compulsive behaviour of their relatives.

Concordance rates don't prove that OCD is caused by genetics. It may be that general anxiety is genetic and that going on to develop OCD itself has other contributing factors, e.g. biochemical or psychological factors.

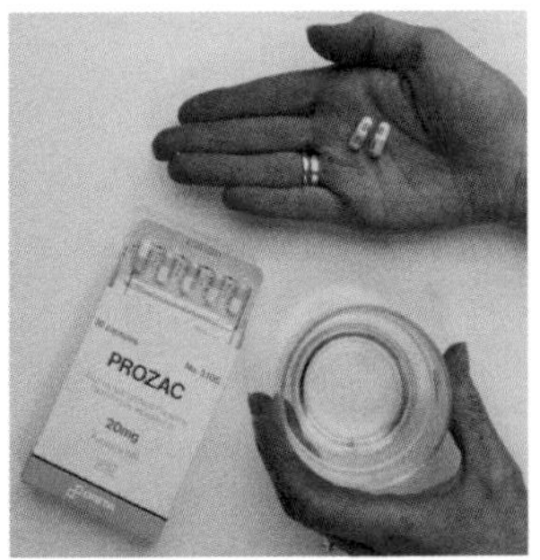

__Figure 1:__ Drug treatments such as SSRIs can be used to treat those with OCD.

Biochemical factors

PET scans have shown that level of the neurotransmitter serotonin is lower in OCD sufferers. Insel (1991) found that a class of drugs called SSRIs, which increase the level of serotonin, can reduce symptoms of OCD in 50 to 60% of cases. Zohar et al (1996) also found that SSRIs alleviated symptoms in 60% of patients with OCD.

SSRIs appear to offer some relief to sufferers of OCD. However, as this is not true in 100% of cases, there must be more to understanding OCD. The link with serotonin is correlational, so it doesn't show cause and effect. It may be that a decreased serotonin level is a symptom of OCD, rather than a cause of it.

Example

Rachman (1998) explains that just because the biochemical treatments for OCD inhibit serotonin reuptake, this doesn't mean we can exclusively conclude that OCD is <u>caused</u> by fluctuating serotonin levels. Also, the fact that other treatments work, means there is probably more to OCD than neurotransmitters.

Tip: SSRIs (selective serotonin reuptake inhibitors) are a type of antidepressant which increase the availability of serotonin by preventing its reuptake. You can read more about how they're used to treat OCD on page 198.

Neurological factors

Some research using PET scans has found that abnormality in the basal ganglia within the brain may be linked to OCD. Max et al (1995) found increased rates of OCD in people after head injuries that caused brain damage to the basal ganglia. Other researchers have found increased activity in this area during OCD-related thoughts and behaviours. OCD is often found in people with other diseases which involve the basal ganglia, e.g. Parkinson's and Huntington's chorea. Rapoport et al (1994) also showed that when patients had their basal ganglia severed from their frontal lobe, their symptoms decreased — but this was only found in those who were experiencing severe OCD to begin with.

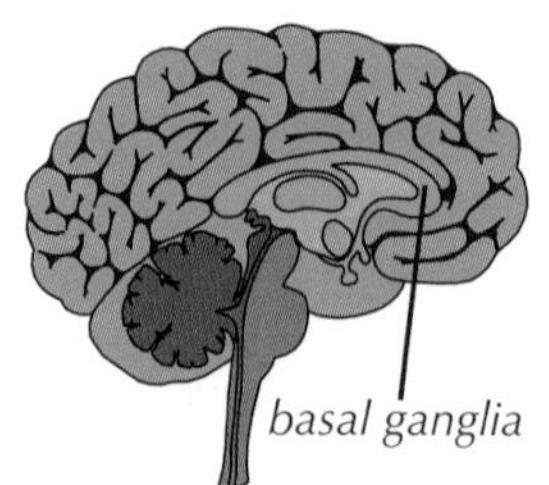

Figure 2: *The basal ganglia.*

Tip: PET scans (see Figure 3) can be used to study brain activity in people with OCD, particularly to highlight activity within the basal ganglia (see Figure 2). Coloured areas show brain activity.

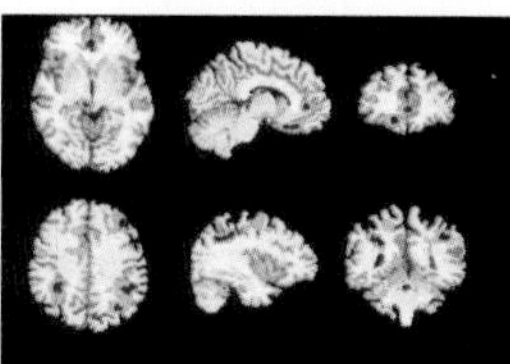

Figure 3: *A PET scan of an OCD patient.*

However, Aylward et al (1996) didn't find a significant difference in basal ganglia impairment between OCD patients and controls. Basal ganglia damage hasn't been found in 100% of people with OCD, so it can't be the full story.

Studying the role of the basal ganglia and other neurological structures is still a pretty new topic of research. As more technological advances are made, more research can be conducted to try to find out the role of the brain in mental health disorders such as OCD.

Psychological factors

Behavioural factors

Behaviourists use both classical and operant conditioning (see pages 107-108) to explain OCD. A person might behave in a certain way by chance when they are feeling anxious. When the anxiety goes away they unconsciously learn to associate the action with the removal of the anxiety. It becomes a reflex response. This is classical conditioning. They then repeat the action when they next feel anxious because they've learnt that it removes anxiety. This is operant conditioning.

Example

- Lotte couldn't remember if she'd turned off her hair straighteners. She began to worry that the house might burn down.
- To avoid this worry in the future, she started to check the hair straighteners repeatedly to make sure they were turned off. This removed her anxiety.
- However, she has now created a ritual to check they're switched off, which could escalate into OCD.

Real World Connection
The biological and psychological explanations for obsessive-compulsive disorder are part of the nature-nurture debate. The nature-nurture debate crops up a lot within psychology. It tries to identify whether the causes of disorders, behaviours or actions are a direct result of our genes and biological make-up (nature) or the environment and social influences in which we're brought up in (nurture). In this case, the biological explanation provides evidence for the nature side of the debate whilst the psychological explanation provides evidence for nurture.

There is research that provides evidence for the behavioural explanation of OCD. Baxter et al (1992) and Schwartz et al (1996) found that behavioural therapy can reduce the symptoms of OCD and change the biochemical factors associated with it. There is also strong support from successful behavioural therapies, such as those reviewed by Marks (1997) involving exposure and response prevention (see page 200).

But there is also evidence against it. Both classical and operant conditioning only explain the compulsive behaviour and not the obsessional thoughts, which are an important aspect of OCD. The behavioural approach also doesn't explain why the compulsions might start in the first place. The behavioural approach is also reductionist — it reduces behaviour to a series of simplistic responses. It also ignores any influence from our genetic make-up.

Real World Connection
Neil (1982) documented cases of sportsmen and women who carried out acts of rituals right before a sporting match or competition. Whilst their behaviour was unconnected and irrelevant to the actual outcome of the match, it can be explained using the behavioural approach. In the past, carrying out the ritual may have resulted in success. Therefore, not doing the ritual may, in their mind, lead to failure — so the compulsive behaviour becomes reinforced. This theory is based on Skinner's (1948) superstition hypothesis, which explains associations that come about from chance but later develop into compulsive behaviours because of the fear of not doing the action.

Psychodynamic theory

Freud claimed that potty training causes conflict and anger in the child when their parents teach them how to use a toilet properly. This is repressed because the parents are more powerful. In adulthood this can resurface, causing anxiety, which is displaced into obsessions and compulsions.

Example

- If parents are too lenient, they can be categorised as being anal-expulsive. According to Freud's theory, this results in a child being wasteful, messy and disorderly.
- If parents are anal-retentive, i.e. strict, they're likely to influence their children into having orderly, rigid and obsessive characteristics.

Evidence for the psychodynamic approach comes from research into stress, which supports the idea that feeling unimportant and out of control may increase the likelihood of developing a mental disorder. Other evidence comes from Adler's (1931) suggestion of a link between developing OCD and having had overbearing parents. In adulthood, engaging in ritualistic behaviours gives the person an opportunity to be very good at something (like hand washing) and so feel an increased level of control.

However, Milby and Weber (1991) found no link between potty training conflicts and developing OCD. Freud based his theories mainly on case studies and therefore, we can't generalise his results to a wider population. Also, his findings are unfalsifiable because we can't prove them wrong. Although some studies have shown that there is a correlation between anal-retentive personalities and the onset of OCD, there are also lots of people who do have these personalities but who don't have the disorder. Salzman (1980) also found that psychoanalysis could be detrimental to those with OCD, which indicates that the psychodynamic theory doesn't fully explain the causes of OCD.

Figure 4: Potty training could result in OCD, according to psychodynamic theorists.

Cognitive factors

The cognitive-behavioural approach to OCD was put forward by Rachman and Hodgson (1980). It suggests that people with OCD process thoughts differently. As a result they're unable to easily dismiss any unwanted thoughts and impulses. This can be made worse if they're feeling stressed or depressed. These unwanted thoughts and impulses cause anxiety, and the sufferer uses compulsive behaviours to remove this. This is the behavioural part of the cognitive-behavioural approach.

Examples

Faulty cognitions can occur in everyday situations:

- On walking past a knife in a kitchen, Brian's level of anxiety increased as he thought "What happens if I pick up that knife and hurt someone?".
- Wendy couldn't leave the room unless she'd turned the light switch on and off seven times. If she didn't do this, she believed that an electrical fault would occur and the house would burn down.
- If Edward didn't touch every door handle before he left, he thought he'd get hit by a bus.

Real World Connection
As mentioned on page 188, one of the differences between OCD and other mental disorders, such as schizophrenia, is the fact that people with OCD are able to distinguish reality from imagination. This is a cognitive symptom and is used as a foundation for the cognitive explanation of OCD. However, with all of the different theories for OCD, it's still difficult to provide an explanation which is clear cut.

Figure 5 illustrates the cycle between obsessions and compulsions found in those with OCD. Cognitive based therapy (on page 158) attempts to break this cycle.

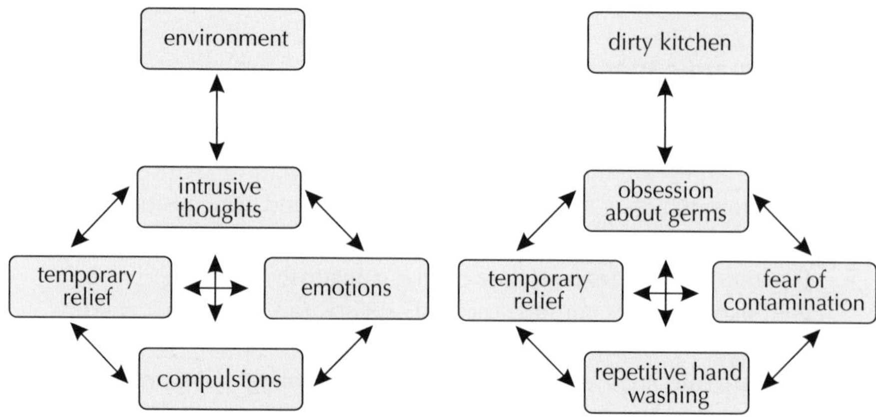

Figure 5: *The cognitive behavioural model illustrates the obsession-compulsion cycle.*

There is a link between depression and OCD. This supports Rachman and Hodgson's idea that feeling stressed or depressed may make people more vulnerable to OCD.

Salkovskis and Kirk (1997) asked OCD sufferers to try to suppress their obsessional thoughts on some days and allow them to surface on others. They reported more distressing thoughts on the days they were deliberately trying to suppress them compared to the other days. However, the cognitive-behavioural explanation describes the difficulty OCD sufferers have in suppressing unwanted thoughts but it doesn't really explain why they have this difficulty. It is also reductionist, claiming that behaviours come purely from faulty cognitions and simplifying complex disorders to faulty processes.

Tip: The diathesis-stress model tries to account for the fact that there is evidence in support of both the biological and psychological explanations for OCD.

The diathesis-stress model

The diathesis-stress model (Figure 6) combines both biological and psychological factors. It suggests that people who are biologically vulnerable to developing a mental disorder may be more likely to develop it if they are subjected to certain social or environmental stressors.

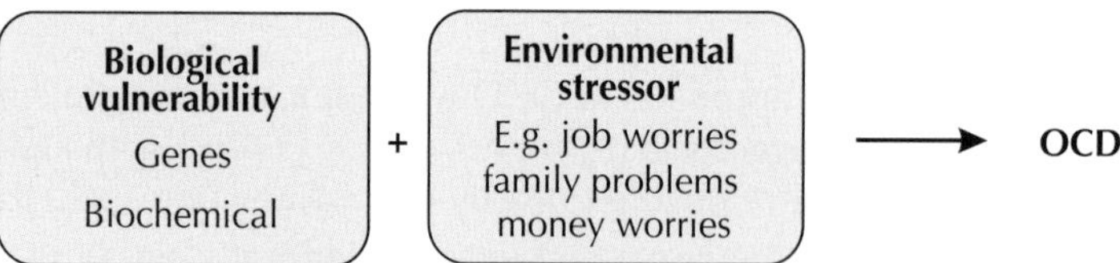

Figure 6: *The diathesis-stress model.*

Lots of research has been conducted in this area. The fact that concordance rates in twin studies (see page 144) aren't 100% indicates that there does seem to be some genetic link, but that the environment must play a role as well. Kleiner and Marshall (1987) investigated patients who had been diagnosed with an anxiety disorder. They found that over 80% of them had been through family problems before developing signs of their own anxiety disorder. Ristvedt et al (1993) also found a significant relationship between those who had undergone elements of emotional stress before they had developed OCD.

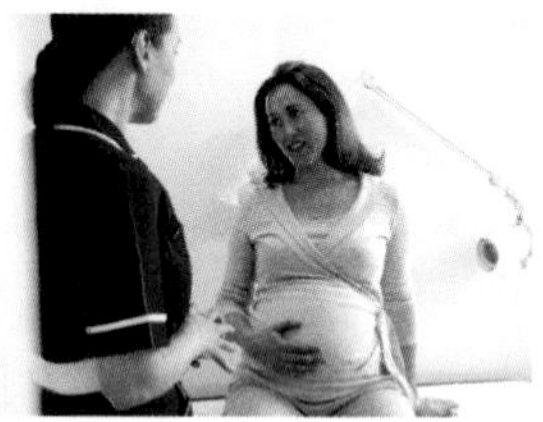

Figure 7: *Stressful life events, such as having a baby, can lead to disorders such as OCD according to the diathesis-stress model.*

However, lots of people experience traumatic events within their lives and yet they don't develop anxiety disorders such as OCD. This must mean there are other factors involved.

Worked Exam-style Question

0 1 Outline and evaluate **one** psychological explanation of obsessive-compulsive disorder. *(8 marks + 8 marks)*

There are several psychological explanations of obsessive-compulsive disorder (OCD). These include behavioural, psychodynamic and cognitive explanations and whilst each have evidence for and against them, it appears that not one of them can fully explain the onset of this disorder.

The behavioural theory of OCD uses classical and operant conditioning as a means of explaining how certain symptoms of the disorder are maintained. People with OCD show two main symptoms — obsessions and compulsions. The behavioural approach suggests that compulsions are reinforced by a series of behaviours. For instance, a person may react in a particular way by accident if they are feeling anxious. When anxiety goes away, they unconsciously learn to associate the behaviour with the removal of the anxiety. It becomes a reflex response by means of classical conditioning. As the individual has learnt that it removes anxiety, they repeat the behaviour next time they feel anxious, by means of operant conditioning.

For example, someone may have forgotten to turn off an electrical appliance. Their anxiety would be diminished if they checked to see if it was turned off. To avoid feeling anxious in the future, they may repeatedly check to see that it has been switched off. When this checking behaviour becomes excessive, it has developed into a compulsion, and therefore may lead to the development of OCD. Support for the behavioural theory of OCD has been found in several studies. Baxter et al (1992) and Schwartz et al (1996) both reported success in the reduction of symptoms of those who underwent behavioural therapy.

However, there is also evidence against the theory. The behavioural explanation focuses on explaining the compulsive part of the disorder, ignoring the obsessions. It is reductionist, simplifying behaviour to a simplistic set of responses. The behavioural approach also doesn't explain why compulsions might start in the first place. There has also been much support for other theories used to explain OCD, particularly biological explanations. Family and twin studies have found some genetic links in developing OCD. However, since the results can't fully explain OCD, we might propose instead that a combination of both biological and psychological factors might best explain the cause and development of anxiety disorders such as OCD.

Exam Tip
This question is asking you to outline and evaluate. Those are two key words which should immediately make you want to write something that will first describe, and then weigh up positives and negatives.

Exam Tip
Don't worry if you can't remember the exact dates of the studies — just try to remember what they involved and what conclusions were drawn from them.

Summary Questions

Q1 a) Name three biological factors that have been used to explain obsessive-compulsive disorder (OCD).

b) Which neurotransmitter is considered to play a role in the biochemical explanation of OCD?

Q2 Which behaviour in children did Freud believe might later lead to obsessions and compulsions?

Q3 Give an example of a faulty cognition that someone with OCD might hold.

Learning Objectives:

- Know about the biological therapies for obsessive-compulsive disorder, including their evaluation in terms of appropriateness and effectiveness.
- Know about the psychological therapies for obsessive-compulsive disorder, for example, behavioural, psychodynamic and cognitive-behavioural, including their evaluation in terms of appropriateness and effectiveness.

Tip: Therapy using drugs is also called chemotherapy.

Tip: A randomised, double blind study is one in which participants are randomly put into groups without either them, or the experimenter, being aware of which experimental group they're in.

Tip: Placebos are just pills that do nothing at all. They're used to test if any effect happens just because people think they're being treated.

13. Treating OCD

OCD has many different treatments... probably because it has many different explanations. Whilst some produce better results that others, it seems that it depends on the individual and what works best for them.

Biological therapy

Drug treatments

The biological approach to treating OCD involves drug therapy. Drug treatments usually work by increasing levels of serotonin in the brain using selective serotonin reuptake inhibitors (SSRIs). These are a type of antidepressant drug that increase the availability of serotonin. SSRIs prevent the reuptake of serotonin in the gap between two neurons. This allows the nervous system to get more benefit from the serotonin as it passes across.

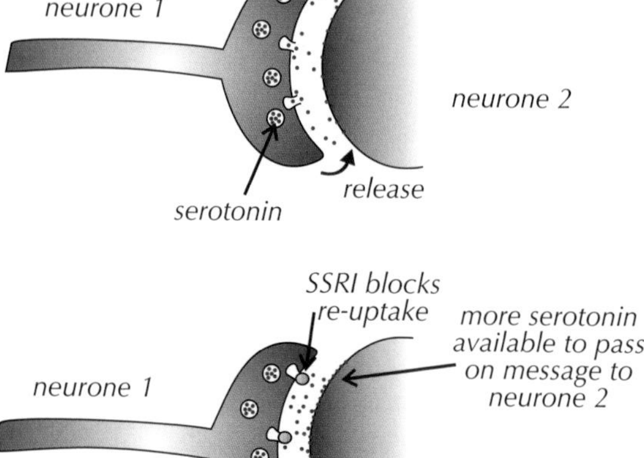

Figure 1: *SSRIs increase serotonin levels in the brain.*

Advantages

Several researchers have found SSRIs to be effective in treating OCD. Thoren et al (1980) found that use of an SSRI was significantly better at reducing obsessional thoughts than a placebo. Research has found that using other antidepressants that don't affect serotonin levels is ineffective at reducing OCD symptoms.

Key study of using biological therapies to treat OCD — Piccinelli et al (1995)

Method:	Piccinelli et al (1995) carried out a meta-analysis, gathering data from all randomised, double-blind studies between 1975 and 1994 that compared the use of drug therapies and placebos as treatment for OCD.
Results:	Drug therapies were significantly more successful at reducing the symptoms of those with OCD in comparison to patients who took a placebo drug.
Conclusion:	Drug therapies are useful in reducing the symptoms of OCD.

Disadvantages

Up to 50% of patients with OCD don't experience any improvement in their symptoms when taking SSRIs. Out of those that do improve, up to 90% have a relapse when they stop taking them. SSRIs have to be taken for several weeks before the patient experiences an improvement in their symptoms.

Side effects of using these types of drugs include nausea and headaches, and sometimes increased levels of anxiety. This can cause people to stop taking their medication.

Psychosurgery

The use of psychosurgery as a treatment for OCD is only really a last resort as it has a controversial past. Before the development of antipsychotic drugs, the 1930s saw lots of research into prefrontal lobotomies and other psychosurgical techniques. Nowadays, an **anterior cingulotomy** can be performed on cases of OCD where drug and other psychological therapies have failed. This involves cutting a lesion in the cingulate gyrus, part of the brain which connects the limbic system with the frontal lobe. Whereas drug treatments take a while to work, psychosurgery offers immediate relief. However, this has only been found to be effective in some cases and it can produce severe side effects such as seizures and, therefore, other treatments are preferable.

In a longitudinal study, Hay et al (1993) looked at over 20 cases of people with OCD who had received psychosurgery as a last resort treatment. They found a significant reduction in the severity of symptoms in 38% of patients. However, Cumming et al (1995) also conducted follow-up research, measuring the symptoms of a set of patients who had undergone psychosurgery. Whilst their symptoms did improve, their performance on tasks which involved problem solving had declined — these patients produced poorer results than a group of matched controls (a group of OCD sufferers who didn't undergo psychosurgery). Therefore, whilst psychosurgery has a place, it should only be used as a last resort treatment.

Real World Connection
There are only two places in the UK that conduct psychosurgery for those with OCD — one is in Wales and the other is in Scotland. Having only two centres goes to show how little it is used as a treatment approach.

Tip: Longitudinal studies are those that follow individuals over a long period of time. They are good because they eliminate any individual variables, such as age, intelligence and social background, which can vary amongst people and influence the results. However, they are often time and cost intensive. The alternative method is a cross-sectional design which uses different participants of different ages who are studied at the same time.

Psychological therapies

Cognitive behavioural therapies

Cognitive behavioural therapy (CBT) can be used as a psychological treatment for OCD. CBT challenges the obsessions by making the person test or question the accuracy of some of their unwanted thoughts.

Example
If a person believes they have to check that their front door is locked 10 times, they could be encouraged to test this by only checking the door once and then going out. When they see that they haven't been burgled, and that the door is still locked, they may question their behaviour.

CBT also uses thought stopping, which means shouting "Stop!" when the patient indicates that they are having the obsessional thoughts or impulses. They then refocus their mind on a more appropriate thought. The idea is that over time the patient will be able to do this by themselves without support. By giving the sufferer information to challenge their obsessions, CBT can help prevent the compulsions.

Figure 2: *CBT can help those with OCD to limit their compulsive behaviours, such as repeatedly checking the front door is locked.*

Advantages

CBT can be used to treat both the obsessions and the compulsions. Franklin et al (2002) found that CBT can be combined with exposure and response prevention (see page 200) to create a treatment that's more effective than either on its own. The patient is more active if they use CBT than if they use drugs. Encouraging people to be active in their treatment might be a more positive way to treat patients.

Disadvantages

CBT can be very challenging for patients — they have to be willing to cope with the increased anxiety that is caused by the treatment. This might be too distressing for some and so drug treatments might be a better option for these patients.

Figure 3: ERP homework tasks might include shaking one person's hand a day without the OCD sufferer feeling they then have to go and wash their hands.

Tip: ERP sessions usually last approximately 90 minutes and patients tend to have around 15-20 sessions.

Real World Connection
Patients with OCD can also be treated with systematic desensitisation. This works by using counter-conditioning so that the person learns to associate a stimulus, such as a dirty kitchen, with relaxation rather than fear. Patients rank feared situations, from the least stressful to the most stressful. The patient then imagines each anxiety-provoking situation, starting with the least stressful. At the same time, they're taught how to use relaxation techniques such as deep breathing. This is repeated until the feared event is only linked with relaxation, and the process is carried out for each feared situation.

Behavioural therapies

Exposure and response prevention (ERP) is commonly used as a behavioural treatment for OCD. Here's how it could go:

With support from a therapist the OCD patient identifies some situations that cause them anxiety. They then rank these situations in order of the anxiety they produce. For example, if the OCD is to do with germs the patient's list might include touching a doorknob, using a communal toilet and shaking hands. The patient is then exposed to the first situation and encouraged not to use the compulsions they usually use in this situation (e.g. using elbows to operate a door handle). Although this causes an increase in anxiety, after a time the anxiety drops as it can't stay high for long periods of time. At the same time the patient is taught to use relaxation techniques, is reassured and is encouraged to take part in different behaviours. Once this is successful they then move on to the next exposure task that they listed.

<u>Advantages</u>

It's been found in studies that ERP was effective in treating around 75% of patients with OCD. For people with mild OCD it's possible to use ERP without a therapist as a self-help technique. Behavioural therapies only take around 3 to 8 weeks.

Key study of using psychological therapies to treat OCD — McLean et al (2001)

Method: McLean et al (2001) compared three groups of over 70 patients with OCD. Group One underwent cognitive behavioural therapy (CBT), Group Two received exposure and response prevention (ERP) therapy, whilst Group Three acted as a control group.

Results: Both CBT and ERP led to a significant reduction in symptoms compared to the control group at the end of the treatment period. However, after three months, Group Two maintained fewer symptoms, although both treatment condition groups were still significantly better than the control group.

Conclusion: CBT and ERP are successful in reducing OCD symptoms. However, ERP appears to be marginally more successful at maintaining treatment in the long term.

Evaluation: There are ethical issues since the groups receive different types of treatment. This could mean that people might be denied a treatment which may be effective for them.

<u>Disadvantages</u>

Behavioural treatment is much less successful in patients whose symptoms are primarily obsessions. The distress caused by resisting compulsions can cause patients to drop out of therapy. It also requires a lot of commitment from the patients — they are expected to complete homework tasks in between each session which can deter some people from completing the therapy.

Psychotherapy

Psychotherapy aims to identify the underlying cause of the mental disorder. This is done using different therapeutic techniques, e.g. dream analysis and free association. When the unconscious conflicts that are causing the problems are made conscious, the therapist and patient can discuss and try to resolve them. This will hopefully lead to the disorder being cured.

Advantages

It aims to understand the underlying cause of the disorder, rather than just focusing on the symptoms.

Disadvantages

Psychotherapy ignores the biological cause of OCD. There's no controlled study that supports the effectiveness of psychoanalysis in the treatment of OCD. Other treatments such as the use of drugs or ERP have much higher success rates.

Figure 4: *Freud was the founder of psychoanalysis.*

Worked Exam-style Question

0 1 Outline **one** biological treatment of OCD.

(4 marks)

Drug treatments are used as a biological treatment for those with obsessive-compulsive disorder (OCD). PET scans have found lower levels of the neurotransmitter serotonin in OCD sufferers. So, drug treatments usually involve using selective serotonin reuptake inhibitors to increase the level of serotonin in the brain. These are a type of antidepressant that prevent the reuptake of serotonin in the gap between two neurones, therefore increasing its availability in the brain and allowing the nervous system to get more benefit from it. This acts to reduce the symptoms of OCD.

Exam Tip

The question only asks you to outline a biological treatment so you don't need to waste your time talking about any studies to support your answer.

Summary Questions

Q1 What is a double-blind study?

Q2 a) Outline how CBT aims to treat OCD.

b) Give one advantage of CBT.

c) Give one disadvantage of CBT.

Q3 a) What does ERP stand for?

b) Describe what happens in ERP.

Q4 How does psychotherapy attempt to treat OCD?

Section Summary

- Clinical psychology is all about diagnosing and treating mental health disorders. Clinical psychologists use interviews, observations and psychological tests to assess patients.
- Twin studies, family studies, adoption studies and animal studies are all used as research methods in clinical psychology.
- Four disorders in psychopathology are schizophrenia, depression, phobic disorders and obsessive-compulsive disorder. They each have different clinical characteristics and symptoms.
- The DSM-IV is the main diagnostic tool used by psychiatrists to diagnose people with these mental health disorders. But, there are problems with validity and reliability when using the DSM-IV.
- There are several explanations for each mental health disorder. Biological explanations include genetic factors, biochemical factors and neurological factors. Psychological explanations for mental health problems include behavioural factors, psychodynamic factors, socio-cultural factors and cognitive factors.
- The diathesis-stress model suggests that psychopathology can be explained by a combined approach which involves a biological vulnerability being triggered by psychological stressors.
- The biological, psychological and behavioural explanations all have strengths and weaknesses. It seems that no single explanation can fully explain the mental health disorders.
- Therapies to treat mental health disorders are also varied. Biological treatments involve drug treatments which affect various neurotransmitters, or the more invasive techniques of ECT and psychosurgery as a last resort. Psychological therapies involve behavioural therapy, cognitive behavioural therapy, psychotherapy and social skills training.
- Each of these therapies have advantages and disadvantages, and most research concludes that there isn't one therapy which 'cures' any mental health problem. Patients often have a combined treatment plan.

Exam-style Questions

0 1 Outline the clinical characteristics of **one** mental health disorder.

(4 marks)

0 2 Outline **one** psychological therapy used to treat this disorder.

(4 marks)

0 3 Evaluate biological explanations for this disorder.

(16 marks)

---

0 4 Discuss the issues surrounding the classification and diagnosis of **one** mental health disorder.

(24 marks)

---

0 5 Discuss how psychological explanations are involved in explaining and treating a mental health disorder of your choice.

(24 marks)

1. The Influence of Media on Social Behaviour

Many young people today spend a lot of time in front of the TV or on computer games and this has led people to suggest that it's having negative effects by increasing violent behaviour. But the opposite may also be true...

Learning Objectives:
- Know the explanations of media influences on pro- and anti-social behaviour.
- Know about the positive and negative effects of computers and video games on behaviour.

The role of the media

Social learning theory (SLT)

SLT suggests that we model our behaviour on behaviour that we observe — whether it's anti-social or pro-social behaviour. There's much debate about whether the media influences our behaviour in this way. A central point to this debate is the effect of observing violence in TV programmes and video games — particularly on children's behaviour. Bandura's Bobo Doll experiments (1961) showed that children who'd watched an adult behaving aggressively towards a doll were more likely to behave aggressively than those who hadn't seen the aggressive behaviour. If the observed behaviour has a positive outcome we are more likely to copy it than if the outcome is negative.

Exam Tip
You only need to answer questions about one contemporary application of psychology. So choose media psychology, the psychology of addictive behaviour or anomalistic psychology and learn everything you need to know about that one.

Key study of behaviour imitation — Bandura (1961)

Method:	36 boys and 36 girls (average age 4 years) were put into two groups. Group 1 watched an adult playing aggressively with an inflatable 'Bobo Doll'. Group 2 witnessed only non-violent play in the adult model. Children were then given a choice of violent and non-violent toys to play with, including the Bobo Doll, and were observed by an unseen researcher.
Results:	The children who witnessed the aggressive behaviour were found to be more likely to behave aggressively in their own play than children who were exposed to a non-violent adult model. Boys were also found to be more aggressive than girls.
Conclusion:	Children learn aggressive behaviour through imitation of others.
Evaluation:	The study doesn't show whether the effects are long-term, and it also lacks ecological validity as it's not a real-life situation. There are also ethical issues surrounding the study as it encouraged violence.

Figure 1: Playing video games may influence a child's behaviour.

Tip: Take a look at the tip on page 53 to see what a Bobo Doll looks like.

Social learning theory also claims that if the model is high status or admired they are more influential.

Social cognitive observation learning theory (SCOLT)

SCOLT expands on SLT by suggesting that children do more than just learn behaviours — they also learn how to think about the world. SCOLT suggests that there are three cognitive structures children develop which influence

Tip: Both SLT and SCOLT are reductionist theories. They explain things through very basic mechanisms. For example, they explain all behaviour as a result of learning from others and ignore any biological explanations.

behaviour. These can be applied to explain the relationship between TV and violent behaviour:

- **Schemas** — Structured mental frameworks containing knowledge about the world. By watching violent TV children may create a schema that says that the world is full of violence.
- **Scripts** — Schemas of particular situations, containing knowledge about expected sequences of behaviour. By watching violent TV children develop scripts that contain aggressive speech and actions.
- **Normative beliefs** — Beliefs and ideas that people have about what is considered appropriate behaviour in their culture. By watching violent TV children start to think of aggressive and violent behaviour as acceptable and 'normal'.

Example

Gerbner et al (1994) reported that children who watched a lot of violent TV were more likely to see other people's behaviour as aggressive.

Real World Connection
Cultural factors may influence how children learn about the world around them.
For example, a community in the !Kung San desert who live without media influences such as TV and video games shows very little aggression. When children do act aggressively towards each other, parents distract them and physically separate them, so the behaviour is not encouraged in any way. This suggests that social learning theory might not apply here.

The influence of violent media

Aggressive behaviour falls outside the social norm — it's considered to be anti-social. Knowing this and still displaying aggressive behaviour can cause someone to feel psychologically uncomfortable. Justification theory suggests violent media can be used to reduce this psychological discomfort. If someone watches violent programmes or plays violent video games, they will become used to seeing aggressive behaviour — they may begin to think that it's normal and acceptable. This helps them justify their own anti-social behaviour and feel less guilty about it. This justification of their anti-social behaviour means that they're more likely to behave that way again.

The effect of television

Lots of studies have examined the link between violence on TV and aggression.

Key study of the effect of television on aggression — Huesmann et al (2003)

Method:	Huesmann et al (2003) conducted a series of natural and longitudinal studies which looked at the relationship between children's television habits when they were younger and their behaviour as adults. They asked over 500 children, who were from 6 to 10 years old, to name their favourite TV shows and characters. After 15 years, almost 400 of the same individuals were asked again to name their favourite TV programmes. Their close friends were also asked to describe the participants' behaviour, and criminal records were later obtained for each participant.
Results:	The results showed a relationship between exposure to TV violence at a young age and the number of criminal convictions in adulthood.
Conclusion:	TV violence is linked to the development of anti-social behaviour and aggression.
Evaluation:	Since this piece of research used a longitudinal method and was only correlational work, there are no ethical issues. However, using a longitudinal method takes a long time, and having a large drop-out rate means the results aren't truly representative of the sample being examined.

Tip: A natural experiment, such as Huesmann et al's (2003) research, doesn't involve the manipulation of any variables — it makes use of a situation which already exists and therefore is a lot more ecologically valid.

Additional study of the effect of television on aggression — Paik and Comstock (1991)

Paik and Comstock (1991) conducted a meta-analysis that summarised the findings of over a thousand studies examining the link between TV violence and aggressive behaviour. The results suggested a strong link between exposure to violent programmes and aggressive behaviour.

Figure 2: *Watching TV can be a huge influence on a child's development.*

The results of these studies show a correlation between exposure to violent TV programmes and aggressive behaviour, but they don't show cause and effect. This means we can't say for sure that watching violence on TV causes aggressive behaviour — it could be that aggressive children are more likely to watch violent programmes. Charlton et al (2000) managed to provide results which supported this case:

Additional study of the effect of television on aggression — Charlton et al (2000)

Charlton et al (2000) studied a population from St Helena in the South Atlantic that hadn't had any influence from TV. Just before TV was introduced, the aggressive actions of children between the ages of 3 and 8 were measured. Five years later, after several years of TV influence, the researchers monitored the same children's behaviour once more.
They found that there was no increase in aggressive behaviours, suggesting that television doesn't have an effect on antisocial behaviour.

Tip: Teachers were used in Charlton et al's research to provide ratings of the children's behaviour. These ratings could be highly subjective and biased.

There have also been studies examining the effect that observing pro-social behaviour on TV has on behaviour.

Key study of the effect of television on pro-social behaviour — Sprafkin et al (1975)

Method: Sprafkin et al (1975) showed 3 groups of children different TV programmes. Group 1 watched a programme where a boy saves a puppy. Group 2 watched a similar programme but with no helping behaviour. Group 3 watched a programme with no interaction between animals and humans. The children could hear the sounds of some distressed puppies and were placed in front of two buttons. They were told that each time they pressed one button they would be given points — the more points they got the bigger the prize they would be given. Pressing the other button wouldn't give them any points but it would alert someone to help the puppies.

Results: Group 1 children were the most likely to spend their time calling for help rather than collecting points.

Conclusion: Pro-social behaviour can be influenced by television.

Evaluation: Since the children were asked to watch a real television programme, the study is valid and more representative of real life than if a specifically designed programme was used.

Real World Connection

In real life, people tend to talk about what they've seen on television. This may affect how much they are influenced by what they've just watched. Fogel (2007) split up a group of 8-12 year olds into two conditions. Group One watched one episode of a TV show with a pro-social message. Group Two watched the same TV show but this was then followed by a 15 minute talk about the show with their parents. The results showed that Group Two were more likely to act in a pro-social way than Group One, following their viewing and discussion.

Many studies don't measure whether pro-social behaviour is a long-term or short-term effect of exposure to such programmes. Sagotsky et al (1981) found that 6 and 8 year olds modelled cooperative behaviour immediately after they witnessed it. However, 7 weeks later, only the older children were still showing the behavioural effects.

Real World Connection
Video games and computers don't always create negative behaviours — Gee (2003) believed that they can be really useful in empowering people and giving them skills to use in life.

The effect of video games and computers

The popularity of video games has stimulated new research into the influence that media has on behaviour. Like other media (e.g. films), games receive age ratings depending on their content. Ratings are determined by things like violence, sexual themes, drug use, criminal behaviour or bad language. It's thought that games may have greater potential to influence behaviour than other types of media due to their interactive nature. Some people believe that violent video games can be held directly responsible for influencing some specific crimes.

Example
The use of violent video games by the Columbine High School shooters has been cited by some people as a reason for the 1999 massacre that killed 13 people and injured 24 others. The families of some of the victims took legal action against the companies that produced them but were unsuccessful.

Tip: The General Aggression Model is used to explain why people might be aggressive following violent video games and TV shows:

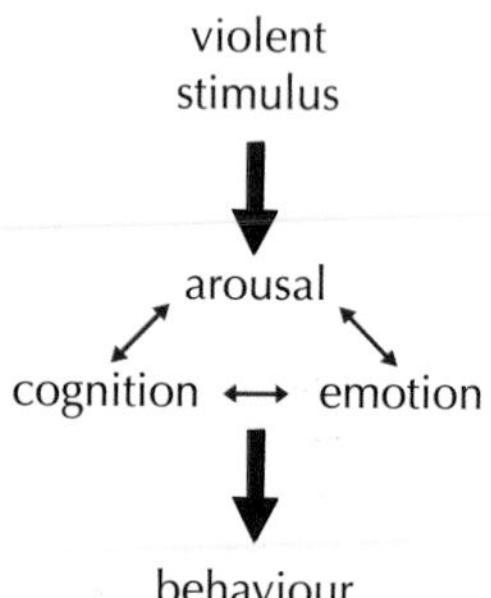

The model states that a violent stimulus, such as watching a violent crime, leads to emotional, physiological (arousal) and cognitive processes (e.g. feeling distress and panic). This then leads to a behavioural response, which could be an aggressive action.

However, many people don't believe that video games can be blamed for crimes. They point out that most people who use the games don't go on to imitate the violent behaviour that they see in them. Greitemeyer and Osswald (2010) found that playing games with a pro-social theme (e.g. saving a city or fighting crime) leads to an increase in pro-social behaviours. Other research has found that playing action video games can help improve speed, accuracy and even the ability to see contrast.

A meta-analysis of early research by Anderson and Bushman (2001) suggests that playing violent video games does increase aggression and decrease pro-social behaviour in young people. Studies have been carried out on the effect that violent video games have on the emotions of people playing them.

Tip: The tendency to expect others to react aggressively during social conflict is sometimes referred to as the 'hostile expectancy bias'.

Key study of video games and emotion — Anderson and Bushman (2002)

Method:	This study was a lab experiment involving 224 participants in two independent groups. Participants played either a violent or non-violent video game and were then asked to 'finish off' three stories from a variety of 'story stems', e.g. one started with a minor car accident. Each participant was asked to describe what the main character would do, say and feel.
Results:	Participants who had played the violent game described the main character as being more aggressive than those who'd played the non-violent game, e.g. shouting at, starting a fight with or stabbing the other driver.
Conclusion:	Playing video games produces aggressive thoughts and emotions in players.
Evaluation:	Low ecological validity may have led the participants to give responses which didn't reflect the way they would

react in real life. Participants might have shown demand characteristics (see page 252) due to their recent exposure to violent scenarios. This was a lab study so there was good control of variables and the results are therefore reliable.

There have been many other research studies investigating the relationship between video game violence and behaviour.

Additional studies of video games and emotion

Carnagey et al (2007) asked participants to play a violent video game for 20 minutes. Following this, the participants, along with a group of controls who had played a non-violent game instead of a violent game, watched a short video showing scenes of real-life violence. The participants and controls then had their heart rate and galvanic skin response recorded. They found that those who had played the violent game had much lower heart rates and skin responses than the control group, suggesting that they had become desensitised to violence.

There are contrasting studies which have shown positive effects of video games. Kestenbaum and Weinstein (1985) found that a group of 208 11-14 year olds were calmer after they had participated in violent video games.

Tip: Galvanic skin response (GSR) measures the electrical conductivity of the skin, which is affected by sweat. More sweat is interpreted as a sign of stress and anxiety.

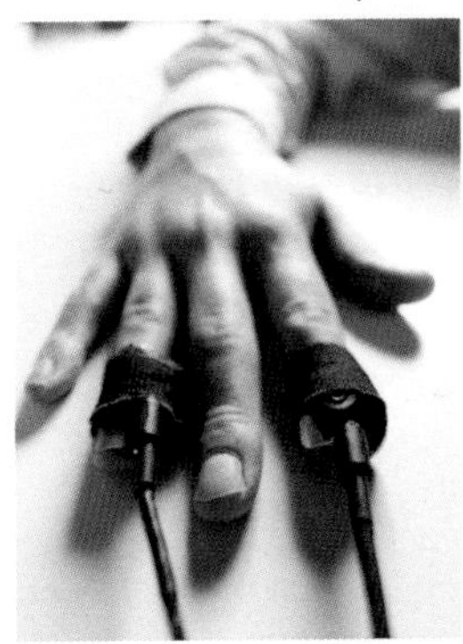

Figure 3: *GSR measures sweat from fingertips.*

Worked Exam-style Questions

0 1 Outline explanations of media influences on anti-social behaviour. *(8 marks)*

There has been lots of research into how much the media influences anti-social behaviour. Two explanations of the media's influence on behaviour are the social learning theory (SLT) and the social cognitive observational learning theory (SCOLT).

SLT suggests that we model our behaviour on others. Bandura (1961) showed in his famous Bobo Doll experiment that after children had seen someone acting aggressively towards a doll, they were then more likely to act aggressively in their own play than those who hadn't seen such behaviour to imitate. Social learning theory also suggests that if the observed behaviour has a positive outcome, we are more likely to copy it than if it has a negative outcome. It's also thought that high status or admired models have more influence.

Another explanation is the social cognitive observational learning theory (SCOLT). SCOLT expands on SLT and suggests that children don't just learn behaviours from viewing others, but they also learn how to think about the world. It suggests that there are three main cognitive structures which influence a child's development within the world. These are schemas, scripts and normative beliefs. In terms of anti-social behaviour, through watching violent TV, schemas will cause a child to believe that the whole world is a violent place. Scripts could cause children to start speaking or acting in an aggressive way after watching violent TV, and normative beliefs could cause children who watch aggressive things on TV to think of this behaviour as 'the norm'.

Tip: Physiological measures, such as heart rate and galvanic skin response tests, provide scientific support for theories.

Exam Tip
This question is worth 8 marks but since Psychology in Action questions are worth 24 marks each, this question would form part of other questions which would total 24 marks.

Exam Tip
This question is only asking you to outline the explanations so don't waste time by evaluating anything you write about. This is just about recalling facts and descriptive details.

Exam Tip
Finish off your answer with a short summary sentence that links back to the question.

■ *These explanations of why anti-social behaviour might come about are supported by various studies.*

---

0 2 Discuss the positive and negative effects of computers and video games on behaviour. *(10 marks)*

Exam Tip
A brief introduction tells the examiner that you've thought about what you're going to say.

■*Many studies have looked at the association between video games and subsequent behaviour, particularly in young people. A lot of people think that video games only produce negative effects, such as making people more aggressive. However, there has been research which has illustrated the positive effects of this type of media, such as pro-social behaviour.*

Pro-social video games have been investigated by Greitemeyer and Osswald (2010). They found that if the video game has a positive, pro-social theme, those that played it were then more likely to show pro-social behaviours. Likewise, research has shown that there are other benefits to playing video and computer games. Certain games can increase speed, accuracy and the ability to see contrast. Similarly, it might not even have to be a pro-social game that influences positive behaviour. ■Kestenbaum and Weinstein (1985) produced results which showed their 11-14 year old participants were calmer after playing a violent computer game.

Exam Tip
A lot of the studies on this topic contradict each other — this means that there's lots of evidence that you could use to support either side of the argument.

However, there is a lot of research which supports the opposite idea that video and computer games can lead to negative behaviour. For instance, Anderson and Bushman (2001) conducted a meta-analysis which showed that there was a positive correlation between violent ■video game playing and aggressive behaviour. Anderson and Bushman (2002) then went on to conduct their own experiment which found that participants who initially played an aggressive video game were more likely to have aggressive emotions and thoughts than a set of control participants who played a neutral video game. However, this was a laboratory experiment and lacks ecological validity since people were asked to complete a task not normally asked of them in real life. Whilst the results are reliable since the variables could be controlled, the participants' behaviour might have been influenced by being in a laboratory setting, or by demand characteristics.

Exam Tip
Don't forget that a positive correlation means that both variables increase together — in this case, as violent video game playing increases, so does aggressive behaviour.

Overall, these studies describing the influences of computers and video games on behaviour suggest that the effect is quite complex.

Summary Questions

Q1 What did Bandura conclude from his 1961 study?

Q2 a) Define 'schema'.
b) Define 'script'.

Q3 Describe the method Huesmann et al (2003) used in their study of the effect of television on aggression.

Q4 Draw a diagram outlining the components that make up the General Aggression Model.

Q5 Name a physiological response that can be measured as a way of detecting arousal levels.

2. Persuasion and Attitude Change

Attitudes are just our views on things, and they can shape how we behave. The media has all sorts of tricks for persuading us to change our attitudes, and therefore our behaviour. Pretty cheeky really.

Persuasion

Our attitudes are our feelings towards something — they can be positive or negative views. Persuasion is changing an attitude, usually using messages about the object, person or concept in question.

The Hovland-Yale model

Carl Hovland researched effective persuasion techniques at Yale University. Hovland argued that a person's change in attitude was a sequential process:

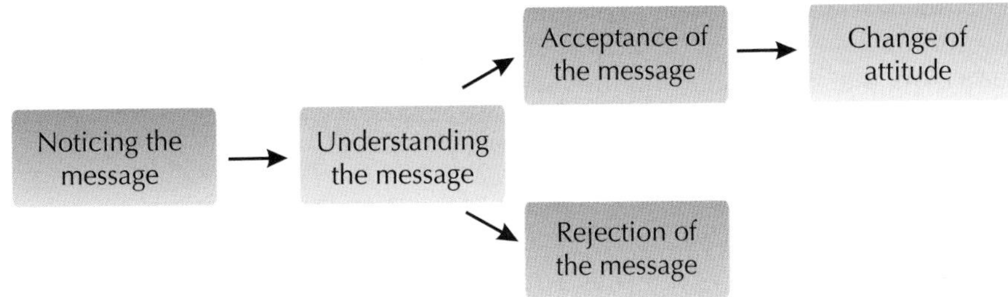

Figure 1: *The Hovland-Yale model.*

Hovland wanted to find out what factors affect the likelihood that a change in attitude will take place. To do this, his team took an experimental approach to studying persuasion, systematically changing one variable at a time. The results of his research became known as the **Hovland-Yale model** (1953) and identified four important components of persuasion:

- The source of the message — e.g. the trustworthiness, expertise and attractiveness of the persuader.
- The message content — e.g. the number, strength, order and emotional appeal of the arguments.
- The recipient — e.g. the age, IQ and personality traits of the person being persuaded.
- The situation — e.g. whether given formally or informally, and whether the message is relevant.

The Hovland-Yale model suggests the key factors involved in creating a change in attitude but doesn't address why these factors are important. The Hovland-Yale model assumes that we always carry out a very careful thought process. More recently, other psychologists have found evidence to suggest that we don't always carry out such a thorough process.

The Elaboration Likelihood model

Petty and Cacioppo (1986) agreed with Hovland that if you try and persuade someone about something, they consider the argument. However, they believed that people don't always consider all of the information available, such as the credibility of the source, as this takes up too much cognitive effort. Petty and Cacioppo (1986) reckoned that a persuasion message can take effect through two processing routes:

Learning Objectives:

- Understand the application of Hovland-Yale and Elaboration Likelihood models in explaining the persuasive effects of media.
- Know explanations for the persuasiveness of television advertising.

Figure 2: *Models who are thought to be attractive can be more persuasive.*

Tip: Critics have argued that it's unclear whether each of Hovland's components of persuasion have equal weightings or if one is more important than the others.

Tip: Hovland based his research on self-report methods. This could mean that his results aren't reliable because people aren't always accurate when they're talking about their own actions and behaviours.

Tip: By suggesting two processing routes, this model improves on the Hovland-Yale model's problem of assuming we always consider everything very carefully.

- The Peripheral Route — low-level mechanisms such as conditioning, use of quick decision-making rules (e.g. 'experts are always right') and attractiveness of the message determine our attitudes. The peripheral route doesn't involve much analysis of the merits of the message itself.
- The Central Route — high-level mechanisms, such as evaluation of the source and content of the message, determine our attitudes. Persuasion via the central route occurs when someone has the time, motivation and ability to analyse the message. When this happens, the likelihood that they'll elaborate on the information that they have increases.

This is known as the Elaboration Likelihood model (ELM). The elaboration-likelihood model is comprehensive and can explain particular experimental findings, but it can't be used to predict them beforehand — it lacks the predictive power which a useful model should have.

Exam Tip
This part of psychology is really applicable to real life. You could pick up loads of AO2 marks in the exam by giving real world examples of how the media tries to persuade the public.

The media's persuasive effect

Both the Hovland-Yale model and the ELM model attempt to explain the process that can lead us to change our attitude about something. It's something that advertisers and the media are pretty keen to understand (for obvious reasons).

Television is used by advertisers, political parties and health organisations to persuade their audience. TV is a really popular way of delivering a persuasion message because of the double whammy of audio and visual information which is delivered, and the potentially huge audience. Different techniques based on models of persuasion are used to make TV persuasion as effective as possible. Here are a few to think about:

Pleasant associations

Products being sold are often teamed with things the audience will automatically feel positive about, such as humour, success and sex. Through classical conditioning, the product may become associated with these things — the audience may be persuaded through the peripheral route that they need to buy it.

Making the message bizarre

Many TV adverts are 'off the wall' and totally unconnected to the product they're advertising. This encourages deep processing of the persuasion message and accesses the central route of persuasion.

Figure 3: *Random pictures, such as yoga bunnies, can actually be useful — they make you process information more deeply.*

Using familiar figures

Celebrities are often used to advertise products and they're usually matched up to the product they're selling. People delivering the message don't actually need to be famous — just recognisable figures.

Examples
- Models advertising beauty products.
- A man in a white coat spouting long words will give an image of scientific credibility.

In this way, advertisers can tap into the peripheral or central route of persuasion by activating mental associations with the personalities used, or increasing motivation to process the message more deeply.

Fear

Adverts often tap into the emotion of fear.

Example

NHS anti-smoking adverts have shown children breathing out cigarette smoke to emphasise the dangers of passive smoking.

Researchers like Meyerowitz and Chaiken (1987) have found that adverts like these, which arouse fear in the viewer, can act as a peripheral cue for persuasion. However, according to Witte et al (1998), if a message creates too much fear, there is a point at which the audience will just switch off.

Figure 4: *Statements can be used on packaging to induce fear and change people's beliefs.*

Repetition

Most adverts are repeated more than once. One reason for this is that peripheral emotional cues (e.g. the Andrex puppy) only last as long as they are memorable — repetition makes them more memorable and eventually automatic. Repeating a message enough also leads to familiarity with it. Researchers have found that, more often than not, familiarity leads to trust and persuasion.

Real World Connection

Zajonc (1968) called the effect of repetition the 'mere exposure effect'. It was found that people grew to like certain words and objects the more they came into contact with them — this could explain why we tend to like songs more once we've heard them several times on the radio.

Worked Exam-style Question

0 1 Outline and evaluate how the Elaboration Likelihood model might explain the persuasive effects of the media.

(8 marks)

In their Elaboration Likelihood model, Petty and Cacioppo (1986) expanded on Hovland's (1953) Hovland-Yale model by suggesting that people don't always think about all the information they're presented with. Instead they are persuaded by media messages through two routes. These two routes are the peripheral route and the central route.

The peripheral route involves low-level mechanisms like conditioning and quick decision-making rules, along with how attractive the message seems. There is not much analysis of the merits of the message itself. The central route involves a lot more evaluation of the source and content of a message. This route is used when we have more time, motivation and ability.

The Elaboration Likelihood model is comprehensive and has been supported by research evidence. It improves on the Hovland-Yale model by acknowledging that we don't always consider everything very carefully. It provides a clear view of how we might be persuaded by the media and be led to change our attitude about something. However, one downfall of the model is that it lacks the predictive power which a useful model should have — it can't predict experimental findings beforehand.

Exam Tip

For key theories and models like the ELM, it'd be great if you could remember who came up with them — in this case, it's Petty and Cacioppo (1986).

Exam Tip

At A2, you're expected to be able to link things together — if you briefly mention how the ELM and Hovland-Yale model relate to each other, you're really showing the examiner that you know your stuff.

Summary Questions

Q1 a) What is persuasion?

b) List the four important components of persuasion in the Hovland-Yale model.

Q2 Aoife has just seen a really good advert on TV. Outline two techniques that may have been used to make it such an effective advert.

3. The Psychology of 'Celebrity'

Learning Objectives:

- Understand the attraction of 'celebrity' including social psychological and evolutionary explanations.
- Know about research into intense fandom, including celebrity worship and celebrity stalking.

People are attracted to all sorts of things — even people they don't know. Psychologists have investigated our fascination with celebrities and have come up with several explanations...

Audiences

The relationships that audiences develop with celebrities are very different from the relationships formed within normal social networks. They are one-sided, with one person knowing lots and the other usually knowing nothing about the other party. The term used to describe this type of relationship is **parasocial**. The study of parasocial relationships between audiences and celebrities has become a branch of social relationship research in its own right. As well as audiences developing relationships with celebrities, many people are attracted to the concept of celebrity and want to be one themselves.

Real World Connection

What is seen as attractive to one person might be different to someone else's idea. This can definitely be the case when comparing what males and females see as the most attractive qualities in each other. McCutcheon (2002) reported that, when asked to comment on celebrities of the opposite sex, over 60% of females with an average age of 20 said that their favourite celebrity was someone glamorous. In comparison, only 25% of men with an average age of 20 had these thoughts about opposite sex celebrities. This shows that attraction might not be based simply on sexual attractiveness. However, the data was taken from first year students from only one US college, so the results might not be representative of the general population.

The evolutionary explanation

There are two main things that the evolutionary explanation tries to account for when explaining why people may be attracted to celebrities.

Creative individuals

Our attraction to creative individuals is explained using ideas of mate selection. Before the invention of the media, including TV and computers, people would have entertained themselves and each other. Therefore, success would be linked to those who were creative and novel. So, the evolutionary explanation for the attraction of celebrity is based on the idea that everyone has a basic selfish drive to ensure that their genes have the best possible chance of being passed on. Celebrity is seen as a way to achieve this and can be looked at from two different perspectives.

- Becoming a celebrity makes a person more desirable. In evolutionary terms, it may result in gaining economic advantage, which may make a person more attractive to others. This then increases their chances of passing on their genes.
- Desirable people become celebrities. Celebrities may be seen as individuals who are hugely popular due to their personality traits. So becoming famous acts as confirmation of having characteristics that others find attractive.

Hartup (1992) researched the characteristics of people who became popular in their own social circles from an early age. The characteristics that were valued included social dominance and athletic ability in boys and prettiness in girls.

Key study of the evolutionary explanation of novelty-seeking behaviour — Shiraishi et al (2006)

Method:	Over 300 Japanese volunteers were asked to complete a personality questionnaire. Their results were compared to the results of a genetic test which indicated their levels of a certain enzyme, MAO-A. MAO-A has been associated with novelty-seeking behaviours.
Results:	There was a correlation between participants who had indications of higher levels of the enzyme and preference for novelty seeking and, therefore, creativity.

Conclusion: There is a genetic explanation for why some people might find creative and novel individuals more attractive, supporting the evolutionary explanation.

Evaluation: The large sample increases the reliability of the results, but because the participants were all Japanese it's difficult to generalise the results — the results might show an effect limited to that one culture.

Celebrity gossip

Celebrity gossip is another thing that the evolutionary approach tries to explain. Dunbar (2004) suggested that gossip is useful to help us form social bonds within our society — a behaviour which would have been useful in our evolutionary past. It would have helped us form relationships and pass on information that would have helped the group survive. Dunbar measured how much time we spend on talking about our social environment and concluded it takes up two-thirds of our everyday conversation.

Figure 1: *Magazines increase our chances to gossip about celebrities.*

Tip: Gossiping is helpful in evolutionary terms because it can strengthen our social bonds with each other.

Key study of the evolutionary explanation of celebrity gossip — De Backer (2007)

Method: Around 800 participants were included in De Backer's (2007) survey. They were asked to report on things such as their interest in celebrities, how they got information about their social world and how many types of media they used on a regular basis.

Results: The more someone engaged in the media, the more interest they had in celebrities. Gossip was a key way to gain information about others in their social group. People who interacted most with the media were more likely to wrongly perceive that celebrities are part of their social group.

Conclusion: Media interaction is linked with an interest in celebrities.

Evaluation: The sample size was large, but self-report questionnaires can be unreliable as they depend on people being honest.

Tip: The evolutionary theory is reductionist — it explains behaviour in a very simple, mechanistic way. By suggesting that our biological drives can explain why we're attracted to certain characteristics, it ignores the fact that we might be influenced by our social environment. For instance, those from a lower social class might find celebrities attractive because they aspire to be as financially successful.

Psychological explanations

Attachment theory

The theories of attachment stem from research conducted by Bowlby, who suggested that people form close attachments with their caregivers. These bonds then influence how they attach and relate to other people in adulthood. In terms of celebrities, attachment theory suggests that children who didn't form close attachments with their caregivers may later develop insecure attachments as adults. They are then more likely to be attracted to celebrities. In one-sided relationships, there is little opportunity for rejection.

Tip: People with insecure attachments can be clingy, needy and want lots of attention.

Key studies of attachment theory

McCutcheon et al (2006) asked over 250 university students to complete questionnaires which examined their personality types and their views on celebrities. They found no relationship between having an insecure attachment and forming parasocial relationships.

The results of Roberts' (2007) study did, however, support the idea that a relationship exists between childhood attachments and parasocial

Tip: You studied attachment at AS so some of the information on Bowlby should seem familiar.

relationships. He asked 200 students (100 males and 100 females) a similar set of questions. A positive correlation between insecurely attached individuals and frequently contacting celebrities was found.

Real World Connection
Celebrity stalking comes up a bit later (see page 215) but it can also be linked to attachment theory. Lewis et al (2001) investigated the characteristics of stalkers in general and found that they often had insecure attachments and were emotionally unstable.

Absorption-addiction model

The absorption-addiction model was created by McCutcheon et al (2002). It says that if people are dissatisfied with their lives, they'll often look for forms of escapism, and this can come through an increased interest in the celebrity world. Three increasingly intensive stages were outlined, ranging from being a harmless fan, to being a stalker.

Positive/active view

Jenkins (1992) and Jenson (1992) came up with the positive/active view which says that parasocial relationships serve a purpose — they help people enhance their lives by social networking (e.g. through fan clubs), by taking a proactive and positive role in society, and by appreciating the skills and work of others.

Tip: The positive/active view suggests that parasocial relationships can actually help people, especially those with low self-esteem. If people can identify with celebrities and view them as people who have succeeded in life, they may see themselves in a more positive light.

Fandom

Wann (1995) studied the active role that audiences play as fans — a social psychological explanation for the attraction of celebrity. This has led to the creation of the term fandom — used to describe a group of fans of a particular celebrity, or the subculture of fans in general. Fandom can provide individuals with:

- Enhanced self-esteem.
- Escape, entertainment and excitement.
- Enhanced family and group affiliation.

The extent to which fandom provides these varies between individuals and contributes to how likely someone is to be a fan. For example, someone whose self-esteem is greatly increased and who finds high levels of entertainment and escape in fandom is likely to find the concept of celebrity more attractive than someone whose self-esteem is only slightly enhanced.

Several aspects of fandom are very social in nature, providing a group of people with a shared focus of interest. Some people believe that 'being a fan' of something can play an important role in adolescence — it might help young people make the transition from parental to peer attachments by providing a common source of gossip.

Figure 2: *Social events, such as concerts, allow us to bond with our peers.*

Three stages of fandom

Explanations of fandom suggest that celebrity worship can be a result of normal instincts and motivations. However, sometimes fandom can take on a more intense form and becomes something which is pathological. McCutcheon (2002) created a **Celebrity Attitude Scale (CAS)** based on the findings of a set of questionnaires which asked participants to score 23 items which described different aspects of celebrity worship. From this, three stages of fandom have been identified:

- Entertainment-social — where the relationship with the celebrity exists as a source of fun, shared with others in a social group.

Example
Milly is a big Meryl Streep fan. She has been to see all of her films and has joined an online fan club.

- Intense-personal — obsessive thoughts begin to arise in relation to the celebrity.

Example

"Justin Timberlake is my soul mate."

- Borderline-pathological — obsessive thoughts begin to give rise to fully-fledged fantasies.

Example

"Justin Timberlake is my boyfriend."

"Justin Timberlake would rescue me if I was in trouble."

It is at this stage that stalking may begin, which involves a level of pursuit that is intimidating.

Stalkers

The word 'stalker' immediately conjures up images of an unattractive and obsessive loner-type, whose walls are decorated with news clippings and photographs of the star who has become the object of their fixation. This image is largely created by the media and contains several misconceptions, which Spitzberg is largely credited with debunking:

Myth: stalking mainly affects celebrities

Stalking involving a well-known person is more likely to be reported in the media than stalking involving a member of the public — so it's clear why this would be assumed. However, it's estimated that around 21% of the population will be pursued at some point.

Myth: stalkers are strangers

In fact, in most cases stalkers have been involved in an intimate relationship with the person they're pursuing.

Myth: stalking ends in violence

News reporting usually focuses on cases where there has been some dramatic ending, and films which portray a sensational account of stalking draw the most attention. However, stalking doesn't usually involve violence.

Examples

- John Lennon's stalker, Mark Chapman, was sentenced to life in prison after shooting the famous Beatles' star. Chapman had become obsessed with John Lennon, and then obsessed about killing him, which led him to carry out his actions.
- Catherine Zeta-Jones was also stalked, but with a less violent ending. Her stalker, Dawnette Knight, sent threatening letters which explained that she loved Michael Douglas and intended to kill Catherine Zeta-Jones in order to marry him.

Worked Exam-style Question

0 1 Outline and evaluate evolutionary explanations used to explain the attraction of 'celebrity'. *(16 marks)*

Evolutionary explanations have been used by psychologists to try and explain attraction to 'celebrity'. There are two key areas psychologists have looked at — the role of creative individuals and the role of celebrity gossip.

Real World Connection

There is lots of research to suggest there may be negative effects of fandom. For example, Maltby et al (2005) investigated the relationship between celebrity worshipping and body image in adolescents. They found that body image in teenage girls was likely to be influenced by the body shape of celebrities, which led to a dissatisfied view of their own body shape. There are much wider implications of this research, including the fact that many eating disorders can start at this time and therefore, celebrity worship could be one factor which may cause the onset of eating disorders.

Exam Tip
A key component of evolutionary psychology is explaining how our ancestors' behaviour might influence our current behaviour.

Exam Tip
It's good to use studies to provide support for theories.

Exam Tip
A lot of psychology research is inconclusive and needs further research — it's a good thing to mention in the summary of a question if you've been evaluating research.

The idea of mate selection has been used to explain why people may be attracted to celebrities. Historically, in times when TV and other media didn't exist, people would rely on others to entertain them. Success would therefore be linked to those who were creative and novel. The evolutionary theory is based on the idea that every person has an unconscious desire to successfully pass on their genes. Therefore, celebrity is seen as a way to achieve this.

Through being creative and novel, celebrity may lead to greater economical success. Once again, this makes the person appear more attractive and so they have a greater chance of passing on their genes. Shiraishi et al (2006) supported this idea with their study of over 300 Japanese volunteers. They found that participants who had a genetic predisposition to produce more of a particular enzyme, MAO-A, were more attracted to people with novelty-seeking behaviours than those who produced less of the enzyme. Since this provides support for a biological explanation for attraction, this adds further support for the evolutionary approach.

Secondly, celebrity gossip can be used to support the evolutionary approach to the attraction of 'celebrity'. Dunbar (2004) suggested that forming social bonds is an important behaviour that would have helped us form relationships and pass on information to aid survival. These days, gossip is a common way of forming social bonds. De Backer (2007) conducted a study with approximately 800 participants. She found that gossip was a key method used to gain information about others in their group, and that those who engaged in the media the most were more likely to wrongly perceive that celebrities are part of their social group. However, whilst De Backer's (2007) study used a large sample, it didn't account for the fact that people could lie on questionnaires and therefore, the results could lack reliability.

Overall, the research for the evolutionary approach to celebrity is still inconclusive. More research is needed to fully understand whether there is any value in explaining attraction to 'celebrity' using these theories.

Summary Questions

Q1 What is a parasocial relationship?

Q2 Describe the method used in Shiraishi et al's (2006) study into the evolutionary explanation of novelty-seeking behaviour.

Q3 How does attachment theory seek to explain someone's obsession with celebrity?

Q4 Jaspreet is dissatisfied with her life and is looking for a form of escapism. Which psychological model explains her interest in the celebrity world?

Q5 Give one way in which fandom might play an important role in adolescence.

Q6 Matthew is a big fan of Tina Turner — he thinks that she wrote about him in her last song and that they're the best of friends, although she doesn't know him. Which stage of fandom is he showing?

Q7 Give three myths about stalking.

4. Models of Addictive Behaviour

You might feel like you're a bit addicted to tea after you have your fourth cup of the day. But some addictive behaviours can be quite serious. Psychologists have tried to explain why and how addiction develops.

Learning Objectives:

- Know about the biological, cognitive and learning approaches to explaining initiation, maintenance and relapse.

Three stages of addiction

Addiction often involves three stages — initiation (e.g. taking up smoking), maintenance (e.g. carrying on smoking even when you have to go outside in the rain) and relapse (e.g. having a cigarette when you'd given up). There are three models that attempt to explain addiction — biological, cognitive and learning.

The biological model

The biological approach includes neurological and genetic explanations for addictions.

Exam Tip
You only need to answer questions about one contemporary application of psychology. So choose media psychology, the psychology of addictive behaviour or anomalistic psychology and learn everything you need to know about that one.

The neurological approach

Both the highs and lows of addiction can be explained at the level of neurons. The neurotransmitter dopamine is released at particular synapses in the brain and affects motivation and pleasure (amongst other things). Some substances (e.g. food and addictive drugs), increase the release of dopamine or prevent its reuptake at synapses.

These both increase dopamine levels in the brain and so dopamine receptors on neurons are stimulated — this gives the person a feeling of pleasure or satisfaction. Once the dopamine has been removed from the synapses (reuptake), this feeling disappears. In order to regain it, the person wants to take more of the substance. If the substance is used repeatedly, the body becomes used to the higher levels of dopamine. The rate at which it's broken down increases and its reuptake also increases. This means that more of the substance is needed to produce the same effect. This is known as tolerance. If the addict then stops taking the substance, they experience effects which are the opposite of the drug's effects. These are called withdrawal symptoms and can be removed by taking more of the substance.

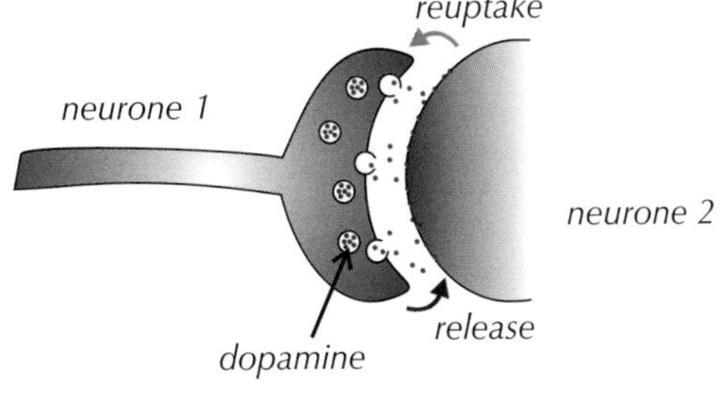

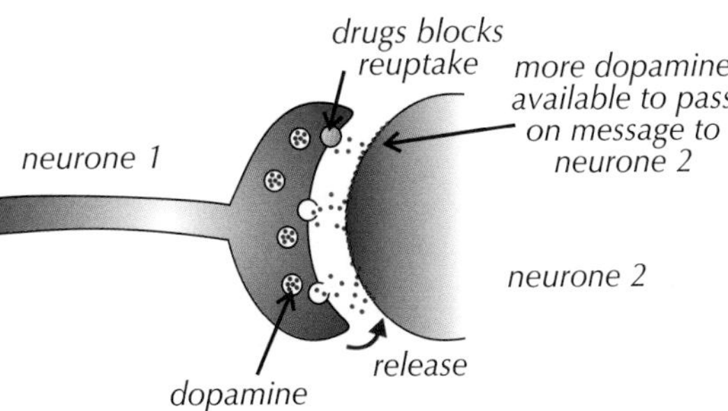

Figure 1: *Certain addictive drugs can increase dopamine levels by preventing its reuptake.*

Tip: This dopamine reward system doesn't cause all people to become addicts though — it may be that some people are more sensitive and vulnerable to its effects than others.

Figure 2: *The nicotine in cigarettes creates more dopamine in the brain.*

Example

Altman et al (1996) conducted various studies and concluded that certain addictive drugs, such as amphetamines, increased dopamine production whilst also blocking its reuptake, further supporting the dopamine hypothesis for drug addiction.

Tip: Although twin studies are useful at providing us with an insight into whether genetic factors might be involved, don't forget that often twins share the same environment — so their surroundings and upbringing might influence their behaviour just as much.

The genetic approach

It's been suggested that predispositions to some addictions are inherited. A review of studies by Sayette and Hufford (1997) concluded that identical (MZ) twins showed a higher rate of concordance for alcoholism than non-identical (DZ) twins, suggesting that alcoholism is controlled to some extent by genes.

Key study of the genetic approach to addiction

Kendler and Prescott (1998) examined the concordance rates in cocaine use in MZ twins and DZ twins. MZ twins showed approximately a 50% concordance rate, whereas DZ twins showed around a 40% concordance rate.

Figure 3: As the concordance rates show, addiction to alcohol isn't exclusively biologically determined — there must be social factors involved as well.

This can explain why, despite the fact that many people drink alcohol on a regular basis, only a small proportion develop an addiction to it. However, there must be an environmental aspect to alcoholism as the MZ twins didn't show 100% concordance. It's also not clear whether the result is just specific to alcoholism, or can be generalised to addiction as a whole.

However, the biological model of addiction doesn't take psychological and social influences into account.

The cognitive model

The cognitive approach looks at the thought processes behind an addiction. These could be shaped by a person's attitude towards the behaviour — e.g. 'alcohol helps me to feel confident and relaxed', their perception of others' opinions — e.g. 'I need to drink to fit in' or an individual's perception of their ability to control their own behaviour — e.g. 'I can't cope in social situations if I don't drink'.

Beck et al (2001) outlined a 'vicious cycle' which explains how addiction can spiral out of control (see Figure 4).

Real World Connection
Using Beck et al's (2001) vicious cycle of addiction, you can see how addiction can get out of control.
For instance, if someone with an alcohol addiction experiences a low mood, they may drink alcohol to cheer themselves up. If they continue to do this, they may experience financial or social difficulties which would make them more stressed and continue to lower their mood. The cycle will go round again. Cognitive therapies can help to break the cycle.

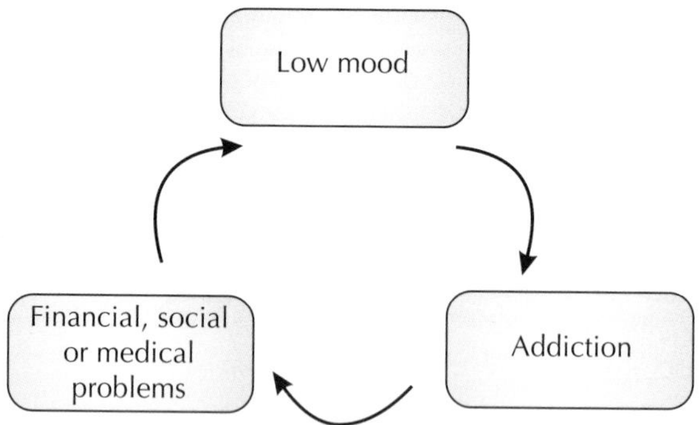

Figure 4: Beck's 'vicious cycle' of addiction.

The cognitive model can be used in therapy sessions to reduce addictive behaviour. Cognitive therapists help the addict to identify the thoughts that trigger their addictive behaviour. They're then taught strategies to change their behaviour, e.g. avoiding certain situations, and practising new thought patterns. Cognitive therapy usually contains a behavioural component which teaches the addict new skills, e.g. alternative relaxation techniques.

Alongside Beck's model of addiction, there are three more models that have been proposed by cognitive psychologists:

- **Self-medication model** — this suggests that individuals resort to addictive behaviours when they get stressed. Addictive behaviours are believed to offer distraction, regulate mood and help people to manage activities such as work, all of which help when someone needs to lift their mood.
- **Expectancy theory** — addicts tend to take a more positive view of the outcomes of their addictive behaviour than non-addicts.

Example

Jim was addicted to alcohol. He thought that alcohol was the one way he could have fun and socialise without feeling anxious.

Andy wasn't addicted to alcohol. He knew that drinking excessively would give him a hangover the next morning.

- **Rational choice theory** — people often conduct a cost-benefit analysis before they undertake certain behaviours. Addicts may believe that the benefits of their behaviour outweigh the costs of being addicted.

Real World Connection

Gambling is an addictive behaviour, and yet the rational choice theory of addiction doesn't explain gambling addiction. Griffiths (1994) compared 30 gamblers who regularly played on fruit machines with 30 people who didn't play regularly. Contrary to the rational choice theory, the regular gamblers made more irrational choices and made more irrational statements than the non-gamblers as a way of justifying their addictive behaviours.

Key study of the cognitive model of addiction — Toneatto and Sobell (1990)

Method:	Toneatto and Sobell (1990) reported the case study of a 47-year-old man who had been gambling for over 25 years. They used a cognitive-based therapy to challenge and alter his beliefs.
Results:	Before therapy, he would gamble on average ten times per month. Six months after therapy, this had decreased to once every two months.
Conclusion:	The cognitive model can explain some types of addiction.
Evaluation:	This was a case study of a single individual and therefore the results can't be generalised to the wider population.

Figure 5: There are many explanations for addictive behaviours, including gambling addiction.

The learning model

The learning approach explains addiction by looking at the role the environment plays in the maintenance and relapse of addictive behaviour.

Repeatedly using a substance, e.g. heroin, in the same environment will lead to associations forming between the substance and the stimuli in the environment, e.g. needles, other addicts (see Figure 6).

Tip: This is an example of classical conditioning.

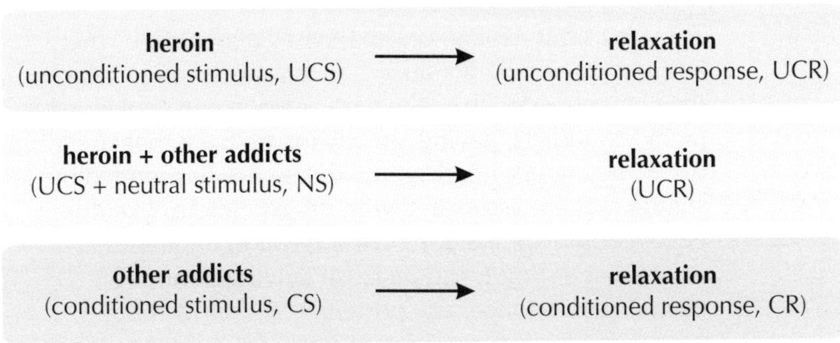

Figure 6: Addictive behaviours can be learnt through conditioning.

Tip: You met conditioning at AS. It's a really important topic so make sure you understand how it works.

When these stimuli are present the body expects to receive the substance and will compensate in advance for certain effects of the drug. For example, heroin addicts feel anxious without the drug, because their body anticipates the increased relaxation that will follow its use. This is known as **classical conditioning**, and is one of the factors that leads to the initiation of addiction, tolerance and withdrawal effects.

- **Addiction** — The environmental stimuli lead to compensatory effects which are often the opposite of the drug effects. The user then wants the substance in order to remove these effects.
- **Tolerance** — Compensatory effects oppose the effect that the substance has on the body, so larger quantities of the substance are needed to create the same effect.
- **Withdrawal symptoms** — If the body experiences compensatory effects but doesn't receive the substance, the person will feel the opposite of how they would if they took the substance.

Operant conditioning can also be used to explain how behaviour might be positively and negatively reinforced, maintaining an addiction.

Example

- Taking drugs may make you feel relaxed and be accepted by your peers — this is positive reinforcement.
- Withdrawal symptoms can lead someone to take more drugs to remove their symptoms — this is negative reinforcement.

There is research evidence for the learning model of addiction.

Key study of the learning model of addiction — Siegel et al (1982)

Method:	This was a lab experiment using independent groups of rats. Two groups of rats were given heroin until they developed a tolerance to it. After 30 days the heroin dose was doubled. For half of the rats, this dose was given in the usual room. For the other half, it was given in a different room.
Results:	32% of the rats that had the double dose in the usual room died, compared to 64% of the rats in the new room.
Conclusion:	Tolerance and withdrawal symptoms are a conditioned response to drug-related stimuli. When there's no familiar stimuli to allow anticipation of the drug, compensatory effects aren't triggered and the body is less prepared to deal with a larger quantity of the drug than usual. This increases the risk of death.
Evaluation:	This result can explain unusual cases of overdose where addicts have died after taking an amount of drugs which they had coped with in the past. Also, it can explain why many ex-addicts, having 'got clean', go back to taking drugs when they return home — there they are surrounded by stimuli that are associated with drugs. Studies like this have real-life applications. As a result of findings that drug-related stimuli can increase cravings, anti-drug campaigns no longer use posters which show drug paraphernalia, e.g. syringes and spoons.

Tip: The learning model is a reductionist approach to explaining addictive behaviour. Although it suggests that we can be influenced by the environment, it ignores biological factors.

Real World Connection

Although it has been rejected as a potential new entry within the revised DSM-IV, 'video game addiction' appears to be a relatively new problem. Psychologists, such as Griffiths (2000), have researched this behaviour which is increasing in frequency and can affect everyday life. It has been likened to behaviours such as gambling, and therefore the same principles can be used to explain it. Chumbley and Griffiths (2006) conducted an experiment to look at reinforcement and punishment and its role in addictive video game behaviour. They found that participants were much more likely to keep playing if they were rewarded little and often. Game makers are aware of this and design their games with such features to boost sales.

Worked Exam-style Question

0 1 Describe and evaluate the learning approach as an explanation of addiction. *(16 marks)*

The learning approach suggests that the environment plays a role in maintaining addictive behaviour and causing relapses. Both classical and operant conditioning are used to explain it.

Firstly, using addictive substances continuously leads people to develop associations between the substance and stimuli in the environment. For instance, for some heroin addicts, seeing a needle will become associated with using the drug. When this stimulus is present, the body expects to receive the drug and starts to react. For instance, heroin addicts feel anxious if they haven't had the drug because their body is waiting for the relaxation it would get immediately following having it. This association is formed through classical conditioning — a previously unconditioned stimulus becomes a conditioned stimulus, leading to a conditioned response.

Operant conditioning can also be used to explain how an addiction might be maintained. It uses the idea of negative and positive reinforcement to explain why behaviours are repeated. For instance, for heroin users, taking drugs is associated with the feelings of relaxation and acceptance from peers — these are seen by the addicts as positive reactions and so behaviour is reinforced. Likewise, through negative reinforcement, unpleasant withdrawal symptoms can be alleviated by taking the drug again.

Many studies support both classical and operant conditioning as explanations for addiction. Siegel et al (1982) studied drug stimuli in rats. Two groups of rats were given heroin until they developed a tolerance to it. After 30 days they were given a double dose, either in the usual room or in a different room. They found that twice as many rats died from this double dose if it was given in a new room. From this, they concluded that when there are no familiar stimuli to allow anticipation of the drug, compensatory effects aren't triggered and so the body is less prepared to deal with a larger than usual quantity of the drug. However, studies like this which use animals have problems as the results can't strictly be generalised to humans, which reduces the support they can give to the learning approach.

One issue of the learning approach is that it is reductionist — it suggests that behaviour is simply a set of responses to the environment and doesn't consider biological factors. Other explanations could improve on the downfalls of the learning approach, for example, the biological model or the cognitive model. However, because the learning model is able to explain maintenance and relapse, it might be that a combination of approaches are necessary to fully explain addiction.

Exam Tip
This question needs you to give a mix of factual and evaluative knowledge. In order to help you structure your answer, it's a good idea to scribble down a quick outline of what you're going to say.

Exam Tip
Giving real world examples counts as evaluating evidence, and being able to extend and apply your knowledge of psychology to the wider world.

Exam Tip
It's always best to explain what you mean when using terms such as 'reductionist' — it shows the examiner that you're able to fully criticise the psychological theories.

Summary Questions

Q1 a) Give one neurotransmitter thought to be involved in addiction.

b) How does the level of this neurotransmitter change when an addictive substance is taken?

c) Outline how these changes are caused.

Q2 How might a cognitive therapist help an addict?

5. Explaining Smoking and Gambling

Learning Objectives:
- Know about the biological, cognitive and learning approaches to explaining initiation, maintenance and relapse, and their applications to smoking and gambling.

Two types of addiction which occur a lot in our society are smoking and gambling — and there can be serious health consequences with both of them.

Smoking addiction

The chemicals in cigarettes can cause diseases such as cancer, emphysema and bronchitis. Despite this, many people smoke and some continue to smoke after being diagnosed with one of these conditions — this is because smoking is addictive. Even though many smokers want to quit, the success rate of those who attempt it is very low. Addiction to smoking can be explained in more than one way:

***Figure 1:** Nicotine is the addictive substance in cigarettes which comes from the tobacco plant.*

The biological approach

There are many chemicals in cigarettes but it's the nicotine that causes addiction. Nicotine stimulates the release of dopamine, increasing the level of dopamine in the brain and providing feelings of pleasure and relaxation (see page 217). If nicotine's taken regularly the body expects it and reduces the amount of dopamine that's released naturally. In order to maintain normal dopamine levels and the effect that they have on the body, nicotine needs to be taken regularly. This reinforces smoking behaviour, leading to more frequent smoking and addiction.

Quitting smoking is very difficult as the body becomes used to nicotine and relies on it to stimulate dopamine release. Quitting deprives the body of nicotine, leading to low dopamine levels until the body readjusts. This causes unpleasant withdrawal symptoms such as anxiety, restlessness, sleep disturbance and weight gain.

The social learning approach

The social learning approach explains why people start smoking. Social learning theory states that new behaviour (in this case smoking) is learned through observation, or modelling. Whether the behaviour is imitated depends on the perceived consequences.

Tip: You can read more about social learning theory on pages 203-204.

Example

If smoking is positively reinforced, e.g. by benefits such as fitting in with peers, then it's likely to be copied. Seeing role models (e.g. parents or celebrities) smoking also encourages people to smoke.

Once someone has started smoking they will experience withdrawal symptoms if they stop. These encourage people to start smoking again (to remove the symptoms). This is known as negative reinforcement. Often, smoking becomes associated with other activities and objects, e.g. alcohol — this is classical conditioning and it makes it difficult to not smoke in certain environments (see page 219).

Tip: Although longitudinal studies take a long time, they're really useful because they give a detailed account of the same group of people over time. However, they're often expensive to run.

Key study of the effects of social learning over time — Akers and Lee (1996)

Method:	A five-year longitudinal study of 454 secondary school students was conducted using self-report questionnaire

surveys. These measured how frequently the students smoked and 'social learning variables'. These were things like whether friends smoked, how often friends smoked, and perceived attitudes of friends and parents towards smoking.

Results: Significant positive correlations were found between the social learning variables and smoking.

Conclusion: Social learning can partly account for whether smoking begins in adolescence.

Evaluation: Methods relying on self report may be unreliable, and correlation doesn't prove that social learning causes smoking to begin. Also, the effect of social learning wasn't analysed to show the relative influence of different variables, e.g. gender or parental vs. peer influence.

The cognitive approach

The cognitive approach explains smoking and gambling addiction in several ways:

- **The perceived effects theory** — Smith (1980) suggested that people often expect certain outcomes from taking addictive substances. The positive expectations about the effects that addictive substances will have play a big part in the initiation and maintenance of use.

Example

- Smokers expect that smoking a cigarette will calm them down.
- Drinkers believe that alcohol will make them relax more and help them to become more confident in social situations.

- **Locus of control** — this uses the idea of attributions to explain addiction. People either have an internal locus of control or an external locus of control and attribute their behaviours to themselves or the outside world. Eiser et al (1987) showed that adolescents who thought of themselves as addicted smokers were more likely to believe that external factors were the cause of their behaviour in comparison to adolescents who didn't perceive themselves as addicted. This supports the idea that thought processes can be used to justify behaviour.

Tip: Other cognitive theories explaining smoking behaviour include the theory of planned behaviour and the theory of reasoned action. These are covered on pages 229-230.

Tip: Someone's locus of control either comes from inside or outside the self.

Internal locus of control (behaviour determined by personal decisions, within your control)

External locus of control (behaviour determined by fate or luck, outside of your control)

The smoking debate

There's been debate over whether smoking is an addiction or a habit. For a long time cigarette companies claimed that people smoked for psychological reasons (smoking for pleasure, which becomes part of a routine), rather than physiological reasons (smoking to avoid the unpleasant withdrawal symptoms caused by changes in the brain). They argued that this meant smoking was a habit rather than an addiction. However, both the physiological and psychological aspects are important in smoking. The physiological impact of withdrawal symptoms is well documented but the effects of psychological dependence shouldn't be underestimated.

Gambling addiction

Addiction to gambling can also be explained by many approaches:

The biological approach

The biological approach explains gambling as an addiction to adrenaline. The stress of awaiting the outcome of a bet triggers the release of the hormone

Figure 2: *Gambling doesn't involve any substance use but can still be addictive.*

adrenaline. This induces an adrenaline rush, making the person more alert and experiencing a 'natural high'. In order to regain this rush, gamblers will place more bets and a physiological addiction may develop. Repeated gambling can cause the body to develop a tolerance to adrenaline. This can lead to more frequent gambling or bets involving more money in order to get the same rush. Other chemicals triggered by stress could also be responsible for gambling addictions. There's some evidence that gambling releases endorphins, chemicals that block pain and negative effects of stress.

Tip: Neuroendocrine measurements record the levels of various hormones and neurotransmitters — in this case, it would record how much adrenaline, dopamine, and cortisol has been released as these are all involved in addiction.

Key study of the biological approach to gambling — Meyer et al (2004)

Method:	Heart rate and neuroendocrine measurements were taken in 14 male, non-substance-abusing, addicted gamblers and 15 non-addicted gamblers when asked to gamble using their own money. Measurements were taken at baseline, and then at 30, 60 and 90 minutes into the game.
Results:	Both groups experienced increased heart rates and increased adrenaline levels during the game, but the increase was significantly greater for the problem gamblers.
Conclusion:	Neurobiological factors are affected more in those who have a gambling addiction than those who don't.
Evaluation:	This study only illustrates a correlational link — it can't confirm a cause and effect relationship.

Real World Connection
Lots of people gamble regularly — playing the lottery, buying an occasional scratchcard, or placing a few bets on upcoming football matches. But there's a point when gambling becomes a problem. The DSM-IV contains criteria which can be used to diagnose someone with 'pathological gambling'. This condition involves a serious disruption to life and can be chronic and progressive. The term 'problem gambling' includes pathological gambling. Problem gambling itself isn't recognised by the DSM-IV but is used to describe the actions of those who experience the negative effects of excessive gambling behaviour.

The psychodynamic approach

The psychodynamic approach suggests gambling is driven by masochism. Bergler (1958) proposed that gamblers gamble to lose, in order to punish themselves. This reduces the guilt they feel from rebelling against their parents during childhood. He suggests that gamblers identify with the casino dealer or roulette wheel, etc. as parental figures. Bergler presented case studies where treatment relevant to his theory was successful in curing some gamblers of their addiction, but scientific evidence is still lacking at the moment.

Tip: 'Masochism' in this context means 'gaining pleasure from losing'.

The cognitive approach

The cognitive approach suggests gambling is driven by faulty reasoning mechanisms. Decision making can be based on rational consideration or quick (sometimes faulty) rules. Wagenaar (1988) identified 16 rules that gamblers commonly use when making decisions. These include:

- The illusion of control — gamblers think of gambling as skill-based. This creates superficially high expectations when in reality the outcomes are often determined by chance alone.
- Representative bias — gamblers believe that random events should look random, e.g. 'tails' seems increasingly likely the longer a run of consecutive 'heads' lasts. Many gamblers believe that the longer a losing streak lasts the more likely a win will follow. This is known as the gambler's fallacy.
- Illusory correlations — gamblers have superstitions which they believe help them succeed, e.g. blowing the dice for a 6.
- Fixation on the absolute frequency of successes — gamblers can recall many past wins, just because they gamble so much. This creates a false image of how often they win.

Worked Exam-style Questions

0 1 Outline the biological approach to gambling addiction.

(4 marks)

Gambling, as an addictive behaviour, can be explained using a biological approach. The approach suggests that a gambling addiction is actually an addiction to adrenaline. The stress of waiting for the outcome of a bet triggers the release of adrenaline, giving someone a 'natural high' — an adrenaline rush. Gambling addicts then want to continue having this 'high' so they place more bets, which eventually results in a physiological addiction. Repeating this behaviour creates a tolerance to adrenaline — the same amount of adrenaline has less of an effect. This can lead to a cycle where the addict gambles more frequently and with higher stakes to recreate this adrenaline rush.

There are also other chemicals which may be involved. Endorphins may also be released when gambling — they block pain and override some of the negative effects of stress.

Exam Tip
When a question asks you to outline a theory, and when it's just worth 4 marks, the examiner is looking for a brief and concise, fact-based answer.

Exam Tip
When you talk about chemicals like hormones and endorphins try to say whether their levels increase or decrease.

---

0 2 Discuss the social learning approach to smoking.

(8 marks)

The social learning approach to smoking suggests that it may be the result of learned behaviours influenced by, and modelled on, the behaviour of others. Whether the behaviour is imitated depends on whether the model is rewarded or punished. For instance, if a behaviour is positively reinforced by benefits such as the model fitting in with peers and gaining friends, then this is likely to encourage someone else to smoke. Alternatively, preventing withdrawal symptoms by continuing to smoke is an example of negative reinforcement, and discourages people from giving up the addictive behaviour.

Akers and Lee (1996) investigated the effects of social learning in a longitudinal study of students. In their five-year study, they found that social learning variables, such as the influence of friends, were positively correlated with smoking and can therefore explain why smoking can start in adolescence. However, there were several flaws with this study. It used a self-report method which means the results may have been unreliable. Also, there is no evidence for a cause and effect relationship as the results merely show a correlational effect. Finally, other variables may have been important in the study, such as gender or parental influence, and may have affected the results. Overall, although there is support for the social learning approach, the results of studies, including Akers and Lee (1996), haven't been conclusive. It may be that the social learning approach isn't the only explanation, so more research is needed.

Exam Tip
Because this question is asking you to discuss an approach, some of your answer should be made up of evaluation.

Exam Tip
Finish off your answer with a brief sentence to summarise all of the points you've made.

Summary Questions

Q1 Name one cognitive theory that can be used to explain smoking addiction.

Q2 What does the psychodynamic approach suggest drives gambling?

Q3 Give an example of an illusionary correlation that a gambler might have.

Learning Objectives:

- Know the risk factors in the development of addiction, including stress, peers, age and personality.
- Understand the media influences on addictive behaviour.

6. Vulnerability to Addiction

Everybody is different, which is why some people become addicts while others don't. Psychologists have investigated why this might be...

Factors affecting addiction

Stress

Stress could be a factor in the development of addiction. Sinha (2007) used brain imaging to investigate the relationship between stress and drug addiction. She found that the same part of the brain was activated during stress as during drug craving. Sinha suggests that stress makes people more vulnerable to reacting to cues associated with drugs. This could make them more likely to develop an addiction.

This research shows an association between stress and addiction — but it doesn't explain it. Drug use might cause altered brain function, or altered brain function might encourage drug use — or there may be another cause, and drug use and altered brain function are both results of this.

Operant conditioning (learning through reinforcement — see p.220) could explain why stress might make people more vulnerable to addiction if the pleasurable effects of the substance reduce the symptoms of stress.

Example

Alcohol is a depressant so it can make a stressed person feel more relaxed. This acts as a positive reinforcement and so they're more likely to repeat the drinking behaviour.

Figure 1: Underage drinking is an issue within the UK, highlighting the fact that age may be a factor that affects addictive behaviour.

Age

Zucker (2008) found that the age of onset of drinking was important. The earlier people start drinking the more likely they are to have drinking problems. Martino et al (2006) carried out a longitudinal study to look at the social factors that affect the drinking habits of adolescents. They concluded that the norms for drinking behaviour are learned through social observations and interactions. The perceived approval or use of alcohol by parents, other important adults and peers increased the likelihood of future decisions to drink and get drunk. Research has shown that although being socially withdrawn can be negative for other reasons, such as loneliness, it actually protects young people from the influence of their peers in relation to addiction.

Tip: Sussman and Ames (2001) conducted a study looking at the effects of peer pressure on teenage addictions. Whilst they did find evidence to support the idea that teenagers were strongly influenced by their peers, there were other factors such as family environment that also correlated with their addictive behaviours.

Key studies of the role of age and peers on addiction

Fergusson and Horwood (1999) found that children who were socially isolated from their peer group at the age of 10 because of social anxiety were less likely to use drugs or drink alcohol when they were 15.

Shedler and Block (1990) found that 18-year-olds who hadn't tried drugs were more likely to be socially isolated, over-controlled by others and anxious.

Sumter et al (2009) found that a person's age affects their ability to resist peer pressure.

Key study of resisting peer pressure — Sumter et al (2009)

Method: 464 children and adolescents were given a questionnaire

	that assessed their ability to resist pressure from their peer group. The questionnaire was written in a style suitable for all ages and used hypothetical everyday situations.
Results:	The participants' answers showed that they were more vulnerable to being influenced by their friends when they were younger. The participants became more resistant as they got older.
Conclusion:	As adolescents become more mature they are less influenced by others. This could explain why early experiences with substances have long-term effects.
Evaluation:	This was a cross-sectional study so individual differences could have affected the results. Carrying out longitudinal research avoids this design flaw, but it takes longer to collect the data. Peer pressure can be both positive or negative when it comes to abusing substances. You're less likely to do it if your friends aren't — but more likely if they are.

Tip: Remind yourself of the advantages and disadvantages of using different research methods within psychology — see pages 254-256.

Personality

Eysenck and Eysenck (1976) outlined three main personality dimensions:

- P for **psychoticism**, which includes being egocentric, aggressive and impulsive.
- E for **extroversion**, which includes being outgoing, happy and sociable.
- N for **neuroticism**, which includes being anxious, moody and irritable.

Eysenck suggested that some personality characteristics make a person more prone to addiction. Francis (1996) found that people with nicotine, heroin and alcohol addictions scored more highly on 'N' and 'P' scales on psychometric tests compared to the E scales.

The exact relationship between addiction and personality is unclear. Being irritable and impulsive could mean you are more likely to use substances such as alcohol or drugs. Or it could be that these personality characteristics make you less able to control your use of the substances. Alternatively it could be that having an addiction leads a person to be moody and impulsive, and makes them less likely to be happy and outgoing.

Tip: Eysenck and Eysenck believed that these personality traits were genetically determined — so you can use this information when talking about the biological approaches to addiction.

Personality disorders and substance abuse

Rounsaville et al (1998) found that people diagnosed with antisocial personality disorder were more likely to be alcoholics compared to those without the disorder. Other research suggests a link between attention deficit disorder and alcohol abuse. Substance abuse is a problem for some people with mental health problems as they may use alcohol and drugs to self-medicate. This makes it difficult to work out where the causal relationship lies. A person with mental health problems might drink or use drugs to help them cope, or using these substances might make them more vulnerable to mental health problems. It's difficult to test this as ethics is a major issue in this area.

Figure 2: *People may self-medicate as they feel drugs can help them cope with other problems.*

The media

The media may influence addictive behaviours by causing an addiction to develop. The growth of mass media has provided people with another reference for their own behaviour. The impact that messages from the media have on individuals varies, depending on the number and strength of messages that they receive from other sources.

Figure 3: Celebrities and others in the media spotlight can act as role models — this is dangerous if they are promoting the use of addictive substances.

One way the media influences behaviour is through reporting the behaviour of celebrities.

Example

Research specifically focusing on the effect that celebrities have on behaviours is lacking, but Boon and Lomore (2001) found that 59% of young people have had their attitudes and beliefs influenced in some way by a celebrity. The media coverage of drug-using celebrities, for example, may make drug use seem glamorous to some people.

This can influence people's perceptions of the consequences of drug use, making them more likely to start using drugs.

More generally, the portrayal of some addictive behaviours in the media may influence people by social learning mechanisms. For example, if the media shows a drug user being rewarded in some way (their behaviour is reinforced), this acts as reinforcement for the viewer as well. This is known as vicarious reinforcement and makes it more likely that they would consider drug use themselves.

The media can also prevent or break an addiction. The large audience reached by mass media means that it can be used to promote positive messages, either to prevent addictions forming or to help people to break their addictions. This may be done intentionally, with the aim being to reduce addictive behaviour. For example, public health interventions often make use of the media in campaigns aimed at reducing addictive behaviours such as smoking, drinking and drug-use. Sometimes media coverage doesn't actively seek to reduce addictive behaviour but may do so unintentionally. For example, watching TV programmes and films that show the negative effects of drug use may reduce the chances of people using drugs.

Real World Connection

There haven't been many studies that have looked specifically at the link between the media and addictive behaviours — this could be because it's difficult to measure the relationship. Atkin and Block (1981, 1984) conducted a series of studies to look at the influence of advertising on drinking alcohol. Although they found small but significant correlations between alcohol consumption and media exposure in both adults and adolescents, their results came from self-report questionnaires which can be unreliable.

Worked Exam-style Question

0 1 Outline **one** risk factor in the development of addiction.

(4 marks)

One risk factor in the development of addiction is personality.
Eysenck and Eysenck (1976) outlined three different personality types — psychoticism, extroversion and neuroticism. They proposed that certain personalities have a tendency to be susceptible to addiction.
Francis (1996) discovered that those with addictions were more likely to score highly on psychotic and neurotic scales than extroverted scales.
Psychotic personalities include those who are egocentric, aggressive and impulsive, whilst neurotic personalities involve anxious, moody and irritable characteristics.

Exam Tip

Since this question only asks for one risk factor, don't waste any time writing about more than one.

Summary Questions

Q1 Give an example of how positive reinforcement might create an alcohol addiction.

Q2 Describe the study by Martino et al (2006).

Q3 a) What did Sumter et al (2009) conclude in their study of peer pressure?

b) Give one criticism of their research.

Q4 Why is it difficult to test the relationship between mental health and substance abuse?

7. Reducing Addictive Behaviour

Health psychologists have an aim to prevent damaging behaviours, such as addiction, even before they begin. They do this using psychological theory.

Learning Objectives:
- Understand the theory of planned behaviour as a model for addiction prevention.
- Know about the types of intervention and their effectiveness, including biological, psychological and public health interventions.

The theory of reasoned action

Fishbein and Ajzen (1975) developed the theory of reasoned action (TRA) model of behaviour. It states that an individual's behaviour, e.g. whether they will give up alcohol, can be predicted by their intention to perform it. Intention is determined by two factors (see Figure 1):

- The person's attitude to the behaviour — this is shaped by their beliefs about the outcome of the behaviour, e.g. 'I'll save money', and their judgement of whether the outcome is positive or negative, likely or unlikely.
- Subjective norms — this describes their expectations of the social consequences of the behaviour, e.g. 'My friends will think I'm boring', and their motivation to follow these norms, e.g. 'I want to be popular'.

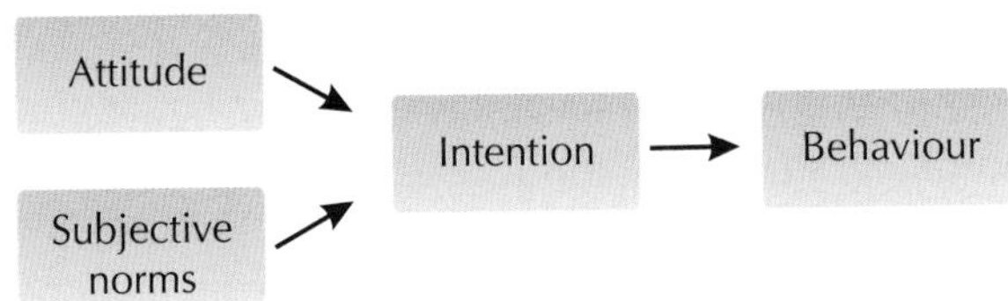

Figure 1: *Attitudes and norms affect intention, which influences behaviour.*

Figure 2: *Some eating disorders can be a result of a food addiction — using preventative theories might help people from becoming obese.*

Examples

Different attitudes and subjective norms might affect the outcome of trying to stop an addictive behaviour, such as smoking.

- Gary wants to save money but is affected greatly by what others think. He is unlikely to give up smoking as he has a low intention.
- Jon is worried about the health effects of smoking and isn't worried by what others think. He is likely to give up as he has a high intention.

Sheppard et al (1988) carried out a meta-analysis and found that the TRA had a strong predictive use — it was pretty good at predicting intentions and behaviour. It's also a useful model for knowing how to alter an individual's intentions and behaviour. However, it's been criticised for neglecting factors such as habits and emotional aspects, which are also important when intentions are being formed.

Tip: Each of the factors in the TRA are weighted depending on the individual. For instance, someone may perceive the negative health effects of smoking as a greater motivator to stop them smoking than the positive effects they'd get from fitting in with their friends who smoked.

The theory of planned behaviour

Ajzen (1991) added a third factor to the TRA — a person's perceived behavioural control, e.g. 'I don't have the willpower to give up alcohol'. This factor increases the model's predictive power. This theory is known as the theory of planned behaviour (TPB). It suggests behaviour is influenced in two ways (see Figure 3):

- Indirectly — if a person believes that the behaviour is too difficult they don't form the initial intention to carry out the behaviour.
- Directly — if the perception of their own level of control is accurate. E.g. if they don't have sufficient willpower, they won't succeed.

Tip: The TPB is a cognitive theory — it deals with mental processes.

Tip: The TPB assumes that people make rational decisions when required.

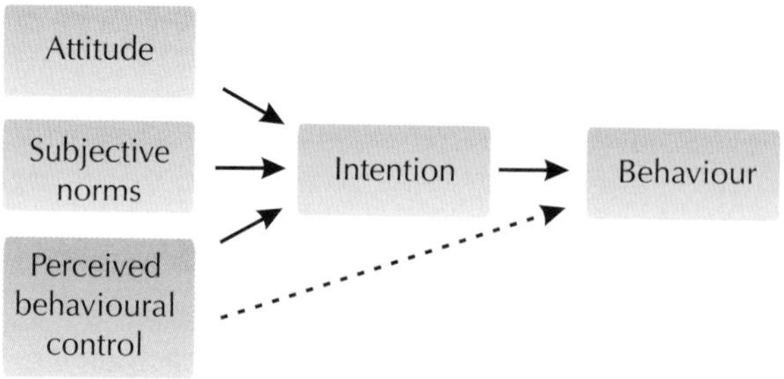

Figure 3: A person's perceived behavioural control can directly affect their behaviour.

Examples

Someone's belief in their ability to change their behaviour might affect the outcome of trying to stop an addictive behaviour.

- Marcus smokes despite knowing his parents disapprove. He believes he'll gain weight if he stops smoking. He also feels he can't control the withdrawal symptoms that would come with giving up. This all means that he's unlikely to form the initial intention to stop smoking.
- Edwige has a new regime to stop smoking. Although she is surrounded by a peer group who smoke, her doctor's support to help her quit has given her a feeling of control over her situation. She has high intentions to stop smoking, so is likely to succeed.

Real World Connection
Skin cancer rates are on the rise and this is partly due to the fact that people are becoming 'addicted' to the sun. White et al (2008) asked over 1000 Australian young people to report on their behaviours and attitudes towards sun protection. They found that the TPB could be applied to predict sun protection intentions and behaviours in young people.

In contrast to the TRA, the TPB takes into account the fact that people don't always have complete control over their behaviour, as there may be obstacles that stand in their way. Norman et al's (1998) study found that perceived behavioural control was a strong predictor of binge-drinking. The TPB could therefore be used to develop intervention strategies and prevention programmes.

Both models ignore the fact that there may be discrepancies between attitude and behaviour and that a person's behaviour is not always a reflection of their intentions. People's actions aren't always rational and based on deliberate decision-making processes. This is especially true for addictive behaviour, which is often irrational.

Tip: One criticism of both the TRA and the TPB is that they don't consider individual variables, such as personality, social environment or demographics (age, gender and social class).

The health belief model

The factors that the health belief model uses as predictors of behaviour include someone's perception of susceptibility and severity — their belief of how likely and serious the threat to their own health is if they don't carry out the preventative health behaviour, e.g. the danger of developing lung cancer as a result of smoking. It also can provide a perception of cost-benefit — they weigh the benefits of the behaviour (e.g. reduces cancer risk) against its costs (e.g. suffering withdrawal symptoms).

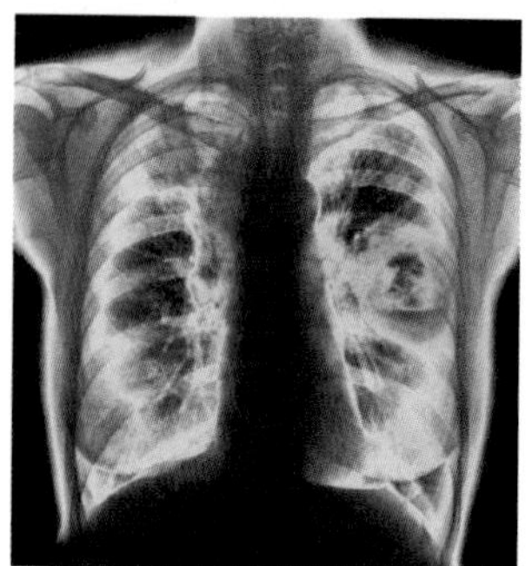

Figure 4: When people understand the severity of the consequences of their actions, such as developing lung cancer, it might help change their behaviour.

The health belief model takes into account factors that encourage people to break their addictive behaviour. These factors are known as cues to action and include experiencing symptoms of health problems or exposure to media campaigns. The model also considers the influence that personal variables, e.g. age, sex, social class and personality traits have on a person's perceptions. The comprehensive nature of the model means that it's an ideal tool for designing individual intervention strategies and highlights the importance of tailoring interventions to an individual's personal profile.

Interventions to reduce addictive behaviours

Biological interventions

The biological approach to reducing drug and alcohol addictions involves a gradual detox, where the quantity of the substance used is reduced over time. Medication may be prescribed to stop addictive behaviour, e.g. Antabuse is prescribed to alcoholics. It causes nausea if it's combined with alcohol, discouraging alcoholics from drinking. The addict will form an association between drinking and nausea — this will continue even when they stop taking Antabuse. This is known as aversion therapy.

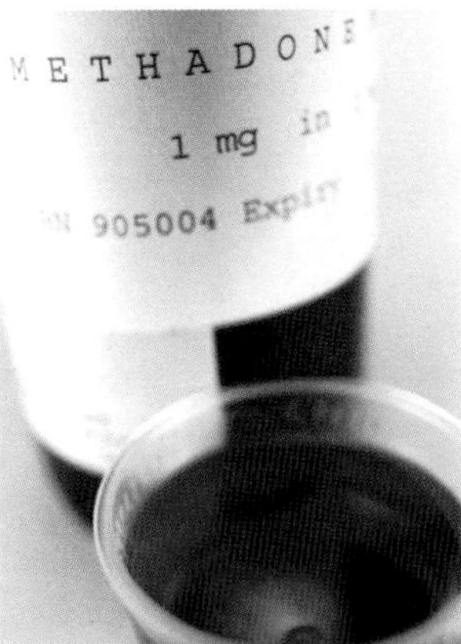

Figure 5: *Methadone is one biological intervention used to reduce heroin addiction.*

Key study of a biological intervention — Meyer and Chesser (1970)

Method:	Meyer and Chesser (1970) carried out an experiment where a group of alcoholics who were prescribed Antabuse were compared to a control group.
Results:	Around 50% of those taking Antabuse stayed teetotal for at least a year — significantly more than in the control group.
Conclusion:	From this study they concluded that an unpleasant response can be conditioned to an addictive behaviour.
Evaluation:	Unfortunately, the results showed that staying teetotal wasn't a permanent behaviour. This means other interventions would be needed for long-term recovery.

However, any medication prescribed has to be carefully controlled so it doesn't become an addiction itself.

Biological interventions can also use **agonists** to help addicts cope with withdrawal symptoms when they stop abusing certain substances.

Tip: Agonists are a type of drug that trigger a response by binding to receptors on cells. Some agonists can replace and replicate the effects of addictive drugs, but with much less harmful side effects. They can be used to wean people off addictive substances slowly and gradually.

Example

Methadone is used as a biological intervention to help heroin addicts become 'clean'. This drug works by stimulating the opiate receptors, which slows down the nervous system, creating similar effects to heroin but in a less dangerous way. Research has found methadone to be an effective way of allowing addicts to wean themselves off heroin. For example, Newman and Whitehill (1979) found methadone to be significantly more successful than a placebo drug when used by a group of heroin addicts.

Tip: Antagonists reduce the effect of addictive drugs and substances.

Antagonists are also used as biological interventions in reducing addictive behaviours. They stop the drug from creating pleasurable feelings after someone has taken the addictive substance, so they prevent reinforcement.

Tip: Antagonists stop any form of reinforcement through operant conditioning. Remind yourself of pages 219-220 to see how conditioning might account for the maintenance of addictive behaviours.

Example

Naltrexone is a drug which stops pathways in the brain from transmitting feelings of pleasure. It's commonly used to treat heroin and alcohol addiction by ensuring that neither drug produces positive side effects for the user. This means there's no longer an association between pleasure and the drug, so no reinforcement or conditioning can take place.

Psychological interventions

The psychological approach consists of a range of therapies that aim to change the way an addict behaves by changing their thought processes. They are based on the behavioural and cognitive approaches which aim to help people to change their thoughts and beliefs in order to change their behaviour.

Cognitive behavioural therapy (CBT) and motivational interviewing (MI) are two types of psychological intervention which combine the behavioural and cognitive approaches. CBT identifies the thoughts that cause the behaviour, e.g. 'I can't cope without cigarettes', and then changes this thought process. This is known as cognitive restructuring. CBT has had some success, e.g. it has enhanced the effectiveness of nicotine replacement treatment for quitting smoking.

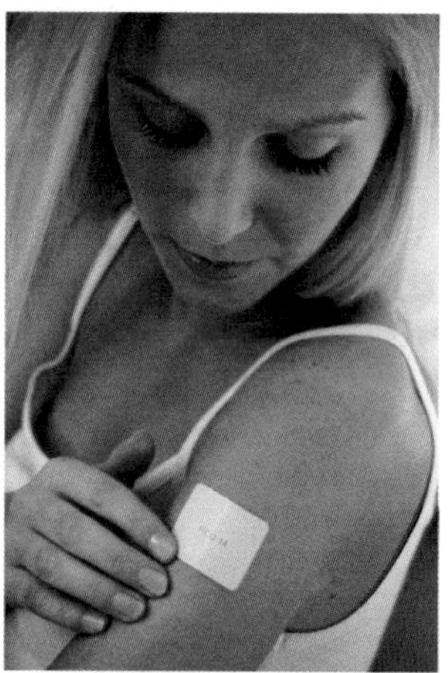

Figure 6: *Cognitive behavioural therapies can work alongside nicotine replacement interventions.*

Real World Connection

Audrain-McGovern et al (2011) compared two groups of teenagers who received different cognitive interventions. Group One received MI whilst the other received structured advice. Although they found that the MI group reduced the number of cigarettes they had on a daily basis, there was no difference between the number of teenagers who actually stopped smoking. Intervention practices may reduce smoking, but they may not be very successful in stopping behaviour.

Key study of CBT as an intervention for addiction — Carroll et al (1994)

Method: Carroll et al (1994) conducted a 12-week study which compared two different intervention practices using two groups of cocaine users. Group One were given a series of CBT sessions whilst Group Two received an alternative form of non-specific psychotherapy.

Results: Both therapies reduced the depressive symptoms of all participants, but CBT was more effective in stopping the addictive behaviour, and was more successful in a follow-up one year later.

Conclusion: CBT is more effective at stopping cocaine addiction than other forms of psychotherapy.

Evaluation: Although CBT is effective, it is still unclear how much more or less effective CBT is than other interventions.

Motivational interviewing (MI) is client-centred, meaning that the patient directs the therapy. With direction from the therapist, they are encouraged to solve their own problems which might be stopping them from changing their behaviour.

Tip: Empathy is really important in motivational interviewing — this is where the therapist tries to see things from the individual's point of view. Empathy provides a non-judgemental environment for the patient which may produce better results.

Key study of MI as an intervention for addiction — Lai et al (2010)

Method: A meta-analysis was conducted to summarise data from studies over a 12-year period which had compared the effectiveness of MI against various other interventions that involved casual advice for smokers.

Results: MI was significantly more effective at encouraging smokers to quit than the other interventions.

Conclusion: MI is an effective method of treatment to help people to stop smoking when given by a healthcare professional.

Evaluation: The results of meta-analyses can be reliable because they combine a lot of data from different studies. However, there may be other confounding variables which weren't accounted for in the meta-analysis — these could have influenced the participants' addictive behaviours.

Public health interventions

Public health interventions address addictive behaviours on a wide scale to reduce their impact on society. For example, to reduce smoking the government banned adverts for cigarettes. They also ran anti-smoking campaigns, placed warning messages on cigarette packs and increased prices. More recently, they've made it illegal to smoke in enclosed public places.

Some public health interventions aren't as straightforward as they sound. It was once proposed in America that the amount of nicotine in cigarettes could be reduced gradually until smokers were no longer addicted. However, in reality smokers might just end up smoking more to get the same effect. The measure would also meet with opposition from smokers.

It's also been suggested that cigarettes containing less nicotine could be made available, so that they won't be as dangerous to addicts. This is based on the idea that if people are going to engage in addictive behaviour, they may as well do it with 'safer' cigarettes.

Figure 7: Messages on cigarette packaging encourage people to quit.

Example

Benowitz et al (2007) believed that if cigarettes decreased their nicotine levels, the number of people who smoke would also decrease.

However, cigarette companies are unwilling to trial these ideas and more evidence would be needed to show how it could work as a potentially successful intervention.

It's difficult to prove the efficacy of public health interventions. One study found 5.1% of smokers gave up smoking after asking their GP for advice — but there's no way of telling if they'd have done that without help:

Key study of doctor's advice — Russell et al (1979)

Method: A group of smokers who were registered at five different London GP practices were divided into four groups. Each group received a different intervention to help them quit smoking. Smoking rates were measured after one month and at a 12-month follow-up. Group One had no intervention, Group Two completed a questionnaire, Group Three received doctors' advice and a questionnaire, whilst Group Four were given doctors' advice and a leaflet with advice on quitting.

Results: Although the rates of quitting were still low (5.1% in Group Four), the groups who had received advice were significantly more likely to quit smoking than the other groups who received no direct help (Groups One and Two).

Conclusion: Interventions, such as receiving advice, do play a role in stopping addictive behaviours.

Evaluation: This research was conducted in 1979 and therefore may not be representative of the modern day, especially with more research into the negative effects of smoking since.

Exam Tip

Giving examples of where psychology has been applied in the real world can help you pick up extra marks in the exam.

Worked Exam-style Question

0 1 Discuss the psychological interventions used to reduce addictive behaviours. *(16 marks)*

Addictive behaviours can be reduced using various intervention

> **Exam Tip**
> Start your answer with a brief introduction that outlines all the areas you'll cover in your answer.

> **Exam Tip**
> You'll have come across CBT in other areas of psychology, particularly in psychopathology.

> **Exam Tip**
> When a question asks you to 'discuss' you need to throw in some strengths and limitations.

> **Exam Tip**
> Finish off your answer by pointing out that there are other interventions which can reduce addictive behaviours. This, like lots of areas in psychology, shows that humans are complex, and due to individual differences everyone responds differently.

techniques — many of these take a psychological approach. Psychological interventions can include behavioural and cognitive-based therapies and each have varying degrees of success.

Two techniques which combine cognitive and behavioural approaches are cognitive behavioural therapy (CBT) and motivational interviewing (MI). Both try to restructure an individual's beliefs and thoughts in order to allow them to make changes to their behaviour. CBT involves a therapist helping a patient to identify which thoughts cause their behaviour. In terms of addiction, this involves the patient trying to figure out what thought processes they experience whenever they engage in the addictive behaviour. When they've identified the thoughts, the therapist then helps the patient to change their thought processes in a method known as 'cognitive restructuring'.

CBT is a successful therapy for reducing addictions. For example, Carroll et al (1994) tested its use in a 12-week study of cocaine users. Half of the participants underwent non-specific psychotherapy whilst the other half engaged in several weeks of CBT. The study found that both therapies were effective in treating depressive symptoms, but CBT was more effective in stopping the addictive behaviour and was also more successful in the long run. However, the fact that both therapies influenced people's feelings suggests that some intervention is better than none. As the study only tested two therapies, however, more research would be needed to see how effective CBT is compared with other methods.

MI is another psychological intervention used to treat and reduce addictive behaviour. This client-centred approach lets the patient change their behaviour by solving their own problems with the therapist's support. Lai et al (2010) conducted a meta-analysis, combining the results of many different studies. They showed evidence for MI as a successful intervention for those with a smoking addiction when administered by healthcare professionals. As this study was a meta-analysis, the results are likely to be reliable since they use data from a large number of studies.

Psychological interventions do appear to be successful in reducing addictive behaviours. However, there is also lots of evidence in support of other intervention techniques such as biological and public health initiatives, which suggests that there may not be one intervention which is better than any other. Perhaps tailoring the intervention programme to individuals would provide the most successful outcome. However, that could be impractical, time-consuming and expensive.

Summary Questions

Q1 The TRA proposes that intention is determined by two factors. Outline one of these factors.

Q2 a) What did Ajzen (1991) add to the TRA to create the TPB?

b) In what two ways does TPB suggest behaviour is influenced?

Q3 Name one personal variable, outlined by the health belief model, which might influence someone's perception of smoking.

Q4 Give one example of a biological intervention used to reduce addictive behaviour.

8. Studying Anomalous Experience

There are some experiences that are really hard to explain. Psychologists call this type of experience an anomalous experience. Read on to find out more...

Anomalous experiences

Something that can't be explained by science is called an anomalous experience. There are many different types:

- **Out-of-body experience** — a sensation of floating around outside of your own body.
- **Near-death experience** — sensations experienced when you're close to death, often interpreted as a glimpse into the 'afterlife'.
- **Spontaneous psychic ability (psi)** — extra-sensory perception, e.g. telepathy, clairvoyance or psychokinesis (altering an object, e.g. moving, bending or softening it using the mind).
- **Past-life experience** — remembering events from a previous existence.
- **Anomalous healing** — healing through unexplainable methods, e.g. by a spiritual healer or through prayer.

Anomalous experiences can't just be immediately rejected — many things that were once considered mysterious, e.g. thunder and lightning, can now be explained scientifically. So it's important that all anomalous experiences are investigated thoroughly — they may one day be explainable, either by what we already know about human behaviour, or accepted as something completely new.

What is parapsychology?

Parapsychology (also called anomalistic psychology) tries to explain paranormal events using scientific methods. Paranormal events are things that can't be explained using our current scientific knowledge. Many critics believe parapsychology to be pseudoscience. Whereas 'science' is objective, replicable, reliable and valid, 'pseudoscience' is often subjective, not replicable, unfalsifiable and unreliable.

Pseudoscience and fraud

Pseudoscience

Explanations based on evidence that's been collected through faulty scientific processes are known as pseudoscience. The results of many demonstrations of so-called anomalous experiences turn out to be caused by methodological issues such as **cognitive bias** and **experimenter effects**.

Cognitive bias

Spontaneous events, such as having a dream come true, are the main reasons why people believe in anomalous experiences. People who believe in such things have been shown to be more susceptible to the illusion of control than people who don't. The illusion of control is a cognitive bias (a faulty judgement) which causes people to believe that they're able to control or influence the outcome of an event over which, in reality, they have no control.

Example

Megan is willing her numbers to be called out in Bingo. If they're not called, she believes she hasn't been concentrating enough.

Learning Objectives:

- Understand pseudoscience and the scientific status of parapsychology.
- Know the methodological issues related to the study of paranormal cognition (ESP, including Ganzfeld) and paranormal action (psychokinesis).

Exam Tip

You only need to answer questions about one contemporary application of psychology. So choose media psychology, the psychology of addictive behaviour or anomalistic psychology and learn everything you need to know about that one.

Tip: There's more about what defines 'science' on page 251. It's helpful to know its characteristics so that you can make a comparison with pseudoscience.

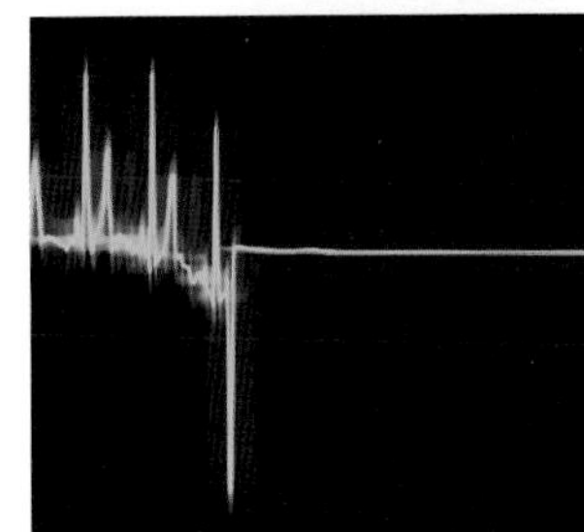

Figure 1: People often report out-of-body experiences if their heart stops during surgery.

Experimenter bias

The outcome of any psychological experiment can be affected by the expectations of the experimenter and how this manifests itself in their behaviour. Certain researchers consistently find significant results using the same methods whilst others consistently fail. This is known as experimenter effects. As a result of this, it's been suggested that only people who don't believe in that particular anomalous experience should be allowed to replicate the experiments. Experimenter effects exist in both directions though, and the expectations of sceptics could affect the experiment just as strongly in the other direction.

Tip: Often, studies that don't show any effects aren't published. This is because they're seen as less interesting. However, this means that there may be a publishing bias in some areas of psychology, suggesting that an effect is stronger than it actually is.

Fraud

Research has also been blighted by cases of fraud, where scientists have deliberately deceived people, invalidating observations and results. Researchers who believe in the anomalous experience are more likely to miss the tricks of fraudsters as they are biased towards results that are consistent with their existing beliefs.

People claiming to have psychic abilities usually demonstrate them most successfully when they have some control over how they show them and the way they are observed. In order to reduce the chances of pseudoscience and fraud being passed off as anomalous experiences, Wiseman and Morris (1995) developed a set of methodological guidelines for research into this area. They include advice on issues such as randomisation of stimuli and preventing 'sensory leakage' (where participants might unintentionally see or overhear stimuli) by soundproofing rooms, etc.

Tip: Although fraud in parapsychology shows the researcher in a bad light, it's also bad for anomalistic psychology as a whole. It could give the impression that researchers have to carry out fraud because their results aren't strong enough to support the theories.

Key study involving fraud — Levy (1974)

Method:	Levy (1974) tested psychokinetic ability in rats. He placed electrodes in the pleasure areas of their brain and connected the electrodes to a computer. The computer used a random event generator to send an impulse along the electrodes 50% of the time. Levy proposed that if the rats wanted to feel more pleasure, they would use some form of psychokinetic ability to influence the random event generator in order to stimulate the electrodes.
Results:	The computer transmitted signals over 50% of the time, indicating that the rats had influenced the random event generator.
Evaluation:	On further investigation from his colleagues, it became evident that Levy had unplugged the random event generator at certain intervals, causing the higher than 50% rate. Although a fraudulent study, this research still raises the problem of generalising results from animals to humans.

Figure 2: *Generalising findings from animals to humans involves many problems — especially if the experiment was fraudulent to begin with.*

Studies into psi

Studies into psi often provoke controversy.

Ganzfeld studies

Ganzfeld studies test participants for **extra-sensory perception (ESP)**. One participant, known as the receiver, is in a state of mild sensory deprivation. This is usually done by covering their eyes with halved ping pong balls, playing white noise through headphones and sitting them in a soundproof room lit with red light. A participant in another room, the sender, then

Tip: There's a high degree of skepticism about psi among scientists and psychologists.

concentrates on a visual stimulus in an attempt to transfer it to the receiver. The receiver is then shown four stimuli — one is the stimulus the sender attempted to transfer by ESP. If the receiver correctly identifies this stimulus it's called a hit. The results and interpretation of Ganzfeld experiments vary:

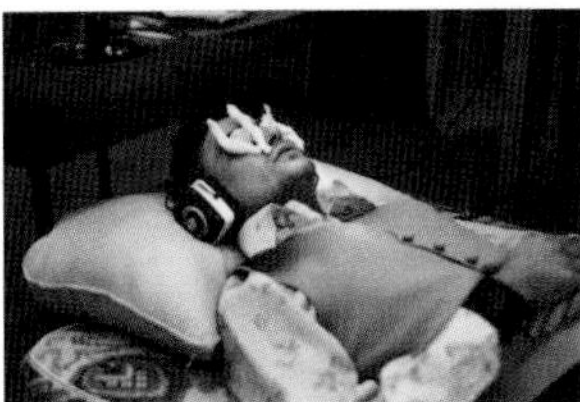

Figure 3: ESP experiments allow for the investigation of anomalous experiences.

Key Ganzfeld studies

A review of 28 Ganzfeld studies by Honorton (1985) showed a 38% hit rate, significantly above the 25% rate of chance. He claimed that this provided evidence for ESP. Hyman (1985) disagreed, criticising the studies for a lack of randomised stimuli, inconsistent judging procedures and selective reporting. After consideration, Honorton and Hyman jointly agreed on suitable conditions to address these flaws and autoganzfeld studies were designed to take these into account. The results of autoganzfeld studies still produced significant results.

A meta-analysis by Milton and Wiseman (1999) of 30 autoganzfeld studies showed no significant evidence for ESP. This analysis was criticised for including studies which deviated from the conventional technique. When the ten studies closest to the original technique were analysed by Bem et al (2001), a significant hit rate was found.

Real World Connection

There have been several famous cases reported in the media of people claiming to have psychokinetic abilities. One of these, written about by Targ and Puthoff (1974), is the case of Uri Geller who is famous for bending spoons.

Psychokinetic ability

Some people claim to have psychokinetic ability, which allows them to move objects using their mind alone. Many people dispute these claims — they believe that tricks are used to make it appear that objects have been altered by psychokinesis. Several magicians have demonstrated how this can be done. Belief in psychokinesis is often explained by cognitive biases such as the illusion of control (see page 224). To establish whether psychokinesis is possible researchers have searched for evidence in laboratory conditions.

One common method is to ask participants to alter the outcome of a computerised random number generator. This allows a lot of data to be collected in controlled conditions.

Example

Holger et al (2006) conducted a meta-analysis on the results of 380 such studies. They did find an effect but it was extremely small — it was probably only reported because of its interesting and controversial nature.

Key study of psychokinetic abilities — Wiseman and Greening (2005)

Method: Wiseman and Greening (2005) wanted to investigate whether psychokinetic abilities are actually the result of the audience's perceptions being influenced by verbal instructions. 46 undergraduate students were split into two groups. Both watched a video of a stationary bent key which they were told had just been bent by a psychic. Group One heard a voice-over describing that the key was still bending, whereas Group Two heard nothing.

Results: Group One were significantly more likely to believe the key was bending and were more confident in their beliefs.

Conclusion: It's possible to create the appearance of psychokinetic effects just through verbal instructions.

Evaluation: This laboratory experiment lacks ecological validity as the task wasn't very realistic.

Worked Exam-style Questions

0 1 Describe the methodological issues associated with parapsychology. *(8 marks)*

There are several methodological issues associated with parapsychology, which include cognitive bias, experimenter bias and fraud. This means that there is a strong argument that parapsychology is pseudoscience, and therefore that more scientifically robust research is required within this area of psychology before it can be treated as valid science. Parapsychology is the study of paranormal events (things that can't be explained using our current scientific knowledge). Trying to create valid and reliable ways to study something this complex has been difficult for psychologists.

Cognitive bias is the idea of a faulty judgement. It can happen when people have an illusion of control; this is where people believe that they're able to control or influence the outcome of an event which, in actual fact, they have no control over. For instance, someone might wish that their lottery numbers are drawn and then, when they're not, they blame themselves for not concentrating enough. People who believe in these anomalous experiences are often much more susceptible to faulty reasoning, which can affect the results of studies.

Experimenter bias is where the results of psychological experiments are influenced by the behaviour of the experimenter, which can be affected by their expectations. Some researchers consistently find significant results, and some consistently fail. This could be the result of experimenter effects, which can work in both directions.

A final issue is fraud, which happens when scientists deliberately report false results, or tamper with their experiments to get the results they want. For instance, Levy (1974) demonstrated that rats were able to show psychokinetic abilities. However, it was later found that he had been manipulating the equipment in order to get the results he needed to support his claim.

All of these issues with the methodology of parapsychology illustrate the potential problems in investigating anomalous experiences. As such, paranormal psychology may still be largely considered a pseudoscience as these issues prevent completely scientific and objective studies.

Exam Tip
Early on in your answer, it's a good idea to define the key words in the question — this shows the examiner that you understand exactly what you're being asked about.

Exam Tip
Then continue by defining each new term you use.

Exam Tip
Including real-life examples in your answer shows that you can apply your knowledge to other situations and contexts.

Exam Tip
Using studies to support your points shows that you've read around the subject.

Summary Questions

Q1 Name three types of anomalous experience.
Q2 Define parapsychology.
Q3 Explain how Levy's (1974) study was fraudulent.
Q4 What do Ganzfeld studies test for?
Q5 What is psychokinetic ability?

9. Explanations for Anomalous Experience

Unlike believers, skeptics think that paranormal activity can be explained rationally, using a variety of factors. Read on to see if you're a believer...

Learning Objectives:
- Understand the role of coincidence and probability judgements in anomalous experience.
- Know the explanations for superstitious behaviour and magical thinking.
- Understand the personality factors underlying anomalous experience.

Coincidence

A coincidence is when events appear to be linked (e.g. dreaming about a car crash and then being involved in one) when in fact the two events are unconnected and occurred closely together purely by chance.

Marks (2000) suggests that coincidence can be explained by subjective validation. Subjective validation is a cognitive bias (an error of judgement caused by faulty thought processes) that means we are more likely to believe in and pay attention to information that has personal relevance. As we concentrate on this personally relevant information (e.g. a dream we had), we don't pay attention to information that feels less relevant to us but is actually more relevant (e.g. the fact that a car pulled out in front of us). So we only see evidence that reinforces our belief in a psychic reason for the coincidence.

Probability judgements

Making a probability judgement involves assessing how likely it is that something will happen. This is usually subjective, so the judgement may differ widely from the actual true statistical probability. According to Wiseman and Watt (2006), probability misjudgements mean that we may believe in a psychic reason for something happening rather than the real reason.

Examples
- Believing that destiny is at play just because you find out that you have the same birthday as the person you fancy. However, the statistical likelihood of them being born on that particular date is the same regardless of whether or not it has personal relevance to you.
- You think it's fate when you run into someone from school when you're on holiday. However, since you'd both have the same school holidays and may have similar social backgrounds, this isn't too unlikely.

Real World Connection
Brugger et al (2002) found that there may be a biological cause for certain people being more susceptible to experiencing anomalous events than others. They discovered that those with higher dopamine levels were more likely to see patterns and coincidences where others didn't. Other biological methods and explanations include overactivity in the right hemisphere of the brain and the role of genes.

Figure 1: *Those with higher dopamine levels were more likely to report UFO sightings and see patterns where they might not exist.*

Superstition

A superstition is a belief that an object or action will affect outcomes when there is no logical reason for it to do so.

Examples
- Believing that wearing your lucky green underpants will mean you pass your driving test — even though passing this test is down to your driving skill and what you wear is irrelevant.
- Believing that Friday 13th will always bring bad luck — even though it isn't any different from other days.
- Believing that picking up a penny from the street will bring you good luck — even though good luck has little to do with picking up a coin.
- Believing that saying 'MacBeth' in a theatre will bring you ill fortune.

Superstitions are the result of cognitive biases such as the illusion of control (see page 224). Lorenz (1963) suggests that superstition is a response

Real World Connection
Superstitions and good luck mascots are used frequently in sporting situations — this could be because the outcome of sports events is often undetermined and, in an effort to regain control, sports people attach cognitive biases to certain behaviours. The 'Fuwa', or panda mascots, for the 2008 Olympic games in China literally translated to meaning 'good luck dolls'.

Tip: 'Compensatory control' could explain what Whitson and Galinsky's participants showed. Because they felt a lack of control in their lives they were attempting to regain some of that lost control by believing in the effectiveness of a superstitious action.

Figure 2: If this group of performers weren't told to 'break a leg' before they went on stage, they might become anxious and be more likely to break the plates... This could make them think that the superstition actually helps.

Tip: Ordinary objects are given 'special properties' in those who experience magical thinking.

we have adapted as a way to cope in some situations where we don't know or don't understand the true causality. It is better for us psychologically to believe in a false relationship rather than not to know what the relationship is at all. Vyse (2000) suggests that in some situations (e.g. job interviews, weddings or sports events), even if people have prepared as much as they could have, there are still some aspects which are out of their control. This means it's difficult to predict the outcome. Using superstition allows people to feel more in control than they actually are.

Key study of superstition — Whitson and Galinsky (2008)

Method:	Over six experiments, the researchers investigated the relationship between the level of control participants felt they had in certain situations and their superstitious beliefs. In one experiment, they asked participants to describe a situation where they felt out of control. They were then shown a scenario which included an actor carrying out a superstitious behaviour, such as tapping something three times. Participants had to rate how likely they thought the actor's superstition influenced the outcome of the scenario.
Results:	Participants who reported high levels of control were less likely to believe in the positive effects of a superstitious action.
Conclusion:	There are cognitive biases which determine how people perceive superstitions.
Evaluation:	Participants were asked to report their feelings of a lack of control which is a very subjective thing to define. This could affect the accuracy of the results. Participants also had to respond to recorded behaviours, which isn't very representative of real life.

Superstitions can be negative (e.g. believing that breaking a mirror brings bad luck) or positive (e.g. believing that lucky charms bring good luck). Positive superstitions may promote optimism and self-efficacy (belief in your ability to do something). This increased belief may increase the changes of the person influencing the situation themselves. This is known as the placebo effect, and it reinforces the initial superstition. However, positive superstitions can still have a negative effect if the person is very dependent on them.

Examples

- Putting your red underpants on by mistake on the day of a test might cause anxiety that impairs performance.
- Accidentally saying 'MacBeth' just before a show might leave actors feeling anxious and unable to perform as well as usual.

Magical thinking

Magical thinking is believing that if you think about something happening, or say that it will happen, it's more likely to actually happen. For example, you might think that wishing that you will win the lottery will make it more likely that you will win. This shows an incorrect understanding of causality. Cognitive bias means you ignore the actual cause (which is pure chance) and believe that your wish manipulates the outcome. Various theories have attempted to explain magical thinking:

- Psychodynamic approach — based on Freud's theories, magical thinking is explained as a defence mechanism brought about by anxiety. Adults revert to a childlike state by projecting their inner thoughts onto the outer world.
- Law of contagion — a belief that if two objects were previously touching, they may share special properties even when they're apart.

Example

Vic is a keen ballerina. She won a pair of Darcey Bussell's old ballet shoes and believes she will dance better whenever she wears them.

Magical thinking can have a positive influence on behaviour, especially through **self-fulfilling prophecies**. Rosenthal and Jacobsen (1968) suggested positive thoughts and expectations about people can lead to those people having a higher sense of achievement and desire to meet those expectations.

Tip: An example of a belief explained by the psychodynamic approach could be that thinking bad things about someone might bring them harm.

Personality factors

Ramakrishna (2001) used students as participants in his research and tested them for their extra-sensory perception (ESP) ability. He reported a positive correlation between scores in ESP tests and some personality traits, including being relaxed, assertive, sociable and talkative. He found a negative correlation between ESP scores and other personality traits, including being withdrawn, suspicious and impatient.

Ramakrishna's study is supported by other research that has found a similar relationship between personality and anomalous experience. However, we can't assume that certain personality factors make anomalous experience more likely (or vice versa).

Real World Connection
Magical thinking can be seen as an adaptive behaviour. Through the law of contagion, these thought processes may have helped us to avoid items which may have been previously contaminated.
For instance, Rozin and Nemeroff (1990) found participants were wary of drinking from a glass that had previously contained a dead cockroach, even if the cockroach had been sterilised.

Neuroticism and ESP

Studies have shown a link between neurotic personalities and paranormal beliefs.

Key study of personality — Williams et al (2007)

Method:	279 Welsh schoolchildren, aged between 13 and 16 years, were asked to complete two questionnaires to categorise their personalities according to Eysenck's definitions and to assess their paranormal beliefs.
Results:	There was a significant relationship between neuroticism levels and paranormal beliefs.
Conclusion:	High levels of neuroticism correlate with paranormal beliefs.
Evaluation:	As the study only involved Welsh schoolchildren, the results can't be generalised to the whole population. Also, it relied on self-report in questionnaires so the participants might not have been completely honest. The results therefore also lack reliability.

Figure 3: *Magical thinking may be adaptive.*

Tip: Eysenck categorised three different types of personality — you can read more about them on page 227.

Extroversion and ESP

Honorton et al (1998) did a meta-analysis of 38 studies testing ESP and extroversion. The experiments included Ganzfeld studies that limit the choice of possible answers, and tests that allowed free choice in the answers. They found that overall extroverts scored more highly than introverts on ESP tests in 77% of the studies. Other research also supports the possibility of a causal relationship between anomalous experiences and extroversion.

However, when ESP is tested in an experimental setting the situation is very artificial. Introverts may feel less comfortable and less able to focus on the task. Extroverts are less likely to feel uncomfortable and so their performance isn't affected. If this is true then the anxiety of taking part in an unfamiliar task could be an extraneous variable that affects introverts more than extroverts.

Haight (1979) conducted spontaneous ESP tests in a social situation so that all participants would feel relaxed whatever their personality type. Introverts and extroverts didn't score differently on these tests.

Creativity and ESP

Moon (1975) found that creative individuals are more likely to believe in paranormal activity and report experiences of ESP than less creative people. This was supported by research by Thalbourne (2001), who conducted a meta-analysis of 15 studies. A standardised measure of creativity was used to assess participants. A significant correlation was found between level of creativity and belief in ESP.

This research into personality factors and anomalous experiences is only able to suggest relationships and doesn't show any causality — other variables besides personality could also be involved.

Real World Connection
'Fantasy proneness' is another factor which can be linked to belief in ESP. It can be used to explain why so many people report paranormal activity such as UFO sightings. Gow et al (2001) compared the personalities of two groups of people. Group One reported to have been abducted by aliens whereas those in Group Two didn't. The results of the study showed that fantasy beliefs were greater in those in Group One — they were more likely to believe objects had thoughts or feelings and were more likely to spend time fantasising during a normal day.

Worked Exam-style Question

0 1 Outline personality factors underlying anomalous experience. *(8 marks)*

Anomalous experiences can be explained using personality factors. Several personality factors have been implicated, including extroversion, neuroticism and creativity. Honorton et al (1998) conducted a meta-analysis which examined the results of 38 different studies which had investigated extroversion and extra-sensory perception (ESP) ability. They found that extroverts scored more highly on tests of ESP than introverts, supporting the idea that personality does influence anomalous experience.

Another personality factor which has been linked to ESP is neuroticism. Support has been given by Williams et al (2007) who conducted a large study of schoolchildren, assessing the personality differences in children who did and didn't believe in paranormal activity. Their study supported a correlation between neurotic personalities and paranormal beliefs.

Creativity may also account for anomalous experiences. Moon (1975) conducted research which showed a correlation between creative people and reported experiences of paranormal activity and ESP. Those who were creative were more likely to believe in paranormal activity and report experiences of ESP than less creative individuals.

Exam Tip
You don't need to include any evaluative comments in your answer as the question only asks you to outline the factors. So don't waste your time on giving information that won't be needed.

Summary Questions

Q1 What is meant by subjective validation?

Q2 Give an example of a probability judgement that could explain anomalous experience.

Q3 How did Lorenz (1963) explain superstitions?

Q4 What is magical thinking?

10. Research into Exceptional Experience

Exceptional experiences can be hard to research. But that hasn't stopped psychologists from trying. Read on to find out about psychic healing and other paranormal phenomena...

Learning Objective:

- Know about psychological research into the explanations for psychic healing, near death and out of body experiences, and psychic mediumship.

Psychic healing

Psychic healers claim they can treat illness and injury without any physical intervention. Instead, the healer moves their hands over the patient's body without making contact. The aim is to transfer a force and restore balance in the patient. Some studies have been done to try to determine whether psychic healing actually works.

Key study of psychic healing — Attevelt (1988)

Method: In an independent groups design, 96 asthma patients were allocated to one of 3 groups — an optimal group, a distance group and a control group. Patients in the optimal group received treatment from a psychic healer in the usual way. The distance group patients were also treated by a healer, but this time from behind a screen. The control group didn't receive any treatment but the screen was present. Distance group and control group patients didn't know which group they belonged to as their physical experiences were the same. Physical and subjective measures of asthma symptoms were taken.

Results: The physical symptoms of asthma (measured by peak flow) improved significantly in all patients.
The optimal group improved significantly more than the other groups on subjective measures of well-being (i.e. they 'felt' an improvement).

Conclusion: The lack of difference between physical symptoms of patients in the different groups shows that improvement was not down to paranormal effects. The subjective improvement in the optimal group patients but not distance group patients shows the influence of psychological rather than paranormal factors.

Evaluation: Participants were randomly allocated to groups after being stratified (see page 254) according to the severity of their asthma. This prevented bias in the groups. The people who took the patients' peak flow measurements didn't know which group each patient belonged to. This also prevented bias. The use of a control group distinguished the psychological effects of visiting a healer from the physiological effects.

Figure 1: Physical measures provide researchers with a more scientific measure of improvement, especially in terms of health.

Additional study of psychic healing — Sicher et al (1998)

Method: In a double-blind experiment, a group of 40 AIDS patients were divided into two treatment condition groups — the first received ten weeks of standard care whilst the second

Tip: Double-blind studies eliminate the possibility of experimenter or participant bias (see page 252).

Tip: This experiment could be considered unethical by those who believe in psychic healing — it isn't fair to deny one group a treatment which might be successful.

received the same ten weeks of standard care plus an additional hour of distant healing each day, six days a week for ten weeks. The number of hospital visits and doctor appointments was monitored alongside illness severity over the duration of the experiment.

Results: Those who received the psychic healing reported a significantly greater improvement to their mood and had fewer hospital stays and appointments

Conclusion: Psychic healing is correlated with feelings of improvement amongst AIDS patients.

Evaluation: There are many other factors which may have affected the outcome of this experiment — personality effects and the gender of the participants may have influenced their improvements. However, because the study was double-blind, the improvement can't have simply been down to the participants knowing which group they were in. The sample used in the study was also small, which means the results could just be due to chance.

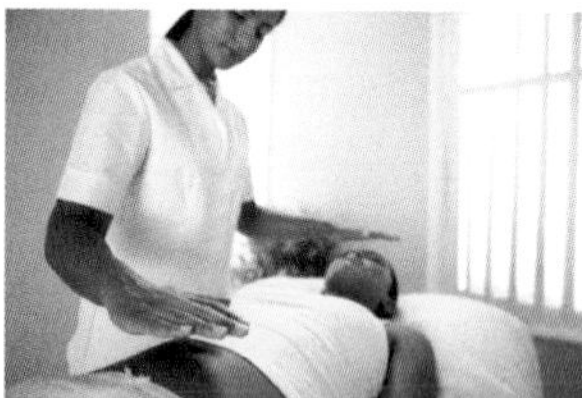

Figure 2: *Psychic healing as an effective treatment has mixed support.*

As with most research in psychology, there are countless experiments which have tried to disprove the theories. Research into psychic mediumship is no exception.

Key study of evidence against psychic healing — Lyvers et al (2006)

Method: Lyvers et al (2006) took a group of 20 back pain sufferers and randomly allocated them to one of two groups. Group One were given psychic healing whilst Group Two were not.

Results: There was no difference in the improvement of back pain between Group One and Group Two. However, their prior belief in whether the treatment would work was significantly correlated to an improvement in their back pain.

Conclusion: There is no evidence for psychic healing but there is evidence for personal beliefs influencing improvement.

Evaluation: A small sample size makes the results of this study hard to generalise to a wider population.

Tip: The placebo effect could underlie a lot of psychic healing research. If people believe strongly enough that treatment will work, it may improve their mood, which could influence their physical improvement.

Out-of-body experiences

An out-of-body experience (OBE) is a sensation of floating outside the body, seeing the world from a different perspective. They're spontaneous and rare events so researching them is difficult. Most evidence is based on case studies.

Tip: Many people remain sceptical about the interpretation of OBEs and much of the research into them has been heavily criticised.

Key study of the case of Miss Z — Tart (1968)

Method: This case study was based on a young woman (Miss Z) who reported experiencing OBEs in her sleep since childhood. Tart brought her into a sleep lab for 4 nights to compare her reports of OBEs with physiological data collected from an EEG that monitored her brain activity. Also, numbers were written down and placed where they couldn't be seen from

	the bed (e.g. lying on top of high shelves). Miss Z was asked to find these target numbers during her OBE, whilst she was physically still in bed.
Results:	Miss Z's OBEs correlated with a particular pattern of non-dreaming, non-awake brain waves. On one occasion, she also correctly identified a 5 digit target number.
Conclusion:	OBEs have a physiological basis.
Evaluation:	The study had to rely on Miss Z's own reports of when and for how long she had left her body. These reports were retrospective and subjective. Tart couldn't be sure that Miss Z hadn't found out the target number conventionally, e.g. from seeing its reflection in the nearby clock face. This study isn't accepted as reliable psychological research by the wider scientific community.

Tip: A lot of research into OBEs relies on self-report. This means it's hard to prove whether or not they happen, so they're unfalsifiable. This provides more support for why the study of parapsychology might be considered pseudoscience.

Some recent studies have induced states similar to OBEs through brain stimulation of participants. This suggests that OBEs could be explained by physiological mechanisms causing a kind of 'waking dream'.

Example

Ehrsson (2007) reproduced the physiological effects of an OBE by giving participants a set of special glasses which caused a visual illusion. The participant could see what was happening behind them, and even though they knew it was a result of the glasses, they still experienced a fear response. This shows that OBEs can feel very real, even if they're illusions.

Near-death experiences

There are obviously ethical issues involved in creating states of near death for the purposes of studying near-death experiences (NDEs). So, like OBEs, most research has to be taken from case studies. From an accumulation of 102 case studies, Kenneth Ring (1980) determined that individuals reporting NDEs don't fit a particular gender, age or religious profile. There also appears to be no link between the reporting of an NDE and a person's attitude towards the paranormal.

Individuals who came close to death or were clinically dead for a period of time report experiences such as moving through a tunnel towards a light, OBEs, reuniting with dead loved ones and feeling total contentment. These experiences were found even when the moments leading up to near-death were particularly nasty. Medication at the time of death did not predict the experience of NDE. Reports of NDEs are more coherent than reports of hallucinations. Individuals who report experiencing an NDE also report life-changing shifts of attitudes, often developing a newly found appreciation of life and loved ones.

Tip: Like OBEs, NDEs are hard to prove and some psychologists question whether they actually occur or not.

Psychic mediumship

Psychic mediumship is the ability to communicate with spirits and transmit messages from the dead to the living. There are a range of methods with which mediums claim they can communicate with the dead, including telepathy and being possessed by spirits that then talk through them. Studies of psychic mediumship are usually based on séances — intentional attempts to communicate with spirits. One of the most famous studies into psychic mediumship is the Scole Experiment.

Figure 3: *Séances, like the one used in the Scole Experiment, are often subject to criticism.*

Key study — the Scole Experiment

The Scole Experiment took place in Norfolk between 1993 and 1998. Researchers including Fontana, Ellison and Keen witnessed 37 séances in rooms that were thoroughly searched beforehand to try to prevent any trickery. A professional magician was also present to identify any attempts at fraud. During the séances a number of paranormal occurrences were reported. These included the materialisation of objects, levitation, patterns of light, voices and the appearance of whole people or body parts.

Some people believe that the Scole Experiment provides evidence of life after death and mediumship. No fraud was identified at any time during the experiment and the professional magician present confirmed that no currently known trickery could have produced the effects that were observed.

However, the experiment has been heavily criticised and isn't widely accepted as evidence for mediumship. The experimental conditions were unreliable — to some extent they were controlled by the mediums. For example, the researchers wanted to use infra-red imaging (as most of the séances took place in darkness) but this was rejected by the mediums as they claimed it would distract them. Also, all the experimenters believed in the paranormal so may have shown experimenter effects (see page 252).

Tip: Sensory leakage happens when information is actually transferred by normal means, rather than through paranormal means. For example, there might be visual or auditory cues that haven't been accounted for.

Key study of psychic mediumship — O'Keeffe and Wiseman (2005)

Method:	Five psychic mediums were asked to take part in this study. They each gave readings to five different participants (sitters). The sitters then rated all of the readings in terms of accuracy.
Results:	All of the sitters rated the readings as being inaccurate, including the reading that they received themselves.
Conclusion:	There is no evidence for psychic mediumship.
Evaluation:	Participants may have been more sceptical than usual due to the nature of the experiment. However, this was a highly controlled experiment which eliminated any effects that may have been caused by sensory leakage.

Tip: The Barnum effect is sometimes referred to as the Forer effect.

Belief in psychic mediumship is often down to the fact that the statements of mediums are often fairly ambiguous and therefore people interpret them to be personally relevant. This is known as the **Barnum effect** and provides one possible explanation for why support for psychic mediumship may exist.

Worked Exam-style Questions

0 1 Outline and evaluate psychological research into the explanations for psychic mediumship. *(8 marks)*

There has been lots of psychological research which has tried to explain psychic mediumship. Psychic mediumship is the idea that people can communicate with spirits, creating a channel from the dead to the living in which messages can cross over. Through séances, people claim to have evidence of psychic mediumship.

However, séances can be very difficult to research so it's also very difficult to find reliable evidence to support psychic mediumship. The Scole Experiment is one psychological study which tried to investigate psychic mediumship. From 1993 to 1998, the researchers examined 37 different séances in rooms which had been previously searched in order to ensure no trickery or deception was being used. To avoid any element of fraud, a professional magician was also present. During the séances, there were many reports of paranormal activity — materialisation of objects, levitation, patterns of light and the appearance of people.

Whilst this evidence could be taken as proof that mediumship exists, the experiment has been heavily criticised. The conditions were unreliable as most of the séance took place in the dark. Also the experimenters strongly believed in paranormal behaviours and this may have resulted in experimenter effects which could have biased the results towards support of mediumship.

Other research has also tried to find support for psychic mediumship and concluded that there is no evidence for it. For example, O'Keeffe and Wiseman (2005) asked five different psychics to give readings for five different participants. The results provided no evidence for their abilities, suggesting that other factors must be involved. However, participants may have been more sceptical than normal given the nature of the experiment.

Overall, the psychological research into the explanations for psychic mediumship has mixed support. Because of this lack of concrete evidence, there may be other explanations which might explain such paranormal behaviours.

Exam Tip
The question asks you to evaluate research into the explanations for psychic mediumship. Each of these studies suggests that experimenter or participant bias could account for psychic mediumship.

Exam Tip
The question is asking you to outline and evaluate the studies — so make sure you write a bit more than just describing the methods.

---

0 2 Outline and evaluate research into out-of-body experiences.
(4 marks)

Out-of-body experiences (OBEs) are difficult to research using robust scientific methods since they rely on individual reports and case studies. This means that the results are often unreliable and also can't be generalised to the wider population. The events themselves are also usually spontaneous and fairly rare.

One study with such problems was conducted by Tart (1968). Tart carried out a case study of Miss Z, a young woman who reported having OBEs on several occasions. When she was monitored in a sleep lab, the results showed that her OBEs correlated with particular sleep patterns. Tart concluded that there is a physiological basis to OBEs. However, the reports from Miss Z were retrospective and highly subjective. Tart's study, along with other issues highlighted above, show that research into OBEs is inconclusive and could be considered to be pseudoscience.

Exam Tip
You need to evaluate in your answer here — that means you should talk about the strengths and weaknesses of the research methods and the conclusions which have been drawn from them.

Summary Questions

Q1 a) Describe the method used by Attevelt (1988) to research psychic healing.

b) What did Attevelt conclude?

Q2 Give one problem associated with studying near-death experiences.

Q3 Name one researcher who carried out a meta-analysis into NDEs.

Section Summary

Media Psychology

- It's been suggested that the media affects behaviour in many different ways. The social learning theory suggests that we model our behaviour on behaviour that we observe, particularly if it has a positive outcome.
- Social cognitive observation learning theory suggests that children don't just learn behaviours. They also learn how to think about the world around them, and their behaviour is shaped through schemas, scripts and normative beliefs.
- Violent media has been linked to aggressive behaviour and studies have looked at the effects of television, video games and computers on antisocial behaviour.
- Several theories have been used to explain how attitudes can change through persuasion. The Hovland-Yale and the Elaboration Likelihood models both look at how people can be persuaded.
- Using pleasant associations, making the message bizarre, using familiar figures, and using tactics such as fear and repetition are all ways in which the media have tried to persuade people.
- Psychologists have looked at why people are attracted to celebrities. By looking at such parasocial relationships, they have come up with several theories. These theories include evolutionary explanations, and psychological explanations such as attachment theory, the absorption-addiction model and the positive/active view.
- Fandom is the term used to describe a group of fans of a particular celebrity, and also the subculture of fans in general. There are three stages of fandom, each more intense than the last — entertainment-social, intense-personal and borderline-pathological.
- There are several myths surrounding stalking behaviour. Stalking doesn't always affect celebrities, it doesn't usually involve strangers and it doesn't always end in violence.

The Psychology of Addictive Behaviour

- Addiction can involve three stages — initiation, maintenance and relapse.
- Psychologists have tried to explain addictive behaviours, such as smoking and gambling. Explanations come from the biological approach, the social learning approach, the cognitive approach and the psychodynamic approach.
- There are several theories which try to explain why some people might be vulnerable to addiction. Factors include stress, age, peer pressure, personality and personality disorders.
- The theory of reasoned action (TRA) model of behaviour predicts that a person's behaviour can be determined by their intention to perform an action. This is shaped by the person's attitude to the behaviour and subjective norms.
- The theory of planned behaviour (TPB) expands on the TRA by including a person's perceived behavioural control. It suggests behaviours can be influenced in two ways — indirectly and directly.
- The health belief model considers someone's perception of susceptibility to health problems and their severity along with a cost-benefit analysis of the behaviour.
- Interventions to reduce addictive behaviours include biological (detox and medication), psychological (cognitive behavioural therapy and motivational interviewing) and public health interventions.

Anomalistic Psychology

- Anomalous experiences can't be explained by science. They include out-of-body experiences, near-death experiences, spontaneous psychic abilities (psi), past-life experiences and anomalous healing.
- Parapsychology involves the study of anomalous experiences. Lots of critics believe it to be a pseudoscience.
- Pseudoscience and fraud can explain why some evidence seems to support anomalous experience. Pseudoscience is research where results are collected through faulty scientific processes, often involving cognitive bias and experimenter effects.
- Psi has been studied using a method known as Ganzfeld studies. These test people for extra-sensory perception (ESP) and involve a participant trying to receive 'images' from another participant via ESP. The evidence so far is mixed.
- Psychokinetic ability allows someone to move objects just by using their mind. Once again, the evidence is mixed.
- Psychologists have tried to explain why people have anomalous experiences — they've suggested these experiences could be due to coincidence, faulty probability judgements, superstition, magical thinking or personality factors.
- Research into exceptional experiences has involved studies into psychic healing, out-of-body experiences, near-death experiences and psychic mediumship. The evidence has been inconclusive and people have been very sceptical about the interpretations of these experiences.

Exam-style Questions

Choose one topic from this section. Answer all questions on the topic you choose.

Media Psychology

0 1 Kate loves to follow the lives of her favourite celebrities, a behaviour that her boyfriend, Matthew, doesn't understand at all.

Outline and evaluate **two** explanations as to why Kate may be more attracted to the idea of 'celebrity' than Matthew.

(4 marks + 6 marks)

0 2 Outline **one** psychological model that has been proposed to explain the persuasive effects of the media.

(4 marks)

0 3 "The reason for the riots that took place in London in August 2011 is that so many young people are watching violent films."

Using your knowledge of psychology, consider to what extent psychologists have shown that this is true.

(10 marks)

The Psychology of Addictive Behaviour

0 4 Shaun is 18. He goes out drinking four nights a week with his friends. He has developed an addiction to alcohol.

Outline **two** factors which may have led to the development of his addiction.

(4 marks)

0 5 Shaun has started to visit a health psychologist who is using an intervention programme to treat his alcohol addiction.

Outline one psychological intervention for reducing addictive behaviour.

(4 marks)

0 6 Discuss models that have been proposed to explain addictive behaviour.

(16 marks)

Anomalistic Psychology

0 7 Outline methodological issues which can arise during the study of paranormal cognition.

(8 marks)

0 8 Lee doesn't believe in paranormal activity but always reads his horoscope in the newspaper. One day it claims, "an old friend will re-enter your life". The very next day, Lee bumps into a childhood friend in the local supermarket.

Discuss explanations of why Lee might start to believe in paranormal activity after this experience.

(8 marks)

0 9 "Parapsychology is not a real science."

Discuss this statement using your knowledge of pseudoscience.

(8 marks)

1. Is Psychology a Science?

This question always causes a bit of a debate. Some aspects of psychology are more scientific than others, making it a difficult question to answer...

Learning Objectives:

- Understand the major features of science, including replicability, objectivity, theory construction, and the use of empirical methods.
- Know about validating new knowledge and the role of peer review.

What is science?

Science is about establishing truths. Scientific research should be objective — independent of beliefs or opinions. So, the methods used should be empirical — based on experimental data, not just theory. The best way to make sure of this is to carry out an experiment that collects quantitative data and has strictly controlled variables. This means that you should be able to establish cause and effect. However, it's hard to make an experiment completely objective.

Tip: To establish 'cause and effect' means to work out if changing one variable causes a direct change in another.

Example

Rosenthal and Fode (1963) showed this in an experiment on psychology undergraduates. They were told to train some rats to run a maze, and that some of the rats were genetically predisposed to be better at learning than others. Actually there was no difference between any of the rats, but the students' results showed that the supposedly more intelligent rats did better in the maze task. This shows how researchers can bring their own biases and expectations to an experiment.

Figure 1: *Rosenthal and Fode (1963) illustrated experimenter bias using rats.*

Popper (a leading philosopher of science) suggested that it's impossible for any research to be totally objective — scientists will always have an expectation about what they think will happen and this will influence their experiments.

Validity and reliability of scientific theories

Scientific theories should have validity and reliability. So, all scientific work must undergo **peer review** before it's published — it's sent to experts in the field (peers) so they can assess its quality. Poor research won't pass peer review so it won't get published. This helps to validate conclusions — it means published theories, data and conclusions are more trustworthy.

Other scientists then read the published research, and try to repeat it. This tests whether the theory is reliable. If it is, then the results should be replicated every time the experiment is done — this shows that the findings aren't affected by time or place. If the replica experiments provide evidence to back it up, the theory is thought of as scientific 'fact' (for now). If new evidence comes to light that conflicts with the current evidence the theory is questioned again. More rounds of testing will be carried out to see which evidence, and so which theory, prevails.

Tip: For more on the scientific process, have a look at the 'How Science Works' section on pages 5-8.

Tip: When other scientists replicate a study they must go about it in exactly the same way as the original experiment. This means that studies must be published with a very detailed method — see page 288 for more info.

Problems with doing research on humans

Psychological research is very different to the research in other sciences — humans are complex, so it's hard to find general laws for their behaviour.

Sampling

Scientists can't study every occurrence of something, so they need to use samples that represent what they're looking at. This is fine if it's something like carbon or gravity. The problem in psychology is that humans vary a lot, and

Figure 2: People vary a lot, making it difficult to generalise findings from studies.

in different ways — e.g. age, gender, culture or class could all be explanations for a person's behaviour. This makes it really difficult to generalise to the whole population from small samples.

Operationalisation

Operationalising variables means defining them in measurable terms. However, human behaviour is often hard to define, so it's questionable whether things like motivation or love can be operationalised accurately. This means that human behaviour is a very difficult variable to control.

Procedures

Experiments focus on just a few specific variables, so they're simplistic compared to real life. The lack of **ecological validity** means you might never see genuine behaviour in a controlled experiment.

Participant variables

People bring their past learning and experiences to experiments.
This can cause:

- **Demand characteristics** — where participants form an idea of what the experiment's about and change their behaviour.
- **The Hawthorne effect** — where people's behaviour changes because they know they're being watched.
- **Social desirability bias** — when people change their behaviour to make themselves look better, e.g. more generous.

Tip: Participants might not change their behaviour on purpose, but if we know that we are taking part in a study we're bound to try and guess what it's about. This can cause us to change our behaviour without realising it.

Experimenter effects

The experimenter can influence participants without meaning to, by giving out subtle clues about how they should behave. This means you can never know for sure if behaviour is genuine.

Scientific approaches in psychology

Some psychological approaches are more scientific than others (see Figure 3).

Tip: A theory is falsifiable if it could in principle be proved wrong. Popper (1969) claimed that a theory is only scientific if it's falsifiable. You can never prove a theory to be right, but you can gain support for a theory each time an attempt to falsify it fails.

Biological

Empirical methods are used which get quantitative data, e.g. brain scans. This means results can be replicated and aren't affected by participant variables such as past experience. The theories are falsifiable.

Behaviourist

It only looks at observable behaviour, not thought processes or emotions, so the methods are empirical. E.g. animal studies get quantitative data and falsifiable theories. However, participant variables can have an impact on results.

Cognitive

Empirical methods are used, e.g. memory tests, so findings can be replicated and the theories are falsifiable. But, it's hard to isolate the variables because it's hard to separate cognitive processes. Also, participant variables can affect results.

Social

Some experimental methods are used which get quantitative data, e.g. Milgram's (1963) study. Other methods are based on observation and get qualitative data, e.g. studies that look at prejudice. This means the variables can be difficult to operationalise and control.

Psychodynamic

Psychodynamic theories are based on abstract concepts that can't be tested, e.g. the unconscious mind. This means they're non-falsifiable.

Very scientific

↑

Biological

Behaviourist

Cognitive

Social

Psychodynamic

↓

Not very scientific

Figure 3: Some approaches are more scientific than others.

The non-experimental research methods (e.g. dream analysis) produce qualitative data and are unreliable, so the findings can't be replicated or generalised.

Worked Exam-style Questions

0 1 Suggest why objectivity can be a problem in psychological research. *(4 marks)*

Psychological research should be ideally objective, as science is about establishing truths. This means that the methods used should be empirical — based on experimental data, not just theory. This is done by carrying out experiments that collect quantitative data and have strictly controlled variables, which allows cause and effect to be established. However, Popper believed that it's impossible to make an experiment completely objective. He thought that researchers will always have expectations about what will happen, and this influences their experiments. This was shown by Rosenthal and Fode (1963). Students were asked to train rats to run a maze, and were told that some of the rats were genetically predisposed to be better at learning than others. The students' results showed that the 'intelligent' rats did better in the task, when actually there was no difference between the rats. This shows how researchers can introduce their own biases and expectations to an experiment.

---

0 2 A psychologist has developed a new theory and wants to publish the results of his research.
Describe the process of validating new knowledge within the field of psychology. *(4 marks)*

All scientific work must undergo peer review before it's published to help ensure it has validity and reliability. Firstly the psychologist's work should be sent to experts in the field (peers) so they can assess its quality. This is known as peer review. Poor research won't pass peer review so it won't get published. This process helps to validate conclusions — it means published theories, data and conclusions are more trustworthy.

Other scientists would then read the published research, and try to repeat it. This tests whether the theory is reliable. If it is, then the results should be replicated every time the experiment is done, showing that the findings aren't affected by time or place. If the replica experiments provide evidence to back it up, the theory is more likely to be thought of as scientific 'fact'. However, if new evidence comes to light that conflicts with the current evidence, the theory is questioned again. More rounds of testing will be carried out to see which evidence, and so which theory, prevails.

Exam Tip
Section C in the Unit 4 exam is called Psychological Research and Scientific Method. It's worth 35 marks in total and is made up of quite a lot of smaller question parts, like the two shown here.

Summary Questions

Q1 Why did Popper think that it's impossible for any research to be totally objective?

Q2 What is meant by the term 'operationalisation'?

Q3 Explain why the biological approach to psychology can be considered scientific.

Learning Objectives:

- Know about selection and application of appropriate research methods.
- Understand the implications of sampling strategies, for example, bias and generalising.
- Know about issues of reliability, including types of reliability, assessment of reliability and improving reliability.
- Know how to assess and improve validity, including internal and external.

2. Designing Psychological Investigations

You can't just wake up one day and do a psychological experiment. Investigations take a lot of planning and designing...

Finding a sample

Research takes samples from a target population. It's really important that the sample is representative of the population. It should include the variety of characteristics that are found in the group, e.g. the group 'student' includes both males and females. If the sample is biased in any way, it's hard to generalise any findings to the whole population.

There are many different ways to select a sample:

Random sample

Everyone in the target group has an equal chance of being selected. Although this is fair and will probably provide a good variety of people, it doesn't guarantee that the sample will be representative — some subgroups could be missed.

Systematic sample

Taking every nth name from a sampling frame (a record of all the names in a population), e.g. every 3rd name from a register, or every 50th name from a phone book. This is useful if there is a sampling frame available, but it isn't truly random or representative, and subgroups may be missed.

***Figure 1:** Systematic sampling is convenient, but doesn't produce a truly random sample.*

Opportunity sample

Studying whoever is available at the time, e.g. students. This is quick, easy and cheap, but it's very unlikely that the sample will be representative.

Self-selected sample

Participants volunteer, e.g. by responding to a newspaper advertisement. This can save time and there may be many replies, producing a large sample. However, it's unlikely to be representative as only certain types of people are likely to volunteer.

Stratified sample

All of the important subgroups in the population (e.g. different age or ethnic groups) are identified and a proportionate number are randomly obtained. This can produce a fairly representative sample, but it takes a lot of time/money to do and subgroups may be missed.

***Figure 2:** Students are often used in psychology studies as they are easy to find.*

Here's a reminder of some of the different research methods used for psychological studies, and their advantages and drawbacks.

Questionnaires

Questionnaires can be face-to-face, on the phone, or via the internet. They are a self-report method, which involves asking participants about their feelings, beliefs and attitudes, etc.

Tip: Most of these research methods should be familiar to you from AS, but you can never have too much information...

Advantage

- They're practical — you can collect a large amount of information quickly and relatively cheaply.

Disadvantages

- Bad questions — leading questions (questions that suggest a desired answer) or unclear questions can be a problem.

- Biased samples — some people are more likely to respond to a questionnaire, which might make a sample unrepresentative.
- Social desirability bias — people sometimes want to present themselves in a good light. What they say and what they actually think could be different, making any results unreliable.
- Ethics — confidentiality can be a problem, especially around sensitive issues which people might not want to discuss.

Other self-report methods include interviews and case studies (see page 279). Self-report methods often provide qualitative data.

Figure 3: *Social desirability bias can be a big drawback of self-report measures.*

Correlational research

Correlational research looks for relationships between variables. **Correlation** means that two variables appear to be connected — they rise and fall together, or one rises as the other falls. BUT it doesn't always mean that a change in one variable causes a change in the other.

Examples

As age increases so might stress (see Figure 4) but ageing doesn't necessarily cause stress.
Or, as it gets sunnier, the number of people getting drunk might increase, but the sun doesn't make people drunk.

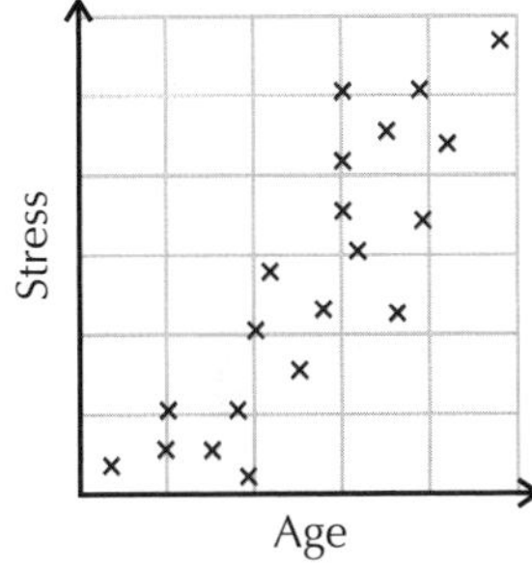

Figure 4: *Scattergram to show the correlation between age and stress.*

Advantages

- Causal relationships — these can be ruled out if no correlation exists.
- Ethics — you can study variables that would be unethical to manipulate, e.g. is there a relationship between the number of cigarettes smoked and incidences of ill health?

Disadvantage

- Causal relationships — these cannot be assumed from a correlation, which may be caused by a third, unknown variable. Sometimes the media (and researchers) infer causality from a correlation.

Laboratory experiments

Laboratory experiments are controlled and scientific. They aim to control all relevant variables except for one key variable, which is altered to see what its effect is. The variable that you alter is called the **independent variable**. Laboratory experiments are conducted in an artificial setting.

Figure 5: *Laboratory experiments lack ecological validity as they often take place in an artificial setting.*

Advantages

- Control — the effects of **extraneous variables** (those that could have an effect in addition to the key variable) are minimised.
- Replication — you can run the study again to check the findings.
- Causal relationships — it should be possible to establish whether change in one variable actually causes change in another.

Disadvantages

- Ecological validity — experiments are artificial and might not measure real-life behaviour.
- Demand characteristics — participants' behaviour changes when they know they're being studied. They may respond according to what they think is being investigated, which can bias the results.
- Ethics — deception is often used, making informed consent difficult.

Tip: Getting informed consent is really important when conducting research. It prevents the people participating in the study from agreeing to do something that they don't feel comfortable with. For more on ethics see pages 260-262.

Figure 6: Field experiments have high ecological validity as they take place in a natural environment.

Field experiments

In field experiments, behaviour is measured in a natural environment — like a school, the street or on a train. A key variable is still altered so that its effect can be measured.

Advantages

- Causal relationships — you can still establish causal relationships by manipulating the key variable and measuring its effect. However it's very difficult to control all the variables in a field experiment.
- Ecological validity — field experiments are less artificial than those done in a laboratory, so they reflect real life better.
- Demand characteristics — these can be avoided if participants don't know they're in a study. They will behave as they usually do in real life.

Disadvantages

- Less control — extraneous variables are often much more likely in a natural environment.
- Ethics — you often can't get informed consent and the participants can't be debriefed. Observation must respect privacy.

Tip: Natural experiments measure, but don't control, variables. They really just take advantage of naturally occurring situations by observing their outcomes.

Natural experiments

A natural experiment is a study where the independent variables aren't directly manipulated by the experimenter. In other words, things are left as they naturally would be.

Advantage

- Ethics — it's possible to study variables that it would be unethical to manipulate, e.g. you can compare a community that has TV with a community that doesn't to see which is more aggressive.

Disadvantages

- Participant allocation — you can't randomly allocate participants to each condition, and so extraneous variables (e.g. what area the participants live in) may affect results. Let's face it — you've got no control over the variables so it's ridiculously hard to say what's caused by what.
- Suitable events can be rare — some groups of interest are hard to find, e.g. a community that doesn't have TV.
- Ethics — deception is often used, making informed consent difficult. Also, confidentiality may be compromised if the community is identifiable.

Tip: Extraneous variables are variables other than the independent variable that could affect what you're trying to measure.

Reliability

Reliability refers to how consistent or dependable a test is. A reliable test carried out in the same circumstances, on the same participants should always give the same results. There are different types of reliability:

Internal reliability

Different parts of the test should give consistent results.

Example

If an IQ test contains sections of supposedly equal difficulty, participants should achieve similar scores on all sections.

The internal reliability of a test can be assessed using the **split-half method**. This splits the test into two halves, e.g. odd and even numbered questions, and the results from each half should produce a high positive correlation.

Tip: A positive correlation means that the two variables rise and fall together. In the split-half method, this means that if the score in one half of the test is low, the score in the other half should also be low.

External reliability

The test should produce consistent results regardless of when it's used.

> **Example**
>
> If you took the same IQ test on two different days you should achieve the same score.

The external reliability of a test can be assessed using the **test-retest method**. This involves repeating the test using the same participants. A reliable test should produce a high positive correlation between the two scores.
A problem with this is that the participants may have changed in some way since the first test, e.g. they may have learnt more. To avoid this, external reliability can be checked using the **equivalent forms test**. This compares participants' scores on two different, but equivalent (equally hard), versions of the test.

Figure 7: A test can be considered reliable if similar scores are produced in the test-retest method.

Inter-rater reliability

The test should give consistent results regardless of who administers it.

> **Examples**
>
> If two researchers give the same person the same IQ test they should both record the same score.
>
> If two researchers are observing mating behaviour in giraffes, they should both record the same behaviours, and therefore get the same results.

This can be assessed by correlating the scores that each researcher produces for each participant. A high positive correlation should be found.

Tip: Inter-rater reliability can also be called inter-observer reliability.

Validity

Validity refers to how well a test measures what it claims to.

> **Examples**
>
> An IQ test with only maths questions would not be a valid measure of general intelligence.
>
> An eye test that only measures long-sightedness (being able to see things far away) is not a valid measure of overall vision.

Tip: Make sure you know and understand the different types of reliability and validity. They've each got quite specific meanings.

There are different types of validity:

Internal validity

The extent to which the results of the test are caused by the variable being measured, rather than extraneous variables.

External validity

The extent to which the results of the test can be generalised, e.g. to a larger population.

Ecological validity

The extent to which the results of the test reflect real life.

Tip: Ecological validity is also known as context validity.

Validity can be assessed in different ways:

- A quick (but not very thorough) way of assessing validity is to simply look at the test and make a judgement on whether it appears to measure what it claims to. For example, an IQ test that just consisted of maths questions could be identified as having low validity by this method.
- Comparing the results of the test with the results of an existing measure (that's already accepted as valid) can help to determine the validity of the test.

- The results of the test can be used to predict results of future tests. If the initial results correlate with the later results it suggests that the test has some validity and can continue to be used.

Improving reliability and validity

There are several ways that the reliability and validity of tests can be improved:

Tip: Having good reliability and validity makes a study more likely to pass peer review, and therefore more likely to be published. See pages 5-6 for more information on the scientific process.

Standardising research

Standardising research involves creating specific procedures which are followed every time the test is carried out. This ensures that all the researchers will test all the participants in exactly the same way.

Examples

Researchers should test participants in the same sequence, at the same time of day, in the same environment, with all participants receiving exactly the same instructions.

This reduces the possibility of extraneous variables affecting the research. Therefore it will help to improve internal validity, external reliability, and inter-rater reliability.

Operationalising variables

Operationalising variables involves clearly defining all of the research variables.

Example

In a study of whether watching aggressive TV influences aggressive behaviour, the terms 'aggressive TV' and 'aggressive behaviour' need to be defined. 'Aggressive TV' could include cartoons or human actors. One of these might influence human behaviour and the other might not — this needs to be taken into account when planning, carrying out and drawing conclusions from the investigation. Similarly, 'aggressive behaviour' could refer to physical and verbal aggression, or just physical aggression.

Figure 8: Aggression must be operationalised in a study measuring 'aggressive TV', as aggression in cartoons is very different to aggression between humans.

Clarifying this from the start improves the reliability and internal validity of the test.

Pilot studies

Pilot studies are small-scale trial runs of the test. They're used to check for any problems before the test is carried out for real. They also give researchers practice at following the procedures. Pilot studies allow the validity and reliability of the test to be assessed in advance, which then gives the opportunity for improvements to be made.

Exam Tip
These questions would make up some of the 35 marks that you can get in Section C of the Unit 4 exam.

Exam Tip
In this section you'll often be presented with a scenario of a study. Read all the information given to you carefully — it's always there for a reason.

Worked Exam-style Questions

Read the text below and answer questions 0 1 and 0 2.

A psychologist is conducting a laboratory experiment to investigate the effect of caffeine on problem solving. Participants were asked to solve one set of maths problems. They were then asked to consume 4 strong cups of coffee. After 15 minutes they were given a second set of maths questions. The questions in each set were of the same difficulty.
A control group was also used in the experiment — participants in this group completed the same sets of maths problems, but drank 4 cups of water in between the tests instead.

0 1 Outline **one** advantage and **one** disadvantage of using a laboratory experiment. *(4 marks)*

An advantage of using a laboratory experiment is that it gives the researcher control over the variables — the effects of extraneous variables (those that could have an effect in addition to the key variable) can be minimised.

A disadvantage of using a laboratory experiment is that it means that the study lacks ecological validity. This is because the experiment is artificial and so might not measure real-life behaviour.

Exam Tip
You're only asked for one advantage and one disadvantage in this question, so don't write more than this — you won't get any extra marks, so it just wastes time.

0 2 The results of the study are shown in the table below.

	Mean score of the experimental group	Mean score of the control group
Set 1	18	15
Set 2	7	2

Explain why the psychologist is concerned about the internal reliability of the study. *(2 marks)*

As the two sets of maths questions were meant to be of the same difficulty, the control group should score similarly on both sets. As the average score of the control group was much lower for the second set of questions, it suggests that the test does not have internal reliability.

Exam Tip
When you're given the results of a study, think about what you would expect the outcome to be. In this question the control group's results should be roughly the same for each set of questions. Because they aren't, this gives you a clue about what's going on.

Exam Tip
Make sure you know the different types of reliability and validity. It's likely that at least one of them will come up in the research methods section.

Summary Questions

Q1 a) What is a stratified sample?
b) Give one advantage of this type of sampling method.
c) Give one disadvantage of this type of sampling method.

Q2 Give one disadvantage of using correlational research.

Q3 What is a natural experiment?

Q4 a) What is external reliability?
b) How could you test the external reliability of a test?

Q5 What is internal validity?

Q6 What is external validity?

Q7 Two psychologists are observing aggressive behaviour in children. One psychologist considers behaviour to be aggressive when a child shouts at another child, while the other researcher only records aggression when a child hits another child.
How could this problem be solved?

Q8 a) What is a pilot study?
b) Give one reason why they are used.

3. Ethics

Ethics is really important in psychology. If guidelines weren't in place a researcher could grab people off the street and stick electrodes in their brains. Actually that probably wouldn't happen, but you get the gist...

Learning Objectives:

- Know about ethical considerations in the design and conduct of psychological research.

Ethics in psychology

Ethics is an important issue in psychology. Psychological research and practice should aim to improve our self-understanding, be beneficial to people and try to improve the quality of life for individuals. As professionals, psychologists are expected to do their work in an ethical manner. Ethical guidelines are formal principles for what is considered to be acceptable or unacceptable. In the UK these are produced by the British Psychological Society (BPS). However, questions are raised about whether the guidelines are adequate and appropriately applied.

Real World Connection

The word 'guidelines' is a bit misleading — it kind of implies that they are just suggestions that researchers should try and follow. In reality they have to be strictly adhered to. There are ethics committees in place to ensure that all psychological research conforms to the ethical guidelines proposed by the BPS. For instance, university psychology students have to submit an ethics proposal to their university ethics committee before being able to do research for their final year project.

Ethical guidelines

Ethical guidelines must be followed during research:

Informed Consent

BPS guidelines state that:

- Participants should always give informed consent.
- They should be told the aims and nature of the study before agreeing to it.
- They should also know that they have the right to withdraw at any time.

BUT if the participant is under 16 years of age they can't give consent (although a parent can).

In naturalistic observation studies, consent is not obtained. In this case the research is acceptable provided that it is done in a public location where people would expect to be observed by others.

Even when informed consent is supposedly obtained, issues may be raised. Menges (1973) reviewed about 1000 American studies and found that 97% had not given people all the information about the research.

Figure 1: It's OK to conduct a naturalistic observation without informed consent in a place where you could expect to be observed.

Deception

If participants have been deceived then they cannot have given informed consent. However, sometimes researchers must withhold information about the study because the participants wouldn't behave naturally if they knew what the aim was. The BPS guidelines state that deception is only acceptable if there is strong scientific justification for the research and there's no alternative procedure available to obtain the data. Researchers can also ask independent people if they would object to the study. If they wouldn't, then the study may be done with naïve participants (although the naïve participants may not agree with others' opinions).

Participants could just be given general details — although if too little is said they may feel deceived, but if participants know too much then they may not behave naturally. The severity of deception differs, e.g. research on memory may involve unexpected memory tests (that participants weren't informed about). This is less objectionable than the deception involved in Milgram's (1963) study.

Tip: There are more details about the Milgram study on the next page. You also covered it at AS, so have a look back if you want more information.

Protection from harm

The BPS guidelines say that the risk of harm to participants should be no greater than they would face in their normal lives. It's hard to accurately assess this. Research procedures can involve physical and psychological discomfort.

Examples

Glass and Singer (1972) exposed participants to noise to make them stressed, and participants in Milgram's research suffered extreme distress.

Some people face risks in their work (e.g. soldiers) but that doesn't mean they can be exposed to risks in research. Researchers don't always know in advance what might be distressing for participants.

Tip: Psychological discomfort includes any negative emotions, for example, stress, embarrassment, distress, anxiety, etc.

Figure 2: Just because some people face risks in their everyday lives doesn't mean they can be subjected to harm for research.

Debriefing

Debriefing is supposed to return participants to the state they were in before the research. It's especially important if deception has been used. Researchers must fully explain what the research involved and what the results might show. Participants are given the right to withdraw their data.

Confidentiality

None of the participants in a psychological study should be identifiable from any reports that are produced. Data collected during research must be confidential — researchers can't use people's names in reports. Participants must be warned if their data is not going to be completely anonymous.

However, some groups or people might be easily identifiable from their characteristics — more so if the report says where and when the study was carried out, etc.

In the past, formal ethical guidelines were not in place or were less strict. Some studies conducted in the past wouldn't be allowed today as they don't adhere to current ethical guidelines:

Examples

Milgram (1963)

In 1963 Milgram conducted a study to investigate obedience. During the experiment, participants were deceived into believing that they were administering electric shocks to another participant. The experiment caused many participants to display obvious signs of stress, such as sweating, groaning and trembling.

This study breaches many of today's ethical guidelines. Participants were deceived as to the true nature of the study, meaning that they couldn't give informed consent. They weren't informed of their right to withdraw from the experiment, and were actually prompted to continue if they did want to stop. Some participants also showed signs of extreme stress during the experiment, so they weren't protected from harm.

Zimbardo et al (1973)

Zimbardo et al carried out a study to investigate conformity. They set up a mock prison to see if people would conform to the assigned roles of prisoner or guard. As the experiment progressed, the guards invented nastier punishments and the prisoners became more passive and obedient. The experiment was abandoned early because some prisoners became very distressed. This raises ethical issues about the protection of participants within the study.

Tip: At the time there were no formal guidelines in place, so technically Milgram didn't break any rules. However, he did take steps to make the study more ethical — e.g. he got the experiment approved by a committee of peers, participants signed consent forms and they were debriefed after the experiment.

Research and sensitive social issues

Findings from psychological research may highlight social issues and create negative effects or reactions in society. Socially sensitive research can be defined as research that may have implications for the individuals in the research, or for groups in society — e.g. the participants' families, or particular cultural groups.

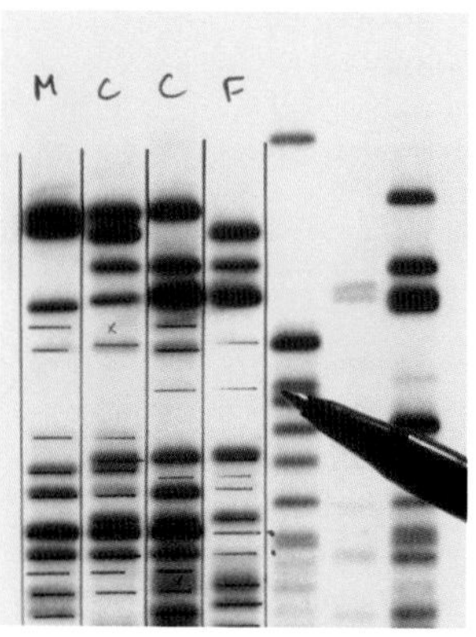

Figure 3: Genetic testing could potentially help people, but it could also lead to social stigma.

Examples

Genetics

- Research into whether there are genetic influences on criminal behaviour raises important questions, e.g. whether genetics could be used as a defence against being convicted for a crime.
- Also, there's the possibility of compulsory genetic testing to identify people with a particular gene. Such screening could also identify genes linked to psychological disorders such as schizophrenia. Although this may potentially help people it could also lead to anxiety and social stigma, especially as people may have a genetic vulnerability for a disorder but not actually develop it.

Using a factor like race as an independent variable

- Some studies using IQ tests have shown possible racial differences in intelligence. The issue is whether this is an appropriate topic for research because of social tensions that the results and conclusions may produce.
- Such research is often discredited because of methodological problems with the IQ tests that were used. For example, they may have been biased towards some social-cultural groups — this shows that we need to be careful about the conclusions that we draw from research methods.

Tip: For more on IQ testing see pages 103.

Worked Exam-style Questions

Read the text below and answer questions 0 1 and 0 2.

A psychologist studied the effect of nicotine withdrawal on anxiety levels. A group of 30 middle-aged, heavy smokers agreed to spend four weeks in a research unit. They were allowed visitors and could spend their time as they wished while in the research unit, but they were not allowed to smoke at any time during the study.
Each day, the participants completed questionnaires assessing their state of mind and anxiety levels. During the study some of the participants experienced severe unpleasant withdrawal symptoms due to the lack of nicotine.

0 1 Outline **one** ethical issue associated with the study.

(2 marks)

During the study, some of the participants experienced severe unpleasant withdrawal symptoms due to the lack of nicotine. This meant that they experienced physical and psychological discomfort, which they would not have experienced if they had not participated in the study. BPS guidelines state that the risk of harm to participants should be no greater than they would face in their normal lives, therefore they study did not protect the participants from harm.

Exam Tip
If you're asked to identify the ethical issues with a study think about the BPS guidelines and see if the study is breaking any. Once you've identified the guideline that a study is breaching, make reference to it in your answer — it illustrates your knowledge to the examiner.

0 2 The psychologist needed to ensure that the participants understood the nature of the study before they agreed to participate.

Write a short consent form for this study.
Include information which allows the participants to make an informed decision about whether to participate or not.

(5 marks)

By signing this form you agree to participate in a study investigating the effect of nicotine withdrawal on anxiety levels. You will be required to stay in a research unit for a total of four weeks. You will be allowed visitors and you can spend your time as you wish, although you will not be able to leave the facility or consume any cigarettes or products containing nicotine during the four-week period. You will also be required to undertake a variety of psychological tests each day.

During the study you may experience unpleasant withdrawal symptoms. Medical staff will be present at all times to assist with any problems this might cause. You have the right to withdraw at any time during the study. All data obtained during the study will remain confidential and you will not be identifiable in the published results.

Exam Tip
Think about all the things that you'd want to know if you were signing up for the study.

Exam Tip
Don't forget to mention that participants have the right to withdraw at any time during the study. This is (or should be) a common feature of all psychological experiments.

Summary Questions

Q1 How old must a person be before they can give their own consent to participate in a psychological experiment?

Q2 Informed consent can't be obtained in naturalistic observations. Where must a naturalistic observation take place in order for it to be ethically acceptable?

Q3 In what circumstances is deception considered acceptable?

Q4 What is the purpose of debriefing?

Q5 a) Outline one ethical issue in the study by Milgram (1963).
b) Outline one ethical issue in the study by Zimbardo et al (1973).

4. Probability and Significance

Probability and significance are pretty key in psychology — they let you know if your results actually mean anything, or if they're just due to chance...

Learning Objectives:

- Understand the major features of science, including hypothesis testing.
- Understand probability and significance, including the interpretation of significance and Type 1/Type 2 errors.

Inferential statistics

You can never be 100% certain that results aren't all down to chance. So instead of 'proving' a hypothesis, you have to be content with finding out whether it's likely to be true. This is called **statistical significance**. If your results are statistically significant, it means that you can read something into them — they're unlikely to be just down to chance. If your results are not statistically significant, it means they could have happened by chance rather than being the effect of changes in your independent variable, so you can't really read anything into them.

Statistical tests

You use statistical tests to find out if your results mean anything. OK, it's not easy, this bit — so stop texting people and concentrate...

Tip: The null hypothesis is what you assume is true during the study. Any data you collect either backs this assumption up, or it doesn't. It's quite usual to have something you don't actually believe as your null hypothesis.

- The first thing you do is write out your **null hypothesis** — this is the theory you want to test. In a statistical test, you assume your null hypothesis is true (for the time being, at least).

  Example

  A null hypothesis might be "rats that eat poison and rats that eat sugar pellets are equally likely to be ill".

- Next you choose a **significance level** — this is a 'level of proof' that you're looking for before you read anything into your results. The smaller the significance level, the stronger the evidence you're looking for that your results aren't just down to chance. A significance level is a probability, and so is a number between 0 and 1. (Probabilities near 1 mean things are very likely, and probabilities near 0 mean things are very unlikely.) Significance levels are always very small — usually 0.05 (5%) or less. (Because a significance level is very small, events with probabilities smaller than the significance level are very unlikely to happen.)

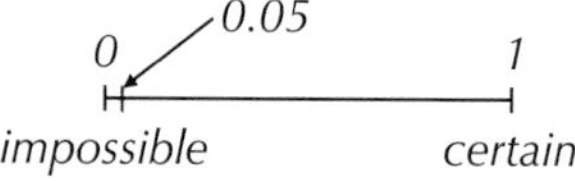

***Figure 1:** Probability number line showing the position of a significance level of 0.05.*

- You then turn all your experimental results into a single test statistic (pages 265-266). Then you can find out how likely this test statistic is (and so how likely your results are), assuming the null hypothesis is true.
- If the probability of getting your results (assuming the null hypothesis is true) is less than the significance level, then they must be really unlikely — and so it's pretty safe to say that your null hypothesis wasn't true after all. This is what stats-folk mean when they talk about 'rejecting the null hypothesis'. (If you reject your null hypothesis, you assume your **alternative hypothesis** is true instead.)
- If you reject your null hypothesis, you can proudly shout out that your results are statistically significant. (So rejecting the null hypothesis above would mean that "rats that eat poison and rats that eat sugar pellets are not equally likely to be ill".)
- If you don't reject the null hypothesis, it means that your results could have occurred by chance, rather than because your null hypothesis was wrong. If this happens, you've proved nothing — not rejecting the null hypothesis doesn't mean it must be true.

Tip: The alternative hypothesis is accepted when your data forces you to reject your null hypothesis. If your null hypothesis was that two variables aren't linked, then your alternative hypothesis would be that they are linked.

- Using a significance level of 0.05 (5%) is okay for most tests. If the probability of your results is less than this ($p \leq 0.05$), then it's pretty good evidence that the null hypothesis wasn't true after all. If you use a significance level of 0.01 (1%), then you're looking for really strong evidence that the null hypothesis is untrue before you're going to reject it.

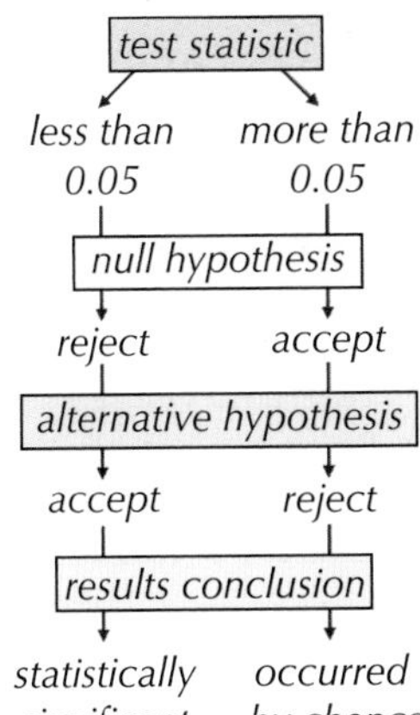

Figure 2: *A flow diagram showing significance testing, e.g. for a chi-squared test.*

Potential error

It's possible to make errors when you're deciding whether or not to reject the null hypothesis. There are two types of potential error:

Type 1 error

A Type 1 error is when you reject the null hypothesis when it was actually true. The significance level gives you the probability of this happening. This is why significance levels are small.

Type 2 error

A Type 2 error is when you don't reject the null hypothesis when it was actually false. This can happen if your significance level is too small (e.g. if you want very strong evidence of the need to reject a null hypothesis and so use a 0.01 significance level).

Choosing significance levels is a compromise — if the level you choose is too big you risk making a Type 1 error. If the significance level you choose is too small, you could make a Type 2 error.

Tip: A very small significance level (e.g. 0.01 or 1%) is used when you need to be very confident in your results, like when testing new theories.

Tip: When $p = 0.05$ the risk of making a Type 1 error is 1 in 20, whereas when $p = 0.01$ the risk is 1 in 100.

Testing significance

Remember that you can never be 100% sure that a hypothesis is correct — it's always possible that results are just due to chance. Significance levels are assigned to establish the probability of the result being due to chance, and if this is acceptably low (e.g. 5%), then you can reject the null hypothesis.

Inferential statistical tests help to decide whether to accept or reject the null hypothesis. However, there are many different tests and it is crucial that you use the correct one for your data. We'll get to the specific tests over the next few pages.

You use inferential tests to calculate what's called an **observed value** (the value you get when you carry out the test on your results). The observed value is then compared against a **critical value**, which is provided for each test in a **critical value table**. This indicates whether or not the results are significant. In some tests, if the observed value is more than the critical value, the results are considered to be significant. In others, the observed value must be equal to or less than the critical value to show significance.

Example

A psychologist investigating eating behaviour is conducting a study to look at the effect of low mood on calorie consumption. His null hypothesis is that low mood will have no effect on calorie consumption and his alternative hypothesis is that low mood will have an effect on calorie consumption.

20 participants kept a food diary and completed various questionnaires rating their mood each day for a period of 4 weeks. Using Spearman's rho correlation coefficient to analyse his data, the psychologist produced an observed value of 0.518. To test the significance of his results, the psychologist must compare his observed value against the critical values for Spearman's rho correlation coefficient.

1. Firstly he must decide if it's a one-tailed or a two-tailed test.

Tip: You should have come across Spearman's rho correlation coefficient at AS. It's a statistical test which allows you to measure the correlation between two variables. See page 269 for more details.

Tip: You need to know the difference between a directional and a non-directional hypothesis when you're doing statistics.

A **one-tailed test** is used when the researcher has predicted a difference and has also stated which way the results will go (i.e. a directional hypothesis, such as 'low mood will increase calorie consumption').
A **two-tailed test** is used when the researcher has predicated a difference, but hasn't stated which way the results will go (i.e. a non-directional hypothesis). The hypothesis in this experiment is non-directional, so a two-tailed test is used.

2. The observed value is then looked up in a critical value table. Some of the critical values for a Spearman's rho correlation coefficient are shown below in Figure 3. As the test is two-tailed, the researcher needs to look at the row of significance levels for two-tailed tests.

Level of significance for two-tailed test				
	0.10	***0.05***	***0.02***	***0.01***
Level of significance for one-tailed test				
N	***0.05***	***0.025***	***0.01***	***0.005***
15	0.443	0.521	0.604	0.654
16	0.429	0.503	0.582	0.635
17	0.414	0.485	0.566	0.615
18	0.401	0.472	0.550	0.600
19	0.391	0.460	0.535	0.584
20	0.380	**0.447**	0.520	0.570
21	0.370	0.435	0.508	0.556
22	0.361	0.425	0.496	0.544
23	0.353	0.415	0.486	0.532
24	0.344	0.406	0.476	0.521
25	0.337	0.398	0.466	0.511

Figure 3: *Critical values of Spearman's rho correlation coefficient.*

3. If the psychologist wants to see if his results are significant at the p = 0.05 level, he should use the column highlighted in purple.
4. N = the number of values in the data set. As there were 20 participants in this study, the critical value at the p = 0.05 level = 0.447.
5. For the data to be significant, the observed value from the Spearman's rho calculation must be greater than or equal to the relevant critical value.

Tip: ≥ means 'greater than or equal to'. ≤ means 'less than or equal to'.

Tip: Here, the observed value must be greater than or equal to the critical value. This isn't the same for all statistical tests though — in some, the observed value must be less than or equal to the critical value.

The observed value in this experiment is 0.518, which is greater than 0.447. This means that the psychologist's results are significant at the p = 0.05 level. Consequently, the researcher can reject his null hypothesis, and accept his alternative hypothesis.

Worked Exam-style Questions

Read the text below and answer questions 0 1 and 0 2.

A psychologist is investigating the effect of age on problem-solving ability in children. Her hypothesis is that as children get older their problem-solving ability increases.
15 children aged between 8 and 12 completed various problem-solving tasks and were awarded a problem-solving score.
Using Spearman's rho correlation coefficient to analyse her data, the psychologist produced an observed value of 0.491.

0 1 State whether the psychologist's hypothesis is directional or non-directional. *(1 mark)*

directional

Exam Tip
The command word 'state' and the fact that the question is only worth 1 mark should tell you that you don't need to go into detail in your answer. Exam technique is really important — see the 'Exam Help' section (pages 296-300) for more hints and tips about doing well.

0 2 The table below shows part of a critical value table for Spearman's rho correlation coefficient. To be a significant result, the observed value must be greater than or equal to the relevant critical value.

Level of significance for two-tailed test				
	0.10	***0.05***	***0.02***	***0.01***
Level of significance for one-tailed test				
N	***0.05***	***0.025***	***0.01***	***0.005***
12	0.503	0.587	0.671	0.727
13	0.484	0.560	0.648	0.703
14	0.464	0.538	0.622	0.675
15	0.443	0.521	0.604	0.654
16	0.429	0.503	0.582	0.635
17	0.414	0.485	0.566	0.615

Exam Tip
Don't forget to use the correct N value — remember, it's the number of values in the data set.

Using the table, state whether or not the psychologist's result was significant at the p = 0.05 level. Explain your answer.

(3 marks)

The psychologist's result is significant at the p = 0.05 level. N = 15 as there were 15 participants. The psychologist's hypothesis was directional, so a one-tailed test is used. This means that the critical value is 0.443. For the data to be significant in Spearman's rho correlation coefficient, the observed value must be greater than or equal to the relevant critical value. The observed value (0.491) is greater than the critical value (0.443), therefore the results are significant at the p = 0.05 level.

Exam Tip
Don't forget to check if it's a one-tailed or a two-tailed test — it all depends on the hypothesis. One-tailed is directional, whereas two-tailed is always non-directional.

Summary Questions

Q1 What does it mean if the results of a psychological experiment are not statistically significant?

Q2 A psychologist is conducting a study on phobias. Her hypothesis is that benzodiazepines will reduce the symptoms of phobias. What is her null hypothesis?

Q3 a) What is a Type 1 error?

b) What is the probability of a Type 1 error occurring when p = 0.01?

Q4 Give an example of when a Type 2 error may occur.

Q5 When is a one-tailed test used?

5. Inferential Statistics

Inferential statistics sound horrible, but they're actually not too bad. Just make sure that you pick the right test for your data and then follow the steps.

Learning Objectives:

- Understand factors affecting choice of statistical test, including levels of measurement.
- Know about the use of inferential analysis, including Spearman's Rho, Mann-Whitney, Wilcoxon and Chi-squared.

Choosing which inferential test to use

Inferential statistics allow you to make an educated guess about whether or not a hypothesis is correct. Deciding which inferential test to use for your data is determined by the following factors:

1. Research design

Research may have either related measures (if a repeated measures or matched participants design was used), or unrelated measures (if an independent measures design was used).

2. Research aims

Some inferential statistics test whether there is a significant difference between two (or more) groups of scores:

Examples

'Did the participants in group A have significantly higher average scores than those in group B?'

'Did the participants in a drug trial show significant improvements in their symptoms after taking the drug?'

This is what happens in an experiment. The independent variable (IV) is manipulated to see if it produces changes in the dependent variable (DV) that are significantly different from the control condition (or other experimental conditions).

Some inferential statistics test to see if there is a significant association between two (or more) variables (i.e. whether they occur together more than would be expected by chance):

Examples

- Whether people's IQ scores increase with the more fish they eat.
- Whether a person's memory increases with age.
- Whether increased exposure to spiders decreases a person's phobia.

Tip: You learnt about descriptive statistics at AS level. These include measures of central tendency (mean, mode and median) and measures of dispersion (range and the interquartile range). Measures of central tendency tell you the 'average' value of your data, while measures of dispersion tell you how spread out your data is. If you can't remember, have a look back to refresh your memory — they'll be useful at A2.

This is what we look for in correlation studies — to see if two variables are positively or negatively associated, more than would be expected by chance factors alone. If they are, a significant correlation has been shown.

Tip: For more on correlation studies see page 269.

3. Level of measurement / type of data

The results of a study can be collected in different ways, which affect how they can be analysed:

- Nominal data
  This is the most basic level of measurement — a frequency count for completely distinct categories.

Examples

In a study where a confederate pretends to need help, you could assign each passer-by to either an 'altruistic' category (if they helped) or a 'non-altruistic' category (if they did nothing).

In an observation of aggression in children you could observe a child over a period of time and using a tally chart, score each time a certain aggressive behaviour is displayed, e.g. 'punching', 'kicking', 'screaming', etc.

Behaviour	Tally
punching	𝍸 II
kicking	II
screaming	𝍸 𝍸 III
hair pulling	𝍸 II
scratching	II

Figure 1: Example of a tally chart used to record nominal data.

- Ordinal data
  All of the measurements relate to the same variable, and measurements can be placed in ascending or descending rank order.

Examples

A rating scale for aggression where 1 = 'not aggressive' and 10 = 'extremely aggressive'. But you can't say a person with a score of 10 is twice as aggressive as a person with a score of 5, just which one was more or less aggressive.

A rating scale for anxiety levels where 1 = 'very relaxed' and 10 = 'very anxious'. But you can't describe someone who scores 10 as 10 times more anxious than someone who scores 1.

Figure 2: *Rating scales are a form of ordinal data. They are often used in observations, e.g. rating aggression in children.*

- Interval data
  Measurements are taken on a scale where each unit is the same size, e.g. length in centimetres. Interval data places participants in rank order according to the differences between them.

Examples

In a race, participant 'F' was quickest, in 15.8 seconds, and participant 'B' was second, in 16.5 seconds.

In a study on the effect of stress on heart rate, participant Z's heart rate was 125 beats per minute (bpm), while participant Y's heart rate was 169 bpm.

Technically, an absolute zero point is needed to make judgements about whether one score is twice that of another. When we have this (e.g. 0 seconds, 0 centimetres, etc.) then we call it a ratio scale.

Types of inferential tests

1. Spearman's rho correlation coefficient

Spearman's rho correlation coefficient is a test statistic used to see if there's a significant association between two variables with ordinal or interval data.

To work out (and then test the significance of) Spearman's rho correlation coefficient, you need values for two different variables (e.g. hours of revision and average test scores for 10 students):

1. The values for each variable are placed into rank order (each variable is ranked separately). The lowest value for each variable gets rank 1 (and in the above example, the biggest value will get rank 10).
2. The difference (d) in ranks for each student's variables is calculated. (So a particular student may have done the most revision, but got the 3rd best results, in which case the difference in ranks will be d = 3 – 1 = 2.)
3. The value of d for each student is squared, then the results are added together (to get $\sum d^2$).
4. Then the special Spearman's correlation coefficient calculation is done, which is $r_s = 1 - \frac{6 \times \sum d^2}{N \times (N^2 - 1)}$
   (where N is the number of students, or whatever).
5. To find out whether the result is significant (and so whether the variables are linked), you compare the outcome of that nightmarish calculation (the observed value) with a critical value that you look up in a statistics table, like on page 266.

Tip: You should have covered Spearman's rho correlation coefficient at AS. It's a number between –1 and +1 that shows the type of correlation and how closely the variables are linked.

Tip: Σ (pronounced 'sigma') just means you add things up.

Tip: r_s is just the shortened way of writing Spearman's rho correlation coefficient.

Figure 3: Spearman's rho is a way of measuring correlation between two variables, e.g. hours of sleep and cognitive function.

Tip: The lowest value for each variable gets rank 1. In this example the biggest value gets rank 10.

Tip: If you have two or more values the same then you have to use an average rank. E.g. if the 3rd and 4th values are the same then you'll use 3.5.

Tip: You just need to find the difference between the ranks, so always subtract the lowest from the highest, e.g. for student B you get d = 1, not d = –1.

Tip: Don't forget to square d — it's easy to forget, but it's an important step.

Example

A psychologist is investigating the effect of sleep on cognitive function. His hypothesis is that students who get more hours of sleep the night before a test will score higher in the test. Students' hours of sleep the night before a test and their test scores are shown below.

- The first thing to do is rank the variables from lowest to highest:

Student	*Hours of sleep*	*Rank*	*Test score (%)*	*Rank*
A	3	2	12	1
B	6	5	71	6
C	9	7	83	7
D	4	3	46	5
E	5	4	38	4
F	13	10	94	9
G	10	8	100	10
H	1	1	15	2
I	8	6	32	3
J	12	9	87	8

- Then work out the difference (d) in ranks for each student's variables.

  Student A — Hours of sleep rank = 2 Test score rank = 1
  d = 2 – 1 = 1
  Student B — Hours of sleep rank = 5 Test score rank = 6
  d = 6 – 5 = 1
  Student C — Hours of study rank = 7 Test score rank = 7
  d = 7 – 7 = 0
  etc.

- Once you have done this for all your data the value of d for each student is squared, then the results are added together (to get $\sum d^2$):

Student	*Hours of sleep*	*Rank*	*Test score (%)*	*Rank*	*d*	*d^2*
A	3	2	12	1	1	1
B	6	5	71	6	1	1
C	9	7	83	7	0	0
D	4	3	46	5	2	4
E	5	4	38	4	0	0
F	13	10	94	9	1	1
G	10	8	100	10	2	4
H	1	1	15	2	1	1
I	8	6	32	3	3	9
J	12	9	87	8	1	1
					$\sum d^2$	22

- The Spearman's correlation coefficient calculation can now be done:

$$r_s = 1 - \frac{6 \times \sum d^2}{N \times (N^2 - 1)}, \quad N = 10$$

$$r_s = 1 - \frac{6 \times 22}{10 \times (10^2 - 1)}$$

$$= \mathbf{0.867} \text{ (3 s.f.)}$$

- The observed value is very close to +1, showing that there is a strong positive correlation between hours of sleep and test score.
- The result of the calculation is then compared with a critical value. For the data to be significant, the observed value must be greater than or equal to the relevant critical value in the table.
  As the hypothesis is directional, a one-tailed test is used:

Level of significance for two-tailed test				
	0.10	***0.05***	***0.02***	***0.01***
Level of significance for one-tailed test				
N	***0.05***	***0.025***	***0.01***	***0.005***
7	714	786	0.893	0.929
8	643	738	0.833	0.881
9	0.600	0.700	0.783	0.833
10	**0.564**	0.648	0.745	0.794
11	0.536	0.618	0.709	0.755
12	0.503	0.587	0.671	0.727

- From the table it can be seen that the critical value for p = 0.05 is 0.564. The observed value (0.867) is greater than this, therefore the results are significant at the p = 0.05 level. The psychologist can reject his null hypothesis and accept his alternative hypothesis.

Tip: N is the number of students in the sample.

Tip: Positive correlation means the variables rise and fall together. A negative correlation would mean that as one variable increases, the other decreases.

Tip: In this example you read the values off the N = 10 row, as there are 10 participants.

Tip: See pages 264-265 for more on how to tell if your results are statistically significant, or just due to chance.

2. The Wilcoxon Signed Ranks test

The Wilcoxon Signed Ranks test is a test of difference for related data. It's used when:

- A hypothesis states that there'll be a difference between two sets of data.
- The data is ordinal or interval.
- The experiment is a repeated measures or matched pairs design.

Example

A psychologist is investigating two methods of memorising. Her hypothesis is that Method 1 will be more effective than Method 2, and her null hypothesis is that there will be no difference between the two methods.

A group does a memory test with the two methods of memorising, in a repeated measures design:

	Participant no.	**1**	**2**	**3**	**4**	**5**	**6**	**7**	**8**
No. words recalled	**Method 1**	6	5	10	6	8	5	9	8
	Method 2	7	7	8	8	7	6	9	9

Tip: See page 269 if you don't know what ordinal data is.

Tip: You should have come across the different types of experimental design at AS. In a repeated measures design the same participants are used in each condition. In a matched pairs design there are different participants in each condition, but they're matched on important variables.

Tip: Always subtract in the same direction, noting if the result is a positive or negative value. Any differences of zero are removed from the results.

Tip: When there are a few of the same number, calculate their mean rank. E.g. here, there are four 1s, which should be rank 1, 2, 3 and 4, so they all get the mean rank 2.5.

Tip: The observed value of T must be less than or equal to the critical value in the Wilcoxon Signed Ranks test. Remember that this isn't the same for all statistical tests. For example, in Spearman's rho, the observed value must be greater than or equal to the critical value. Make sure you use the correct rule for the test that you're using.

- The difference between each participant's two scores is calculated:

Participant no.	**1**	**2**	**3**	**4**	**5**	**6**	**7**	**8**
Difference	1	2	2	2	1	1	0	1
Sign (+/-)	-	-	+	-	+	-		-

- The differences are given a rank to show their order — the lowest gets rank one. Ignore +/- signs.

Difference	1	2	2	2	1	1	0	1
Rank	2.5	6	6	6	2.5	2.5		2.5
Sign (+/-)	-	-	+	-	+	-		-

- Total the ranks for the positive differences and for the negative differences. The smallest is the observed value of 'T'.

  Total negative differences
  = 2.5 + 6 + 6 + 2.5 + 2.5 = **19.5**

  Total positive differences
  = 6 + 2.5 = **8.5**

  So, the observed value of T = **8.5.**
- The observed value must be less than or equal to the critical value to be significant.
- Critical values for each number of participants can be found in a special table that you'll be given.
- *N* is the number of differences calculated from the table — in this case it's 7 because you don't include any differences that are zero.
- As the psychologist's hypothesis is directional, a one-tailed test is used:

Level of significance for two-tailed test				
	0.10	***0.05***	***0.02***	***0.01***
Level of significance for one-tailed test				
N	***0.05***	***0.025***	***0.01***	***0.005***
5	0			
6	2	0		
7	3	2	0	
8	5	3	1	0
9	8	5	3	1
10	10	8	5	3
11	13	10	7	5
12	17	13	9	7
13	21	17	12	9

- From the table you can see that the critical value for p = 0.05 is 3. The observed value for T (8.5) is more than this, therefore the results are not significant at the p = 0.05 level. The psychologist can accept her null hypothesis and reject her alternative hypothesis.

3. The Mann-Whitney U Test

The Mann-Whitney U Test is a test of difference (or of similarity) for unrelated data. It focuses on ranks and is used when you have ordinal or interval data. Take a look at the following example:

Tip: Unrelated data means that an independent groups design is used. In this type of research design different participants are used in each group and the groups can be unequal in size.

Example

Two groups took part in a study investigating whether drinking a vitamin drink once a day for 4 weeks improved performance on a verbal memory test compared to a group who had not had any vitamin drinks.

Number of words recalled								
	Vitamin group	19	13	9	12	21	15	14
	No vitamin group	7	5	10	8	6	11	18

- Firstly, the data needs to be ranked. It's ranked regardless of the group each score is in. Start with the lowest score (in the example it's 5) and give it a rank of '1'. Then the next lowest score gets a rank of '2' and so on.
- If some of the data values are the same then you have to use an average rank. E.g. if the 3rd and 4th values are the same then you'll use 3.5.

Tip: If you do have to give an average rank, remember to 'skip out' the next rank — e.g. if the 3rd and 4th values are the same then you'll use 3.5 for both of them. They are sharing ranks 3 and 4, so the next rank you'll give is 5 (not 4).

Number of words recalled								
	Vitamin group (A) (rank)	19 (13)	13 (9)	9 (5)	12 (8)	21 (14)	15 (11)	14 (10)
	No vitamin group (B) (rank)	7 (3)	5 (1)	10 (6)	8 (4)	6 (2)	11 (7)	18 (12)

- Look at the ranks associated with the vitamin group's scores and add them up. Then do exactly the same for the no vitamin group:

  Sum of ranks in vitamin group (R_A)
  = 13 + 9 + 5 + 8 + 14 + 11 + 10
  = **70**

  Sum of ranks in no vitamin group (R_B)
  = 3 + 1 + 6 + 4 + 2 + 7 + 12
  = **35**

- When you think about it, if the vitamin group really did show better verbal recall then their scores will be higher than the no vitamin group. This means that the ranks of the scores in the vitamin group will also be higher. The Mann-Whitney U test then uses the following scary-looking formulas:

$$U_A = N_A N_B + \frac{N_A(N_A + 1)}{2} - R_A \qquad U_B = N_A N_B + \frac{N_B(N_B + 1)}{2} - R_B$$

Tip: Don't be scared by the formulas — it's just a case of plugging the numbers in.

N_A is the number of people in group A
N_B is the number of people in group B
R_A is the sum of the ranks for scores in group A
R_B is the sum of the ranks for scores in group B

$$U_A = (7 \times 7) + \frac{7(7 + 1)}{2} - 70 \qquad U_B = (7 \times 7) + \frac{7(7 + 1)}{2} - 35$$

$U_A = \mathbf{7}$ $\qquad$ $U_B = \mathbf{42}$

- You need to select the smaller of these, 7, and call it 'U'.
- The observed U must be less than or equal to the critical value to be significant.

Tip: $p = 0.01$ is just one level of significance that can be used. See page 264 for more on significance levels.

- Critical values can be found in a table that you'll be given in the exam. For example this table shows the critical values for U for a one-tailed test at $p = 0.01$:

		N_1				
		5	**6**	**7**	**8**	**9**
N_2	**5**	1	2	3	4	5
	6	2	3	4	6	7
	7	3	4	6	7	9
	8	4	6	7	9	11
	9	5	7	9	11	14

Tip: Remember, N_1 is the number of people in group A, and N_2 is the number of people in group B.

- As N_1 and N_2 are both 7, the critical value is 6. In the Mann-Whitney U test, the observed U value must be less than or equal to the critical value. As $U = 7$ here, it can be concluded that there's no significant difference between the two groups.

4. The chi-squared test

Tip: An independent samples design means that there are different participants in each group.

The chi-squared test is used with nominal data and independent samples. There's no better way of explaining this than showing you an example. So, hey presto...

Example

A student is interested in seeing whether finding reality TV programmes entertaining is related to being either male or female. His results are shown in the table below.

Tip: Check out page 264 for a refresher on null hypotheses.

- The chi-squared test tests the null hypothesis. In this example, the null hypothesis would be that there's no association between finding reality TV entertaining and being male or female — this is shown by the expected frequencies. Under the null hypothesis, the expected frequencies show that equal amounts of men and women find reality TV entertaining, and equal amounts do not.

	Men	Women	Totals
Finds reality TV entertaining (expected frequency)	19 (27)	35 (27)	54
Does not find reality TV entertaining (expected frequency)	41 (33)	25 (33)	66
Totals	60	60	120

- The expected frequencies are worked out using the following formula:

$$E = \frac{\text{row total} \times \text{column total}}{\text{overall total}}$$

- The chi-squared (χ^2) is calculated using yet another scary-looking equation:

$$\chi^2 = \Sigma \frac{(O - E)^2}{E}$$

O is the observed frequency

E is the expected frequency

Tip: Don't forget to square your result for (O - E) before you divide it by E — it's an easy mistake to make, and will mess up your results if you don't do it.

- So, for each pair of observed and expected frequencies, take the expected score away from the observed score, square this and then divide by the expected score.
- Do this for all the observed and expected pairs. For example:

Finds reality TV entertaining

Men

$$\frac{(19-27)^2}{27} = \mathbf{2.37}$$

Women

$$\frac{(35-27)^2}{27} = \mathbf{2.37}$$

Does not find reality TV entertaining

Men

$$\frac{(41-33)^2}{33} = \mathbf{1.94}$$

Women

$$\frac{(25-33)^2}{33} = \mathbf{1.94}$$

- Then add up all your answers (that's what the Σ means).
  $\chi^2 = 2.37 + 2.37 + 1.94 + 1.94$
  $\chi^2 = \mathbf{8.62}$
- You can then use a critical value table to see if this is significant. But first you've got to work out the **degrees of freedom** (as if you hadn't done enough already).
- Degrees of freedom (df) = (No. of rows – 1) × (No. of columns – 1)
- In this example $df = (2-1) \times (2-1) = 1$

Level of significance for two-tailed test					
df	***0.20***	***0.10***	***0.05***	***0.02***	***0.01***
1	1.64	2.71	3.84	5.41	6.64
2	3.22	4.60	5.99	7.82	9.21
3	4.64	6.25	7.82	9.84	11.34
4	5.99	7.78	9.49	11.67	13.28
5	7.29	9.24	11.07	13.39	15.09
6	8.56	10.64	12.59	15.03	16.81
7	9.80	12.02	14.07	16.62	18.48
8	11.03	13.36	15.51	18.17	20.09

- For the chi-squared result to be significant, χ^2 needs to be greater than or equal to the critical value. In this example, the results are significant as the critical value at $p = 0.05$ is 3.84, which is less than 8.62. This means that the null hypothesis is rejected.

Tip: Don't worry about degrees of freedom too much. You don't need to know what it means for the exam — you just need to be able to calculate it, so that you know which row of the critical values table to look at.

Choosing which test to use

It's really important to choose the right test for the job. You need to think about things like the research aims, the level of measurement or types of data, and the research design that is being used in the experiment. The flow diagram in Figure 4 (see the next page) can help you to decide which test you need to use in different situations.

When looking up critical values it's important to remember to look back to the hypothesis. You need to know whether it's directional or non-directional, so that you can tell whether your test is one-tailed or two-tailed.

It's also important to remember to check whether your observed value

Tip: Remember, a directional hypothesis states which way the results will go, whereas a non-directional hypothesis doesn't.

needs to be greater than or less than the critical value for the test you are doing — it differs for each statistical test.

Exam Tip
It's really important that you know which statistical test to use when. In the research methods section of the exam you may be given a description of an experiment (including its research design, hypothesis, etc.) and be asked which test you'd use to analyse the data.

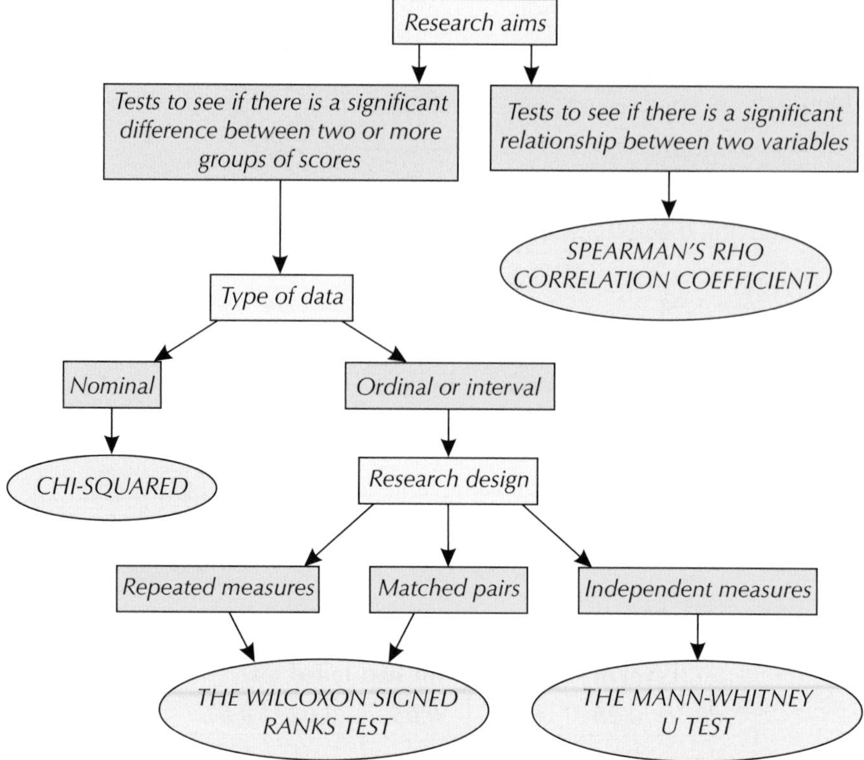

Figure 4: *Flow diagram for deciding which statistical test to use.*

Worked Exam-style Questions

Read the text below and answer questions 0 1 and 0 2.

A psychologist is investigating whether playing violent video games increases aggression in children.

A group of 8 children play a violent video game for one hour, and are then observed playing together for one hour. They are given an 'aggression rating' based on the behaviours that they display. A week later the children play a non-violent video game and are observed and rated again.

The researcher's hypothesis is that ratings of aggression will be higher after playing the violent game than after playing the non-violent video game.

0 1 Identify an appropriate statistical test that the psychologist could use to see if his results were statistically significant. Explain your answer. *(3 marks)*

The Wilcoxon Signed Ranks test. This statistical test would be used as it tests whether there is a significant difference between two groups of scores. The data in the experiment was ordinal and a repeated measures design was used.

Exam Tip
It's really important to know which test to use in a situation. You need to think about the experiment's aim, the type of data used and the research design. The flow diagram in Figure 4 (see above) is really useful for this type of question, so make sure you know it.

0 2 After analysing the results, the psychologist calculates an observed value of 1.
Using Table 1, state whether the psychologist's results are statistically significant at the p = 0.05 level.
Explain your answer. *(3 marks)*

Level of significance for two-tailed test				
	0.10	***0.05***	***0.02***	***0.01***
Level of significance for one-tailed test				
N	***0.05***	***0.025***	***0.01***	***0.005***
7	3	2	0	
8	5	3	1	0
9	8	5	3	1
10	10	8	5	3
11	13	10	7	5

Table 1. Observed value must be less than or equal to the relevant critical value for statistical significance.

As the hypothesis was directional a one-tailed test is used. There were 8 participants (N = 8), so the critical value at p = 0.05 is 5.
The observed value of T (1) is less than the critical value so it can be concluded that the psychologist's results are statistically significant.

Exam Tip
Make sure to look at the hypothesis so you know if you need to use a one-tailed or a two-tailed test.

Summary Questions

Q1 What is ordinal data?

Q2 A psychologist's hypothesis is that babies will prefer sweet foods to bitter foods.

a) Is her hypothesis directional or non-directional?

b) Should she use a one-tailed test or a two-tailed test when analysing her results?

Q3 A scientist conducts a study to see if there is a significant association between two variables. Which statistical test should he use to analyse his results?

Q4 A scientist conducts a study to see if there is a significant difference in blood pressure between people who smoke and people who don't smoke. Participants were matched on variables such as age, sex, weight, etc. Which statistical test should he use to analyse his results?

Learning Objectives:

- Know about the analysis and interpretation of qualitative data.

6. Analysis of Qualitative Data

Enough of the numbers. It's time for some qualitative data. Qualitative data includes things like words, sounds, videos, pictures, etc.

Observational Methods

1. Naturalistic observation

Participants are observed in their natural environment, normally without their knowledge.

Several design issues are involved:

- Sampling of Behaviour
  Researchers may use **event sampling**, where they only observe and record the particular events of interest. **Time-interval sampling** is used if the observation is over a long period of time.
- Recording Behaviour
  Researchers may make notes, or complete pre-made forms to record how often something happens. A problem with this method is that researchers may miss some behaviours or disagree over behaviours, so video or audio recordings may be made.
- Rating Behaviour
  Behaviours need to be described and placed into categories, e.g. solitary play, cooperative play, etc. Researchers can do a frequency count of how many times each behaviour is observed.

Figure 1: *Naturalistic observations have high ecological validity as participants are observed in their natural environment, without their knowledge.*

Advantages

- The observation is in the participants' natural environment so there is **ecological validity**.
- Participants don't know they're being observed so should behave naturally and not show **demand characteristics**.

Disadvantages

- There is no control over any of the variables so **cause and effect** relationships cannot be established.
- Observers may be biased in how they interpret behaviours. So, it's important to establish **inter-observer reliability** by comparing two or more observers' recordings to ensure that they're similar.
- For ethical reasons naturalistic observations can only be done where people would expect to be observed.

Tip: Learning the advantages and disadvantages of each type of observational method will come in useful in exam questions where you're asked to evaluate.

Tip: See page 257 for more on inter-observer reliability — it's also known as inter-rater reliability.

2. Participant observation

An observer joins the group they are studying. They may be known to the group or hidden.

Advantage

- Insights about groups may be found that other methods couldn't show.

Disadvantages

- It can be more difficult to record data.
- 'Hidden' observation raises ethical issues.
- If the researcher is known to the group then they won't behave naturally.
- The researcher may get emotionally attached to the group, and become biased.

Figure 2: *Participant observation may involve a researcher posing as a football fan to investigate aggression in crowds — it allows them to get in amongst the action.*

3. Interviews

The structure of an interview can vary.

- Fully structured — a set sequence of questions with closed answers, i.e. multiple-choice (this is quantitative).
- Informal/Unstructured interviews — the interviewer asks questions with no set structure and answers are open, i.e. the person being interviewed can respond in any way.

There are advantages and disadvantages to both methods:

- Fully structured interviews are quick and easily analysed, but the structure limits how the interviewee responds.
- Unstructured interviews can provide lots of detailed, insightful qualitative data, but this is hard to analyse.

To compromise, both open and closed questions can be used.

Researchers must make sure that questions are not:

- ambiguous, e.g. "Do you exercise frequently?" How often is frequently?
- double-barrelled (combining more than one issue in a single question), e.g. "Do you prefer rugby to football and do you think goal-line technology should be used equally in both sports?
- leading, e.g. "You do like Celine Dion, don't you?"

Figure 3: *Informal interviews often make use of open questions, providing rich, detailed data.*

4. Case studies

These involve the detailed study of an individual or small group, using many different methods.

Examples

Interviews (structured and/or unstructured), observations, psychometric tests (e.g. intelligence tests), experiments, etc.

Advantage

- Lots of data may be obtained, providing detail that other methods can't give. This may give insight into unique cases and unusual situations which may help to develop theories, e.g. case studies on children who were socially deprived have shown its effects on their development.

Disadvantages

- Researchers have very little control over variables in the study and can mistakenly identify causal relationships.
- Results can't be generalised to the rest of the population.

Tip: You might remember some case studies from AS, such as the case of Genie reported by Curtiss (1977) and the case of the Czech twin boys reported by Koluchova (1976).

Analysing qualitative data

Once quantitative data is collected it can be easily and objectively analysed. However, qualitative data (such as an interview transcript) is much more difficult to analyse objectively.

Qualitative analysis involves subjective decisions. It can involve making summaries and identifying key themes and categories.

Examples

Analysis of a transcript or video involves identifying statements — e.g. feelings, jokes, criticisms, etc.

Tip: An interview transcript is an exact record of a conversation. It includes things like pauses, "erms", coughing and laughter. Words are written as they are spoken, i.e. slang terms and abbreviations are used, (e.g."yeah", "'cause", "nah", etc.) and the tone of the speaker is noted.

Different researchers may read different things into the statements. Such analysis may give the basis for hypotheses, e.g. about what may be found in other sources or other things the participant may say — the hypothesis formation is therefore grounded in the data (but could still be subjective).

Criticisms

- How do you decide which categories to use and whether a statement fits a particular category?
- How do you decide what to leave out of the summary, or which quotations to use?
- These are subjective decisions and researchers may be biased, possibly showing statements or events out of context.

Strengths

- Qualitative analysis preserves the detail in the data.
- Creating hypotheses during the analysis allows for new insights to be developed.
- Some objectivity can be established by using triangulation — other sources of data are used to check conclusions (e.g. previous interviews). With more sources researchers can cross-check their interpretations.

Tip: When you're collecting quantitative data, the theory is the starting point. With qualitative data, the theory often comes after you've conducted the research.

Content analysis

Content analysis is a way to quantify qualitative data. When analysing a transcript, **coding units** can be established, e.g. 'references to cultural stereotypes'. Theses phrases are given **operationalised definitions**, e.g. 'defining a cultural stereotype'. A frequency count of how many times each coding unit occurs in the transcript can be done, producing quantitative data, which can then be statistically analysed.

Tip: You should have covered content analysis at AS, so you can look back if you want a reminder.

Example

A psychologist is investigating cultural stereotypes. Using open questions, she interviews 150 London residents about their thoughts on people coming from all over the world to London on holiday. She records their answers and produces a transcript of each participant's interview.

- To analyse the transcript, the psychologist establishes coding units, for example 'references to cultural stereotypes'. These phrases are given operationalised definitions, e.g. 'defining a cultural stereotype'.
- A frequency count of how many times each coding unit occurs in the transcript can then be done. For instance, each time a statement such as "British people like tea and the Queen", "Italians are good cooks", or "Brazilians are good at football" appear they are recorded.
- This produces quantitative data, which can be statistically analysed.

Tip: Care is needed to avoid bias when defining coding units, or deciding which behaviours fit particular units.

Strengths

- A clear summary of the patterns in the data may be established.
- Statistics provide a more objective basis for comparisons and statistical tests may show, for example, that a coding unit is significantly more frequent in one source of data than in another.

Criticisms

- Subjective judgements are still made to define coding units.
- Reducing the data to particular coding units removes detail, and the true meaning of things may be lost when taken out of context.

Worked Exam-style Questions

Read the text below and answer questions 0 1 and 0 2.

A psychologist is studying the breakdown of relationships.
He conducts fully structured interviews with 30 men and 30 women who have recently come out of a long-term relationship. He asks a series of closed questions about the reasons for their break-up.

0 1 Outline **one** advantage and **one** disadvantage of using a fully structured interview consisting of closed questions.

(2 marks)

An advantage of using fully structured interviews with closed questions is that the data is quick and easy to analyse.

A disadvantage of using fully structured interviews with closed questions is that the interviewee is limited in how he/she can respond.

Exam Tip
Just give one advantage and one disadvantage. You won't get extra marks for writing more than that, so it's a waste of your time in the exam.

0 2 In a second interview, the psychologist asked a series of open questions about the reasons for the breakdown of the participant's relationship, and recorded their responses.
A transcript of the interview was made, in order for content analysis to take place.
Describe how the psychologist could carry out content analysis to analyse the transcript. *(3 marks)*

The psychologist could establish coding units, for example 'references to boredom with the relationship' and 'references to the existence of an attractive alternative relationship'. These coding units must all be given valid operationalised definitions — this means providing a clear definition of each coding unit.

A frequency count of how many times each coding unit occurs in the transcript can then be done, producing quantitative data, which can be statistically analysed.

Exam Tip
Try and give examples of the points you are making. It gives a more full explanation, showing the examiner that you know what you're talking about.

Summary Questions

Q1 What is event sampling?

Q2 Give one disadvantage of naturalistic observations.

Q3 a) What is participant observation?
b) Give one advantage of participant observation.

Q4 Give three types of questions that researchers should avoid when conducting interviews.

Q5 a) What is a case study?
b) Give one advantage of using a case study.
c) Give one disadvantage of using a case study.

Q6 Give one strength of using qualitative data.

7. Presenting Data

Learning Objectives:

- Know about appropriate selection of graphical representations.

Once you've got your data, you want to be able to show it to the world. It's graph time. Get excited — they're prettier and more fun than stats...

Presenting data

Qualitative data from observations, interviews, surveys, etc. (see pages 279-280) can be presented in a report as a 'verbal summary'. The report will contain summaries of what was seen or said, possibly using categories to group data together. Also quotations from participants can be used, and any research hypotheses that developed during the study or data analysis may be discussed.

When quantitative data is collected (or produced from qualitative data, e.g. by a content analysis — see page 280), it can be summarised and presented in various ways. Read on...

Figure 1: *Presenting your data graphically allows others to easily interpret the results of your study.*

1. Tables

Tables are a good way to summarise quantitative data. They can be used to clearly present the data and show any patterns in the scores. Tables of 'raw data' show the scores before any analysis has been done on them (see Figure 2).

Tip: For more examples of raw data tables see pages 270 and 274.

	Quality (score out of 10)		
Type of ice cream	Tastiness	Thickness	Throwability
Chocolate	9	7	6
Toffee	8	6	7
Strawberry	8	5	4
Earwax	2	9	8

Figure 2: *Table to show the qualities of different types of ice cream.*

Other tables may show descriptive statistics such as the mean, range and standard deviation.

2. Bar charts

Bar charts (bar graphs) are usually used to present 'non-continuous data' — when a variable falls into categories rather than being measured on a numbered scale. The bar chart in Figure 3 shows the number of words recalled by two different groups in a memory experiment.

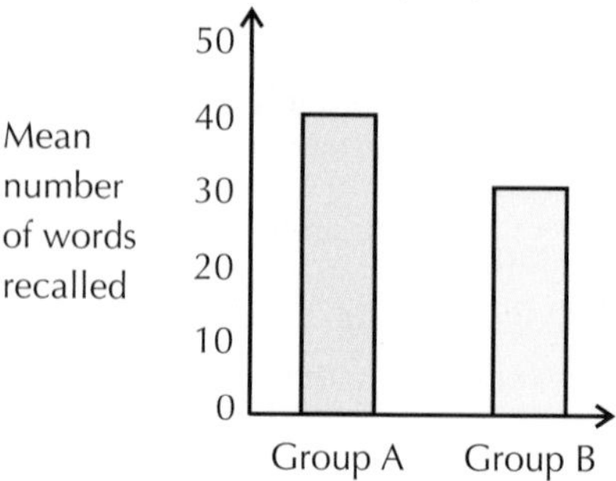

Figure 3: *Bar chart showing the mean number of words recalled by two groups in a memory experiment.*

Note that the columns in bar charts don't touch each other. Also, it's preferable to always show the full vertical scale, or clearly indicate when it isn't all shown (otherwise it can be misleading) — see Figure 4.

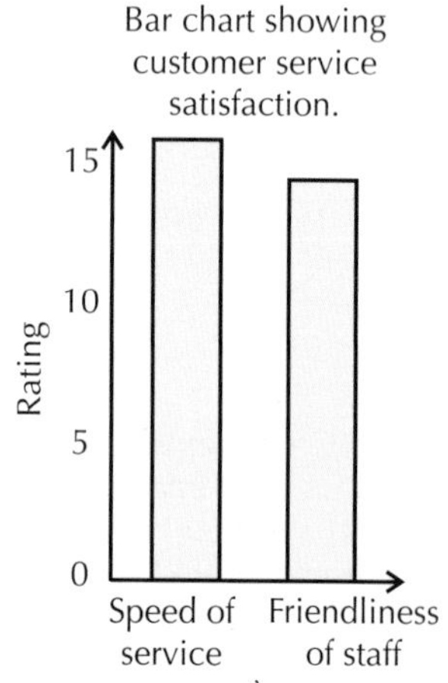

Figure 4: *Not showing the full vertical scale can be misleading. Customer service may look good in this graph, but in fact the rating scale went up to 100 — not such great service now.*

3. Histograms

Histograms show data measured on a 'continuous' scale of measurement. The histogram in Figure 5 shows the time different participants took to complete a task.

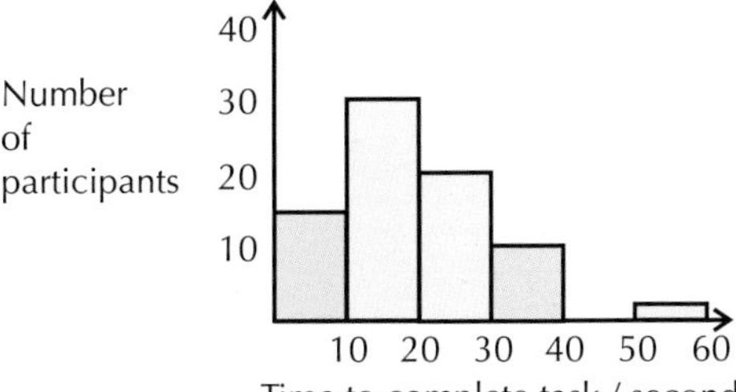

Figure 5: *Histogram showing the time participants took to complete a task.*

Each column shows a class interval (here, each class interval is 10 seconds), and the columns touch each other. All intervals are shown, even if there are no scores within them. When the columns are all the same width, it's the height of the column that shows the number of values in that interval.

Tip: Histograms are for when you have continuous data. This includes things like height, temperature and time — things that fall on a scale. Non-continuous data includes things like exam grades, types of ice cream and names of football teams — things that fall into distinct categories.

4. Frequency polygons

Frequency polygons are good for showing more than one set of data. They are similar to histograms, but use lines to show where the top of each column would reach. It can be useful to combine two or more frequency polygons on the same set of axes — then it's easy to make comparisons between groups, as shown in Figure 6.

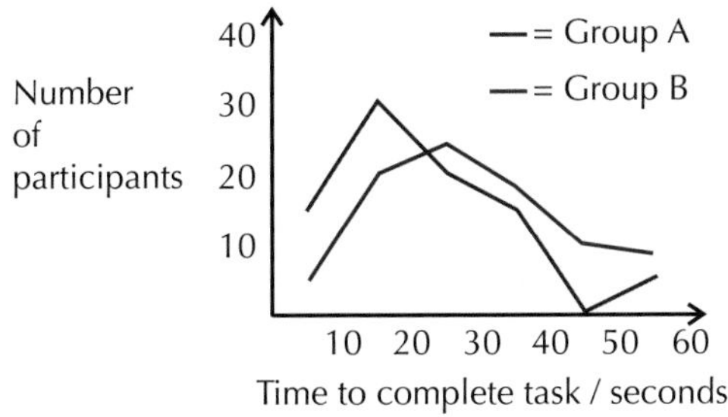

Figure 6: *Frequency polygon showing the time participants in two groups took to complete a task.*

Tip: Frequency polygons are used for continuous data.

5. Scattergrams

Scattergrams show relationships between co-variables. **Correlation** is a measure of the relationship between two variables.

Examples

How closely exam grades are related to the amount of revision done.

How age is related to intelligence.

How depression increases with decreased levels of the hormone serotonin.

Correlational analysis will give you a correlational coefficient — these range from –1 (a perfect linear negative relationship) to +1 (the same, but positive) — see Figure 7.

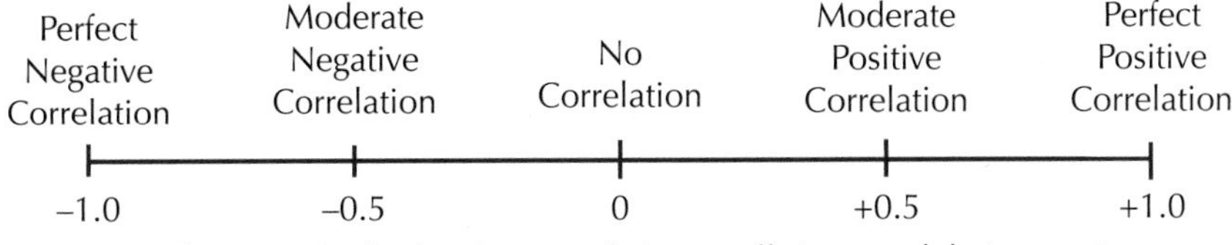

Figure 7: *Scale showing correlation coefficients and their meanings.*

Tip: Correlational analysis can't establish 'cause and effect' relationships — it can only show that there's a statistical link between the variables. Variables can be closely correlated without changes in one causing changes in the other — a third variable may be involved.

However, care must be taken when interpreting correlation coefficients — high correlation coefficients could be down to chance. To decide whether a correlation is significant, you have to compare your correlation coefficient to a table of critical values (see page 266).

In a correlational study data can be displayed in scattergrams:

Tip: Scattergrams can also be called scatter graphs or scatter diagrams — they're all the same thing.

1. Positive correlation

This means that as one variable rises, so does the other (and likewise, if one falls, so does the other).

Example

Hours of study and average test score — the correlation coefficient is roughly 0.75 (close to +1).

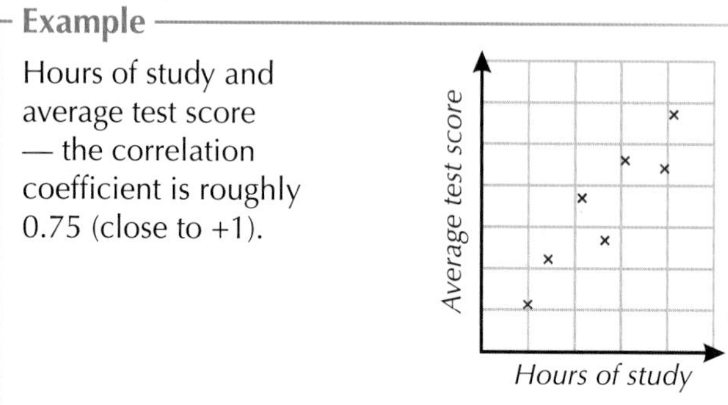

2. Negative correlation

This means that as one variable rises, the other one falls (and vice versa).

Example

Hours of TV watched each week and average test score — the correlation coefficient is roughly –0.75 (close to –1).

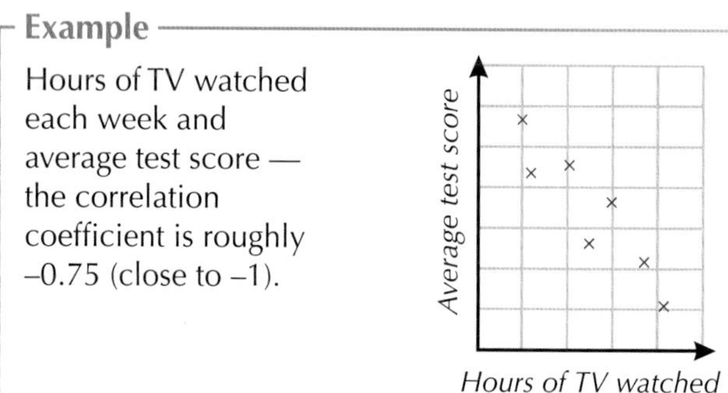

Figure 8: In this example, TV watching and test scores share a negative correlation.

3. No correlation

If the correlation coefficient is 0 (or close to 0), the variables aren't linked.

Example

A student's height and their average test score — the correlation coefficient is roughly 0.01 (close to 0).

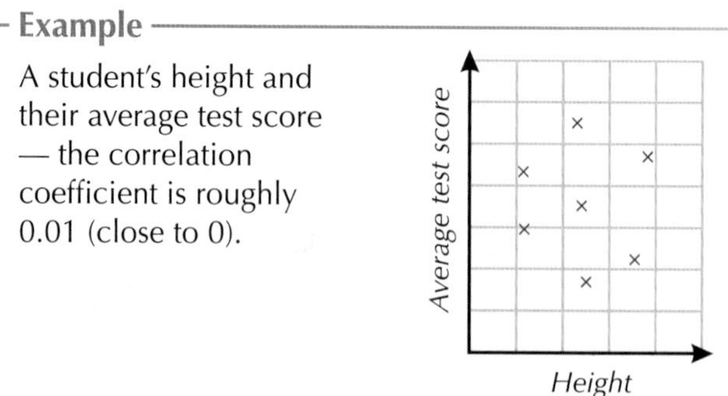

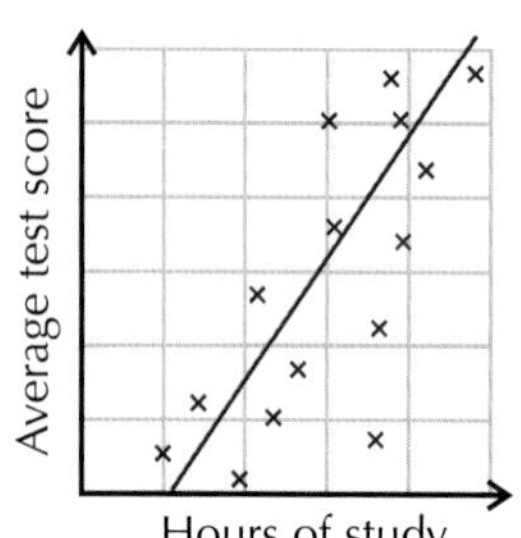

Figure 9: Scattergram showing hours of study plotted against average test scores. The red line is the line of best fit.

Line of best fit

If there's a relationship between variables, you can draw a **line of best fit** to show the trend (see Figure 9). This is a line that fits the general pattern of the data and that passes as close to as many of the points as possible. You should end up with roughly the same number of points plotted on each side of your line.

Worked Exam-style Questions

Read the text below and answer questions 0 1 to 0 4.

A psychologist is studying the effect of anxiety on sleep. 10 participants completed a questionnaire assessing their level of anxiety each day for a 2-week period. They were also asked to record the number of hours of sleep they had each night. The participants' average anxiety and hours of sleep scores are shown in the table below.

Participant	A	B	C	D	E	F	G	H	I	J
Average anxiety level rating (/10)	5	5	2	7	2	6	1	9	8	8
Average number of hours of sleep per night	9	7	8	8	10	6	10	4	4	5

0 1 Use the data in the table to draw a scattergram. Include axis labels and give the scattergram a title.
(4 marks)

0 2 Draw a line of best fit on your scattergram.
(1 mark)

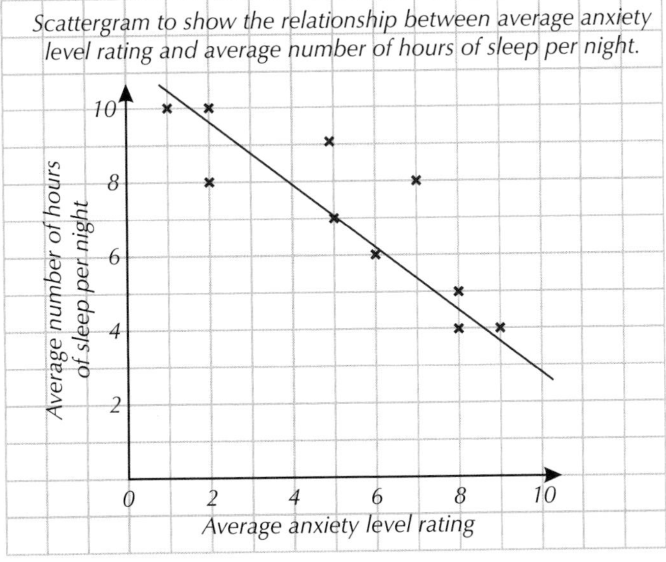

> **Exam Tip**
> Section C of the exam ('Psychological Research and Scientific Method') consists of more questions worth less marks than other sections in the exam. The topic carries 35 marks in total.

> **Exam Tip**
> For full marks in question 01 you need to accurately plot the data points, label the axes correctly and give your scattergram an appropriate title. Believe it or not, you also get a mark for drawing a scattergram, so don't go drawing a bar chart. Be careful though — forgetting your title or not labelling the axes is an easy way of throwing marks away.

0 3 Using your graph, describe the relationship between average number of hours of sleep per night and average anxiety levels.
(2 marks)

Average number of hours of sleep per night is negatively correlated with average anxiety levels. As the average number of hours of sleep per night increases, the average anxiety level rating decreases.

0 4 The psychologist is also interested in sleep apnoea. This is a condition where an individual's airways become blocked whilst they are sleeping, which can cause them to wake up.

Some sufferers visited a sleep laboratory to have their sleep patterns assessed throughout the night.
One participant's results are shown in the table below.

Time	Number of times participant awoke
11:00 - 00:00	0
00:00 - 01:00	2
01:00 - 02:00	5
02:00 - 03:00	4
03:00 - 04:00	2
04:00 - 05:00	0
05:00 - 06:00	3
06:00 - 07:00	1
07:00 - 08:00	0

Use the data in the table to draw a histogram.
Label the axes and give the histogram a title.

(4 marks)

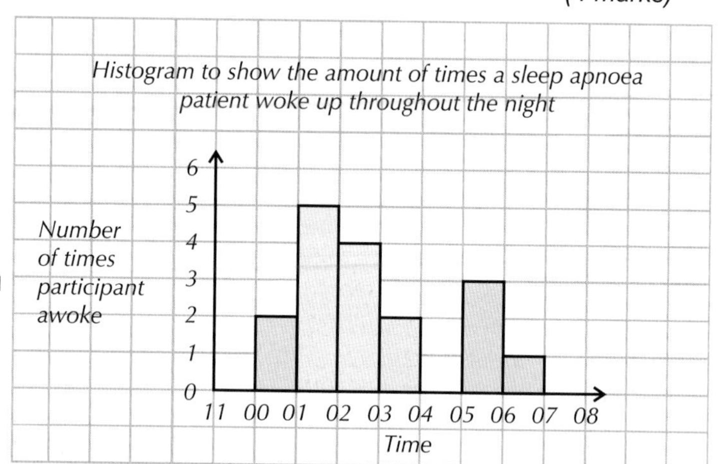

Exam Tip
Remember that in a histogram each column shows a class interval and the columns touch each other. It's a bar chart if there are gaps between the columns.

Summary Questions

Q1 Suggest how a psychologist might present their qualitative data.

Q2 What sort of data is displayed in a bar chart?

Q3 Height, temperature and time are examples of which type of data — continuous or non-continuous?

Q4 Can 'cause and effect' relationships be established by correlational analysis? Explain your answer.

Q5 What sort of relationship between two variables do the following correlation coefficients represent?

a) 1

b) 0.02

c) –0.5

8. Reporting on Psychological Investigations

Psychologists have to write up their studies in a certain way, following specific conventions so that other psychologists know exactly what's gone on.

Learning Objectives:
- Know about conventions of reporting on psychological investigations.

Reports of psychological studies

Reports of psychological studies have a specific structure:

1. Title

The first thing a report needs is a title. It should say what the study's about and include the **independent variable** (IV) and the **dependent variable** (DV).

Examples

'An Investigation into the Effect of Hunger on Reaction Times'

'Does Consumption of Alcohol Decrease People's Social Inhibitions?'

'An Investigation into the Effect of Age on Moral Understanding'

'Can Leading Questions Affect Our Ability to Accurately Recall Events?'

Tip: Reports must follow specific conventions to aid peer review (see pages 5-6). If a paper wasn't written properly it would probably be rejected even if it contained brilliant new data.

Tip: The IV is the variable that is manipulated by the researcher. The DV is the variable that you think is affected by changes in the IV. So in the first example, the DV would be reaction time, and the IV would be hunger.

2. Abstract

The abstract's a concise summary of the report (often no more than 120 words), telling the reader about the research and findings without them having to read the whole report. It should include brief descriptions of the aims and hypotheses of the study, the method, and a summary of the results. The abstract should also contain interpretations of the findings and any significant flaws in the study. A lot to fit into a small space...

Example

The following abstract is taken from a study by Baron-Cohen et al (1985):

'We use a new model of metarepresentational development to predict a cognitive deficit which could explain a crucial component of the social impairment in childhood autism. One of the manifestations of a basic metarepresentational capacity is a 'theory of mind'. We have reason to believe that autistic children lack such a 'theory'. If this were so, then they would be unable to impute beliefs to others and to predict their behaviour. This hypothesis was tested using Wimmer and Perner's puppet play paradigm. Normal children and those with Down's syndrome were used as controls for a group of autistic children. Even though the mental age of the autistic children was higher than that of the controls, they alone failed to impute beliefs to others. Thus the dysfunction we have postulated and demonstrated is independent of mental retardation and specific to autism.'

Tip: You can read about Baron-Cohen et al's (1985) study of theory of mind on page 135. Try and pick out the hypothesis, method and summary of the results in their abstract.

3. Introduction

The introduction is a general overview of the area being studied, including existing theories. It should also discuss a few studies closely related to the current study.

Tip: The introduction should give the reader a good background into the area of research, allowing them to understand why the study was conducted.

4. Aim and Hypotheses

The aim is a sentence stating the purpose of the study.

Examples

'To investigate whether reaction times are affected by hunger levels.'

'To investigate whether alcohol decreases people's social inhibitions.'

Tip: See pages 287-288 for more on hypotheses.

The hypothesis is what's actually going to be tested, and should include the independent variable and the dependent variable.

Examples

'There is no relationship between hunger levels and reaction time.'

'Alcohol will decrease people's social inhibitions.'

5. Method

Tip: Having a detailed method section allows other scientists to read the research and try to repeat it. If the results are replicated each time the experiment is done then the results are considered reliable. See page 251 for more on testing scientific theories.

The method describes how the research was carried out. Someone should be able to replicate the study by following the method, so it needs to be detailed. The method should include information on:

1. The design of the investigation, for example:
   - The research method used, e.g. field experiment, interview.
   - The research design, e.g. repeated measures, and any potential problems with the design.
   - How variables and order effects were controlled, e.g. counterbalancing, randomisation.
   - How word-lists, questions, etc. were chosen.
   - How ethical issues were dealt with.
2. The procedure used:

   This should be a blow-by-blow account of what happened each time a participant took part. It should start with how the researcher and the investigation were introduced to the participant and how informed consent was obtained. It needs to include:
   - What was said to the participants (the standardised instructions).
   - How the study was carried out.
   - How the participants were debriefed.
   - How the data was recorded.

Tip: Standardisation makes sure all conditions are kept the same in a study, ensuring that each participant has the same overall experience.

3. The use of participants, for example:
   - The number of participants used.
   - The demographics of the participants, e.g. age, employment, gender, etc.
   - The sampling method used (see page 254).
   - How participants were allocated to conditions.
4. The resources used, for example:
   - The materials used, e.g. questionnaires, pictures, word lists, etc.
   - Any apparatus used — it's often useful to include diagrams or photographs of these.

6. Results

***Figure 1:** Descriptive statistics provide a visual summary of the results for the reader.*

The results of the study can be reported as descriptive or inferential statistics. Descriptive statistics include tables, graphs and charts (see pages 282-284). Inferential statistics (see pages 268-276) involve doing statistical tests on the data.

The results section needs to include:

- explanations of why certain tests were chosen, e.g. because the study was looking for a correlation.
- the results of the test — including the observed value, the critical value and level of significance.

7. Discussion

The discussion covers a range of things including:

- An explanation of the findings — summarising the results and relating them to the aim and hypothesis. The **null hypothesis** should be accepted or rejected in the discussion. Any unexpected findings should also be addressed and explained here.
- The implications of the study — for example, whether the study relates to real-life situations, e.g. interviews, exams, etc.
- The limitations and modifications of the study — any problems or limitations need to be explained, along with modifications that could improve the study.
- The relationship to background research — the results need to be related to the background research covered in the introduction. The data should be compared to other data, and comments made on whether or not the findings of the study support the findings of other studies.
- Suggestions for further research — at least two ideas for further research should be included.

Tip: The discussion can be thought of as an evaluation of the study — what did it show, what does it mean, what went wrong, what could be done better, what's next etc.

8. References

The references section contains a list of all the books, articles and websites that have been used for information during the study. It allows the reader to see where the information on the research and theories mentioned in the report (e.g. in the introduction) came from. References should be presented in alphabetical order of first author's surname.

Figure 2: References allow the reader to refer to other authors' work and to read around the topic.

9. Appendices

Any materials used, e.g. questionnaires or diagrams, can be put in the appendix. Raw data and statistical test calculations also go here.

General Tips

- The report should be written in the third person.

Example

'The participants were asked to recall numbers' rather than 'I asked the participants to recall numbers'.

- The language used should be formal.

Example

'The participants in the study were an opportunity sample', rather than 'the participants were basically anyone we could get hold of.'

Worked Exam-style Questions

Read the text below and answer the following question.

A psychologist conducted an investigation into the effect of age on conservation (the ability to understand that a set quantity stays the same even if it looks different). Her hypothesis was that children under seven years of age will be unable to complete a conservation task. The psychologist wrote to a selection of primary schools asking for volunteers. One hundred participants were selected. These were 50 males and 50 females, aged between five and nine. They were divided

Exam Tip
There's a lot of information in this question but it's all there for a reason. Make sure you read it through carefully.

into five equal groups according to age (20 five-year-olds, 20 six-year-olds, etc.). Participants were shown two identical glasses containing the same volume of liquid. The psychologist poured the liquid from one glass into beaker A, a short, fat beaker. She poured the liquid from the other glass into beaker B, a tall, thin beaker. Participants were then asked which beaker contained more liquid, or if they thought that the beakers contained the same volume of liquid.

Exam Tip
When answering this question, think whether you would be able to repeat the experiment based on what you have written. If not, think about what other information you need to include.

0 1 Write a method section for the report of the psychologist's study. Your answer should contain details of the experimental design, participants, procedure and resources.
Include enough detail to allow the study to be replicated.

(10 marks)

The study was a laboratory experiment using an independent measures design. One hundred participants between the ages of five and nine years were selected from a variety of primary schools using volunteer sampling. The participants were split into five equal groups according to age, and each group had an equal gender split, e.g. Group A consisted of 20 five-year-olds, 10 of whom were male and 10 of whom were female, etc. As the participants were children, consent was obtained from their parents.

Exam Tip
You could also use headings in your answer to break the method section down into design, participants, procedure and resources. Either way is fine — you've just got to make sure you've included all of the important details that someone would need to know about in order to carry out the study.

The participants were tested individually. They were shown two identical glasses which contained the same volume of liquid. The researcher then poured all of the liquid from one glass into beaker A, and all of the liquid from the other glass into beaker B. Beaker A was short and wide. Beaker B was tall and thin. Participants were then asked, "Which beaker contains more liquid, or do they contain the same amount of liquid?" The participants' answers were recorded.

The experiment required two identical glasses filled with the same volume of water, and two beakers — one short and wide, the other tall and thin.

Read the text below and answer the following question.

A psychologist was investigating whether alcohol has an effect on reaction time. His hypothesis was that consumption of alcohol would decrease a person's reaction time. He recruited participants by placing an advert in a university asking for volunteers to participate in a study of the body's response to alcohol. The participants were taken to a quiet room and were asked to complete a reaction time test involving pressing a button every time a light flashed on a computer screen in front of them. Participants then returned to a waiting room where they were given two large glasses of wine (4 units in total) to drink.
Fifteen minutes after drinking the wine they returned to the test room and the reaction test was repeated.
It was found, on average, that consumption of 4 units of alcohol increased reaction time by 0.4 seconds. This difference was found to be statistically significant at the $p = 0.05$ level.
The discussion of the study noted that the study lacked ecological validity, but that important implications regarding the dangers of drink-driving were raised. The psychologist suggested that further research was required in order to more accurately assess the dangers

of drink-driving, for instance looking at how alcohol affects coordination.

0 2 Write an abstract of the study for a scientific report.

(8 marks)

This study aimed to investigate whether alcohol affects reaction time. A repeated measures design was used, in which university student volunteers completed a basic reaction test involving reacting to a light flashed on a screen. Participants repeated the test 15 minutes after consuming 4 units of alcohol.

It was hypothesised that consumption of 4 units of alcohol would slow an individual's reaction time. It was found that consumption of 4 units of alcohol increased reaction time by 0.4 seconds and that these results were statistically significant at the $p = 0.05$ level. Although the experiment lacked ecological validity, it has important implications regarding the dangers of drink-driving.

Exam Tip

Remember an abstract should ideally be no more than 120 words. Don't waffle on or you'll lose marks for not producing a 'concise summary' of the study.

Exam Tip

In an abstract you need to summarise the aim, hypothesis, method, results, interpretations of the findings and any significant flaws in the study. Make sure you include all of these to get the marks — a good abstract will contain all of these things but be very concise.

Summary Questions

Q1 What should you include in the introduction of a psychological report?

Q2 When writing a psychological report, what is the aim used for?

Q3 Give three pieces of information about the participants that should be included when writing the methods section.

Q4 What three things should be included in the results section about the results of the statistical test?

Q5 List three things that should be included in the discussion.

Q6 Give one thing that could be included in the appendix of a psychological report.

Section Summary

- Scientific research should always have validity and reliability and be objective. This is checked by the process of peer review. Once a piece of research has passed peer review, other scientists try to replicate the findings. If the research proves replicable it's accepted as 'fact' for now.
- There is debate over whether psychology is a science or not. Some psychological approaches are more scientific than others.
- Research samples should be representative of the population, so that results can be generalised to the target population. There are many different ways to select a sample, including random sampling, systematic sampling, opportunity sampling, self-selected sampling or stratified sampling.
- Different research methods can be used in psychological investigations. These include questionnaires, correlational research, laboratory experiments, field experiments and natural experiments. They all have their own advantages and disadvantages.
- There are different types of reliability. Internal reliability ensures that different parts of a test give consistent results and can be assessed using the split-half method. External reliability ensures a test produces consistent results regardless of when it's used and can be assessed using the test-retest or the equivalent forms method. Inter-rater reliability ensures that a test gives consistent results regardless of who administers it and can be assessed by correlating the scores awarded by each researcher.
- Validity refers to how well a test measures what it claims to. There are three different types of validity — internal, external and ecological. Validity can be assessed in different ways.
- Both reliability and validity can be improved by standardising research, operationalising variables, and running pilot studies.
- Ethics is an important consideration when designing a psychological experiment. Various ethical guidelines produced by the British Psychological Society must be followed when conducting psychological investigations in the UK. Researchers must also be aware of possible sensitive social issues.
- Calculating statistical significance allows you to assess how likely your results would be if the null hypothesis were true. If your results are statistically significant you can reject your null hypothesis. If they are not statistically significant then you accept your null hypothesis.
- When deciding whether to accept or reject your null hypothesis, there's a chance that you might make an error. This is known as potential error and there are two types — Type 1 and Type 2 errors.
- Inferential statistics allow you to calculate an observed value. This is compared to a critical value which indicates whether or not your results are significant.
- Choosing which inferential test to use for your data is determined by factors such as the research design, the research aims, and the type of data. Inferential tests include Spearman's rho correlation coefficient, the Wilcoxon Signed Ranks test, the Mann-Whitney U test and the chi-squared test.
- Qualitative data is produced by observational methods such as naturalistic observation, participant observation, interviews and case studies. The data can be converted into quantitative data using content analysis — this can then be statistically analysed.
- Qualitative data can be presented as a 'verbal summary'. Quantitative data can be presented in tables, bar charts, histograms, frequency polygons and scattergrams.
- Specific conventions must be followed when writing a report on a psychological investigation. Psychological reports must include a title, an abstract, an introduction, an aims and hypotheses section, a method section, a results section, a discussion, references and an appendix. Reports should use formal language and be written in the third person.

Exam-style Questions

Read the text below and answer questions 0 1 to 0 3.

A psychologist is studying the effects of a new drug. He believes that the drug could be used to decrease food cravings in patients suffering from bulimia nervosa. The psychologist obtained a list of bulimia nervosa patients and contacted every 50th person from the register.
The study investigated whether an experimental group taking the drug each day for 4 weeks had a reduction in food cravings compared to a control group who did not take the drug.
At the end of the 4 weeks both groups of participants completed a self-report questionnaire assessing their food cravings. Their results are shown in the table below:

Food cravings score	**Drug group**	3	4	2	5	2	1	4
	Control group	7	8	7	10	9	6	10

0 1 What sampling technique was used by the psychologist?

(1 mark)

0 2 Suggest **one** disadvantage of this type of sampling method.

(1 mark)

0 3 Identify an appropriate statistical test that the psychologist could use to analyse the results. Explain your answer.

(4 marks)

Read the text below and answer questions 0 4 to 1 0.

A psychologist is interested in seeing whether wanting to get married is related to being either male or female. His hypothesis is that more women want to get married than men.

The psychologist obtained his participants by placing an advert on a popular dating website asking for volunteers to participate in a psychological study on attitudes towards relationships.
The psychologist conducted 120 interviews consisting of open questions. He then analysed the interview transcripts using content analysis. His results are shown in the table below.

	Men	**Women**	**Totals**
Wants to get married (expected frequency)	24 (31.5)	39 (31.5)	63
Doesn't want to get married (expected frequency)	36 (28.5)	21 (28.5)	57
Totals	60	60	120

The psychologist analysed his results using the chi-squared test.

He calculated that $\chi^2 = 7.52$

Exam-style Questions

0 4 What sampling technique was used by the psychologist?

(1 mark)

0 5 Give **one** advantage and **one** disadvantage of this sampling method.

(2 marks)

0 6 Describe how the psychologist might have used content analysis to analyse the interview transcripts.

(3 marks)

0 7 State whether the psychologist's hypothesis is directional or non-directional.

(1 mark)

0 8 Write out the psychologist's null hypothesis.

(1 mark)

0 9 Using Table 1, state whether the psychologist's results are statistically significant at the p = 0.05 level. Explain your answer.

(3 marks)

Level of significance for one-tailed test					
df	**0.10**	**0.05**	**0.025**	**0.01**	**0.005**
Level of significance for two-tailed test					
df	***0.20***	***0.10***	***0.05***	***0.02***	***0.01***
1	1.64	2.71	3.84	5.41	6.64
2	3.22	4.60	5.99	7.82	9.21
3	4.64	6.25	7.82	9.84	11.34
4	5.99	7.78	9.49	11.67	13.28
5	7.29	9.24	11.07	13.39	15.09
6	8.56	10.64	12.59	15.03	16.81
7	9.80	12.02	14.07	16.62	18.48

Table 1. Value of χ^2 needs to be greater than or equal to the critical value for statistical significance.

Exam-style Questions

10 Write an abstract of the study that would be suitable for a published report.

(8 marks)

Read the text below and answer questions **11** to **14**.

A psychologist is conducting a study to investigate the relationship between intelligence and brain size. Participants underwent MRI scanning to measure their brain size and also completed an IQ test to assess their intelligence level. The results of the study are shown in the table below.

Participant	A	B	C	D	E	F	G
Brain size (cubic centimetres)	1360	1280	1267	1420	1275	1254	1425
IQ score	89	97	74	119	113	110	80

11 Use the data in the table to draw a scattergram.
Label the axes and give the scattergram a title.

(4 marks)

12 Using your graph, describe the relationship between brain size and intelligence.

(1 mark)

13 Outline **one** advantage and **one** disadvantage of using correlational research.

(2 marks)

14 Explain how the external reliability of the IQ test could be assessed.

(3 marks)

Exam Help

You're almost there... the end is in sight. Just two exams to go and you'll have done everything you need to do for A2-Level psychology. These next few pages tell you exactly what to expect and are full of useful tips and advice about how to approach exam questions in the most sensible way.

The exam papers

You'll have to do two exams for A2 psychology — Unit 3 and Unit 4. So far so good. Both exam papers are broken down into sections.

Unit 3

Unit 3 (Topics in Psychology) is made up of eight topics. There'll be questions on each of the following topics:

- Biological Rhythms and Sleep
- Perception
- Gender
- Relationships
- Aggression
- Eating Behaviour
- Intelligence and Learning
- Cognition and Development

Don't worry though — you just need to choose **three** of these topics to answer questions on. The questions for each topic are worth a total of **24 marks** and could be either a single question or several smaller questions.

The exam lasts for an hour and a half.

Unit 4

Unit 4 is split into three sections:

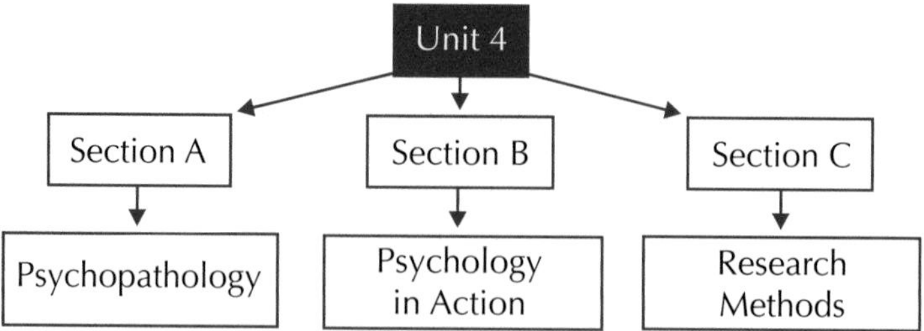

- Section A is on Psychopathology and you'll have to answer questions on one topic out of a choice of four. There are a total of **24 marks** available for each topic.
- Section B is on Psychology in Action — here, you need to pick one topic out of three — with a total of **24 marks** up for grabs in each topic.
- Section C has one compulsory question on Research Methods. It's worth **35 marks** and is split into several parts.

The exam lasts for two hours.

Exam Tip
Make sure you know exactly what each unit covers — you don't want any surprises on the day of the exam.

Exam Tip
You won't be asked anything from Unit 3 in the Unit 4 exam. Similarly, none of the Unit 4 stuff will come up in your Unit 3 exam. This means you can learn it in two separate chunks. However, if you really want to impress the examiner in your Unit 4 exam, you could bring relevant examples from Unit 3 into your answers.

Exam Tip
In the Unit 3 exam, the questions for each topic are worth the same number of marks so make sure you don't spend too long on the first two topics and run out of time for the last topic. For Unit 4, the marks are distributed a little differently — you'll need to spend about 35 minutes on Section A, 35 minutes on Section B and then about 50 minutes on Section C.

Command words

Exam questions contain content words and command words. The content words give away what the topic of the question is. A command word gives you an instruction of exactly what you need to do to answer the question. It's really vital that you know what they mean so that you can write the correct things in your answer.

Command word:	What it means:
Give/Name/ State	Give a brief one or two word answer, or a short sentence.
Describe	Give details of something — it might be a theory, concept or a study.
Outline	This requires less detail than 'describe' — it's more of a brief summary of something. Just give details of the main or important features. You don't need to go into too much depth.
Identify	This will often just require a single point without any explanation. Sometimes 'state' might be used instead.
Explain	If a question asks you to explain something, it means you need to give reasons for it and say why it is the case.
Discuss	This is asking for an answer that is a bit like a debate. The idea is that you'll build up an argument for and against something. You need to give evidence and examples for what you're saying, and support your points with explanations. This sort of question tends to be worth quite a lot of marks.
Evaluate	Evaluating something means weighing it up. You need to weigh up the advantages and disadvantages, positives and negatives, or strengths and weaknesses. It's important to keep your answer balanced — don't just concentrate on one side.
Consider	This is quite similar to 'evaluate' — your answer will involve weighing up the point that you've been asked to consider. Again, keep your comments balanced.

Command words can sometimes be combined together in a question. For example, examiners will often ask you to 'outline and evaluate' or 'describe and explain' something. Don't let this put you off — just break the question down into bits. Start your answer with the outline or describe bit, and then move on to your evaluation or your explanation.

How much to write

The number of marks that a question is worth gives you a pretty good clue of how much to write. It's not all about writing lots though — you'll have to present your answers in a well structured and reasoned way and back up your points with evidence in order to really impress the examiners. In the Research Methods Section (Unit 4) there's no point writing a huge answer for a question that's only worth a few marks — it's just a waste of your time. For the longer essay-style questions, make sure that you've written enough to get good marks, but don't waffle.

Exam Tip
Some questions may not use a command word, instead asking What? Why? etc. Here, make sure you understand exactly what you're being asked and, as always, make sure you keep your answer focused on the question.

Exam Tip
The more questions you practise, the quicker you'll get at figuring out what you need to do.

Exam Tip
For higher scoring questions, marks will be given in bands. You'll start by getting marks for the breadth of knowledge you show, but then also for the depth and quality of your answer.

Planning an answer

Examiners will stick to their mark scheme pretty strictly. So they won't give you extra marks for writing loads if it doesn't answer the question — to them it's just pointless and irrelevant information.

Also, when you're writing your answers, try to structure them in an organised way. If there's one thing that examiners find worse than a load of pointless information, it's being unable to make head nor tail of an answer — it just makes it really difficult for them to mark.

Before you start, it's worth jotting down a quick plan of what you want to write so that you don't just end up with a really jumbled answer.

Example

If a question asks you to outline and evaluate a study, your plan might look something like this:

1. Brief description of the method, results, conclusion
2. Strengths of the study design
3. Weaknesses of the study design
4. Brief summary of main points to conclude

Exam Tip
It's fine to write a plan like this before you start a question. Just put a line through it when you're done so that the examiner knows that it's not part of your answer.

Time management

This is one of the most important exam skills to have. How long you spend on each question is really important in an exam — it could make all the difference to your grade.

It doesn't matter if you leave some questions out to begin with. For example, if you're stuck on a question that's worth only a few marks, don't spend ages trying to answer it — you can always come back to it if you have time left at the end when you've bagged loads of other marks elsewhere.

Figure 1: *Make sure you don't lose track of time when you're in the exam.*

Applying your knowledge

You need to be able to apply your knowledge to questions in the exam.

Example

You could be asked how the cognitive approach can be used to explain a certain psychopathological disorder. It's no good just explaining what the cognitive approach is — you won't get very many marks. You need to talk about how the cognitive approach can be applied to the particular context in the question.

You'll have gathered that to get the higher grades, your answer needs to show detailed and accurate knowledge. Basically, you need to show the examiner that you understand stuff really well. Picking out studies and theories to support your answers is great — but keep it all relevant to the question.

Exam Tip
Exam questions are sometimes put into a context — you'll need to work out which bit of your psychological knowledge to use in your answer.

Quality of written communication (QWC)

In some of these questions, you get marks for QWC. It assesses things like:

- whether your scribble, sorry, writing is legible
- whether your spelling, punctuation and grammar are accurate
- whether your writing style is appropriate
- whether you organise your answer clearly and coherently
- whether you use specialist psychology vocabulary where it's appropriate.

Exam Tip
You'll be marked on the quality of your written communication in your answers to all three topics you choose in Unit 3. In Unit 4 you'll only be marked on the quality of your written communication in Section A.

On the front of the paper, you'll be told which of the questions this is being assessed in. However, stop right there. This doesn't mean that you don't need to think about it in all the other questions though. If your writing is easy to read and your answers make sense it makes the examiner's job much easier.

Assessment objectives

Just as in AS, there are three assessment objectives covered by the two units — AO1, AO2 and AO3. The way that a question is worded can give away which assessment objective is being tested.

AO1 is about the facts and theories

These questions test your knowledge and understanding of science. You get marks by recalling and describing psychological knowledge, such as theories, studies and methods. For example, you might get asked to describe a theory of depression. To get the marks, you'd simply need to describe what the theory proposed and describe its key features. What you don't need to do is evaluate the theory — that'd just be a waste of time that you could use elsewhere, and you wouldn't get any extra marks.

Tip: The questions in the exam won't be labelled AO1, AO2 or AO3, but you can use the information on these pages to work out which assessment objective a question covers.

Examples

AO1 Questions

- Outline the clinical characteristics of one eating disorder.
- Outline the problems of validity when diagnosing schizophrenia.

Exam Tip
If a question only has AO1 marks, there's no point writing anything that would get you AO2 or AO3 marks. For example, if a question asks you to outline the experimental design of a study, don't go into its strengths and weaknesses. It won't get you any more marks as it's not actually answering the question.

AO2 gets you to apply your knowledge

AO2 questions are slightly different in that they get you to apply your knowledge and understanding of science. It's likely that these questions will begin with 'discuss' or 'evaluate'. Rather than just recalling stuff, e.g. listing relevant experiments, you've got to apply your knowledge to the situation in these questions. So, you'd need to use the experiments you've come up with to support your argument. You also might have to apply your knowledge to situations you've not come across before. For example, you could be asked to assess the validity, reliability or credibility of a study that's new to you.

Examples

AO2 Questions

- Discuss the biological explanations of gender development.
- Evaluate explanations of one eating disorder.

AO3 is about 'How Science Works'

'How Science Works' focuses on how scientific experiments are carried out. You need to be able to suggest appropriate methodology and know how to make sure measurements and observations are valid and reliable. You could also be asked to analyse and evaluate the methodology and results of a study described in the exam. When you're doing this, don't forget about things like ethics and safety.

Tip: Have a look at pages 5-8 for more on How Science Works and Unit 4: Section 11 for more on research methods.

Examples

AO3 Questions

- Explain why the researcher should use a chi-squared test to analyse the data.
- Discuss how ethical considerations might influence the running of an experiment.

Question wording

The wording of the question can tell you what to do. For example, if the question simply asks you to 'describe' or 'outline' something, you know it's an AO1 question. So you don't need to go into evaluating and explaining stuff. Both AO2 and AO3 questions could ask you to evaluate something — but it's what you're asked to analyse that tells you which assessment objective is being covered:

- If the question asks you to evaluate a theory, it's an AO2 question.
- If you're asked to evaluate the method or results of a study, you know it's an AO3 question.

Exam Tip
Underlining key words in the question can help to make sure you keep your answer focused on the right things.

Assessment objective weighting

Each unit has a different weighting of assessment objectives. In Unit 3, most of the marks come from AO2, and the least from AO3.
In Unit 4 there's much more emphasis on AO3.

Exam Tip
With lots of marks up for grabs, it's tempting to write as much as possible. But remember it's a waste of time writing about everything you know if it's not answering the question.

		Assessment Objective		
		AO1	AO2	AO3
Weighting (%)	Unit 3	16.7	25.0	8.3
	Unit 4	11.5	16.7	21.8

Figure 2: *Table to show the weighting of the three assessment objectives in the Unit 3 and 4 exams.*

What to avoid

It's important to remember that it's not just a case of blindly scribbling down everything you can think of that's related to the subject. Doing this just wastes time, and it doesn't exactly impress the examiner. You only get marks for stuff that's relevant and answers the question. So, read the question a couple of times before you start writing so that you really understand what it's asking.

Figure 3: *You won't have a dictionary or a computer in the exam to help you with neat spelling or writing. Make sure that you write properly though so you don't lose unnecessary marks.*

Armed with all your new-found knowledge and by following all the tips and hints in this book, exam success is just around the corner...

Answers

Unit 3

Unit 3: Section 1 — Biological Rhythms and Sleep

1. Biological Rhythm Cycles

Page 12 — Summary Questions

Q1 E.g. the menstrual cycle / Seasonal Affective Disorder.

Q2 e.g. light

Q3 They both influence the timing of biological rhythms which tell us when we need to sleep. Endogenous factors may completely determine a cycle through biological influences such as the suprachiasmatic nucleus, the pineal gland or melatonin. Exogenous factors, e.g. light, exist outside the body and act like a prompt or as a mechanism to 'fine-tune' biological rhythms.

You not only need to know the difference between endogenous and exogenous factors, but also how they interact.

Q4 a) Because Declan has travelled to a different time zone, from east to west, his body clock is now out of sync with the local timing.

You should be able to give examples of psychology in a real life setting — make sure you can talk about things like jet lag and shift patterns.

b) E.g. he should force himself to stay awake.

Q5 E.g. they cannot be accurately generalised to humans.

2. Sleep States

Page 17 — Summary Questions

Q1 Rapid eye movement sleep is the active stage of sleep where metabolic rate increases and dreams occur.

Q2 Core sleep is made up of stage four slow wave sleep (SWS) and rapid eye movement (REM) sleep. It is used for body restoration. Optional sleep is made up of all other sleep stages and it is not necessary, although having it can help to conserve energy.

Q3 Any three from, e.g. EEGs / EOGs / EMGs / self reports / observations.

Q4 Stage two.

Make sure you know the characteristics of each stage of sleep. Generally, the higher the sleep stage, the larger the waves and the deeper the sleep.

Q5 E.g. the restoration theory suggests that sleep restores the body's ability to function after being busy during the day. Shapiro et al (1981) found that long-distance runners had more slow wave sleep after a race, implying that exercise increased the need for bodily restoration. But Horne and Minard (1985) found that although people who undertook physical and cognitive tasks fell asleep more quickly, they didn't sleep for longer. To further support the restoration approach, Horne and Pettitt (1985) looked at the effect of rewards on sleep deprived people. They showed that if a sleep deprived person is offered a reward to complete a task, they will perform just as well as people who have had sleep but had no reward incentive. However, the sample size for this study was very small, making it hard to generalise the results to the wider population. The experiment also lacked ecological validity as the auditory tasks were not tasks people would do in everyday situations.

3. Disorders of Sleep

Page 21 — Summary Questions

Q1 a) Primary insomnia isn't linked to any existing condition, whereas secondary insomnia is the result of an existing physical or psychological condition.

b) E.g. disruptions to circadian rhythm, through jet lag, shift work or sleeping at irregular times. / Using stimulants such as caffeine or nicotine.

c) E.g. they may have a physical complaint such as arthritis, diabetes or asthma. / They might have a psychological condition such as depression, post-traumatic stress disorder or generalised anxiety disorder. / They may be suffering from stress or anxiety. / They may be taking a medication where the side-effects include sleep deprivation.

Make sure you know several examples before you go into the exam to show the examiner you are able to distinguish between primary and secondary insomnia.

Q2 secondary insomnia

Q3 E.g. there are many variables that can cause or influence the condition / some of the variables are hard to control / a lot of the research is correlational rather than showing cause and effect.

Q4 a) E.g. day-time sleepiness / weak muscles (cataplexy) / dream-like imagery.

b) Because the concordance rate is fairly low, although there must be some genetic link, there must also be environmental influences. It could be that a virus may trigger a genetic predisposition to narcolepsy.

Page 22 — Exam-style Questions

01 Maximum of 24 marks available.
HINTS:

- Give a brief introduction to biological rhythms — outline what they are and give some examples.
- Outline how the research has been carried out. Explain that a lot of biological rhythm research has been conducted on animals. This means the findings cannot be accurately generalised to humans.
- Studies of humans have often used artificial light in a laboratory setting. Although this is useful research, people may sleep differently when under observation, and when in a different place, so the results may not be completely reliable or valid.
- Include some examples of research into biological rhythms.
- You also need to evaluate the research. Talk about how the research still does not account for individual differences which might greatly impact biological rhythms.
- Finish your answer by summarising everything you've written — draw an overall conclusion about what the research has found.

02 Maximum of 24 marks available.
HINTS:

- This question is pretty straightforward — it's just asking you to talk about two different theories of sleep. Make sure you choose two theories that you know well, and start by outlining them.
- You then need to go on to evaluate the theories. Give examples of studies which either support of contradict your chosen theories. This is a good way of pointing out a theory's strengths and weaknesses.

- You could also compare and contrast the two theories that you've chosen. For example, you could point out how one study makes up for the other study's failings, and vice versa.
- Finish with a brief summary of the main points of your answer — but don't just repeat everything you've previously said.

Unit 3: Section 2 — Perception

1. Theories of Perception

Page 26 — Summary Questions

Q1 Any one from, e.g. horizon ratios / optic flow patterns.

Q2 Visual illusions such as the Necker cube can provide support for Gregory's theory. Palmer's (1975) experiment scientifically investigated his theory, providing more support.

You could give an example of a visual illusion, and even draw it to show how it applies to Gregory's theory.

Q3 top down

Make sure you know the differences between Gregory and Gibson's theories.

2. Development of Perception

Page 31 — Summary Questions

Q1 a) She's trying to investigate depth perception in infants to determine if it is an innate process or if it develops over time.

The important aspect of this study was that it used babies to see whether depth perception is innate. It provides evidence for the nature-nurture debate within perceptual development.

b) Babies can perceive depth so depth perception is innate and the result of nature, not nurture.

c) E.g. the validity of the results is questionable as the infants could have learnt depth perception in their first few months of life. / The study may be ethically questionable as it involves putting infants in a potentially stressful situation.

Q2 The process whereby we understand that, despite a rotated shape looking different and resulting in a different image forming on the retina, it hasn't actually changed shape at all.

3. Face Recognition and Visual Agnosia

Page 36 — Summary Questions

Q1 E.g. he could be experiencing prosopagnosia.

There are obviously lots of things that could be wrong with Steven, but the question is given in the context of face recognition and visual agnosia, so we know it must be related to the topic somehow.

Q2 a) Any two from, e.g. structural encoding / expression analysis / facial speech analysis / directed visual processing.

b) Any two from, e.g. structural encoding / face recognition units / person identity nodes / name generation.

The question just asks you to name two components, so there's no need to explain them here, but make sure you do know what they all mean for the real exam.

Q3 a) Bruce and Young stated that the process of face recognition involves several different components that all work together. The more cues we have, such as the context of the rest of the face, the more likely we are to recognise a face's features.

b) Bruce and Young proposed that face recognition is different from object recognition. In this case, it would mean that whilst face recognition is impaired if faces aren't given in context, it should be different for houses. It would be expected that there would be no difference in Adam's ability to recognise house parts in isolation and whole houses. This effect was shown by Tanaka and Farah (1993).

Page 37 — Exam-style Questions

01 Maximum of 4 marks available.

E.g. A condition where people have difficulty recognising familiar faces. It's usually caused by brain damage, but sometimes it can be present from birth. There are also several types and it seems to exist on a scale, from very severe (not being able to recognise your own face or those of loved ones) to more mild.

02 Maximum of 20 marks available.

HINTS:

- Start your answer by explaining that much of the research has involved case studies of prosopagnosia patients.
- Talk about how the studies have provided support for or have contradicted Bruce and Young's model of face recognition.
- Outline and evaluate particular examples of case studies, and explain how they've contributed to our understanding of perception.
- Finish your answer with a summary — you might conclude that research into face recognition still needs to be developed further in order to fully understand our perceptual abilities and how the process works.

Unit 3: Section 3 — Relationships

1. Formation, Maintenance and Breakdown

Page 41 — Summary Questions

Q1 E.g. contact / physical appearance / similarity.

Q2 Potential people to form a relationship with.

Q3 E.g. dissatisfaction or boredom with the relationship. / Breaking agreed rules (e.g. being faithful, confidentiality). / Interference from other relationships (e.g. family or friends). / Abuse (e.g. violence, drugs, alcohol). / An attractive alternative relationship exists. / Costs outweigh benefits. / Conflict or dispute (e.g. over finances). / Jealousy over a real or imagined rival.

Q4 resolution

It won't take you long to learn Lee's stages of relationship breakdown — and it's certainly handy to know them for the exam.

Q5 a) The intra-psychic phase.

b) The dyadic phase.

c) The social phase.

Examiners love testing your ability to apply psychological theories to 'real life' scenarios. So, don't get worried if you see questions disguised in a context — you just need to work out which bit of psychology to use.

2. Reproductive Behaviour

Page 45 — Summary Questions

Q1 E.g. in the species of antelope, the large horns of the male antelopes are used in combat with other males when competing for the female antelope. Because of this, males with the largest horns have a higher chance of reproducing and passing their genes on to the next generation than other males. This means that the characteristic evolves in the species even though it reduces the survival chances of the males. This evolution of characteristics is known as intrasexual selection.

Reproductive and mating behaviour isn't just studied in humans — there are lots of examples of animal behaviour which are really interesting.

Q2 Intrasexual selection is the evolution of characteristics that are attractive to a mate. Intrasexual selection is the evolution of characteristics that enable an individual to compete with their rivals.

Both intersexual and intrasexual selection increase an animal's chance of reproducing and therefore passing on their genes to the next generation.

Q3 a) intrasexual selection

b) Release large amounts of sperm during ejaculation.

Q4 Any time, effort and energy that a parent puts towards the conception, gestation and rearing of a child that reduces their ability to invest in other offspring.

Q5 E.g. men only need to be involved at conception whilst women also have to invest during pregnancy and after birth, e.g. in breast feeding. / The number of children women can have is limited so they're likely to invest heavily in the survival of each one. Men can have many more children so investment in each individual is less important.

Q6 Men are more willing to engage in one-night stands and to have sex with lots of different partners, whereas women are more choosy. Trivers argued that this was because the parental investment per child is usually much lower for men than for women. Men need to make as many offspring as possible whereas women need to find a mate with good genes and who will protect their offspring.

3. Adult Relationships

Page 50 — Summary Questions

Q1 Secure / insecure-resistant / insecure-avoidant.

Q2 It gives opportunities to develop the skills needed to form successful adult relationships.

Q3 a) E.g. any two from: individuals are seen as part of an interdependent social group. / Obligations to others and the good of the group are very important. / Relationships are more likely to be non-voluntary (e.g. arranged marriages), where marriage joins families as well as individuals. / Extended families are more likely to live together, providing support for each other.

b) Eastern

The specification doesn't specifically ask you to know about individualistic and collectivist cultures but it does want you to know about cultural differences — so it's great if you can use the proper terms.

Q4 E.g. Gupta and Singh (1982) conducted a longitudinal study of 100 couples in India. 50 had arranged marriages and 50 had romantic marriages. They found that couples 'loved' each other more at the start of romantic marriages but then this decreased. The reverse trend was seen in arranged marriages. / Xiaohe and Whyte (1990) found that women in love matches in China were more satisfied with their relationships that women in arranged marriages.

Q5 Factors such as religion may influence divorce, e.g. within the Catholic Church, divorce isn't recognised. Other cultural factors can also influence divorce — in China, it is often seen as shameful.

Page 51 — Exam-style Questions

01 Maximum of 24 marks available.

HINTS:

- Start your answer by pointing out that there are several different theories of the formation and maintenance of relationships and say which ones you're going to discuss.
- Talk about the reward/need satisfaction theory to explain that relationships may be formed for selfish reasons — so that we satisfy our needs.
- You could also talk about theories such as Byrne and Clore's (1970) Reinforcement-Affect theory and the matching hypothesis.
- Go on to talk about the social exchange theory by Thibault and Kelly (1959) which suggests a cost and reward system as a base for relationships. You'll get extra marks if you expand on this theory and talk about other economic theories such as the Equity theory.
- Use research and studies that you've read about to support each of the theories — briefly outline the studies and say how they support the theories.
- You also need to evaluate the theories. Point out their strengths and weaknesses, and support your answer with examples and research where possible.

02 Maximum of 24 marks available.

HINTS:

- This is a 'discuss' question — it gives you quite a lot of freedom when writing your answer, but it's really important to remember to stay focused on what the question is asking you.
- Start by outlining what is meant by cultural factors. This could include the differences between individualistic and collectivist cultures or religions. It's important to show the examiner that you know what the key terms in the question mean.
- Next, you could talk about how these cultural factors affect specific parts of relationships. For example, you could focus on the duration of relationships and attitudes towards marriage and divorce.
- Support your answer with plenty of psychological research. If you know a study that provides evidence for the point you're making then use it. You don't need to go into too much detail about it — just outline what was done, what it showed, and link it back to the point you are making.
- For a really well-rounded answer, write a concluding statement at the end which refers back to the question.

Unit 3: Section 4 — Aggression

1. Social Theories of Aggression

Page 56 — Summary Questions

Q1 The theory that states when we're an anonymous part of a crowd, we're more likely to be disinhibited and display aggressive behaviours.

Q2 If children were anonymous (in costumes, masks or large groups) they were more likely to steal money and sweets while trick-or-treating.

Q3 An independent measures design.

Q4 There was an overall significant correlation between watching violent television and films and violent behaviour.

The correlation for men was slightly stronger than for women, and those who watched violent cartoons and fantasy programmes also showed more aggressive behaviour than people who watched other types of films and programmes.

Q5 Aggression within an institutional environment, e.g. in prison or in the military.

Q6 24 male undergraduate students

Q7 E.g. aggression in the police force / the military.

2. Biological Explanations of Aggression

Page 60 — Summary Questions

Q1 The amygdala, within the limbic system, and the temporal lobe.

Q2 Any one from: testosterone / cortisol.
It's also a good idea to make sure you know whether it's high or low levels of these hormones which increase aggressive behaviour in humans.

Q3 Van Goozen et al (1994) used a repeated measures design where they asked 35 female-to-male and 15 male-to-female transsexuals to complete a questionnaire to assess proneness to aggression. They completed the questionnaires before and after hormone treatment to 'change' their sex. Male-to-female participants were given anti-androgens and female-to-men participants were given testosterone (androgens) for 3 months.

3. Evolutionary Explanations of Aggression

Page 64 — Summary Questions

Q1 An individual will be more likely to pass on their genes if they're able to gain the upper hand in competition for food, mates or territory.

Q2 a) Men's jealousy is innately triggered by the threat of uncertainty over the paternity of children produced within the relationship. However, women are more threatened by emotional infidelity as it could mean being left for another woman, and so reducing the resources available to her children.

b) The validity of the results is questionable because the hypothetical nature of the scenarios in the questionnaires and the limited multiple choice answers means that the responses may not accurately reflect what participants would actually do in real life.

Q3 Being associated with the winning team would give them increased status and make them more attractive to potential partners. This, therefore, increases the likelihood of their genes being passed on, so the behaviour has survival value.

Q4 E.g. Podaliri and Balestri (1998) investigated the behaviour of Italian football supporters. They found that aggressive chants and behaviours strengthened the cultural identity of the different supporters, so that the differences between the groups were emphasised.

Page 65 — Exam-style Questions

01 Maximum of 8 marks available.
HINTS:

- Since this is an outline question, you just have to write a brief description of how hormones and neural mechanisms are thought to be linked with aggression.
- Split your answer into two — talk about the two factors in two separate paragraphs so that your answer is really clear.
- For neural mechanisms, point out that certain brain areas have been linked to aggressive behaviour, and for hormones, point out that changes in the levels of particular hormones have been implicated in aggression.

02 Maximum of 16 marks available.
HINTS:

- Start off your answer by briefly identifying the neural and hormonal mechanisms involved in aggression — e.g. the temporal lobe, the limbic system and the amygdala, along with testosterone and cortisol.
- You need to spend the rest of your answer evaluating these proposed mechanisms.
Do this by discussing studies that have either provided evidence to back up or disprove the theories.
- You could also introduce some alternative theories into your evaluation — use them to form an argument about whether or not the biological theories are superior.
- Finish your answer with a brief conclusion to sum up your ideas.

03 Maximum of 24 marks available.
HINTS:

- Start off by pointing out that jealousy is a type of aggression that can arise from a partner's infidelity.
- Go on to explain how infidelity can be seen as an evolutionary advantageous strategy — for example, males can increase the quantity of offspring carrying their genes and females can improve the quality of their offspring.
- Include some studies in your answer to support the evolutionary theory. For example, you could use Buss et al's (1992) study of sex differences in jealousy or Haden and Hojjat's (2006) study.
- Make sure that a large proportion of your answer focuses on evaluating the explanations, as this is where the majority of the marks come from. You can do this by discussing how well studies support (or contradict) the theories, and also by comparing the explanation against alternative explanations.
- Finish your answer with a brief summary — round up the points you've made with an overall conclusion to close your answer nicely.

04 Maximum of 24 marks available.
HINTS:

- The first part of your answer should point out that the social approach involves several different theories, including the deindividuation theory and the social learning theory.
- Choose which theories you're going to cover in your answer, and spend some time outlining them.
- Then talk about research which either supports, or contradicts, your chosen theories. This will form some of the evaluation of the social approach.
- Other evaluation points can come from comparing the social approach to other explanations — it might be that other explanations can account for factors that the social explanation can't account for, or vice versa.
- Round off your answer by summarising what you've said and providing an overall conclusion. You might also point out that behaviour is really hard to define with just one approach — lots of different approaches provide plausible explanations and it might be that a combination of all of them is best for explaining why people act aggressively.

Unit 3: Section 5 — Eating Behaviour

1. Factors Influencing Eating Behaviour

Page 70 — Summary Questions

Q1 Any one from, e.g. a reduced appetite or bad diet, caused by lack of motivation, is a common symptom of depression / people may binge eat or comfort eat when feeling stressed or sad.

Q2 An eating disorder where people survive on a highly restricted diet to try and avoid anything they think might be 'unhealthy'.

Q3 a) Any one from, e.g. constant monitoring may leave Gina feeling stressed so she may secretively binge eat as a defence mechanism / she may have developed a lower metabolic rate through extreme dieting so eating normally means she converts more calories to fat than before.

b) Any one from, e.g. motivation / willpower / informing friends and family / joining a weight loss group.

2. Biological Explanations of Eating Behaviour

Page 75 — Summary Questions

Q1 The process that keeps conditions in the body constant.

Q2 a) E.g. Baylis et al (1996) made two symmetrical lesions in the ventromedial nucleus (VMN) of 13 rats. They compared these rats with age-matched controls.

The question only asks for the method, so don't get carried away and start talking about the results and conclusion.

b) Any one from, e.g. a small sample was used so results can't be generalised / only one breed of rat was used so results can't be generalised / other tissues around the VMN may have been damaged so we don't know if it's purely the impact of the VMN.

Q3 The ventromedial nucleus (VMN).

Q4 It detects a drop in blood sugar and causes neurons to fire, creating hunger sensations, and driving the person to eat.

3. Anorexia Nervosa

Page 80 — Summary Questions

Q1 a) Amenorrhoea is when a female stops menstruating due to their low body weight.

b) Any two from, e.g. low weight / body-image distortion / anxiety.

Q2 Anorexics often have abnormally high levels of serotonin which makes them a lot more anxious. Serotonin levels increase with food intake which may be why anorexics may feel better through starvation.

Q3 E.g. it may be a reaction to sexual abuse / it may reflect a reluctance to take on adult responsibilities / it may reflect low self-esteem / it may be a battle against controlling parents.

4. Bulimia Nervosa

Page 83 — Summary Questions

Q1 Any two from, e.g. it may be a reaction to sexual abuse / it may be a result of emotional damage caused by poor relationships with parents / it may be a defence mechanism to help guard against trauma.

Q2 Any three from: bingeing / purging / frequently bingeing and purging / distorted self-evaluations / separate condition from anorexia nervosa.

Q3 Bingeing is eating a large quantity of food in a short time frame. During a binge the person feels out of control. Purging is preventing weight gain by getting rid of food from the body. This may involve vomiting, using laxatives, not eating for a long period or excessive exercise.

Don't forget that 'bingeing', 'purging' and 'bingeing and purging' are listed as three separate characteristics of bulimia nervosa used to diagnose the illness.

Q4 Before a person develops bulimia nervosa, they may have disordered eating habits. Part of the disordered eating may involve overeating to compensate for restricting their food intake. This results in positive reinforcement — praise for weight loss and satisfaction from indulgence. However, overeating may lead to anxiety (punishment), which is then reduced by purging (negative reinforcement). This makes the purging behaviour more likely to happen again.

5. Obesity

Page 87 — Summary Questions

Q1 Using the body mass index (BMI) scale. Someone obese would have a BMI of 30 kg/m^2 or higher.

Q2 Obesity increases the risk of illnesses like heart disease, diabetes and cancer.

At A2-Level, the examiner would like to know that you can apply what you're learning to real life situations.

Q3 leptin

Q4 Any one from, e.g. parents or teachers may use sweets to reinforce behaviour. / Parents may praise children for clearing their plate. / Advertisers use brightly coloured packaging/friendly characters/free gifts. / Celebrations are always accompanied by food.

Page 88 — Exam-style Questions

01 Maximum of 8 marks available.
HINTS:

- Choose one eating disorder from anorexia nervosa, bulimia nervosa and obesity and define it. List the symptoms and characteristics that are needed for someone to be classified with the disorder.
- This is a simple 'outline' question, so you don't need to take the answer any further, say, by suggesting the causes of your chosen disorder.

02 Maximum of 16 marks available.
HINTS:

- Start off your answer by restating to the examiner which disorder you are going to talk about in your answer.
- Describe the different explanations for this disorder — this should include both psychological and biological theories.
- For each theory, include some evaluation. Give examples of research to either support or contradict the theory, or you could point out how parts of one theory can improve on problematic parts of other theories.
- Your evaluation could also include how no one approach fully explains eating disorders.
The evolutionary approach is deterministic, doesn't consider free will and also doesn't take into account cultural and social influences on eating behaviour.
The psychodynamic approach is unscientific and the behavioural approach is reductionist.
- Finish with a conclusion which states that there isn't one theory which successfully explains the eating disorder — there are good points to all of them and therefore, it may be a mix of all approaches that best explains the behaviour.

03 Maximum of 8 marks available.
HINTS:

- There are lots of different things could talk about in this answer. However, it's only worth 8 marks so you need to keep your answer concise. Don't try to write about every possible thing that's relevant.
- You could talk about cultural influences and how these may have developed over time. Within the Western world, the idea that 'thin is beautiful' is a concept that has become increasingly popular over the last 40 years. This isn't the case in all cultures though.
- Religion is also a key influence in eating behaviour and can affect attitudes.
- Mood is another factor — this can cause people to eat more, but it can also cause people to adopt unusual behaviours which might stop them from eating.
- You don't need to explain or evaluate these factors — just stick to what the question asks for.

04 Maximum of 8 marks available.
HINTS:

- Start by describing the evolutionary theory for food preferences that states we may prefer calorie rich food because we have descended from hunter-gatherers who needed to ensure they had enough energy to keep them going.
- Then explain that a burger is more calorie rich than a salad and would provide us with this much needed energy.
- Finish off your answer by mentioning that we don't really face food shortages in our culture so Roz's food choice is actually just a result of our evolutionary past.

05 Maximum of 8 marks available.
HINTS:

- Start your answer by very briefly outlining the ideas that have been suggested about the functions of the LN and the VMN. Then you can talk about the research that has already been conducted into the neural mechanisms of eating behaviour.
- You could also mention the role of ghrelin in eating behaviour.
- Then you need to move on to the main part of your answer — the evaluation. Talk about how neither study is conclusive and how there appear to be other brain areas which are also relevant in eating behaviour.
- They also only test on animals and so generalising to humans is hard.
- Finish off your answer by saying whilst research has provided some evidence for neural mechanisms involved in controlling eating behaviour, there are no definite answers and so more research is necessary.

Unit 3: Section 6 — Gender

1. Psychological Influences on Gender

Page 93 — Summary Questions

Q1 The way someone acts and identifies themselves — the behavioural characteristics that make a person masculine or feminine.

Q2 a) A basic gender identity.
b) The concept of an in-group and an out-group.

Q3 E.g. Rekers and Kilgus (1997) studied families where offspring had gender dysphoria. They found that 80% of the gender dysphoria sufferers had mothers with mental health problems, 45% had fathers with mental health problems and 37% had absent fathers. But since not all children who experience these problems go onto develop gender dysphoria, there must be other factors. / Cole et al (1997) asked 318 males and 117 females who had all been diagnosed gender dysphoria to complete a set of questionnaires to monitor their mental health. They found that less than 10% of them had another mental health disorder, which isn't significantly different from the general population. The researchers concluded that gender dysphoria should therefore be classified as a separate mental health disorder.

2. Biological Influences on Gender

Page 97 — Summary Questions

Q1 a) Males have one X and one Y chromosome — XY.
b) A disorder where males are born with XXY sex chromosomes — they have an extra X chromosome. Males with this syndrome are sterile and usually less muscular with less facial and body hair. They can have trouble using language to express themselves and may have trouble with social interaction.

Q2 Evolutionary theory states that traditional gender roles developed through evolution. Women typically stayed at home to rear the offspring while men went out to hunt and provide for the family. This is the reversal of roles for Laura and Frank in the example.

Once you know all about a theory, you can apply your knowledge to any type of question.

Q3 Money and Ehrhardt suggest that once a baby is born people react to it differently depending on whether it is male or female. This means that the child learns different attitudes and behaviours.

Q4 A sample of women were asked to play with an unfamiliar baby using a variety of toys available. The babies were dressed in gendered clothing and given either a male or female name. The adults were likely to offer gender stereotyped toys to the baby they played with. They also spoke differently to the babies depending on their gender label. The results concluded that people's behaviour towards babies alters depending on the babies' perceived gender.

3. Social influences on gender

Page 101 — Summary Questions

Q1 Any one from: e.g. Rubin et al's (1974) study found that fathers used words like 'soft' and 'beautiful' to describe newborn daughters and 'strong' and 'firm' to describe sons. / Culp et al (1983) found that women talked more to babies dressed as girls and smiled more to babies dressed as boys. / Hron-Stewart (1988) found adults were quicker to comfort a crying baby girl than a crying baby boy.

Q2 Williams (1986) compared the population of a town in Canada, Notel, which had previously had no access to TV to another town, Multitel, which already had TV.
At the start, gender stereotyping was greater in Multitel than Notel. However, when TV was introduced to Notel, gender stereotyping in Notel children became more common and more like that of Multitel children. This suggests the media do appear to influence sex role stereotypes in children.

Page 102 — Exam-style Questions

01 Maximum of 8 marks available
HINTS:

- You could start your answer by talking about different gender roles, e.g. women staying at home with children and men going to work.
- Go on to suggest how these gender roles may have ensured the survival of our ancestors, by dividing up behaviours into complementary roles.
- You could also talk about Trivers' (1972) theory which suggested that women invest more in offspring than men do and so they often discriminate more then choosing a mate. These different gender roles might have come about from our ancestors as women would have developed characteristics such as coyness, whereas men would have to compete and so would be more aggressive.

02 Maximum of 16 marks available.
HINTS:

- Start your answer by briefly explaining that biological influences on gender development, include genes and hormones.
- You could use syndromes like Klinefelter's syndrome to back up the genetics part of the biological explanation, and CAH to back up the hormone part of the explanation.
- You can also use alternative explanations to provide a comparison, and therefore more evaluation, of the biological approach. For example, you could use the positives or the shortcomings of alternative theories, such as the evolutionary theory or the biosocial theory, as evaluation points.

- You could also bring in issues and debates, such as whether a biological explanation is reductionist.
- Finish off your answer with a brief, overall summary to round it off nicely.

Unit 3: Section 7 — Intelligence and Learning

1. Theories of Intelligence

Page 106 — Summary Questions

Q1 Any two from: numerical / verbal / spatial / word fluency / memory / perception / reasoning.
Make sure you know the details of each of the theories of intelligence — you never know which one might come up in the exam.

Q2 Crystallised intelligence and fluid intelligence.

Q3 Any one from: Sternberg's (1985) triarchic model of intelligence / Gardner's (1985) theory of multiple intelligences.

Q4 a) Visual-spatial intelligence.
b) Logical-mathematical intelligence.
This question is just testing that you know the eight kinds of intelligence that Gardner named. Don't worry that the question is asking you about two people you've never met...

2. Animal Learning and Intelligence

Page 112 — Summary Questions

Q1 a) When a previously extinct CR is produced in response to the CS.
b) When the CR (e.g. salivating) isn't produced as a result of the CS (e.g. bell).
Make sure you're able to describe each of the principles of classical conditioning, not just list them.

Q2 a) E.g. being told by the teacher that you'll have no extra homework if you pass your test.
b) E.g. giving out a detention after someone has handed in homework late.
It's really useful to be able to give real-life examples of the theory — it shows you understand it.
c) Reinforcement encourages behaviour whereas punishment discourages future behaviours.

Q3 Machiavellian intelligence is the ability to manipulate social situations to reach a goal.
For an animal to do this, it must have a theory of mind — the ability to imagine the world from the perspective of others.

Q4 This occurs when an individual copies behaviour that it sees another individual receive a benefit from.

3. Human Intelligence

Page 116 — Summary Questions

Q1 E.g. by using a complex set of navigational skills to forage for food, they would have increased their intelligence. / Their use of problem solving skills to open nuts would have increased their intelligence.

Q2 Any one from: ecological demands / social complexity / brain size.

Q3 E.g. Bouchard et al (1990) conducted a large scale twin study looking at the correlation in IQ between identical and non-identical twins raised apart and together. They found that there was a correlation of approximately 0.7 for identical twins raised apart and roughly 0.9 for those identical twins raised together. This suggests that IQ is influenced by both genes and environment.
There are plenty of other studies that you could have used, including Bouchard and McGue (1981), so don't panic if you used a different one.

Q4 E.g. Sternberg et al (2001) showed that Kenyan children knew more about herbal medicines than Western children, although they didn't perform well on IQ tests. / Sternberg and Yang (1987) suggested that Asian cultures see intelligence as an understanding of others, whereas Western cultures use quantitative skills such as verbal and numerical reasoning. / Das (1994) found that Buddhists and Hindus were likely to attribute intelligence to feelings of awareness, mental effort and recognising others.

Page 117 — Exam-style Questions

01 Maximum of 8 marks available.
HINTS:
- You could either answer about Sternberg's triarchic model or Gardner's multiple intelligences theory.
- You're asked to outline the theory, so you just need to give brief descriptions of the key features of your chosen theory.
- Don't include any evaluation of the theory — you won't get any marks for it.

02 Maximum of 16 marks available.
HINTS:
- Start your answer by briefly describing what the information processing approach to intelligence is. You could mention Sternberg and Gardner's theories as examples.
- However, you need to spend the majority of your answer evaluating the theory. Pick out its good and bad points. Also, if you compare it to the psychometric approach, you'll be able to show how the information processing approach is good, but also how it doesn't explain everything in regards to intelligence.

03 Maximum of 24 marks available.
HINTS:
- Start by talking about the role of genetics in intelligence.
- Expand on this point by exploring the studies involved in trying to determine the role of genetics. For example, twin studies such as those by Bouchard et al (1990) can be used as evidence that there is some genetic link — but point out that because the correlation is never 1 there must be an environmental factor too.
- You could also use cross-cultural examples to illustrate the fact that as intelligence is dependent somewhat on the culture it is measured in, there does seem to be an environmental component.
- Finally, you could also talk about theories other than genetics that may explain intelligence. This could be factors such as the environment, brain size or social complexity.

Unit 3: Section 8 — Cognition and Development

1. Development of Thinking

Page 125 — Summary Questions

Q1 E.g. the child has some language, but makes logic mistakes. They typically can't do the 'three mountains task' or conservation tasks. The child shows egocentrism, irreversibility and centration.

Q2 Children at the formal operational stage used systematic testing of different mixtures to find the answer, whereas children at the concrete operational stage used a random approach.

Q3 The difference between the problem solving a child can do on their own and the problem solving they can do with a more able peer or adult.

Q4 Children completed jigsaws of increasing levels of difficulty with guidance from their mother. They were observed during this, and the hardest jigsaw they completed was recorded. They then returned a week later and attempted a new set of jigsaws alone.

Q5 Vague syncretic, complex, potential concept, mature concept.

2. Applying the Theories to Education

Page 129 — Summary Questions

Q1 A review of primary level education in 1967, which made recommendations for UK schools.

Q2 a) E.g. a teacher, an adult or a more cognitively advanced child.
b) The expert guide makes suggestions or demonstrates the task to a child in order to provide a framework by which the child learns to do the task. At first the child might need lots of help, but as they learn less help is needed and they can carry on learning independently.

Q3 a) Thirty children aged 3–5 were given the task of building a model and were observed. A tutor gave help to each child according to how well they were doing — the help was either in the form of showing or telling.
b) Wood et al's (1976) study found that scaffolding allowed the children to complete a task they wouldn't have been able to do alone. The effectiveness of the scaffolding was influenced by various factors, e.g. how the tutor simplified the task, and how they helped them identify important steps. Showing was used most when helping younger children, whilst telling was used more with the older children. Also, the older the child was the less scaffolding was needed for them to complete the task

Q4 The idea that children should learn by exploring and discovering facts.

Q5 E.g. it can be very time-consuming to continually assess the ZPD of all the children in a class. / Providing enough appropriate challenges and finding appropriate expert peer tutors can be a problem.

3. Development of Moral Understanding

Page 133 — Summary Questions

Q1 Joe's father promised that if Joe earned $50 he could go to camp, but then changed his mind and asked Joe for the money. Joe only gave him $10 and went to camp with the other $40. Alex, Joe's younger brother, knows the truth. Should he tell their father?

Q2 preconventional morality, conventional morality and postconventional morality

Q3 72 American boys aged 10, 13 and 16.

Q4 a) E.g. participants had to come up with the responses themselves, rather than choosing from a list of possible responses. This meant that the responses were not influenced by any pre-existing ideas that Kohlberg may have had.
b) E.g. when sorting the participants' responses into levels, Kohlberg may have shown some investigator bias. / It lacked ecological validity as the dilemmas were hypothetical. / The participants were all males so the findings can't be generalised to females. / The sample of American boys meant it was culturally biased so can't be generalised to more collectivist cultures. / It didn't allow for emotions such as guilt and empathy to be displayed.

Q5 a) a meta-analysis
b) Kohlberg's stages 1-4 are universal, but stages 5-6 are not.

Q6 Some morally-driven people are not motivated by duty or by right and wrong, but behave morally because it makes them feel good.

4. Development of Social Cognition

Page 138 — Summary Questions

Q1 Any three from, e.g. being able to distinguish between self and others. / Being able to refer to self and others with appropriate language. / Knowledge of experiences, abilities, motivations, etc. / Ideas about their body image.

Q2 Nose-touching increased during the second observation in the older children. Below 18 months the children typically ignored the mark.

Q3 a) From about two years old.
b) At the categorical self stage, we start to use language to describe ourselves, using culturally defined categories, e.g. age, male/female, tall/short, etc. We are also described by other people in this way, which can influence our idea of ourself.

Q4 He told children a number of stories involving dilemmas. For example, one was about Holly, a girl who liked to climb trees but whose father had made her promise that she wouldn't. Holly's friend then asks her to rescue his cat from a tree. Selman asked the children various questions about how the characters would feel and what they should do, etc. He then analysed their responses and used them to develop a model of perspective taking.

Q5 a) undifferentiated and egocentric
b) Up to six years old.

Q6 From about fourteen, children understand that third-party perspectives can be influenced by factors such as social or cultural values. They can see a situation from a variety of different perspectives, e.g. moral, legal, etc.

Q7 E.g. using multi-cultural materials and having class discussions can expose children to different perspectives, which may help to promote their perspective-taking ability.

5. The Mirror Neuron System

Page 142 — Summary Questions

Q1 frontal, temporal, parietal, occipital

Q2 a) Electrodes were inserted into individual neurons in the premotor cortex of macaque monkeys. When the monkeys reached for food, the activity in the neurons was recorded.
b) The neurons were active when the monkeys reached for food, but also, unexpectedly, active when they observed someone else reach for food.
c) The experiment involved inserting electrodes into animals' brains.

Q3 Areas of the frontal cortex and the parietal cortex.

Q4 In one condition participants played a piece of music on a silent piano and in the other condition participants imagined themselves playing the same piece of music.

Q5 During the first year of life.

Q6 E.g. that mirror neurons have an innate basis. / That imitation doesn't necessarily involve mirror neurons.

Page 143 — Exam-style Questions

01 Maximum of 24 marks available.
HINTS:

- Start off by outlining Vygotsky's theory — summarise the main points of his theory.
- Be careful not to go into too much detail — the 'outline' part of the question is only worth 8 marks, so don't spend forever on it.
- Next you need to evaluate Vygotsky's theory. This part of the question is worth 16 marks. There are loads of points you can make here, but you shouldn't just write everything you know — make sure your points are focused and well ordered.
- Try and back up the points you make with experimental research. For example, you could talk about Vygotsky's idea that language is a driving influence on cognitive development and then bring in Berk's (1994) study as an example that provides support for Vygotsky's theory.

- Finish your answer with a summary to draw together the conclusions you came to during the evaluation.

02 Maximum of 8 marks available.
HINTS:
- Start off your answer by briefly outlining what it means to have a sense of self.
- Then describe studies investigating sense of self. Lewis and Brooks-Gunn (1979) and Povinelli et al (1996) are good examples of studies to talk about. Say what the studies involved, what the results were, and what conclusions were drawn.
- This is a 'describe' question. Don't evaluate the studies — you won't get any marks for it.

03 Maximum of 16 marks available.
HINTS:
- In this answer, you need to keep focused on the strengths and weaknesses of the theory — don't just start describing the theory.
- You can evaluate just the theory itself, or you could also evaluate the methodology of the study that he based his theory on (as this will have influenced how reliable/valid his theory is).
- Use other research to provide evidence to support or disprove the theory too — for example, you might use a study where the results didn't fit with Kohlberg's theory.
- Remember, in an evaluation you don't just have critical — you should weigh up both the positives and the negatives.
- Finish off with a brief summary of the conclusion that you've come to in your answer.

Unit 4

Unit 4: Section 9 — Psychopathology

1. Clinical Psychology

Page 147 — Summary Questions

Q1 Studying, explaining and treating emotional or behavioural disorders.
Q2 Any one from, e.g. interviews / observations / psychological tests.
Q3 a) Information collected during direct observation.
b) Information collected from other studies.
Q4 Any one from, e.g. they aren't always valid as they don't report all of the variables that may be contributing to a disorder. / They rely on comparing people who are already diagnosed with the disorder so it's hard to tell the difference between whether something is genetic or environmentally caused.
Q5 Any one from: they can highlight whether something seems to be genetically or environmentally determined. / They are ethical since they rely on situations that already exist and so don't need to split up families. / They allow researchers to observe cases for long periods of time so lots of detail can be obtained.
Although the question only asks you to give one strength, make sure you know why it's a strength.
Q6 E.g. Lipska et al (1993) studied schizophrenia in rats. This lab experiment created lesions in rats' brains to see if they developed symptoms similar to those found in people with schizophrenia. They found that damage to the hippocampus did play a role in the development of schizophrenia.
You'll never be asked directly to outline a specific example of a study. But it's a good idea to make sure you know one study for each type of study, because they could come in useful for the exam.

2. Schizophrenia

Page 151 — Summary Questions

Q1 a) Any two from: delusions / thought control / language impairments.
b) Any two from: stereotyped behaviours / psychomotor disturbance / catatonic stupor.
Q2 a) E.g. hallucinations / delusions / jumbled speech.
b) positive
Positive and negative symptoms are referred to a lot within schizophrenia research — make sure you know the difference between the two.
Q3 How far the classification system produces the same diagnosis for a particular set of symptoms.
Reliability and validity are two completely different concepts but they often pop up together.

3. Explanations of Schizophrenia

Page 156 — Summary Questions

Q1 Any one from, e.g. post-mortems / PET scans.
Q2 The hypothesis which states that synapses that use dopamine as a neurotransmitter are overactive in the brains of people with schizophrenia.
Q3 Any one from, e.g. non-schizophrenics can also have enlarged ventricles. / There's conflicting findings amongst schizophrenic patients. / The findings are correlational, so they don't show cause and effect.
Q4 Any two from, e.g. behavioural factors / psychodynamic factors / socio-cultural factors / cognitive factors.
Q5 a) E.g. concordance rates of twin studies are not 100%.
b) Any one from, e.g. job worries / family problems / money worries.

4. Treating Schizophrenia

Page 160 — Summary Questions

Q1 Patients are given tokens which reinforce socially desirable behaviours — they can then exchange these for something they want, like sweets or cigarettes.
It's easier to understand treatments if you understand the theories behind them.
Q2 a) Patients can be helped by identifying and changing their 'faulty cognitions'.
Don't forget that a lot of people with schizophrenia these days are treated with a combination of biological and psychological therapies — for example, CBT and drug therapy.
b) Any two from, e.g. it only treats the symptoms and doesn't address the cause of the disorder. / It's difficult to measure the effectiveness of CBT because it relies on self-report and is therefore less objective. / Patients can become dependent on their therapist.
Q3 A therapy that allows patients to observe others who act appropriately, and then through modelling, reinforcement and role play learn how to act in certain situations.
Q4 Any one from, e.g. it aims to treat the cause of the disorder, not just the symptoms. / Patients have more control over their treatment than with other therapies.

5. Depression

Page 164 — Summary Questions

Q1 Caused by internal factors, e.g. neurological factors.
Q2 It involves an alternation between two mood extremes (mania and depression). The change in mood often occurs in regular cycles of days or weeks. It's also known as bipolar disorder.
Depression is often referred to as either bipolar or unipolar depression so be sure to know which is which.

Q3 Any two from: extreme feelings of sadness, hopelessness and despair / diurnal mood variation / anhedonia.
There are some technical terms used here — diurnal and anhedonia. If you use these correctly, the examiner will be really impressed. Make sure you spell them correctly though.
Q4 How similar the cause of the disorder is for each sufferer.
Q5 a) major depression and dysthymia
b) E.g. the length of time the symptoms persist for and the level of depression felt by the sufferer. Major depression affects the person's everyday functioning, whereas those with dysthymia have a less deep depression and sometimes a relatively 'normal' mood.

6. Explanations of Depression

Page 169 — Summary Questions

Q1 Any one from, e.g. McGuffin et al (1996) carried out a twin study which found if one identical twin had major depression, the concordance rate was 46% for the other twin to have the disorder. In non-identical twins, the concordance rate was around 20%. / Wender et al's (1986) adoption study found that biological parents were eight times more likely to have depression than the children's adoptive parents. / Gershon's (1990) family study found that the rates of depression were significantly higher in those with biological relatives who also had the disorder than those with no family history.
There are lots of different studies to choose from here — all you have to do is outline the findings of one.
Q2 Kety's (1975) theory which states that serotonin controls the levels of the neurotransmitter noradrenaline. A low level of serotonin causes the level of noradrenaline to fluctuate — low levels of noradrenaline then cause depression, while high levels cause mania.
Neurotransmitters can be a bit complicated to get your head round, but they're really important when you're looking at the explanations for psychopathology.
Q3 Seligman restrained dogs so that they couldn't avoid receiving electric shocks. Later, when they could actually avoid the shocks, they didn't even try.
Q4 E.g. there isn't any research evidence to support Freud's theory so it's unfalsifiable. / It ignores the significance of other factors in causing depression, e.g. biological factors.
Q5 E.g. a biological vulnerability and an environmental stressor. / Biological factors and psychological factors.

7. Treating Depression

Page 174 — Summary Questions

Q1 Any two from: monoamine oxidase inhibitors (MAOIs) / tricyclic antidepressants (TCAs) / selective serotonin reuptake inhibitors (SSRIs) / serotonin and noradrenaline reuptake inhibitors (SNRIs).
Q2 a) E.g. it aims to treat the cause of the disorder, not just the symptoms. / Patients have more control over their treatment than with other therapies.
b) E.g. it can be distressing to recall traumatic events. / It's difficult to prove the effectiveness of psychotherapy. / There's a risk of patients developing false memories. / Other treatments, e.g. cognitive behavioural therapies, have been found to be more effective.
Knowing the advantages and disadvantages of different treatments is essential. You can't weigh them up against each other otherwise.
Q3 The ABC model claims that disorders begin with an activating event (A) which leads to a belief about why it happened (B), which could be rational or irrational. The belief then leads to a consequence (C) which produces an appropriate or inappropriate action. To treat depression, CBT aims to change inappropriate and irrational beliefs which cause depression, i.e. the B part of the model.
Q4 E.g. Brandsma et al (1978) found CBT was effective for people who put a lot of pressure on themselves and feel guilty about being inadequate. / Dobson (1989) conducted a meta-analysis that confirmed CBT is successful in the short term, producing a higher success rate than drug or behaviour-based treatments. / Hollon et al (2005) found those who underwent CBT had a lower relapse rate than those who had only taken antidepressants.

8. Phobic Disorders

Page 177 — Summary Questions

Q1 An extreme, irrational fear of a particular object or situation.
Q2 Blood-injection-injury type.
Q3 The fear of open spaces.
Q4 Any two from: a significant prolonged fear of an object or situation. / An anxiety response if exposed to the phobic stimulus. / A realisation that the fear is irrational and out of proportion to any actual danger. / Avoidance of the phobic stimulus. / Disruption to daily life.
Q5 a) How similar the cause of the disorder is for each sufferer.
b) How useful the diagnostic categories are for predicting the right treatment.

9. Explanations of Phobias

Page 182 — Summary Questions

Q1 The limbic system.
Q2 A loud noise was made every time Little Albert played with a white rat. He then began to associate the rat with the frightening noise, and showed fear when he saw the rat. The white rat turned from a neutral stimulus to a conditioned stimulus.
It's fine to sketch a quick flow diagram to work out what stimuli are causing what responses.
Q3 E.g. the research on upbringing is correlational. / It relies on people's memory, which can be inaccurate. / Other factors may be responsible, e.g. some people may have a biological pre-disposition that makes them more likely to develop phobias.
You can also use the strengths of one approach as limitations for a different approach, or vice versa.
Q4 It suggests that some people may have a biological vulnerability for a phobic disorder that will be triggered by a certain stressor.

10. Treating Phobic Disorders

Page 187 — Summary Questions

Q1 a) They increase the activity of the neurotransmitter GABA, which produces feelings of calmness.
b) Any one from, e.g. they cause side effects like drowsiness. / They can cause physical and psychological dependency, so they can't be used long-term. / The symptoms of phobias often return when people come off medication. / Drug therapy only treats the symptoms of the disorder, not the cause.
Q2 a) A behavioural therapy which works by using counter-conditioning so that the person learns to associate the phobic stimulus with relaxation rather than fear through gradual stages.
b) Any one from: exposure therapy / social skills training.
Q3 Any one from, e.g. Santacruz et al (2006) found that play therapy was successful in treating children with a darkness phobia, compared to a control group of children who were not treated with this form of psychotherapy. / Knijnik et al (2004) investigated people with generalised social anxiety and found that those who had received psychotherapy improved a lot more than those who hadn't.
You could also talk about any other study you've learnt that talks about the success of psychotherapy.

11. Obsessive-Compulsive Disorder

Page 192 — Summary Questions

Q1 a) E.g. excessive worrying about catching germs (an obsession) may lead to excessive hand washing (a compulsion).

Make sure you know the difference between obsessions and compulsions. It'd be a good idea to have an example ready to illustrate how they differ as well.

b) For obsessions, any one from: persistent and recurring thoughts, images or impulses that are unwanted and cause distress to the person experiencing them. / The thoughts, images or impulses are more serious than just worrying too much. / The person actively tries to ignore the thoughts, images or impulses but is unable to. / The person is aware that the thoughts, images or impulses are created by their own mind and aren't the result of thought insertion.
For compulsions, any one from: the person repeats physical behaviours or mental acts that relate to an obsession. Sometimes the person has rules that they must follow strictly. / The compulsions are meant to reduce anxiety or prevent a feared situation — in reality they're excessive or wouldn't actually stop a dreaded situation.

c) More than an hour each day.

Q2 a) E.g. having all the tins in your food cupboard facing forward in exactly the same way. / Having everything on your desk arranged in a neat order in the right places.

b) E.g. checking, contamination and hoarding.

Q3 How useful the diagnostic categories are for predicting the right treatment.

Q4 The fourth edition of the American Psychiatric Association's Diagnostic and Statistical Manual of Mental Disorders.

12. Explanations of OCD

Page 197 — Summary Questions

Q1 a) Genetic factors, biochemical factors and neurological factors.

b) serotonin

Although you've not been asked to expand in this question, it'd be good to know whether there is too much or too little of this neurotransmitter in people with OCD.

Q2 potty training

Q3 E.g. on walking past a knife in a kitchen, someone with OCD may become anxious, thinking "What happens if I pick up that knife and hurt someone?". / Someone with OCD might not be able to leave the room unless they'd turned the light switch on and off a certain number of times. If they didn't do this, they might believe that an electrical fault might cause a fire. / Someone with OCD might have to touch every door handle before leaving the house. If they didn't do this, they might think that they'll get hit by a bus.

13. Treating OCD

Page 201 — Summary Questions

Q1 A study where participants are put into groups, but neither they nor the researchers are aware of which experimental group the participants are in.

Q2 a) It challenges the obsessions by testing or questioning the accuracy of an individual's thoughts and behaviours. By giving the sufferer information to challenge their obsession, CBT can help prevent the compulsions.

b) Any one from, e.g. it can be used to treat both the obsessions and compulsions. / The patient is more active in their treatment if they use CBT than if they use drugs.

c) E.g. it can be challenging for patients — the treatment causes increased anxiety and distress.

Q3 a) Exposure and response prevention.

b) With support from a therapist, the patient identifies some situations that cause them anxiety. They then rank these situations in order of the anxiety they produce. The patient is exposed to the first situation and encouraged not to use the compulsions they usually use in this situation. At the same time, the patient is taught to use relaxation techniques. Once this is successful, they then move on to the next exposure task that they listed.

Q4 E.g. it aims to identify the underlying cause of the mental disorder, using therapeutic techniques such as dream analysis and free association. When the unconscious conflicts that are causing the disorder are made conscious, the therapist and patient can discuss and try to solve them.

Page 202 — Exam-style Questions

01 Maximum of 4 marks available.
HINTS:

- You simply need to briefly describe the characteristics of the disorder you choose.
- Don't go into too much detail as there are only 4 marks up for grabs.
- You could include signs and symptoms of the disorder, diagnostic criteria from the DSM-IV, or details of the disorder's incidence and prevalence.

02 Maximum of 4 marks available.
HINTS:

- Again, this only requires a brief outline of the therapy you have chosen.
- Give details of what the therapy involves, but don't go into any evaluation of how effective it is.

03 Maximum of 16 marks available.
HINTS:

- It'd be a good idea to start off by creating a quick plan of what you're going to say.
- Point out that there are several explanations within the biological approach, and then begin to discuss each of them. This will involve a brief outline of the explanation and some analysis of its pros and cons. Use evidence to support what you're saying where possible.
- For example, you could talk about the genetic factors, biochemical factors and neurological factors.
- You could finish this answer by suggesting that more research is needed within the biological field as more technological advances are made, e.g. in the field of MRI and PET scans.

04 Maximum of 24 marks available.
HINTS:

- This question will need some careful structuring as it covers quite a lot of ideas.
It's worth writing down a plan of what you want to cover before you start.
- Start your answer by talking about the DSM-IV as a diagnostic tool.
- The answer is looking for a discussion about reliability and validity, so define what these terms mean so that it's clear to the examiner that you know what you're talking about.
- Then relate the definitions of reliability and validity to problems when diagnosing mental health disorders.
- Explain why reliability might be an issue when diagnosing health disorders. You could give an example of research which has investigated this problem.

- Then explain why validity might be an issue when diagnosing health disorders. Again, you could give an example of research which has investigated this problem.
- Finish off your answer with a brief summary of the conclusions you've drawn during your discussion.

05 Maximum of 24 marks available.
HINTS:

- There's a lot to cover in this answer, so make a quick plan of what you want to say so that you can structure your answer logically.
- Don't forget to say which disorder you've chosen and always make it clear which explanation or treatment you're talking about.
- First outline the theories used to explain the disorders, such as behavioural, psychodynamic and cognitive factors. Then move onto the evidence for and against each explanation.
- Then talk about the treatments that are based on each of these explanations. Include evidence for and against each treatment.
- Finish off your answer with a short summary to round it off nicely. Don't just repeat what you've said — come to a conclusion such as the fact that the psychological approach can't yet fully explain the disorder and that there isn't yet a single treatment that is 100% effective.

Don't forget to make sure your spelling and grammar is correct. It'll need to be of a decent standard to get you the marks that you deserve if you've written some really good answers.

Unit 4: Section 10 — Psychology in Action

1. The Influence of Media on Social Behaviour

Page 208 — Summary Questions

Q1 Children learn aggressive behaviour through imitation of others.
Q2 a) A structured mental framework containing knowledge about the world.
b) A schema of a particular situation, containing knowledge about expected sequences of behaviour.
Q3 Over 500 children, who were from 5 to 8 years old, were asked to name their favourite TV shows and characters. After 15 years, almost 400 of the same individuals were asked again to name their favourite TV programmes. Their close friends were also asked to describe the participants' behaviour, and criminal records were obtained for each participant.
Q4

violent stimulus
↓
arousal
cognition ↔ emotion
↓
behaviour

You won't get asked specifically about the GAM in the exam, but it is worth remembering the model to help you answer questions on why people might be aggressive.

Q5 Any one from, e.g. heart rate / galvanic skin response.

2. Persuasion and Attitude Change

Page 211 — Summary Questions

Q1 a) E.g. changing an attitude, usually using messages about the object, person or concept in question.
b) The source of the message / the message content / the recipient / the situation.
The Hovland-Yale model is on the specification, so you really do have to know the details of how it explains persuasion.
Q2 Any two from, e.g. pleasant associations — products are often paired with things which an audience automatically feels positive about. / Making the message bizarre — images of something unconnected can encourage deep processing of the persuasion message and access the central route of persuasion. / Using familiar figures — celebrities provide people with mental associations and increase motivation to process the message more deeply. / Fear — this can act as a peripheral cue for persuasion. / Repetition — this makes the message more memorable, familiar and eventually automatic.
It's questions like these that really give you a chance to apply psychology to real life, showing you know how to integrate what you've learnt with everyday examples.

3. The Psychology of 'Celebrity'

Page 216 — Summary Questions

Q1 A one-sided relationship, with one person knowing lots and the other knowing nothing about the other party.
Q2 Over 300 Japanese volunteers were asked to complete a personality questionnaire. Their results were compared to a genetic test which indicated their levels of a certain enzyme, MAO-A, which has been associated with novelty-seeking behaviours.
Q3 E.g. the attachment someone forms with their caregiver influences how they attach and relate to other people in adulthood. Attachment theory suggests that children who didn't form close attachments with their caregivers may later develop insecure attachments as adults. They are then more likely to be attracted to celebrities — in one-sided relationships, there is little opportunity for rejection.
Q4 The absorption-addiction model.
Q5 E.g. it might help young people make the transition from parental to peer attachments by providing a common source of gossip.
Q6 intense-personal
It might be easier to think of some examples, such as the one in the question, to help you remember the different stages of fandom.
Q7 Stalking mainly affects celebrities. / Stalkers are usually strangers. / Stalking often ends in violence.

4. Models of Addictive Behaviour

Page 221 — Summary Questions

Q1 a) E.g. dopamine
b) The level increases.
c) Any one from, e.g. the release of dopamine is increased. / Dopamine's reuptake at synapses is prevented.
Q2 E.g. they may help them to identify the thoughts that trigger their addictive behaviour. They may then teach the addict strategies to change their behaviour, e.g. by avoiding certain situations and practising new thought patterns.
You could even mention that cognitive therapy may contain a behavioural component, teaching the addict new skills such as alternative relaxation techniques.

5. Explaining Smoking and Gambling

Page 225 — Summary Questions

Q1 E.g. the perceived effects theory / locus of control.
Make sure you know the details of these theories too.

Q2 Gambling may be driven by masochism — the idea that gamblers gamble to lose in order to punish themselves and reduce the guilt they feel from rebelling against their parents during childhood.

Q3 E.g. blowing the dice will make it more likely to land on a 6.

6. Vulnerability to Addiction

Page 228 — Summary Questions

Q1 E.g. alcohol can make someone who is stressed feel more relaxed. They're more likely to repeat this behaviour after being positively reinforced.

Q2 Martino et al (2006) carried out a longitudinal study to look at the social factors that affect the drinking habits of adolescents. They concluded that the norms for drinking behaviour are learned through social observations and interactions.
This question asks you to describe the study — that means the method and what they found.

Q3 a) As adolescents become more mature they are less influenced by others. This could explain why early experiences with substances have long-term effects.
b) E.g. as it is a cross-sectional study individual differences could have affected the results. / Peer pressure can be both positive or negative when it comes to abusing substances.
When criticising studies, you can talk about the method in general or be more specific about issues such as reliability and validity.

Q4 E.g. it's difficult to assess where the causal relationship lies in the case of a person with mental health problems. They might drink or use drugs to help them cope, or using these substances might make them more vulnerable to mental health problems. Ethics is also a major issue here, preventing many ways of testing this.

7. Reducing Addictive Behaviour

Page 234 — Summary Questions

Q1 Any one from: the person's attitude to a behaviour, which is shaped by their beliefs about the outcome of the behaviour and their judgement of whether the outcome is positive or negative, likely or unlikely. / Subjective norms, which describe a person's expectations of the social consequences of a behaviour, and their motivation to follow these norms.

Q2 a) perceived behavioural control
b) Indirectly — if a person believes that the behaviour is too difficult they don't form the initial intention to carry out the behaviour, and directly — if the perception of their own level of control is accurate.

Q3 Any one from, e.g. age / sex / social class / personality traits.

Q4 E.g. Antabuse / methadone / naltrexone.
Medication works in different ways to treat addiction — make sure you know the differences between agonists and antagonists.

8. Studying Anomalous Experience

Page 238 — Summary Questions

Q1 Any three from, e.g. out-of-body experience / near-death experience / spontaneous psychic ability / past-life experience / anomalous healing.

Q2 The area of psychology which looks at things that can't be explained using our current scientific knowledge.

Q3 Levy had unplugged the random event generator and so had only been recording the electrode activity for some of the time — most likely, when the electrodes were active.

Q4 Extra-sensory perception (ESP).
Make sure you also know how Ganzfeld experiments are conducted.

Q5 The ability to alter or move objects using your mind alone.

9. Explanations for Anomalous Experience

Page 242 — Summary Questions

Q1 A cognitive bias that means we are more likely to believe in and pay attention to information that has personal relevance.

Q2 E.g. believing that destiny is at play if you find out that you have the same birthday as someone you fancy / believing it is fate when you run into someone from school when on holiday.

Q3 Lorenz suggests superstition is a response we have adapted as a way to cope in some situations where we don't know or don't understand the true causality.
You could link this to what you know about the evolutionary approach in psychology.

Q4 E.g. believing that if you think about something happening, or say that it will happen, it's more likely to actually happen.

10. Research into Exceptional Experience

Page 247 — Summary Questions

Q1 a) It was an independent groups design where 96 patients were split into three different groups. The optimal group received treatment from a psychic healer in the usual way. The distance group received treatment from a psychic healer but from behind a screen. The control group received no treatment. Physical and subjective measures of asthma symptoms were taken.
It's useful to know the method that a study uses as it provides you with information to evaluate the study.
b) Improvement was not down to paranormal effects. The subjective improvement in the optimal group patients but not the distant group patients shows the influence of psychological rather than paranormal factors.
Remember — evaluation points can be good, as well as bad.

Q2 E.g. there are ethical issues involved — you couldn't create a state of near-death for the purposes of studying near-death experiences.

Q3 Kenneth Ring

Pages 249-250 — Exam-style Questions

01 Maximum of 10 marks available.
HINTS:
- Start off your answer by identifying the two different approaches you're going to talk about in your answer. These could include evolutionary and psychological explanations.
- For each approach, start off by giving a brief description of what it proposes.
- Then evaluate it by giving evidence to either support or oppose it.

02 Maximum of 4 marks available.
HINTS:
- You could answer about either the Hovland-Yale model or the Elaboration Likelihood model.
- As the question is only worth four marks, don't spend too long on it — there's no need to go into massive detail. Also, don't include any evaluation.

03 Maximum of 10 marks available.
HINTS:
- Begin by outlining some of the psychological theories about how the media might lead to anti-social behaviour. This could include the social learning theory (SLT), the social cognitive observation learning theory (SCOLT) and the general aggression model (GAM).
- The main part of your answer, however, should focus on the evidence for the theories.
- That will help you to argue to what extent the statement is true. You might find that the evidence is inconclusive.

- Finish off by coming to a conclusion which summarises your answer. If you've decided that the research is still undecided about whether the media could have had an influence on the riots, say that more research is needed.

04 Maximum of 4 marks available.
HINTS:

- Begin your answer by identifying the two factors that you're going to talk about in your answer. You could choose from age, stress, peer pressure, personality factors, personality disorders or the media.
- You could provide an example of each of your chosen factors to show the examiner that you understand how they might relate to Shaun's problem.
- For example, you might talk about stress and suggest that Shaun might suffer from high levels of stress. As alcohol is a depressant, it could make him feel more relaxed. This would act as positive reinforcement and so he's more likely to repeat the behaviour.
- This question is worth four marks — that's only two marks per factor, so keep your answer short and concise.

05 Maximum of 4 marks available.
HINTS:

- Choose one psychological intervention that you understand well. You could go for cognitive behavioural therapy or motivational interviewing.
- Simply describe what the intervention involves, and how it's carried out.
- You don't need to include any evaluation — and you won't get any extra marks for it if you do.

06 Maximum of 16 marks available.
HINTS:

- This question is very open-ended, so you've got a lot of choice about what to write about.
- As the command word is 'discuss', you need to build up a comparison of the models against each other. So don't just describe each model separately — make sure you evaluate them too, and compare and contrast their strengths and weaknesses.
- This is the sort of question where it would be a very good idea to quickly scribble out a plan before you start. Jot down the key things that you want to cover — that way, you'll stick to answering the question and won't go off on a tangent.

07 Maximum of 8 marks available.
HINTS:

- This question asks you to 'outline' issues, so just talk about the facts — you don't need to support your comments with, say, studies.
- It'd be good to define paranormal cognition in your opening paragraph so the examiner knows that you understand what it is.
- The answer asks for methodological issue*s*, so you need to talk about more than one, e.g. cognitive and experimenter biases.
- Describe how each methodological issue can lead to controversial results.

08 Maximum of 8 marks available.
HINTS:

- Start your answer by outlining which explanations of anomalous experiences you're going to talk about in your answer. These could include coincidence, probability misjudgements, magical thinking or personality factors.
- Relate each of the factors back to the context of the question — i.e. say why each factor explains why Lee is likely to believe in paranormal activity.
- Finish off your answer by summarising your main points. You could point out that what Lee experienced was unlikely to be due to paranormal activity, but that there are explanations for why he might assume that it was.

09 Maximum of 8 marks available.
HINTS:

- Start your answer with a brief explanation of what is meant by 'parapsychology' and 'pseudoscience'. It's good to show that you know what you're talking about.
- To answer the question, you could talk about research which has been classed as fraudulent or has used faulty scientific methodology.
- You could also talk about studies of parapsychology which have taken place using stricter scientific methods (e.g. autoganzfeld studies), and whether these have still found significant results.
- Round off your answer with a brief summary of your conclusions.

Unit 4: Section 11 — Research Methods

1. Is Psychology a Science?

Page 253 — Summary Questions

Q1 Scientists will always have an expectation about what they think will happen, and this will influence their experiments.

Q2 Defining variables in measurable terms.

Q3 Empirical methods are used which get quantitative data, which means results can be replicated and aren't affected by participant variables such as past experience. The theories are falsifiable.

2. Designing Psychological Investigations

Page 259 — Summary Questions

Q1 a) A sample where all of the important subgroups in the population (e.g. different age or ethnic groups) are identified and a proportionate number are randomly obtained.
b) E.g. it can produce a fairly representative sample.
c) E.g. it can take a lot of time/money to do. / Subgroups may be missed.

Q2 Causal relationships cannot be assumed from a correlation, as the correlation may be caused by a third, unknown variable.

Q3 A study where the independent variables aren't directly manipulated by the experimenter.

Q4 a) When a test produces consistent results, regardless of when it's used.
b) E.g. using the test-retest method, where the test is repeated using the same participants. A reliable test should produce a high positive correlation between the two scores. / Using the equivalent forms test, where participants' scores on two different, but equivalent, versions of the test are compared.

Q5 The extent to which the results of a test are caused by the variable being measured, rather than extraneous variables.

Q6 The extent to which the results of a test can be generalised, e.g. to a larger population.
Make sure you've got your head round all the different types of reliability and validity.

Q7 By operationalising variables so each researcher has a clear definition of the behaviour they should be recording.

Q8 a) A small-scale trial run of a test.
b) E.g. pilot studies are used to check for any problems before the test is carried out for real. / They give researchers practice at following the procedures used in a study. / They allow the validity and reliability of the test to be assessed in advance, which then gives the opportunity for improvements to be made.

3. Ethics

Page 263 — Summary Questions

Q1 16 years old

Q2 In a public location where people would expect to be observed by others.

Q3 If there is strong scientific justification for the research and there's no alternative procedure available to obtain the data.

Q4 To return participants to the state they were in before the research. The researchers fully explain what the research involved and what the results might show. Participants are given the right to withdraw their data.

Q5 a) E.g. Participants were deceived as to the true nature of the study, meaning that they couldn't give informed consent. / Participants weren't informed of their right to withdraw from the experiment, and were actually prompted to continue if they did want to stop. / Some participants showed signs of extreme stress during the experiment, so they weren't protected from harm.

b) E.g. Some prisoners became very distressed so they were not protected from harm.

For this question it helps to think about the British Psychological Society's ethical guidelines — you can then work out which guideline(s) each study would have breached.

4. Probability and Significance

Page 267 — Summary Questions

Q1 They could have happened by chance rather than being the effect of changes in the independent variable, so you can't really read anything into them.

Q2 Benzodiazepines will have no effect on the symptoms of phobias.

Q3 a) A Type 1 error is when you reject the null hypothesis when it was actually true.

b) 0.01, or 1 in 100

Q4 When your significance level is too small — for instance if you use a 0.01 significance level because you want very strong evidence of the need to reject a null hypothesis.

Q5 When the researcher has predicted a difference and also has stated which way the results will go. / When the researcher has used a directional hypothesis.

Knowing when to use a one-tailed test and when to use a two-tailed test is really important in statistics. Remember it's all to do with the hypothesis.

5. Inferential Statistics

Page 277 — Summary Questions

Q1 Data where all of the measurements relate to the same variable, and measurements can be placed in ascending or descending rank order.

Q2 a) directional

b) one-tailed

Q3 Spearman's rho correlation coefficient

Q4 The Wilcoxon Signed Ranks test.

If you're presented with a description of a study, read it carefully. You need to be able to pick out the experiment's aim, the type of data collected and the research design to know which is the correct test to pick.

6. Analysis of Qualitative Data

Page 281 — Summary Questions

Q1 A type of naturalistic observation where researchers only observe and record the particular events of interest.

Q2 E.g. there is no control over any of the variables so cause and effect relationships cannot be established. / Observers may be biased in how they interpret behaviours. / For ethical reasons naturalistic observations can only be done where people would expect to be observed.

Q3 a) An observational method where an observer joins the group they are studying. They may be known to the group or hidden.

b) E.g. insights about groups may be found that other methods couldn't show.

Q4 E.g. ambiguous questions, double-barrelled questions and leading questions.

Q5 a) The detailed study of an individual or small group.

b) E.g. lots of data may be obtained, providing detail that other methods can't give.

c) E.g. researchers have very little control over variables in the study and can mistakenly identify causal relationships. / Results can't be generalised to the rest of the population.

Q6 E.g. qualitative analysis preserves the detail in the data. / Creating hypotheses during the analysis allows for new insights to be developed. / Some objectivity can be established by using triangulation — with more sources researchers can cross-check their interpretations.

7. Presenting Data

Page 286 — Summary Questions

Q1 E.g. as a verbal summary.

Q2 non-continuous data

Q3 continuous

Q4 No, correlational analysis can't establish 'cause and effect' relationships — it can only show that there's a statistical link between the variables. Variables can be closely correlated without changes in one causing changes in the other, as a third variable may be involved.

Q5 a) a perfect linear positive correlation

b) no correlation

c) a moderate negative correlation

8. Reporting on Psychological Investigations

Page 291 — Summary Questions

Q1 You should provide a general overview of the area being studied, including existing theories. You should also discuss a few studies closely related to the current study.

Q2 It states the purpose of the study.

Q3 E.g. the number of participants used. / The demographics of the participants, e.g. age, employment, gender, etc. / The sampling method used. / How participants were allocated to conditions.

Q4 The observed value, the critical value and level of significance.

Think about the information you need to know when assessing if your results are statistically significant.

Q5 E.g. an explanation of the findings. / The implications of the study. / The limitations and modifications of the study. / The relationship to background research. / Suggestions for further research.

Q6 E.g. any materials used (e.g. questionnaires or diagrams) / raw data / statistical test calculations.

Pages 293-295 — Exam-style Questions

01 Maximum of 1 mark available.
systematic sampling ***(1 mark)***

02 Maximum of 1 mark available.
E.g. it isn't truly random or representative. / Subgroups may be missed ***(1 mark)***.

03 Maximum of 4 marks available.
The Mann-Whitney U Test ***(1 mark)***. This statistical test is chosen as it tests to see if there is a significant difference between two groups of scores ***(1 mark)***. The data is ordinal ***(1 mark)***, and an independent groups design is used ***(1 mark)***.

04 Maximum of 1 mark available.
self-selected sampling ***(1 mark)***

05 Maximum of 2 marks available.
Advantage: e.g it can save time / there may be many replies, producing a large sample ***(1 mark)***.
Disadvantage: e.g. the sample is unlikely to be representative as only certain types of people are likely to volunteer ***(1 mark)***.

06 Maximum of 3 marks available.
HINTS:

- In your answer make sure you talk about coding units, operationalised definitions and the frequency count of each coding unit. You should also refer to the fact that content analysis converts qualitative data into quantitative data, which can then be statistically analysed.
- Make sure you apply the scenario in the question to your answer, e.g. give an example of a coding unit that might be used by the psychologist.

07 Maximum of 1 mark available.
directional ***(1 mark)***

08 Maximum of 1 mark available.
There will be no difference in the number of men and women wanting to get married ***(1 mark)***.

09 Maximum of 3 marks available.
degrees of freedom = (2 – 1) × (2 – 1) = 1 ***(1 mark)***
As the hypothesis was directional a one-tailed test is used, so the critical value at p = 0.05 is 2.71 ***(1 mark)***.
The observed value of χ^2 = (7.52) is greater than the critical value so it can be concluded that the psychologist's results are statistically significant ***(1 mark)***.

10 Maximum of 8 marks available.
HINTS:

- All the information you need is in the text, and in the answers that you've already worked out.
- Make sure you include a brief description of the study's aim, hypothesis and method, along with a summary of the results, interpretations of the findings and any significant flaws in the study.
- Make sure that your abstract is no more than 120 words. You'll be penalised for writing too much as then you wouldn't be producing a concise summary.

11 Maximum of 4 marks available.

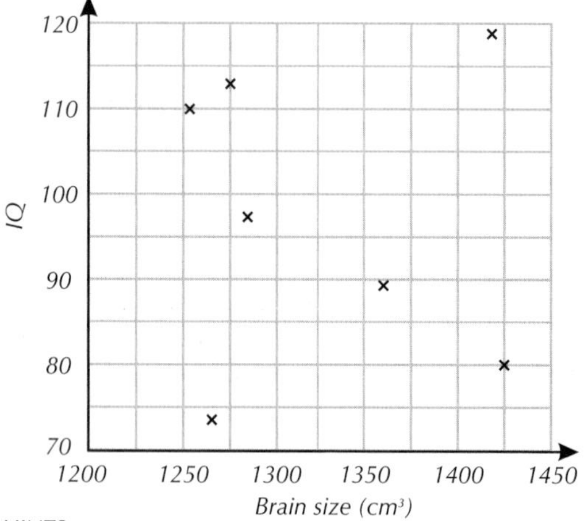

HINTS:

- Don't forget to give your graph a title and label the axes. Make sure you include the units too.
- Make sure you use a suitable scale for both axes too. Think about the highest value each scale needs to go up to and how much space you have.
- Mark the points with neat crosses using a nice sharp pencil — it'll make your graph neater, and easier for the examiner to read.

12 Maximum of 1 mark available.
The graph shows no correlation between brain size and intelligence ***(1 mark)***.

13 Maximum of 2 marks available.
Advantages: e.g. causal relationships can be ruled out if no correlation exists. / It allows variables to be studied that would be unethical to manipulate, e.g. is there a relationship between the number of cigarettes smoked and incidences of ill health? ***(1 mark)***
Disadvantages: e.g. causal relationships cannot be assumed from a correlation. The correlation may be caused by a third, unknown variable. ***(1 mark)***.

14 Maximum of 3 marks available.
If a test is externally reliable it should produce consistent results regardless of when it's used ***(1 mark)***. The external reliability of the IQ test could be assessed using the test-retest method ***(1 mark)***. This involves repeating the IQ test using the same participants. If the test is reliable it should produce a high positive correlation between the two scores ***(1 mark)***.

Glossary

A

ABC model
Ellis's (1962) model that claims that disorders begin with an activating event (A), leading to a belief about why this happened (B), which leads to a consequence (C).

Abstract
A concise summary of an investigation which appears in a psychological report.

Accommodation
The process of altering an existing schema to fit new experiences.

Active sleep
REM sleep. Characterised by dreaming and an increase in brain activity, metabolism and muscle paralysis. During this stage people experience rapid eye movements and vivid dreaming.

Adaptive response
A behaviour that has developed over time in reaction to certain stimuli in order to help an organism survive.

Addiction
Physical or psychological dependency on a substance or a habit, e.g. gambling. It can involve three stages — initiation, maintenance and relapse.

Adipose tissue
Fatty tissue in the body.

Adoption study
A study that looks at people who have been adopted. It examines concordance rates to determine the relative influences of genetic and environmental factors on a particular characteristic.

Adrenaline
A hormone secreted by the adrenal glands, often in times of stress or anxiety.

Aetiological validity
How similar the cause of a disorder is for each sufferer.

Affordance
When an object 'lends itself' to a certain task and its characteristics suggest how it can be used.

Agonist
A type of drug which triggers a response by binding to receptors on cells. Some agonists can replace and replicate the effects of addictive drugs, but with much less harmful side effects. They can be used to wean people off addictive substances slowly and gradually.

Agoraphobia
The fear of open spaces.

Amenorrhoea
The state when a female has stopped menstruating due to low body weight.

Amphetamine
A drug that increases dopamine function, sometimes causing schizophrenia-like symptoms in people without schizophrenia.

Amygdala
A part of the limbic system in the brain, believed to be strongly involved in aggressive behaviour.

Analytical intelligence
See componential intelligence.

Androgens
A group of hormones, including testosterone — the male sex hormone involved in the development of male characteristics.

Anhedonia
No longer enjoying activities or hobbies that used to be pleasurable.

Anomalous experience
An experience that can't be explained by science.

Anomalous healing
An anomalous experience which involves healing through scientifically unexplainable methods, e.g. by a spiritual healer or through prayer.

Anorexia nervosa
One of the most common eating disorders in the UK — symptoms include low weight, body-image distortion, anxiety and amenorrhoea.

Antagonist
A drug that reduces the effect of another substance. Some antagonists can stop addictive drugs from creating pleasurable feelings, so they can prevent the reinforcement of drug taking through operant conditioning.

Anterior cingulotomy
A last resort treatment for depression. It involves cutting a lesion in the cingulate gyrus, part of the brain which connects the limbic system with the frontal lobe.

Antimicrobial
Something that kills microorganisms like bacteria.

Antisocial personality disorder
A personality disorder in which the sufferer disregards the needs of others.

Anxiety disorder
The term used to describe a mental health disorder where anxiety is the main symptom.

Anxiolytic drug
A drug (e.g. a tranquilliser), such as a benzodiazepine, that reduces anxiety by increasing the activity of the neurotransmitter GABA.

Aphagia
Failure to eat.

Arranged marriage
Where a husband or wife is chosen for a person, rather than them choosing for themselves.

Assimilation
The process of taking new experiences into an existing schema.

Attention deficit disorder
A personality disorder characterised by hyperactivity and poor concentration.

Auditory hallucination
Hearing something that isn't there.

Autoganzfeld study
An updated version of a Ganzfeld study which has had the flaws of the original method addressed and removed.

Aversion therapy
Removal of an undesired behaviour by associating it with unpleasant feelings.

B

Bar chart
A way of presenting non-continuous data, where the height of the bars shows frequency.

Barnum effect
When people believe that a statement (e.g. a horoscope) applies personally to them, mistaking it for psychic mediumship, when it is actually an ambiguous or vague statement that applies to many people.

Basal ganglia
Part of the brain which may be linked to OCD.

Behavioural inhibition system
A circuit in the limbic system in the brain that's linked to anxiety.

Benzodiazepine
An anxiolytic drug (e.g. a tranquilliser) which reduces anxiety by increasing the activity of the neurotransmitter GABA.

Biosocial approach
An approach which uses a combination of biological and social factors to explain behaviour.

Bipolar depression
See manic depression.

Bodily kinaesthetic intelligence
The use of the body, e.g. athletic and dance ability. One of Gardner's multiple intelligences.

Body mass index (BMI)
A measurement of height relative to weight used to class people into weight bands.

Body-image distortion
A distorted view of oneself. Usually found in those with eating disorders who believe they're overweight when they're actually very thin.

Borderline-pathological fandom
A stage of fandom where obsessive thoughts begin to give rise to fully-fledged fantasies.

Bottom up process
Processes that build up an overall picture from combining lots of different parts. Information is put together to make sense of it.

British Psychological Society (BPS)
An organisation that oversees psychological research in the UK. The BPS has developed ethical guidelines to help psychologists resolve ethical issues in research and to protect participants.

Bulimia nervosa
A common eating disorder in the UK — symptoms include bingeing, purging, frequent bingeing and purging and a distorted self-evaluation.

C

CAH
Congenital adrenal hyperplasia — a syndrome where the sufferer is born with much more testosterone than normal, leading to early sexual development in males and masculinised females.

Case study
The detailed study of an individual or small group using many different methods including interviews, observations, psychometric tests, experiments, etc.

Cataplexy
A condition characterised by weak muscles.

Catatonic schizophrenia
A subtype of schizophrenia where the patient's movement and behaviour is disturbed.

Catatonic stupor
Lying rigidly and not moving for long periods of time, despite being conscious.

Categorical self
A stage in the development of social cognition which occurs from about two years. Here we use language to describe ourselves using culturally defined categories, and are described by other people in this way.

Causal relationship
Where a change in one variable causes a change in another.

Celebrity Attitude Scale (CAS)
A scale created by McCutcheon (2002) based on a questionnaire about celebrity worship.

Central route
One of the two processing routes outlined by Petty and Cacioppo (1986). It suggests that high-level mechanisms, such as evaluation of the source and content of the message, determine our attitudes to a message.

Centration
Where a child focuses on a small aspect of a task, rather than the task as a whole.

Circadian rhythm
A biological rhythm that occurs once every 24 hours.

Checking
A type of OCD behaviour which includes repeatedly checking things, e.g. that the lights are off or that you have your purse.

Chi-squared test
A statistical test used with nominal data and independent samples to see if there is a significant difference between two or more groups of values.

Cholecystokinin (CCK)
A hormone related to satiety.

Classical conditioning
A type of learning where associations are made between different things in our environment.

Clinical psychology
The area of psychology which focuses on studying, explaining and treating mental health disorders.

Cognitive behavioural therapy (CBT)
A psychological therapy based on the assumption that patients can be helped by identifying and changing their 'faulty cognitions'.

Cognitive bias
An error of judgement caused by faulty thought processes.

Cognitive developmental theory
First proposed by Piaget, it is the theory that suggests children's thoughts and views on the world change as they develop.

Cognitive system
A system involving memory, attention and planning that is used to analyse and process incoming information.

Cognitive triad
Beck's (1963) model which identifies three types of negative, automatic thought linked to depression.

Coincidence
When events appear to be linked, but in fact the two events are unconnected and occur closely together purely by chance.

Collectivist society
A type of society common in non-Western cultures. Features of collectivist societies are that the individual is seen as part of an interdependent social group. Obligations to others and the good of the group are very important.

Comorbidity
Where one disorder exists alongside another one.

Complex stage
Vygotsky's second stage of cognitive development. At this stage strategies are used in problem solving but they are not used successfully.

Componential intelligence
One of the three components of intelligence in Sternberg's triarchic model. The ability to solve problems, see solutions, monitor and plan.

Compulsions
Physical or mental repetitive actions.

Concordance rate
The likelihood that someone will show a characteristic if another family member has it.

Concrete operational stage
Piaget's third stage of cognitive development. It occurs between 7–11 years and is when a child's use of logic improves and they can do conservation tasks. They no longer show egocentrism, irreversibility and centration but can't yet use abstract reasoning.

Conditioned stimulus
A stimulus used in classical conditioning that comes to bring about a particular response.

Confidentiality
Keeping information private.

Congenital
Something (often a disorder) that is present at birth.

Conservation
The understanding that a set quantity stays the same, even if it looks different.

Contamination
A type of OCD behaviour that involves a fear of catching germs.

Content analysis
A method of turning qualitative information into quantitative data so that it can be statistically analysed. It typically involves doing a frequency count of how many times a coding unit appears in the data, producing quantitative data.

Contextual intelligence
One of the three components of intelligence in Sternberg's triarchic model. The ability to adjust to different environments and contexts.

Conventional morality
Kohlberg's second level of moral understanding, which consists of the morality of interpersonal cooperation stage and the social-order orientation stage.

Core sleep
REM sleep and stage 4 slow wave sleep used for body restoration.

Correlation
The extent to which two variables rise and fall together, or that one rises as the other falls.

Correlational research
A research method which looks for relationships between variables.

Counter-regulation effect
When dieters give in to total indulgence after failure and eat more.

Creative intelligence
See experiential intelligence.

Critical value
A value which you compare the observed value from a statistical test against. This indicates whether or not the observed value is statistically significant.

Critical value table
A table containing values which you compare the observed value from a statistical test against to see if the observed results are statistically significant.

Cross-cultural study
A study that looks at the same thing across different cultures. It allows us to see whether something is biologically or environmentally determined.

Cross-sectional study
An experimental design that assesses a common factor across different people of different ages.

Crystallised intelligence
One of two types of intelligence in Cattell's psychometric approach. It requires people to use their previous knowledge and learning.

Debriefing
A way of returning participants to the state they were in before the research. It's an opportunity for the researchers to fully explain what the research involved and what the results might show.

Deception
Misleading or withholding information from participants.

Defence mechanism
An unconscious process for protecting our instinctive thoughts and actions.

Deindividuation theory
The theory that states when we're an anonymous part of a crowd, we're more likely to be disinhibited and display aggressive behaviours.

Delusion
Believing something that isn't true.

Demand characteristics
This is where participants form an idea of what an experiment's about, and change their behaviour to fit their interpretation.

Dependent variable
The variable that you think is affected by changes in the independent variable.

Depth perception
Being able to visually distinguish between objects which are close or far away. Also being able to see things in 3D.

Descriptive validity
How similar individuals diagnosed with a disorder are.

Diathesis-stress model
A model that combines both biological and psychological explanations for a disorder. It suggests people have a biological vulnerability for a disorder, and that certain psychological stressors can trigger its onset.

Differentiated and subjective
Selman's second stage of perspective taking. From five to nine, children understand that other people have different perspectives because they have access to different information. However, only their own perspective is seen as important and they can't take the perspective of the other person.

Direct theory of perception
Gibson's (1979) theory which states that stimuli provide visual information which the cognitive system then processes to make sense of a situation. Stored knowledge isn't used to understand what is being perceived.

Directed visual processing
Processing of specific features (e.g. whether a person has a beard).

Directional hypothesis
A hypothesis that predicts a difference or correlation between two variables and states which way the results will go (e.g. which of two values will be greater).

Discrimination
This is when stimuli similar to a conditioned stimulus don't produce the conditioned response.

Discussion
A section within a psychological report discussing the findings, implications and limitations of the study. It can also include comments on related background research and suggestions of possible modifications and further research.

Disorganised schizophrenia
A subtype of schizophrenia where patients' speech and behaviour is often disorganised, and mood is flat or inappropriate.

Diurnal mood variation
Changes in mood throughout the day, e.g. feeling worse in the morning.

Dizygotic twins (DZ)
Non-identical twins.

Dopamine
A neurotransmitter involved in the reward, pleasure and motivation system of the brain.

Dopamine hypothesis
The theory that states schizophrenia is linked to increased dopamine activity in the brain.

Dream analysis
Psychoanalytic treatment that is based on the idea that a certain part of the mind keeps repressed thoughts in the unconscious. Freud believed these repressed thoughts are likely to appear in dreams, so patients' dreams were analysed.

DSM-IV
The fourth edition of the American Psychiatric Association's Diagnostic and Statistical Manual of Mental Disorders.

Ecological demands
Environmental factors which cause a species to evolve and adapt their behaviour.

Ecological validity
The extent to which the results of an experiment reflect what would happen in natural settings.

Economic theory
A theory explaining why we form relationships. Economic theories consider relationships to be a trading process.

Effeminate behaviour
Stereotypically feminine behaviours and mannerisms.

Egocentrism
Where a person can only view the world from their own viewpoint — they're not sensitive to the fact that others may have different views or thoughts.

Elaboration Likelihood model
Petty and Cacioppo's (1986) model which suggests that people can be persuaded using two processing routes — the peripheral route and the central route.

Electroconvulsive therapy (ECT)
Therapy used to relieve depression and schizophrenia in extreme cases and as a last resort. It causes a seizure by passing a voltage of around 250 V through a person's brain.

Electroencephalogram (EEG)
A technique used to measure electrical activity in the brain. It can be used to record sleep stages.

Elementary function
A type of mental function described by Vygotsky that includes innate reflexes, sensory abilities and certain types of memory.

Emotional blunting
Not reacting to typically emotional situations.

Emotional infidelity
The act of forming a deep emotional attachment with someone else other than your partner.

Emotional intelligence (EI)
The ability to recognise and manage your own emotions and those of other people.

Empirical evidence
Scientific evidence that's obtained through rigorous testing.

Empirical method
A scientific method based on experimental data, not just theory.

Enactive mode
Bruner's first mode of knowledge representation. In this mode, knowledge is only in the form of physical actions, i.e. learning by doing.

Endogenous depression
Depression caused by internal factors, e.g. neurological factors.

Endogenous pacemaker
A biological structure or mechanism within the body that influences biological rhythms.

Endorphins
Chemicals that block pain and some of the negative effects of stress.

Entertainment-social fandom
A stage of fandom when a relationship with a celebrity exists as a source of fun, shared with others in a social group.

Equity theory
A type of economic theory which states that people expect relationships to be fair and equal. They want to receive rewards from relationships that are in balance with the rewards they provide for the other person.

Equivalent forms test
A method used to check the external reliability of a set of results. It compares participants' scores on two different, but equivalent, versions of the test.

Event sampling
A way of sampling behaviour during an observation where researchers only observe and record the particular events of interest.

Evolutionary adaptive strategy
A strategy that helps organisms survive and therefore makes them more likely to reproduce and pass on their genes.

Evolutionary theory
An approach which states that behaviour has adapted over time, as a result of the environment, to aid survival.

Existential self
A stage in the development of social cognition which occurs from about three months old. Here we learn to distinguish self from non-self, and find out that we exist separately from other things.

Exogenous zeitgeber
An influence from outside of the body that acts like a prompt to trigger a biological rhythm.

Expectancy theory
A cognitive theory of addiction which states that addicts tend to take a more positive view of the outcomes of their addictive behaviour than non-addicts.

Experiential intelligence
One of the three components of intelligence in Sternberg's triarchic model. The ability to react to stimuli and develop ideas, either new or familiar.

Experimenter effect
Where the experimenter influences participants without meaning to, by giving out subtle clues about how they should behave.

Exposure and response prevention (ERP)
A behavioural treatment used for OCD. Patients identify situations that cause them anxiety. They're then exposed to the situation whilst using relaxation techniques to overcome their fear.

Exposure therapy
A behavioural therapy which involves exposing the patient to the phobic stimulus straight away, without any relaxation or gradual build-up.

Expression analysis
The analysis of facial features to work out a person's emotional state.

External reliability
A type of reliability. If a test has external reliability it should produce consistent results regardless of when it's used.

External validity
The extent to which the results of a test can be generalised, e.g. to a larger population.

Extinction
This is when a conditioned response isn't produced as a result of the conditioned stimulus, because the conditioned stimulus has been repeatedly presented without the unconditioned stimulus following it.

Extra-sensory perception (ESP)
Perceiving information not through the normal senses, such as through telepathy.

Extraneous variable
Any variable (other than the independent variable) that could affect what you're trying to measure.

Extroversion
One of Eysenck and Eysenck's (1976) personality dimensions. It includes being outgoing, happy and sociable.

F

Face recognition
The ability to identify faces based on appearance. This allows us to form relationships and function socially.

Face recognition units
Units that contain information about the structure of familiar faces.

Facial speech analysis
Facial movements (e.g. lip movements) that are used to help interpret speech.

Falsifiable
If something is falsifiable it could in principle be proved wrong.

Family study
A research method used to find out if genetic factors influence the development of a disorder. It compares concordance rates in families to see how likely it is that someone will have a disorder if others in their family have it as well.

Fandom
A group of fans of a particular celebrity, or the subculture of fans in general.

Faulty cognitions
Thoughts that are irrational or wrong.

Field experiment
A research method where behaviour is measured or recorded in a natural environment. A key variable is altered so that its effect can be measured.

Field of availables
Potential people to form a relationship with.

Field of desirables
A narrow group of potential people to form a relationship with, produced after applying certain filters to a field of availables.

Filter model
Kerckhoff and Davis's (1962) explanation of the development of relationships. We narrow down choices of potential partners from an initial group of people by applying a series of filters.

Fluid intelligence
One of the two types of intelligence in Cattell's psychometric approach. It requires people to use reasoning and information processing, with no prior knowledge needed.

Formal operational stage
Piaget's final stage of cognitive development. It occurs from 11 years and is when a child is much more advanced, and can use abstract reasoning in problem solving. They can also use hypotheses and theoretical principles, and deal with hypothetical situations.

Fraud
An act of deliberately deceiving others. In psychology, this involves invalidating observations and results.

Free association
Psychoanalytic treatment where the patient is given a cue word and asked to say any ideas or memories that come into their mind.

Frequency polygon
A type of line graph useful for showing continuous data.

Frugivore
Fruit-eating creatures.

Functional Magnetic Resonance Imaging (fMRI)
A brain scanning technique used to analyse brain activity by monitoring blood flow to different areas of the brain.

G

Galvanic skin response
A change in the electrical conductivity of the skin, which is affected by sweat.

Gambler's fallacy
The thought that many gamblers hold when they believe that the longer a losing streak lasts the more likely a win will follow.

Gamma-aminobutyric acid (GABA)
The neurotransmitter involved in anxiety. It produces feelings of calmness.

Ganzfeld study
A psychological study which tests participants for extra-sensory perception (ESP).

Gender
The way someone acts and identifies themself — the behavioural characteristics that make a person masculine or feminine.

Gender consistency
A stage in Kohlberg's theory of gender consistency. It's when an individual is aware that gender remains fixed in different situations.

Gender dysphoria
Also known as gender identity disorder. It is a mental disorder which causes a person to feel that they're biologically one gender but psychologically the other.

Gender identity
A stage in Kohlberg's theory of gender consistency. It's when a child thinks that their gender can change, e.g. by wearing opposite sex clothing, but they're aware that they're male or female.

Gender schema theory
A theory which combines cognitive developmental theory and social learning theory to suggest how gender stereotyping helps children learn what is and what isn't appropriate for their gender.

Gender stability
A stage in Kohlberg's theory of gender consistency. It's when an individual realises that their gender will remain fixed over time (e.g. boys will become men).

Gender typical behaviour
Behaviour that is seen to be stereotypically masculine or feminine.

General aggression model (GAM)
A model which explains how a violent stimulus can lead to emotional, physiological and cognitive arousal which then determines behaviour.

General intelligence ('g')
The genetically determined and unchangeable intelligence that everyone has, proposed by Spearman in his psychometric approach.

Generalisation
This is when stimuli similar to an original conditioned stimulus produce the conditioned response.

H

Hawthorne effect
This is where people's behaviour changes because they know they're being watched.

Health belief model
A model used to predict behaviour. It suggests unhealthy behaviour is the result of someone's perception of their susceptibility to a threat and its severity.

'Heinz dilemma'
A moral dilemma story famously used by Kohlberg in his 1963 study of moral understanding.

Higher function
A type of mental function described by Vygotsky that includes complex tasks like language comprehension and decision-making.

Higher order conditioning
This is when a new conditioned stimulus produces the conditioned response because the animal associates it with the original conditioned stimulus.

Histogram
A way of presenting continuous data.

Hoarding
A type of OCD behaviour that involves keeping useless or worn-out objects, such as old newspapers or junk mail.

Homeostasis
The process that keeps conditions in the body constant.

Horizon ratio
A perceptual cue where objects that are the same height are cut in the same place by the horizon, regardless of how far away they are.

Hopelessness theory of depression
Abramson et al's (1978) theory which stated depressed people may see failure as internal, global and stable.

Hovland-Yale model
The model outlined by Carl Hovland which illustrates how a person's change in attitude is affected by the source of a message, the message content, the recipient and the situation.

Huntington's chorea
A rare and inherited brain disorder caused by damage to the basal ganglia.

Hyperphagia
Overeating.

Hypersomnia
Sleeping a lot more than usual.

Hypocretin
A chemical made by the hypothalamus, involved in regulating arousal levels and linked to narcolepsy.

Hypothalamus
A small area of the brain responsible for homeostasis and regulating things like temperature, circadian rhythms and feeding.

I

Iconic mode
Bruner's second mode of knowledge representation. In this mode, knowledge is stored in the form of mental images involving different senses.

Identity crisis
A stage in adolescence described by Erikson which involves trying out different roles until we find our true identity.

Illusion of control
A cognitive bias which causes people to believe that they're able to control or influence the outcome of an event over which, in reality, they have no control.

Illusory correlation
A faulty reasoning mechanism involving superstitions which gamblers believe will help them succeed.

Inappropriate emotion
Displaying feelings that don't match the situation.

In-depth and societal-symbolic
Selman's final stage of perspective taking. From about fourteen, children understand that third-party perspectives can be influenced by factors such as social or cultural values. They can see a situation from a variety of different perspectives.

In-group
A group of people who share the same interests, characteristics, etc.
For example, for boys, playing with cars and trucks might be an in-group activity.

Independent groups design
A type of experimental design that has different participants in each group.

Independent variable
A variable directly manipulated by the researcher.

Indirect theory of perception
Gregory's (1966) theory which states stimuli don't provide the cognitive system with enough information for it to make sense of a situation. Stored knowledge is used to understand what is being perceived.

Individualist society
A type of society common in Western cultures. In individualist societies, the emphasis is on the individual's freedom, achievements and rights.

Infant studies
Research that involves studying babies. The studies can be used to look at the developmental aspects of certain conditions, behaviours or processes.

Inferential statistics
Statistics that allow you to tell if your data is significant.

Information processing approach
A psychological approach to intelligence focusing on the use of a set of cognitive processes.

Informed consent
When participants agree to being studied knowing the full aim of the research.

Infradian rhythm
Biological rhythms that occur less than once every 24 hours.

Initiation
The act of taking up, or starting, an addictive behaviour.

Innate
An ability that is inbuilt — something someone has been born with.

Inner speech
Self-talk that has become internalised.

Insomnia
A sleep disorder characterised by difficulty falling asleep, difficulty staying asleep or both.

Institutional aggression
Aggression within an institutional environment, e.g. in prison or in the military.

Intense-personal fandom
A stage of fandom where obsessive thoughts begin to arise in relation to a celebrity.

Internal reliability
If a test is consistent within itself and is measuring the same thing throughout.

Internal validity
The extent to which the results of a test are caused by the variable being measured, rather than extraneous variables.

Inter-rater reliability
A test of external reliability. In an observation, if different assessors agree, i.e. both give the same score, then the inter-rater reliability is high.

Interpersonal intelligence
Social skills, empathy and the ability to cooperate with others. One of Gardner's multiple intelligences.

Intersexual selection
The evolution of characteristics that are attractive to a mate (e.g. the peacock's tail). Animals with more attractive characteristics are more likely to mate, and will therefore pass on their genes to their offspring.

Interval data
Data which falls on a scale where each unit is the same size.

Intervention strategy
A plan to stop a behaviour before it becomes a problem.

Intrasexual selection
The evolution of characteristics that enable an individual to compete with their rivals. Animals with 'better' characteristics are able to survive to reproduce and pass on their genes to their offspring.

Intrapersonal intelligence
Associated with self-understanding, feelings, motivations and objectives. One of Gardner's multiple intelligences.

Jet lag
The experience that comes from travelling long distances at high speed because your body clock is out of sync with local timing.

Klinefelter's syndrome
A condition where males are born with an extra X chromosome, leaving them sterile, less muscular and less facial and body hair. They also experience difficulties in expressing themselves and interacting socially.

Knowledge acquisition component
One of Sternberg's cognitive processes underlying intelligence. It involves processes used to learn new information.

Laboratory experiment
A research method where research is conducted in an artificial setting in a controlled and scientific way. The aim is to control all relevant variables except for the independent variable, which is altered to see what effect it has.

Lateral nucleus (LN)
Part of the hypothalamus believed to be involved in food regulation. It detects a drop in blood sugar and causes hunger signals.

Learned helplessness
A theory coined by Seligman (1975) outlining the behaviour that occurs when people learn not to try because they believe they'll never succeed.

Learning approach
A psychological approach to intelligence which suggests behaviour is developed by reinforcement.

Leptin
A protein produced by adipose tissue to signal that fat reserves in the body are full.

Lesion
A change, brought about by surgery, injury or disease, in the structure of a body organ.

Limbic system
Part of the brain that contains the hypothalamus, thalamus, amygdala and hippocampus. It's thought to be involved in mental health disorders such as schizophrenia and anxiety disorders and has been linked to aggressive behaviour.

Line of best fit
A line drawn on a scattergram that fits the general pattern of the data and that passes as close to as many of the points as possible. It helps the reader visualise the correlation between two variables.

Locus of control
An expression of how much personal control people believe they have over the events in their lives. A person can have either an internal or an external locus of control.

Logical-mathematical intelligence
An ability in mathematics and logical and abstract reasoning. One of Gardner's multiple intelligences.

Longitudinal study
A study that follows the same participants over a long period of time.

Machiavellian intelligence
The ability to manipulate social situations to reach a goal.

Magical thinking
Believing that if you think about something happening, or say that it will happen, it's more likely to actually happen.

Maintenance
The act of carrying on with an addictive behaviour.

Major depression
Also known as unipolar disorder. An episode of depression that can occur suddenly.

Malnutrition
When your body doesn't have enough vitamins or minerals to function properly.

Mania
A behavioural state characterised by over-activity, rapid speech and feeling extremely happy or agitated.

Manic depression
Also known as bipolar disorder. The alternation between two mood extremes (mania and depression).

Mann-Whitney U test
A statistical test used with ordinal and unrelated data to see if there is a significant difference between two or more groups of values.

Matched pairs design
A type of experimental design where there are different participants in each condition, but they're matched on important variables (like age, sex and personality).

Mature concept stage
Vygotsky's final stage of cognitive development. At this stage lots of strategies are used at the same time in problem solving. Thinking becomes mature and developed.

Melatonin
A hormone secreted by the pineal gland, which seems to induce sleep.

Meta-analysis
A research method used in psychology where the results of lots of different studies are combined to look for an overall effect.

Metacomponent
One of Sternberg's cognitive processes underlying intelligence. It involves the planning and control processes used in problem solving and decision making.

Mirror neurons
Brain cells that are involved in performing an action, but that are also active when you observe someone else doing the same action.

Monoamine oxidase inhibitor (MAOIs)
A type of antidepressant that increases the availability of serotonin and noradrenaline by preventing their breakdown.

Monozygotic twins (MZ)
Identical twins.

Motivational interviewing
A client-centred form of therapy where the patient is directed by the therapist and is encouraged to solve their own problems which might be stopping them from changing their behaviour.

Müller-Lyer illusion
An optical illusion which shows two lines that appear to be different lengths due to inward or outward facing arrow heads.

Musical intelligence
Abilities relating to sound, rhythm and tone. One of Gardner's multiple intelligences.

Mutation
An alteration or change to DNA.

N

Name generation
A process that helps us to retrieve the name of a familiar person and relate it to their face.

Narcolepsy
A neurological disorder causing sudden episodes of daytime sleepiness, leading to a person falling asleep for a short period of time (seconds or minutes).

Natural experiment
A research method that measures variables that aren't directly manipulated by the experimenter.

Naturalistic intelligence
The ability to understand and act in the natural world. One of Gardner's multiple intelligences.

Naturalistic observation
An observational method where participants are observed in their natural environment, normally without their knowledge.

Near-death experience
An anomalous experience which involves sensations experienced when you're close to death, often interpreted as a glimpse into the 'afterlife'.

Necker cube
A visual illusion used to support Gregory's indirect theory of perception.

Negative correlation
A type of correlation in which as one variable rises, the other falls.

Negative reinforcement
When an action is more likely to be repeated because the action prevents a negative event or experience from occurring.

Negative symptom
See Type 2 symptom.

Neural mechanisms
Parts of the brain which control behaviours, such as eating.

Neuroticism
One of Eysenck and Eysenck's (1976) personality dimensions. It includes being anxious, moody and irritable.

Nicotine
The addictive chemical in cigarettes, contained in tobacco.

NMDA
A toxin used in certain studies to make lesions in the lateral nucleus of rats.

Nominal data
Data which can be split up into completely distinct categories. A frequency count can be used.

Non-directional hypothesis
A hypothesis that predicts that there will be a difference or correlation between two variables, but doesn't state which way the results will go (e.g. which variable will be larger).

Noradrenaline
A neurotransmitter.

Normative beliefs
Beliefs and ideas that people have about what is considered appropriate behaviour in their culture.

Null hypothesis
A hypothesis that you assume is true during a study. Any data you collect either backs this assumption up, or it doesn't. It's quite usual to have something you don't actually believe as your null hypothesis.

O

Obesity
When someone has a body mass index over 30 kg/m^2.

Object permanence
The understanding that an object exists even if it can't be seen, e.g. if you put a towel over a toy, the toy is still there.

Objectivity
Not allowing beliefs or opinions to bias scientific research.

Observed value
The value calculated when a statistical test is carried out on the results of an experiment.

Obsession
Intrusive and persistent thoughts, images and impulses.

Obsessive-compulsive disorder (OCD)
A type of anxiety disorder that has two parts — obsessions and compulsions.

Oedipus conflict
Freud's theory which claimed young boys are attracted to the opposite sex parent and fear the same sex parent.

Oestrogens
Female sex hormones involved in the development of female characteristics.

One-tailed test
A test used when the researcher has predicted a difference and has stated which way the results will go (i.e. a directional hypothesis).

Operant conditioning
A type of learning where an individual learns to associate their own behaviour with a particular consequence.

Operationalisation
Clearly defining variables so they can be reliably measured.

Opportunity sampling
A method of selecting a sample where anyone who is available at the time is used.

Optic array
The pattern of light that enters the eye, allowing things to be seen.

Optic flow pattern
Changes in the optic array as we move. It explains the feeling that objects that are close us seem to be moving quickly, whilst those far away seem to move much more slowly.

Optical illusion
Images which trick the brain into either faulty or multiple interpretations. They can be used to look at perceptual processes.

Optional sleep
All sleep stages except for stage four and REM sleep. It can help to conserve energy.

Ordinal data
Data where the measurements relate to the same variable, and can be placed in ascending or descending rank order.

Orthorexia
An eating disorder where people survive on a highly restrictive diet to try and avoid anything they think might be 'unhealthy'.

Out-group
A group of people who share different interests, characteristics, etc. from you and the rest of your in-group.

Out-of-body experience
An anomalous experience which involves the sensation of floating around outside of your own body.

P

Paranoid schizophrenia
A subtype of schizophrenia where patients experience hallucinations and delusions whilst their cognitive abilities remain unaffected.

Parapsychology
An approach in psychology which tries to explain the unexplained using scientific methods.

Parasocial relationship
A one-sided relationship with one person knowing lots and the other usually knowing nothing about the other party.

Parental investment
Any time, effort and energy that a parent puts towards the conception, gestation and rearing of a child that reduces their ability to invest in other offspring.

Parkinson's disease
A neurological and degenerative disorder which involves damage to the basal ganglia.

Participant observation
An observational method where an observer joins the group they are studying. They may be known to the group or hidden.

Past-life experience
An anomalous experience which involves remembering events from a previous existence.

Peer pressure
The influence of other people of the same age and social group.

Peer review
Where scientific reports are sent to experts in the field (peers) so that their quality can be assessed before they're published. This helps to validate conclusions — it means published theories, data and conclusions are more trustworthy.

Perceived behavioural control
A person's perception of how able they are to carry out certain behaviours.

Perceived effects theory
A theory of addiction which states that people often expect certain outcomes from taking addictive substances.

Perception
The process of giving meaning to stimuli.

Performance component
One of Sternberg's cognitive processes underlying intelligence. It involves the processes that allow us to carry out actions, e.g. memorising, calculating, etc.

Peripheral route
One of the two processing routes outlined by Petty and Cacioppo (1986). It suggests that low-level mechanisms such as conditioning, use of quick decision-making rules and attractiveness of the message determine our attitudes to a message.

Permissive amine theory
Kety's (1975) theory which states that serotonin controls the level of noradrenaline. A low level of serotonin causes the level of noradrenaline to fluctuate. Low levels of noradrenaline cause depression and high levels cause mania.

Perspective-taking
The ability to understand that other people's perspectives can differ from your own.

Person identity nodes
Units that contain information known about a person (e.g. their job, interests).

Persuasion
The act of changing, or trying to change, an attitude.

Phobia
An extreme, irrational fear of a particular object or situation. It is an example of an anxiety disorder.

Pilot study
A small-scale trial run of a test to check for any problems before the test is carried out for real.

Pineal gland
A gland in the brain that secretes melatonin — a hormone which seems to induce sleep.

Phase advance
When the body-clock and our sleep-wake cycle is moved backwards. For instance, travelling west to east or getting up and going to bed earlier.

Phase delay
When the body-clock and our sleep-wake cycle is moved forwards. For instance, travelling east to west or getting up and going to bed later.

Placebo effect
A medical improvement caused by a patient's belief that a treatment will work, rather than through any direct effect of the treatment.

Plowden report (1967)
A review of primary level education that made recommendations for UK schools.

Positive correlation
A type of correlation in which the variables rise and fall together.

Positive reinforcement
When an action is more likely to be repeated because it has a good outcome through a reward.

Positive symptom
See Type 1 symptom.

Postconventional morality
Kohlberg's final level of moral understanding, which consists of the social-contract orientation stage and the universal ethical principles stage.

Potential concept stage
Vygotsky's third stage of cognitive development. At this stage successful strategies are used in problem solving but only one at a time.

Practical intelligence
See contextual intelligence.

Preconventional morality
Kohlberg's first level of moral understanding, which consists of the punishment and obedience orientation stage and the instrumental purpose orientation stage.

Predictive power
How likely it is that a psychological model can predict future occurrences.

Preoperational stage
Piaget's second stage of cognitive development. It occurs between 2–7 years, and is when a child has some language, but makes logic mistakes. They show egocentrism, irreversibility and centration.

Preparedness theory
The theory which states humans have evolved a genetic predisposition to fear dangerous objects or situations in order to survive.

Prevention programme
A programme used to deter problematic behaviour, such as addiction, from happening in the first place.

Primary data
Information collected during the researcher's direct observations, e.g. test results, answers to questionnaires, observation notes.

Primary insomnia
Insomnia that is not linked to any existing physical or psychological condition.

Primary mental ability
Thurstone's different types of intelligence. These are numerical, verbal, spatial, word fluency, memory, perception and reasoning.

Pro-social behaviour
Behaviour with the positive intention of helping others.

Probability judgement
An assessment of how likely it is that something will happen.

Prosopagnosia
A condition where people have difficulty recognising familiar faces.

Pseudopatients
Participants in an experiment who pretend to act as patients.

Pseudoscience
Explanations based on evidence that's been collected through faulty scientific processes.

Psychic healer
A person who claims to be able to treat illness or injury without any physical intervention.

Psychic mediumship
The ability to communicate with spirits and transmit messages from the dead to the living.

Psychokinesis
An anomalous experience which involves affecting objects using the mind.

Psychological androgeny
A trait shown by people who don't fit gender stereotypes — they aren't stereotypically masculine or feminine.

Psychometric approach
A psychological approach to intelligence that involves measuring differences between people.

Psychomotor disturbance
Not having control of your muscles.

Psychopathology
The psychological study of mental disorders.

Psychosurgery
Brain surgery involving destruction or separation of parts of the brain.

Psychotherapy
A psychological therapy with the aim of identifying the underlying causes of a mental disorder. It uses techniques such as dream analysis and free association.

Psychoticism
One of Eysenck and Eysenck's (1976) personality dimensions. It includes being egocentric, aggressive and impulsive.

Q

Questionnaire
A type of self-report method that involves asking participants questions about certain topics.

R

Random sampling
A method of selecting a sample where everyone in the target group has an equal chance of being selected.

Rapid eye movement (REM)
A stage of sleep also known as active sleep. Muscles are paralysed and this is a time of vivid dreaming.

Rational choice theory
A cognitive theory of addiction which states that people often conduct a cost-benefit analysis before they undertake certain behaviours.

Reactive depression
Depression caused by external events.

Reductionist
When a theory breaks something down into small, basic, distinct parts or processes.

References
A section within a psychological report listing all the books, articles and websites that have been used for information during the study.

Regression
Going back to a less developed mental state.

Reinforcement-Affect theory
A type of reward/need satisfaction theory proposed by Byrne and Clore (1970). It suggests that both operant and classical conditioning play a part in relationships — we learn to associate people with positive or enjoyable situations, even if they are not directly rewarding us in these instances.

Relapse
The act of going back to an addictive behaviour after it has been previously stopped.

Related measures
Research where a repeated measures or matched participants design is used.

Reliability
If a test is consistent and measures what it's supposed to then it is reliable.

Repeated measures design
A type of experimental design where participants take part in all conditions.

Replicability
Whether the results of a study can be repeated when it is carried out again. It's a test of whether a theory or an experimental method is reliable.

Representative bias
A faulty reasoning mechanism where gamblers believe that random events should always look random.

Residual schizophrenia
A subtype of schizophrenia where patients are generally getting better but continue to experience negative symptoms. These patients don't show any sign of psychotic symptoms.

Restoration approach
A theory of sleep which states sleep is needed to restore the body's ability to function after being busy in the day.

Retina
The light sensitive layer at the back of the eye. It receives visual information and sends it to the brain.

Reward/need satisfaction theory
A theory explaining why we form relationships. It states that we form friendships and relationships to receive rewards or reinforcement from others. Relationships provide rewards that satisfy our social needs.

Ritualistic behaviour
Behaviour that follows simple and repetitive patterns.

S

'Sally-Anne task'
A study carried out by Baron-Cohen et al (1985) to test if children had Theory of Mind.

Sampling
Choosing a number of participants from the population that are representative of the target group.

Satiety
A bodily response that tells us when we feel full.

Scaffolding
When a teacher, another adult, or a more cognitively advanced child acts as an expert to guide an individual by making suggestions or doing demonstrations. This provides a framework by which the individual learns to do a task.

Scattergram
A way of plotting points and visualising relationships between variables.

Schema
All the information you know about an object, action or concept which helps you to organise and interpret information.

Schizophrenia
A thought process disorder characterised by disruption to a person's perceptions, emotions and beliefs.

Script
A schema of a particular situation containing knowledge about an expected sequence of behaviour.

Second-person and reciprocal
Selman's third stage of perspective taking. Between seven and twelve, children can put themselves in someone else's shoes and view a situation from another's perspective. They also realise that other people can do the same.

Secondary data
Information collected from other studies.

Secondary insomnia
Insomnia that is the result of existing physical or psychological conditions.

Selective breeding
Breeding specific organisms to ensure certain genes are passed on to the offspring.

Selective serotonin reuptake inhibitor (SSRI)
An antidepressant that increases the availability of serotonin by preventing its reuptake.

Self-efficacy
Belief in your ability to do something.

Self-medication
Administering drugs and treatment to yourself.

Self-medication model
A cognitive model of addiction which suggests that individuals resort to addictive behaviours when they get stressed.

Self-recognition
Used as evidence of intelligence. The idea that an animal can recognise themselves and therefore show that they're self-aware.

Self-report
A method of collecting data which involves asking participants about their feelings, beliefs and attitudes, etc.

Self-selected sampling
A method of selecting a sample where participants volunteer, e.g. by responding to a newspaper advertisement.

Self-talk
When a child talks out loud to regulate and direct themselves.

Sense of self
The ability to distinguish between self and others and to refer to each with appropriate language. It also involves having knowledge of our experiences, abilities, motivations, etc., having ideas about body image and being able to see yourself as others see you.

Sensorimotor stage
Piaget's first stage of cognitive development. It occurs between 0–2 years, and is when a child's knowledge is limited to what their senses tell them when they're exploring their surroundings.

Sensory leakage
When information is unintentionally transmitted by normal methods (e.g. visual and auditory cues) rather than by paranormal activity.

Serotonin
A neurotransmitter associated with eating behaviour, anxiety and depression.

Serotonin and noradrenaline reuptake inhibitor (SNRI)
An antidepressant that prevents the reuptake of serotonin and noradrenaline, so increases their availability.

Sex Role Inventory
A questionnaire developed by Bem (1974) which can be used to see how stereotypically masculine or feminine someone is. It's also known as the Bem Sex Role Inventory (BSRI).

Sexual infidelity
The act of sexual intercourse with someone else other than your partner.

Sexual selection
The evolution of characteristics which increase our mating potential.

Shape constancy
A visual constancy in which the shape of the image on the retina changes, but the brain doesn't interpret this as the object changing shape.

Shift work
Working patterns that usually involve people working through the night at some point.

Significance level
The 'level of proof' that you're looking for before you can read something into your results. It's the probability of making a type 1 error if the null hypothesis is true.

Size constancy
A visual constancy whereby the brain processes an image and is able to identify the object as being closer rather than larger.

Sleep apnoea
A sleep disorder where the person's airways become temporarily blocked whilst they are sleeping, causing their breathing to be interrupted.

Sleep hygiene
Controlling for situations and circumstances that might cause sleep problems, such as avoiding caffeine and creating a comfortable sleeping environment.

Sleepwalking
A sleep disorder characterised by normal movements and walking despite the brain being in a state of sleep. It is associated with stage three and stage four sleep.

Social cognition
The cognitive processes that underlie social interactions. Social cognition includes things like understanding ourselves, others and how we fit into society.

Social cognitive observation learning theory (SCOLT)
A theory which suggests that children learn how to think about the world by observing others.

Social complexity
The social world of a species which includes interactions and relationships with others.

Social desirability bias
This is where people change their behaviour to make themselves look better, e.g. more generous.

Social drift hypothesis
The hypothesis which states there are more people with schizophrenia in deprived areas because having schizophrenia gives them a lower social status.

Social exchange theory
A type of economic theory proposed by Thibaut and Kelley (1959).
It suggests that people try to maximise rewards from a relationship and minimise costs. If the relationship is to continue, then the rewards must not be outweighed by the costs — we should end up in profit.

Social learning theory
A theory which suggests that behaviours are learnt directly through reinforcement (reward and punishment) and indirectly by seeing other people being rewarded or punished for their behaviour.

Social neuroscience
A discipline in psychology which involves a combination of biological and social concepts and theories.

Social phobia
The fear of being in social situations. It's usually down to the possibility of being judged or being embarrassed.

Social skills training
A form of behavioural therapy which allows patients to observe others who act appropriately. Through modelling, reinforcement and role play, they can then copy the behaviour so that they know how to act in certain situations.

Social withdrawal
Not taking part in or enjoying social situations.

Spearman's rho correlation coefficient
A statistical test used to see if there is a significant association between two variables.

Specific phobia
A phobia which involves the fear of specific objects or situations.
It contains five subtypes — animal, environmental dangers, blood-injection-injury, situational and 'other'.

Sperm Competition Theory
A theory proposed by Short (1979) which provides an explanation for males evolving to release large amounts of sperm during ejaculation.

Spontaneous psychic ability (psi)
An anomalous experience which involves extra-sensory perception, e.g. telepathy, clairvoyance or psychokinesis.

Spontaneous recovery
This is when a previously extinct conditioned response is produced in response to the conditioned stimulus.

Spiral curriculum
Bruner's idea that difficult concepts can be introduced at an appropriate level from an early age. The concepts can be repeatedly revisited, each time in more depth until a more complete and in-depth understanding is reached.

Split-half technique
When a questionnaire is randomly split in two to see if all participants score similarly on both halves.
If they do, the questions measure the same thing, and therefore have good internal reliability.

Statistical significance
If your results are statistically significant it means that they are unlikely to be just down to chance if the null hypothesis is true.

Stereotyped behaviour
Continuously repeating actions, which are often strange and don't have a purpose.

Stimulus
A change in an organism's environment that causes a response.

Stratified sampling
A method of selecting a sample where all of the important subgroups in the population are identified and a proportionate number from each subgroup are randomly obtained.

Structural encoding
The process in face recognition where physical features are interpreted to determine basic information.

Structural model
A model made up of lots of different components that shows the structure of a system.

Subjective validation
A cognitive bias where we're more likely to believe in and pay attention to information that has personal relevance.

Submission
Displaying exaggerated and ritual signs of defeat in order to deter further aggression.

Superstition
A belief that an object or action will affect an outcome when there is no logical reason for it to do so.

Suprachiasmatic nucleus (SCN)
Part of the hypothalamus that acts as an internal clock.

Survival reflex
An innate and unconscious change in behaviour in order to help us survive.

Symbolic mode
Bruner's final mode of knowledge representation. In this mode we develop the ability to think in symbolic ways. Language and thinking become strongly linked, which allows us to mentally manipulate concepts and ideas, and to think in abstract ways.

Symmetry and orderliness
A type of OCD behaviour that involves getting objects lined up 'just right'.

Systematic desensitisation
Wolpe's (1958) behavioural therapy which works by counter-conditioning patients to allow them to associate the phobic stimulus with relaxation rather than fear.

Systematic sampling
A method of selecting a sample where every n^{th} member of a population is selected from a sampling frame.

Tardive dyskinesia
Involuntary, repetitive movements.

Telepathy
The ability to transmit messages via thoughts alone.

Testosterone
The male sex hormone involved in the development of male characteristics. It is an androgen and is believed to be involved in aggression.

Texture gradient
When objects are far away they take up less of the optic array and are closer together than objects that are near.

Theory of mind
The ability to understand that other people have minds with knowledge, feelings, beliefs, motivations, intentions, etc.

Theory of planned behaviour (TPB)
A model of behaviour which expands upon the theory of reasoned action but also includes a person's perceived level of control.

Theory of reasoned action (TRA)
A model of behaviour which states that an individual's behaviour can be predicted by their intention to perform it.

Third-person and mutual
Selman's fourth stage of perspective taking. Between ten and fifteen years old, children develop the ability to take the perspective of a third impartial person who's viewing an interaction between other people.

Thought control
A symptom of schizophrenia where the patient believes that their thoughts are being controlled.

'Three mountains task'
A study carried out by Piaget and Inhelder in 1956 to test egocentrism in children.

Thrifty gene
A gene that would allow hunter-gatherers to put on weight quickly when food was plentiful.

Time-interval sampling
A way of sampling behaviour during an observation where you choose to observe only at set time intervals.

Tolerance
When the body becomes used to a substance, and taking the same amount of a drug no longer has the same effect.

Token economy
A programme based on the behavioural model which uses rewards and reinforcement to encourage 'normal' behaviour.

Top down process
Processes that work by looking at the object as a whole and then breaking it down into parts, using prior knowledge to help.

Triarchic model of intelligence
Sternberg's information processing approach which suggests there are three different aspects to intelligence.

Tricyclic antidepressant (TCA)
An antidepressant that increases the availability of serotonin and noradrenaline by preventing their reuptake.

Twin study
A method used to find out if genetic factors influence the development of a disorder. It compares concordance rates in identical and non-identical twins.

Two-tailed test
A test used when the researcher has predicted a difference, but hasn't stated which way the results will go (i.e. a non-directional hypothesis).

Type 1 error
When you reject the null hypothesis when it was actually true.

Type 1 symptom of schizophrenia
A symptom where people experience something, feel that something is happening to them, or display a certain behaviour — e.g. a hallucination, delusion, jumbled speech.

Type 2 error
When you don't reject the null hypothesis when it was actually false.

Type 2 symptom of schizophrenia
A symptom where people don't display 'normal' behaviour —
e.g. they're withdrawn, unresponsive and show a lack of emotion.

Ultradian rhythm
Biological rhythms that occur more than once every 24 hours.

Unconditioned stimulus
A stimulus that causes an automatic, and reflexive, response or behaviour.

Undifferentiated and egocentric
Selman's first stage of perspective taking. Up to about six years of age, children can separate self and other, but in a physical sense only. They don't perceive any psychological differences, seeing the other person in the same way they see an object.

Undifferentiated schizophrenia
A subtype of schizophrenia where patients show signs of schizophrenia but they don't show enough of one behaviour to categorise them fully.

Unfalsifiable
Something that is impossible to prove wrong.

Unipolar depression
See major depression.

Unrelated measures
Research where an independent measures design is used.

Vague syncretic stage
Vygotsky's first stage of cognitive development. At this stage problem solving is by trial and error with no understanding of the underlying concepts.

Validity
Whether something actually measures what it sets out to measure.

Ventricle
A hollow area of the brain.

Ventromedial nucleus (VMN)
Part of the hypothalamus believed to be involved in food regulation. It provides the signal to stop eating.

Verbal-linguistic intelligence
Speaking, reading, writing and the ability to learn languages. One of Gardner's multiple intelligences.

Vicarious learning
Learning indirectly by observing others being punished or rewarded for their behaviour.

Vicarious reinforcement
When an individual copies behaviour that it sees another individual receive a benefit from.

Visual constancy
The process whereby we know size and shape stay the same regardless of the angle at which an object is seen from.

Visual-spatial intelligence
An ability in mental visualisation and art. One of Gardner's multiple intelligences.

Wilcoxon Signed Ranks test
A statistical test used with related, ordinal data to see if there is a significant difference between two or more groups of values.

Withdrawal symptoms
Uncomfortable physical and psychological symptoms that occur when a person stops taking a substance that they're addicted to.

'Yo-yo' dieting
Diets that result in continuous alternating weight gain and weight loss.

Zone of proximal development (ZPD)
The difference between the problem solving a child can do on their own and the problem solving they can do with a more able peer or adult.

Acknowledgements

AQA Specification reference points are reproduced by permission of Assessment and Qualifications Alliance.

Data acknowledgements

p 266, p 267, p 271 Journal of the American Statistical Association by AMERICAN STATISTICAL ASSOCIATION Copyright 1972 Reproduced with permission of TAYLOR & FRANCIS INFORMA UK LTD - JOURNALS in the format Textbook via Copyright Clearance Centre.

p 272, p 277 Journal of the American Statistical Association by AMERICAN STATISTICAL ASSOCIATION Copyright 1965 Reproduced with permission of TAYLOR & FRANCIS INFORMA UK LTD – JOURNALS in the format Textbook via Copyright Clearance Centre.

p 274 Fundamentals of behavioural statistics (3rd ed.), R. Runyon and A. Haber (1976), copyright The McGraw-Hill Companies, Inc.

p 275, p 294 Fisher & Yates, Statistical Tables for Biological, Agricultural and Medical Research, Pearson Education Ltd., Longman Group UK Ltd. 1974 6e.

p 287 Abstract reprinted from Cognition, 21 (1), Simon Baron-Cohen, Alan M. Leslie, Uta Frith, Does the autistic child have a "theory of mind"?, pages 37–46, (1985), with permission from Elsevier.

Photograph acknowledgements

Science Photo Library

Cover Photo Pasieka, p 3 (top) Thierry Berrod, Mona Lisa Production, p 6 Patrice Latron/Look At Sciences, p 7 BSIP, PDA, p 8 Klaus Guldbrandsen, p 9 Adam Jones, p 10 Louise Murray, p 12 Cordelia Molloy, p 13 Southern Illinois University, p 14 John Serrao, p 15 Deep Light Productions, p 18 Patrick Landmann, p 19 Fisher/Custom Medical Stock Photo, p 23 Jens Lucking, p 24 Mike Miller, p 26 Science Photo Library, p 27 Science Source, p 28 Paul Rapson, p 30 Deep Light Productions, p 33 Sam Ogden, p 34 Zephyr, p 38 Simon Potter, p 42 (bottom) Chassenet, p 44 (bottom) Bernhard Lang, p 53 Mauro Fermariello, p 55 Gustoimages, p 57 Ria Novosti, p 59 Andy Harmer, p 61 George D. Lepp, p 63 Alexis Rosenfeld, p 66 David Munns, p 69 (top) Ian Hooton, p 69 (bottom) Peter Menzel, p 72 George Steinmetz, p 73 Maximilian Stock Ltd, p 76 Oscar Burriel, p 77 Chris Sattlberger, p 78 Chris Martin-Bahr, p 81 Sheila Terry, p 84 Christophe Vander Eecken, p 85 Oak Ridge National Laboratory/US Department of Energy, p 86 Library Of Congress, p 89 Ghislain & Marie David De Lossy, p 90 Stefanie Aumiller, p 91 Ghislain & Marie David De Lossy, Cultura, p 95 Matthew Oldfield, p 98 Spencer Grant, p 99 AJ Photo, p 100 Phil Boorman, p 103 Sam Falk, p 104 Ghislain & Marie David De Lossy, Cultura, p 105 Peter Muller, p 107 Science Source, p 108 Walter Dawn, p 109 Bob Gibbons, p 110 (top) Louise Murray, p 110 (bottom) Adam Jones, p 111 Nigel Cattlin, p 113 Georgette Douwma, p 115 Simon Fraser, p 118 (top) Bill Anderson, p 118 (bottom) Doug Goodman, p 120 Lew Merrim, p 121 (top) Ria Novosti, p 123 (top) Tim Hall, Cultura, p 126 (bottom) Martin Riedl, p 134 Thierry Berrod, Mona Lisa Production, p 139 Simon Fraser, p 140 Will & Deni Mcintyre, p 144 Thierry Berrod, Mona Lisa Production, p 147 Will & Deni Mcintyre, p 148 CC Studio, p 149 (top) US National Library of Medicine, p 149 (bottom) Grunnitus Studio, p 153 (bottom) Sovereign, ISM, p 155 Colin Hawkins, p 157 Science Photo Library, p 158 William Lingwood, p 159 Mauro Fermariello, p 162 Jim Varney, p 163 Mark Thomas, p 166 Cordelia Molloy, p 167 Crown Copyright/Health & Safety Laboratory, p 168 Kevin Curtis, p 170 Cordelia Molloy, p 172 Maiwolf, p 173 Daniel Sambraus,Thomas Luddington, p 176 Mark Thomas, p 177 BSIP Krassovsky, p 179 (top) Pasieka, p 179 (bottom) Coneyl Jay, p 180 Simon Booth, p 181 Nick Dolding, p 184 Michael Donne, p 186 Lea Paterson, p 188 Johnny Greig, p 189 Lea Paterson, p 190 Jerry Mason, p 191 Louise Murray, p 193 Damien Lovegrove, p 194 Wellcome Dept. of Cognitive Neurology, p 195 Alex Bartel, p 196 Janie Airey, p 199 Elsa M Megson, p 200 Colin Hawkins, p 201 National Library of Medicine, p 203 Ciot, p 205 Ian Hooton, p 207 Tek Image, p 209 Ian Hooton, p 211 Tony Craddock, p 214 BSIP Chassenet, p 217 Saturn Stills, p 218 Ria Novosti, p 219 Martin Riedl, p 222 Wayne Hutchinson, Visuals Unlimited, p 223 Rosenfeld Images Ltd, p 226 Jim Varney, p 227 Ian Hooton, p 229 Life In View, p 230 Simon Fraser, p 231 Cordelia Molloy, p 232 BSIP, Laurent, p 233 Gustoimages, p 235 Pasieka, p 236 Science Source/USDA, p 237 (top) Dr Rob Stepney, p 237 (bottom) Adam Hart-Davis, p 239 John K. Davies, p 240 Peter Menzel, p 241 Gustoimages, p 243 Gavin Kingcome, p 244 Adam Gault, p 251 Will & Deni Mcintyre, p 255 (bottom) ARS Information Staff/US Department of Agriculture, p 262 David Parker, p 298 Gustoimages, p 300 Mauro Fermariello.

iStockphoto

p 3 (bottom) Dem10, p 4 LeggNet, p 39 TatyanaGl, p 40 jhorrocks, p 43 (top) Zero Creatives, p 43 (bottom) Digitalskillet, p 44 (top) Clerkenwell_Images, p 46 EJWhite, p 48 Damircudic, p 49 Zarinmedia, p 52 Erlucho, p 96 Graphixel, p 121 (bottom) Damircudic, p 123 (bottom) Jojof, p 126 (top) Bowden Images, p 127 Miklav, p 130 Aluxum, p 135 Matspersson0, p 137 Fertnig, p 141 Dolgachov, p 146 Eyecrave, p 161 Tony Baggett, p 169 Williv, p 185 Shironosov, p 210 Rzdeb, p 213 Mediaphotos, p 228 Arsenik, p 246 Ratstuben, p 252 Ozgurdonmaz, p 254 (top) Jhorrocks, p 254 (bottom) Damircudic, p 255 (top) Paulaconnelly, p 256 Gemenacom, p 257 Bluberries, p 258 Serow, p 260 Andreaskermann, p 261 Rockfinder, p 269 Willsie, p 270 Kali9, p 278 (top) Track5, p 278 (bottom) Adamkaz, p 279 Ruslan Dashinsky, p 282 Lilcrazyfuzzy, p 284 Kupicoo, p 288 Spinka, p 289 Anthiacumming.

Other

p 153 (top) Drs E Fuller Torrey and Daniel Weinberger

Every effort has been made to locate copyright holders and obtain permission to reproduce sources. For those sources where it has been difficult to trace the originator of the work, we would be grateful for information. If any copyright holder would like us to make an amendment to the acknowledgements, please notify us and we will gladly update the book at the next reprint. Thank you.

Index of Names

Index

N

O

P

Q

R

S

T

U

V

W

Z